Human Behavior, Communities, Organizations, and Groups in the Macro Social Environment

SECOND EDITION

Karen K. Kirst-Ashman
University of Wisconsin-Whitewater

THOMSON

BROOKS/COLE

Australia • Brazil • Canada • Mexico • Singapore • Spain
United Kingdom • United States

THOMSON

BROOKS/COLE

Human Behavior, Communities, Organizations, and
Groups in the Macro Social Environment
Second Edition
Karen K. Kirst-Ashman

Social Work Editor: Dan Alpert
Development Editor: Tangelique Williams
Assistant Editor: Ann Lee Richards
Editorial Assistant: Stephanie Rue
Technology Project Manager: Julie Aguilar
Marketing Manager: Meghan McCullough
Marketing Communications Manager: Shemika Britt
Project Manager, Editorial Production: Tanya Nigh
Creative Director: Rob Hugel
Art Director: Vernon Boes

Print Buyer: Judy Inouye
Permissions Editor: Bob Kauser
Production Service: ICC Macmillan Inc.
Photo Researcher: Terri Wright
Copy Editor: Richard Camp
Cover Designer: Paula Goldstein
Cover Image: Stephan Daigle, Getty Images
Cover Printer: West Group
Compositor: ICC Macmillan Inc.
Printer: West Group

Printed in the United States of America
1 2 3 4 5 6 7 11 10 09 08 07

Library of Congress Control Number: 2007920375

ISBN-13: 978-0-495-09514-9
ISBN-10: 0-495-09514-1

Thomson Higher Education
10 Davis Drive
Belmont, CA 94002-3098
USA

For more information about our products, contact us at:
Thomson Learning Academic Resource Center
1-800-423-0563
For permission to use material from this text or product, submit a request online at
http://www.thomsonrights.com.
Any additional questions about permissions can be submitted by e-mail to
thomsonrights@thomson.com.

To Mabel F. Scholtka, my dear aunt and the nicest person you could ever want to meet

Contents

Preface

Focusing on empowerment, this book explores human behavior in task groups, organizations, and communities. The text has undergone a major expansion, with the intent to provide a sound knowledge base for understanding how the macro social environment works and make it easier for students to apply theory in subsequent practice courses. Theories and major concepts concerning communities, organizations, and groups are explained. This content has been significantly expanded since the first edition. An ecosystems perspective is emphasized. A strengths perspective, empowerment, and resiliency are underlying themes throughout the book. Applications of how macro systems operate and impact human behavior are examined. Critical thinking questions are posed throughout to stimulate students' understanding of content and exploration of issues. A new chapter on social justice and global development has been added.

Primary emphasis is also placed on values and ethics, diversity, populations-at-risk, and the promotion of social and economic justice. Numerous case examples are presented of how communities, organizations, and groups can enhance people's optimal health and well-being. These include how macro systems affect the lives and behavior of people of color, women, lesbian and gay people, and people with developmental disabilities.

A major concern in social work education today is the strong tendency for students to veer away from thinking about how communities and organizations affect human behavior. Instead, students are frequently drawn to the perceived psychological drama and intensity of more clinically oriented practice with individuals, families, and treatment groups. This book relates content about the macro social environment directly to generalist social work practice. Applications of content to practice settings are integrated throughout. Students should clearly understand why a macro focus is a necessity in practice, in addition to their acquisition of micro and mezzo skills.

This book is especially written for undergraduate and graduate courses in human behavior and the social environment (HBSE) that incorporate content on communities, organizations, and task groups. It can be used independently to teach human behavior in the HBSE context from a macro perspective, or in conjunction with other textbooks such as *Understanding Human Behavior and the Social Environment* (Zastrow & Kirst-Ashman, 2007) that include content on bio-psycho-social development throughout the lifespan. The intent here is to emphasize the dynamic interaction among systems in the macro social environment and provide breadth and depth of insight into the functioning of communities, organizations, and task groups.

A major thrust of this text is to present the material in a readable fashion. It uses numerous case applications and jargon-free language so that the reader can readily grasp theory and concepts. The three adjectives the author hopes best describe this text are relevant, practical, and readable. The macro social environment and the social forces acting upon it are clearly defined. Theory and major concepts are presented in a straightforward and thought-provoking manner. Applications to actual macro practice situations are emphasized throughout, as is the importance of client system empowerment.

CSWE EDUCATION POLICY AND ACCREDITATION STANDARDS

The book is written to comply with the Council on Social Work Education's Educational Policy and Accreditation Standards that require the following content be covered in HBSE courses (CSWE, 2001, IV.D.):

- Content on the reciprocal relationships between human behavior and social environments.
- Empirically based theories and knowledge that focus on the interactions between and among individuals, groups, societies, and economic systems.
- The range of social systems in which individuals live (individual, family, group, organizational, and community).
- Ways social systems promote or deter people in maintaining or achieving optimal health and well-being.

The book incorporates subject matter responding to required foundation curriculum content on values and ethics, diversity, and populations-at-risk and social and economic justice, reflecting CSWE's intent that the educational experience provide the student with "the opportunity to be aware of personal values; develop, demonstrate, and promote the values of the profession" and begin to analyze "ethical dilemmas and the ways in which these affect practice, services, and clients" (CSWE, 2001, IV.A.). To enhance this process, critical thinking questions are posed throughout. The book also seeks to "integrate content that promotes understanding, affirmation, and respect for people from diverse backgrounds" and to emphasize "the interlocking and complex nature of culture and personal identity (CSWE, 2001, IV.B.). It also promotes the goal that "social services meet the needs of groups served and are culturally relevant" (CSWE, 2001, IV.B.). Another of the book's goals is to "integrate content on populations-at-risk, examining the factors that contribute to and constitute being at risk" as well as to integrate "social and economic justice content grounded in an understanding of distributive justice, human and civil rights, and the global interconnections of oppression," providing foundation content for students "to advocate for nondiscriminatory social and economic systems" (CSWE, 2001, IV.C.).

Additionally, this book aims to achieve purposes specified by CSWE through the following means (CSWE, 2001, I.C.):

- Developing knowledge
- Promoting interprofessional and interdisciplinary collaboration
- Preparing social workers to practice with individuals, families, groups, organizations, and communities
- Preparing social workers to practice without discrimination, with respect, and with knowledge and skills related to clients' age, class, color, culture, disability, ethnicity, family structure, gender, marital status, national origin, race, religion, and sexual orientation
- Preparing social workers to alleviate poverty, oppression, and other forms of social injustice
- Preparing social workers to recognize the global context of social work practice

NEW ADDITIONS

As noted briefly earlier, major additions include an emphasis on the strengths perspective and the addition of questions to stimulate critical thinking throughout the book. An additional chapter on social justice and global development has also been added. Specific content has been added in the following respective chapters.

Chapter 1:

- Multiple diagrams illustrating a wide range of concepts
- Professional roles
- Critical thinking
- Empowerment, the strengths perspective, and resiliency
- Sexual orientation and the expression of gender
- Competencies for cultural competence
- Common elements in oppression

Chapter 2:

- Expanded content on social exchange and cognitive-behavioral theories
- Empowerment and feminist theories related to group functioning
- Verbal and nonverbal behavior in task groups
- Cross-cultural differences in communication
- The communication of group norms to members
- Task-oriented and relations-oriented roles
- Ways power can be used in groups
- Types of leadership
- Empowerment by group leaders

Chapter 3:

- Barriers to successful teamwork
- Variables characterizing team empowerment
- Team empowerment
- Committee empowerment through good leadership
- Types of social action groups
- Political action organizations advocating for GLBT people

Chapter 4:

- Elaboration of classical organizational theories including scientific management, the administrative theory of management, and bureaucracy
- Neoclassical organizational theory
- Feminist theories
- Chaos theory
- Culture-quality theories

Chapter 5:

- The relationship among mission statements, goals, and objectives to achieve goals
- Updating of TANF

Chapter 6:

- Interpersonal communication within social service agencies
- The perceptual process during communication
- Interpersonal barriers to communication including noise, personality factors, individual errors in perception, and lying and distraction
- New figures depicting the perceptual process and the communication process
- Means for enhancing ethical communication in agencies
- The importance of power in organizations
- Various types of power
- Organizational politics and their potential effects on workers' behavior
- Dynamics contributing to political behavior
- Tactics for using agency politics for positive change
- The use of unethical agency politics

Chapter 7:

- Newer approaches to management and worker empowerment including constructing a culture of caring, the learning organization, teamwork and team empowerment, managing diversity, and client system empowerment by management
- Leadership styles
- Women in social services management
- Servant leadership

Chapter 8:

- Greatly expanded content on community theories
- Structuralist theories and social action
- Content on manifest and latent functions, positive and negative social functions, social dysfunctions, social problems, and social disorganization in the context of functionalist theories.
- Conflict theories with content on class conflict and interest group conflict.
- Symbolic interactionist theories with content on deviant behavior and labeling theory
- Empowerment theories emphasizing the strength perspective and resiliency
- Greatly expanded content on non-geographical communities including discussion of professional communities, spiritual communities, ethnic communities and communities of people of color, and communities based on sexual orientation
- Rural communities with content on population trends, employment issues, inherent problems, and generalist practice within rural communities
- Ethical issues involved in dual relationships in rural communities
- Advantages for social workers in rural environments
- Social work in urban communities including content on inherent problems and social work practice within these communities

Chapter 9:

- Community assessment and data-gathering methods
- Mapping community assets, including releasing individual capacities, mapping assets of associations, organizations, and institutions, and data collection approaches

Chapter 10:

- Qualities of strong neighborhoods
- Inclusion of a neighborhood groups and value implementation approach to describing and understanding neighborhoods
- Ethnicity and social class in neighborhoods, including the strengths of ethnic and cultural solidarity, and segregation
- Projects that can enhance neighborhood strengths including murals, gardens, and community playgrounds

- Processes of change in neighborhoods, including those based on the invasion-succession, life cycle, and political capacity models
- Specification of the types of activities neighborhood centers can sponsor to improve living conditions for neighborhood residents

Chapter 11:

- Expanded and new content on African American grandparents providing care for grandchildren
- Expanded and new content on Hispanics including language and terms used, oppression, and traditional family values involving the importance of family, personalismo, machismo and marianismo, and spirituality
- The autistic spectrum
- Today's empowerment approach when working with people who have disabilities

Chapter 12:

- The context of the global environment in which we live
- Social justice and its significance for international social work practice
- The social issues of poverty and economic justice, global conflict, and the forced migration of people in need
- Community development and its theoretical foundations
- Examples of community development practice
- Social development
- A feminist perspective on global development
- International social work
- International social work and social welfare organizations
- International nongovernmental organizations
- Social work values and cross-cultural values in global perspective
- Cultural differences existing in organizational contexts

ACKNOWLEDGEMENTS

The author wishes to express her heartfelt appreciation to Nick Ashman, who cooked for and supported her throughout the writing process. The author also expresses indebtedness to Dan Alpert, Executive Editor, Tanya Nigh, Senior Content Project Manager, Stephanie Rue, Editorial Assistant, and the other staff at Brooks/Cole who encouraged her to pursue this endeavor, provided ongoing help and support, and expressed infinite patience while she worked to get it done. Sincere appreciation is extended to Vicki Vogel for her expert work on the index and Karen Thomson for her excellent assistance. Much gratitude is expressed to Santosh Vasudevan, Project Manager, who conscientiously supervised the book's production. Many thanks to Mary Ann Suppes, who provided encouragement and creative ideas for the initial conceptualization of content. Thanks also to Bradley Blaeser for his innovative ideas concerning and work in neighborhood development.

The author would also like to thank the following reviewers of this book for their help and input:

Beverly C. Favre, Southern University at New Orleans

Kristina M. Hash, West Virginia University

Adelle Sanders, Governor's State University

Judi Egbert, Ball State University

Marcia Bombyk, Eastern Michigan University

Francis Origanti, Creighton University

Jade Stanley, Northeastern Illinois University

Laura Lowe, Texas Tech University

Felix O. Chima, Prairie View A & M University

Jay Bishop, University of Maryland, Eastern Shore

Jay Metzger, Nazareth College

Janet Nes, University of St. Francis

Susan Cody-Rydzewski, LaGrange College

Ardyth L. Krause, University of Wisconsin, Eau Claire

Stacey Kolomer, University of Georgia

Sondra Floyd, University of Kentucky

Nancy Francisco Stewart, Jacksonville State University

Luther Brown, Castleton State College

Karen Randolph, Florida State University

Gail Leedy, University of Wyoming

Jennifer Brougham, Arizona State University

MaryAnn Overcamp-Martini, University of Nevada, Las Vegas

Lonnie R. Helton, Cleveland State University

Batya Hyman, Salisbury University

Janice M. Whitfield, Western Illinois University

Michael R. Daley, University of South Alabama

Debra Lavendar-Bratcher, Wayland Baptist University

Steven Applewhite, University of Houston

Pam Black, Eastern Kentucky University

Sheli Bernstein-Goff, West Liberty State College

Carolyn D. Haney, University of Wyoming

Gemma Beckley, Rust College

Carlene Quinn, Indiana University

Dianne Thompson, Columbia College

Introduction to Human Behavior in the Macro Social Environment

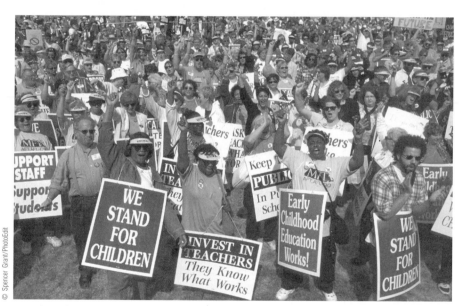

Social workers can address important social issues in the macro social environment.

1

CHAPTER CONTENTS

- *A social worker employed by a large public social services department hears increasing numbers of complaints from clients about drug houses popping up in their residential neighborhoods. The worker identifies clients and other concerned citizens in the communities and organizes a community meeting. She then assists community residents in formulating a plan to band together, identify drug house locations, and establish a procedure to report such houses to the authorities.*
- *The main tasks of a Foster Care Unit are to assess potential foster parent applicants, monitor placement and manage cases as they move in and out of foster care, and train foster parents in parenting and behavior management skills. The unit social workers hold bi-weekly meetings where they discuss how to improve agency service provision. The workers take turns organizing the meetings and running the discussions.*
- *A social worker employed by a neighborhood center determines that the range of workers and other professionals working with various adolescent clients within the community are not communicating with each other. For example, school social workers have no established procedure for conveying information to protective services workers who, in turn, do not communicate readily with probation and parole workers. This is despite the fact that most of these professionals are working with many of the same clients. The neighborhood-center social worker decided to pull together representatives from the various involved agencies and establish more clearly defined communication channels.*
- *A social worker employed by a large private family-services agency specializes in international adoptions, especially those involving the states in the former Soviet Union. He discovers that many of the adoptive children are experiencing health problems resulting from early nutritional deprivation. The worker feels that the problem goes beyond one or two cases, and reflects a serious pattern. No referral process is in place to automatically assess adoptive children and refer them to needed resources, including designated medical specialists. The worker begins to establish a systematic process for assessment and referral.*
- *Agency administration asks one of three social workers in a large residential health care complex for older adults to assess the effectiveness of its social services program.*
- *A social worker at a public assistance agency is terribly troubled by the conditions of the agency's waiting room for clients and by the tedious process required for clients' intakes. She explores the issue, develops a proposed plan for improvement, and makes an appointment to speak with the agency's executive director about it.*
- *A local charitable funding organization decides to cut off its funding contribution to a Planned Parenthood agency that has three satellite clinics in addition to its larger, centrally located main clinic.[1] The result*

[1] Planned Parenthood agencies assist people in making decisions about pregnancy and promote birth control and contraception.

would be a severe cutback in services including the closure of at least two of its satellite clinics. A huge number of clients would find it difficult if not impossible to receive adequate services. A social work counselor at one of the clinics, with the support of her supervisor, gathers facts to support her argument that funding is necessary and arranges a meeting with the funding organization's leaders to discuss the cuts and try to persuade these leaders to change their minds.

- *A juvenile probation officer is distressed by a proposed legislative action to delete a vocational training program for juvenile offenders because of its expense. He talks to other workers and administrators in his state agency, and gathers facts and statistics that support the program's cost-effectiveness. He then begins calling and writing involved legislators and sets up a meeting with the chairperson of the legislative committee that recommended the program's deletion. Additionally, he contacts other concerned social workers and encourages them to participate in similar activities.*

- *A group of community residents approach a social worker about starting a Neighborhood Watch program.[2] The worker provides them with both encouragement and some information about how to go about it.*

None of the vignettes above involve direct service to clients. Yet, all are examples of social workers undertaking necessary activities as part of their daily role in providing effective service. Each scenario describes how social workers can help people within the context of larger macro environments, namely, organizations and communities. Generalist social work is much more than working with individual clients and families. It also is working in and with larger systems.

People do not function in a void. They interact dynamically on many levels, assuming structured behavior patterns and having active involvement in various interpersonal relationships. Mary Beth is a sister, a mother, an aunt, a member of Mothers Against Drunk Driving (MADD), a Republican, a member of St. Mary and St. Antonious Coptic Orthodox Church, and a dentist, all at the same time. Understanding everything about human behavior, with all its complexity, is a vast task.

Social workers practice *in agency organizational settings* to help clients *who live in communities*. The work environments of social work practitioners provide the structure and resources allowing them to help clients. A healthy organizational work environment permits social workers to function effectively and get things done for clients. An unhealthy work environment (for example, one with few resources, poor morale, or policies not supportive of clients) interferes with social workers' performance and their potential to assist clients. Clients, in turn, live in communities that enjoy various degrees of prosperity

---

[2] Neighborhood Watch programs involve neighborhood residents coming together and making a commitment to prevent crime in their neighborhood. They devise a system for observing any suspicious behavior, especially on the part of strangers, and for alerting the proper authorities in order to deter crime. Members also usually educate new people moving into the neighborhood about the program and publicize that the program exists via window decals and signs.

and offer their citizens diverse levels of resources, support, and safety. Social workers must understand and negotiate the mazes of these macro environments in order to do their jobs effectively.

This book focuses on understanding human behavior in the *macro* social environment. How do communities, organizations, and groups serve as the background for human behavior? How do individuals and macro systems reciprocally influence each other? How do these organizations and communities operate to keep themselves and society going? What are the internal environment of communities, organizations, and the groups within them like? Exactly how and why do the answers to these questions affect how social workers can do their jobs?

Several terms reflect the meaning of macro, including: large scale; affecting many people; emphasis on social, political, and economic forces; and a focus on community. It is social workers' responsibility to seek changes in the macro social environment that improve services, increase resources for clients and citizens, and change policies to implement improvements. This contrasts with a *micro* perspective, which emphasizes the actions and personal issues of individual clients. Micro practice skills focus on treatment of individuals that helps them solve their problems.

Communities, organizations, and the task groups functioning within them are important in understanding human behavior because they consist of individuals. Comprehending the nuances of behavior involves not only the psychological makeup of individuals and the interpersonal dynamics of intimate relationships but also the interaction of these individuals with all the macro systems with which they're in contact.

This chapter will:

- Define the macro social environment.
- Introduce material addressed by the remainder of the book.
- Define generalist practice and explain the relationship between its major concepts and the macro social environment; these concepts include work within an organizational structure, using a seven-step planned change process, targeting any size system for change, adopting a wide range of professional roles, applying critical thinking skills, and focusing on empowerment, the strengths perspective, and resiliency.
- Examine ecosystems theory and explain the concepts involved that are derived from systems theories and the ecological perspective.
- Discuss people's involvement with multiple systems in the macro social environment.
- Provide a brief history of social work practice in the macro social environment.
- Discuss human diversity and empowerment in the macro social environment, explaining culture, cultural competency, oppression, population-at-risk, and the promotion of social and economic justice.
- Address four competencies involved in cultural competence.
- Introduce critical thinking questions that will be raised throughout the book.

WHAT IS THE MACRO SOCIAL ENVIRONMENT?

The *social environment* is the sum total of social and cultural conditions, circumstances, and human interactions that encompass human beings. The *macro* social environment, for our purposes, is the configuration of communities, organizations, and groups within the latter that are products of social, economic, and political forces and social institutions. The following breaks down the definition of the macro social environment into various facets and explains what each means.

The macro social environment involves communities, organizations, and groups and how these systems affect people. A *community* is "a number of people who have something in common that connects them in some way and that distinguishes them from others"; the common feature might be a neighborhood where people live, an activity people share such as jobs, or other connections like ethnic identification (Homan, 2004, p. 9). Later chapters discuss various aspects of communities including theories, community empowerment, and neighborhood empowerment.

Organizations are "(1) social entities that (2) are goal directed, (3) are designed as deliberately structured and coordinated activity systems, and (4) are linked to the external environment" (Daft, 2004, p. 11). In other words, organizations are structured groups of people who come together to work toward some mutual goal and perform established work activities that are divided among various units. Organizations have a clearly defined membership in terms of knowing who is in and who is out. Later chapters explore different facets of organizations and how they can operate to benefit or detract from clients', citizens', and employees' best interests and optimal well-being.

Social services include the work that social work practitioners and other helping professionals perform in organizations. Goals include improving people's health, enhancing their quality of life, increasing autonomy and independence, supporting families, and helping people and larger systems improve their functioning in the macro social environment (Barker, 2003). That is quite a mouthful. In essence, social services include the wide range of activities that social workers perform in their goal of helping people solve problems and improve their personal well-being.

A *social agency*, or *social services agency*, is an organization providing social services that typically employs a range of helping professionals including social workers in addition to office staff, paraprofessionals (persons trained to assist professionals), and sometimes volunteers (Barker, 2003). Social agencies generally serve some designated client population experiencing some defined need. Services are provided according to a prescribed set of policies regarding how the agency staff should accomplish their service provision goals.

A *group* is "a collection of people, brought together by mutual interests, who are capable of consistent and uniform action" (Barker, 2003, p. 184). Our concern with groups involves their significance in the context of communities and organizations. Communities and organizations are made up of groups, which, in turn, are composed of individuals. Chapters 2 and 3 will describe various types of groups and focus on the operation of task groups in the macro social environment.

Social forces are values and beliefs held by people in the social environment that are strong enough to influence people's activities, including how government is structured or restricted. Key words here are "values" and "beliefs." For example, social forces fire the debate between anti-abortion and right-to-choice factions over the abortion issue.

Economic forces are the resources that are available, how they are distributed, and how they are spent. The key word here is "resources." They involve how taxes are spent at the national level and how salaries are distributed to an agency's workers.

Political forces are the current governmental structures, the laws to which people are subject, and the overall distribution of power among the population. Political forces are reflected in laws and public policies. Here the key word is "government." Elected politicians make decisions about what rules should govern public behavior and how to distribute resources. Consider the public welfare grant program Temporary Assistance to Needy Families (TANF) established by political forces. The program, discussed more thoroughly in a later chapter, structures how needy children and their families are treated.

Often, issues, programs, or situations reflect a blend of forces. For instance, the complicated issue of national health insurance, making health care available to all citizens, has been debated for decades. Social forces reflect values on health and good medical care. However, another value is the ability to choose. Many people fear that a national health care policy will cause them to lose their ability to select a health care provider. Economic forces are also involved, as making national health care available for all would be very expensive. Currently, people who hold "good" jobs usually have health insurance provided primarily, and sometimes totally, by their employers. Some people fear that a national policy would cause them to lose resources in the form of health care benefits. Health care resources would have to be shared by more people and, therefore, easy access would be more difficult for some. Political forces clearly are involved in the national health care arena as political debate continues.

Social forces converge over time to form social institutions. A *social institution* is an established and valued practice or means of operation in a society resulting in the development of a formalized system to carry out its purpose. Examples of social institutions are "religion, the family, military structure, government, and the social welfare system" (Barker, 2003, p. 404). See Figure 1.1.

Social institutions establish expectations and requirements for expected behavior, and govern these through policies and laws. Communities provide the macro environments for social institutions to be upheld. Organizations carry out policies and distribute services social institutions deem necessary. Decision-making groups and administrators in organizations and communities implement policies and distribute services based on social institutions.

For example, consider public education in the United States. The right of all U.S. citizens to receive public education until age 18 is a social institution.

Figure 1.1
Social, Eco-
nomic, and
Political Forces
Result in For-
malized Social
Institutions That
Affect Individuals

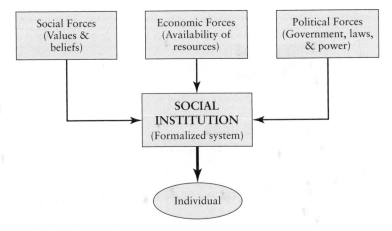

Individual schools are organizations that comply with this concept. Individual communities make decisions regarding how schools will accomplish their educational goals. Community residents determine whether new schools will be built or old ones will suffice. They decide what content will be taught to students in family life education courses and whether or not to offer music or art.

Intricate interconnections exist among social forces, social institutions, communities, organizations, and groups carrying out public directives. Sometimes, forces and institutions are not clearly distinguishable from each other. All are collectively intertwined to make up the macro social environment.

Note that the macro social environment may include macro systems of various dimensions depending on your focus of attention. It may include small groups in organizations, neighborhoods, towns, cities, large metropolitan areas, counties, states, nations, and the global macro social environment.

THE MACRO SOCIAL ENVIRONMENT AND GENERALIST SOCIAL WORK PRACTICE

Social workers help people in need using a wide range of methods. They counsel individuals, work with families, run various types of groups, help cli-ents in their communities, and strive to improve the organizations in which they practice. It is the ethical responsibility of professional social workers to address problems and issues in the macro social environment and to initiate and implement positive change (National Association of Social Workers [NASW], 1999). To do all this requires acquisition of a wide range of skills. Regardless of who their clients are or what their goals might be, social workers must follow an orderly process to get things done that stresses professional core values. This perspective is referred to as generalist practice.

Generalist practice, occurring *within an organizational structure,* is the application of an extensive and diverse knowledge base, professional values, and a wide range of skills by using a *seven-step planned change process* to *target any size system for change* within the context of three dimensions (Kirst-Ashman & Hull, 2002, 2006a, b). First, it requires the assumption of a *wide range of professional roles.* Second, it involves the *application of critical thinking skills* to the planned change process. Third, it emphasizes *client empowerment.* The following sections will address each of these concepts.[3]

WORK WITHIN AN ORGANIZATIONAL STRUCTURE

One important concept in the definition of generalist practice is that practitioners *work within an organizational structure.* Social workers are employed by social service agencies. Agencies are integral parts of larger communities in the macro social environment. Workers, thus, must understand how social service organizations and communities function both together and independently. Practitioners must know how organizational and community systems work in order to improve how they provide resources and services.

Note that the terms *generalist social worker, worker, generalist practitioner,* and *practitioner* will be used interchangeably throughout this book to refer to professionals undertaking generalist social work practice.

USING A SEVEN-STEP PLANNED CHANGE PROCESS

A second basic concept in the definition of generalist practice involves the structured change process. *Planned change* and *problem-solving* are often used interchangeably in social work. Some feel the term "change" has more positive connotations than the term "problem." Regardless of whether social workers are working with individual clients, families, large communities or any other client systems, they follow the basic seven-step process portrayed in Figure 1.2 to solve a problem or pursue a positive change (Kirst-Ashman & Hull, 2006a, b):

Step 1. *Engagement* is the process of establishing a positive professional relationship between the worker and the client. It may include greeting the client, portraying appropriate verbal and nonverbal behavior, listening to the client's issues, discussing agency services, and identifying client expectations (Kirst-Ashman & Hull, 2006b).

An example of engagement in an organization is a worker approaching the administration with a new idea about how to distribute information to clients

---

[3] Most of these concepts are taken directly from *Educational Policy and Accreditation Standards,* developed by the Council on Social Work Education (CSWE) (CSWE, 2001).

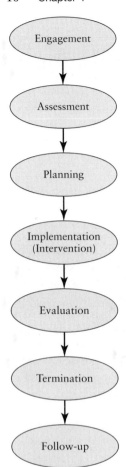

Figure 1.2
The Planned
Change Process
in Generalist
Practice

about the agency's services. A community example is a social worker attending a meeting at a senior citizen's center, introducing herself, and presenting some ideas about developing recreational activities.

Step 2. *Assessment* is the identification of the "nature and extent of client needs and concerns, as well as critical information about client resources and supports and other environment factors" so that a helping plan can be devised and implemented (Blythe and Reithoffer, 2000, p. 551). From the perspective of this book, assessment is the most significant step in the planned change process. This book's purpose is to provide information so that you as a social worker can understand what's going on in the organization where you work, other organizations with which you have contact, and the community in which all the organizations function. It should provide information for how you should think about proceeding to make and undertake effective plans.

Step 3. *Planning* is the process of identifying goals, rationally considering various ways to implement them, and establishing specific steps to achieve them. Since this and the following steps involve learning skills that are taught in practice courses, they will only be briefly mentioned here.

Step 4. *Intervention* is the actual doing or implementation of the plan. It concerns applying the skills you will learn in practice classes to achieve goals.

Step 5. *Evaluation* is the appraisal of the effectiveness of the plan and its implementation. How well did the plan work? To what extent were goals achieved?

Step 6. *Termination* is the ending of the social worker–client relationship. Virtually all relationships come to an end. Clients move. Workers get different jobs. Goals are attained and there's no longer any need for worker–client contact.

Step 7. *Follow-up* is the retrieval of information about a client's functioning after the intervention has been terminated. Follow-up may provide information about the intervention's effectiveness after the fact or it may be useful to determine if the client has new needs.

TARGETING ANY SIZE SYSTEM

The second relevant concept in the definition of generalist practice involves *targeting any size system for change*. The important thing is that generalist practitioners work with and on the behalf of systems of all sizes, including individuals, families, groups, organizations, and communities. At the community macro level, a worker might help a group of neighborhood residents develop a plan for identifying and getting rid of drug houses or start a summer recreation program for youth. At the organizational macro level, a social worker might advocate on clients' behalf with administrators to change a restrictive policy. Similarly, an agency worker might lead a task group to develop a training program for teaching workers new skills to work with involuntary or angry clients.

Theoretical or conceptual perspectives provide symbolic representations or pictures for how to view the world—in this case, the macro world of communities, organizations, and groups. Because the environment is so important in the analysis and understanding of human behavior, conceptual perspectives must be clearly defined. Social work focuses on the interactions between individuals and various systems in the environment. Because of the importance of both systems terminology and the terminology used to refer to the social environment (based in the ecological approach), the following section will explore the foundation theory upon which this book is based, namely, ecosystems theory.

Ecosystems Theory and the Macro Social Environment

The *Encyclopedia of Social Work* states that "ecosystems theory unquestionably provides the most comprehensive framework for understanding behavior. . . . Social workers often view it as an organizing framework rather than a theory of behavior or development" (Beckett & Johnson, 1995, p. 1394; Compton, Galaway, & Cournoyer, 2005; Mattaini & Meyer, 2002; Poulin, 2005). They continue that "according to ecosystems theory, psychological processes are manifestations of complex biological, interpersonal, cultural, legal, economic, organizational, and political forces" which "work together to influence human behavior throughout the life span" (p. 1391). Social systems theory can serve as a "way of thinking" or "a theory about theories" (Anderson and Carter, 1999, p. xix). Ecosystems theory is "systems theory used to describe and analyze people and other living systems and their transactions" (Beckett & Johnson, 1995, p. 1391; Zastrow & Kirst-Ashman, 2004). In other words, terms proposed by ecosystems theory can be used to characterize and explain the behavior of individuals, groups, organizations, or communities even when discussing the application of other theories. Ecosystems theory provides a general perspective and vocabulary for describing systems' functioning in the macro social environment. In essence, ecosystems theory serves as an umbrella encompassing other theories.

This book will define and explore both systems and ecological concepts that relate to understanding human behavior within the macro social environment. Later chapters will introduce additional theories relating to groups, organizations, and communities. These are included to help you gain a variety of perspectives for understanding macro systems.

Ecosystems Theory: Basic Terms Taken from Social Systems Theories

A number of terms based in social systems theories are extremely important in understanding ecosystems theory and its relationship to social work practice. They include *system, boundaries, subsystem, homeostasis, role, relationship, input, output, feedback, interface, differentiation, entropy, negative entropy,* and *equifinality.*

System A *system* is a set of elements that are orderly, interrelated, and a functional whole. An individual person is a system with biological, psychological, and social qualities and characteristics. Examples of systems are Slab City, WI; a large urban department of social services; a tiny two-person, part-time counseling center in a town of 2,356 residents; Washington, DC; Buzzard, Saskatchewan; and a local chapter of Gamblers Anonymous.

Boundaries *Boundaries* are borders or margins that separate one entity (for example, a system) from another. For instance, your skin provides a boundary between you as an independent, living system and the external environment. Boundaries determine who is a member of a system and who is not. If you haven't paid your dues to the National Association of Bungee Jumpers, the National Rifle Association, or your social work student club, you are not a member of that system. You are not within that particular system's boundaries. You are either in it or not.

Subsystem A *subsystem* is a secondary or subordinate system. It may be thought of as a smaller system within a larger system. The social work program, for example, is a subsystem of your college or university. Similarly, each member of the Denver Broncos is a subsystem of the team system.

Homeostasis *Homeostasis* is the tendency for a system to maintain a relatively stable, constant state of balance. If something disturbs the homeostatic system, that system will strive to return to its prior stable state. Members of the group Neighborhood Warriors on Trash maintain homeostasis as long as they can relate well enough to stay together and pick up garbage, their designated purpose. The system, in this case, the group, must maintain some kind of homeostasis to function.

Homeostasis, however, does not mean that all group members will like each other or even talk to each other. Harry, for example, can't stand Izod, whom he feels bullies other group members by telling them the best way to organize trash collection. However, Harry feels the group and its purpose are important enough to continue his support and involvement. He simply ignores Izod. Homeostasis merely means maintaining the status quo. Sometimes, that status quo can be ineffective, inefficient, or seriously problematic.

Another example is a community that strives to maintain its homeostasis despite having corrupt political leaders. Community members may hesitate to depose their leaders because potential replacements scare residents even more. At least the residents already know about the leaders they have. The unknown is scary even though it might be better. It also might be worse.

Roles A *role* is "a socially expected behavior pattern determined by an individual's status" and expectations in a particular group or society (Mish, 1995, p. 1014). In other words, each individual involved in a system assumes a role within that system. For instance, you assume the role of student in class. Expectations include performing required work, receiving grades the instructor assigns, and working toward your degree. If you hold a job, you assume the role of employee with whatever work expectations that job role involves. In a community, the mayor assumes a role with the decision-making responsibilities required in such a position.

Relationships   A *relationship* is the dynamic interpersonal connection between two or more persons or systems that involves how they think about, feel about, and behave toward each other. For example, a social worker may have a professional relationship with her agency supervisor. Ideally, their communication and interaction maximizes the worker's effectiveness.

Relationships may exist between systems of any size. Workers within an agency have relationships with each other. Likewise, one agency or organization has a relationship with another. A local church may establish a relationship with a community Boys' Club. Together they could recruit and train volunteers, share activity space, and cosponsor community activities for the community's male youth.

Input   *Input* is the energy, information, or communication flow received from other systems. You receive input from instructors regarding class assignments. Elected officials receive input from constituents when they vote on whether or not to support a referendum that allows building a nuclear plant. As an employee, you receive input in the form of a paycheck, not necessarily a big enough paycheck, but it is still input. Other examples include a person who breaks both arms after falling with her new 800-pound hog motorcycle who will require substantial input by others to help her take care of daily personal tasks. Still another example of input is information received from the Atlanta Centers for Disease Control about new HIV mutations.

Output   *Output,* on the other hand, is what happens to *input* after it's gone through and been processed by some system. It is a form of energy going out of a person's life or taking something away from it. For instance, a Moose Lodge may "adopt a highway" and take responsibility for cleaning up two miles of a local road. Another form of output is paying money to purchase a 2001 Honda Civic coupe. Yet another form of output is the progress made with a client. Pablo, a worker, can expend time and energy, use his knowledge and skills, and work with a client, Astrid, to achieve the goal of finding employment. The intervention's output is Astrid's employment and her level of satisfaction with it.

At times these terms are confusing. For example, in the case above, Pablo provides Astrid with his input (time, energy, knowledge, skill, and expertise). Astrid then, hopefully, has output (attaining her goal of finding a job). However, if we focus on Pablo instead of Astrid, we can apply the terms differently. Pablo's *input* includes his salary, ongoing skill development, and help from supervisors. Pablo's *output,* on the other hand, is the time, energy, knowledge, skill, and expertise he exercises to achieve intervention goals. How terms are applied and used depend on which individual, subsystem or element of the systems involved is the focus of attention. One person's input is another's output.

A related issue critically significant in social work practice is whether the output is worth all the input. Are treatment results worth how much the treatment costs? Does a community program to fight crime (that requires significant financial input) have adequate results (output) to justify how much it costs? If ten officers are hired to implement the program, how successful must the program be? Is it successful if crime is cut by 10 percent? Or 30 percent? What about 2 percent?

Many times it's difficult to measure input and output in equal units. If money is the only measurement of inputs and outputs, it makes it easier. If a stockbroker invests more (input) than he earns (output), he is losing money and better change his investment strategy. In social services, it is often difficult to measure the value of a service or the extent it adds to peoples' quality of life. For example, is a hospice program geared to enhancing the comfort of terminally ill people worth the expense? The input in terms of financial resources for treatment, care, housing, and medicine can be substantial. However, the value of such care to a dying person (the output) may be priceless.

The bottom line concerns whether the community or agency is using its resources efficiently and effectively. Or, can those resources be put to a better use by providing some other more effective and efficient service?

Negative and Positive Feedback   *Feedback* is a special form of input where a system receives information about that system's own performance. As a result of *negative feedback,* the system can choose to correct any deviations or mistakes and return to a more homeostatic state.

For example, Natasha, a community resident, might give negative feedback to Boris, another, about how Boris' small children regularly run out into a busy street while playing and riding bikes. As Natasha feels it is very dangerous for Boris' children, she gives Boris feedback about the problem. Hopefully, Boris will use this negative feedback to correct it.

Positive feedback, also valuable, is the informational input a system receives about what it is doing correctly in order to maintain itself and thrive. Receiving a significant pay raise resulting from an excellent job-performance review provides positive feedback to a worker that she is doing a good job. Likewise, an agency receiving a specific federal grant gets positive feedback that it has developed a plan worthy of such funding.

Interface   An *interface* is the point where two systems (including individuals, families, groups, organizations, or communities) come into contact with each other, interact, or communicate. An interface may be the interaction and communication between an agency supervisor and her supervisee. It may also be your communication with an instructor regarding expectations for some class assignment. A board of directors may be the interface between a community and a residential treatment center for adolescents with serious emotional and behavioral problems. Such a board is usually composed of volunteers who are influential in the community and serve to oversee agency policies, goals, and how the agency is generally run.

During an assessment of a client system's strengths, needs, and problems, the interface must be clearly in focus in order to target the appropriate interactions for change. For example, a young single mother of three is homeless and desperately needs services. The interface between her and the macro systems providing human services includes those services for which she might be eligible. The interface also involves her interactions with social workers helping to provide those services.

Differentiation   *Differentiation* is a system's tendency to move from a simple to a more complex existence. As you grow older, get wiser, have more varied experiences, meet increasing numbers of people, and assume more responsibilities in general, your life gets more complicated. You experience differentiation. Likewise, as a social agency grows over time, it will likely develop more detailed policies and programs. A women's center might start out with one support group for battered women run by one volunteer. If that support group is a success, years later it may expand and differentiate into an entire program where eight groups addressing other issues commonly experienced by women are run by paid program staff and supervised by a director. Similarly, as laws and clarifications to laws proliferate in the legal system, that system differentiates and becomes more complex.

Entropy   *Entropy* is the natural tendency of a system to progress toward disorganization, depletion, and death. The idea is that nothing lasts forever. People age and eventually die. After early periods of growth and differentiation, agencies grow old, often obsolete, and disappear. As history moves on, older agencies and systems are eventually replaced by new ones.

Negative Entropy   *Negative entropy* is the process of a system toward growth and development. In effect, it is the opposite of entropy. Individuals develop physically, intellectually, and emotionally as they grow. Social service agencies grow and develop new programs and clientele. A sheltered workshop that provides supervised training and vocational guidance for people with cognitive disabilities begins in one small building with twenty clients. Negative entropy characterizes the agency as it grows to serve over one hundred clients and adds new programs. These include an information and referral helpline, a volunteer program called Special Friends that is similar to Big Brothers/Big Sisters programs, and a wide range of supervised recreational activities.

Equifinality   *Equifinality* refers to the fact that there are many different means to achieve the same end. It is important not to get locked into only one way of thinking. In any particular situation, alternatives do exist. Some may be better than others, but, nonetheless, there are alternatives. For example, a community may need funding to start up a new community center for holding community meetings and housing social and recreational events. The end goal is establishment of a place to conduct community activities. However, there are many ways to attain this goal. A citizen group may apply for grants from public and private sources, the community may undertake a massive fundraising campaign on the center's behalf, or residents might work with county and state leaders to solicit support.

Ecosystems Theory: Basic Terms Taken from the Ecological Perspective

Ecosystems theory incorporates basic ecological concepts in addition to those proposed by systems theories. The ecological perspective "emphasizes understanding people and their environment and the nature of their trans-actions" (Barker, 2003, p. 136). We have established that concepts from both systems theories and the ecological perspective provide useful means for social workers to view the world. Both approaches focus on systems within the environment and how these systems interact with and affect people, resulting in ecosystems theory.

Some would say that subtle differences exist between the approaches and the terms inherent in each. Shriver (2004) explains: "The ecological perspective . . . explicitly defines the environment as including physical (nonhuman) elements. Social systems [theories] . . . are less explicit about the place and role of nonhuman elements in the environment. Some would also argue that social systems and ecological approaches differ in their conceptualizations of boundaries and exchange across boundaries. Recognizing these areas of disagreement, we will consider these two perspectives similar enough to be treated together here." (p. 124) Hence, we will conceptualize this as ecosystems theory.

The following concepts derived from the ecological perspective are important facets of ecosystems theory: *social environment; transactions; energy; input; output; interface; adaptation; person-in-environment fit; stressors, stress, and coping; relatedness; interdependence;* and *personal characteristics including competence, self-esteem, and self-direction.* As noted above, input, output, and interface are terms used in both approaches. See Highlight 1.1 for a brief summary of terms. To avoid redundancy, please refer to the earlier descriptions of these terms within the context of social systems theories.

The Social Environment   The *social environment* involves the conditions, circumstances, and human interactions that encompass human beings. Persons are dependent upon effective interactions with this environment in order to survive and thrive. The social environment includes the actual physical setting that society provides. This involves the type of home a person lives in, the type of work that's done, the amount of money that's available, and the laws and social rules by which people live. The social environment also includes all the individuals, groups, organizations, and systems with which a person comes

| Highlight 1.1 | **Summary of Some of the Major Concepts in Systems Theory and the Ecological Perspective** |

Some Major Concepts in Systems Theory	Similar Concepts in Both	Some Major Concepts in the Ecological Perspective
System	Input	Social Environment
Boundaries	Output	Energy
Subsystem	Interface	Adaptation
Homeostasis		Person-in-Environment Fit
Roles		Stress, Stressors, & Coping
Relationships		Relatedness
Negative Feedback		Interdependence
Positive Feedback		
Differentiation		
Entropy		
Negative Entropy		
Equifinality		

into contact. Families, friends, work groups, organizations, communities, and governments are all involved.

The *macro social environment* extends beyond the individual's interaction with immediate friends, relatives, and other individuals. We have established that it is the configuration of communities, organizations, and groups within the latter that are products of social, economic, and political forces and social institutions.

People communicate and interact with others in their environments. Each of these interactions or types of interactions are referred to as *transactions*. Transactions are active and dynamic. That is, something is communicated or exchanged. They may be positive or negative. A positive transaction may be the revelation that you won the lottery. Another positive transaction might be that you are named state social worker of the year. A negative transaction, on the other hand, might be receiving news your house burnt down or was ruined in an earthquake, destroying almost all your personal possessions. Another negative transaction is a huge fight with your significant other in which you discover your partner is having an affair.

Energy *Energy* is the natural power of active involvement between people and their environments. Energy can take the form of input or output. Use of these terms in the ecological perspective resembles that in systems theories.

Adaptation   *Adaptation* is the capacity to adjust to surrounding environmental conditions. It implies an ongoing process of change. A person must adapt to new conditions and circumstances in order to continue functioning effectively. An individual diagnosed with severe rheumatoid arthritis must adapt to new, less difficult levels of physical activity. The individual must also adapt to the process of taking required medications and performing the appropriate exercises to maximize comfort, endurance, and agility. Another example is a family whose primary breadwinner is laid off from a high-paying industrial job after a serious dip in the economy. Family members must adapt to a less costly lifestyle until input returns to its former level when the breadwinner gets a new job.

Environments also adapt and react to people. Consider the destruction of Brazil's rainforest to supply lumber and provide farmland. Many questions have been raised concerning the potential effects of this damage and the extinction of plant and animal life. Questions even have been asked about the impacts on global weather as oxygen-producing plants are destroyed. Plants, animals, and humans must all adapt to new conditions, positive or not, if they are to survive.

Person-in-Environment Fit   *Person-in-environment fit* is the extent to which "an individual's or a collective group's needs, rights, goals, and capacities" match or fit the environment's abilities to meet that person's or group's physical, social, and cultural needs (Germain & Gitterman, 1995, p. 816). Sometimes, person-in-environment fit is amazingly good. Other times, it is exceedingly poor. Many variables are involved in how an environment meets individual and groups needs.

The person-in-environment fit would likely be poor for a person using a wheelchair whose home is a third-story apartment without elevators or ramps. Likewise, Nassir is a Muslim person of color who is just beginning to learn English and lives in a neighborhood composed almost exclusively of Roman Catholic white people. The extent to which Nassir suffers neighbors' discrimination and rejection because of his differences negatively affects his person-in-environment fit. On the other hand, the extent to which neighbors accept and appreciate his differences enhances that fit.

Stress, Stressors, and Coping   Because they are so interrelated, stress, stressors, and coping will be addressed here together. A *stressor* is "a demand, situation, or circumstance" that results in physiological and/or emotional tension, in other words, stress (Zastrow & Kirst-Ashman, 2004, p. 528). *Stress*, then, is the resulting physiological and/or emotional tension produced by a stressor that affects a person's internal balance. Stressors include any of a wide range of variables and circumstances: traumatic events such as sudden deaths or discovery of fatal disease; potentially troublesome life transitions such as adolescence or old age; and other changes in living patterns like divorce. Even positive events such as getting a job, moving to a new home, or falling in love can be stressors. Adapting to new circumstances, regardless of what they are, can cause stress.

Coping is a form of adaptation where "efforts to regulate immobilizing, negative feelings" and problem-solving strategies are applied "to handle the demands posed by the life stressor" (Germain & Gitterman, 1995, p. 817). A parent must cope with the worry and distress caused by a sick child. From a macro perspective, an agency must cope with strict government regulations about service provision. A community must cope with state and federal funding cuts.

Social workers help people cope with problems and issues. Assessing people's coping skills, whether they are part of a group, organization, or community, is a critical aspect of preparing for generalist intervention.

Relatedness   *"Relatedness"* is the condition of being attached to others in friendships, social networks, kinship, and other positive relationships in the social environment (Germain & Gitterman, 1995, p. 817). People need to feel they belong and have support from others. Think of your first day of class as a freshman and all the unknowns you had to face. To what extent did you feel a sense of relatedness to the college environment? To what extent has your sense of relatedness changed from then until now? How many more people do you know now? How many friends have you made? With how many instructors' expectations have you learned to cope? To what extent do you feel a relatedness with the college or university?

Similarly, residents may experience various degrees of relatedness with their community. They may know most of the neighbors, be a member of a neighborhood association, and participate regularly in community events. On the other hand, residents may know no neighbors, lack involvement in any community activities, and feel isolated and alone. Whether an individual is a member of a group, an employee in an organization, or a neighborhood resident, that person must experience a positive sense of relatedness in order to achieve good person-in-environment fit. Assessing people's relatedness in their immediate social environment provides social workers with important clues for how to help clients get their needs met. A client's relatedness can pose many strengths upon which to draw in solving problems. Supportive people in the environment can be called upon to provide emotional, financial, housing, baby-sitting, and day care, support. If they have substantial support systems, how can these systems be used to the best advantage? If social support is sadly lacking, how can it be improved? Later, we will discuss further how groups, organizations, and communities can serve to enhance or detract from people's sense of relatedness and their overall well-being.

Interdependence   A related concept to relatedness is *interdependence,* the mutual reliance of each person upon each other person. An individual is interdependent or reliant upon other individuals and groups of individuals in the social environment. Likewise, these other individuals are interdependent upon each other for input, energy, services, and consistency.

People can't exist without each other. To get a roof over your head, you need shelter in the form of a room, apartment, flat, duplex, or house to rent,

Highlight 1.2 | Personal Characteristics

Germain and Gitterman (1995) cite three basic concepts inherent in the ecological approach that involve personal characteristics (p. 818). *Competence* is the assumption that people are naturally "motivated to affect their environment in order to survive" (Germain & Gitterman, 1995, p. 181). People should have opportunities throughout life to effectively manipulate, improve, and thrive in their environment. The implication is that social workers should nurture people's natural tendency to work and succeed in their environment. This applies to people from all walks of life. For example, impoverished people living in a border shantytown require opportunities to improve their living conditions. In addition to food and clothing, needs include financial resources for building materials, skilled help regarding how to improve dwellings, and education to establish a higher standard of living.

Self-esteem is "the extent to which one feels competent, respected, and worthy" (Germain &

Gitterman, 1995, p. 818). Each individual must feel important. In the university setting, I always try to demonstrate respect and consideration for janitors and administrative assistants. Their jobs are necessary to keep the university running. They deserve to feel important and to have self-esteem, even though their job positions and salaries fall low on the status ladder of higher education.

Self-direction is the ability to take control over one's life and make decisions that are as responsible as possible, while still respecting other people's rights (Germain & Gitterman, 1995, p. 818). This concept is almost synonymous with self-determination, a core concept in social work values. People have the right to make their own decisions and control their own behavior within their environment as long as their actions don't harm others. Thus, practitioners must vigilantly assess the extent to which people's involvement in groups, organizations, and communities allow them to demonstrate self-direction.

buy, or build from scratch. Landlords and property owners need people to build the houses. Builders and contractors need plumbers, electricians, carpenters, roofers, plasterers, appliance installers, and woodworkers, among others, to complete housing that's livable by today's standards. All these skilled tradesmen need others to teach them the necessary skills. People don't pick up such skills out of nowhere. Furthermore, someone else has to make the bricks or cut and finish the lumber. And somebody else yet has to plant and grow the trees. Still somebody else supplies the tree farmer with seeds and farming equipment. Regardless of job type, everyone needs farmers or farm labor to produce their food. And on it goes. People are interdependent.

All of the terms discussed thus far that are taken from the ecological perspective involve the essence of dynamic interactions between and among people. Highlight 1.2 cites three personal characteristics that also affect human interaction in the social environment.

People's Involvement with Multiple Systems in the Social Environment

We have established that people are constantly and dynamically involved in interactions with other systems in the social environment. There is constant activity, communication, and change. Understanding human behavior seeks to answer the question, "What is it in any particular situation that causes a

Figure 1.3
An Individual
Micro System

Personality

Emotion   Strengths

Beliefs   Weaknesses

Behavior   Goals

Interests

MICRO SYSTEM
(An Individual)

problem or creates a need?" Ecosystems theory provides a perspective for social workers to assess and understand many aspects of a situation by looking at the various systems involved. A number of useful terms for conceptualizing interaction include *target of change, micro system, mezzo system, macro system, client system,* and *macro client system.*

Generalist social work practitioners work on the behalf of individuals, families, groups, organizations, and communities. Any of these systems may be a *target of change,* the system that social workers need to change or influence in order to accomplish goals. It is helpful to think of different systems as micro, mezzo, or macro systems.

A *micro system* is an individual. We have established that a system is a set of elements that are orderly, interrelated and a functional whole. In a broad sense, this definition applies to individual persons. Hence, a person is also a type of system, for our purposes, a *micro system.* Individual systems entail all the many aspects of personality, emotion, beliefs, behavior, interests, goals, strengths, and weaknesses that make a person unique. Targeting a micro system for change involves working with an individual, identifying issues and strengths, and enhancing that person's functioning. Figure 1.3 illustrates the complexity of any individual micro system.

A *mezzo system* refers to any small group. Figure 1.4 reflects how individuals make up mezzo systems. In the macro environment, groups include those involved with organizations or communities.

A *macro system* is any system larger than a small group. This book, of course, focuses on organizations and communities.

Macro settings are made up of individuals and groups of individuals. Thus, workers must use their skills in developing relationships, interviewing, and problem-solving with individuals and groups who are responsible for making decisions about communities' and organizations' policies and activities. Workers can undertake projects, seek policy changes, and develop programs within the macro context. (Note that the explanation of specific skills for effecting macro-level change is beyond the scope of this book and is saved for future practice classes). Figure 1.5 depicts an organizational macro system that is made

Figure 1.4
Micro Systems
Make Up Mezzo
Systems

Figure 1.5
Organizations
Are Macro
Systems

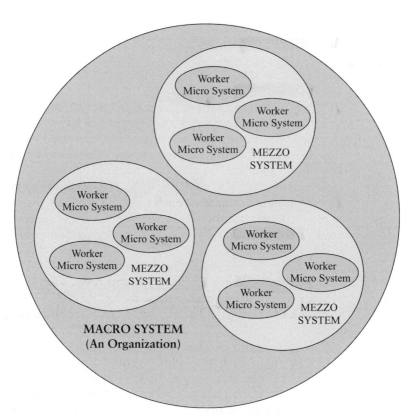

Figure 1.6
Communities
Are Macro
Systems

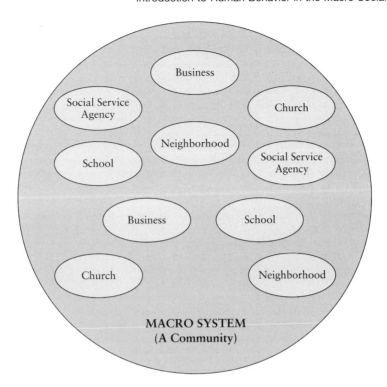

up of various groups and units (mezzo systems) that, in turn, are made up of individual workers (micro systems). Figure 1.6 illustrates a community macro system which is a complex, interconnected array of various smaller macro systems and groups (for example, neighborhoods, businesses, social service agencies, schools, and churches).

The *client system* is any individual, family, group, organization, or community who will ultimately benefit from social work intervention. Figure 1.7 portrays how social workers, client systems, and macro systems operate within the social environment. A client system may be micro, mezzo, or macro. The client system and the social worker work together for change, reflected by their close contact or interface. Arrows leading from the social worker/client system to the organization and community macro systems depict how social workers and clients work together with these macro systems in the social environment on the behalf of clients. The two-way arrow between the organization and community macro systems reflect how organizations and communities are integrally involved with each other.

Macro client systems include communities, organizations, and larger groups of clientele with similar issues and problems. The concept of macro intervention concerns agency or social change that affects larger numbers of people than an individual client or family. For example, a social worker might work with a community to establish a *food bank* (a program where

Figure 1.7
Social Workers
Help Clients
Negotiate
the Social
Environment

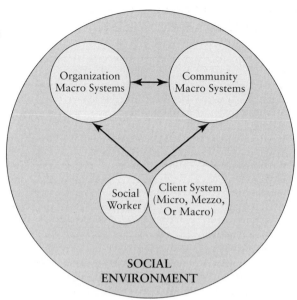

surplus food is collected from restaurants, cafeterias, grocery stores, individuals, and anywhere else it might be available, and redistributed to places such as soup kitchens serving people in need). A practitioner might also work with a social services organization to create a new position for an interpreter to serve as translator for a large population of Hmong clients who recently immigrated from Southeast Asia. Highlight 1.3 describes a history of generalist practice with and within communities serving various macro client systems.

A WIDE RANGE OF PROFESSIONAL ROLES

Another concept important in the definition of generalist practice involves the assumption of a wide range of professional roles. Such roles when working with macro systems include the following (Kirst-Ashman & Hull, 2006b, pp. 21–26; Yessian & Broskowsky, 1983, pp. 183–184):

- *Advocate:* One who steps forward on the behalf of the client system in order to promote fair and equitable treatment or gain needed resources.
- *Mediator:* One who resolves arguments or disagreements among micro, mezzo, or macro systems by assuming a neutral role.
- *Integrator/Coordinator:* One who oversees the process of assembling different elements to form a cohesive whole, product, or process (for example, a new agency policy) and subsequently watches over its functioning to make sure it's effective.

| **Highlight 1.3** | **The History of Generalist Practice with and within Communities** |

Macro practice is generalist social work practice intending to affect change in large systems, including communities and organizations. Historically, *community organization* has been the term used to refer to macro practice in social work. The methods and directions of social work practice have changed and evolved, just as the economic and social realities of the times have drastically changed. However, reviewing the historical perspective on community practice helps us to understand the significance of community assessment and work today.

Past major methods of community organization engaged in by social workers have included social action, social planning, and locality development (Rothman, 2001). *Social action* is coordinated effort to advocate for change in a social institution to benefit a specific population (for example, homeless people), solve a social problem, enhance people's well-being, or correct unfairness (for example, racism) (Kirst-Ashman & Hull, 2006a, b). (*Racism* is the belief that people of different races are inherently different and that some races are superior to others.) Social action applies macro-practice skills to advocate for people in local, state, national, and global communities. Frequently, social action can be used to remedy imbalances of power.

Social planning involves "a technical process of problem-solving with regard to substantive social problems, such as delinquency, housing, and mental health" (Rothman, 2001, p. 31). The emphasis here is to call in experts or consultants to work, usually with designated community leaders, to solve specific problems. People in the general community would have little, if any, participation or input into the problem-solving process. For example, a city might call in an urban renewal expert to recommend what should be done with a deteriorating area in the community.

Locality development emphasizes "community change . . . pursued optimally through broad participation of a wide spectrum of people at the local community level in determining goals and taking . . . action" (Rothman, 2001, p. 29). The idea is to involve as many people as possible within the community in a democratic manner to define their goals and help themselves. Locality development fits extremely well with social work values. Individual dignity, participation, and free choice are emphasized.

Today, *macro practice* is still a major thrust of generalist social work. The basic concept of community is just as important as ever. Most macro practice today takes place within an organizational context. Necessary skills are those that involve changing agency or public social policies, initiating and conducting projects within agency or community contexts, and planning and implementing programs.

- *General Manager:* One who assumes some level of administrative responsibility for a social services agency or other organizational system.
- *Educator:* One who gives information and teaches skills to other systems.
- *Analyst/Evaluator:* One who determines the effectiveness of a program or agency for an organization or community.
- *Broker:* One who links any size system (individuals, families, groups, organizations, or communities) with community resources and services.
- *Facilitator:* One who guides a group experience.
- *Initiator:* One who calls attention to an issue or problem.
- *Negotiator:* One who acts to settle disputes and/or resolve disagreements, acting on the behalf of one of the parties involved.
- *Mobilizer:* One who identifies and convenes community people and resources and makes them responsive to unmet community needs.

APPLICATION OF CRITICAL THINKING SKILLS

Critical thinking is yet another important concept in the definition of generalist practice. *Critical thinking* is (1) the careful scrutiny of what is stated as true or what appears to be true and the resulting expression of an opinion or conclusion based on that scrutiny, and (2) the creative formulation of an opinion or conclusion when presented with a question, problem, or issue. Critical thinking concentrates on "the process of reasoning" (Gibbs & Gambrill, 1999, p. 3). It stresses *how* individuals think about the truth inherent in a statement or *how* they analyze an issue to formulate their own conclusions. As Gibbs & Gambrill (1999) so aptly state, "Critical thinkers question what others take for granted" (p. 13). This is an essential concept when trying to understand what's going on in the macro environment in which you work as a social worker.

Two dimensions included in the definition of critical thinking are significant. First, critical thinking focuses on the questioning of beliefs, statements, assumptions, lines of reasoning, actions, and experiences. You read a "fact" in a book or hear about it from a friend or an instructor. Critical thinking focuses on *not* taking this "fact" at face value. Rather, it entails assuming the following Triple A approach to seriously examine and evaluate its validity:

1. *Ask* questions.
2. *Assess* the established facts and issues involved.
3. *Assert* a concluding opinion.

For example, a friend and fellow student might tell you, "Gasoline prices will never go down again." To what extent is this statement really true? To find out, first you could *ask* questions about what the statement is really saying. What does "never" mean? Does it include differences in price from day to day, or between one gas station and another or one area of the country and another? What future economic factors might influence the cost of gas? Is it possible to predict the future accurately as if looking into a crystal ball? What experiences has your friend had to come to such a conclusion?

Second, *assess* the established facts and issues involved by seeking out information to answer the questions. What is the track record of the average daily gas price in your area? To what extent has it fluctuated over time? What variables might affect the cost and potentially decrease its cost—discovery of new oil fields, drilling in Alaska, development of alternative fuels, increased use of public transportation, regulation of gas costs by the government?

Third, *assert* a concluding opinion. To what extent do you agree with your friend's statement? Or, would you prefer to assume a more optimistic stance and wait and see?

Critical thinking can be applied to virtually any belief, statement, assumption, line of reasoning, action, or experience proposed as being true. Consider the following statements that someone might maintain as "facts":

- Rich people are arrogant.
- Politicians are crooks.
- It is physically impossible for pigs to look up into the sky.

- Rats and horses can't vomit.
- A duck's quack doesn't echo, and no one knows why.[4]

These statements are silly (although some may be true), but the point is that critical thinking can be applied to an infinite array of thoughts and ideas. For each of the statements above: (1) what questions would you *ask;* (2) how would you *assess* the established facts and issues involved; and (3) what concluding opinion would you finally *assert?*

The second facet of the definition of critical thinking is the creative formulation of an opinion or conclusion when presented with a question, problem, or issue. Instead of being presented with a proposed "fact" to be scrutinized for its validity, you are asked your opinion about an issue, assumption, or action. Examples include:

- Should murderers receive the death penalty?
- Should national health care be made available to all citizens who need it and be paid for by the government?
- What is the best way to eliminate poverty in this nation?

Consider answering the last question. It could be posed as a term paper question in one of your courses. First, what questions about it would you *ask?* What are the reasons for poverty in a rich industrialized country? What social welfare programs are currently available to address poverty? What innovative new ideas for programs might be tried? Where might funding for such programs be found? How much money would it take to eliminate poverty, and who would pay for it?

Second, what facts and issues would you seek to address and *assess?* You probably would first seek to define poverty—what makes a person or family considered "poor?" What income level or lack of income is involved? You then might research statistics, costs, and studies concerning the effectiveness of various programs intended to reduce poverty. You might also investigate innovative ideas. Perhaps, there are proposals for programs that you feel look promising. You might explore what various programs cost and how they are funded. Note that these suggestions only scratch the surface of how you might examine the issue.

Third, *assert* your opinion or conclusion. To what extent do you think it is possible to eliminate poverty? What kinds of resources and programs do you think it would take? What do you feel citizens and their government should do about poverty?

Critical thinking enhances self-awareness and the ability to detect various modes of distorted thinking that can trick people into assuming truth (Gibbs & Gambrill, 1999). The following are among the many traps to avoid by using critical thinking (Ruscio, 2006, pp. 6–10):

- *Outward appearance of science.* A supposed "fact" may superficially be cited in the context of scientific proof. How many times have you seen

---

[4] The last three statements were received in an email from Keith McClory on January 12, 2002.

some well-groomed man wearing a doctor's lab coat appear in a television commercial and state that this weight-loss supplement's effectiveness has been scientifically proven many times over? What questions might you ask about this? What tests were run to prove this effectiveness? Was the supplement taken by people who also were implementing other weight-loss approaches, including exercise and diet restrictions? Is the professional-looking person on TV telling the truth or being paid to read from a script? A related issue involves dietary supplements of all kinds that are supposed to do miraculous things for your health. Current federal standards allow "for anyone to sell almost any drug to the public, as long as he or she refers to the drug as a dietary supplement and does not make specific health claims about its effects. . . . Unproven remedies . . . are now officially tolerated under the guise of dietary supplements. . . . Vague wording and the sheer number of people who routinely violate . . . [legislative] provisions . . . have resulted in insufficient enforcement of even these weak standards" (Ruscio, 2006, p. 65). Hence, we really don't know the extent to which various supplements are helpful or harmful.

- *Absence of skeptical peer review.* Has the fact been evaluated by credible professionals who support its validity? There is an almost infinite number of websites on the internet addressing almost any topic you could think of and claiming almost any "fact" to be true. A scary thing is that it's almost impossible to tell which sites have well-established validity and credibility and which do not. Usually, websites ending in *.edu* or *.gov* enhance credibility potential because they're supposed to be initiated by formal educational or governmental organizations. But, how do you know for sure?

- *Reliance on personal experience and testimonials.* A woman enthusiastically proclaims, "This exercise equipment gave me awesome abs and made me look twenty years younger!" Because an approach worked for one person doesn't mean it will work for all. Perhaps that woman worked out with the equipment three hours a day for the past year. How has diet and stress management contributed to her youthful appearance? How old is she anyway, and can she prove it? Is she telling the truth? What scientific evidence is available to document the effectiveness of the equipment?

- *Wishful thinking* (p. 43). Hoping that something is so can provide a powerful incentive to believe in it. For example, consider the idea, "Putting magnets on your head can cure headaches." It would be nice to find an automatic cure for headaches that did not involve imbibing some substance. However, Ruscio (2006) explains:

> What about the alleged healing power of magnets as they interact with our bodies? The suggestion for how a magnetic field might be useful in curing disease is that it increases the flow of blood (which contains iron) to a targeted area, thereby bringing extra nutrients and carrying away the waste products of our metabolism. This theory, too, is directly contradicted by known facts. Blood, as with other bodily tissue and fluids, consists primarily of water. Thus, the fact that water is slightly repelled by a magnetic field is especially

relevant. Why? Because the primary constituent of the human body—including not only our blood but also, as in most forms of life, all of our tissues and fluids—is water. We are therefore weakly repelled by magnetic fields. In principle, a strong enough magnet could be used to levitate a person, as has been done with drops of water, flowers, grasshoppers, and frogs. The small amounts of iron in our blood's hemoglobin do not exist in sufficiently dense quantities to offset the repulsive effect of the much larger amount of water. Therefore, to the extent that magnets have *any* influence on our blood—and this influence is minimal—they will drive blood *away* from the targeted areas." (pp. 82–83)

- *The "ancient wisdom" fallacy* (p. 59). "That must be the right way to do it because we've always done it that way." Ruscio (2006) points out that this type of argument can have dangerous consequences, because "if beliefs are granted truth owing merely to their age, this would provide justification for sexism, racism, anti-Semitism, and a host of other repellent notions that have been widely held throughout human history" (p. 59).
- *The popularity fallacy* (p. 59). "Everybody else is doing it, so it must be right." I once had a classmate, age 26 no less, who said in an election year that he was going to vote for the current president because that president had already been elected, and all those people who voted for him surely couldn't be wrong. I stared at him in total disbelief. How could he be so naïve? How could he not think for himself? And, at his age? He obviously believed in the popularity fallacy.

Because of the importance of critical thinking in social work and in generalist practice, as well as in understanding macro systems and the social environment, a wide range of critical thinking questions will be posed throughout this book.

 Critical Thinking Questions 1.1

What do you think about critical thinking? Do you use it often? If so, to what extent have you found it useful?

FOCUS ON EMPOWERMENT AND THE STRENGTHS PERSPECTIVE

The final vital concept in the definition of generalist practice and an ongoing theme throughout social work is *empowerment*, the "process of increasing personal, interpersonal, or political power so that individuals can take action to improve their life situations" (Gutierrez, 2001, p. 210). The empowerment approach is a perspective on practice that provides "ways of thinking about and doing practice" (Lee, 2001, p. 32). Throughout the assessment process and our quest to understand human behavior in macro systems, it's critical to emphasize, develop, and nurture strengths and positive attributes in systems of all sizes to empower people. Empowerment aims at enhancing individuals', group's, families', and communities' power and control over their destinies. Empowerment involves social workers striving to improve people's:

- *Positive sense of self-worth and competence* ("I am important." "I am capable of getting things done.")
- *Ability to influence the course of one's life* ("I have control over what I do." "I can make and follow plans to accomplish my goals.")
- *Capacity to work with others to control aspects of public life* ("I am an important part of my community and other larger systems, and can work with others to improve our quality of life." "In collaboration with others, I can make improvements in my community, in the organization where I work, and in other groups to which I belong.")
- *Ability to access the mechanisms of public decision making* ("I can influence community and organizational decision makers." "My vote counts.") (Walsh, 2006, p. 21; Lee, 2001).

Walsh (2006) explains:

Many clients do not, or perceive that they do not, have power, either over themselves, their significant others, or the agencies and communities in which they reside. This sense of powerlessness underlies many problems in living. It can be internalized and lead to learned helplessness and alienation from one's community. An empowerment orientation to practice represents the social worker's efforts to combat the alienation, isolation, and poverty . . . in clients' lives by positively influencing their sense of worth, sense of membership in a community, and ability to create change in their surroundings. (p. 21)

Empowerment in generalist practice involves critical thinking about how macro systems affect people (Lee, 2001). To what extent are people getting the resources and support they need from their communities and organizations within their communities? Why or why not?

The Strengths Perspective

Focusing on strengths can provide a sound basis for empowerment. Sometimes referred to as the *strengths perspective*, this orientation focuses on client resources, capabilities, knowledge, abilities, motivations, experience, intelligence, and other positive qualities that can be put to use to solve problems and pursue positive changes (Sheafer & Horejsi, 2003).

Assessment of human behavior establishes the basis for understanding people's problems and issues, and subsequently helping them improve their lives. Social workers address people's problems everyday, but it's the identification of people's strengths that provides clues for how to solve these problems and improve their life situations. Saleebey (2002) cites the following principles involved in the strengths perspective:

- *Every individual, group, family, and community has strengths.* Even during people's darkest times, it's important to identify and emphasize strengths. Strengths include intelligence, good character, close family, good friends, spiritual faith, a job, a place to live, talent, personality, and any other positive thing you can think of.
- *Trauma and abuse, illness and struggle may be injurious, but they may also be sources of challenge and opportunity.* Think of one of the worst experiences you've ever had. Regardless of how terrible it was at the time, were you able to turn it around and learn something from it? To some extent, did it make you a stronger or wiser person?
- *Assume that you do not know the upper limits of the capacity to grow and change and take individual, group, and community aspirations seriously.* It's impossible to foresee the future and know all the opportunities you will encounter and the barriers you will face. A strengths perspective emphasizes that it's important to set goals and to eagerly pursue opportunities when they occur.
- *We best serve clients by collaborating with them.* Saleebey (2002), a social worker, reflects about a client he knows:

  "Mrs. Johnson knows more about thriving in a public housing project than anyone I can think of. Over the course of 35 years, she successfully raised 11 children. She maintained a demeanor of poise, and she demonstrated intelligence and vigor, even as her community underwent dramatic, often frightening changes. Her contributions to the community are, simply put, amazing. She has much to teach us and other residents of her community. I certainly would not presume to work on Ms. Johnson but would be privileged to work with her" (p. 16).

- *Every environment is full of resources.* Resources can provide great strengths. One of social workers' major roles is to link clients with the resources they need to empower them to improve their lives.
- *Caring, caretaking, and context are key.* Social workers care about others. They are concerned about the environment or context in which people live. They recognize that communities and social service organizations should, respectively, take care of their citizens and the people they serve (pp. 14–18).

Individuals, families, groups, organizations, and communities all have strengths. It's a goal of generalist practice to identify these strengths and use them to solve problems and make effective plans to enhance people's well-being. To orient you to the process of identifying strengths, Highlight 1.4 asks a number of questions about your own personal arsenal of strengths.

| Highlight 1.4 | **What Are Your Strengths?** |

Individual Strengths

- What do you see as your most significant personal strengths?
- What challenges have you overcome about which you're especially proud?

Family Strengths

- What strengths do you see in your own family?
- In what ways does your family put these strengths to use?
- In times of trouble, how does your family contribute to your own personal sense of strength?

Group Strengths

- To what social, work, and other types of groups do you belong?
- Do you have special people upon whom you can rely? If so, who are they and in what ways do they support you?

- What are the strengths inherent in these groups?
- How do these group strengths contribute to your own personal sense of strength?

Organizational Strengths

- To what organizations do you belong (for example, clubs, work settings, churches, recreational groups, sports groups, volunteer groups)?
- What are the strengths in these organizations?
- How do these organizational strengths contribute to your own personal sense of strength?

Community Strengths

- What are the strengths in the community where you live?
- How do these strengths contribute to your own quality of life?

Resiliency: Using Strengths to Combat Difficulty

A concept related to the strengths perspective and empowerment is resiliency. *Resiliency* is the ability of an individual, family, group, community, or organization to recover from adversity and resume functioning, even when suffering serious trouble, confusion, or hardship. Whereas the "strengths perspective focuses on capabilities, assets, and positive attributes rather than problems and pathologies," resiliency emphasizes the use of strengths to cope with adversity and survive, despite difficulties (Gutheil & Congress, 2002, p. 41).

Norman (2000) provides an illustration of the concept of resiliency:

> When a pitched baseball hits a window, the glass usually shatters. When that same ball meets a baseball bat, the bat is rarely damaged. When a hammer strikes a ceramic vase, it too usually shatters. But when that same hammer hits a rubber automobile tire, the tire quickly returns to its original shape. The baseball bat and the automobile tire both demonstrate resiliency." (p. 3)

Resiliency involves two dimensions—risk and protection (Norman, 2000). In this context, *risk* involves "stressful life events or adverse environmental conditions that increase the *vulnerability* [defenselessness or helplessness] of individuals" or other systems (p. 3). *Protection,* on the other hand, concerns those factors that "buffer, moderate, and protect against those vulnerabilities" (p. 3).

Perez-Koenig (2000) describes an example of an organization in a community that builds on the strengths and resiliency of Hispanic youth. The

Unitas Extended Family Circle (UEFC) conducts outreach to Hispanic youth in the South Bronx of New York City. UEFC "recognizes the devastating effects of urban ghettos on people, particularly children and youth, and firmly believes in the healing power of all people, in their strengths, capacities, aspirations, and the availability of internal and external resources" (Perez-Koenig, 2000, pp. 143–144). It builds on

protective factors

> strengths that emanate from the Hispanic culture's core values of "personalismo" [that is, "valuing and building interpersonal relationships" (Santiago-Rivera, Arredondo, & Gallardo-Cooper, 2002, p. 44)] and respect, familism [that is, "a preference for maintaining a close connection to family" (Santiago-Rivera et al., 2002, p. 42)] and spirituality. Each individual is respected and valued, regardless of status. Respect emphasizes "being" and "who," rather than competition and "what." There is a substantial reverence for life, and for living in the moment. Familism locates the family, rather than the individual, as the most important social system. The family is a source of identity and support. Familism for most Hispanics includes the entire extended family. This extendedness emphasizes strong feelings of identification, loyalty, and solidarity. Extended family refers not only to the traditional kin, related by blood or marriage, such as aunts, uncles, and cousins, but also includes non-blood, non-marriage related persons who are considered family—compadres and comadres (godfathers and god-mothers) and hijos de crianza (children who are raised as members of the family). The extended family provides an indispensable source of instrumental and expressive support. . . .
>
>   . . .UEFC invites children and adolescents to become members of make-believe small families and of the large, agencywide, extended family. . . . Through corrective make-believe family relationships (in small groups as well as in the larger group of the community) participants develop better adaptive or coping mechanisms. . . . The large family circle is decentralized into small symbolic families, to permit an individual sense of belonging without anonymity. . . . UEFC meetings reinforce in each participant their identity as a member of this extended family (a make-believe extended kinship network), as well as their membership in their small symbolic families. The use of rituals, stories, group discussions, and clear norms and rules maintain a milieu necessary for healing relationships to be experienced in an emotional climate of mutual trust and peaceful, nonviolent transactions. (Perez-Koenig, 2000, pp. 145–149)

The importance of spirituality which "lies at the core of the Hispanic culture" is stressed (Perez-Koenig, 2000, p. 146). In addition,

> The make-believe parents, aunts, and uncles (caretakers) participate in an ongoing weekly training program led by a professional social worker. The goal of these sessions is to enable "helpers of children" to learn interpersonal skills which will encourage children to be effective, happy, and cooperative. In the training program they learn skills to raise children's self-esteem and feelings of competency; skills to communicate effectively with children; skills to help children resolve conflicts and solve problems. (Perez-Koenig, 2000, p. 149)

The formulated families meet weekly. Children are encouraged to share their feelings and ideas. Caretakers work to meet children's and adolescents' needs by nurturing them, teaching them communication and problem-solving skills, and providing an environment where they feel important and safe. The basic idea is to enhance children's natural resiliency by stressing and developing their strengths.

OTHER IMPORTANT PRINCIPLES CHARACTERIZING SOCIAL WORK IN THE MACRO SOCIAL ENVIRONMENT

Empowerment implies that people lack power and thereby need it increased. Several designated groups of people suffer from stereotypes, discrimination, and oppression. A *stereotype* is a fixed mental picture of a member of some specified group based on some attribute or attributes that reflect an overly simplified view of that group, without consideration or appreciation of individual differences" (Kirst-Ashman, 2007, p. 57). *Discrimination* is "the act of treating people differently based on the fact that they belong to some group" rather than on their individual merit (Kirst-Ashman, 2007, p. 57). *Oppression* is the act of "placing extreme limitations and constraints on some person, group, or larger system" (Kirst-Ashman, 2007, p. 57). It is social work's task to empower clients in general, and members of oppressed groups in particular. Several concepts relating to this issue are *human diversity, oppression, populations-at-risk, culture, cultural competence,* and *the promotion of social and economic justice.* These ideas are basic to understanding the ongoing dynamics in the macro social environment.

Human Diversity

Human diversity refers to "the range of differences between people in terms of race, ethnicity, age, geography, religion, values, culture, orientations, physical and mental health, and other distinguishing characteristics" (Barker, 1995, p. 172). Lum (2004) explains:

> *Diversity* emphasizes *the similarities and differences among ethnic and cultural persons and groups.* The diversity of the United States includes differences in ethnicity, gender, sexual orientation, and age. In speaking of diversity, we recognize *the similarities that bind us together and respect the differences among cultures* in our country." (p. 5)

Social work by nature addresses virtually any type of problem posed by any type of person from any type of background. To help people, practitioners must be open-minded, nonjudgmental, knowledgeable, and skilled to work with any client. Social work education is charged with teaching knowledge, skills, and values concerning "clients' age, class, color, culture, disability, ethnicity, family structure, gender, marital status, national origin, race, religion, sex, and sexual orientation" (Council on Social Work Education [CSWE], 2001, 3.3). Highlight 1.5 discusses sexual orientation and the expression of gender as aspects of human diversity.

| Highlight 1.5 | **Sexual Orientation and the Expression of Gender** |

Sexual orientation, a significant aspect of diversity, is sexual and romantic attraction to persons of one or both genders. Terms concerning sexual orientation are important to understand. Puglia and House (2006) explain:

> Language is important for what it communicates as well as what it implies. Throughout their lives, gays, lesbians, and bisexuals hear biased and offensive street language such as "queer," "faggot," "homo," "dyke," and "queen." This language affects the self-esteem of gays, lesbians, and bisexuals, stigmatizes them, and is just as offensive to these populations as ethnic slurs are to various ethnic populations" (p. 516).

People having a sexual orientation toward the same gender are generally referred to as *gay* if they are male and *lesbian* if they are female. However, many people use the term gay to refer both to lesbians and gay men. The older term referring to same-gender sexual orientation is *homosexual.* People having a sexual orientation toward persons of the opposite gender are *heterosexual,* also referred to as *straight.* People sexually oriented toward either gender are referred to as *bisexual.*

It's difficult if not impossible to state exactly how many people are lesbian or gay. Many lesbian and gay organizations maintain that gays and lesbians make up 10 percent of the population. One lesbian and gay organization is called "The Ten Percent Society." After reviewing a number of more recent studies, McAnulty and Burnette (2003) conclude that it appears that about 5 percent of all men are gay and 3 percent of all women are lesbians. Regardless of whether lesbian and gay people make up 1 or 10 percent of the population, they are a sizable minority group.

Intersex and Transgender People

In an overly simplistic, naïve view of the world, one might think, "You're either a male or you're a female. Period." However, in reality neither gender nor sexual orientation are such simple concepts. Money (1987) proposes eight factors of gender that

more fully portray some of the complexity of gender. The first six are physical variables that include chromosomal predisposition to gender; the presence of either ovaries or testes; exposure to male or female hormones prior to birth; brain differentiation resulting from hormones prior to birth; the presence of female or male internal reproductive organs; exterior genital appearance; and the production of either male or female hormones during puberty. The two psychological variables are the gender assigned at birth ("It's a boy" or "It's a girl") and the person's *gender identity* (one's perception of oneself as being either "female" or "male").

About 2 percent of people are born with contradictions among Money's first six physical variables, such as some mixture of male and female predisposition and configuration of reproductive structures (Blackless, et al., 2000). Such a person is referred to as *pseudohermaphrodite* or *intersex.* A true *hermaphrodite* is a person "born with fully formed ovaries and fully formed testes, which is very, very rare" (Carroll, 2005, p. 70).

Another variation in the expression of gender involves *transgenderism,* including "people whose appearance and/or behaviors do not conform to traditional gender roles" (Crooks & Baur, 2005, p. 63), "who live full- or part-time in the other gender's role" (that is, their non-biological gender), "and derive psychosocial comfort in doing so" (Carroll, 2005, p. 85). Among these people are *transsexuals,* people who feel they are imprisoned in the physical body of the wrong gender. Since their gender identity and sense of self are at odds with their biological inclination, they often seek to adjust their physical appearance closer to that of their gender identity through surgery and hormonal treatment. Many transsexual people prefer to be referred to as transgendered people. The word "transsexual" emphasizes "sexual," whereas "transgender" emphasizes "gender" identity, which they say is the real issue.

Because lesbian, gay, bisexual, and transgender people face some of the same problems, when referring to them as a group, we will use the term LGBT (i.e., lesbian, gay, bisexual, and transgender) (Morrow, 2006).

continued

Highlight 1.5 | *continued*

Homophobia

A major problem LGBT people face is *homophobia,* the irrational "hatred, fear, or dislike" of gay, lesbian, and bisexual people (Morales, 1995, p. 1089). Although not all LGBT people suffer from the impacts of homophobia in all its forms everyday, all LGBT people must endure some forms at some times (Tully, 2001). In order to help LGBT people cope with the results of homophobia, social workers must understand their life situations and environmental issues.

LGBT people may suffer from homophobia in at least three ways, one of which is *overt "victimization";* Dworkin (2000) remarks:

Anti-LGB[T] violence is more common than most people realize. . . . All the symptoms commonly associated with posttraumatic stress [a condition in which a person continues to reexperience some traumatic event like a bloody battle or a sexual assault] are likely to follow a physical or verbal attack, in varying degrees of intensity, depending on the circumstances of the attack and the vulnerability of the victim. In a 4-year study of hate crimes against LGB[T] people, Herek et al. [1997] found that stress,

depression, and anger lingered for as long as 5 years after the attack. In addition to post-traumatic symptoms, an LGB[T] client can experience anxiety about his or her sexual identification [Bridgewater, 1992]." (p. 170)

A second way LGBT people encounter homophobia involves *covert victimization,* where discrimination occurs that is not obvious. For instance, Erik, a 21-year-old gay man and college student, applies for a part-time job at Bubba's Big Burgers, a local fast-food restaurant. Bruce, the manager, somehow finds out that Erik is gay. He chooses to hire another applicant for the position who is heterosexual (or so Bruce thinks) because that applicant is more "appropriate."

A third way LGBT people suffer from homophobia involves internalizing it (Dworkin, 2000; Tully, 2001). If the majority of those around them are homophobic, making fun of and severely criticizing LGBT people, it's fairly easy for LGBT people to start believing it themselves. Results may include "low self-esteem, depression, suicidal ideation, substance abuse, isolation, self-loathing . . . or acting out" (Tully, 2001, p. 610).

Culture

The term culture is often used with respect to the macro social environment. *Culture* is "a way of life including widespread values (about what is good and bad), beliefs (about what is true), and behavior (what people do every day)" (Macionis, 2005, p. 470). It involves "the sum total of life patterns passed on from generation to generation within a group of people and includes institutions, language, religious ideals, habits of thinking, artistic expressions, and patterns of social and interpersonal relationships" (Hodge, Struckmann, & Trost, 1975; Lum, 1999, p. 2). Aspects of culture are often related to people's ethnic, racial, and spiritual heritage.

Culture is evident in both communities and organizations. For example, a geographic community's culture may be based on Hispanic, Jewish, African-American, or white Anglo customs and expectations. Or, it may reflect a mixture of cultural traditions and heritages.

Organizations also have culture. On one level, organizational culture involves the diversity and backgrounds of its staff. On another level, *organizational culture* is defined as "the set of key values, beliefs, understandings, and norms that members of . . . an organization share" (Daft, 2003, p. 747). Later chapters discuss organizational culture further.

Cultural Competence

Social workers must develop cultural competence in order to work effectively with clients from various cultural, ethnic, and racial backgrounds.

Cultural competence is "the set of knowledge and skills that a social worker must develop in order to be effective with multicultural clients" (Lum, 1999, p. 3). Cultural competence, strongly supported by the NASW Code of Ethics (NASW, 1999, 1.05), involves several dimensions (Lum, 2005; NASW, 1999, 1.05). Workers should strive to develop an awareness of personal values, assumptions, and biases. They should establish a positive approach toward and an appreciation of other cultures. They should work to understand how their own cultural heritage and belief system differs from and may influence interaction with clients who have a different cultural background. Workers should recognize the existence of stereotypes, discrimination, and oppression for various diverse groups. They should develop a nonjudgmental attitude and learn about the cultures of their clients. Finally, practitioners should develop attitudes that respect differences and effective skills for working with people from other cultures.

Sue (2006) suggests that social workers should have four competencies (that is, appropriate skills, knowledge, ability, and understanding) in the area of cultural competence.

Competency One: Becoming Aware of One's Own Assumptions, Values, and Biases about Human Behavior   What biases, stereotypes, and beliefs do you hold about various diverse groups? Everyone has them. Social workers must take care not to make automatic assumptions about diverse groups in the social environment. They must strive to appreciate human differences yet view each client system as an individual. It's an ongoing, endless process to identify, clarify, and evaluate your own values.

 Critical Thinking Questions 1.2

Do you automatically make assumptions about any particular group based on their race, culture, gender, sexual orientation, religion, economic status, or ability level? If so, what are these assumptions? To what extent are they fair or accurate?

Competency Two: Understanding the Worldview of Culturally Diverse Clients   Before social workers can work objectively and effectively with clients, they must strive to become aware of the lens through which they view the world. *Worldview* concerns "one's perceptions of oneself in relation to other people, objects, institutions, and nature. It relates to one's view of the world and one's role and place in it" (Leashore, 1995, p. 112). Slattery (2004) explains:

> Our worldview influences whether we see the glass as half full or half empty or even whether it contains fluid at all. . . . [It] is a way of organizing and distilling huge

amounts of complex material into simple and understandable forms, which allows us to respond to the world more rapidly and efficiently. Imagine the feeling of having to pay attention to every piece of information that was received every minute of the day. The sound of the rain on the window, the temperature of the room, the feel of a book, the sound of pages being turned, and one leg on the opposite knee with one foot on the floor. The amount of information sensed at any moment is overwhelming. So, we perceive only part of it and use a still smaller portion. . . . Our worldview serves as a filter, accepting information that makes sense and discarding information that does not fit. (pp. 88–89)

Social workers must be aware of their own values and biases so that they don't impose their ideas on clients. They must also explore carefully with clients the clients' own worldviews. It is a practitioner's job to try to view the social environment from the client's perspective in order to help that client make the most effective decisions.

 Critical Thinking Questions 1.3

How would you describe your own worldview? What are the major values and beliefs that support this worldview?

Competency Three: Developing Appropriate Intervention Strategies and Techniques   Sue (2006) explains:

> Social work and social workers must begin the process of developing appropriate and effective helping, teaching, communication, and intervention strategies in working with culturally diverse groups and individuals. This competency means . . . systems intervention as well as traditional one-to-one relationships. Additionally, it is important that the social worker have the ability to make use of indigenous helping/healing approaches and structures that may already exist in the minority community . . . The concept here is to build on the strengths of a community and to empower . . . [its residents] in their ability to help themselves . . . Effectiveness in helping clients is most likely enhanced when the social worker uses intervention modalities and defines goals that are consistent with the life experiences and cultural values of clients. (p. 27)

Competency Four: Understanding Organizational and Institutional Forces that Enhance or Negate Cultural Competence   Communities may not be tolerant or supportive of various diverse groups. "In many cases, organizational customs do not value or allow the use of cultural knowledge or skills. Some social service organizations may even actively discourage, negate, or punish multicultural expressions. Or client problems may be the result of institutions that oppress them. Thus, it is imperative to view cultural competence for organizations as well. . . . Developing new rules, regulations, policies, practices, and structures within organizations that enhance multiculturalism is important" (p. 28).

Oppression

We have established that oppression is the act of placing extreme limitations and constraints on some person, group, or larger system. Essentially, oppression involves conditions where "one segment of the population acts to prevent another segment from attaining access to resources"; often the dominating group tries to inhibit the other group's freedom or look for ways to "devalue them" (Van Soest & Garcia, 2003, p. 35). People with lesser power, usually falling into some category of distinguishable characteristics (for example, race, religion, political party, age, or disability), are denied rights, treated unfairly, or put down by a group holding greater power.

Van Soest and Garcia (2003) introduce at least three elements that are common to all oppression:

> First, oppression always bestows power and advantage on certain people who are regarded as the norm and denied to others based on status as the 'other' or different. The defined norm (i.e., White, male, heterosexual) is the standard of *rightness* against which all others are judged; the 'other' (i.e., not White, not male, not heterosexual) is not only different from the norm, but is also believed and perceived to be inferior and deviant, which then justifies conferring advantage on those who fit the norm and disadvantaging the other. . . .
>
> A second element common to all oppressions is that they are held in place by ideology [i.e., a systematic manner of thinking, in this case, about people and their behavior] and violence or the threat of violence. The ideology on which racial oppression is based is that of superiority based on race (i.e., White supremacy). Likewise, the ideology on which sexual oppression is based is that of superiority based on gender (i.e., male) and the basis for homosexual oppression is an ideology of superiority based on sexual orientation (i.e., heterosexual). Violence is used to enforce and maintain all oppressions. Violence comes in many forms and may be physical and direct (e.g., lynching, rape, battering, gay bashing), or personal and psychological (e.g., name-calling based on dominant ideology and negative stereotypes). Violence may be indirect and/or institutionalized. For example, it may be associated with high poverty rates, the predominance of men of color in the criminal justice system and on death row, and the reality of police brutality.
>
> A third common element of all oppressions is that they are institutionalized. This means that racism, sexism, and heterosexism are built into the norms, traditions, laws, and policies of a society so that even those who have non-racist, non-sexist, and non-heterosexist beliefs are compelled to act in accordance with institutional interest. (pp. 35–36)

A major thrust of social work is to combat oppression and advocate on the behalf of oppressed groups. Advocacy is the act of speaking up, pushing for change, or pleading clients' causes. The NASW Code of Ethics specifies that social workers should never "practice, condone, facilitate, or collaborate with any form of discrimination on the basis of race, ethnicity, national origin, color, sex, sexual orientation, age, marital status, political belief, religion, or mental or physical disability" (NASW, 1999, 4.02). It is workers' responsibility to actively thwart any cruelty, unfairness, or discrimination they observe. This standard places the ultimate responsibility upon the individual worker to make certain that service is provided fairly and people are treated justly. This doesn't relinquish the responsibility of agency administrators. However, individual professional social workers also have responsibility to advocate for and pursue positive change.

 Critical Thinking Questions 1.4

When you think of the word "oppression," what groups come to mind? What are the reasons that you feel these people are oppressed?

Populations-at-Risk

Populations-at-risk are populations or groups of people who share some identifiable characteristic that places them at greater risk of social and economic deprivation and oppression than the general mainstream of society. Because our job as social workers involves getting people resources and helping to solve their problems, we will likely work primarily with populations-at-risk. These may include client groups characterized by "age, class, color, culture, disability, ethnicity, family structure, gender, marital status, national origin, race, religion, sex, and sexual orientation" (CSWE, 2001, 1.2). It follows that we need information and insight concerning these populations' special issues and needs. Social workers must be able "to identify how group membership influences access to resources," understand "the dynamics of such risk factors," and develop skills to enhance equitable distribution of resources and help people in need (CSWE, 2001, 4.2).

Promotion of Social and Economic Justice

Social work education is also charged with focusing on the promotion of social and economic justice. *Social justice* involves the idea that in a perfect world, all citizens would have identical "rights, protection, opportunities, obligations, and social benefits" (Barker, 2003, p. 28). Similarly, *economic justice* concerns the distribution of resources in a fair and equitable manner. Social work education programs are required to provide "content related to implementing strategies to combat discrimination, oppression, and economic deprivation and to promote social and economic justice" (CSWE, 2001, 4.2).

In real life, social and economic justice are hard goals to attain. Rarely are rights and resources fairly and equitably distributed. Even the definitions of "fair" and "equitable" are widely debated. What does "fair" mean? Does it mean that all people should receive the same income regardless of what work they do, or even whether or not they have jobs at all? The point is that social workers must be vigilantly aware of the existence of injustice. It is our ethical responsibility to combat injustice whenever it is necessary and possible to do so.

The NASW Code of Ethics stresses that workers' ethical responsibility to the broader society is to advocate and work for people's general welfare. This responsibility reflects the basic core of social work, although most job descriptions do not specifically reflect this. The Code reads, "Social workers should promote the general welfare of society, from local to global levels, and the development of people, their communities, and their environments. Social workers should advocate for living conditions conducive to the fulfillment of basic human needs and should promote social, economic, political, and cultural values and institutions that are compatible with the realization of social justice" (NASW, 1999, 6.01).

The Code continues that as part of their professional responsibility, social workers should pursue social and political action seeking fair and equal access to resources and opportunities. They should actively support policies to improve the human condition and promote social justice for all. Practitioners should especially work to enhance opportunities for "vulnerable, disadvantaged, oppressed, and exploited people and groups" (NASW, 1999, 6.04b). Social workers should support conditions and policies that respect cultural diversity. Similarly, they should work to prevent and eliminate conditions and policies discriminating against or exploiting people, especially vulnerable populations. Chapter 12 discusses social justice in the context of the global macro environment.

 Critical Thinking Questions 1.5

Should poor people holding minimum wage jobs that don't offer health insurance have free access to public health care?

Should gay people be allowed to legally marry?

In what ways does the concept of social justice relate to the answers you gave to these questions?

SUMMARY

This chapter introduced content addressed in the remainder of the book. The macro social environment was described. Generalist social work practice and its relationship to the macro social environment was explained. Major concepts inherent in the definition of generalist social work include working within an organizational structure; using a seven-step planned change process; targeting any size system for change; using a wide range of professional roles; applying critical thinking skills; and focusing on empowerment, the strengths perspective, and resiliency.

Ecosystems theory was explored. Basic terms derived from systems theories included system, boundaries, subsystem, homeostasis, roles, relationship, input, output, interface, differentiation, entropy, negative entropy, and equifinality. Terms taken from the ecological perspective included the social environment, energy, input, output, interface, adaptation, person-in-environment fit, relatedness, and interdependence. Finally, people's involvement with multiple systems in the social environment was discussed, and micro, mezzo, and macro systems were defined and described.

Other important concepts characterizing social work in the macro social environment include human diversity, culture, cultural competence, oppression, populations-at-risk, and the promotion of social and economic justice.

CHAPTER 2

Human Behavior in Groups: Theories and Dynamics

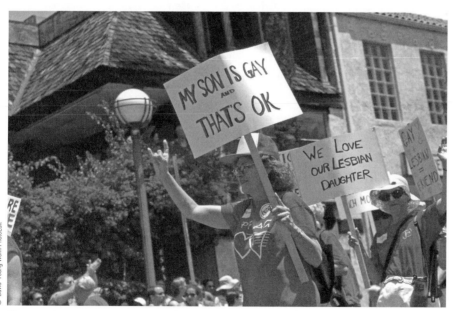

Communication, cooperation, and conflict may be part of the dynamic group process.

© David Young-Wolff/PhotoEdit

CHAPTER CONTENTS

Theoretical Perspectives on Groups

Field Theory

Social Exchange Theory

Learning Theory

HIGHLIGHT 2.1   *Analysis of a Conversation According to Social Exchange Theory*

HIGHLIGHT 2.2   *An Example of Negative Reinforcement in a Macro Setting*

Cognitive-Behavioral Theory

HIGHLIGHT 2.3   *An Example of Punishment in a Macro Setting*

Psychoanalytic Theory

HIGHLIGHT 2.4   *Case Example—Id, Ego, and Superego*

Systems Theory

Objectives of Groups

Balance Between Task and Socio-Emotional Functions

Group Functioning

Empowerment Theory

Social Justice

Consciousness Raising

Mutual Aid

Power

Multicultural Socialization

Feminist Theories

Using a "Gender Lens"

The End of Patriarchy

Empowerment

Consciousness Raising

The Personal Is Political

The Importance of Process

Unity in Diversity: "Diversity Is Strength"

Validation

Understanding Groups in the Macro Social Environment: Group Dynamics

Communication

Positive Verbal Communication in Effective Task Groups

Nonverbal Communication in Task Groups

Cross-Cultural Differences in Communication

Barriers to Communication

Self-Disclosure

HIGHLIGHT 2.5   *Case Example—Self-Disclosure*

Interpersonal Interaction

Norms

HIGHLIGHT 2.6   *Case Examples—Interpersonal Interaction*

Roles

Group Cohesiveness

Power and Status

Possible Sources of Power in Groups

Leadership

Types of Leadership

Leadership Skills

HIGHLIGHT 2.7   *Empowerment by Group Leaders*

Stages of Task Group Development

Stage 1: Task Group Composition

Definition of the Group's Purpose

The Group's "Social Context"

Group Size

Stage 2: Beginnings

Stage 3: Assessment

Stage 4: Stabilization and Working

Stage 5: Endings and Evaluation

Chapter Summary

LaTonya, the university's Social Work Club (SWC) president, called the full membership meeting to order. SWC had much to accomplish tonight. The goal was to identify a range of volunteer activities in which members could participate. At the last meeting, the club passed the requirement that all members participate in at least thirty hours of volunteer activities. Now it was up to the club to identify volunteer possibilities in the university's small town and help members get involved.

The SWC board consisted of LaTonya, Bert (vice-president), Ernie (secretary), Sallie (treasurer), and Morticia (activities director). Board meetings were held every other Tuesday night, with full membership meetings on alternate Tuesdays.

LaTonya felt the SWC board generally got along well except for periodic minor conflicts between herself and Bert. Bert liked to vie for power and control of both board and membership meetings. LaTonya felt Bert somewhat resented that she had been elected SWC president.

LaTonya, however, had assessed their interpersonal dynamics the first time the newly elected board met. From the second board meeting on, whenever Bert got on a control kick, LaTonya tactfully cut him off, regained control, and got the meeting back on track. After all, interpersonal feuding just consumed unnecessary energy and ate away at SWC's process and effectiveness. LaTonya took her role as president very seriously. She and the SWC membership had a lot to do tonight to get the volunteer program on its feet and running.

The above scenario highlights how groups consist of people having unique personalities, issues, and concerns. On the one hand, a group must accomplish its purpose as a unified entity. On the other, individual members come to a group with their own desires and needs. As in organizations and communities, human behavior in groups is complex.

A *group* is at least two individuals gathered together because of some common bond, to meet members' social and emotional needs, or to fulfill some mutual purpose. Social work practitioners must understand human behavior in groups for many reasons. Working with others to get something done is a core component of generalist social work practice in organizations and communities.

Schopler and Galinsky (1995) cite four main reasons why groups are relevant in social work. First, sharing *common interests and pursuits* provides a group of individuals with support, information, and motivation. It is also likely that a group of people can exert greater influence on the social environment than a single individual.

Second, groups enhance *creative and problem-solving potential*. They "provide an arena in which members can exchange ideas and opinions, review the problems they face, engage in new experiences, and develop new approaches" (Schopler & Galinsky, 1995, p. 1130). Exposure to perspectives different than one's own can initiate ideas and enhance creativity.

A third reason groups are important involves *small-group forces*. Working together in a group, members exert social pressure and influence on each other. A group member is accountable to other members for assuming responsibility and getting things done. In this way members can empower each other to make progress and achieve goals.

The fourth reason groups are important to social work is *convenience.* When a number of individuals are involved in decision-making, planning, advocating, or intervening, groups often provide the most efficient way of communicating, solving problems, and making decisions.

Chapter 3 will describe the types of groups relevant to generalist social work practice. A number of theoretical perspectives can conceptualize any group's functioning regardless of type. Theory provides a framework for understanding how groups work. Additionally, some concepts characterize interpersonal group dynamics such that you can use them in conjunction with any theoretical perspective. The greater your comprehension of group functioning, the more effectively you will lead or participate in groups.

This chapter will

- Explain major theoretical perspectives on groups, including field, social exchange, learning, psychoanalytic, systems, empowerment, and feminist theories.
- Examine basic concepts inherent in interpersonal group dynamics, including communication, interpersonal interaction, norms, roles, group cohesion, power and status, and leadership.
- Describe phases of task group development, including composition, beginnings, assessment, stabilization and working, and endings and evaluation.

THEORETICAL PERSPECTIVES ON GROUPS

Theoretical perspectives provide avenues for understanding how communities, organizations, or groups function. Theories about groups discussed here include field, social exchange, learning, psychoanalytic, and systems theories.

Field Theory

According to *field theory,* initially developed by Kurt Lewin (1951), a group should be viewed as an entity moving through its immediate environment in pursuit of its goals. A major strength of field theory is that it stresses the importance of examining the relationship of the group to its environment (Garvin, 1987; Martin, 2003). Picture a bowling ball rolling down an alley or a soccer ball speeding down a field. Each rolls or reacts within its own context or field. Movement involves the force and direction with which it was hit and the ruts, gutters, or impediments encountered along the way. This is overly simplistic, however, as field theory sees groups as dynamic entities whose members constantly adapt to their environments. Observing bowling or soccer balls when not moving is about as dynamic as watching rocks.

Field theory emphasizes how groups function in order to achieve designated goals. It views groups as progressing or failing to progress because of positive and negative forces acting on them both internally and externally in the environment. These forces can either help or hinder the group's advancement. Field theory predicts that groups experiencing numerous positive forces, rewards, and encouragements will continue functioning. Groups encountering primarily negative forces will probably fail if positive forces don't counterbalance the negative. Such forces that push toward or pull one away from involvement and participation are called *valences* (Martin, 2003).

An important concept in field theory in *cohesion,* the collective sum of forces affecting individuals that encourage them to remain group members (Garvin, 1987; Toseland & Rivas, 2005). Examples of positive forces might be how much group members like each other and enjoy each others' company, or members' commitment to the group's purpose. Negative forces might include inconvenient meeting times or other pressures on members' time external to the group.

Field theory views leadership within a group as being democratic, authoritarian, or laissez-faire (Lewin, Lippitt, & White, 1939; Toseland & Rivas, 2005). Leadership, discussed more thoroughly later on, significantly impacts how the group functions and moves along toward accomplishing goals. *Authoritarian* leaders take control of group functioning and make decisions with little or no input from other group members. Needless to say, group members may seriously resent this approach. They may balk at group goals, behave in ways that obstruct group progress, or quit the group altogether. On the other hand, some groups may require such strong leadership when members lack necessary knowledge, skill, or direction.

In contrast, *democratic* leaders maximize member input and participation. They emphasize open discussion of issues, even uncomfortable ones such as disagreements among group members or hostility toward the group leader. Advantages of a democratic approach are equal input for all and open knowledge of the issues. Disadvantages include the fact that members may not really be equal in terms of motivation, competence, skills, or participation.

Finally, *laissez-faire* leaders assume a laid-back, nondirectional approach where the group is left to function or struggle on its own. This approach usually doesn't work unless group members are highly knowledgeable, competent, and independent, requiring little guidance to accomplish tasks.

Field theory also introduced a number of concepts regarding the importance of internal group interaction. *Roles* are expected behavior patterns based on individuals' status or position within the group. *Norms* are collective rules and expectations held by group members concerning what is appropriate behavior within the group.

Power is the ability to move people on a chosen course to produce an effect or achieve some goal (Homan, 2004). *Consensus* is the extent to which group members concur about group goals and other aspects of group interaction. *Cohesion* is the extent to which group members are attracted to and feel closeness to other group members. (Note that the concept of cohesion here is similar to its conception in field theory which refers to the collective sum of forces affecting individuals that encourage them to remain group members.)

Social Exchange Theory

Field theory views a group as a single entity, stressing its functioning as a unit. Although some attention is given to interpersonal dynamics within the group, the focus remains on how the group functions as a unit. *Social exchange theory*, on the other hand, stresses the importance of the individual within the group context. It views the group as the place where social exchange takes place, which involves both rewards and costs. *Rewards* are "the pleasures, satisfactions, and gratifications a person enjoys from participating in a relationship" (Families.com, 2006). Individual group members continue in the group because they receive social rewards for group membership. This membership is based on receiving more rewards than experiencing costs. *Costs* include negative experiences, "the energy invested in a relationship," or the loss of rewards because of making ineffective choices (for example, spending time talking with a group member you don't like much instead of one you do) (Families.com, 2006).

Garvin (1987) explains:

> People enter into social interactions with the expectation of rewards. Because each person in the interaction has the same motivation, it logically follows that each must offer something of value to the other in the exchange. . . . What an individual offers another in an exchange—whether energy, time, or resources—is referred to as a "cost."

Social exchange theory focuses on interactions between and among individuals. Each interaction can be broken down into a series of behaviors and responses. Each behavior or response is evaluated in terms of how rewarding or punishing it is to the other member of any pair of members in the group. When group members experience more rewards and fewer costs, the social exchange is likely to be positive and to reinforce group participation.

Several assumptions are inherent in exchange theory (Families.com, 2006). First, relationships have an interdependent dimension. That is, the ability of each participant to receive rewards is dependent on that person's ability to bestow rewards. If you can't give rewards to others, they probably won't give any to you. Second, the process of social exchange is governed by values and expectations such as fairness and the importance of a mutual sense of give and take. It follows, then, that giving rewards should result in eventually receiving rewards. Third, "trust and commitment" develop as more social exchanges occur over time, which tends to "stabilize" relationships. As people get to know each other and expectations become established, relationships become more predictable. Highlight 2.1 analyzes a conversation according to social exchange theory.

Learning Theory

Learning theory is a theoretical orientation that conceptualizes the social environment in terms of behavior, its preceding events, and its subsequent consequences (Zastrow & Kirst-Ashman, 2004). It posits that behavior can be learned and, therefore, that maladaptive behavior can be unlearned. Learning

| Highlight 2.1 | **Analysis of a Conversation According to Social Exchange Theory** |

Francine and Horace, members of a volunteer community group whose goal is to maintain cleanliness on four city block sidewalks, have the following conversation. Each response is followed by a brief analysis according to social exchange theory.

Francine says to Horace, "Did you finish your assigned block yet?" *(Neutral question, although a minor cost to Francine in terms of effect expended)*

Horace responds, "Heck, yes. I appreciate your suggestions about removing the dog dirt. I just don't know why people keep big dogs in the city." *(Reward for Francine; minor cost for Horace for effort expended)*

Francine states, "Yeah, that Super Duper Pooper Scooper really works. Will you be cleaning your assigned sidewalks on a weekly basis?" *(Minor cost to Francine for effort expended)*

Horace replies, "Nah, once a month is plenty. Don't want to wear myself out." *(Cost to Francine because it's not what she wants to hear; minor cost to Horace for effort expended)*

Francine vehemently states, "What! This neighborhood will be a pig sty if you don't assume your responsibility and do it every week." *(Cost to Horace because Francine criticized his behavior; cost to Francine because of her anger and for effort expended)*

Horace huffily retorts, "You can't tell me what to do. This is a voluntary neighborhood group. One more crack like that and I quit." *(Cost to Horace because of his anger; cost to Francine because she doesn't want Horace to quit, as she would probably have to do his work)*

"I'm sorry," Francine humbly replies. "I just get so upset when people mess up the neighborhood so." *(Reward for Horace because he appreciates Francine's apology; cost to Francine because of the effort it took to apologize)*

"Oh, don't worry about it," Horace says. "We're all in this together. You're probably right. I'll do my part and clean up at least every two weeks. The Super Duper Pooper Scooper does make it easier." *(Reward to Francine because she appreciates Horace's effort; cost to Horace for effort expended)*

---

theory provides a framework for understanding how behavior develops. Like social exchange theory, learning theory focuses on individual group members rather than the entire group's process and functioning. It is usually applied to treatment groups, specifically therapy, for individual clients rather than task groups in macro settings. However, because of learning theory's significance in understanding human behavior and the increasing body of research documenting its effectiveness in many settings, it merits brief discussion here (Kazdin, 2001; Sundel & Sundel, 2005).

Learning theory proposes three primary means of affecting people's behavior within groups. First, *respondent conditioning* refers to the elicitation of behavior in response to a specific stimulus. If a group member suddenly screams, "FIRE!" (a stimulus), other group members will probably run for their lives out of the room (response). Another example is a group of social workers receiving in-service training on solving ethical dilemmas. When the group leader gets up and goes to the chalkboard (stimulus), other group members dig out notebooks from their briefcases to take notes (response).

A second type of learning is *modeling,* the learning of behavior by observing another individual engaging in that behavior. For example, a social worker leads an educational group of community residents interested in writing their legislators about some hot political issue. The worker can serve as a model

| **Highlight 2.2** | **An Example of Negative Reinforcement in a Macro Setting** |

An example of negative reinforcement in a macro setting involves a group of community leaders. An ancient tradition for the group is to read both the meeting's minutes and any new reports at the beginning of the meeting. Because this is so excruciatingly dull, most group members come about 45 minutes late, or don't show up at all. Matt Tress, the group's chairperson, decides that reading all that boring material is a waste of time and is really turning people off. Matt sent a written announcement to all group members stating that minutes and new reports will no longer be read during meetings because it wastes precious time. Rather, members are expected to read the material in advance of meetings so that it can be addressed. It was amazing how group members started showing up on time after only a meeting or two when the meetings dealt with business items instead of boring reading. Halting readings (removing a negative event) reinforced group members' punctuality and attendance (increased frequency of behavior).

by writing to designated legislators herself. She can model what to write and how to say it.

A third type of learning is *operant conditioning,* "a type of learning in which behaviors are altered primarily by regulating the consequences which follow them" (Kazdin, 2001, p. 458). One type of behavioral consequence is *reinforcement,* a procedure or consequence that increases the frequency of the behavior immediately preceding it. *Positive reinforcement* is the positive event or consequences that follow a behavior and act to strengthen or increase the likelihood that the behavior will occur again. Consider an agency task group working to establish a new recording format for monitoring clients' progress. Karl, one group member, states to Max, another, "Thanks so much for sharing your ideas. They're great." Max likes the compliment, which is positive by nature. If Karl's response increases Max's future sharing of ideas, it is positive reinforcement.

Negative reinforcement is the removal of a negative event or consequence that serves to increase the frequency of a particular behavior. First, something must be removed from the situation. Second, the frequency of a particular behavior is increased. In this manner, positive and negative reinforcement resemble each other. Both function as reinforcement that, by definition, serves to increase or maintain the frequency of a behavior. Highlight 2.2 provides an example of negative reinforcement in a Macro Setting.

Learning theory describes another type of consequence, *punishment,* which is the presentation of an aversive event or the removal of a positive reinforcer that results in the decrease in frequency or elimination of a particular behavior. In a way, punishment is the opposite of reinforcement in that it weakens or decreases the frequency of behavior instead of increasing it. Highlight 2.3 provides an example of punishment in a macro setting.

Cognitive-Behavioral Theory   Cognitive-behavioral theory combines components of learning theory and cognitive theory. Behavioral theory (also known as behavioral therapy) involves the practical application of learning theory principles to changing behavior. Cognitive theory emphasizes people's ability to make rational decisions and alter their behavior.

| **Highlight 2.3** | **An Example of Punishment in a Macro Setting** |

Consider a group supervisory meeting where Yaakov, a social services supervisor, is holding a group supervisory meeting with his financial assistance workers. Yaakov often tends to drone on when trying to make a point. Akuba, one of the workers, interrupts, tactfully in her perception, and asks a question for clarification before discussion moves on and the question becomes irrelevant. Obviously annoyed, Yaakov sharply retorts, "Never, never interrupt me again in the middle of a thought!"

Akuba learns. She never, ever interrupts Yaakov again. In fact, she hesitates to speak to him at all unless she has to. Yaakov's sharp rebuttal is punishment because Akuba's interrupting behavior never occurs again (decreased frequency or, in this case, elimination of behavior).

Four basic assumptions are involved in cognitive-behavioral theory (Vourlekis, 1999). First, it's relatively optimistic. It asserts that people are capable of making positive changes if obstacles in the environment don't prevent them from doing so.

Second, people are not considered dry sponges that automatically soak up any bit of information and knowledge with which they come into contact. Rather, people continuously process information, make choices about beliefs, and construct their own worldview.

Third, the act of thinking (*cognition*) mediates or affects people's behavior. Mental processes like selective attention, coming to conclusions, and judgment "influence one's motivation to act, shape the nature of one's action, and color one's feeling about the action after the fact" (p. 179). Note that cognition's role in influencing behavior is "not a one-way street" (p. 179). Other variables including "behavioral consequences, adequacy of performance, [and] physiological states . . . also influence thinking" (p. 179).

Fourth, "the three subsystems" of cognition, emotion, and behavior "provide feedback to each other; all may contribute to a given outcome or state, and change in one may lead to change in the others" (p. 180). If you feel depressed (emotion), you might think very negative thoughts about yourself (for example, "I'm such a rotten person") (cognition), and may avoid friends to isolate yourself (behavior). Similarly, if you studied very hard and received 98% after taking a recent exam (behavior), you might think very positive thoughts about yourself (for example, "I'm so smart") (cognition), and feel extremely happy (emotion). Hence, the three subsystems can affect each other.

Cognitive-behavioral theory has been used extensively in treatment groups. As with learning theory, it has rarely been applied to task groups and other groups operating in macro settings.

Rose (1998) describes the application of cognitive-behavioral therapy in group therapy with troubled youth. Great emphasis is placed on modeling positive behavior such as coping strategies to deal "with problematic situations, inducing anger, stress, or other strong emotions, that young people confront every day" (p. 10). Positive reinforcement is used to reinforce positive behaviors. Such reinforcers might include "praise, tokens, points, goods, small objects, activities," and whatever else might be both manageable and valued by group members (p. 22). Finally, cognitive restructuring involves "a set of procedures used to replace self-defeating, illogical, or automatic patterns of thinking that interfere with social functioning with self-enhancing or logical ones" (p. 23). Many other techniques are also applied, but these are beyond this book's scope. Our focus is on groups in macro versus treatment contexts.

Psychoanalytic Theory

Psychoanalytic theory emphasizes the impact of early life experiences on current feelings and behavior. It has been applied to individual and group situations, although it is primarily used in treatment instead of macro contexts. Because of its significance in the conceptualization of group work, however, it merits some attention here.

Psychoanalytic theory focuses on three major aspects of group functioning (Garvin, 1987). The first is how group members act out in the group context unsettled issues encountered early in life, usually within their own families. Yalom (1985) comments, "Without exception, patients enter group therapy with the history of a highly unsatisfactory experience in their first and most important group—the primary family" (p. 15). For example, a group member may have had difficulties communicating with his father, who ruled the family with an iron fist. That group member might then view "the group leader as the all-powerful father figure who reigns supreme over group members," (Toseland & Rivas, 2005, p. 58).

A second aspect of group functioning emphasized by psychoanalytic theory is the attention given to the emotional reactions "by group members both to each other and the leader" (Garvin, 1987, p. 688). These may include "helpless dependence" on the leader(s) who group members see as being very powerful; "blind defiance of the leaders" who members may see as threatening their rights and autonomy; "bitter competition" among group members vying for attention from the leader(s) and other group members; the quest for forming subgroups of allies gaining power against the group leader(s) or other members; and extreme selflessness when trying to meet other group members' needs at the expense of their own (Yalom, 1985, p. 15).

Psychoanalytic theory's third focus on groups involves "the distorted perceptions members may have of each other and of group events because of forces in the personality" (Garvin, 1987, p. 688). Psychoanalytic theory poses a number of concepts used to explain such personality forces. For instance, it views people as experiencing frequent conflict among three levels of consciousness—the id, the ego, and the superego. The *id* is the primitive force hidden in the unconscious arena of the brain that represents basic primitive drives such as hunger, sex, and self-preservation. The *ego* is the rational component of the mind that evaluates consequences and determines courses of action in a logical manner. The *superego* is the conscience which decides what actions and behavior are right and wrong. Highlight 2.4 presents a case example illustrating these concepts.

| **Highlight 2.4** | **Case Example—Id, Ego, and Superego** |

Pearl, a member of a community action group to prevent drug abuse, provides an example of how these three mental dimensions might conflict. She attends a planning meeting to designate responsibilities for implementing a drug-prevention program. Unfortunately, she was so busy she skipped both breakfast and lunch, so she is ravenously hungry at the 1:30 P.M. meeting. Her id tells her to leave the meeting and get something to eat immediately. However, her ego tells her it isn't socially appropriate to leave the meeting abruptly and get something to eat. She should have thought ahead rationally and brought a sandwich. Finally, her superego says she must stay and participate to the best of her ability because of her strong belief in controlling illegal drug use. The right thing to do is to help the community's children and, although almost starving, remain at the meeting.

Another concept important in understanding a psychoanalytic perspective on group functioning is the *defense mechanism,* any unconscious attempt to adjust to conditions such as anxiety, frustration, or guilt that are painful to experience. For example, without realizing it, in order to cope with her anxiety about group involvement, a group member is excessively quiet and withdrawn (a defense mechanism).

Psychoanalytic theory emphasizes careful scrutiny of individual members' feelings, behaviors, and interactions. These are then closely examined while the group leader and other members give feedback. The intent is for group members to attain *insight,* an understanding of their motivations, emotions, behaviors, and issues, a primary goal of the group process.

Systems Theory

Garvin (1987) maintains that "in a sense, all small-group theories may be thought of as systems oriented inasmuch as they portray the small group as an organic entity with boundaries, purposes, and mechanisms for attaining change while maintaining stability" (p. 687). We have established that systems theories provide an exceptionally useful means for understanding human behavior in many contexts, including the interactions of individuals, groups, families, organizations, and communities in the macro social environment.

A group is a *system,* a set of related elements that are orderly and interrelated and a functional whole. The group is distinguished by *boundaries,* repeatedly occurring patterns that characterize relationships within the group system and give that system its particular identity. Think of the group as a living cell having a membrane or boundary around it. This boundary determines who is a group member and who is not.

Subsystems are subordinate or secondary systems within the group system. For example, two group members may form a special friendship that distinguishes their relationship from that of others in the group. They then become a subsystem.

Group systems strive to maintain a state of *homeostasis,* the tendency for a system to maintain a relatively stable, constant state of balance. Groups must maintain some homeostasis—or status quo—in order to survive and thrive.

Group members assume roles within the group. A *role* is "a socially expected behavior pattern determined by an individual's status" and expectations within a particular group or society (Mish, 1995, p. 1014). Group members may assume roles such as leader, emotional supporter, idea person, task director, and so on.

Group members have relationships with each other. A *relationship* is the dynamic interpersonal connection between two or more persons or systems that involves how they think about, feel, and behave toward each other. Relationships among various group members may be cooperative, friendly, helpful, hostile, or strained, depending on group members' patterns of interactions.

Objectives of Groups   Group systems strive to attain four primary objectives (Bales, 1950; Garvin, 1987; Parsons, Bales & Shils, 1953; Toseland & Rivas, 2005). First, they seek *integration,* the means whereby group members fit and work together. Group members must get along and communicate well enough to get things done.

Second, group systems pursue *pattern maintenance,* the means by which the group adheres to its basic processes and procedures. Group members establish procedures and expectations for ongoing interaction, such as how members should relate to each other, how decisions are made, or how members are given opportunities to voice opinions.

Third, group systems strive for *goal attainment,* achievement of their ultimate tasks and goals. Group systems exist for a purpose. To be worthwhile, the group must achieve its goals.

Fourth, group systems seek *adaptation,* the group's capacity to adjust to surrounding environmental conditions through an ongoing process of change. For example, if the building in which the group meets is condemned to be torn down, the group must adapt by finding another meeting location.

Balance Between Task and Socio-Emotional Functions   Bales (1950) sees group systems as striving to maintain a balance between two basic functions: task functions and socio-emotional functions. This is true both for task and treatment groups. Task functions, which pursue goal attainment and adaptation, include exchanging information, establishing plans, and evaluating progress toward goals. They concern work and responsibility in groups. Socio-emotional functions, on the other hand, represent the feeling and emotional needs of group members. Such functions, geared to maintaining the group system's integration and pattern maintenance, are positive when they "reduce tensions, seek agreement, or show solidarity" (Garvin, 1987, p. 687). Negative socio-emotional functions, on the other hand, increase conflict, tension, and disagreement.

Group Functioning   Homans (1950) stressed that the following four concepts are critical in understanding a group system's functioning:

1. *Activities* are the happenings and actions conducted in a group.
2. *Interactions* are the reciprocal behaviors and communications engaged in by group members.
3. *Sentiments* are the emotional feelings and reactions manifested by group members.
4. *Norms* are the expectations held by group members regarding how they should behave in the group.

Homans maintained that these four dimensions are critical to a group system's ongoing health and well-being. Furthermore, he developed an ecosystems approach to viewing these dimensions. He stressed how a group system functions along these dimensions in reaction to its internal and external environments. Group system activities, interactions, sentiments, and norms are oriented to and affect the internal group environment when they relate to group members' adaptation to each other. These same variables are oriented to and affect the external environment when group members must adapt to pressures posed by that environment.

For example, consider a group planning a soup and sandwich supper fundraising project to raise money for a community's homeless population. Group activities, interactions, sentiments, and norms may focus on the internal group relationships and process when two members are fighting about which one has the best chunky chicken soup recipe. The internal group environment is the focus of attention. However, when the planning group finds out that its treasurer has absconded with its funds (to pay for the food) and run off to Mexico, it must turn its attention to the external environment. Its activities, interactions, sentiments, and norms now must focus on obtaining new funding to do the supper.

Empowerment Theory

We have defined *empowerment* as the "process of increasing personal, interpersonal, or political power so that individuals can take action to improve their life situations" (Gutierrez, 2001, p. 210). Groups provide "the optimum medium for empowerment on all levels" (Lee, 2001, p. 291). "An empowering perspective on group work also involves linking group techniques to women's social, historical, and political environments to affect change" (Gutierrez & Lewis, 1999, p. 69). Groups using an empowerment approach can strive "to change oppressive cognitive, behavioral, social, and political structures or conditions that thwart the control people have over their lives, that prevent them from accessing needed resources, and that keep them from participating in the life of their community" (Breton, 2004, p. 59). We will discuss five dimensions regarding how empowerment theory applies to groups. These include social justice, consciousness raising, mutual aid, power, and multicultural socialization (Breton, 2004; Gutierrez & Lewis, 1999; Lee, 2001).

Social Justice *Social justice* involves the idea that in a perfect world, all citizens would have identical "rights, protection, opportunities, obligations, and social benefits" (Barker, 2003, p. 28). An underlying theme of empowerment theory is that society is structured so that some groups are oppressed and denied their right to resources, free choice, and equal opportunity. Action groups can be formed to address these issues and advocate for positive change. (Of course, treatment groups also can and should assume an empowerment approach, but here we're focusing on macro settings.)

Consciousness Raising *Consciousness raising* is the process of enhancing people's awareness of themselves, of others, or of issues in the social environment. It occurs when they either have not thought of these ideas before or have made superficial assumptions about them, not having used critical thinking to evaluate the ideas' validity. People often have a tendency to blame oppressed groups for their oppression. People may think that it's the group members' fault that they are subject to social injustice. People feel group members should've worked harder. Or that they're too stupid to do better. Or that they're immoral. Because the oppressed group members are part of the macro social environment, they may also fall into the trap of blaming themselves (Breton, 2004; van Wormer, 2004).

Consciousness raising helps people ask themselves questions about their personal predicament. Facts and ideas are brought to their attention regarding why they in addition to numerous others are experiencing social injustice. This process helps people link issues like poverty and racism to the social, political, and economic configurations in which they live. Essentially, consciousness raising empowers people to view themselves more positively and realistically. Through consciousness raising they identify their strengths and see their capabilities for action. They become stronger, both personally and politically. Consciousness raising "provides group members opportunities to begin to see themselves as members of a community and eventually to fully participate in the life of that community"; they "begin to identify themselves as citizens—political beings—who, in a democracy, have the right and responsibility to participate on the sociopolitical scene, to be heard, and to influence policies so that they can access the resources they need" (Breton, 2004, pp. 60, 63).

Mutual Aid Empowerment stresses how group members can help and empower each other through *mutual aid,* the act of providing support, feedback, and information within a group context (Breton, 2004; Lee, 2001). Group members may see themselves as "a group of peers perceived as equal partners striving and helping each other to gain control over their lives" (Breton, 2004, p. 67). They view each other "as active and having power to make a difference in the group, as social beings who need to belong and as social learners who help each other in learning. They establish bonds, empathy, and identification. Differences are supported and a balance is sought between the needs of the individual and the needs of the group" (Lee, 2001, p. 293).

Power Potential power discrepancies exist within any group (Gutierrez & Lewis, 1999). Some members may be more assertive, knowledgeable, skilled, or have greater status for any variety of reasons. If a leader has been designated in a group or if a leader emerges, there is a natural power discrepancy that may work against mutual aid and empowerment.

Five styles of communication in groups affect the potential for empowerment through mutual aid in a group (Lee, 2001, pp. 294–295; Goldberg, Wood & Middleman, 1989). First, the *Maypole* demonstrates a communication pattern where the leader (for example, a social worker) remains at the center of the group, controlling the members and paying attention to each individual separately. Group interaction among members is discouraged. The second communication pattern involves the *Round Robin*, where the leader maintains control but each group member takes turns speaking. A third type, the *Hot Seat*, involves the leader maintaining control by directing all attention to one group member (in the hot seat) while the other members watch. The fourth communication style is the *Agenda-Controlled*, where the leader maintains strict order by using Robert's Rules of order or some other structured form of running a meeting. The final communication style is the *Free Form*, where no leader emerges and group members feel free to contribute at will.

The most empowering communication style is the *Free Form*, where members empower themselves and are free to support each other (Lee, 2001; Goldberg, Wood & Middleman, 1989). A disadvantage of this style might be a lack of structured order. It's possible that group members can get off track, thus interfering with the achievement of group goals. Gutierrez and Lewis (1999) propose two solutions. First, co-leadership may be established where two group members take turns leading the group. This may prevent a dominant and controlling leader from emerging. A second suggestion is for all group members to rotate the leadership role. Group members can learn from others who can model leadership approaches, and power is distributed more equally among members. Greater empowerment of each member should result.

Multicultural Socialization Empowerment in any group also involves multicultural understanding and socialization. Group leaders and members should strive to identify, be sensitive to, and appreciate any differences that might exist among members in terms of "ethnicity, race, gender, sexual orientation, class, and ability" (Gutierrez & Lewis, 1999, p. 69). Heterogeneous groups can empower all members only if leaders and members "are willing to explicitly and repeatedly identify (1) the sources of diversity within the group, (2) the different approaches that can be used to resolve target problems, (3) the different resources brought to the group setting of both leaders and members and, in particular, (4) the potential for bicultural or multicultural socialization of group members" (Gutierrez & Lewis, 1999, p. 71). (*Socialization* is the process by which a group or society conveys its knowledge, values, beliefs, and expectations to its members.)

Use of false assumptions and stereotypes can hastily serve to "turn off" group members, disrupting group cohesion and empowerment. (*Group cohesion* is the extent to which group members feel that they belong in a group and desire to continue being members.) "For example, irreparable damage could result from conduct as blatant as a group facilitator asking a Puerto Rican group member if she would prepare tacos for the last group meeting (tacos are not even a staple dish in Puerto Rico)" (Gutierrez & Lewis, 1999, p. 70).

 Critical Thinking Questions 2.1

To what extent do you feel you have multicultural knowledge and awareness? In what group situations involving people from diverse backgrounds, if any, might you feel uncomfortable and why? What things might you do to enhance your own multicultural knowledge, awareness, and sensitivity?

Another example of insensitivity concerns sexual orientation (Gutierrez & Lewis, 1999, p. 74) (*Sexual orientation* is the "pattern of sexual and emotional attraction based on the gender of one's partner" [Strong, et al., 2005, p. G-12].):

Jiwan and Imani, the two lesbian women in Liz and Anna's group, sat together during the first group meeting. No mention of it was made. As the second group convened, however, these same two women moved to occupy adjacent seats. Jean . . . [another group member], said aloud to Anna, "Why is it that the lesbians always sit together?" Liz overheard the remark and responded, "Probably for the same reasons that all the heterosexual women have sat together." Somewhat perplexed, Jean then looked around the room at how others had chosen to arrange themselves and found that group members had indeed organized themselves in this fashion. She responded, "I never thought of it that way before?" Liz and Anna then began the group with a discussion of choices and their multiple interpretations, using the seating experience as an illustration. As all members of the group began to understand their collective lack of comfort in this new situation, they also began to gain additional information about choices others made that they had previously misunderstood. Seating options in later group sessions began to vary from the pattern exhibited during the first two weeks. [In other words, after addressing and thinking about this aspect of diversity, sexual orientation no longer dictated who sat together and who did not.] (Gutierrez & Lewis, 1999, pp. 74–75).

Feminist Theories

Feminist theories involve "the liberation of women and girls from discrimination based on gender. The goal of feminist theory and practice is women's self-determination." *Self-determination* is each individual's right to make his or her own decisions (Kirst-Ashman & Hull, 2006b, p. 51). "For some feminists this means securing equal rights for women within existing institutions—from marriage and the family to government policy and law. For others it means fundamentally changing these institutions" (Kirk & Okazawa-Rey, 2004, p. 4). Many feminist theories "were developed in the context of women's organizing for change—for the abolition of slavery, for women's suffrage, for labor rights, the civil rights of people of color, women's rights, and GLBT (gay, lesbian, bisexual, and transgender) rights. Feminist theories have been concerned with fundamental questions: Why are women in a subordinate position in our society and, indeed, worldwide? What are the origins of this subordination, and how is it perpetuated?" (Kirk & Okazawa-Rey, 2004, p. 12).

Note that there is a range of feminist theories that emphasize various concepts (Kirk & Okazawa-Rey, 2004, pp. 13–15). The following are a few examples. *Liberal feminism* "grew out of one of the most significant strands of U.S. political thought, liberalism, a theory about individual rights, freedom, choice, and privacy" (p. 13). *Socialist feminism* "grew out of Marxist theories of the economy" and is "particularly concerned with the economic-class aspect of women's lives" (p. 13). *Radical feminism* emphasizes how "male domination manifests itself in women's sexuality, gender roles, and family relationships, and it is carried over into the male-dominated world of work, government, religion, and law" (p. 14). *Postmodern feminism* stresses "the particularity of women's experiences in specific cultural and historical contexts" (for example, racial and class contexts) (p. 14).

For our purposes, we will arbitrarily select some of the major themes characterizing most feminist theories and apply them to group functioning. These include using a "gender lens" (Gutierrez & Lewis, 1998, p. 100), the "end of patriarchy," "empowerment," "consciousness raising," "the personal is political," the importance of "process," "unity in diversity," and "validation of the nonrational" (Bricker-Jenkins & Lockett, 1995, p. 2531; Gutierrez & Lewis, 1998; Lee, 2001). We addressed some of these themes earlier when discussing empowerment theory. However, in the context of feminist theories, the focus here is their application to women's lives.

Using a "Gender Lens"   Using a "gender lens" to view the plight of women in the macro social environment assumes that sexism is relevant to the experiences of many women and is the basis for many of women's difficulties (Gutierrez & Lewis, 1998, p. 100). Such a gender lens emphasizes that women are not only part of the larger community, but that they themselves make up a community of women within that larger community. In essence, this establishes a new way of looking at the world, with women and their issues becoming the focus of attention (Bricker-Jenkins & Lockett, 1995).

The End of Patriarchy   *Patriarchy* generally refers to "control by men of a disproportionately large share of the power" (Mish, 1995, p. 852). It may involve men having more money and economic opportunity, having superior authority over women, or having inheritance follow a male line of descent. Feminist theories refute the concept as inherently oppressive and unfair. They maintain that women should have equal rights, responsibility, and opportunity, and call for a "fundamentally transformed, nonexploitive social order" (Lee, 2001, p. 175).

Empowerment   Feminist empowerment involves women coming together concerning a common cause and promoting "human liberation" (Lee, 2001, p. 175). The emphasis, of course, is the empowerment of women. "Power" is "reconceptualized as limitless" and conceived of as being collectively shared and used; having equal power is stressed so that no one would have "power over" others (Bricker-Jenkins & Lockett, 1995, p. 2531).

Consciousness Raising   Consciousness raising, an important principle in empowerment theory, is just as significant from a feminist perspective. *Consciousness raising* is the development of "critical awareness of the cultural and political factors that shape identity, personal and social realities, and relationships" and of one's position and opinions with respect to these issues (Bricker-Jenkins & Lockett, 1995, p. 2533). It involves undertaking a serious examination of a woman's self and her feelings about a range of issues involving women. Women must become aware of the issues engulfing them in their environment before they can take steps to address them. Bricker-Jenkins and Lockett (1995) suggest that a basic approach for consciousness raising entails asking oneself a series of questions and considering potential answers. Questions include

- "Who am I?" What are my needs, my desires, my visions of a life that is safe, healthy, and fulfilling?
- "Who says?" What is the source of my self-definition and that of my reality? Does it conform to my experience of self and the world?
- "Who benefits from this definition?" Does it conform to my needs, my 'truths?' Is it possible for me to live by these definitions? If not . . .
- "What must change, and how?"(p. 2535)

Answers to these questions should focus on defining a woman's self-worth, what she values, and how fairly the world is treating her. If she determines that her treatment is unfair or inadequate because she is a woman, how can she make changes in her macro environment to receive better or more fair treatment? Consciousness raising thus can become a foundation of empowerment. First, a woman explores herself. Next, she examines issues and appraises her status. Finally, she proposes plans to improve her life and her environment.

For example, LaShondra is a single mother of two children, ages 2 1/2 and 4. She can support her children well enough by working as an optometrist's assistant. However, she must work some evenings in addition to 9:00–5:00 on most weekdays. One of her problems is finding adequate and flexible daycare. Another problem is receiving court-mandated child support payments from her ex-husband. He just can't seem to hold down a job for very long. Still another problem is her high rent for a tiny apartment due to lack of adequate affordable housing. Other problems include lack of a social life and difficulties in obtaining credit to buy a sorely needed new car. Her "ex" ruined her credit rating while they were married.

Alone, LaShondra feels stuck. She views her problems as personal and individual. She tends to blame herself after the fact for making the "wrong decisions." However, talking to other women, getting information, and discussing issues can help to raise LaShondra's consciousness. She can become aware of how she is not alone, but shares her plight with many other women in similar boats. She can come to realize that many things in her world are not her fault. Rather, they result from basic social conditions working against her.

The final facet of consciousness raising involves proposing and working toward positive changes in the macro environment. With others, LaShondra can confront community leaders and politicians about the lack of adequate child care. Can community funds be directed to help subsidize centers? Can she and other local women establish their own center, together paying for staff and volunteering their free time to help cut costs?

How can LaShondra and other women not receiving child support from itinerant ex-husbands or ex-partners seek their fair share? Is there some community agency available to help them search for missing fathers and demand payment? If not, why not? Can such a service be developed?

LaShondra discovers that other community women share similar concerns regarding the lack of adequate reasonable housing. How can the community address this problem? Can community leaders help? Can private developers be encouraged or subsidized to build housing that community mothers need?

Together, LaShondra and other women can address their social issues. Can they organize and sponsor community events to fulfill social needs and decrease isolation? Can they form clubs or groups to help them "get out" regularly?

Finally, can LaShondra and other community women work together to find ways to establish credit? Can they as a group approach local banks and businesses to discuss the issues? Can processes be established to determine when credit problems are not their fault but rather the fault of ex-spouses?

The Personal Is Political   Grasping the concept that *the personal is political* is a major aspect of consciousness raising from a feminist perspective. "Personal problems and conditions have historical, material, and cultural bases and dimensions" (Bricker-Jenkins & Lockett, 1995, p. 2531). GlennMaye (1998) defines the personal and political facets of consciousness raising:

> The personal dimension of consciousness raising involves (1) identifying one's own feelings, perceptions, and needs from the vantage point of one's own experiences, (2) naming or defining one's experiences in one's own language, and (3) telling one's own life story.... The political dimension of consciousness raising involves (1) linking one's personal experiences to one's position as a woman in a male-dominated society, (2) identifying oneself as a woman who shares a common fate with all women, and (3) taking action to change oneself and the social structures that oppress women.
>
> The personal and the political aspects of consciousness raising cannot really be separated. They exist as . . . [an intellectual, logical process of reasoning] in which personal experience and social reality are discovered, tested, and recreated. The full meaning of feminist consciousness resides in apprehending the complex reality of one's situation as a woman with the faith in one's ability and right to a fully human existence." (p. 37)

Thus, a feminist perspective proposes that all woman are "connected," that "there are no personal private solutions," and that "personal growth" can only be attained "through political action" (Bricker-Jenkins & Lockett, 1995, p. 2531).

The Importance of Process   Feminist theories emphasize that the process of *how* things get done is just as important as *what* gets done (Butler & Wintram, 1992; Bricker-Jenkins & Lockett, 1995). A traditional patriarchal perspective that stresses male dominance focuses on the significance of end results and goal achievement. For example, consider a wealthy male politician who readily gets elected to the position of state senator after spending a huge amount of money on his political campaign. A patriarchal perspective emphasizes the importance of having won the election. It does not focus on how the election was won. Attention centers neither on the amount of money that was spent nor what contributions the senator received from large corporations expecting to receive privileged treatment.

Feminist theories stress that decision making should be based on equality and the participation of all. All group members' input is important. No one should have power over another. Feminist theories focus on aspects of process such as making certain all participants have the chance to speak and be heard, adhering to principles of ethical behavior, working toward agreement and consensus, and considering personal issues as important.

Unity in Diversity: "Diversity Is Strength"   Feminist theories stress unity and harmony, on the one hand, and appreciation of diverse characteristics on the other (Bricker-Jenkins & Lockett, 1995). Gutierrez and Lewis (1998) explain that "efforts are made to bridge differences between women based on such factors as race, class, physical ability, and sexual orientation with the principle that *diversity is strength*" (p. 101). Related concepts are "sisterhood" and "solidarity" (Bricker-Jenkins & Lockett, 1995, p. 2531). Women working together can achieve a better quality of life for all. In order to remain unified, women must appreciate each other's differences. Diverse characteristics are sought out and welcomed. New ideas to improve old ways of doing things are encouraged.

Validation   *Validation* is the process of accepting a person and a person's actions as justifiable and relevant. A feminist perspective does not exclude the importance of "rationality, analytical skills, order, and efficiency" (Lee, 2001, p. 175). However, it also includes validation of the nonrational, that is, aspects of life and human interaction that go beyond structured scientific reasoning (Bricker-Jenkins & Lockett, 1995). Feelings, emotions, and intuition are taken into account (Lee, 2001). Spirituality is another dimension given precedence. *Spirituality* "includes one's values, beliefs, mission, awareness, subjectivity, experience, sense of purpose and direction, and a kind of striving toward something greater than oneself" (Frame, 2003, p. 3).

Parsons, Gutierrez, and Cox (1998) comment on the importance of "validation through collective [or group] experience":

> In collective experience, the self and others recognize shared experience; i.e., that some of one's perceptions about oneself and the surrounding world are indeed valid and therefore legitimate to voice. This recognition contributes to a collective view that reduces self-blame, increases the tendency to look beyond personal failure as the cause of the problem at hand, brings about a sense of shared fate, and raises consciousness. Collective experience can motivate one to seek change beyond the individual level toward other systems, such as the family or community." (pp. 4–5)

 Critical Thinking Questions 2.2

To what extent do you agree with the concepts inherent in feminist theories? To what extent do you feel you are or are not a feminist and why?

 Critical Thinking Questions 2.3

Of all the theories discussed here (field, social exchange, learning, psychoanalytic, systems, empowerment, and feminist), which concepts do you think are most relevant in understanding how groups work? Explain why.

UNDERSTANDING GROUPS IN THE MACRO SOCIAL ENVIRONMENT: GROUP DYNAMICS

What goes on in task groups? What do you need to know about groups to understand how groups work so you can be an effective group member or leader? At least seven concepts tend to characterize groups—communication, interpersonal interaction, norms, roles, group cohesion, power and status, and leadership.

Communication

Communication, the exchange of information, is the heart of a group. Communication may be *verbal,* using spoken or written words, or nonverbal. *Nonverbal behavior* includes any means by which information is conveyed not using spoken or written words. Group members must communicate effectively in order to get things done.

Wheelan (1999) explains:

> You would be surprised at the number of groups . . . encountered whose members receive feedback about group performance but do not use that feedback to implement constructive changes. In most cases, this is due to a simple flaw in the group's internal processes. Groups that do not utilize feedback constructively usually do not

have a mechanism [or procedure] in place to evaluate the validity of the feedback and to make decisions about what changes they should make based on that feedback. An example of such a mechanism might be that internal and external feedback is sought on a regular basis and that the feedback is discussed and evaluated at the beginning of the next meeting. If the feedback is judged to be valid and helpful, members discuss ways to improve team performance, decide what changes to make, and implement those changes.

This may seem like an elaborate process, but in reality it usually takes 10 minutes or less. The trick is to collect the feedback from internal members at the end of one session and discuss it at the beginning of the next. Feedback from external sources should be collected between meetings. (p. 43)

Positive Verbal Communication in Effective Task Groups   Wheelan (1999) describes four aspects that tend to characterize verbal behavior in effective task groups functioning in macro settings (Wheelan, 1999). First, they should "have an *open communication structure* that . . . [encourages] all members to participate. Individuals are listened to regardless of their age, title, sex, race, ethnicity, profession, or other status characteristics. This enhances productivity since all ideas and suggestions get heard" (p. 42).

Second, effective groups regularly seek out feedback about the efficiency and success of their process and output. In successful groups, members accurately can evaluate themselves, their interaction, and their results. They ask for feedback both from each other and from outside sources with whom the group is involved.

Third, in effective task groups, members provide each other with feedback that is practical and useful. Useful feedback satisfies one of two criteria. First, it can help the group achieve its goals. Second, it can provide information to members about improving their individual performance within the group.

Fourth, effective task groups actually put to use both the internal and external feedback they receive. Group members not only seek out and obtain information about group functioning, but they implement recommendations to improve the group's performance.

Nonverbal Communication in Task Groups   We've established that nonverbal behavior includes any means by which information is conveyed not using spoken or written words. Eye contact, facial expressions, body positioning (for example, relaxed or extremely tense), and posture all can convey vital information among group members. Nonverbal communication can give important clues about what's really going on in group members' heads. Sometimes a group member will say one thing but mean another and provide nonverbal evidence for the latter. For example, a task group member might say while grimacing and looking desperately at her watch, "That's a great idea, but we should really save our discussion for when we have more time." The nonverbal cues may indicate that the member really means that she's quite annoyed that the other group member introduced the topic so late in the meeting. She really doesn't think it's a "great idea" at all.

Carroll, Bates, and Johnson (2004) discuss the importance of nonverbal communication, particularly from the perspective of group leaders. (This information is just as important for group members who are not leaders to comprehend what's really going on in a group.) They write:

> Nonverbal behavior is a particularly important source of information for group leaders. Alertness and sensitivity to nonverbal data can provide group leaders with a rich source of interactive material. The thumb tucked tightly inside a fist, a flexing jaw muscle, arms folded tightly across the chest, the drumming of an index finger . . . all represent important messages to group leaders. Although leaders may not always respond immediately to verbal or silent signals such as tight fists, drumming fingers, excessive yawns, inappropriate smiles, or a flushed neck, leaders observe and draw tentative meaning from them. When verbal and nonverbal cues . . . [do not coincide], when the tone of voice insinuates one thing while the words say another, when lips are smiling but hands are clenched, the leader is watchful. The language of nonverbal communication in a group is rich with silent signals that can be received by a leader's [and other group members'] sensitive antennae. The leader "hears" as many of these signals as possible, then responds selectively and in a responsible manner.
>
> Group leaders [and other group members] also may note changes of posture, rates of speech, direction of gaze, length of messages and silences, and changes in facial expression" to provide indications of what members are thinking. (p. 68)

Cross-Cultural Differences in Communication   Note that it's important to be sensitive to cultural differences concerning the meaning of specific nonverbal and verbal behaviors in task group settings. Corey, Corey, and Callanan (2007) explain:

> Many cultural expressions are subject to misinterpretation, including appropriate personal space, eye contact, handshaking, dress, formality of greeting, perspective on time, and so forth. Mainstream Americans frequently feel uncomfortable with periods of silence and tend to talk to ease their tension. In some cultures silence may be a sign of respect and politeness rather than a lack of a desire to continue to speak. Silence may be a reflection of fear or confusion, or it may be a cautious expression and reluctance [to participate further in discussion.] (pp. 125–126)

Eye contact provides an example of diverse cultural expectations for this type of nonverbal behavior. Cormier and Hackney (1999) explain:

> In some cultures . . . eye contact is appropriate when listening. In other cultures, an individual may look away as a sign of respect or may demonstrate more eye contact when talking and less eye contact while listening. Good eye contact [in mainstream American culture]—eye contact that reinforces . . . [attentiveness and makes] communication easier—lies somewhere between the fixed gaze and 'shifty eyes,' or frequent breaks of eye contact. (p. 37)

For instance, Chinese people speaking together "use much less eye contact, especially when it is with the opposite sex"; thus, a male group participant's direct eye contact with a Chinese woman might be "considered rude or seductive in Chinese culture" (Zhang, 2003, p. 47; Ivey and Ivey, 2003, p. 47).

Barriers to Communication   A number of barriers can interfere with communication and group progress. Sometimes, the communication sender is unclear, vague, or evasive in terms of what she's saying. For example, a group member says, "That idea is interesting." What does "interesting" mean? What do you mean when you say you got an "interesting" birthday gift? Is it good or bad? Are you happy or unhappy?

Other times, communication barriers are due to the communication's receiver. The receiver may be biased against the sender, more interested in other concerns, or floating off somewhere in Never Never Land. For example, a group member sends the following communication to another group member, "Time is short. We must come to a decision quickly. How do you vote, yes or no?" The receiving group member responds, "Huh?" The receiver had been thinking about how his parking meter was probably overdue and how he hoped he wouldn't get a parking ticket. The last one he got was for $65.

Still other times, communication barriers exist in the group environment, either internally or externally. Examples are noise and distractions in the hallway, phones ringing, or outbursts, interruptions, and whispering by other group members. A screaming child outside might distract group members who wonder what's happening to him. A communication receiver might be unable to clearly hear a sender's message because other group members are rudely talking about their social plans for Friday night. A fire alarm might disrupt the group altogether.

Communication is effective in groups when senders' intents, that is, what they wish to convey, match their impacts, that is, what the receiver understands. Groups work most effectively when members pay attention and strive to clarify and understand what each other means.

Self-Disclosure   One other aspect of communication worthy of note is *self-disclosure,* the sharing of personal feelings and information. Self-disclosure can enhance group members' feelings of belonging and acceptance in a group. It forms the basis for members getting to know and trust each other.

Some research indicates that self-disclosure can improve members' positive feelings about themselves (Anderson, 1997). Yet other research reveals that self-disclosure has no clear relationship with the group's achievement of goals (Anderson, 1997).

Corey and Corey (2006) urge that group members use care when self-disclosing. For example, going into intimate detail of some former experience not really related to the group or the group's purpose may detract from the group's effectiveness and annoy other members. These authors make some suggestions for using self-disclosure. Group members should only self-disclose when the information has direct bearing on the group's purpose. Members should use careful discretion regarding what they really want to share with others and what is too private or irrelevant to reveal. Finally, self-disclosure is often more appropriate after a group has been meeting for a while instead of during its initial sessions. Highlight 2.5 provides a case example of self-disclosure.

| Highlight 2.5 | Case Example—Self-Disclosure |

Mindy and Mort are members of a community group in the small town of Big Littlehorn that is trying to raise community residents' awareness about the need for a new elementary school. Big Littlehorn has begun to serve as a bedroom community for a nearby metropolitan area. Mindy self-discloses to Mort, "Thanks for volunteering to talk to the town board chairperson. It's always so difficult for me to talk to community leaders." Here she takes a personal risk of possible criticism by confessing to Mort a weakness of hers. Mort responds, "Oh, no problem. I like talking to that guy and pushing him a little. He always thinks he knows everything." Mort's response to Mindy is pleasant, implies warmth, and avoids criticism. As a result, Mindy's and Mort's relationship is enhanced just a little bit by providing mutual support that increases trust.

Interpersonal Interaction

Interpersonal interaction is the result of verbal and nonverbal communication, expressed emotions and attitudes, and behavior between or among persons. It is much more complicated than communication because emotions, attitudes, and behaviors in addition to reciprocal responses are integrally involved. Interpersonal interaction can reflect mutual respect, liking, dislike, resentment, admiration, encouragement, discouragement, approval, disapproval, or mistrust. Through interaction, group members express ideas, emotions, and attitudes to each other. Highlight 2.6 provides a case example involving interpersonal interaction in a group.

Norms

Norms are unwritten, collective rules and expectations held by group members concerning what is appropriate behavior within the group. In essence, norms are "codes of conduct" about what is and is not supposed to be done within the group's interaction (Aldag & Kuzuhara, 2005; Johns, 1996, p. 241). An example of a group norm is a shared expectation that only one group member speaks at a time. Members should not interrupt each other. Another norm may be that all issues discussed within the group are confidential and, therefore, should not be shared outside of the group. Cathy's breaking of this norm was described in Highlight 2.6, an illustration of interpersonal interaction in the group context.

Norms are communicated to group members in at least three basic ways (Dumler & Skinner, 2005). First, a group leader may simply and explicitly state the unwritten rules. Second, group members may discuss among themselves and verbally identify norms. Third, incidents occurring in the group's history may shape norms. Dumler & Skinner (2005) propose the following four examples of how events happening in and to a group can mold group norms, (p. 167):

1. *Leadership "rotation."* One example involves an early point in a group's history where a group member aggressively tries to establish control and

| Highlight 2.6 | Case Examples—Interpersonal Interaction |

One group, a foster care unit, provides an example of contrasting interpersonal interaction by various members. The unit is made up of a social work supervisor, Ada, and her five supervisees, Tom, Dick, Harry, Mary, and Herman. Tom, Dick, Harry, and Mary almost worship Ada. They respect her expertise, appreciate her support, and genuinely like her. Herman, on the other hand, harbors bitter resentment toward Ada because she had been chosen unit supervisor over him. Herman typically pouts during group meetings, interspersing occasional negative or critical comments. The other group members simply ignore him.

Another example of how interpersonal interaction affects group process is a group of community residents on a search committee for the neighborhood's youth recreational center. Applicants include both community residents and candidates from other parts of the city. In order to maintain fairness, avoid hurt feelings, and fulfill legal responsibilities, group members agree that all comments made within the group will go no further.

One group member, Cathy, makes a few comments to Ludwig, one of the applicants from the community who happens to be a good friend of hers. Cathy informs Ludwig of the criticisms made by other group members, implying he shouldn't get his hopes up too high about getting the job. Ludwig irately calls the group members who had criticized him, tells them of Cathy's communication, and angrily complains.

Thereafter, Cathy's credibility within the group is totally blown. When confronted, Cathy refuses to acknowledge that she is the one who blew the whistle to Ludwig. She won't admit to doing it, but she won't admit to not doing it either. Ludwig told groups members she was the one who informed him. Worse yet, group members no longer trust that group discussion will be kept confidential. Productive conversation about the pros and cons of each candidate is severely inhibited. Eventually, the position is filled, for better or worse. However, the other group members swear they will never again serve on another committee with Chatty Cathy.

become the group's forceful leader. Other group members resent this tack and seek to prevent such an occurrence in the future. Thus, they establish a group norm that leadership will be formally rotated every time the group meets. Such rotation, of course, could also be specified for every month, every other group meeting, or some other designated rotation.

2. *The importance of "timeliness" and punctuality.* Consider a group that misses the important deadline of submitting a report to the agency's executive director (the person highest in the agency's power structure). As a result, the agency director chews out the group mercilessly about how the agency's funding depends on getting information to funding sources in a timely manner and that this should NEVER happen again. The group then may establish the norm that deadlines absolutely must be met and excuses for lateness will not be tolerated.

   A similar issue involves being late for meetings. If one or two group members typically saunter into meetings 5 or 10 minutes late, the rest of group is forced to wait, collectively wasting a significant amount of their time. As a result, the group may establish the norm that meetings will start on time. Period. Anyone coming in late will just have to miss anything transpiring during the beginning of the meeting.

3. *Expectations for "loyalty."* In the Highlight 2.6 case example where confidentiality was broken, the group might have openly discussed, changed,

and established a new norm requiring loyalty to the group in the form of confidentiality. *Confidentiality* is the ethical principle that workers should not share information provided by or about a client unless that worker has the client's explicit permission to do so.

4. *The pursuit of "fairness."* Consider a social work unit in a public welfare department. Historically, the first person putting in a request for vacation days automatically gets the days requested. Only a limited number of workers can be on vacation at any one time because enough staff must remain to serve clients adequately. Some of the unit workers who had children in elementary school were unable to put in requests very early because of their children's as-yet-unscheduled sports and other activities. The social work unit group determined that the norm governing the vacation request process was unfair and instituted a new one. The new norm established a process where names were rotated on a list. The worker having first choice for vacation this year would be rotated to having last choice next year, thereby giving all workers a chance at getting the vacation days they wanted.

Note that norms, even once established, are not necessarily static; they often change over time as group purpose, membership, and needs change. Consider an agency work group formed to discuss fund-raising mechanisms. Initially, the group maintains a formal dress code norm, the expectation that members wear three-piece suits or their equivalent during meetings. As group members get to know each other better and become more comfortable, they start attending group meetings in more comfortable informal attire. The dress code norm changes from formal suits to sweatshirts and jeans.

Roles

Roles are expected behavior patterns based on individuals' position or status within the group. Two types of roles are necessary in order to achieve group goals effectively on an ongoing basis (Aldag & Kuzuhara, 2005). First, *task-oriented roles* are those with the purpose of conducting tasks to achieve goals. Group members "who initiate tasks, gather information for use by the . . . [group], offer suggestions, and help motivate others" are performing task-oriented roles (p. 446). *Relations-oriented roles* are those with the purpose of keeping group members happy and satisfied with group progress and interaction. Group members "who keep the group harmonious, assist in helping members resolve disputes, and encourage members as they face barriers are engaging in relations-oriented roles" (p. 446). Sometimes, group members also assume *self-oriented roles*, where these members seek their own satisfaction and control, often without concern for other group members' well-being (Aldag & Kuzuhara, 2005, p. 446). For example, a group member might try to bully other group members into accepting himself as group leader. People assuming self-oriented roles often disrupt the group's ability to work together and get things done.

Roles may be formal or informal. A formal role is that of a committee chairperson assigned by the agency's executive director. Another formal group role is that of a secretary elected by a group majority vote.

Informal roles vary widely. A group member with established expertise might serve as the group expert on certain matters. A member with a well-developed sense of humor might become the group clown, helping the group dissipate anxiety and interact more comfortably. Group leaders might also develop informally. On a court jury, for example, a task-oriented person with good listening, communication, and organizational skills might emerge as leader by group consent.

Group Cohesiveness

Group cohesiveness is the extent to which group members feel close to each other or connected as group members. It makes sense that in most groups, cohesiveness doesn't occur immediately but rather develops over time (Corey & Corey, 2006). Indicators of cohesiveness include good attendance and punctuality, efforts by group members to maintain confidentiality and make each other feel safe, use of good listening skills and support among group members, and a willingness to provide feedback and share perceptions about other members' issues (Corey & Corey, 2006).

Group cohesiveness obviously facilitates a group's ability to function effectively. Effects include members' increased willingness to participate in group activities and functions, encouragement of nonconforming members to get with the program and cooperate, and increased success at achieving goals (Dumler & Skinner, 2005; Johns, 1996).

Power and Status

Related concepts to interpersonal interaction and cohesiveness in groups are power and status. *Power* is the potential ability to move people on a chosen course to produce an effect or achieve some goal (Homan, 2004; Martinez-Brawley, 1995). *Status,* a concept closely related to power, is the relative rank assigned members within the group. People with higher status usually have more power, and those with lower status lesser power. People with more power and higher status can exert greater influence on what a group does.

Aldag and Kuzuhara (2005) describe the three ways that power can be used in groups:

- **Power over.** This is power used to make another person act in a certain way; it may be called *dominance*.
- **Power to.** This is power that gives others the means to act more freely themselves; it is sometimes . . . [referred to as a type of *empowerment*]. . . .
- **Power from.** This is power that protects us from the power of others; it may be called *resistance*. (p. 366)

They indicate that "these uses of power suggest that power is more than just a way to change others' behaviors (although that function is certainly important). It may also be used to help others act more freely or to prevent others from forcing us to do things we don't want to do" (p. 366).

Possible Sources of Power in Groups   There are five possible sources of power in groups: legitimate, reward, coercive, referent, and expert (Aldag & Kuzuhara, 2005; Capuzzi & Gross, 2006; Dumler & Skinner, 2005; French & Raven, 1968). Each can contribute to a group member's potential to influence the group.

Legitimate power is that attained because of one's position and vested authority. Police officers, judges, and state governors have some degree of legitimate power because of their positions.

Reward power is that held because of the ability to provide positive reinforcement or rewards to others. Examples of rewards are raises, "A's" on papers, allowances, promotions, days off, awards, and social praise.

Coercive power is the capability of dispensing punishments or negative reinforcement in order to influence other members' behavior. Bosses wield coercive power over their employees by reprimanding them or by imposing limitations on what they're allowed to do. In addition to legitimate power, police officers have coercive power over speeders by giving expensive speeding tickets. The head nurse on a mental institution's ward can exert coercive power over uncooperative patients by restricting privileges.

Referent power is that held as a result of other group members' respect and high esteem. A military hero might have referent power in his platoon because of great acts of bravery. Famous actors and actresses, some high-level politicians, famous authors, and well-known playwrights have referent power to the extent that they are admired and command respect.

Finally, *expert power* is that based on established authority or expertise in a particular domain. A famous family therapist and author of many books on family therapy may have expert power among a group of social work practitioners who work with families. Likewise, a successful investment counselor volunteering to assist a group of urban residents get their financial affairs in order has expert power within that group.

Leadership

Leadership is the act of exerting influence on other group members to direct their behavior, activities, attitudes, or interaction. Leadership may be formally assigned or informally established. The new executive director of a community mental health center has power based on her formal status, that is, legitimate power. Depending on her qualifications and the parameters of her job description, she may also possess reward, coercive, referent, or expert power.

Informal leaders who gradually develop within a group context might establish their status through referent and expert power. Group members might discover over time that a particular member is exceptionally responsible, conscientious, considerate of others' feelings, and organized. Such a person might emerge as a group leader by consensus or majority agreement.

Types of Leadership   There are two types of leadership often occurring in groups—task leadership and social-emotional leadership (Johns, 1996). These are similar to the types of roles group (task-oriented and relations-oriented) that members can assume in order to enhance group functioning. An individual becomes a *task leader* when she has some established power and focuses her attention on organizing group members to attain group goals. *A social-emotional leader,* on the other hand, functions as group leader concerning emotional issues. He might be the person most liked in the group, or maybe the one providing support to other group members, praising input, suggesting compromises when differences arise, mediating conflicts, or enhancing morale. Another term for social-emotional leadership is group maintenance leadership (Schopler & Galinsky, 1995).

Leadership Skills   In addition to power base, effective leaders require three skills: promoting group functioning; collecting and assessing information; and taking action (Toseland & Rivas, 2005). Promoting group functioning centers on involving and motivating group members. Attending and responding skills are important. Basic communication skills such as simple encouragement are important. For example, sometimes a simple one-word response of nonverbal head nod while maintaining eye contact is enough to encourage a group member to continue. Another effective communication skill is *rephrasing,* stating what another person says, but by using different words than those used by that person. One other useful communication skill is *clarification,* making certain that what a group member says is understood. This is often done by asking a question about a statement. The group leader must make group members feel they are important group participants. Highlight 2.7 discusses ways that group leaders can empower group members.

The second skill in successful group leadership is collecting and assessing information. This involves soliciting necessary information from group members, synthesizing its meaning, and analyzing its importance. For example, an agency group is established to develop an *in-service training program.* This is a program provided by an employing agency, usually conducted by a supervisor or an outside expert, designed to help agency staff improve their effectiveness (e.g., providing education about specific treatment techniques) or better understand agency functioning (e.g., educating staff about new legal issues or policy changes). An effective group leader asks members "the right questions" to elicit the necessary information. The group leader should help the group address what types of training agency staff require, how the group should solicit this information from staff, who could provide training, and what scheduling would be most convenient. The leader should help the group summarize information and prioritize tasks. Such action includes "pointing out patterns in the data, identifying gaps in the data, and establishing mechanisms or

| **Highlight 2.7** | **Empowerment by Group Leaders** |

Toseland and Rivas (2005) emphasize that it's critical for group leaders to share power and encourage member participation beginning at the very first meeting. They cite at least five ways that leaders can empower members to become involved, take responsibility for group activities, and feel that they are important contributors to the group:

1. A group leader should promote communication *among group members* instead of structuring communication primarily *between him or herself and a member.* Members directing attention only to the group leader gives that leader great power and control over what happens in the group. When group members communicate with each other, it decreases the leader's power in a positive way. Relationships may then develop among members, they may feel freer to share ideas with each other, and they may be more willing to work productively together.

2. A group leader should seek "members' input into the agenda for the meeting and the direction the group should take in future meetings" (p. 94). Asking for input implies that the leader respects what group members have to say. A leader who responds to group members' suggestions by incorporating their input can empower group members and make them feel that their participation in the group really matters.

3. A group leader should support group members who have natural leadership potential when they "make their first, tentative attempts at exerting their own influence in the group" (p. 95). A leader should not hoard power and abruptly halt other group members' access to it. Rather, a leader should appreciate group members' strengths and energy, encouraging the use of these qualities to further fulfill group goals.

4. A group leader should support "attempts at mutual sharing and mutual aid among members" (p. 95). We've discussed *mutual aid*—the act of providing support, feedback, and information within a group context—in the context of empowering groups and group members. Spending group time in this way can enhance development of relationships, trust, and competence in working together.

5. A group leader should "model and teach members selected leadership skills early in the life of the group" (p. 95). A good group leader can use the group context to teach group members effective leadership skills by utilizing such skills during the group process.

plans for obtaining data to complete the assessment" (Toseland & Rivas, 2005, p. 111).

The third type of skill necessary for effective leadership is taking action, that is, those skills that are those geared to developing plans and assisting group members in plan implementation. An effective leader should encourage members' input, assist them in communication with each other (both of which are discussed in Highlight 2.7), provide direction when necessary, keep the group on task, and resolve conflicts as they arise.

STAGES OF TASK GROUP DEVELOPMENT

Groups usually proceed through a number of stages as they develop through time. These include composition, beginnings, assessment, stabilization and working, and endings stages (Corey & Corey, 2006; Schopler & Galinsky, 1995; Toseland & Rivas, 2005).

Stage 1: Task Group Composition

Whether individuals are appropriate for membership in any particular group depends on that group's purpose. Shulman (1992) emphasizes "that there be some common ground between their individual needs and the purpose of the group" (p. 303). In treatment groups, it makes sense to select members who are working on common problems or addressing similar issues. For example, a support group for people with multiple sclerosis might focus on experiences commonly encountered by persons with the disease and how such experiences best be dealt with. (*Multiple sclerosis* is a disease where the central nervous system slowly deteriorates resulting in paralysis, numbness, muscle tremors and weakness, visual impairments, and speech problems [Barker, 2003; Mish, 1995].) Likewise, a treatment group for people with schizophrenia would focus on their common issues and problems. (*Schizophrenia* is a mental disorder where people experience a range of cognitive and emotional problems, including "delusions," "hallucinations," "disorganized speech," "grossly disorganized or catatonic behavior," and "other negative symptoms" (American Psychiatric Association, 2000, p. 297). The disorder lasting at least six months, interferes with people's ability to function in occupational or interpersonal settings.)

Composing task groups in the macro environment requires different considerations. Task groups may be either formal or informal. Formal groups requiring structured representation in membership include delegate assemblies, committees composed of elected representatives, and task forces appointed by administration. Because informal groups are "groups that emerge naturally in response to the common interests of organizational members," there may be great diversity in membership (Johns, 1996, p. 233).

Definition of the Group's Purpose   A major consideration in task group composition is definition of the group's purpose to determine who will be the most useful group members. (Aldag & Kuzuhara, 2005; Fatout & Rose, 1995; Toseland & Rivas, 2005). For example, two social workers bring a group of community members together to address the community issue of sexual assault. Who would logically support or be interested in addressing this issue? Who might have expertise to help define the problems involved and develop plans? Who has potential resources to contribute for plan implementation? The workers identified a number of potential group members including the local physician who examines sexual assault survivors; a police officer who has access to legal statistics and is often the first one called to the crime scene; upstanding community leaders, such as the bank president, who lend credibility to the issue and have significant access to resources; and women's studies faculty from the local university, who have natural interest in this women's issue.

The Group's "Social Context"   Another factor to consider regarding group composition is the "social context" of the group (Fatout & Rose, 1995, p. 33). One aspect is location and sponsorship (Toseland & Rivas, 1995). Is an agency sponsoring the meeting? If so, what agency representation is required? What resources will the agency provide? If no agency is technically sponsoring the meeting, where in the community will group meetings be held?

The perceptions held by others in the external environment about the issue and the group's purpose is another aspect of social context. With respect to the community group formed to address sexual assault identified above, is public sentiment sympathetic to or blaming of assault survivors? Will the community likely support or resent the group and its purpose?

Group Size   Group size is still another element of group composition (Fatout & Rose, 1995; Toseland & Rivas, 2005). There appears to be no magical answer regarding the best size of a group (Corey & Corey, 2006). The trick is to include enough people to generate ideas and get work done, but not so many that the group process becomes unmanageable. Group membership should reflect a broad enough range of abilities and behavior "to ensure a breadth of perspective and capability for solving problems" (Schopler & Galinsky, 1995, p. 1135).

As groups increase in size, they tend to become more formal and develop structures resembling those in larger organizations (Fatout & Rose, 1995). For example, a social work student club may have very informal interactions when there are only five members. However, when the group expands to 35, the membership elects officers and follows more formal procedures for running meetings such as parliamentary procedure (a highly structured technique designed to make decisions and conduct business).[1]

Stage 2: Beginnings

During the beginnings stage, group members get to know each other and begin establishing the group's interpersonal dynamics. Initially, introductions are in order. Members begin addressing trust issues so that group cohesion is enhanced. They discuss the group's purpose and goals to establish the group's ongoing direction. A group usually seeks a consensus regarding goals so that it may begin identifying the tasks necessary to achieve those goals. Contracting involves establishing agreements about individual and group responsibilities. Goals, procedures, roles, and basic arrangements such as regularity of meetings and meeting place are established.

The beginnings period allows the group to structure itself in terms of leadership and division of responsibility (Corey & Corey, 2006). In some groups, one strong authoritarian leader will emerge. Other groups will assume

---

[1] It should be noted that parliamentary procedure can be and often is used with any size group. Major concepts include "motion" (a proposal submitted to the group that requires action), "second" (an indication of approval of a proposed motion), "amend" (to add, delete, or substitute words or portions of a motion), "majority vote" (greater than one-half of the total of persons voting or ballots cast), and "table" (a motion to postpone action indefinitely on a motion already on the floor) (Kirst-Ashman & Hull, 1997, p. 111).

a much more democratic perspective, more evenly distributing responsibility for maintenance and tasks.

Stage 3: Assessment

We have established that effective group leaders conduct ongoing assessment of group dynamics and functioning. Assessment is cited as stage three because it should begin when the group is formed.

Assessment involves all of the concepts described earlier in the discussion of group dynamics. Leading a group requires focusing attention on communication, interpersonal interaction, norms, roles, cohesion, power, and status. As group interaction is ongoing, so is assessment. A leader's role involves making certain the group gets along well and remains on task. Assessment of group functioning is important both during initial group involvement and as an ongoing maintenance task.

Conflict, referred to as *storming*, often characterizes both this phase and the beginnings phase of the group (Johns, 1996, p. 235; Schriver, 2004, p. 400). Members may experience disagreement regarding where they think the group should go or how it should be run. It is important for leadership to address such conflicts in order for the group to continue and accomplish its goals.

Stage 4: Stabilization and Working

Stabilization and working is the task group's productive period. Order must be established for the group to function and progress. Sometimes, the stabilization process is referred to as *norming,* where "mechanisms for resolving conflict, working together as a group, and accomplishing the group purpose" are established (Johns, 1996, p. 235; Schriver, 2004, p. 400). Group members must come to a consensus about how disagreements will be handled so that they may proceed with their assigned tasks.

During the working phase, group leadership must pay special attention to meeting preparation, clear designation regarding how and when tasks will be performed, empowering participants, enhancing motivation, minimizing conflict, keeping members on track, and evaluating the progress of both individuals and the entire group (Toseland & Rivas, 2005). Sometimes, this is referred as the *performing* phase of the group, where the focus is on completing tasks (Johns, 1996, p. 235; Schriver, 2004, p. 400).

Stage 5: Endings and Evaluation

Not all groups terminate. Some are ongoing, such as a city council or a civic association like the Jaycees. Even with ongoing groups, membership usually changes. People move away, lose interest, or must attend to other priorities. Endings for individual group members and full groups happen inevitably, just like death.

Some approaches help to facilitate endings in groups. First, leadership can help prepare group members by talking about the group's termination ahead of time. This dulls the surprise factor when a group abruptly ends. It also gives members time to think about the group's end ahead of time, deal with their feelings, and think of alternative ways for spending their time.

Another suggestion for helping groups end is to encourage the sharing of ending feelings (Anderson, 1997). Group members can get negative feelings such as regret and loss out in the open, in addition to receiving emotional support from other group members.

Finally, evaluating and summarizing the group's accomplishments is helpful (Anderson, 1997; Schopler & Galinsky, 1995). Especially with a successful group that accomplished many or most of its goals, giving the group and members credit for their achievement can be very rewarding. In the event that goals were not achieved, the group might discuss reasons why and suggest alternative methods to achieve goals in the future.

CHAPTER SUMMARY

This chapter examined human behavior in groups functioning in macro settings. Theoretical perspectives on groups were explained, including field, social exchange, learning, psychoanalytic, systems, empowerment, and feminist theories. Group concepts operating regardless of theoretical perspective were defined and discussed. These included communication, interpersonal interaction, norms, roles, group cohesion, power and status, and leadership.

Five stages of task group development were examined and suggestions for effective group functioning provided. Stages included (1) task group composition, (2) beginnings, (3) assessment, (4) stabilization and working, and (5) endings and evaluation.

3 CHAPTER

Types of Groups in the Macro Social Environment

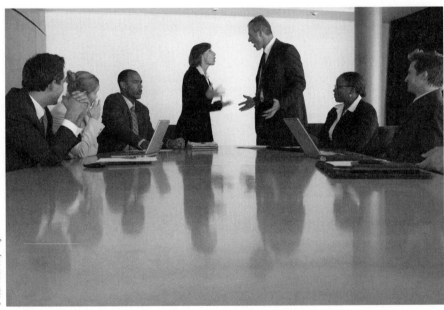

© Nick White/Getty Images

Many types of organizational and community groups function in the macro social environment.

CHAPTER CONTENTS

Sunshine is the social worker on a homeless shelter's assessment team. Other team members are a physician, nurse, psychologist, in-house living supervisor, and vocational counselor. Together, the team works with incoming homeless families, conducting individual and family assessments. Their initial plans involve meeting families' immediate health and survival needs. Long-term planning focuses on permanent housing, access to health care, vocational planning, and counseling needs. Sunshine's been working with the group for almost six years now. She thinks they function together pretty well, as they're used to each other's little personality quirks.

Aaron, a social worker at a group home for adults with chronic mental illness,[1] is leading a treatment conference on behalf of Harry, one of the group home's residents. Aaron is responsible for calling together the home care supervisor, psychiatrist, and daytime care counselors to discuss Harry's case. Aaron will formulate an agenda for the meeting, lead the discussion, solicit feedback from participants, assist the group in establishing intervention plans, and write up the final report including recommendations.

Giovanna, the supervisor of a hospital social work unit, is a member of an administrative group comprised of the hospital director, the head nursing supervisor, and the physical therapy supervisor. Their purpose is to evaluate the hospital's policies regarding job expectations for members of each professional group and make recommendations for changes.

Javier, a school social worker, was elected by the other workers in his school district to serve as a delegate to the state's School Social Work Advocacy Association. This group meets in the state capitol four times each year to identify common issues, discuss concerns, and make recommendations to state legislators that advocate for school policy improvements.

Ginny, a school worker at a large residential facility for people with cognitive disabilities, is a member of the agency's Facilities Improvement Committee. The group includes representatives from various other agency units such as adult care counselors and educational specialists. The group's task is to evaluate the adequacy of living conditions for residents. Plans include assessment of various institutional facets including: furniture and paint conditions throughout the institution; food preparation and quality; transportation availability for residents (for example, to meet health care and recreational needs); regularity of treatment plan updates; and general staff conduct toward residents. Ultimately, the group will make recommendations to the agency's administration for improvements.

Jude, a social worker at a county social services department, organized a group of neighborhood center residents to advocate for a summer sports and recreation program for community youth. The social action group's goal is to persuade elected county officials to divert some funds to the center so that volunteers might develop and run the program.

---

[1] Mental illness or mental disorder is any of a wide range of psychological, emotional, or cognitive disorders that impair a person's ability to function effectively. Causes may be "biological, chemical, physiological, genetic, psychological, or social" (Barker, 2003, p. 269). *Chronic* mental illness means that it is ongoing or long lasting.

Each scenario above illustrates how social workers can be involved in task groups. Social workers, of course, also run treatment groups. For example, a worker might run a group for adult survivors of sexual abuse, adult children dealing with their parents' deteriorating health, or children struggling with their parents' divorce. Or, a worker might lead a group to educate teens about HIV transmission, new parents about the behavioral management of their children, or unemployed adults about job possibilities in their community.

Because groups vary so radically in size, purpose, and process, there are many ways to categorize them. Most of the ensuing discussion will address task groups because of their significance in the macro social environment.

This chapter will:

- Explain the relevance of groups for generalist practice in the macro social environment.
- Define task groups, including teams, treatment conferences, administrative groups, delegate councils, committees, and social action groups.
- Discuss barriers to successful teamwork and team empowerment.
- Address empowerment through good committee leadership.
- Define treatment groups, including therapy, support, educational, growth, and socialization groups, and address the differences between treatment conferences and treatment groups.
- Examine how social action groups empower their members to alter the external social environment through increasing understanding, inspiring others, conscious raising, providing mutual support, and using cooperation.

TASK GROUPS

Task or *work groups* are those applying the principles of group dynamics to solve problems, develop innovative ideas, formulate plans, and achieve goals. Task groups in the macro social environment are formed to meet the needs of individuals, families, groups, organizations, or communities. For example, an agency task group might focus on developing treatment strategies to meet the needs of Eastern European immigrants seeking agency resources. This targets helping individuals and families. Another task group might include social services personnel and representatives from community neighborhoods to coordinate a neighborhood watch program aimed at preventing crime. This task group works on behalf of various neighborhood groups and the entire community. Still another organizational task group consists of representatives from various departments to review the agency's policy manual and recommend changes. This task group serves the organization.

There are six main types of task groups, including teams, treatment conferences, administrative groups, delegate councils, committees, and social action groups (Fatout & Rose, 1995; Toseland & Rivas, 1995). Teams and treatment conferences are groups formulated to meet clients' needs, while the others usually address organizational needs (Toseland & Rivas, 2005).

Teams

A *team* is a group of two or more people gathered together to work collaboratively and interdependently to pursue a designated purpose. Within the macro environment of social service provision, team members function together to improve client treatment and service provision. Note that not just any old work group is a team. A team consists of committed members working in unison on the behalf of clients (Johnson & Johnson, 1997).

Teams, then, differ from other types of work groups in two major ways (Johnson & Johnson, 1997; Katzenbach & Smith, 1993). First, teams depend on each other and clearly acknowledge that fact, whereas other work groups often consist of members working more independently of each other. Second, teams emphasize achievement of team goals, whereas other work groups tend to focus on achievement of individual tasks and goals within the group context. A good way for conceptualizing an effective team is to think of a successful sports team; "such teams are small groups made up of highly skilled individuals who are able to meld these skills into a cohesive effort" (Johns, 1996, p. 256). Team members have a unified identity and see themselves as a unit working together to achieve mutual goals.

Teams may be formed either internally within an agency environment or they may include representatives from other systems in the macro environment external to the agency. Six types emerge (Compton et al., 2005).

First, a team may consist solely of social work practitioners from the same agency. An example is a team of social workers in a Veteran's Administration hospital where social workers assigned to the temporary housing unit for homeless vets, a substance abuse counseling unit, and the hospital surgical unit work together on the behalf of a homeless vet who is an alcoholic and has serious kidney malfunctioning.

A second type of team is also one composed solely of social workers, but they come from a variety of agencies within the community. An example involves social workers from various agencies including a community recreational center, the school, protective services, and a shelter for victims of domestic abuse. These workers come together as a team to establish a service plan for a family with children ages 7, 9, and 11 and a physically abusive father.

A third type of team involves professionals from a variety of disciplines within the same agency. An example is a social worker, psychiatrist, nursing supervisor, and an occupational therapist[2] working in a nursing home. Together, they function as a team to develop residents' plans involving medication, exercise, activities, and counseling.

A fourth type of team also includes a variety of professionals, but they come from different agencies. Consider a young man with a cognitive disability who lives in a group home and needs to establish a vocational plan for his

---

[2] Occupational therapy is "therapy by means of activity, especially creative activity prescribed for its effect in promoting recovery or rehabilitation" (Mish, 1995, p. 804). It often focuses on enhancing fine motor coordination (such as eye/hand coordination) and sensory integration (the ability to take in, sort out, and connect sensory information gathered from the external environment).

future. The group home social worker forms a team with an independent psychologist who does ability and achievement testing along with a vocational rehabilitation counselor from a sheltered workshop to establish a plan.

A fifth type of team involves social work practitioners working together with indigenous helpers or paraprofessionals within the parameters of the same agency. An *indigenous worker* is a community member who either volunteers or is employed to assist professionals. Tasks may include conducting basic problem assessments, providing necessary information about available services, or connecting people with services (Barker, 2003). A *paraprofessional* is a person with specialized skills and training who assists a professional in conducting his or her work. Examples include paralegals and physicians' assistants (Barker, 2003). This type of team might include an agency social worker and a foster parent working together to establish a service plan for a child in foster care (Compton et al., 2005).

The final type of team also involves social work practitioners working with indigenous workers or paraprofessionals, but who come from outside the agency's parameters. An example is a social worker employed by a homeless shelter who forms a team with volunteer community residents to raise funds for area homeless people. Highlight 3.1 discusses barriers to successful teamwork and team empowerment.

Treatment Conferences

Treatment conferences are groups who meet to establish, monitor, and coordinate service plans on the behalf of a client system (Fatout & Rose, 1995; Toseland & Rivas, 2005). They may also be called case conferences, case staffings, treatment staffings, or, simply, staffings. A treatment conference may be conducted by a team, if the group meets the definition of a team, namely, that members are interdependent and work together toward a unified goal.

However, treatment conferences often differ from teams in at least three ways (Toseland & Rivas, 2005). First, group members might not have established a working relationship as a unit. Second, treatment conferences might be held infrequently, such as at six-month or one-year intervals, preventing the bonding necessary to establish a team. Third, treatment conferences might involve a different configuration of participants at each meeting since long periods of time pass, clients' needs change, and staff come and go.

Treatment conferences may involve internal agency professionals and staff, or they may include professionals and staff from other agencies. It depends on which agencies and staff are involved in service provision. Usually, the involvement of all service providers, regardless of their agency affiliation, is encouraged.

Sometimes, clients and their families are invited to attend treatment conferences. Other times, clients are invited to attend only a portion of the conference. Some agencies indicate that having clients and other outsiders present interferes with the frank presentation of information about clients and their families. Other agencies feel that content may be too emotionally stressful for clients and their families to hear.

| Highlight 3.1 | **Barriers to Successful Teamwork and Team Empowerment** |

Sometimes a social worker may be hesitant to participate on a team. Compton and her colleagues (2005) propose a scenario that might be used to describe such unwillingness:

> A man crossing the street was hit by a truck. When passers-by rushed over to help, they saw the man crawling away as fast as he could, on hands and one knee, dragging one leg helplessly. They said, "Where are you going? Don't you realize you've just been hit by a truck? You need help." The man replied, "Please leave me alone. I don't want to get involved." (p. 293)

The following four dynamics can become obstacles to team participation (Compton et al., 2005, pp. 293–294):

1. *The Myth of Good Intentions.* "Social workers sometimes assume that good intentions and a cooperative attitude are sufficient to ensure effective teamwork. If we are friendly, respectful, and considerate of others, surely good interdisciplinary collaboration must follow? This rests on the assumptions that getting along with others is a relatively simple and natural ability, that teamwork depends primarily on personal characteristics, and that specific knowledge and skills are nonessential" (p. 293). Instead, a team effort should be conducted carefully as it is a complex process "that involves a great deal more than good intentions and desirable personal qualities. . . . [K]nowledge and skills for

effective teamwork must be learned and refined" (p. 293).

2. *Helplessness in the Face of Authority.* Some social workers practice in settings dominated by other professions. For example, primary and secondary schools are governed by educators, and health care personnel preside over hospital or other health care settings. Being in the minority might discourage a social worker from speaking up and actively contributing on a team. Social workers should be encouraged to develop confidence in their knowledge and skills, and to assertively contribute to the team's process of goal achievement.

3. *Professional Boundaries.* "Professionals who serve on helping teams tend to have both distinct and common areas of expertise. Indeed, some tasks can be completed by team members from several professions or disciplines. Because of the overlapping responsibilities associated with these common tasks, specific negotiation is required to avoid misunderstanding, conflict, and duplication of effort. Some professionals, including certain social workers, view their turf as large and expansive. They may consign other team members from other professions and disciplines to peripheral roles. Some other professionals may eschew specialization and insist that all members of the team—regardless of discipline—can deal effectively with any problem. Neither extreme seems especially productive. Teams reflect diverse talents

Case Example of a Treatment Conference   The following is an example of a treatment conference in a diagnostic and treatment center for children with multiple physical and psychological disabilities. The client Timmy, 3, has severe cerebral palsy, a disability resulting from damage to the brain before, during, or shortly after birth that results in problems with muscular coordination and speech (Mish, 1995). Timmy has very little control of his extremities, torso, face, and mouth. He has some limited control of his eyes.

After Timmy is referred for assessment, extensive testing is performed by speech, occupational, and physical therapists. A physician conducts a thorough physical examination and orders relevant tests. Sometimes, a geneticist is involved to establish the etiology of the disorder. However, Timmy experienced oxygen deprivation at birth due to the umbilical cord being wrapped and abilities. Effective service often requires a combination of specialized and general expertise. Teams benefit from recognition and use of members with special competence and clarification about who should do what within those common areas that overlap" (p. 293). Therefore, it's important to discuss and specify who will assume what role in getting things done.

4. *Professional Differences.* Professionals from different disciplines may assume different perspectives on the "right" way to accomplish goals. For example, consider a doctor and a social worker who are dealing with an older adult who broke her hip and now must find an alternative supportive living environment. The doctor and other health care personnel might stress her physical needs, her physical limitations, and her medication. A social worker, on the other hand, would probably focus more keenly on the patient's ability to fit into and be comfortable in whatever environment she enters (person-in-environment fit). For instance, who might serve as her support system? How will she get around to conduct her daily living affairs, such as grocery shopping and washing clothes? Who could she call upon to help her in the event of an emergency?

Even professionals from the same discipline— including social work—might have very different perspectives on how to do things. One social worker might be very behaviorally oriented and feel that all goals and means to achieve them should be clearly defined and started immediately. Another social worker might assume that it's much more important to spend time talking about things and examining goals carefully before proceeding. Have you ever worked on a group project for some class where you and some of the other group members had totally different ideas about how the project should proceed? It is suggested that team members "should recognize the inevitability . . . of diverse perspectives and opinions, and learn to negotiate them, in the best interests" of whomever the team is trying to help or whatever goals it's trying to accomplish (p. 294).

Team Empowerment

Hellriegel and Slocum (2007) emphasize that effective teams are empowered by having high degrees of at least three variables. First, teams are empowered by members who actually feel the team is *effective*. Members are motivated when they feel their work is worth it. To what extent are team members confident in their ability and power to achieve goals? A second variable empowering teams is the extent to which members feel their work and *goals are valuable*. To what extent do they feel they can really make an impact? To what extent is what they're doing important to others? A third empowering variable involves the extent to which team members feel they have *adequate autonomy* and can exercise their own judgment, even though the team must function as a unit. Team members should not feel ignored, bullied, or overly pressured. They should feel their voices are heard as they work with others to compromise and get things done.

Critical Thinking Questions 3.1

Have you ever been a member of a team or task group? If so, what were the circumstances? What variables acted as barriers to effective teamwork? What factors helped to empower the group to achieve its goals?

around his neck. Since the etiology of the disability has been established, the program director, a physician, determines that a genetic assessment is unnecessary. A psychologist conducts perceptual and ability testing. Finally, a social worker carries out a family assessment.

All evaluators subsequently attend the treatment conference. This particular group cannot be considered a team, because it does not work together on a regular basis. For example, there are five occupational therapists and three social workers. The configuration of participants for any particular client varies drastically as only one professional per discipline is involved with each case. During the treatment conference, participants share their findings and prepare a treatment plan. For children like Timmy who require ongoing treatment and therapy, an annual treatment conference is automatically scheduled. Only those professionals involved in ongoing treatment attend later treatment conferences. For instance, a speech therapist would no longer be involved with the case if the child did not require speech therapy. Since Timmy has such extensive treatment needs, professionals from all disciplines will be involved in future conferences.

 Critical Thinking Questions 3.2

The agency in the above case example of a treatment conference has a policy that excludes parents and clients from treatment conferences because of reasons mentioned earlier. Is this appropriate? Is this ethical? How does client exclusion relate to self-determination (each individual's right to make his or her own decisions), an important professional value in social work? To what extent do clients have the right to know about and be involved in their own and their family's assessment and intervention planning? What is your recommendation—inclusion or exclusion?

Treatment Groups Versus Treatment Conferences   Note that agencies, in addition to providing treatment to individuals and families, can also offer counseling and help to a group of people gathered together at the same time. Such groups are called *treatment groups*. The major difference between task groups and treatment groups is that the task group's aim is to achieve a desired goal or to implement a change in the group's *external* environment. A treatment group's purpose, on the other hand, is to alter group members' behavior or attitudes in the *internal* group environment for therapeutic, educational, supportive, or social reasons (Fatout & Rose, 1995; Toseland & Rivas, 2005). Treatment groups involve clients and establish treatment goals for those clients. Task groups form goals to make changes or implement goals outside of the group (for example, in the agency or the community). Highlight 3.2 describes five primary types of treatment groups. That content is included here to describe a common aspect of service provision in social service agencies.

Be careful not to confuse treatment groups with treatment conferences. Treatment conferences may be composed of staff and clients with the goal of *externally* monitoring the treatment process. Treatment groups provide treatment *internally* and directly to clients.

Highlight 3.2 | Treatment Groups

Treatment groups help individuals solve personal problems, change unwanted behaviors, cope with stress, and improve quality of life. Efforts focus on clients solving their personal problems, enhancing personal qualities, or providing each other with support. Toseland and Rivas (2005) divide treatment groups into five primary types: therapy, support, education, growth, and socialization.

Therapy Groups

Therapy groups help members with serious psychological and emotional problems change their behavior. Led by an expert therapist, emphasis is on "remediation and rehabilitation" (Toseland & Rivas, 2005, p. 25). Examples of therapy groups are those formed to treat "depression, sexual difficulties, anxiety, and psychosomatic disorders"* (Corey & Corey, 1997, p. 11).

Support Groups

Support groups consist of participants who share common issues or problems and meet on an ongoing basis to cope with stress, give each other suggestions, provide encouragement, convey information, and furnish emotional support (Barker, 2003). Such groups vary greatly in process and structure. They may either be run by a trained social worker or by members themselves. Examples include a group of persons living with AIDS, recovering alcoholics, adult survivors of sexual abuse, and veterans experiencing posttraumatic stress disorder.

Support groups differ from therapy groups in two major ways. First, support groups place greater emphasis on members supporting and helping each other. This contrasts with how a therapy group focuses on the leader assisting members in solving serious personal problems. The second way support groups differ from therapy groups is their emphasis on ongoing coping and support instead of alleviating psychological difficulties.

Case Example: Therapy Groups for Women Living with Depression and Anxiety

An example of a therapy group is one run in a mental health setting for women living with depression and anxiety (Stauffer, Pehrsson, & Briggs, 2006, p. 359). Stauffer and his colleagues (2006) describe such a group:

A group of women sat waiting for the first session of an anxiety and depression group to begin.

Angie looked at her fingers guiltily. Despite her best efforts, she had bitten down to the quick of her exposed and raw nailbeds. She did feel good, though, about keeping her appointment for the "class to help me with my nerves."

Across the waiting room, Susan leaned against a wall, restless and fidgeting nervously. Thoughts raced through her mind as she wondered, 'How has life come to this?'

As Kat hunched in a chair near the exit, her stomach churned with hunger. She had virtually stopped eating a month ago. What little she did eat she vomited. Kat read books and watched television many hours a day to stop worrying about everything. She often drank wine to forget and to sleep.

Tricia sat in a corner chair wracked with guilt, believing she was failing her struggling family. "This is a waste of time and money," she thought, while considering her family needs. Yet she lacked the energy to move. She felt exhausted all the time.

Keely sat in a corner opposite Tricia with reddened eyes, trying to hold back tears. She cried easily and too often. Life overwhelmed her. She no longer felt connected to friends and family. Although her involvement in her church had been substantial and important to her, more recently she felt isolated and detached from everyone and everything. (p. 359)

The following are five examples of goals such a group might establish for its members (Stauffer et al., 2006). First, participants might learn to carefully examine their own behavior for symptoms of depression and replace old behavior patterns with new, more functional ones. Second, members might work on decreasing negative thinking about themselves and substituting more positive, objective thinking about their strengths. Third, these women might learn relaxation and stress-reduction techniques. Fourth, participants might provide a supportive environment where they feel free to express their concerns. Fifth, members may use the group as a forum for practicing "positive and assertive communication" that they then could apply to other settings in their lives (p. 362).

continued

Highlight 3.2 | *continued*

Case Example: Support Groups for GLBT People
Examples of support groups include those benefiting GLBT (gay, lesbian, bisexual, and transsexual) people. Finnegan and McNally (1996) indicate that "lesbians and gay men are often traumatized by the emotional, and sometimes physical, abuse visited on them by a virulently homophobic culture" (p. 117). Due largely to such oppression, lesbian and gay people are at special "risk for conditions such as depression, substance abuse, suicide, homelessness, and injury or death from perpetrators of hate crimes" (DeLois, 1998, p. 65).

Communities and agencies can establish support groups to address any number of issues, depending on needs. Several themes often emerge in gay men's support groups, including the following (Ball & Lipton, 1997; Puglia & House, 2006):

- Dealing with the stigma and shame associated with being gay that is imposed by the encompassing society
- Coming out, the "ongoing developmental process of gay identity formation organized around revealing and accepting one's sexual orientation" (Ball & Lipton, p. 265)
- AIDS/HIV
- Family issues such as acceptance or lack thereof by their family of origin
- Relationships and intimacy in a society that doesn't foster gay relationships
- The resolution of ethnic and cultural identities with the many issues involved

Similarly, Engelhardt (1997) describes common themes addressed in lesbian women's support groups:

- "Management of oppression, stigma, and difference."
- The "invisibility of the lesbian woman's experience."
- "Safety and vigilance issues . . . ranging from verbal harassment to physical assault."
- "Lesbian relationships and sexual expression."
- "Living with dignity as a declared lesbian woman" (pp. 281–283).

Educational Groups
Educational groups provide information to participants. Information may be of virtually any kind. Examples of educational groups include an infomational meeting of parents of children having a rare genetic disorder characterized by extremely frail bones that are easily broken (osteogenesis imperfecta); teens receiving sex education; a presentation by an employment counselor to a group of adults interested in finding jobs; and a group of older adults in a nursing home requesting information about their prescribed drugs.

Toseland and Rivas (2005) explain the functioning of educational groups:

All educational groups are aimed at increasing members' information or skills. Most groups routinely involve presentations of information and knowledge by experts. They also often include opportunities for group discussion to foster learning. When leading educational groups, workers concentrate on both the individual learner and the group as a whole as vehicles for learning, reinforcement, and discussion.

Members of educational groups are bonded by a common interest in the material to be learned and by common characteristics, such as being an adolescent, a prospective foster parent, a union worker, or a board member. In composing educational groups, workers consider each member's knowledge of the subject matter and level of skills and experience so that all members can derive the most benefit from the learning experience. (p. 24)

Growth Groups
Growth groups are those aimed at expanding self-awareness, increasing potential, and maximizing optimal health and well-being. Growth groups often emphasize exploring hidden thoughts and emotions in addition to disclosing these to other group members for feedback. Examples include a group of heterosexual singles exploring their attitudes about the opposite gender; "a values clarification group for adolescents"; and a group of gay men focusing on gay pride issues (Toseland & Rivas, 2005, p. 25).

Case Example: Growth Groups for African American Juvenile Offenders

Harvey (1997) describes the development and implementation of growth groups for African American juvenile offenders that use an Afrocentric approach. *Afrocentricity* is a worldview that emphasizes the history, culture, and experiences of people who have black African ancestry as a basis for understanding how the world functions and how people are treated (Barker, 2003). These growth groups provide a good example of how a macro system can develop a program to enhance the well-being of a population-at-risk. Here, a type of "treatment group" can also address broader needs (that is, fighting oppression, increasing social awareness, and enhancing self-confidence) in a macro context.

Leashore (1995) comments on the status of African American citizens in the United States:

> African Americans have fought and endured institutionalized racism, discrimination, and oppression . . . Amid inhumane assaults and against great odds it is remarkable that they have made substantial improvements in advancing the quality of their lives, as well as the lives of Americans in general. However, improvements for African Americans have been uneven, and African Americans continue to differ on many socioeconomic indicators when compared with whites. (p. 107)

Making up almost 12.8 percent of the U.S. population, African American people continue to suffer a range of injustices; when compared with whites, the following is true (U.S. Census Bureau, 2005):

- Children are much more likely to live in poor families.
- Infant mortality is almost two and a half times that of whites.
- African Americans are almost one third less likely to graduate from college.
- Income levels are significantly less.
- African Americans are much more likely to be incarcerated in the criminal justice system. African Americans make up almost 40 percent of people in correctional facilities and almost 40 percent of people on death row.

The purposes of forming Afrocentric growth groups of African American juvenile offenders include enhancing members' self respect; establishing a stronger identity with African heritage and culture; developing ties with a positive peer group; widening vocational aspirations; and strengthening the ability to make socially responsible decisions (Harvey, 1997). In addition to providing a treatment context where they work on developing personal strengths, these groups address and help members cope with broader social issues.

Young African American offenders are viewed within their macro context. Poverty, marital and family dissolution, white oppression and discrimination, the strong social pressure of negative street-corner peer groups and gangs, and lack of career hopes all contribute to an environment where crime becomes a logical means of survival. These young men typically express a number of themes (Harvey, 1997):

- Adults around here do it, so why shouldn't I?
- Violence is a way of life. If you don't stand up for yourself, you're history.
- How can I be moral and still survive the horrendous peer pressure to be bad?
- You have to be strong and not express emotion to get any respect and protect yourself (p. 166).
- Shouldn't women be treated as inferior and be handled with violent behavior?
- Police are the bad guys.
- How can I deal with whites' racist treatment?
- I don't know that much about African culture.

An Afrocentric approach emphasizes both spirituality and connectedness with others in the environment, including individuals, family, and community. Its goal is to engender self-understanding, self-respect, and "a strong sense of responsibility for the well-being and harmonious interconnection between self and others" (Harvey, 1997, p. 163; Nobles, 1976). The Afrocentric approach rests on seven basic principles, called the Nguzo Saba (Harvey, 1997, Karenga, 1965, 2000). These include (1) "unity" with "the family, community, nation, and race," (2) "self-determination," (3) "collective work and responsibility," (4) "cooperative economics" (to own and operate business for profit), (5) "purpose"

continued

Highlight 3.2 | *continued*

(to develop a positive and great community), (6) "creativity," and (7) "faith" ("to believe in our parents, our teachers, our leaders, our people, and ourselves, and in the righteousness and victory of our struggle") (Harvey, 1997, p. 163).

Growth groups, then, are designed to provide members with "a positive perspective on African and African-American culture, assist them in developing their own African-American group identity, and provide them with tools to deal with the oppressiveness of white supremacy" (Harvey, 1997, p. 164). Groups consist of 15 boys ages 14 through 18 who are on probation. Offenses include dope dealing, sexual assault, car theft, armed robbery, burglary, and numerous other criminal acts.

Group co-leaders include social workers or people with other types of expertise such as that in African studies, music, or theater. Group process involves the acquisition of skills such as positive interpersonal interaction, relationship building, communication, and introspection. Groups stress enhancing members' self-concepts, developing "constructive lifestyles and positive solutions to life problems," and appreciating their cultural heritage and personal strengths (Harvey, 1997, p. 167).

During the initial eight-week group phase, co-leaders teach members about group process, the Afrocentric perspective, and the important formalized rites of passage involved in group membership. Group members then participate in a weekend retreat where co-leaders and a group of older adult men decide which 15 young men will be included in the group. Chosen members then undergo an initiation ritual where they

pledge to uphold the principles of Nguzo Saba, are given an African name, and are presented a "special identifying symbol" they are expected to wear at all group meetings. No new members are admitted after this point (Harvey, 1997, p. 167).

Groups then meet weekly for 90 minutes, as members develop their group identity, learn, and develop skills. Group activities may include videos and music, depending on the topics addressed. Guests are invited to speak on various topics, called "modules," that stress the importance of African and African American culture (Harvey, 1997, p. 168). Modules, which last from four to six group sessions, address any number of topics ranging from African American culture to relationships between men and women to dealing with racism.

Upon completion of all modules, group members participate in another weekend experience, where they demonstrate their newly learned skills and prepare for the final special recognition ceremony. This ceremony becomes the culmination of the group experience, where members demonstrate before their families and community what they have achieved. They proclaim their sacred name and "receive a symbol and a certificate of sacred transformation" (Harvey, 1997, p. 168).

We have established that this process intends to enhance group members' self-respect, sense of African American identity, and sense of responsibility for and belonging to the African American community. It is hoped that other anticipated effects will include crime reduction, improved school attendance, better grades, and increased employment. Initial results were promising

Administrative Groups

A social service organization's administration is expected to "set goals; acquire funds and physical facilities; hire people with the necessary skills; design mechanisms for assigning, monitoring, and coordinating work; determine whether the organization is accomplishing what it has set out to do; and introduce changes when needed" (Gummer & Edwards, 1995, p. 57; Turem, 1986). To do this, lines of authority are usually described in a hierarchical fashion, as illustrated by an organizational chart described in Chapter 6. Most often, decision-makers are clustered into groups so they can communicate about what's happening in the organization, make decisions, and coordinate their leadership.

(Harvey, 1997). Family members reported improved behavior at home, and group members expressed enhanced self-respect and appreciation of African heritage.

Socialization Groups

Socialization groups help participants improve interpersonal behavior, communication, and social skills so that they might better fit into their social environment. Social activities and role plays are often used for group members to practice new social skills. Examples of such groups include an urban neighborhood's youth activities group, a school-based group of shy teens working to improve interpersonal skills, and a Parents Without Partners group sponsoring various social activities, such as parties and outings (Toseland & Rivas, 2005).

Corey (2004) explains the process involved in leading socialization groups (Rose, 1986):

> Before beginning the social skills training process, the group leader discusses with the members the general purposes of the group and the main procedures that are likely to be used. The members are given a variety of examples and are encouraged to ask questions. The group leader attempts to draw on the experiences of those members who have used these procedures themselves. If the members have had no prior experience with role playing, the leader generally provides them with some training. Then situations are given to the group, and experienced members from previous groups are asked to demonstrate how to role play. Once members learn role-playing skills, they are then trained to develop situations that lend themselves to social skills training. After the group is trained in the

development of problem situations, the members are asked to keep a diary of situations as they occur during the course of the week. Each week at least one situation of each member is handled by the group.

> Either the therapist or some group member models the desired verbal and nonverbal behaviors in a brief demonstration. Clients then practice their roles in the situation by using the agreed-on behaviors. If clients have trouble using a strategy during the rehearsal, they can be coached by the group leader or other members. When coaching is used, it is generally eliminated in later rehearsals. After each rehearsal, clients receive feedback from the group pertaining to their strengths and weaknesses. Clients assign themselves homework to carry out in the real world. As they complete these assignments, they are asked to observe themselves in new situations and to keep a diary of problems. Behavioral procedures such as modeling, rehearsal, and homework are used to restructure cognitions. (pp. 373–374)

Groups Serving More Than One Purpose

Sometimes, a treatment group will serve more than one function and not fit neatly into a designated category. For example, consider a group of young adults with cognitive disabilities formed to improve group members' assertiveness skills. The group serves as a growth group because it expands members' self-awareness, a socialization group to improve social skills, an educational group to provide members with assertiveness training, and a support group for members to help and encourage each other.

---

[*] Psychosomatic disorders are physical symptoms (for example, stomach aches, numbness, pain) caused by emotional problems.

Clusters of Supervisors and Administrators   One common type of administrative group "is composed of supervisors, department heads, or other administrative staff" (Fatout & Rose, 1995, p. 21). Such an administrative group usually meets on a regular basis to discuss issues and develop plans for running various aspects of the organization. An example of an administrative group in a residential treatment center for girls with serious behavioral and emotional problems is the assistant director, social work director, home care staff director, and on-grounds school principal. An example in a sheltered workshop serving people with cognitive disabilities is the activities director, vocational director, social work supervisor, and transportation manager.

Boards of Directors   A *board of directors* is another type of administrative group. It is a group of people authorized to formulate the organization's mission, objectives, and policies and to oversee the organization's ongoing activities. A board of directors also has ultimate control over the agency's higher administration, including its executive director or chief executive officer. Boards are usually made up of respected volunteers recruited from the community on the basis of "their power, status, and influence in the community; their expertise; and their representation of particular interest groups and constituencies" (Toseland & Rivas, 2005, p. 38). Examples of boards of directors include one overseeing a large private substance abuse treatment center and another governing an organization running seven hospices. (A *hospice* is a nonhospital facility where people having terminal illnesses can die as comfortably as possible with the best quality of life possible.)

Advisory Boards   Another type of administrative group is an organization's *advisory board*. Group members are recruited because of their expertise and interest in the agency's services. Unlike a board of directors, it has no formal power. However, it provides agency personnel with expert information and recommendations for improving organizational performance. An example of an advisory board is a group of field instructors and agency administrators who meet twice annually to give feedback and suggestions to a social work program regarding its effectiveness, curricula, and reaccreditation needs.

Delegate Councils

A *delegate council* is a group of representatives from a series of agencies or units within a single agency. Representatives may be elected by their constituencies or appointed by agency decision-makers. Typical goals include enhancing cooperation and communication among professionals in different units or agencies, reviewing issues relevant to service provision, enhancing management approaches, and pursuing social action goals (Toseland & Rivas, 2005).

An example of a delegate council is a group of representatives from four private social service agencies in three states. Each agency provides a range of services including mental health counseling, substance abuse counseling, group homes for people with various disabilities, residential treatment centers for troubled youth, recreational programs for families, and foreign adoptions. In two agencies, administrators appointed five representatives each. In the other two agencies, representatives were elected by staff in their respective six service divisions. One recent delegate council conference focused on integrating quality management principles throughout the agencies' administrative structures.

Another example of a delegate council is a group of professionals working in rape crisis centers throughout the state. Each agency designates a representative to meet in the council to discuss education and treatment issues in addition to interagency cooperation.

Committees

A *committee* is a group of persons "delegated to consider, investigate, take action on, or report on some matter" (Mish, 1995, p. 231). Committees are common entities in organizations. They consist of volunteers, appointees, or elected representatives who meet to address any significant issue concerning the organization's functioning. Sometimes committees are ongoing; other times, they are temporary or ad hoc. Examples of committees include a group of staff representatives appointed to investigate, assess, and make recommendations about the quality of food served residents in a nursing home. Another example is a large county department of social services that establishes a committee of unit representatives to develop a plan for coordinating and scheduling scarce meeting space within the facility. As the agency was housed in an old Grumbles department store building built many decades earlier, adequate meeting rooms were rare.

Highlight 3.3 discusses how a good leader can empower a committee and enhance its functioning.

Social Action Groups

Social action groups are formed to engage in some planned change effort to modify or improve aspects of their macro social or physical environment (Fatout & Rose, 1995; Toseland & Rivas, 2005). They may consist of professionals, clients, community residents, or some combination of these groups. Social workers can use social action groups to connect people with necessary services and resources, address and solve problematic situations, and alter conditions in the macro social environment to enhance living conditions and quality of life.

Social action groups in communities often involve one of three dimensions—"geographic, issue, or identity" (Staples, 2004, p. 344). First, a group from a *geographical area* (for example, a neighborhood, a town, a county, a state, or even a whole region) might band together and address issues of concern to them all. Such problems might include "housing, education, recreation, employment, environmental issues, transportation, or health care" (p. 345). One example is a group of agency workers and community residents collaborating to raise funds to establish a neighborhood park. Another example is the Coalition for a Better Acre, a group of primarily Central American and Cambodian residents who live in one of the poorest neighborhoods of Lowell, Massachusetts. Their goal is social action for neighborhood improvement through cleanup, increasing inexpensive housing availability, and development of programs serving young people.

A second dimension often fueling community social action groups concerns specific social *issues*, regardless of particular geographic residence. Such issues might include "clean elections, tax reform, women's rights, environmental justice, or elderly issues" (p. 345). One example of such a social action

| **Highlight 3.3** | **Empowerment through Good Leadership** |

Brody (2005) stresses how good leadership can help committees and other task groups function more effectively. When a social worker has been designated, appointed, or elected as a committee leader, six tactics facilitate successful meetings:

1. The leader should clearly state the purpose of the meeting immediately at the beginning. All committee members should be on track and know generally what to expect.

2. An agenda for the meeting should be prepared in advance of the meeting and distributed ahead of time to all committee members. An *agenda* is a prioritized list of topics to be covered at the meeting (Kirst-Ashman & Hull, 2006b). Agenda items are usually one to a few words that alert committee members to discussion topics. This allows them to think about the issues ahead of time and possibly bring information that they feel applies to the topic.

3. Ground rules should be clearly explained right at the outset of a committee meeting. The leader (or chairperson) "identifies expectations on how members are to interact with each other and how the business of the meeting would be conducted. This includes clarifying the process for decision making" (Brody, 2005, p. 359). For example, *Robert's Rules of Order* (Robert, 1971) illustrate one method of running meetings with highly structured techniques such as formal motions ("proposed actions that the group is asked to support") and voting procedures (Kirst-Ashman & Hull, 2006a).

4. Committee members should get specific assignments so that their understanding of what they need to do by the next meeting is perfectly clear. Sometimes, a leader will ask for volunteers to complete assignments or volunteers will suggest their own assignments. Other times, a leader may make assignments. But a leader should be very careful that committee members are really willing to carry them out, or they probably won't get done.

5. An effective leader should deal with any conflict emerging in the group. Conflicts may arise because of interpersonal or emotional issues occurring among members, differences of opinion regarding how the group should proceed, or competition for control of the group. A good leader will address the conflict and seek a compromise without taking sides.

   Wheelon (1999) remarks, "Some groups navigate their conflicts well, and others disband or become dysfunctional by dealing with their differences ineffectively. What do successful teams do to promote positive conflict resolution? Members of successful teams communicate their views clearly and explicitly. They avoid generalizations and are specific in their communication. They talk about trust and cooperation during the discussion" (p. 65). They also will argue their points straightforwardly so that the group may come to some resolution. A good leader will facilitate this process.

6. Finally, an effective leader will periodically summarize the discussion throughout the committee's meeting. This helps to establish a consensus regarding where the group is going and keep the group on track.

group is a coalition of social work practitioners working to improve professional social work licensing standards in their state. Another example is the Massachusetts Senior Action Council (MSAC), which involves members throughout the state. Its goal is social action to improve living conditions for senior citizens, improved and better-maintained senior housing, improved prescription drug coverage, and "a managed-care patients' bill of rights" (p. 346). (*Managed care* is "a generic label for a broad and constantly changing mix of health insurance, assistance, and payment programs that seek to retain quality and access while controlling the cost of physical and mental health services" [Lohmann, 1997, p. 200].)

The third focus involving community social action groups is *"identity,* for instance, ethnicity, religion, sexual orientation, or physical or mental disability. The Latino Immigrant Committee in Chelsea, Massachusetts, is composed primarily of recent immigrants from El Salvador, Honduras, Guatemala, Colombia, Chile, and Nicaragua. A core group of 30 people is most active and has engaged in social action focused on discriminatory treatment at the local branch of the post office, on worker safety at a local meat processing plant, on gang violence, on immigrant rights, and on increased participation in the political process" (Staples, 2004, p. 346).

Note that sometimes the distinctions among these three dimensions are not that clear. The MSAC example that addresses the concerns of older people might also he considered an issue of identity. However, the point is that social action groups are formed to improve social and economic policies, as well as to enhance people's overall well-being.

SOCIAL ACTION GROUPS AND EMPOWERMENT

Social action often means pushing a macro system to change, moving against the mainstream, or making demands on scarce resources. To do this requires substantial effort. Expenditure of output or effort requires adequate energy or strength. Social action groups can be used to empower group members internally and, thus, enhance their strength for altering the external environment (Carr, 2004; Cox, 1991; Fisher, 2001; Staples, 2004).

Increasing Understanding

First, communicating with other group members about their perceptions of problems and issues can greatly expand group members' understanding of these issues (Carr, 2004). The depth of understanding and insight increases as group members share personal insights about how relatives and friends view these issues.

For example, consider a group of neighborhood residents and agency social workers formed to evaluate the adequacy of neighborhood housing and the extent to which it complies with established building codes. Horace, one group member, lives with his family in a rented home with horribly drafty windows. He understands that problem from personal experience. However, as other group members share their perceptions, Horace's understanding of such problems significantly deepens.

Quanisha, another group member, talks of how her seven-year-old son, paraplegic from an accidental bullet to the spinal cord during a neighborhood gang battle, can't get into their rented home without being carried. Ramps are nonexistent. Quanisha indicates that she can cope with the situation now while the boy is small. However, the bigger he gets, the harder it is to move him.

Robert, still another group member, tells how his aging parents, who live in a rented home next door to him, have broken windows whose cracks are plastered with masking tape, making it almost impossible for his parents to see outside. Additionally, their two outside doors don't close properly, so that in winter the place is like a wind tunnel. Robert's parents are afraid to tell the landlord, as they fear he will get mad and evict them. In similar cases, neighborhood landlords found reasons to evict tenants or simply shut the properties down, saying that the upkeep wasn't worth the meager rent they received.

Horace's understanding of the neighborhood housing problems and issues is greatly expanded by hearing about other residents' issues and experiences. His individual view is multiplied many times so that he now better understands the nuances and complexities of the housing problem.

Inspiring Others

A second way that social action groups can empower group members is how "members who have survived or overcome aspects of powerlessness can inspire and motivate others" (Carr, 2004; Cox, 1991, p. 82). This can include serving as a role model, providing emotional support, and sharing relevant skills and knowledge.

For example, Thelma is part of a social action group aimed at increasing voter registration and education about issues in her community. She shares with the group how she was once totally apathetic regarding voting. At the time, she thought no matter how she felt or what she did, it really didn't matter. She felt like a tiny gold fish in Lake Ontario. Thelma then told of how her neighbor Louise got her involved in the social action process. Louise recruited Thelma to get out, pound the pavement, and encourage community residents to vote. Louise also helped Thelma dispense brochures about issues affecting the community. At first Louise accompanied Thelma to visit community residents. As Thelma gained experience and confidence, she soon went out by herself.

Thelma now helps other action group members become empowered to carry out the group's tasks. She gives them tips about how to handle crabby and irascible residents. She often accompanies new members when they start out. In essence, Thelma provides a significant role model of empowerment for other group members.

Consciousness Raising

A third way social action groups can empower members is through consciousness raising, a concept introduced and discussed in Chapter 2 (Carr, 2004; Cox. 1991). Social workers can encourage group members to relate their personal problems and issues to what's happening around them in the macro social environment (Carr, 2004). For example, Chapter 2 established that group members, like many people in American culture, may feel that poverty is the result of personal failure rather than an institutionalized socioeconomic condition of unfairness and lack of equal opportunity. A social worker might assist group members in looking beyond their own circumstances by asking questions.

"Why does poverty, then, affect, so many people?" "Why are so many poor people working, yet still can't make it?" "Why are so many children and older adults poor?" In this way, group members might begin to view poverty as a structural problem that the political and economic system needs to address.

 Critical Thinking Questions 3.3

Consider a social action group working to improve state laws regarding how sexual assault perpetrators and survivors are treated. The group discusses the history, legalities, and oppressive issues involved. In this way, action group members enhance their awareness of issues they never considered before. For example, how fair is it that wives cannot legally prosecute their husbands for sexually assaulting them? When prosecuting an assault case, how rational is it to explore the survivor's detailed sexual history with the perpetrator and with other sexual partners? How significant is the amount of force the perpetrator used against the survivor (for example, use of a weapon or gang rape)? How relevant is the amount of resistance offered by the survivor to protect herself?

Providing Mutual Support

Provision of mutual aid or support among action group members is a fourth means of group empowerment. Chapter 2 also introduced and discussed this important concept involved in empowerment. The group context "provides a medium of mutual social-emotional support for members in their struggle to cope with and bring about change in both the personal and political aspect of the problem" (Carr, 2004; Cox, 1991, p. 82). Consider an action group working on getting signatures for a petition to improve the quality of health care provided by a managed care organization. When the group experiences extreme resistance on the part of that organization's administration to its recommendations, group members can turn to each other for support, encouragement, and the generation of new ideas.

Another example is an action group of single mothers receiving public assistance whose purpose is to improve benefits, educate recipients regarding their rights, and inform members and others of community resources. Group members become increasingly supportive of each other in addressing related personal problems such as difficulties with men, dealing with substance abuse, "sharing economic resources, providing small loans or child care," and participating in recreational activities with each other (Cox, 1991, p. 85).

Using Cooperation

A fifth means of empowerment within social action groups is ongoing communication and cooperation concerning the macro change process (Carr, 2004; Staples, 2004). It's often easier to work with others toward a designated goal than to pursue it in isolation. The planned change effort is usually uneven, having ups and downs in terms of making progress. New impediments can emerge in the political environment. Action group members can work together to adjust to changes in the environment, alter plans accordingly, and continue monitoring progress toward goals.

For example, school social workers from secondary schools in a large metropolitan area form a social action group to seek increased funding for students' extracurricular activities. With shrinking budgets, one special activity after another has been eradicated. These include band, drama club, play productions, debate, golf, and tennis. The workers feel young people require positive activities to experience healthy growth and development. Without such activities, the teachers feel teens are much more likely to turn to gangs, drugs, and crime.

Parents form a similar social action group with the same concerns about their children's school activities. The social workers' group invites the parents' group to merge with it, thereby enhancing both groups' mutual power and influence. Both groups must adjust to the new changes in membership. For example, parents provide a different perspective concerning expectations and needs. The social workers' group will need to learn to encompass this new perspective. Together, social workers and parents develop new cooperative goals.

When the state legislators abruptly decrease property taxes, and, hence, the amount of resources available to schools, the social action group must respond accordingly. With continuously shrinking state funding, the group starts exploring new alternatives. One idea is to form a fundraising Booster Club that sponsors pancake breakfasts and charity concerts, in addition to sending members door-to-door to solicit funds.

The point is that conditions often are in flux for social action groups. A strength of a group context is that members can help each other work out new alternatives and plans of action for accomplishing goals. The group can monitor its progress in a coordinated fashion without full responsibility falling on an individual member.

CHAPTER SUMMARY

Task groups are the foundation for generalist social work in organizations and communities. Task groups include teams, treatment conferences, administrative groups, delegate councils, committees, and social action groups. Barriers to successful teamwork and team empowerment are discussed. The difference between treatment conferences and treatment groups is explained, and types of treatment groups are mentioned.

Empowerment through good leadership is addressed.

How social action groups empower their members to alter the external social environment is explored. Important aspects include increasing understanding, inspiring others, consciousness raising, providing mutual support, and using cooperation.

Knowledge and Theories About Organizations

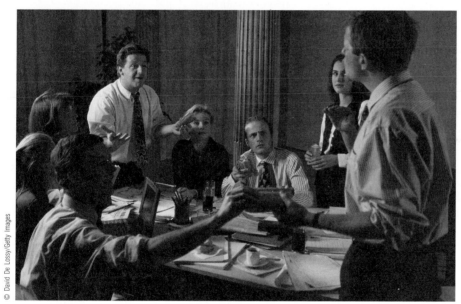

CHAPTER 4

Organizational systems are composed of many subgroups.

CHAPTER CONTENTS

Beverly Hill received her social work degree last month and was ecstatic. She just got the job of her dreams as a counselor at Gridlock Meadows (GM), a residential treatment center for adolescent males with serious behavioral and emotional problems. She would be doing individual and group counseling with residents, providing consultation for behavioral planning on two residential units, and running some parent groups. Beverly loved working with young people and their families. She couldn't wait to start. It was too good to be true.

Three weeks after her first day on the job, Beverly knew the job was too good to be true. She was seriously wondering whether accepting the position was such a good idea. Her experiences at GM were unlike any she had before in work, educational, or volunteer positions. Every morning when she arrived at GM, she felt like she was in jail. GM required all employees to sign in and out. One minute late meant being docked a half hour's pay.

But that was only a minuscule part of the problem. Beverly felt she couldn't breathe without her supervisor Bambi's approval. Bambi insisted on attending all Beverly's adolescent and parent group sessions and proceeded to take over running them. Beverly had little chance to get a word in edgewise.

Every progress note, letter, and report Beverly wrote, Bambi insisted on seeing, approving, and initialing. Beverly felt like Bambi thought her an incompetent idiot. Beverly had little chance to get a cup of coffee without Bambi's explicit approval.

When Beverly gently approached Bambi about these and several other similar issues, Bambi blew up. "How dare you contradict me after being here a measly couple of weeks," she exclaimed. "You're under a strict three-month probationary period. I can fire you anytime. You'd better start paying attention to company policy and watch your Ps and Qs."

Beverly never thought an organization could be run like that. She felt thwarted and trapped. She didn't know if she could work under such circumstances even for a short time. Maybe she should quit and start her job search over again. Now, she felt she knew much more when considering a job about what to look for in an agency and how it was run. She would give the possibility of quitting very serious thought.

Organizations–including social service agencies–vary dramatically in structure and managerial style. Perhaps, Beverly would not have been so shocked had she better understood organizational dynamics and the potential problems she might encounter. No organization is perfect. Some organizations are more productive and better places to work than others.

Holland (1995) describes human behavior in organizations: "Organizations are made up of people who use skills and resources to perform tasks and produce services, coordinated by systems of communication and authority. The behavior of an organization's members is the vehicle for implementing the organization's purposes" (p. 1789).

Social service organizations, as macro systems in the social environment, have major impacts on clients and other community residents. They establish services and develop means to deliver them. Because the organizational environment provides the context and structure for social workers to provide services, it is critical for workers to understand organizations' internal functioning.

Despite the difficulties, people within organizations can work to improve organizational effectiveness and efficiency. Social workers have the serious ethical responsibility to enhance agency functioning. The National Association of Social Workers (NASW) Code of Ethics states that "social workers should work to improve employing agencies' policies and procedures and the efficiency and effectiveness of their services" (NASW, 1999, 3.09b).

We have established that this book does not try to teach *how* to do social work practice and implement changes in communities, organizations, or groups. However, it does intend to provide a *foundation* upon which to build such system-changing skills. Before you can plan and implement changes in organizations on clients' and communities' behalf, you must understand how these macro systems work. This and the next three chapters will address a range of problems and issues relevant to how organizations function in the macro social environment.

This chapter focuses primarily on organizations related to social services. However, much of the content also is relevant to understanding any type of organization as a macro system. This chapter will:

- Define organizations.
- Describe organizations providing social services.
- Discuss several organizational theories, including classical organizational theories (scientific management, the administrative theory of management, and bureaucracy), neoclassical organizational theories, human relations theories (Theory X and Theory Y), feminist theories and organizations, the cultural perspective, economics theory, chaos theory, contingency theory, culture-quality theories, and ecosystems theories.
- Demonstrate the application of systems concepts to organizations and social agencies.

DEFINING ORGANIZATIONS

Organizations are "(1) social entities that (2) are goal directed, (3) are designed as deliberately structured and coordinated activity systems, and (4) are linked to the external environment" (Daft, 2007, p. 10). Four elements stand out in this definition.

First, organizations are *social entities*. That is, organizations are made up of people with all their strengths and failings. Organizations dictate how people should behave and what responsibilities employees must assume as they do their jobs. Individuals bring to their jobs their own values and personalities. Thus, patterns of behavior develop in organizational environments, which a later chapter discusses further.

Second, organizations are *goal-directed*. They exist for some specified purpose. An organization specializing in stock brokering subsists to help clients develop financial packages that make money. Social service organizations exist to provide services and resources to help people with designated needs. An organization must clearly define its goals so that workers can evaluate the extent to which it achieves these goals.

The third key concept in the definition is that organizations are *deliberately structured and coordinated activity systems*. Activity systems are clusters of work activities performed by designated units or departments within an organization. Such systems are guided by a technology, the practical application of knowledge to achieve desired ends. Organizations coordinate the functioning of various activity systems to enhance efficiency in attaining desired goals. Organizations have structures that include policies for how the organization should be run, hierarchies of how personnel are supervised and by whom, and different units working in various ways to help the organization function.

An intake unit for a large county Department of Social Services is an example of an activity system. Workers under supervision process new cases by following established procedures, obtaining required information, and making referrals to the appropriate service providers.

Another example is a family services organization that has a number of activity systems including one staff unit providing marriage and family counseling, another providing family life education,[1] and still another focusing on community activities aimed at family advocacy, recreation, and support (Barker, 2003). Each unit pursues different functions in order to achieve the agency's general goal of providing family services.

Of course, organizations other than those providing social services also have activity systems. For example, consider a factory, also an organization, that specializes in producing customized wash baskets. One activity unit is responsible for designing baskets, one for manufacturing them, and another for marketing them.

The fourth concept inherent in the definition of organizations is *linkage to the external environment*. Thus, an organization is in constant interaction with other systems in the social environment, including individuals, groups, other organizations, and communities. Agencies providing social services interact dynamically with clients, funding sources, legislative and regulatory agencies, politicians, community leaders, and other social service agencies.

ORGANIZATIONS PROVIDING SOCIAL SERVICES

This and the next three chapters focus on organizations that provide social services to clients. *Social services* include the tasks that social work practitioners

---

[1] Family life education "is a leader-directed group-learning service" used to help parents "increase their knowledge, develop skills, and examine their attitudes, with the goal of adjusting to, coping with, and growing during normal, predictable life transitions" (Riley, 1995, p. 960).

and other helping professionals perform with the goal of improving people's health, enhancing their quality of life, increasing autonomy and independence, supporting families, and helping people and larger systems improve their functioning in the social environment (Barker, 2003). That is quite a mouthful. In essence, social services include the wide range of activities that social workers perform in their goal of helping people solve problems and improve their personal well-being.

Social services may be *institutional,* that is, those provided by major public service systems that administer such benefits as financial assistance, housing programs, health care, or education (Barker, 2003). They might also include *personal social services* that address more individualized needs involving interpersonal relationships and people's ability to function within their immediate environments. Such services usually target specific groups (such as children or older adults) or particular problems (such as family planning or counseling) (Barker, 2003).

Social Agencies

A *social agency,* or *social services agency,* is an organization providing social services that typically employs a range of helping professionals, including social workers in addition to office staff, paraprofessionals (persons trained to assist professionals), and sometimes volunteers (Barker, 2003). Social agencies generally serve some designated client population who experience some defined need. Services are provided according to a prescribed set of policies regarding how the agency staff should accomplish their service provision goals. Highlight 4.1 discusses some related terms.

A number of different concepts can characterize social agencies. For example, social agencies can be either public, private, or proprietary. *Public* social agencies are run by some designated unit of government and are usually regulated by laws impacting policy. For example, a county board committee oversees a public welfare department and is responsible for establishing its major policies. (Of course, such a committee must function in accordance with state or federal governments, which often provide at least some of the money for the agency's programs.)

Private social agencies, on the other hand, are privately owned and run by people not employed by government. They are nonprofit social agencies. That is, they are run to accomplish some service provision goal, not to make financial profit for private owners. They usually provide some type of personal social services. Funding for services can include tax moneys, private donations, grants, and service fees. A board of directors presides over a private agency, formulating policy and making certain that agency staff run the agency appropriately.

Proprietary, or *for-profit,* social agencies provide some designated social services, often quite similar to those provided by private social agencies. However, a major purpose for the existence of a proprietary social agency is to make a profit for its owners.

| **Highlight 4.1** | **Common Terms** |

Note that the terms "social services," "human services," and sometimes "social welfare" are often used interchangeably when referring to organizations, agencies, and agency personnel. Human services are "programs and activities designed to enhance people's development and well-being," including the provision of financial help and social support when they're needed (Barker, 2003, p. 204). Since the terms social services agency, social services organization, and social agency mean essentially the same thing, these three terms will be used interchangeably.

Social welfare is the "nation's system of programs, benefits, and services that help people meet those social, economic, educational, and health needs that are fundamental to the maintenance of society" (Barker, 2003, p. 6). Social welfare, then, is a broad concept related to the general well-being of all people in a society. Inherent in the definition are two basic dimensions: (1) what people get from society (in terms of programs, benefits, and services) and (2) how well their needs (including social, economic, educational, and health) are being met.

ORGANIZATIONAL THEORIES

Organizational theories are ways to conceptualize and understand how organizations function by stressing specific concepts and explaining how these concepts relate to each other (Hodge, Anthony, & Gales, 2003, p. 18). They provide a lens through which to view the organizational environment and direct you as to which aspects of that environment should be your focus of attention. The remainder of this chapter explores a range of ways in which organizations can be viewed and examined.

Organizational behavior "is the study of human behavior in the workplace, the interaction between people and the organization, and the organization itself. The major goals of organizational behavior are to explain, predict, and control behavior" (Dubrin, 2002, p. 2). What components in the organizational environment are significant to those who work there? What issues do they face and how do they tend to react? *Management* "is the attainment of organizational goals in an effective and efficient manner through planning, organizing, leading, and controlling organizational resources" (Daft, 2003, p. 5). Here attention is focused on the interaction between managers, those in power, and workers, those who directly accomplish the organization's goals through doing various tasks. Later chapters will further explore organizational behavior, dimensions and structure of the organizational environment, and management.

In order to work within organizations, evaluate them, and sometimes work to change them, it is helpful to understand the major theories regarding how organizations operate. Such a perspective is also useful to determine what kinds of organizational structures are most effective for specific client situations.

Many organizational theories have been borrowed from the business and management literature. Businesses and social service organizations have much in common. Both need resources, namely money, to function.

Likewise, both produce results or products via some kind of process. For example, a business might manufacture the product of burglar alarms. A social services organization might furnish the product of improved family functioning.

There is a wide range of theories concerning how organizations work. Some of them directly contradict others, probably because there is such a vast array of organizational structures, functions, and goals. There are tremendous differences among social service organizations in terms of structure and function, and more so among all types of businesses and organizations. The important thing for you is to think about how organizations work, because you will be working in one.

Some theories emphasize similar dimensions such as expectations for staff treatment, the importance placed on profits, or the degree to which new ideas are encouraged. However, each theory stresses various concepts somewhat differently.

One means of considering the wide variety of organizational theories is to place them on one of two continuums (Burrell & Morgan, 1979; Netting and O'Connor, 2003). One is adherence to traditional rigid structure, on the one hand, versus seeking fundamental change for the better on the other. The second continuum involves a focus on human individuality and well-being on one side, and a focus on objective, efficient completion of tasks on the other.

The following theories are reviewed here. Classical organizational theories developed early in the last century include scientific management, the administrative theory of management, and bureaucracy. They reflect rigid structure in addition to emphasis on productivity and task completion. Neoclassical organizational theory portrays a later shift in perspective to theory that's more oriented toward human relationships and motivation. Human relations theories and feminist theories stress the importance of the human component in organizational functioning. Feminist theories, of course, focus on the empowerment of women. The cultural perspective emphasizes the importance of expectations in the organizational environment and culture to maintain the organization's the status quo. Economics theory focuses on productivity and task completion, yet emphasizes flexibility. Chaos theory reflects more divergent perspectives that emphasize the complexity of variables involved in organizations. Contingency theory stresses careful analysis of all variables to determine those that relate directly to an issue or problem (which could involve either "personal" or "situational factors") (Vecchio, 2006, p. 11). Culture-quality theories, characterizing the end of the last century, emphasize the importance of establishing a positive organizational culture that promotes worker motivation and improves the quality of their work. Finally, ecosystems theory provides a perspective for understanding organizational functioning that fits well with social work. It provides a structured way of viewing organizations, yet focuses on how change might occur. It also can involve both the importance of human well-being and the accomplishment of organizational tasks and goals.

Classical Organizational Theories

Classical management theories emphasize that specifically designed, formal structure and a consistent, rigid organizational network of employees are most important in having an organization run well and achieve its goals (Hodge et al., 2003; Holland & Petchers, 1987; Sarri, 1987). In general, these early theories saw each employee as holding a clearly defined job and straightforwardly being told exactly how that job should be accomplished. These schools of thought call for minimal independent functioning on the part of employees. Supervisors closely scrutinize the latter's work. Efficiency is of utmost importance. Performance is quantified (that is, made very explicit regarding what is expected), regulated, and measured. How people feel about their jobs is insignificant. Administration should avoid allowing employees to have any input regarding how organizational goals can best be reached. Rather, employees should do their jobs as instructed and as quietly and efficiently as possible. Early proponents of these theories included Frederick W. Taylor, Henri Fayol, and Max Weber (Champoux, 2003; Netting & O'Connor, 2003).

Scientific Management   Frederick W. Taylor introduced the concept of *"scientific management"* (Champoux, 2003, p. 11). Developed in the early twentieth century, it reflected a time when there was often great hostility between management and employees. Management pushed employees to work as hard as possible to maximize company profits. In response, employees, to protect themselves, worked as slowly and did as little as possible. They figured that working faster and becoming more productive would endanger their own and other workers' jobs if management could get more work out of fewer people. Management sought high profits and workers wanted high wages. Both were working against each other.

Four principles characterize Taylor's "scientific management" style (Champoux, 2003):

1. Jobs and tasks should be studied scientifically to "develop" and "standardize" work procedures and expectations.
2. Workers should be chosen on a scientific basis to maximize their potential for being trained and turned into productive employees.
3. Management and employees should cooperate with each other and work together following standardized procedures.
4. Management should make "plans" and "task assignments," which workers should then "carry out" as instructed (p. 12).

The Administrative Theory of Management   Also in the early twentieth century, Henri Fayol proposed an *administrative theory of management* (Champoux, 2003). His ideas focused on the administrative side of management rather than the workers' performance. He proposed five basic functions that management should fulfill, including "planning, organizing, command, coordination, and control" (Champoux, 2003, p. 12). He concluded that all managers should abide by the following six basic principles, although he did indicate that they should use discretion (the opportunity to make independent judgments and decisions) concerning the intensity of their actions (Champoux, 2003):

1. *Division of labor.* Workers should be divided up into units so that they might perform specialized instead of more general tasks. He posed that specialization would lead to greater productivity.
2. *Authority and responsibility.* Management should have the authority to give orders to workers, oversee their activity, and make them comply with these orders. In response, workers would assume responsibility for completing their assigned work.
3. *Centralization.* Depending on what would maximize productivity, management should centralize authority (that is, place decision-making power and responsibility at the top of the organization's power hierarchy) or decentralize such authority (give power and responsibility to lower-level managers and workers in the organization's power hierarchy).
4. *Delegation of authority.* Upper-level management should have the responsibility of delegating responsibility and work assignments to managers and workers lower in the power hierarchy. Management should carefully analyze organizational processes and delegate authority as it saw fit.
5. *Unity of command.* Each worker should have one designated supervisor to whom he or she should report. This should avoid confusion and give consistent messages and orders to workers.
6. *Unity of direction.* Each unit in the organization (which is specialized under the division of labor) should have a single designated goal. This also should avoid confusion and inconsistency.

In essence, these principles should work together. High-level management should give authority to lower-level management (authority and responsibility) as it saw fit (centralization or decentralization; delegation of authority). Workers should be specialized (division of labor) and work in designated units. There should be a clear hierarchy of authority regarding who is responsible for each worker (unity of command) and each unit (unity of direction) to avoid confusion, enhance consistency, and maximize productivity.

Bureaucracy Initiated by Max Weber in the early twentieth century, "bureaucracy is an administrative structure with well-defined offices or functions and hierarchical relationships among the functions. The offices or functions have clearly defined duties, rights, and responsibilities. Each office or function is designed without regard for who will hold the office. Relationships within a bureaucracy are impersonal. Decisions are made according to existing rules, procedures, and policies. Bureaucracies attain goals with precision, reliability, and efficiency" (Champoux, 2003, p. 14).

In summary, traditional bureaucracies emphasize the following:

- Highly specialized units performing clearly specified job tasks
- Minimal discretion on the part of employees
- Numerous specific rules to maintain control

The Social Security Administration, the Detroit Department of Social Services, and the Federal Bureau of Investigation are examples of large bureaucracies. A later chapter will address what it's like to work in an organization with a bureaucratic style of management.

Neoclassical Organizational Theories

Originating during the mid-twentieth century, neoclassical theories were reactions to classical management thought and represented "a transition in the theoretical movement from the overly simplistic, mechanistic perspectives of the classical theorists to more contemporary thinking about complex organizations" (Netting & O'Connor, 2003, p. 106). They addressed problems and omissions in classical theories. Criticisms of classical theories involved lack of attention to human needs and individuality, coordination of work and goals among various bureaucratic units, the importance of relationships among organizations in the larger macro environment, and the need to comprehend the decision-making processes in organizations (Netting & O'Connor, 2003, pp. 105–106).

Champoux (2003) describes the ideas expressed by one of the leaders of this movement, Chester I. Barnard. Barnard defined an organization as a deliberately structured system of tasks and activities undertaken by two or more people. The implication is "that any system of two or more people with consciously coordinated activities is an organization. Organizations are based on cooperation and have a conscious, deliberate purpose" (p. 16). In order to achieve coordination and cooperation, organizations "offer inducements in exchange for contributions. *Inducements* include salary and fringe benefits. *Contributions* are things such as the work to be done. Barnard felt a person joined an organization when the inducements exceeded the contributions" (p. 16). Management's goal should be maintenance of this balance.

Barnard proposed that organizations functioned on the basis of two types of motivation—motivation to participate and motivation to perform (Champoux, 2003). "*Motivation to participate* is the motivation of an individual to join and stay with the organization and perform at a minimally acceptable level" (p. 16). Various organizations maintain different expectations regarding what is minimally acceptable performance. It is the responsibility of managers to balance inducements and contributions to retain staff and motivate them to complete their work. After management attends to workers' motivation to participate, they then should direct their attention to workers' motivation to perform; *motivation to perform* involves inducements to produce contributions that are greater than minimal performance expectations (p. 16).

Barnard's contributions changed how organizations were viewed from the classical organizational perspectives in several ways (Champoux, 2003).

First, he emphasized deliberately coordinated tasks that required cooperation between two or more people. Thus, the theoretical focus was changing from production results to how people work together in an organizational environment. Second, he stressed the need to induce people by providing incentives (salary and benefits) to reinforce their contributions (work performance). This began to change the focus from controlling worker behavior and performance to motivating workers to perform. An emphasis on motivation reflected the beginning of a shift toward considering workers as individuals with emotions, needs, and desires instead of as mindless entities requiring control and direction.

Human Relations Theories

Human relations theories reflect the result of this shift to focus on "human relations" within the organizational environment. As Netting and O'Connor (2003) reflect:

> It was at this stage that classical organizational theory was actually displaced, making room for the more creative approaches to understanding organizations. At this juncture, theorists realized that organizations were much more than variables to manipulate in order to change behavior of organizational members. Instead, organizations were understood as contexts within which behavior occurs. The people and the organization represent mutual, interactive influences through which people are shaped by the organization and the organization is shaped by the people within its boundaries. (p. 107)

Human relations theories emphasize "the role of the informal, psychosocial components of organizational functioning" (Holland & Petchers, 1987, p. 206; Vecchio, 2006). The idea is that satisfied, happy employees will manifest the most productivity. Important concepts include "employee morale and productivity"; "satisfaction, motivation, and leadership"; and "the dynamics of small-group behavior" (Sarri, 1987, p. 31). Organizational leaders should strive to enhance their workers' morale. Thus, effective leadership is important.

Likewise, the immediate work group, a mezzo system, is critical in human relations theories. Employees should be encouraged to work cooperatively together and participate in group decision-making. Employers should encourage employee input concerning organizational policies and practices.

Theory X and Theory Y   The management styles of administrators and supervisors in organizations have considerable impact on the productivity and job satisfaction of employees. Douglas McGregor (1960) developed two theories of management style. He hypothesized that management thinking and behavior are based on two different sets of assumptions, which he labeled Theory X and Theory Y. Theory X reflects aspects of classical scientific management in its focus on hierarchical structure, providing a contrasting approach to Theory Y, which focuses on human relations. These theories are addressed here because they emphasize the treatment of employees.

Theory-X managers view employees as being incapable of much growth. Employees are perceived as having an inherent dislike for work, and it is presumed that they will attempt to evade work whenever possible. Therefore, X-type managers believe that they must control, direct, force, or threaten employees to make them work. Employees are also viewed as having relatively little ambition, wishing to avoid responsibilities, and preferring to be directed. X-type managers therefore spell out job responsibilities carefully, set work goals without employee input, use external rewards (such as money) to induce employees to work, and punish employees who deviate from established rules. Because Theory-X managers reduce responsibilities to a level where few mistakes can be made, work can become so structured that it is monotonous and distasteful. The assumptions of Theory X, of course, are inconsistent with what behavioral scientists assert are effective principles for directing, influencing, and motivating people.

In contrast, Theory-Y managers view employees as wanting to grow and develop by exerting physical and mental effort to accomplish work objectives to which they are committed. Y-type managers believe that the promise of internal rewards, such as self-respect and personal improvement, are stronger motivators than external rewards (such as money) and punishment. A Y-type manager also believes that under proper conditions, employees will not only accept responsibility but seek it. Most employees are assumed to have considerable ingenuity, creativity, and imagination for solving the organization's problems. Therefore, employees are given considerable responsibility in order to test the limits of their capabilities. Mistakes and errors are viewed as necessary phases of the learning process, and work is structured so that employees can have a sense of accomplishment and growth.

 Critical Thinking Questions 4.1

Compare and contrast classical organizational theories and human relations theories. What are the strengths and weaknesses of each?

Feminist Theories and Organizations

Chapter 2 discussed feminist theory with respect to groups and established that there are a range of feminist theories that emphasize various concepts (for example, women's individual rights, economic status, or cultural contexts). Feminist theories emphasize interpersonal relationships and respect for each other's right to be heard and contribute. Five basic feminist concepts will be applied here in the context of organizations.

- *Using a "gender lens"* (Gutierrez & Lewis, 1999, p. 100). Feminist theories focus on the rampant sexism existing in the macro social environment and the need to stress women's conditions, needs, and opportunities. Therefore, within organizational contexts, management and workers must be vigilant regarding the treatment of women in a fair, nondiscriminatory manner.

- *Empowerment.* Power should be distributed and equalized to whatever extent possible within an organization. This would support a decentralized organizational structure that provides great discretion on the part of workers throughout the organization. Organizations should also empower women to be promoted and assume leadership positions (Netting & O'Connor, 2003).

- *The personal is political* (Bricker-Jenkins & Lockett, 1995, p. 2531). Feminist theories emphasize that women become aware of their own opinions, feelings, and situation (consciousness raising). They stress that the condition of women goes beyond one's personal situation and that women should strive to improve conditions for all women. The implication is that workers should strive to improve conditions and combat sexism wherever it occurs in an organization, not just on their own personal behalf.

- *The importance of process.* Feminist theories emphasize that the process of *how* things get done is just as important as *what* gets done. The implication in an organizational context is that management should involve workers in decision making and planning to the greatest extent possible. Workers should feel like important participants in the organizational environment.

- *"Diversity is strength"* (Bricker-Jenkins & Lockett, 1995, p. 2531). Feminist theories stress unity and harmony, on the one hand, and appreciation of diverse characteristics on the other. Women should appreciate each other's differences and work together for the benefit of all. In organizational contexts, diversity (for example, gender, race, ethnicity, age, and sexual orientation) should not only be appreciated but actively sought out and encouraged.

Powell and Graves (2003) recommend that "*all* organizations—large or small, public or private, profit or nonprofit—set the goals of being nondiscriminatory, diverse, and inclusive in their employment practices. . . . [Organizational] communications should convey the message that promoting nondiscrimination, diversity, and inclusion are important organizational goals. These communications may include speeches by top executives, with transcripts or videos available to internal and external groups, newsletters, status reports, recognition events, special awards, and publicity for employees who have done good work toward these goals. The mission statement [a declaration of an organization's purpose and goals] of the organization should state that the organization regards achievement of these goals as critical to its success" (pp. 231–232).

Critical Thinking Questions 4.2

How do men fit into the application of feminist theories to organizations?

Cultural Perspective

Organizational culture is "the constellation of values, beliefs, assumptions, and expectations that underlie and organize the organization's behavior as a group" (Holland, 1995, p. 1789). The cultural perspective on organizations assumes that each organization develops a unique mixture of values, standards, presumptions, and practices about how things should be done that eventually becomes habit (Hodge et al., 2003; Holland, 1995).

Management and other personnel may not be consciously aware that such patterns and expectations have developed. They become ingrained in established means of accomplishing tasks and goals. If it worked before, it'll work again. "If it ain't broke, don't fix it." The result is the establishment of an ideological structure that frames how organizational members think about the organization and how it should work. This perspective not only guides people's view of current practices but also shapes how they think about new issues. Employees tend to view new ideas by shaping them to conform to old, "tried and true" practices.

An advantage of the cultural perspective may be that performance becomes predictable, thus requiring less effort to develop new approaches. However, a disadvantage is that such an established view may squelch innovative ideas. There's pressure to retain the old way of thought. For example, an energized worker in a social services organization might come to a staff meeting with a brilliant new treatment approach (in his opinion). The cultural perspective suggests that staff will tend not to evaluate the new approach fairly and impartially. Rather, they might nod pleasantly in feigned mild agreement and proceed to recycle the new approach into the same old routine.

It should be noted that the organization's culture might support "innovation" and "risk-taking" instead of the status quo (Johns, 1996, p. 289). If this were the case with the group discussed above, staff would enthusiastically welcome the new treatment idea the worker presented. Personnel would shy away from old techniques and search for new ones. In this case, the advantages and disadvantages would be reversed. An advantage, then, would be development of fresh, more effective intervention modalities. A disadvantage would be lack of stability and predictability.

Economics Theory

Economics theory emphasizes how organizations should proceed in whatever way necessary to maximize profits or output (Hodge, et al., 2003: Holland, 1995). Serious attention is paid to the relationships between inputs or investments and the resulting outputs or production. Efficiency is paramount. Emphasis is placed on evaluating processes and programs to determine which is the most cost effective, that is, which produces the most results for the least money.

Economics theory also frames the transactions between management and employees (Hodge, et al., 2003). Just as the organization is viewed as being out to get as much as it can, so are the employees. Thus, management must assume that employees will act in their own best interests rather than the organization's. Management's responsibility is to ensure that procedural structure is sufficient so that employees have difficulty acting selfishly. For example, installation of a time clock would monitor employees who for their own convenience preferred to come in late and get out early.

In some ways, the economics theory resembles classical scientific management approaches. Efficiency is emphasized and employees are closely supervised. However, economics theory stresses the examination of numerous alternatives to achieve the same end. Flexibility and creativity may provide potential means to higher productivity for less cost. In contrast, the classical scientific management approaches focus on structured, established ways to accomplish tasks, such as has often been demonstrated in traditional bureaucracies. Change is often the enemy because it tends to interfere with following established procedures.

Economics theory obviously poses difficulties for social workers who maintain professional values and ethics. It places primary emphasis on profit and productivity. How do you translate into dollars the gain of saving a 3-year-old from neglect and abuse? Or how do you determine the cost effectiveness of helping an adult with bulimia nervosa control the disorder? (*Bulimia nervosa* is a condition occurring primarily in females that is characterized by uncontrolled overeating followed by purging activities such as self-initiated vomiting and the use of diuretics, as well as excessive guilt and shame over the compulsive behavior.)

Chaos Theory

Today's macro global environment is unstable and unpredictable in many ways; from this perspective, organizational management "can no longer maintain an illusion of order and predictability" (Daft, 2007, p. 27). Organizations now function in a world that goes beyond the straightforward, simple control of product production, service provision, or interpersonal dynamics and motivation. Chaos theory focuses on the much broader complexity of all variables affecting an organization's ability to function.

Chaos theory "is the branch of mathematics for the study of processes that seem so complex that at first they do not appear to be governed by any known laws or principles, but which actually have an underlying order. . . . Examples of chaotic processes include a stream of rising smoke that breaks down and becomes turbulent, water flowing in a stream or crashing at the bottom of a waterfall, electroencephalographic activity of the brain, changes in animal populations, fluctuation on the stock exchange, and the weather. All of these phenomena involve the interaction of several elements and the pattern of their changes over time as they interact" (Krippner, 1994, p. 49; cited in Schriver, 2004, p. 140). Chaos theory seeks patterns that occur in nature, while intricate and multifaceted, actually form some complex, ordered arrangement (Krippner, 1994; Schriver, 2004).

Daft explains (2007):

The science of *chaos theory* suggests that relationships in the complex, adaptive systems—including organizations—are nonlinear and made up of numerous interconnections and divergent choices that create unintended effects and render the universe unpredictable. The world is full of uncertainty, characterized by surprise, rapid change, and confusion. Managers can't measure, predict, or control in traditional ways the unfolding drama inside or outside the organization. However, chaos theory also recognizes that this randomness and disorder occurs within certain larger patterns of order. The ideas of chaos theory suggest that organizations should be viewed more as natural systems than as well-oiled, predictable machines.

Many organizations are shifting from strict vertical hierarchies to flexible, decentralized structures that emphasize horizontal collaboration [cooperation among organizational units with equal power in the organizational power structure], widespread informal sharing, and adaptability. (pp. 27–28)

Chaos theory contrasts starkly with organizational theories that emphasize predictability and standardized production of goods or provision of services. Rather, it stresses "the importance of recognizing the positive aspects of change and flexibility" (Schriver, 2004, p. 456). Although chaos theory can be abstract and difficult to apply because of it's inherent unpredictable nature, viewing organizations from this perspective does have several advantages (Schriver, 2004). First, chaos theory allows for the identification and appreciation of creativity and positive change. Because it emphasizes all variables affecting an organization, creativity can gain precedence. Second, in a similar fashion, chaos theory also allows for the expression and appreciation of human diversity. An excellent source of "creative disorder" is work force diversity: "Organizational culture traditionally works to smooth out, if not eliminate, difference, but public managers can endeavor to counter this tendency by flexible job assignments, creating diverse work groups, and recognizing the unique contributions of individual women and men" (Evans, 1996, p. 491, cited in Schriver, 2004, pp. 456–457). Finally, chaos theory can focus attention on the "multiple layers and complexity of organizational life" instead of limiting the focus on only a few aspects of that life (Schriver, 2004, p. 457).

Contingency Theory

Contingency theory maintains that each element involved in an organization depends on other elements; therefore, there is no one generally best way to accomplish tasks or goals (Daft, 2007; Hodge et al., 2003). Each organization with its units or subsystems is unique. Thus, the best way to accomplish goals is to make individual determinations in view of the goal's context. Contingency theory maintains that "employee behavior is too complex to be explained by only a few simple and straightforward principles. Instead, [it seeks] to identify the factors that are jointly necessary for a given principle to hold. Contingency researchers recognize the interdependency of personal and situational factors in the determination of employee behavior" (Vecchio, 2006, p. 11).

Different means are required to solve various problems depending on all of the variables involved. The best approaches for organizations to take are ones reflecting a good fit with those in the external environment. Daft (2007) explains:

> For example, some organizations experience a certain environment, use a routine technology, and desire efficiency. In this situation, a management approach that uses bureaucratic control procedures, a hierarchical structure, and formal communication would be appropriate. Likewise, free-flowing management processes [with few standardized routines and much worker discretion] work best in an uncertain environment with a nonroutine technology. The correct management approach is contingent on the organization's situation. (p. 27)

A strength of this theory is its flexibility. It can be applied to any situation in any organization. However, a potential weakness is its lack of direction. The core idea suggests that all variables should be evaluated and any may be significant. Where does one start when evaluating a problem or planning a procedure? Staff? Input? Output? Process? It's difficult to determine.

Culture-Quality Theories

Theories stressing organizational culture and quality improvement characterized the final two decades of the twentieth century and paved the way for future approaches (Vecchio, 2006). These views

> focused on how to build a strong set of shared positive values and norms within a corporation (that is, a strong corporate culture) while emphasizing quality, service, high performance, and flexibility. Simultaneously, Western industry developed an interest in designing an effective response to growing global competition. High quality was seen to be related to high employee commitment and loyalty, which were believed to result, partially, from greater employee involvement in decision making. In order to establish new mechanisms for employee involvement, changes were seen as being necessary in existing corporate cultures, and the establishment and maintenance of new cultures became the goal. Some organizations now seek to have employees openly discuss aspects of corporate culture and suggest techniques for achieving a culture that emphasizes greater teamwork and cooperation. (Vecchio, 2006, p. 12)

One application of culture-quality theories is total quality management, described in a later chapter. Theory Z, described in Highlight 4.2, provides an example of a theory emphasizing culture and quality (Vecchio, 2006).

Ecosystems Theories

Chapter 1 established that ecosystems theory serves as an umbrella approach for defining and understanding the functioning of macro systems, including organizations. We have established that ecosystems theory assumes a systems theory perspective but integrates a number of relevant ecological concepts. Other theories can be explained using concepts and terms inherent in ecosystems theory.

Highlight 4.2 | **Theory Z**

Theory Z proposes a theoretical perspective relating to organizational culture and quality based on five assumptions initiated in Japanese industry. Developed by Ouchi (1981), these assumptions about human behavior within organizations clash poignantly in several ways with many traditional assumptions about organizational behavior espoused by U.S. and Canadian organizations (Ouchi, 1981; Schriver, 2004). Note that we are emphasizing differences between Theory Z and traditional organizational perspectives here. The organizational management scene constantly changes. Any particular agency can adopt a hybrid combination of theoretical assumptions and management styles.

First, Theory Z views workers as lifetime employees instead of people having a series of short-term jobs in different organizations over a career's time. It emphasizes job security as a major component of employee satisfaction and, hence, motivation for productivity.

A second presumption in Theory Z is that employees undergo long periods of evaluation and are not promoted quickly. This is in contrast to U.S. organizations, which tend to evaluate regularly and after relatively brief periods of time. For example, it is not uncommon for workers in social service agencies to undergo a six-month probationary period during which management can discharge them with relative ease. Also in contrast to Theory Z, U.S. workers hope for promotions more quickly in order to progress along salary and career paths.

Theory Z's third assumption is that workers progress down career paths that aren't specialized. Job descriptions are more flexible and management views employees as being capable of performing any job when they receive relevant training (Keys, 1995a). U.S. workers, on the other hand, are oriented to receive specialized training for specific jobs. Changing career paths in mid-stream is usually considered the exception rather than the rule.

Collective decision making is a fourth tenet of Theory Z. Instead of higher levels of management imposing decisions on employees, groups of workers collectively address issues and arrive at some consensus regarding how to proceed. Such work groups are called *teams, quality circles,* or *quality control circles* (Keys, 1995a, 1995b; Schriver, 2004).

In contrast, U.S. organizations historically have emphasized decision making on the individual level. Each employee has discretion for performing his job as he sees fit as long as he remains within the boundaries of his job description. Job descriptions usually describe the general goals and tasks inherent in a particular job. Similarly, individuals in higher levels of U.S. management are generally given greater individual power to affect the work of employees below them in the organizational power structure. The Chief Executive Officer of a U.S. organization might decide that Fridays are casual days where employees should not wear high heels, ties, or three-piece suits. She could make such a decision independently and would expect employees to follow her directive automatically.

A fifth assumption in Theory Z (one related to collective decision making) is collective responsibility. Theory Z emphasizes the importance of all workers being responsible for the successful functioning of the organization. High-level management does not drop arbitrary decisions and policies upon workers without extensive worker input. Since employees have a lifetime job, "everyone must agree with decisions because everyone may very well have to live with the decision for the rest or their working lives" (Schriver, 2004, p. 459). In contrast, U.S. organizations have traditionally emphasized individual responsibility. Each employee is responsible for making his own decisions within the parameters of his job expectations.

Schriver (2004) identifies a drawback of Theory Z, namely, that it assumes a "homogeneous internal organizational culture" (p. 459). Decision making by consensus assumes that opinions don't differ too much, or workers could never reach an agreement. This can conflict with the concept of cultural diversity and respect for a wide range of values and opinions.

It is interesting that Theory Z principles reflected in quality management historically have been used in many Japanese businesses but not in Japanese social service agencies (Keys, 1995a). Later content will discuss further the differences between organizations providing social services and those producing material products. With the current turbulent global economic environment, it is unclear to what extent Japanese businesses will continue maintaining a Theory Z approach (Schriver, 2004).

Ecosystems theories focus on how organizations take resources (input) and process them into some kind of product or service (output) (Holland, 1995). They emphasize how all parts of the organization (subsystems) are interrelated and function together to produce output (Holland & Petchers, 1987; Hodge et al., 2003).

Ecosystems theories stress the interactions of the various subsystems involved. Additionally, the importance of the environment and the impacts of other systems upon the organization are also stressed. In some ways, ecosystems theories are more flexible than many other theories. Irrational, spontaneous interactions are expected rather than ignored. Ecosystems theories emphasize constant assessment and adjustment.

Viewing Organizations from an Ecosystems Perspective   Social workers want to provide clients the best services they can. Because practitioners generally work under the auspices of organizations, they want those organizations to be as effective as they can be. Other organizations with which clients have transactions should also be as effective as possible. The underlying theme is to provide the best resources and services possible to help clients.

For whatever reasons, organizations may not provide the best service possible. An agency director may make decisions in the best interest of a grant funding source instead of clients. Procedures may be out of date and bogged down. Resources might shrink so critical decisions must be made about which programs to support and which to cut. The NASW Code of Ethics states that social work practitioners should advocate for "open and fair" resource allocation procedures: "When clients' needs can be met, an allocation procedure should be developed that is non-discriminatory and based on appropriate and consistently applied principles" (NASW, 1999, 3.07b). Thus, practitioners have an ethical responsibility to advocate on the behalf of clients when those clients are not being served adequately. Social workers are expected to work with larger systems to improve service provision. If the agency isn't doing its job well enough, then it's the worker's responsibility to initiate and undertake positive changes. In order to undertake such change, you must understand how organizations function as systems. Highlight 4.3 applies ecosystems concepts both to organizations and social service agencies.

Which Organizational Theory Is Best?

No one really knows which organizational theory is best. As time passes, theoretical perspectives rise and fall in terms of their popularity. Daft (2007) reflects: "Today, almost all organizations operate in highly uncertain environments. Thus, we are involved in a significant period of transition, in which concepts of organization theory and design are changing as dramatically as they did with the dawning of the Industrial Revolution" (p. 27).

Most organizations probably reflect a mixture of concepts derived from various theories. It is outside the scope of this text to explore organizational theory beyond providing a foundation to help you understand human behavior within the context of organizational macro systems.

| # Applying Ecosystems Concepts to Organizations and Social Service Agencies

Ecosystems concepts can be applied to social service and other organizations such as businesses and industry. We've established that they help structure ways to think about how any organization works. Organizations in general take *input,* process it, and produce some *output.* Input is the energy, information, or communication flow received from other systems. Output is what happens to input after it has gone through and been processed by some system.

Consider an industrial organization that manufactures earplugs called Plugitup. Plugitup is a *system,* a set of elements that are orderly and interrelated and a functional whole. The system's purpose is for its elements, including employees, management, and machinery, to work together to manufacture earplugs. The system is delineated by its *boundaries,* the repeatedly occurring patterns that characterize the relationships within a system and give that system a particular identity. People working for Plugitup are within the system's boundaries. People not working there are outside those boundaries. Boundaries determine who is and is not part of the system. Within these boundaries are various *subsystems,* secondary or subordinate systems. These include employees working on the plant floor, engineers, and management.

Plugitup's *input* is raw materials necessary for producing earplugs. Their processing involves converting raw materials into a liquid formula, pouring it into molds, and refining the final product in preparation for sale. Plugitup's *output* is the final earplug products ready for sale.

As does any company, Plugitup has a *relationship* with its consumers. A relationship is the dynamic interpersonal connection between two or more persons or systems that involves how they think about, feel about, and behave toward each other. To establish *homeostasis*—the tendency for a system to maintain a relatively stable, constant state of balance—the company must preserve lines of communication with its public and respond to the public's wants.

A *role* is "a socially expected behavior pattern determined by an individual's status" and expectations in a particular group or society (Mish, 1995, p. 1014). Part of Plugitup's management's role is to monitor public demand. Management finds that the public desires more variety in earplugs than it did two decades

ago. It sponsors market surveys to get *feedback* from consumers. Feedback is a special form of input by which a system receives information about that system's own performance. Sometimes consumers give *positive feedback,* the informational input a system receives about what it is doing correctly in order to maintain itself and thrive. For example, consumers say they particularly love fluorescent orange earplugs. This tells Plugitup what it is doing well and encourages the company to continue producing orange ones. *Negative feedback,* on the other hand, is informational input received by a system that criticizes some aspect of its functioning. For instance, consumers might indicate that the earplugs are too small for people with exceptionally large ear canals. Plugitup would then have to address the issue of earplug size. It might start offering earplugs that are more flexible in terms of size or provide a range of earplug sizes.

That there are many ways of producing and marketing earplugs reflects *equifinality,* the fact that there are many different means to the same end. Earplugs can be made in various colors and shapes, and with varying pliability. Various production procedures can be employed. In Plugitup's case, the end or goal is to produce marketable earplugs regardless of the final product's specifications and how that product is made. Therefore, instead of manufacturing only one type of earplug as it originally did decades ago, the company sustains six different lines of earplugs using somewhat different production procedures. This reflects *differentiation,* a system's tendency to move from a more simplified to a more complex existence.

The *interface* between the company and earplug consumers is the stores selling earplugs to the public. An interface is the point where two systems (including individuals, families, groups, organizations, or communities) come into contact with each other, interact, or communicate.

If Plugitup's management does not effectively respond to public demand, the company may experience *entropy,* the natural tendency of a system to progress toward disorganization, depletion, and death. Rather, management strives to achieve *negative entropy,* the process of a system toward growth and development. Company management wants to continue growing and increasing earplug profits.

continued

Highlight 4.3 | *continued*

[handwritten: Social svc org. version of ecosys. perspective]

Now compare Plugitup with a counseling center called Happyhelp. Happyhelp is a *system* whose purpose is to help clients solve problems. People working for Happyhelp are within the system's *boundaries*. People not working for Happyhelp are not part of the system. Various *subsystems* including social workers, accounting staff, support staff, and management work within Happyhelp's boundaries to provide service.

Happyhelp's *input* into the helping process includes its staff and all their skills. Plugitup's process is the conversion of raw materials into earplug products. Happyhelp's process is the application of intervention skills to help clients with many different problems, including depression, mental illness, eating disorders, and substance abuse. Happyhelp's *output* is the extent to which clients' goals are achieved and problems alleviated.

Relationships are formed between Happyhelp's social workers and its clients. Relationships are also formed among staff and between practitioners and management. Practitioners' *role* includes helping clients work on and solve problems. Role expectations include having effective skills in addition to conducting oneself professionally and ethically. Goals include helping clients regain their *homeostasis* so that they might maintain stable and productive lives. Happyhelp also strives to maintain its own homeostasis so that it can continue to function as a helping agency. Happyhelp seeks to avoid *entropy* because it wants to continue functioning as a productive system. Thus, it strives for *negative entropy* by adding new staff and innovative programs. Such development reflects *differentiation* as service provision becomes more complex.

The *interface* is the contact between client and social worker, the agency's representative. Workers provide clients with *feedback* about their thoughts and behavior. Workers endeavor to give *positive feedback* to clients whenever possible to reinforce clients' strengths and positive efforts.

Various Happyhelp social workers use different treatment approaches and techniques to help people solve problems. This reflects *equifinality*, as there are many different ways to conceptualize issues and pursue goals.

Because of its flexibility and the complexities of working with real clients, this book will primarily view organizations from an ecosystems perspective. As we have discussed, various organizational theories emphasize different aspects of organizations in terms of how you should view their functioning and what you should consider most significant. Regardless of the theory chosen, you can use an ecosystems approach to readily describe the processes involved in organizational life. The *Encyclopedia of Social Work* portrays all management approaches within the context of systems theories (Austin, 1995). Each management theory can be examined using concepts inherent in ecosystems theories. Additionally, accreditation standards for social work programs emphasize the concept of work with "systems of all sizes" (Council on Social Work Education (CSWE), 1992a, B5.7.6, B6.9; CSWE, 1992b, M5.7.6, m6.11).

Critical Thinking Questions 4.3

Which organizational theory or theories do you think are most effective and practical? What are your reasons for thinking so? What concepts do you think are most important? What type of organizational environment would you prefer to work in? What experiences in working for businesses or organizations have you had that influence your opinions?

CHAPTER SUMMARY

This chapter provided a theoretical foundation for understanding organizations and how they function. Organizations and social service agencies were described, and a range of theories were reviewed.

These theories included classical organizational theories that reflect rigid structure in addition to emphasis on productivity and task completion. Examples are scientific management, the administrative theory of management, and bureaucracy. In contrast, neoclassical organizational theory represents a later shift in perspective to theory that's more oriented toward human relationships and motivation. Human relations theories and feminist theories stress the importance of the human component in organizational functioning. Feminist theories, of course, focus on the empowerment of women. The cultural perspective emphasizes the importance of expectations in the organizational environment and culture to maintain the organization's status quo.

Economics theory focuses on productivity and task completion, yet emphasizes flexibility. Chaos theory reflects more divergent perspectives that emphasize the complexity of variables involved in organizations. Contingency theory stresses careful analysis of all variables to determine those that relate directly to an issue or problem involving either personal or other organizational factors. Culture-quality theories, characterizing the end of the last century, emphasize the importance of establishing a positive organizational culture that promotes worker motivation and improves the quality of their work. Finally, ecosystems theory provides a perspective for understanding organizational functioning that fits well with social work. It provides a structured way of viewing organizations, yet focuses on how change might occur. It also can involve both the importance of human well-being and the accomplishment of organizational tasks and goals.

5 CHAPTER | Social Service Organizational Settings, Goals, and Environmental Contexts

© Wally McNamee/CORBIS

Organizations respond to human needs. Here people demonstrate on the behalf of
Social Security to emphasize the importance of saving it.

CHAPTER CONTENTS

A pink slip. Perry could not believe it. He went to his mailbox today at work just like he did every weekday, and there it was. The pink slip said he was being laid off in two weeks.

Perry had been a social worker for a Protective Services unit at Rutabaga County Department of Social Services for four years. Although very demanding, he loved his job. He worked in a special program stressing family preservation that emphasized keeping families together if at all possible. It involved intensive work with families over limited time periods. Perry's goal was to help families get back on their emotional feet and function permanently without social service assistance.

With a relatively small caseload of families, he could provide the intensive services families at risk of child abuse or neglect desperately needed. Sometimes, he served as an educator, providing help with child management, anger control, or budgeting. He usually served as counselor and support system, focusing on family strengths and assisting with members' problem solving. Other times, he was a broker, linking families with needed resources like health care or grants for paint and home repairs to comply with building codes. He even helped families paint rooms and fix windows to avoid having children removed for neglect because of inadequate housing conditions. The intent was to help families in crisis and under extreme economic and emotional pressure become stronger, healthier, and independent. As a result, the risk for child abuse or neglect was significantly decreased and the need for placement of children in foster care at the county's great expense eliminated. Perry felt he had provided enormous help to many families over the years.

In the past, getting people off expensive assistance and service-provision roles had delighted county administrators gravely focused on budget crises. The external environmental climate, however, had abruptly changed. Severe budget cuts forced agency administrators to make tough decisions. They decided Perry's family preservation program was much too expensive to continue. He served too few clients to warrant his salary. Perry no longer had a job. His clients would no longer receive the service they needed.

It was not Perry's fault that he lost his job. Nor was it his fault that he could no longer help his clients as he had in the past. His agency's external environment had shifted and resources had been reduced. The result was a change in the agency's goals that no longer made his program a priority. Forces in the external environment had direct impacts on his agency's ability to provide services.

Chapter 4 discussed organizational theories and some basic knowledge about organizations. This chapter will continue examining organizations within the social environment, both internally and externally. Two important concepts concerning the internal environment are agency setting and organizational goals. A range of variables in the external environment directly affect structure and human behavior in the internal environment.

This chapter will:

- Examine primary and secondary agency settings.
- Define and discuss organizational missions statements, goals, and objectives for achieving goals.

- Discuss goal displacement.
- Explore the external macro environment of organizations, including resources, legitimation, client sources, and relationships with other organizations.
- Examine the impact of social and economic forces on social service organizations.
- Provide case examples concerning working in a secondary setting, goal displacement, personnel resources, and competitive relationships among organizations.
- Examine how federal social legislation, Temporary Assistance to Needy Families (TANF), and managed care impact agency service provision.
- Explore ethical issues in managed care.

THE IMPORTANCE OF ORGANIZATIONS FOR SOCIAL WORKERS

Organizations are particularly important to practitioners for three basic reasons. First, they employ workers. An organization's policies, goals, and restrictions will directly affect what work practitioners can and cannot do with clients. The second reason for an organization's significance is that frequently the organization and not the client will be the source of problems. Workers, therefore, need to evaluate how well their organizations are functioning in order to do their own work effectively. Third, Hasenfeld (1984) stresses the importance of organizational analysis prior to undertaking any macro-level changes. We have established that the NASW Code of Ethics obligates social workers to advocate and work for improvements in their agency settings when necessary.

Meenaghan (1987) eloquently states that the profession has come "to believe that social workers should be trained to see how their agency functioned as a complex organization, what external forces could and would influence and constrain it, and how social workers could act positively, even initiating events in the agency's environment" (p. 83). Social workers must understand their agencies' internal environments and how they work in order to enhance agency functioning and effectiveness. This section's purpose is not to provide a detailed explanation of organizational behavior. Rather, it is to alert new social workers to internal organizational factors that can affect their ability to do their jobs. Two primary concepts important in understanding the internal environment of organizations are agency settings and organizational goals.

It is necessary to briefly comment about the terms used in this book. Organizational theories are taken primarily from the business and management literature. However, they may apply to all organizations, including social services agencies. For our purposes, we will use the terms "organization," "social services agency," "social service agency," "social agency," and "agency" interchangeably. The chapters on organizations in this book focus on the social services agencies in which social workers practice and clients receive services.

AGENCY SETTINGS

Social workers usually work within one of two types of organizational settings, primary or secondary. Each type of setting has implications for effective practice and for how workers experience their work environment.

Primary Settings

Primary settings are those agencies where social work is the main or primary profession employed. Most public social service agencies are primary settings. It is common for the administrators, supervisors, and most of the workers to be social workers with social work degrees and titles. While there may be other occupations or professions present (for example, homemaker service providers[1] or psychologists), they represent a minority of the staff.

Because most of the staff and administrators are social workers, they tend to share similar professional values and perspectives. Their education and training are typically similar. One benefit of these settings is that workers never have to explain what social workers do. Everyone knows and understands the social work role. This cannot be said for secondary settings.

Secondary Settings

Secondary settings are characterized by the presence of a variety of professional staff. The main service provided by the agency is not social services. Typical examples are hospitals and schools. In a hospital, medical care of patients is the primary service. Medically trained personnel (for example, nurses and physicians) comprise the largest segment of the professional staff. Most of the administrative staff and supervisors will have a medical background. Social work is just one of several ancillary professions contributing to the overall goal of medical care provision. Other professions include dietitians, pharmacists, and chaplains, to name a few.

The wealth of disciplines and professional perspectives can produce a challenging environment for social work. Typically, social workers must learn the language (for instance, medical terminology or relevant abbreviations) used by the other professions. Unlike primary settings, a secondary setting like a hospital is usually operated within a definite pecking order controlled by other professions. Physicians are at the top of that hierarchy. Social workers are not. This sometimes means that social work values and perspectives will clash with those of the physicians and other medical personnel. Highlight 5.1 provides an example illustrating how this can work.

---

[1] A homemaker service provider helps clients remain in their own homes by providing necessary services such as meal preparation, laundry, shopping, cleaning, or transportation (Barker, 2003, p. 199).

| **Highlight 5.1** | **Case Example—Working in a Secondary Setting** |

Cristina, a hospital social worker, was working with Tyrone, a 61-year-old patient with Parkinson's disease, along with his family. *Parkinson's disease* is "a chronic progressive nervous disease chiefly of later life . . . marked by tremor and weakness of resting muscles and by a shuffling gait" (Mish, 1995, p. 845). Tyrone had been hospitalized for a malfunctioning of his kidneys that had nothing to do with his Parkinson's disease. However, nurses referred Tyrone to Cristina when they observed him falling several times while walking from his bed to the bathroom. These nurses felt that Tyrone would have difficulty returning home without special equipment such as a walker or a wheelchair. They indicated he might even require some special placement instead of returning to his home.

Cristina met with Tyrone. She found it very difficult to understand him, as the Parkinson's disease was seriously affecting his ability to formulate words. However, with some difficulty she was able to discuss his situation with him. He stated vehemently that he wanted to return home. He emphasized how the disease "wasn't that bad." He stressed that he would be all right now that the kidney problem had subsided, if he could just get home!

Cristina also spoke alone with Tyrone's wife, Ursula, age 59. Ursula felt that Tyrone was denying the seriousness of his condition. She said that his muscular control and balance had deteriorated significantly in the past four months. Ursula told Cristina that Tyrone had been a university professor in engineering at a prestigious private college. She explained that it was very difficult for him to admit to his increasingly serious weakness. Ursula also expressed concern about her ability to care for him adequately at home. Tyrone was a large hulk of a man. Ursula indicated that it was impossible for her to lift him if he should fall. She felt that someone needed to be with him at all times. Yet, she hesitated to take him out of the home and place him in a health care facility. She felt it might break his spirit and his heart.

Cristina met with Tyrone and Ursula individually one more time and, finally, together for their last encounter. She discussed with them a variety of possibilities. These included obtaining supportive equipment, widening the doorways in their home, installing ramps for wheelchair accessibility, and

referring them to various other supportive service providers. The latter included a beeper Tyrone could use to call for help in the event he fell. Additionally, Cristina began arranging for a visiting nurse to assist Ursula with Tyrone's care and to provide respite care one afternoon each week to give Ursula a break.

Cristina felt good about her work with Tyrone and Ursula. She felt she had helped them establish a viable plan for the present. It could maintain Tyrone in his own home until his increasing disability required more extensive treatment and, possibly, placement in some special facility. Cristina had already contacted the recommended services to establish their availability and viability in Tyrone's case. The next step was to finalize the plans and put them into place before Tyrone's upcoming discharge.

Cristina came to work the next morning and went around as usual checking her patients' charts to see what was happening and monitor progress. When she got to Tyrone's room, it was empty. Initially, Cristina assumed that a nurse or volunteer had taken him for a walk in order to get some daily exercise.

However, Cristina was shocked as she found and read his chart. It stated he was being transported this very day to a health care facility. What about the plans she had made with Tyrone and Ursula? What about Tyrone's adamant feelings about remaining in his own home? In disbelief she stared at the signature of Tyrone's attending physician, Dr. Strangelove. Dr. Strangelove had totally ignored all that she had written in the chart about Tyrone's discharge planning. A deepening fury began to paint her emotions. How dare Dr. Strangelove do this! How dare he act as if she did not even exist.

Luckily, Cristina became so busy that day that she had little more time to think about Tyrone, Ursula, or Dr. Strangelove. By the next morning she had simmered down quite a bit. After all, Tyrone and Ursula had the right to choose their own destinies. She was just there to help them if she could.

When she later talked to the head nurse about the matter, Cristina was enlightened about what it meant to work in a secondary setting. She abruptly found out that the physician's word ruled in a medical facility. Apparently, Dr. Strangelove was personal

continued

friends with Ursula's son Devin, who was also a physician. Dr. Strangelove and Devin sat down first with Ursula and later with Tyrone to discuss their feelings about Tyrone's condition and his and Ursula's future. Both physicians felt strongly that it was ridiculous for Tyrone to return home. Both felt it was far beyond Ursula's marital responsibility to "sacrifice" herself for Tyrone. They apparently had urged and eventually persuaded Ursula to pursue placing Tyrone in a residential facility. It was the head

nurse's opinion that Tyrone felt too weak to fight all three of these people and voice his own desires. So, defeated, he complied with their recommendations.

Cristina was not convinced that the decision was the correct one for either Tyrone or Ursula. However, she understood that they had every right to make their own decisions, regardless of the dynamics involved in the decision-making process. Cristina also learned that she had significantly less status than physicians did in this secondary setting.

MISSION STATEMENTS, GOALS, AND OBJECTIVES

Every social services agency should develop a *mission statement,* a declaration of the organization's purpose that "establishes broad and relatively permanent parameters within which goals are developed and specific programs designed" (Kettner, Moroney, & Martin, 1999, p. 95). It also includes what client populations are to be served and provides general guidance for what needs should be met.

For example, Lad Lake, Inc., a private nonprofit social services agency, has a mission statement saying it "provides living and learning environments for at-risk youth and families in preparation for responsible living in our communities" (Lad Lake, Inc., undated). This is a broad statement that encompasses a range of programs including the following:

- A residential treatment center for adolescents with severe behavioral and emotional problems.
- Special education programs and an alternative school in the community.
- Independent living services to support children transitioning out of the foster care system as they approach age 18.
- Outreach services offering "guidance, therapy, and even friendship" to young people and families (p. 19).
- An in-home therapy program.
- A mentoring program serving youth ages 7 to 21 "with a history of substance abuse, truancy, disorderly conduct, or an unstable family life" (p. 23).
- A "Brighter Future Initiative" program offering "intervention services" to youth " who have committed their first minor delinquent offense" and to their families (p. 23).
- Parent training classes.
- A number of other creative initiatives (Lad Lake, 2005).

Other examples of mission statements, suggested by Kettner et al., include a family service agency whose mission is "to promote family strength and stability in a manner that allows each individual to achieve his/her potential while, at the same time, supporting strong and productive interrelationships among family members," or an agency offering services to alcohol and drug addicts whose mission is "to promote and support the achievement of a positive and productive lifestyle for those formerly addicted to chemical substances (1999, p. 95). The key to a mission statement, they argue, is that it "should focus on what lies ahead for its clients/consumers if the agency is successful in addressing their problems and meeting their needs" (Kettner et al., 1999, p. 95).

Organizational Goals

Mission statements identify the organization's basic goals. Kettner et al. offer this definition of *goals*: "Goals are statements of expected outcomes dealing with the problem that the program is attempting to prevent, eradicate, or ameliorate. Goals need not be measurable or achievable. They simply provide programmatic direction" (Kettner et al., 1999, pp. 95–96).

Organizational goals serve at least three major purposes (Etzioni, 1964). First, they provide guidelines for the kinds of functions and activities organizational workers are supposed to pursue. Second, organizational goals "constitute a source of legitimacy which justifies the activities of an organization and, indeed, its very existence" (p. 5). Third, goals can "serve as standards by which members of an organization and outsiders can assess the success of the organization—i.e., its effectiveness and efficiency" (p. 5).

How does an organization establish its mission statement and goals? According to Holland and Petchers:

> Official goals represent a translation of social welfare legislation and policy direction into programmatic action or activities. Official goals also indicate value choices and ideological and theoretical stances about human needs or problems. Goals that the organization sets for itself form criteria by which the organization may be evaluated and held accountable. (1987, p. 207)

Social service organizations and agencies, then, formulate goals in order to address any of a wide range of needs and problems concerning human well-being. Social service organizations are supposed to use their resources to address these needs and remedy problems. The establishment of goals directs this process.

In order to understand an organization's functioning, it is helpful to think in terms of "official" goals and "operative" goals (Perrow, 1961, p. 856). *Official* goals "are the general purposes of the organization as put forth in the charter [often called a *mission statement*], annual reports, public statements by key officials and other authoritative pronouncements; *operative* goals, on the other hand, "designate the ends sought through the actual operating policies of the organization" (p. 856).

Why must we make the distinction between official and operative goals? The problem is that "official goals may predict little about organizational behavior" (Hasenfeld, 1983, p. 87). In other words, official goals may have very little to do with an agency's actual operative goals. Reasons for this will be discussed more thoroughly later when we address the concept of goal displacement.

Goals provide social services agencies with general direction concerning *what* should happen, but not with specific guidance regarding *how* it should be done. Highlight 5.2 discusses how agencies structure the process of carrying out goals by identifying objectives.

Multiple Goals

Social service organizations usually are complex entities. Therefore, they frequently aim to accomplish multiple goals (Austin, 2002; Ginsberg, 1995). There are a number of reasons for this. First, agencies must hold themselves accountable to legislative requirements and constraints. For instance, an organization providing group homes for children with cognitive disabilities must conform to a range of state licensing rules that mandate the minimum standards for service provision. These include the maximum number of clients in any particular residence, the amount of space required per child, the staff-to-client ratio, how the kitchen and dining areas should be equipped, and even the requirement that toilet seats be open or split in the front instead of closed.

Multiple goals also occur because many social service agencies may serve a range of client groups. For example, one organization may provide daycare services, vocational training, adoption services, and foster care all at the same time. Lad Lake, Inc., described earlier, provides another example of an organization sponsoring a wide range of programs pursuing many goals. Each segment of the agency pursues its own goals within the context of the larger organizational environment that has more encompassing organizational goals.

Additionally, organizations may be held accountable to different segments of the public, each making its own demands upon agency performance and subsequently its goals. Such publics can include "other human service organizations, interest groups, legislative bodies, and professional associations" in addition to clients being served (Ginsberg, 1995; Hasenfeld, 1983, pp. 90–91). For example, a child advocacy group may pressure a social services agency specializing in helping survivors of domestic violence to increase its standards for temporary shelter of mothers and their children. Likewise, professional organizations may require the same agency to provide minimum in-service training sessions for staff in various job positions. We have established that in-service training is instructional programming provided by an employer that brings in experts to help employees develop skills and understanding intended to help them improve their work performance. Hence, the agency must pursue both of these goals in addition to many other goals established for numerous other reasons.

| Highlight 5.2 | **Objectives Indicate How to Achieve Goals** |

Goals are general statements about what an organization wants to accomplish. They usually don't specify exactly how to achieve them. *Objectives* are smaller, behaviorally specific subgoals that serve as stepping stones on the way to accomplishing the main goal. Brody (2005) explains:

> Typically, goals represent long-term endeavors, sometimes as long as three to five years, and may even be timeless. Examples of these goals statements would be "improving access to health care services for low-income persons" or "reducing racism in our community."

Objectives represent relevant, attainable, measurable, and time-limited ends to be achieved. They are relevant because they fit within the general mission and goals of the organization and because they relate to problems identified by the organization. They are attainable because they can be realized. They are measurable because achievement is based upon tangible, concrete, and usually quantifiable results. They are time limited (usually a year); this time frame helps the organization demonstrate concrete results within a specified period. (pp. 58–59)

Kettner and his colleagues (1999) recommend that the following questions be asked in order to establish "clear, specific measurable, time-limited, and realistic" objectives that the agency is committed to achieve:

- Is the objective clear? Does it mean the same thing to anyone who reads the statement?
- Does the objective specify results to be achieved, including numbers and changes in conditions?
- Is the objective written in such a way that it can be measured? Are measurement criteria incorporated into the objective?
- Does the statement indicate a time limit within which or a target date by which the objective will be achieved?
- Is the objective realistic given our technology and knowledge as well as available resources? (p. 97)

Brody (2005) identifies four basic types of objectives used in social service agencies—*impact, service, operational,* and *product*:

> *Impact objectives* specify outcomes to be achieved as a result of program activities. They detail the return expected on the organization's investment of time, personnel, and resources.

The following are examples:

- To place 20 children in adoptive homes in one year
- To secure jobs for 35 juvenile delinquents in 5 months
- To increase the number of foster children reunited with their natural parents from 40 to 50 by June 30 . . .

Service objectives are the organization's tally of activities provided or services rendered. Sometimes these are referred to as *activity* or *process* objectives. Examples include the following:

- To serve 300 clients in the program year
- To conduct 680 interviews
- To provide 17 neighborhood assemblies
- To interview 20 children needing foster homes . . .

Operational objectives convey the intent to improve the general operation of the organization. Examples include the following:

- To sponsor 4 in-service training workshops for 40 staff
- To obtain a pilot project grant of $10,000 within 6 months
- To increase the number of volunteers by 150
- To reduce staff turnover from 20% to 10% annually

Operational objectives are essential to enhance the way an organization functions. They are a means to the end for which the organization was established. By providing in-service training, for example, an organization improves the way it serves its target populations.

Product objectives are designed to provide a tangible outcome to benefit a target population or a community. . . . The following are examples of product objectives:

- To obtain passage of House Bill 41
- To develop a neighborhood family support system
- To review and critique a specific piece of legislation
- To open four schools in the evening for recreation
- To provide a media effort on teen pregnancy prevention . . .
- To sponsor a communitywide campaign on mental health (pp. 59–60)

Goal Displacement

A major problem encountered by workers in organizations involves *goal displacement*. Goal displacement was originally defined as "substitution of a legitimate goal with another goal which the organization was not developed to address, for which resources were not allocated and which it is not known to serve" (Etzioni, 1964, p. 10). Holland and Petchers (1987) interpret this meaning by stating that "goal displacement often occurs when the means to a goal becomes the goal itself explaining that in recent years, "goal displacement has become a serious concern in human service organizations" (p. 208).

In other words, goal displacement occurs when an organization continues to function but no longer achieves the goals it's supposed to. A typical scenario in social service organizations is when the rules and following those rules become more important than providing services to clients.

It should be noted that goal displacement can also involve positive changes in goals. A classic example is the March of Dimes, which began as an organization dedicated to raising money to eradicate polio, historically a major childhood disease. With the discovery of a polio vaccine, the disease ceased to be a major health problem in the United States and Canada. Instead of going out of business, however, the organization shifted its goal to raising money to combat birth defects. The new goal had one advantage over the polio-related goal. Instead of focusing on a single disease, the organization now directed its attention to a large category of problems. With such a broad scope, the organization would probably never run out of new childhood health problems to combat. Therefore, it would be unlikely that it would ever again face a similar dilemma of goal displacement.

This commentary is not intended to be critical of the March of Dimes, or any other organization. It is a fact of organizational life that agencies rarely go out of existence. Once a goal is achieved, most organizations do not disappear. Instead, they shift their attention to new goals. This process only becomes a problem when the means to the goals assume a life of their own. When this happens, agencies may place greater emphasis on getting the files up-to-date than on providing effective service to clients.

People's access to resources has major impacts on the options available to them and, in effect, how they behave. Poverty and lack of resources will be at the root of many of your clients' problems. Therefore, it is crucial to understand how organizations affect resource provision and clients. Such a background can enable you to identify ways to make changes in systems so that your clients are better served.

For instance, consider the example concerning the county social services department in Highlight 5.3. As a worker in that agency, there are several things you might target for change. These include working with other workers and administration to shorten significantly the tedious forms. You might also explore ways to get information out to community residents regarding the documentation and needed information they must bring when applying for services. Simple things like putting up clearly visible signs instructing people

| Highlight 5.3 | An Example of Goal Displacement—Process Supersedes Progress |

A large county Department of Social Services (previously referred to as "the public welfare department") comes to mind. It is located in the shell of an old department store with high ceilings and a myriad of small worker cubicles somewhat resembling a mammoth beehive. All outside windows have been sealed with bricks because of "the heating and ventilation problems." No one really knows what that means. However, everyone inside the building knows that the building's interior is isolated from the outside world.

When entering the main door of the building, it is extremely difficult to figure out where to go for what kind of services. This is true even if you're a professional social worker, let alone if you're a client entering the building for the first time. Consider what it would be like if you were a client applying for services from this agency. You probably have to stand in line for fifteen or twenty minutes simply to get the information you need to find out where to go.

When you finally wander into a waiting area for the services you need, you have to stand in line again for another twenty minutes or so to get the forms you must fill out for the services you need. You then take the twenty pages of complicated forms, which you must fill out meticulously, and take a seat. The chairs are made of hard plastic. There are large "dust bunnies" (sometimes referred to as "dinosaur dust bunnies") rolling around your feet. It then takes approximately an hour to fill out the forms. This is assuming you can read well in English. You probably do not understand some of the questions, so you leave the spaces blank. You then take the forms up to the desk, where they are placed in a pile. You must wait your turn in order to see an intake worker (that is, someone who begins the process to provide services). You wait two to three hours.

Finally, your name is called and you are instructed to go to Cubicle 57 to see Ms. Hardmoney. You enter Cubicle 57 and see Ms. Hardmoney sitting at her desk and reading your forms. You then begin a discussion with her concerning the additional information she needs in order to process your application for services. It seems, she indicates, that a number of critical elements of information are missing. Look at those blanks. She then says you must get the critical information before you can continue the application process. The critical information is somewhere at home. Well, that's all right. Just go home, get it, and start this whole process over again tomorrow. At least you know where the waiting room is now.

In this example, the organization was supposed to be providing services to people in need. However, the complicated process, commonly called "red tape," became much more important to the organization's staff than whether clients received needed services or not.

where to go when they first enter the building might be helpful. Even advocating for waiting room chairs made to make people comfortable might be useful.

Ecosystems Theory, Organizations, and Goal Displacement

We have established that it is helpful to view social service organizations in terms of ecosystems theories' concepts. Many of the notions involved are similar to those used in reference to business and industry. For example, in industry, resources or *input* are *processed* by the organizational system, which turns out some product or *output*. Figure 5.1 illustrates this sequence as "ecosystems concepts." Essentially, the same thing happens in social service organizations. They take resources (*input*) and, in response to social forces and institutionalized values, apply some *process* (procedures for

Figure 5.1
The Process
of Goal
Displacement

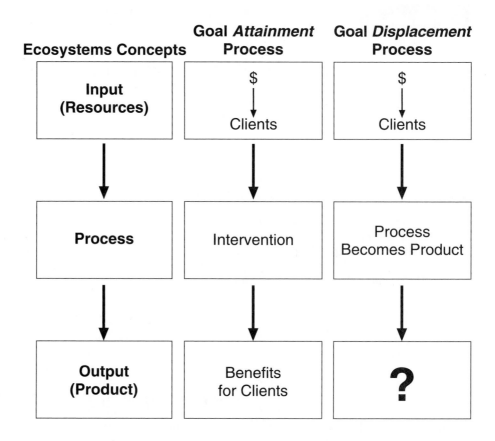

providing services) to produce *output* (actual service provision or some other benefits for clients).

Often when goal displacement occurs, however, the emphasis is placed on the process rather than the product. The organizational system begins to consider the rigid process of providing services as its major function. The *process*, rather than effective provision of services, then becomes the organization's *product*.

Goal attainment comprises what is supposed to happen through the intervention process. Illustrated in Figure 5.1, the input (in the form of resources) is supposed to be used on the behalf of clients in the intervention process. Hence, "$" refers to resources with an arrow pointing to "clients" in the top box in the goal attainment process. The result is supposed to be positive benefits for clients. Thus, an arrow points from the "$ to clients" box to the middle box that refers to the "intervention process." The intervention process involves whatever treatment process or technology the organization uses to help its clients. Finally, an arrow points from the "intervention" box down to the "benefits for clients" box, illustrating what is supposed to happen in an agency's goal attainment process.

Figure 5.1 also illustrates *goal displacement* on the far right. Here, input (in the form of resources) is used to maintain the *process* of what is done with those resources. In essence, the process becomes the *product*. The positive impacts upon clients are somehow lost and forgotten as agency personnel strive to maintain and complete the process. Figure 5.1 depicts this with arrows leading down from the "$ to clients" box to the "process becomes product" box. The arrow leading from the latter box down to the "?" box reflects how the actual results for clients become relatively unimportant and possibly unknown.

Goal Displacement and Generalist Practice

This discussion's intent is to enhance your awareness of problems often encountered in organizational service provision. Understanding the dynamics of organizational behavior is a prerequisite to changing an organization's behavior for the clients' benefit. When a social service agency ceases to serve clients as effectively as possible, it is your job as a generalist practitioner to try to improve service provision. This may involve advocating with administrators for a new program, suggesting and promoting agency policy changes, or initiating a fund-raising project to provide Christmas toys for needy families.

THE ENVIRONMENTAL CONTEXT OF SOCIAL SERVICE ORGANIZATIONS

The environmental context in which a social services organization functions is critically important to the organization's ability to pursue and attain its goals. It is essential for you to understand at least four environmental dimensions impacting organizations. They include available resources, legitimation, client sources, and relationships with other organizations (Holland & Petchers, 1987).

Resources

Hasenfeld (1984) refers to "resources inputs" as "those external units which provide the target agency with [1] its financial basis and those units which provide [2] its personnel" (p. 24). First, a social services agency must have money to function. It needs to pay staff salaries, rent and/or for building maintenance, for supplies, telephone, and a myriad of other expenses.

The second type of resource critical for a social services agency involves personnel. What kind of staffing does the agency have? What are their professional credentials? Are staff qualified and plentiful enough to carry out their duties effectively? Highlight 5.4 provides a case example involving personnel resources.

| Highlight 5.4 | Case Example—Personnel Resources |

A debate raged in one state between professional social workers, on the one hand, and certain county social services agency administrators, on the other. (It might be noted that many of the latter administrators were not social workers by profession.) The battle ensued when professional certification for social workers was first initiated in the state. Most professional social workers adamantly maintained that it was critically important for workers calling themselves "social workers" to have graduated from accredited social work programs and have the requisite experience.

Some rural county social service agency administrators, on the other hand, staunchly maintained that there were not enough graduates from professional social work programs to fill all of the positions available in their rural agencies. They declared that the only workers they could attract to fill their agencies' job positions were graduates having other degrees, such as those in sociology and psychology. These administrators emphasized that most social work graduates were attracted to the state's larger, more exciting urban areas.

Much to the dismay of professional social work educators, a faction of sociologists teaching in local universities supported the county administrators' view and politically lobbied on the former's behalf. In reality, these sociologists were concerned that graduates with sociology degrees would be able to find employment as easily as graduates with social work degrees. To a great extent, this approach coincided with the sociologists' own interests, namely, to maintain a higher number of sociology majors.

Most professional social workers and social work educators were appalled. None of the sociology programs were accredited. Therefore, these programs were held accountable to no standards such as those mandating the teaching of practice skills, the infusion of professional values and ethics throughout the curriculum, a substantial field internship, and a focus on human diversity. All social work programs, on the other hand, were required to adhere faithfully to such standards.

Upon further investigation, the state association of social workers established that the major reason the complaining rural county administrators were unable to recruit social work graduates was that these administrators paid near-to-minimum-wage salaries. Additionally, the state Social Work Education Association determined that virtually hundreds of graduates were being turned out from several state universities within 100 miles of these counties. In reality, there were plenty of graduates available to fill positions, that is, if the counties would pay salaries appropriate for professional social workers.

This environmental dimension substantially affected the ability of county social service agencies to provide professional services. If agencies were not required to hire professional social workers, but could employ sociology or psychology graduates, regardless of their training in skills and values, quality of service would be seriously curtailed. The agencies' personnel resources would directly affect the agencies' ability to provide service to clients.

Legitimation

A second environmental dimension impacting social service agencies is *legitimation.* We have already briefly mentioned the importance of legislative requirements and constraints with respect to an agency's organizational goals. Legitimation is the condition where the external environment provides an agency with the appropriate status or authorization to perform agency functions and pursue agency goals. An agency must be legally viable. Once established, the agency must continue to abide by the rules upon which its existence is based.

Consider, however, if an agency does not follow the appropriate rules and regulations. For example, a health care center for older adults failed to follow the rules concerning maintenance of its bedridden patients, especially those with Alzheimer's disease. Clients' relatives visiting the center reported to the state's licensing agency that they had observed a number of seriously disturbing incidents during their visits. These observations included clients having wallowed in their own feces for over a day, staff slapping clients in the face when these clients refused to cooperate, and employees depriving clients of food to punish them for poor behavior. Needless to say, once the health care center's practices became known and were investigated by state authorities, the agency was closed. It no longer possessed the legitimation and accountability needed to support its existence.

Client Sources

The third environmental dimension affecting agencies involves the availability of clients. This "array of client sources, which ranges from groups or programs that serve as client referral mechanisms to individuals who directly seek out services for themselves," is critical to an agency's existence and functioning (Holland & Petchers, 1987, p. 208). In other words, an agency cannot last very long without enough clients to sustain it.

One agency, for example, provided special therapy services (including social work, occupational, speech, and physical) to school children in a variety of rural counties. The counties initially did not each have enough clients to hire their own full-time therapists. Therefore, each county respectively purchased from the agency whatever therapists' time was needed.

For instance, a social worker or occupational therapist might serve clients in a particular county only one or two days each week. Because of a limited number of clients, this might be all the service that the county needed. Together, the counties provided enough work for the agency to maintain several full-time therapists in each discipline. However, new state requirements to provide adequate service to children were put into place. More children became eligible for service. The counties also began to develop enhanced assessment techniques and procedures. As a result, a number of counties subsequently identified enough of their own clients to hire their own full-time therapists. Hence, the agency providing special services no longer had access to enough clients in enough counties. It simply had to shut down.

Relationships with Other Organizations

The fourth environmental dimension affecting organizations involves relationships with other agencies in the macro environment. Analysis of this organizational environment is essential to understand any particular organization's functioning. How does the social service agency interact with other organizations within its macro environment? Such relationships may fall under the category of *uninvolved, complementary,* or *competitive* (Holland & Petchers, 1987, pp. 208–209).

Uninvolved Relationships Among Organizations   Organizational involvement can be placed on a continuum (Emery & Trist, 1961). At one end of this continuum are agencies that are integrally involved with each other and, in essence, can't function without each other. Such complementary relationships are discussed below. On the other end of this continuum lie agencies that have virtually nothing to do with each other except for brief, haphazard encounters. Therefore, there is little need to focus much attention on such *uninvolved* relationships. Finally, in the middle of this continuum lie those organizations that are competitive with each other. This latter type will also be discussed below.

"Complementary" Relationships Among Organizations   The "availability of complementary services" involves how organizations often need each other to work together (Holland & Petchers, 1987, p. 208). Agencies are not islands. Often, they cannot function in isolation. They need referral sources for clients. Alternately, they need appropriate resources to which they can refer clients whose needs they cannot meet.

Consider a sheltered employment facility where adults with cognitive disabilities are trained in basic work skills and function under comprehensive supervision. Such an agency needs other agencies that run group homes and institutional facilities where clients can reside when not at work. If clients have nowhere to live, then they can't take advantage of the sheltered employment facility activities.

Another example is an organization providing in-service treatment for alcoholic clients. This organization receives virtually all of its referrals from local family services agencies providing family counseling and local hospitals. Without the cooperation of these referral agencies, the inpatient program would cease to exist. Likewise, the local family services agencies and hospitals would be unable to serve alcoholic clients adequately if the in-service alcohol treatment program did not exist.

"Competitive" Relationships Among Organizations   Social service agencies may compete with each other for clients. If the number of clients is relatively limited, the competition may be quite fierce. We have established that agencies need clients to survive and thrive. Highlight 5.5 provides a case example of competitive relationships among organizations.

THE IMPACT OF SOCIAL AND ECONOMIC FORCES ON SOCIAL SERVICE ORGANIZATIONS: THE SHIFTING MACRO ENVIRONMENT

Organizations function within the larger macro environment and must respond to shifting social and economic forces. Social forces include societal expectations regarding who is eligible to receive benefits and what types of benefits are appropriate. People vote for politicians who support their ideas and, hopefully, will implement social policies agreeing with these conceptions. Economic forces involve how many resources are allocated to agencies for service

| Highlight 5.5 | **Case Example—Competitive Relationships Among Organizations** |

One state supported a number of privately run residential treatment centers for boys, ages 12 to 17, who had serious behavioral and emotional problems. The state purchased services from these agencies because the state did not provide these services itself. *Purchase-of-service* involves a financial agreement or contract where one agency, often a public agency, agrees to purchase services from another agency. It may be cost effective for the public agency to purchase the services from the other agency rather than to develop and provide those services itself. The agency from which services are purchased then assumes responsibility for developing and overseeing service provision.

For many years the state and counties provided enough clients to maintain all of the centers. No new centers opened because the number of agencies approximately matched the number of clients. No new agencies were needed. The status quo, or homeostasis, was maintained.

However, when the state decided to build and open its own extremely large treatment complex, the number of clients available to privately run treatment centers was significantly decreased. Thus, approximately half of the residential centers were forced to close. They could not solicit enough clients to sustain themselves. The other half of the centers that continued to exist did so because they quickly decided to specialize their services. For instance, one center specialized in serving clients who had dual diagnoses of both behavioral disorder and cognitive disability. Another center specialized in boys needing treatment because they had been sexually abused.

The new state treatment complex was not large enough to accommodate all of the state's clients who needed treatment. These clients had to go somewhere. The state determined that it was in the state's best fiscal interest to continue purchasing services for some clients who fell in certain categories. The fact that various centers decided to specialize in treating certain problems facilitated the state's decision-making process concerning which clients to treat in its own facility and which to refer elsewhere. Children with special needs and problems were referred to those centers that specialized in the treatment of those respective needs and problems.

---

provision. Social service agencies can only provide resources that are available and administer services in legally prescribed ways.

Social and economic forces may affect social service provision in at least three major ways. First, resources and funding may be limited. For example, a funding cut may result in the elimination of one of several programs in a domestic abuse shelter. Second, policies, regulations, and the wishes of political leaders determine what agencies can and cannot do. For instance, a child protection agency may be required by law to address a child maltreatment complaint within twenty-four hours. Third, social service agencies may be pressured to conform to public expectations. For example, the encompassing community might expect a large private mental hospital to sponsor an annual triathlon for fund-raising.

As population continues to expand worldwide, resources continue to shrink. Decreasing resources means that funding and financial support become more and more difficult to get. It also means that competition becomes more and more intense. It then makes sense that organizations producing higher-quality products (more effectively) at lower costs requiring lesser input (more efficiently) will be more likely to survive than those that are less effective and efficient. Likewise, social service organizations providing more effective and efficient services will probably outlive less effective and efficient counterparts.

Understanding social and economic forces affecting social service organizations provides insights into organizational behavior and individual behavior within organizations. Whenever possible, social workers have a professional obligation to improve organizational systems' performance and enhance service provision to clients. This is difficult to do within the macro context because social service organizations' external environment is constantly in flux. Social forces impact other macro organizations and influence political policies which, in turn, modify the availability of funding. Thus, as Holland and Petchers (1987) explain:

> Financial support from public and private sources must be sought, maintained, and protected while community expectations and priorities shift from one problem or need to another. Legal requirements and policies regulating operations undergo modification. Service technologies evolve in new directions, not always in consonance with consumer or public preferences. (p. 208)

Funding mechanisms vary widely. Social and economic forces jar social service organizations with unpredictability, suddenness, and severity. Thus, to survive and effectively meet their goals of helping clients, these organizations must maintain keen awareness of external influences and their effects. Organizations must also readily react to changing needs and demands. Two major social and economic thrusts seriously impacting and, in many ways, restricting service provision today are federal social legislation and managed care.

Federal Social Legislation Reflects Major Social and Economic Forces

Federal social legislation has major effects on what programs social service agencies can provide. Therefore, when legislation changes, agency services are identified and limited by that legislation. The underlying theme is that social legislation may significantly enhance or severely cut benefits to people in need. Agencies and their workers must comply with regulations whether they like them or not and whether they think such regulations are fair or not.

The current major public assistance program for children and families living in poverty is Temporary Assistance to Needy Families (TANF), which replaced the former program Aid to Families with Dependent Children (AFDC) in 1996. TANF was created by the Personal Responsibility and Work Opportunity Reconciliation Act of 1996 (also known as PRWORA). In February 2006, President George W. Bush signed into law the Deficit Reduction Act (DRA) of 2005. The result is a $39 billion cut in federal spending over the subsequent five years (Keene, 2006). Also included is a five-year extension of TANF (Child Welfare League of America [CWLA], 2006).

It's important to review the history of public assistance to understand the issues involved. Americans have a long-established record of ambivalence about providing poor people with financial assistance. Karger and Stoesz (2006) explain:

> On the hostility side, the argument goes like this: If privilege is earned by hard work, then people are poor because they are lazy and lack ambition. To those driven by the American spirit of competitiveness, the refusal of the poor to compete is a serious character flaw. On the other hand, only a few paychecks separate the welfare recipient from the average citizen—thus the compassion. Although democratic capitalism is based on the belief that hard work guarantees success, real life often tells a different story. (p. 271)

AFDC, originally established as Aid to Dependent Children (ADC) by the Social Security Act of 1935, was a program providing payments funded by federal and state governments to children deprived of parental support because a parent was absent from the home, had died, or was incapable of managing the household for physical or mental reasons. Most families receiving benefits were single mothers whose partners were not in the home.

AFDC established eligibility standards based on "family composition, income level, age of the children, and the applicant's willingness to participate in a welfare-to-work program and to cooperate with the welfare department to obtain paternity and child support" (Abramovitz, 1995, p. 184). Eligible families passed an income test, that is, an eligibility guideline that establishes the maximum amount of income a family may earn without losing benefits. Those who made too much money were ineligible for benefits.

Eligible families could potentially receive financial assistance for many years in addition to Medicaid,[2] food stamps,[3] and partial financial support for housing, "although a few states deduct[ed] the value of food stamps and housing grants from AFDC payments" (Abramovitz, 1995, p. 186). Note that how long families continued receiving public assistance is a matter of strong debate. Facts indicate that before TANF, half of all AFDC recipients left welfare rolls within one year, the number rising to 70 percent after two years (Karger & Stoesz, 2006).

A number of issues characterize the public assistance debate concerning the effectiveness, fairness, and humaneness of TANF and its effects on children and families in need. They include adequacy of funding, time limits, work requirements, child care, education and training for better jobs, job quality and availability, health insurance after TANF, encouraging healthy marriages, and equitable treatment by states.

Adequacy of Funding DiNitto (2005) describes some aspects of TANF spending. Note that the 2006 Deficit Reduction Act allows for no increase in

---

[2] *Medicaid* is a program funded by federal and state governments that pays for medical and hospital services for eligible people who are unable to pay for these services themselves and are determined to be in need.

[3] *Food stamps* are coupons distributed through a federal program to people in need who use them like cash to purchase primarily food, plants, and seeds (Barker, 2003).

TANF funding for five subsequent years (CWLA, 2006). First, TANF requires states to spend at least 75% of what they spent on AFDC in 1994. States can then choose to contribute more if they wish. However, most states have continued to fund TANF at the 1994 level; although some have increased benefits, five states and the District of Columbia essentially decreased benefit levels. When adjusting for inflation, the real dollars allocated to recipients has significantly decreased over time. After adjustments, the actual monthly benefits per family in 2002 ($355) were 121 percent lower than those in 1969 ($803 in 2002 dollars) (Karger & Stoesz, 2006, p. 273).

With state budgets continuing to shrink, it's highly unlikely that states will divert proportionately more funding than they have in the past to address additional public assistance needs. Instead, they are likely to supply only the minimal funding required, which means fewer resources for potential recipients. TANF also permits states to impose tighter restrictions regarding who is eligible for benefits. Many social service agencies providing benefits have serious concerns about these restrictions and the negative effects on clients. Will TANF benefits be adequate during tough economic times? "TANF now assists fewer than half of the families with children who qualify" (Center on Budget and Policy Priorities [CBPP], 2006; Karger & Stoesz, 2006). Additionally, "PRWORA allows states to impose a family cap, which denies assistance to children born into families who are already receiving public assistance" (Karger & Stoesz, 2006, p. 278).

 ## Critical Thinking Questions 5.1

Do you feel that children and families living in poverty should be supported by the government? If so, to what extent and under what circumstances? If not, why not?

Time Limits   TANF also establishes time limits for receipt of benefits (ACF, 2005). Clients must find work within 2 years of beginning the program (or less if the state so chooses) and can receive no more than 5 years of benefits in their lifetime. Beyond 5 years, states may opt to extend assistance to no more than 20% of their caseload, or they may continue funding recipients through state funds alone. This is a huge change from AFDC, through which "people received assistance as long as they satisfied the program's eligibility rules, which were set by the individual states under federal guidelines" (Abramovitz, 1997, p. 312). "Seventeen states or jurisdictions have TANF time limits of less than five years", but nine other states have continued providing benefits funded solely by the state after the five years were up (DiNitto, 2005, p. 238). A concern is that agencies may have to turn away people in desperate need because these people have depleted their time allocation. What happens when time limits run out?

Critical Thinking Questions 5.2

Should time limits be imposed upon how long a recipient can receive assistance? If so, what should they be?

Work Requirements   According to the CBPP:

> Under the DRA, states must have 50 percent of all adults receiving TANF assistance—and 90 percent of two parent households receiving assistance—in a set of work activities defined in the law. The work requirements are lower for states that reduce their TANF caseloads below 2005 levels, but few states are likely to accomplish this unless they choose to restrict poor families' access to assistance, given that caseloads already are at historic lows. (2006)

States face financial penalties if they don't comply. It is predicted that only four states will be able to meet the standard that requires work participation in 90 percent of two-parent households (Keene, 2006).

Critical Thinking Questions 5.3

Should public assistance recipients be required to work? If so, what do you think this requirement should be?

Child Care   TANF maintains strict work requirements to make people eligible for financial assistance compared to AFDC. Single parents must work at least 30 hours per week, and two-parent families must total 35–55 weekly work hours, depending on their situation (ACF, 2005; Workworld.org, 2006). This is increased from the 20 hours originally established in 1997 (Abramovitz, 1997). Questions concern how parents will cope with child care needs, work stress, homemaking responsibilities, and parenting.

TANF will not allow mothers with children age 6 or older to cite lack of adequate child care as their rationale for not working outside the home (Karger & Stoesz, 2006; Marx, 2004). Although states are not required to provide child care for working parents as AFDC did, states are allowed to transfer up to 30 percent of TANF funds for its provision; $2.6 billion was spent on child care in 1999, but this decreased to only $1.9 billion in 2002 (DiNitto, 2005, p. 243). Slashing child care expenditures has been connected to economic declines and resulting state budget deficits (DiNitto, 2005). When states need money to provide cash assistance and health care to recipients, child care may get a much lower priority.

The Deficit Reduction Act reauthorized the child care program with few changes and marginal funding increases; child care funding was increased less than 5 percent in 2006 and will have no increase in 2007 to 2010 (CWLA, 2006).

Critical Thinking Questions 5.4

Who will provide all the additional child care services for newly working mothers?
Will funding be adequate in view of the huge potential influx of children requiring care?
What if no adequate day care is available?
Will centers accept infants or toddlers who are not yet toilet-trained, children many current child care facilities reject?
How will these services be monitored for adequacy, safety, and quality?
How will parents adjust to separation from their children?
How will children be affected by limited access to their single parent?
How does this policy affect children's welfare?

Education and Training for Better Jobs   States spend comparatively small amounts on providing education and training for participants. According to DiNitto, less than 2 percent ($462 million) of the total TANF budget was used to enhance skills in 2002, and similar amounts ($584 million) were spent on transportation and supportive services (2005, p. 243). How can former TANF recipients seek better jobs and experience upward mobility with little or no education and training? In contrast, pregnancy prevention programs received over a sevenfold increase from 1999 to 2002, resulting in 2.6 percent of total TANF funding (DiNitto, 2005, p. 243).

Critical Thinking Questions 5.5

To what extent should the public pay for education and training for public assistance recipients?

Job Quality and Availability   About 75 percent of TANF recipients are working when they leave welfare rolls (Waller, 2002). According to Karger and Stoesz:

> Between 50 and 70 percent of welfare leavers remain poor two to three years after leaving welfare. Forty-two percent of welfare leavers remain poor five years after leaving welfare compared to a 55 percent poverty rate in the first year after leaving welfare. . . . On average, household income of welfare leavers averaged about $1,000 a month. (2006, p. 280)

Gilbert and Terrell contend that the nature of jobs available to welfare recipients is the primary reason for this: "Many, roughly a third, are part-time jobs. Others are low-wage, low-benefit, dead-end jobs—clerks, burger-flippers, telephone sales reps—paying close to the minimum wage. Families, in addition, also face new job-related expenses in the form of transportation, day care, clothing, and meals" (2005, p. 268).

Realistically, how good are the benefits and potential for upward mobility offered by most low-paying jobs? Research also indicates that as the economy slowed between 1999 and 2002, TANF recipients had increasing difficulty finding jobs and also were more likely to return to TANF; a higher percentage of people became "disconnected leavers" who were neither employed nor recipients of assistance, possibly because of TANF's benefit time limits (Loprest, 2003).

 Critical Thinking Questions 5.6

What could be done to improve the quality of jobs for public assistance recipients?

Health Insurance After TANF   Only about a third of employed former-TANF recipients had employer health insurance benefits in 2002 (Loprest, 2003). This is due to getting low-paying or minimum wage jobs that have poor or no benefits. After leaving TANF, families can continue receiving Medicaid for 12 months if their income does not surpass 185 percent of the poverty line (DiNitto, 2005, p. 235). For many families, what happens after that? To what extent does TANF force single mothers to deprive themselves of future health care by accepting low-paying jobs without benefits—the only jobs they can get?

 Critical Thinking Questions 5.7

Should health insurance be made available to all citizens like it is in many other industrialized countries? If so, how should it be paid for?

Encouraging "Healthy Marriages"   TANF's stated goals are as follows:

1. Assisting needy families so that children can be cared for in their own homes
2. Reducing the dependency of needy parents on government benefits by promoting job preparation, work and marriage
3. Preventing incidence of out-of-wedlock pregnancies
4. Encouraging the formation and maintenance of two-parent families (U.S. Administration for Children and Families [ACF], 2005).

Three of these goals relate directly to the support of "healthy marriages" (ACF, 2006). The initiative designed by President George W. Bush and administered by the Administration for Children and Families provides funding for "marriage education services" to married couples and initiatives to promote "responsible fatherhood" (ACF, 2006).

Critical Thinking Questions 5.8

To what extent does the government have the right to try to coerce people into marriage? Explain your answer?

Equitability Among States   TANF "eliminated the federal income test that previously determined eligibility for AFDC" (Abramovitz, 1997, p. 312). Instead, TANF permits states to establish their own eligibility rules. However, with budget pressures, states could establish eligibility levels so low that only the very poorest of the poor would receive benefits. Additionally, benefit levels vary appreciably from state to state, which raises questions regarding the program's fairness (DiNitto, 2005; Waller, 2002). In 2003, maximum benefits for a family of three ranged from $170 per month in Mississippi to $923 per month in Alaska (DiNitto, 2005, p. 236).

In contrast to AFDC, TANF limited the amount of federal funding given to states and allowed states greater discretion in benefit distribution. Gilbert and Terrell (2005) explain:

> Under AFDC, welfare was, by and large, the monthly cash benefit. But under TANF, states employ their welfare spending for a multitude of antipoverty purposes—many, indeed, not targeted specifically on welfare recipients. Some states, for example, have invested in wage supplements through a state version of the Earned Income Tax Credit in order to increase salaries for low-wage earners. Others, such as New York, have created public jobs. Still others have expanded day care and transportation and counseling services and have intensified job training. (p. 261)

Critical Thinking Questions 5.9

To what extent should benefits provided to public assistance recipients be equal in all the states?

What Is the Answer?   We have touched upon only a few of the many issues involved in TANF. Legislation governs programs and service provision in the macro social environment. The following are suggestions to consider when making future legislative decisions:

1. Provide adequate funding and build in adjustments for inflation in future years.
2. Reduce current weekly work requirements.
3. "Require states to emphasize education and job training" that can lead to career advancement and better occupational opportunities.

4. Increase the opportunities that can be involved in "work" to include "participation in an education program" leading to a degree or involvement in vocational or technical training so that recipients have access to a better, more productive future.

5. Eliminate time limits or make them more flexible so that recipients can actually have enough time to become educated and develop career skills.

6. Abolish "marriage promotion" pressures which have "not been proven to be an effective measure in reducing poverty and enabling welfare recipients to become economically self-sufficient."

7. "Increase child care funding" to support working parents and their children (Women Work!, 2006).

 Critical Thinking Questions 5.10

How would you restructure the public assistance system if you had the power? What are your values concerning what's important?

Managed Care Reflects Social and Economic Forces

Managed care is another major social and economic force that affects many agencies' service provision. It is "an integral aspect of social work practice in many settings" including health, mental health, family, child welfare, and a wide range of other public social service settings (Corcoran, 1997, p. 191). Although "there is no standard definition of managed care" (Edinburg & Cottler, 1995, p. 1639), we can say that managed care is "a generic label for a broad and constantly changing mix of health insurance, assistance, and payment programs that seek to retain quality and access while controlling the cost of physical and mental health services" (Lohmann, 1997, p. 200). An identified group or range of health practitioners and mental-health care providers contract with social service agencies that employ them to provide health care for agency workers at a negotiated rate. One intent is to save agencies the cost and inconvenience of administering employees' health insurance plans.

Poole (1995) asserts that "the purpose of direct social work practice in health care is to enhance, promote, maintain, and restore the best possible social functioning of clients, families, and small groups when their ability to do so is affected by actual or potential stress caused by illness, disability, or injury" (p. 1159). Social work roles supported by managed care include social assessments, intervention planning and implementation, "case consultation, health education, discharge planning, information and referral, financial assistance, advocacy, case management," "agency planning, community planning, resource development," and "legislative reform" (Poole, 1995, p. 1159).

Thus, managed care programs and the policies they develop concerning how services are provided have tremendous impact on what agencies and their workers can do.

Two primary principles promoted by managed care are *retention of quality and access* while *controlling cost*. That is, health and mental-health services should be of high quality and readily accessible to clients, on the one hand. Yet, they should be very cost-effective, on the other.

Managed care "fundamentally transformed" traditional relationships between clients and workers (Lohmann, 1997, p. 201). Historically, social workers in agency settings established treatment plans in conjunction with clients, in addition to stressing informed consent and confidentiality to comply with ethical standards. Managed care takes these decisions out of workers' and clients' hands and puts them into the hands of removed third-party decision makers. A managed care representative, often a utilization reviewer or case manager, then reviews documentation and regulates "the services that clients receive, especially what specific services will be provided and at what cost" (Corcoran, 1997, p. 194). To Lohmann (1997), managed care "represents the complete (and seemingly sudden) triumph of financial management concerns over virtually all other professional considerations" (p. 202).

Physicians indicate that the quality of health care has decreased since the advent of managed care due to "limitations on diagnostic tests, length of hospital stay, and choice of specialists" (DiNitto, 2005; Karger & Stoesz, 2006; Mooney, Knox, & Schacht, 2007, p. 57). Karger and Stoesz (2006) explain further:

> Managed care plans generally make access to specialists difficult for consumers. Plans do this by pressuring primary physicians not to refer or by limiting specialist care to one or two visits. Some managed care plans are reluctant to cover costly procedures or experimental treatments, especially those relating to cancer. Some plans refuse to pay for medical care clients receive while out of state, even if it was required in an emergency. Other enrollees complain that managed care forces them to use only primary care physicians, hospitals, and specialists that are on an approved list, which restricts their freedom of choice. (p. 320)

Highlight 5.6 discusses some ethical issues in managed care.

Managed Care and Advocacy in Social Work Practice   It's useless to get depressed about the managed care environment. It's here (Karger & Stoesz, 2006). Rather, practitioners must respond to the potential ethical dilemmas posed. Edinburg and Cottler (1995) suggest:

> Perhaps the most important role for social workers will be as advocates for patients and families in dealing with managed care delivery systems. Patients and families will need to know what their entitlement benefits are and how to obtain proper services. Social workers will also need to continue to advocate for improving the health care system by serving on advisory committees and lobbying their legislators. (p. 1641)

| **Highlight 5.6** | **Ethical Issues in Managed Care** |

Generalist practitioners must work within social service agencies that employ them. They are supposed to follow agency and other regulatory policy. However, they are also responsible for maintaining ethical practices and making certain clients' needs are met. Several ethical issues may be raised concerning managed care and how it affects agency service provision.

The first involves the potential conflict between "the gatekeeping role of some managed care organizations and client self-determination" (Corcoran, 1997, p. 196). When subject to managed care, clients no longer have the right to choose their service provider. Rather, the managed-care utilization reviewer makes this determination. Redmond (2002) reflects how "hospital social workers face serious ethical dilemmas when patients are forced out of the hospital before they or their families are ready or when resources have not been put into the home" (p. 23).

Similarly, managed care may conflict with the ethical principle of informed consent. Corcoran (1997) remarks:

> Informed consent requires that the client know in advance the clinical procedures, the risk of those procedures, and the available alternative

procedures. Managed care may destroy informed consent by restricting the available procedures to a limited number. For example, a managed care company may determine the preferred practice and the preferred providers, with little consideration or disclosure of alternative procedures. (p. 196)

Managed care also has the potential to violate client confidentiality (Corcoran, 1997). Social workers are bound by the code of ethics, which emphasizes how "social workers should respect clients' right to privacy" and "should not solicit private information from clients unless it is essential to providing service" (NASW, 1996, 1.07a). However, the code also indicates that social workers may disclose confidential information "when regulations require disclosure without a client's consent" (NASW, 1999, 1.07b). If a managed care organization demands information before providing services, what should the worker do? The code does not discuss the validity of "regulations," which managed care organizations can often establish themselves. What if the worker does not agree with the organization's demand for information and feels the regulations violate clients' rights to privacy? Workers may be required to report confidential information, whether they feel it's ethical or not.

At least five specific provisions could improve legislation to protect clients and their rights ("Managed Care," 1998):

- Guarantee patients the right to choose a doctor outside their health plans' networks if they agree to share the cost of services.
- Ensure patients access to detailed information about coverage, treatment options.
- Require companies to cover emergency care without prior authorization.
- Make health plans comply with state and federal laws that protect the confidentiality of . . . health information.
- Require companies to set up procedures under which providers could appeal denials of coverage. (p. 1)

 Critical Thinking Questions 5.11

How would you structure the managed care system if you had the power to do so?

CHAPTER SUMMARY

This chapter described primary and secondary settings in social service agencies. Organizational mission statements, goals, and objectives to achieve goals were defined and explained. The relationship among systems theories, organizations, and goal displacement was discussed.

The environmental context of organizations was addressed including the importance of resources, legitimation, and client sources. Relationships with other organizations include uninvolved, complementary, and competitive relationships.

The impacts of social and economic forces upon social service organizational functioning was emphasized. Federal social legislation was explored, with a focus on Temporary Assistance to Needy Families (TANF). TANF issues addressed included adequacy of funding, time limits, work requirements, child care, education and training for better jobs, job quality and availability, health insurance after TANF, encouraging healthy marriages, and equitable treatment by states. Suggestions for improved legislation were proposed. Managed care as a major force affecting life in the macro social environment was defined and some of its problems identified. Ethical issues were raised and approaches for advocacy proposed.

Organizational Structure and Dynamics

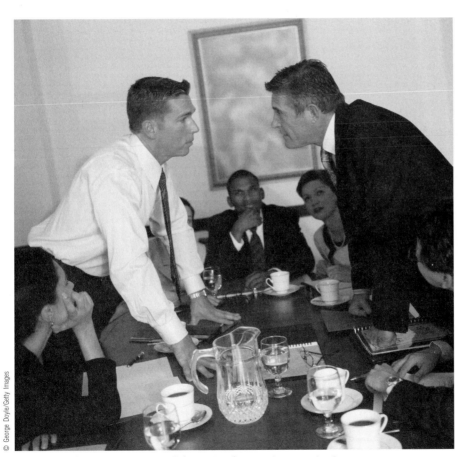

CHAPTER 6

Interpersonal communication and dynamics characterize organizations.

CHAPTER CONTENTS

"I just can't tolerate Mr. Biff," Brunhilda proclaims to Stanwood, one of her social work colleagues in a large private social services organization providing numerous services including counseling, substance abuse programs, vocational training, and community-based facilities for people with developmental disabilities. Mr. Biff, whose real name is Bufford Bifford, is the manager of the agency's accounting department. Mr. Biff is very impressed with his own accomplishments, but unfortunately has extremely poor social interaction skills. With a superior demeanor, he typically commands Brunhilda and other social workers to scurry about and do his bidding when he determines that some billing matter needs immediate attention. He expects workers to drop everything else they're doing and obey his command on the double.

Stanwood tries to soothe Brunhilda's ruffled feathers. "After all," he stresses, "Mr. Biff is not our immediate supervisor" Social workers must maintain positive working relationships with other agency staff, including Mr. Biff, because financial accountability is so important. However, other staff like Mr. Biff have little direct power over what social workers in the agency can, cannot, will, or will not do. Social workers must work directly with their own supervisor to develop appropriate treatment and referral plans and respond to agency needs. Stanwood urges Brunhilda to "be cool." He adds, "Our own supervisor is a pretty good egg. The bottom line is you don't have to obey Mr. Biff. You could just choose to smile, nod, and ignore him. You know, there are no jerk-free work environments."

This vignette does not imply that all organizational environments have Mr. Biffs, although many probably do. However, it focuses on the importance of agency expectations, structure, and interpersonal dynamics when you're trying to get your job done. Depending upon your agency environment, you can feel supported and energized or angry and thwarted.

Simply put, management is "the art of getting things accomplished in organizations through others" (Johns, 1996, p. 10). Managers in organizations accomplish this by setting goals for the entire organization or agency units, acquiring and allocating resources, coordinating employees' work, monitoring progress, and improving efficiency and effectiveness where possible (Daft, 2003; Daft & Marcic, 2004). This says *what* management does, but it doesn't say *how* managers do it. This is where management style comes in. Equifinality applies here in that there are many ways to manage an organization.

Ginsberg (1995) maintains "that strict adherence to a hierarchy often is dysfunctional, and the bureaucratic element of organizations can be harmful" (p. 15). However, he continues that "the principle of maintaining some unity of command is important, and failure to maintain a division of labor can lead to conflict and to some functions not being performed. The need for an organizational structure that separates tasks and maintains distinct responsibilities is probably as important as it always was" (p. 15).

Thus, elements of organizational structure are necessary to hold an agency together regardless of variations in management style, that is, how staff and clients are viewed and services provided. This chapter investigates organizational culture, structure, and interpersonal dynamics. Chapter 7 will further explore management approaches and means of empowering staff.

This chapter will:

- Describe organizational culture and structure, and discuss how lines of authority and channels of communication are involved.
- Discuss the pros and cons of centralized and decentralized organizations.
- Examine interpersonal communication within social service agencies.
- Describe the perceptual process during communication.
- Identify interpersonal barriers to communication, including noise, personality factors, individual errors in perception, and lying and distraction.
- Propose means for enhancing ethical communication in agencies.
- Describe the importance of power in organizations.
- Identify the various types of power.
- Explain organizational politics and their potential effects on workers' behavior.
- Explore the dynamics contributing to political behavior.
- Suggest tactics for using agency politics for positive change.
- Discuss the use of unethical agency politics.

ORGANIZATIONAL CULTURE

Organizational culture is "the constellation of values, beliefs, assumptions, and expectations that underlie and organize the organization's behavior as a group" (Holland, 1995, p. 1789). Daft (2004) continues that these "underlying values may pertain to ethical behavior, commitment to employees, efficiency, or . . . [client] service, and they provide the glue to hold organization members together. An organization's culture is unwritten but can be observed in its stories, slogans, ceremonies, dress, and office layout" (pp. 19–20).

Organizational culture, then, involves many facets. For example, what kind of attire is expected and considered appropriate within the organization's cultural environment—suits or jeans? A hospital social worker might choose to dress more formally because the environment is full of uniformed professionals. Contrasting informal dress might appear "unprofessional." A residential treatment center for males with behavioral disorders, on the other hand, might manifest a very informal organizational culture, at least concerning dress. The latter culture expects social workers and counselors to participate in a range of activities, including informal group sessions in the living units, recreational activities, and administration of consequences for poor behavior. It makes sense to dress comfortably and informally in such an environment.

Another facet of organizational culture is the agency's "personality." Each agency has its own personality. That is, it is more formal or informal, structured or unstructured, innovative or traditional than other agencies. From the first day of work within an agency, it is important to explore and begin understanding that agency's character. How much freedom do workers have in conducting daily professional activities? What tasks are considered the most important (for example, documentation of treatment effectiveness, other record-keeping, administrative conferences, or number of hours spent with clients)?

Organizational culture is a common concept addressed in studying organizations, regardless of the theoretical perspective assumed. The cultural theoretical perspective on organizations discussed in Chapter 4, of course, emphasizes culture as the primary dimension for understanding organizational functioning. Other theories give the concept of culture less emphasis in relationship to the numerous other dimensions involved in organizations.

ORGANIZATIONAL STRUCTURE

Organizational structure is "the manner in which an organization divides its labor into specific tasks and achieves coordination among these tasks" (Johns, 1996, p. 490). All large agencies (and many smaller ones, as well) have *a formal* structure specifying how management thinks the organization should be run. Most often formal structure is explicated in an organizational chart showing who reports to whom (Daft, 2004; Hodge et al., 2003). Such charts depict designated lines of authority and communication within the agency. A later section of this chapter will discuss organizational charts more thoroughly. Frequently, the agency operates in accordance with this chart, at least with respect to some functions, such as how information is disseminated either from the top down or bottom up. For example, a social work supervisor might be expected to give appropriate information directly to supervisees. Likewise, those supervisees might expect the supervisor to convey their concerns up the administrative ladder. Highlight 6.1 discusses an important dimension of agency structure—the degree to which the organization is centralized or decentralized.

Agencies also develop *informal* structures and lines of communication. For example, it is typical for an agency to structure its units so that all workers in the unit report to one supervisor. Consider the case of the Humdrum County Foster Care Unit. Five workers and a supervisor comprise this unit. When workers have questions or problems, they are supposed to bring these to Henry, the Foster Care Unit Supervisor. Often, however, Henry's supervisees discuss their cases with other workers in the unit or with Tiffany, the senior worker in the agency's Adoptions Unit. This means that the Foster Care Unit Supervisor is deprived of information that might be important to doing his job.

While superficially confiding in Tiffany may seem like a bad arrangement, it has some beneficial aspects. Workers who are sometimes uncomfortable talking with their supervisor can get help from other more experienced workers. Maybe Henry is not competent to provide answers or is too lazy or busy to take the time? Tiffany might be an extremely knowledgeable, pleasant person who likes to help her colleagues. Sharing ideas and problems helps to produce a camaraderie among the workers. This decreases their stress levels and often leads to better job performance. Human relations

Highlight 6.1	**Pros and Cons of Centralized Versus Decentralized Organizations**

One other aspect of agency structure merits brief commentary. A continuum can depict organizations and their degree of centralization. On one far side are extremely centralized organizations. These organizations resemble those run according to classical scientific management theories. Their lines of authority are clearly established. There is a strict hierarchy designating who has power over whom. The units in centralized organizations are clearly defined and cleanly separated. Workers have little discretion to make their own decisions. Responsibilities are defined and overseen from above.

A probation and parole department provides an example of centralization. Clients assigned to workers in a designated unit reflect very similar characteristics. Procedures and treatment plans are relatively uniform in approach. Clients and workers must abide by clearly defined rules and regulations. Little worker discretion is possible.

On the opposite side of the centralization continuum are extremely decentralized organizations, contrasting sharply with centralized organizations in flexibility. Decentralized organizations provide and encourage broad worker discretion. They likely serve a wide variety of clients with vastly different problems, issues, and backgrounds. Workers in such organizations need discretion to make plans for viable solutions. For example, extreme decentralization might characterize a community crisis-intervention organization. Clients coming in for help might have problems ranging from depression to illness to job loss to executive-level stress. Workers need a broad range of discretion to address a wide variety of problems.

theories stress the importance of such interpersonal communication and support in organizations.

The point here is not to praise or criticize the existence of informal structures and communication channels. Instead, it is to acknowledge that they do exist and are a reality with which practitioners must deal within a social agency's context. In practice, being aware of both formal and informal avenues within an agency strengthens social workers' ability to do their job. Once practitioners know the options and alternatives, they can make more-informed choices. This is, after all, a major goal of the intervention process.

Three concepts are especially significant when appraising agency's formal and informal structures. These are *lines of authority*, *channels of communication*, and *dimensions of power*.

Lines of Authority

All large agencies (and many smaller ones) have a formal structure. An agency's formal structure involves *lines of authority* (Daft, 2004; Johns, 1996). For our purposes, authority concerns the specific administrative and supervisory responsibilities of supervisors involving their supervisees. Authority entails who is designated to supervise whom. Agency policy usually specifies in writing these lines of authority.

We have established that often an agency's formal structure is explained in an organizational chart. Job positions held by individual staff members are portrayed by squares or circles that are labeled according to their respective job positions. A formal hierarchy of authority in an organizational chart is depicted by vertical lines leading from supervisors down to supervisees (Daft, 2004; Jansson, 2003). Generally, job positions higher on the chart have greater authority than those placed lower on the chart. Lines drawn from higher figures to lower figures identify the supervisors of staff holding job positions located lower on the chart and having less responsibility and power. In essence, these lines represent "who is directly responsible for whom" (Lauffer et al., 1977, p. 31). The formal organizational structure as demonstrated by an organizational chart, then, dictates how control and supervision are supposed to flow.

The chart in Figure 6.1 reflects the hierarchy of authority for the Idle Ness Center for Diagnosis and Treatment, an agency providing assessment and therapeutic treatment to children with multiple developmental and physical disabilities. Parents bring children with a wide range of physical and behavioral difficulties to the agency to assess the children's abilities in a variety of areas, plan treatment programs, and provide the appropriate therapies.

Rectangles in Figure 6.1 designate those job positions having some degree of administrative responsibility within the agency system. The bolder the rectangle, the more authority and responsibility the position entails.

The Executive Director has the most authority and is responsible for the overall performance of the Idle Ness Center. Below him are five agency directors, including the Medical Director (a physician), and those for accounting, maintenance engineering, food services for clients and staff, and transportation services for clients. Each director (except accounting) is, in turn, responsible for the supervision of other staff further down the hierarchy of authority. The Medical Director is responsible for overseeing the entire clinical program, including the work of the various departmental supervisors. Departments include occupational therapy, physical therapy, speech therapy, psychology, and social work. Circles at the very bottom of the chart represent line staff who are providing services directly to clients.

By examining this chart, it is painfully clear how this agency is run, correct? If you look at the Social Work Department, there are two direct service workers who report directly to their Social Work Supervisor. It is obvious how these social workers go about their business of providing services to clients, look to their own supervisor for direction, and live happily ever after, right? The chain of command is so blatant you may think this entire discussion borders on, if not engulfs itself in, monotony.

The "catch" is that formal organizational charts depict lines of *formal* authority within agencies. Such formal lines of authority dictate how communication and power are *supposed* to flow. Sometimes, an agency's actual chain of command follows the formal chart fairly closely. Equally often, however, agencies develop *informal* channels of communication and power that are very different from those stated on paper. As an example, we will explore the Idle Ness Center's informal channels of communication and dimensions of power.

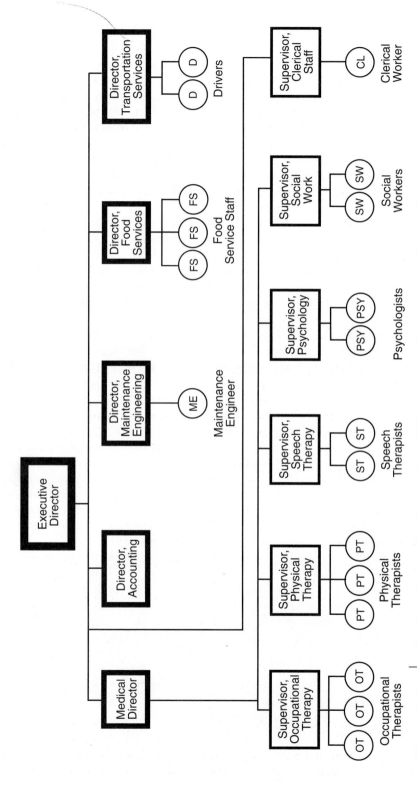

Figure 6.1 | Idle Ness Center for Diagnosis and Treatment—Example of a Formal Organizational Chart

Channels of Communication

All agencies have "multiple networks of communication by which members relay and receive information" (Resnick & Patti, 1980, p. 51). *Communication,* of course, is "a process by which information is exchanged between individuals through a common system of symbols, signs, or behavior" (Mish, 1995, p. 233). Communication, then, involves the many nuances regarding how information is conveyed verbally and nonverbally. It entails subtle inflections, comfort level between communicators, and multitudes of minute gestures. Communication will be explored further later in the chapter.

Formal lines of authority might imply that such communication channels are supposed to flow harmoniously and synchronously along with these lines of authority. In other words, supervisees are *supposed* to communicate primarily with their identified supervisors for direction and feedback. Likewise, supervisors are *supposed* to communicate directly with their supervisees and the managers who supervise them. As we will see, this is not the case in the Idle Ness Center.

Power in the Formal Structure

Power is the potential ability to move people on a chosen course to produce an effect or achieve some goal (Homan, 2004; Martinez-Brawley, 1995). Like channels of communication, dimensions of power are supposed to follow the established lines of authority. In the organizational chart, those in supervisory positions above their employees are supposed to have actual power (that is, clear-cut influence and control) over those employees. In real-life agency environments, this may or may not be the case. Note that many other facets of power and organizational politics will be explored later in the chapter.

Example of Informal Structure: The Idle Ness Center

Direct your attention to the Social Work and Psychology Departments illustrated in Figure 6.2. We will concentrate on this smaller portion of the organizational chart concerning the informal structures of communication and power within the agency. Figure 6.2 contrasts the formal and informal structures for these two agency departments. The *real* channels of communication and dimensions of power among supervisors and direct service staff are very different than those illustrated in the formal organizational chart. The real relationships reflect the personalities and interactions among people who have unique perspectives and identities, strengths, weaknesses, problems, and needs of their own.

The formal structure pictures Ellen, the Psychology Department Supervisor, as being responsible for the administration and supervision of both LaVerne and Shirley's job performance. Both the latter have a master's degree in psychology. Likewise, the formal structure portrays Roseanne, the Social

Figure 6.2
Organizational
Charts Con-
trasting Formal
and Informal
Structures in
Agencies

Formal Structure of Authority in Two Agency Departments

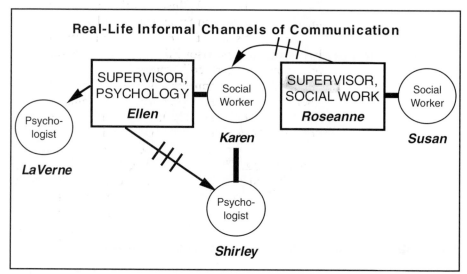

Real-Life Informal Channels of Communication

Work Department Supervisor, as having direct supervisory authority over both Karen and Susan, each of whom has a master's degree in social work.

The lower box portrays the real-life informal structure of these departments. Karen, one of the social workers, has become good friends with Ellen, the Psychology Department Supervisor. Both single, they frequently socialize together and even vacation together. Their positive relationship is reflected by the bold line connecting them in Figure 6.2.

Karen, on the other hand, gets along terribly with Roseanne, her own supervisor. It is difficult to define what "having a personality conflict" really means. However, this concept could be used to define Karen's and Roseanne's relationship. For whatever reason, they do not personally like each other. Additionally, Karen views Roseanne as basically being incompetent, lazy, and interested in doing as little work as possible. On the other hand, Roseanne perceives Karen as an overly energetic, impulsive "go-getter" who acts "just like a bull in a china closet." Both interact as little as possible with each other. Most communication between them takes place in memo form, with Roseanne issuing Karen direct commands regarding what should and should not be done. Figure 6.2 illustrates Roseanne and Karen's relationship by the arrow that swoops up from Roseanne and down again to Karen. Communication and power consistently flows downward from Roseanne to Karen in a dictatorial, hierarchical fashion. Cross lines on the arrow indicate conflict.

Roseanne, on the other hand, has much in common with Susan, the other social worker. They frequently spend much time together and go out to lunch. Roseanne views Susan as a calmly competent worker who communicates well and provides enjoyable company. In effect, Roseanne treats Susan like a friend and equal. Figure 6.2 illustrates this relationship with the thick linear bond linking Roseanne and Susan horizontally.

Now, let's investigate the informal relationship within the Psychology Department. Supervisor Ellen sees LaVerne, one of her supervisees, as a competent professional colleague. Hence, Figure 6.2 portrays LaVerne slightly below Ellen. The connecting arrow flows from Ellen down to LaVerne because Ellen maintains her supervisory and administrative status with respect to LaVerne. They essentially like each other on a professional basis. However, neither considers herself a personal friend of the other.

Ellen, on the other hand, perceives Shirley, her other supervisee, in a much different light. Ellen regrets hiring Shirley and has begun to document Shirley's difficulties in performance in preparation for "letting her go" (dismissing her or firing her from the agency). Thus, Shirley is positioned significantly below Ellen, the arrow connecting them running from Ellen down to Shirley. The chain of communication and power clearly positions Ellen in the more powerful, communication-controlling position, and Shirley in an inferior, less powerful, communication-receiving status.

However, the plot is even more complicated. Karen, who is substantially younger than Ellen, is about the same age as Shirley, who is also single. Karen and Shirley have much in common and have established a firm friendship. They, too, occasionally spend time and socialize with each other. Thus, a bold vertical line connects them. This indicates that they consider each other equals, friends, and colleagues. This is despite the fact that Ellen and Shirley's relationship is poor and quickly deteriorating. Cross lines on the arrow again indicate conflict.

Karen is in an uncomfortable and tenuous position. On the one hand, she values her friendship with Ellen. She also sees Ellen as a professional ally within the agency who provides her with some leverage against Roseanne. On the other hand, Karen likes Shirley. Karen understands that Ellen is not perfect (nor is she). Thus, Karen can listen to Shirley's complaints against Ellen and provide some sympathy. Karen, however, must take extreme care not to speak against either Ellen or Shirley to the other. It is not easy to maintain such a balancing act.

The point here is neither to praise nor criticize the existence of informal structures of communication and authority. Instead, it is to acknowledge that they do exist and pose a reality to deal with in any agency, including yours. In practice, being aware of both formal and informal agency structures may strengthen your ability to do your job. Once you know the options and alternatives open to you, you can make better informed, more effective choices.

What eventually happened at the Idle Ness Center described above? Shirley quit and left for another position in a different state. Shirley and Karen soon lost contact. Six months later, Karen also left the agency for another social work position that more closely matched her more energetic, enthusiastic style. She became a counselor for teens with serious behavioral and family problems. Karen and Ellen continued to maintain their personal friendship for many years after Karen left the agency. No one knows what became of Roseanne, Susan, or LaVerne.

Informal assessment of your agency environment can help you determine how you can best do your job. It can help you to decide the extent to which you "fit in" or should look for another job somewhere else.

The next sections of the chapter will explore in greater depth the processes of interpersonal communications, power, and politics as they occur in social service agencies.

 Critical Thinking Questions 6.1

Have you ever worked in an environment where the actual channels of communication differed significantly from those proposed by the formal agency structure? If so, in what ways did they differ?

INTERPERSONAL COMMUNICATION IN SOCIAL SERVICE ORGANIZATIONS

We've established that communication is "the process of transmitting information from one person to another" (Williams, 2006, p. 448). Such transfer occurs in the context of the perception of both the person sending information and those receiving it. The sender's *intent* is the information that the sender is trying to communicate. The receivers' *impact* is what the receivers actually comprehend.[1] The communication's effectiveness involves the extent to which the sender's intent matches the receiver's impact. The receiver may *perceive*

---

[1] The concepts of *intent* and *impact* were taken from the film *Behavioral Interviewing with Couples*, available from Research Press, Dept. 98, P.O. Box 9177, Champaign, IL 61826.

what the sender is saying in a very different way than what the sender is trying to say.

Williams (2006) explains:

> *Perception* is the process by which individuals attend to, organize, interpret, and retain information from their environments. And since communication is the process of transmitting information from one person or place to another, perception is obviously a key part of communication. However, perception can also be a key obstacle to communication. (p. 449)

People are exposed to multiple stimuli at the same time. They may be talking on the phone while reading their email while someone knocks at their door. They thus must filter all the input they're getting and focus on what they perceive as the most significant or attention-grabbing aspects of that communication. People participating in the same group or watching the same event may have totally different perceptions or be in total disagreement about what's occurring.

Williams explains:

> For example, every major stadium in the National Football League has a huge TV monitor on which fans can watch replays. As the slow motion videotape is replayed on the monitor, you can often hear cheers *and* boos [at the same time], as fans of both teams perceive the same replay in completely different ways. This happens because the fans' perceptual filters predispose them to attend to stimuli that support their team and not their opponents. (2006, p. 449)

The filtering process involves four phases (Williams, 2006):

> *Attention* is the process of noticing or becoming aware of particular stimuli. Because of perceptual filters, we attend to some stimuli and not others. *Organization* is the process of incorporating new information (from the stimuli that you notice) into your existing knowledge. Because of perceptual filters, we are more likely to incorporate new knowledge that is consistent with what we already know or believe. *Interpretation* is the process of attaching meaning to new knowledge. Because of perceptual filters, our preferences and beliefs strongly influence the meaning we attach to new information (e.g., 'This must mean that top management supports our project.'). Finally, *retention* is the process of remembering interpreted information. In other words, retention is what we recall and commit to memory after we have perceived something. Of course, perceptual filters also affect retention, that is, what we're likely to remember in the end. [Figure 6.3 depicts the process of perception.]
>
> In short, because of perception and perceptual filters, people are likely to pay attention to different things, organize and interpret what they pay attention to differently, and, finally, remember things differently. Consequently, even when people are exposed to the same communications (e.g., organizational memos, discussions with . . . [supervisors] or . . . [clients]), they can end up with very different perceptions and understandings. (pp. 449–450)

Just as families or couples have misunderstandings (potentially resulting in fights), so do people communicating in organizations have problems "hearing" the meaning of what others are saying. For example, a supervisor may say to

Figure 6.3
The Process
of Perception

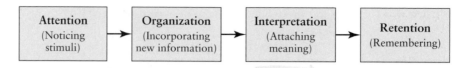

her social work supervisees, "The agency director is coming to talk to us tomorrow." One of the workers may perceive that she said, "The director probably wants to break some bad news to us." A second worker might think, "The director's going to pat us on the back for the nice job we did on that fund-raising dinner." Still another worker may interpret, "The director's coming and I never can understand a thing she says because she's such a jumbled speaker."

Interpersonal Barriers to Communication in Agencies

At least four barriers can inhibit effective communication in social service organizations. These include noise, personality factors, individual perceptual errors, and lying and distortion (Hellriegel & Slocum, 2007, p. 328). Figure 6.4 illustrates how each of these barriers can negatively impact effective communication. They distort the congruence between the sender's *intent,* what the sender wants to communicate, and the receiver's *impact,* what the receiver actually interprets.

Noise   The first barrier to effective interpersonal communication in agencies is *noise,* "any interference with the intended message" while a sender is trying to get his or her message across (Hellriegel & Slocum, 2007, p. 328). We've already established that people in work settings must sift through multiple stimuli to focus on, organize, interpret, and retain what has been said. Distractions can involve any number of circumstances. Several people may be talking at once. Someone may drop a large metal box filled with office equipment. Outside an office window, a car may crash into a lamp post.

Personality Factors   Personality factors are the second type of barrier to effective interpersonal communication (Dumler & Skinner, 2005). We all know people who are popular and other people whom everybody tries to avoid. Personality factors are a major dimension in any interpersonal relationship, including those developed in organizations. This is true both for social workers providing direct service and for people holding management positions. Five personality factors can either enhance or interfere with effective communication (Hellriegel & Slocum, 2007):

1. "*Emotional stability* refers to the degree to which a person is relaxed, secure, and unworried" (p. 47). People with high levels of emotional stability can be described as calm, unexcitable, level-headed, and steady in their interpersonal interactions. They are easier to work with than people who "fly off the handle" when the least bit flustered.

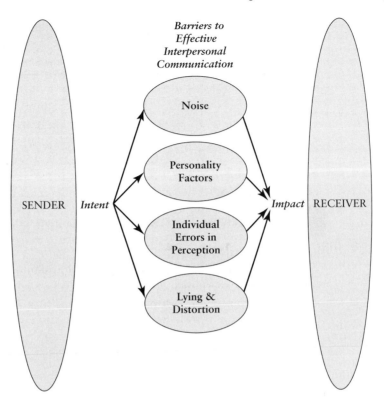

Figure 6.4
Barriers to Effective Interpersonal Communication

2. "*Agreeableness* refers to a person's ability to get along with others." Highly agreeable people are often described as "cooperative, kind, understanding, and good natured" in their interactions with others (p. 47). On the other hand, people with low levels of agreeableness are frequently characterized "as short tempered, uncooperative, and irritable" (p. 47). People who are highly agreeable are better at forming relationships with others. Other people are more likely to feel comfortable with them instead of being defensive and are more likely to communicate openly their feelings and ideas.

3. "*Extraversion* refers to a person's comfort level with relationships" (p. 47). Extraverts (people who are socially outgoing) eagerly seek out and socialize with others. They generally develop good interpersonal skills and nurture relationships. Introverts (people who are socially withdrawn), on the other hand, tend to isolate themselves and avoid interaction with others.

4. "*Conscientiousness* refers to the number of goals on which a person focuses" (p. 47). A conscientious person places importance on achieving goals and getting things done. Conscientious people are often described as organized, self-disciplined, and thorough. They take their responsibilities seriously and can be depended upon to carry out their tasks. A person who lacks conscientiousness tends to assume a laid-back attitude where

promptness and attention to detail are not all that important. It's much more difficult to work with, communicate with, and trust unreliable people than conscientious people.

5. "*Openness* refers to a person's curiosity and range of interests. People with high levels of openness are willing to listen to new ideas and to change their own ideas, beliefs, and assumptions in response to new information" (p. 47). An open person actively seeks out others' ideas and is open-minded about trying to understand them. An individual who lacks openness can be described as closed-minded and unreceptive to new ways of thinking and doing things.

 Critical Thinking Questions 6.2

How would you describe yourself in terms of emotional stability, agreeableness, extraversion, conscientiousness, and openness? How do these personality variables relate to how you see yourself interacting with others in a work setting?

Individual Errors in Perception   Individual errors make up the third category of perceptual mistakes involved in agency interpersonal communication. As people organize and interpret information, inaccuracies and errors in both perception and judgment may occur (Dumler & Skinner, 2005; Hellriegel & Slocum, 2007, p. 78).

Accuracy of judgment is important because perceptions affect how people are treated in organizations. For example, a supervisor who attends to or emphasizes the wrong factors in a supervisee's performance could cause an inaccurate perception of how well that employee is functioning in the agency. This could result in a poor performance review of that employee instead of a good one. (Note that this book uses the terms *employee* or *worker* to refer to people who directly serve clients and other staff generally at the bottom of an organizational chart. The terms *manager* and *supervisor* refer to people higher in the organizational chart who have supervisory responsibility and authority over other employees. Specific agencies may choose one of the latter two terms over the other in their job titles and descriptions. The term *manager* can also refer to people in management higher in the organizational structure who have direct authority over supervisors or other managers.)

Another example of inaccurate judgment involves an employer interviewing a potential employee for a job. The interviewer may selectively focus on characteristics that are insignificant or simply miss out on the interviewee's best qualities because of perceptual errors and erroneous judgment. Several errors commonly occur in such job interview situations (Hellriegel & Slocum, 2007, p. 79). First, *similarity error* happens when interviewers place too much importance on the similarities and differences between themselves and the interviewees. People are naturally drawn to others whom they perceive as being similar to themselves. Once, a job candidate was interviewing for a social work position. The candidate had mentioned on his resume that one of his personal areas of interest was flying airplanes recreationally. It just so happened that the interviewer was also a recreational flier. They "hit it off" immediately while talking about flying and the candidate was hired. The candidate, who was qualified for the job along with many others, felt strongly that having flying in common with the interviewer gave him an edge over other candidates and got him the job.

Contrast error, a second type of error of judgment, involves placing too much emphasis on how a job candidate compares with other candidates in the pool of those who applied. Every job search has a pool of candidates who apply. (Sometimes, no one applies and the job search must be done over.) It's unpredictable who will be in the pool. Pools vary dramatically regarding the quality of applicants. An average candidate (in terms of qualifications such as education, experience, and interpersonal skills) may look terrible in a pool composed applicants with stellar qualifications but look terrific compared to a group of very poorly qualified candidates.

Third, *first-impression error* happens when, for whatever reason, an interviewer formulates an initial impression based on the perceptions of some variables and then refuses to change that impression. For example, an interviewee might be wearing orange earrings, a color the interviewer despises. It's neither fair nor logical, but the interviewer forms a negative impression of the interviewee right from the beginning of the interview. This view may be highly resistant to change, regardless of the interviewee's relevant qualifications.

Hellriegel and Slocum (2007) suggest guidelines to help make more accurate judgments in job interviewing situations: "(1) Avoid generalizing from an observation of a single trait (e.g., tactful) to others traits (e.g., stable, confident, energetic, dependable); (2) avoid assuming that a behavior will be repeated in all situations; and (3) avoid placing too much reliance on physical appearance" (p. 79).

Critical Thinking Questions 6.3

We probably all have been interviewed for a job at some time or another. Some of us have had many job interviews. If you've had such experience, picture a specific situation where you were interviewing for a job. To what extent do you think the interviewer's perceptions of you and your abilities were accurate? To what extent do you think that the interviewer made similarity, contrast, or first-impression error? Did you get the job? Why or why not?

Highlight 6.2 reviews several other specific perceptual errors that can occur in interpersonal communication in an agency context.

| Highlight 6.2 | Specific Types of Individual Perceptual Errors in Agency Settings |

Some other specific types of inaccurate judgments can occur in agency settings that interfere with effective interpersonal communication. These include stereotyping, the halo effect, projection, and assumptions about ethnicity and culture.

Stereotyping

We've established that a *stereotype* is "a fixed mental picture of a member of some specified group based on some attribute or attributes that reflect an overly simplified view of that group, without consideration or appreciation of individual differences" (Kirst-Ashman, 2007, p. 57). For example, if an agency worker maintains the stereotype that women make poor supervisors regardless of their practice and interpersonal skill levels, that worker will probably resent a woman being hired as his or her supervisor. Similarly, consider a young employee who automatically assumes that a person in his or her 70s is probably "getting senile." That young employee is unlikely to place any confidence in colleagues over 70. Additionally, the employee will likely have perceptual distortions about the abilities and strengths of senior clients.

Halo Effect

"The *halo effect* refers to evaluating another person solely on the basis of one attribute, either favorable or unfavorable" (Hellriegel & Slocum, 2007, p. 80). For example, if Jadwiga, an agency worker, perceives her colleague Mohammad as having trouble being punctual in meeting deadlines, that impression may color her impression of other aspects of Mohammad's personality and behavior. Jadwiga may display impatience whenever Mohammad volunteers to get something done for their social work department (a group of social workers clustered together under one supervisor in the organizational power structure and organizational chart). She may not listen to Mohammad's contributions during staff meetings, because she automatically assumes he's a poor worker. She may perceive everything Mohammad does negatively even when his work is done well and punctually.

Projection

"Projection is the tendency for people to see their own traits in other people" (Hellriegel & Slocum, 2007,

p. 81). This is especially true for negative traits including hostility, vengefulness, miserliness, disorganization, or the need to control others. In effect, projection reverses the truth. For example, consider a worker who savers manipulating colleagues to do work for him. He may also project this trait onto his colleagues and feel that they are trying to manipulate him into doing their work.

Assumptions about Ethnicity and Culture

Hellriegel and Slocum (2007) explain how perceptions are influenced by ethnicity and culture:

> Interpretation occurs when an individual gives meaning to observations and their relationships. Interpretation organizes our experience and guides our behavior. Read the following sentence and quickly count the number of Fs:
> FINISHED FILES ARE THE RESULT OF YEARS OF SCIENTIFIC STUDY COMBINED WITH THE EXPERIENCE OF YEARS.
>
> Most people who do not speak English see all six Fs. By contrast, many English speakers see only three Fs; they do not see the Fs in the word *of*. Why? Because English-speaking people do not think that the word *of* is important for them to understand the meaning of the sentence. We selectively see those words that are important according to our cultural upbringing. (pp. 81–82)

The role of culture is important in organizational settings concerning both staff and staff/client interactions. For example, differences in cultural perceptions exist regarding what is appropriate behavior for people in the United States compared to those in Saudi Arabia (Hellriegel & Slocum, 2007, p. 80). A common behavior in the United States is to shake hands upon meeting. In Saudi Arabia, a male should not shake hands with a female unless she extends her hand first. Verbal greetings are appropriate. Under no circumstances should a male being introduced to a female greet her by kissing her. In the United States, it is generally customary to open a gift in front of the gift giver when it is received. Arabian people do not do so in organizational settings, but open gifts later when the giver is no longer present. Gifts involving alcohol or pork should never be given to Arabian people.

Critical Thinking Questions 6.4

Have you had interactions in work settings that involved inaccuracies of judgment such as stereotyping, the halo effect, projection, or ethnic and cultural assumptions? If so, what were they? Did they involve misperceptions on your part or on the part of other staff? If you could go back and improve the communication and interaction both on your part and on the part of the other people who were involved, what would you change?

Lying and Distortion   A fourth barrier to effective interpersonal communication in agencies, unfortunately, involves lying and distortion (Hellriegel & Slocum, 2007, p. 329). *Lying* is the use of communication to deceive information receivers into believing something that is not true. In contrast, honesty involves stating what one considers to be true in the most straightforward manner possible. *Distortion,* "as defined by Hellriegel and Slocum," represents a wide range of messages that a sender may use between the extremes of lying and complete honesty" (2007, p. 329). The intent is to slant information in a particular direction.

The NASW *Code of Ethics* instructs social workers to "act honestly and responsibly and promote ethical practices on the part of the organizations with which they are affiliated" (NASW, 1999). Furthermore, it directs social workers not to "participate in, condone, or be associated with dishonesty, fraud, or deception" (NASW, 1999, 4.04).

However, just as organizations are imperfect, so are the people who work in them. The *Code of Ethics* cannot guarantee that all professionals will always function in an ethical manner. We address the issues of lying and distortion because you may be confronted with these in the agency where you work.

Hellriegel and Slocum (2007), commenting from a business management perspective, note that "the use of vague, ambiguous, or indirect language doesn't necessarily indicate a sender's intent to mislead" (p. 329). In fact, they continue:

> This form of language may be viewed as acceptable political behavior. Silence may also be a form of distortion, if not dishonesty. Not wanting to look incompetent or take on a manager [or supervisor] in a departmental meeting, a subordinate may remain quiet instead of expressing an opinion or asking a question. (p. 329)

Sometimes, distortion provides a means of *"impression management*—the process by which a sender knowingly attempts to influence the perceptions that the receivers form." The following are three tactics reflecting forms of impression management (Hellriegel & Slocum, 2007, pp. 329–330):

1. *Ingratiation* is the act of seeking acceptance and support through deliberate efforts such as "using flattery, supporting others' opinions, doing favors," or "laughing excessively at others' jokes."

2. *Self-promotion* is the act of describing oneself in an unwarranted and overly positive manner. It might be considered a form of bragging.

3. *Face-saving* is behavior that attempts to avoid being accountable for the full consequences of one's negative behavior, decisions, and performance. People using face-saving strategies will try to make their actions look better than they really are. This might involve making excuses for why things turned out badly, blaming others for negative results, minimizing negative consequences by disguising them as not really being that bad, or denying that the problem really exists at all.

Lying is clearly unethical. Levels of distortion are more complex. For example, you don't necessarily say to someone you really don't like, "I really can't stand you. Shut up." In this instance it's not that you're lying. Rather, it does not necessarily facilitate an agency's functioning to say every negative thing that comes to mind. However, on the continuum from mild distortion to lying, the more distortion strategies approach lying, the more unethical they are. The more that distortion and lying occurs in an agency environment, the worse the agency's potential for effective interpersonal communication. Highlight 6.3 suggests tactics for enhancing ethical communication in agency settings.

 Critical Thinking Questions 6.5

To what extent do you feel distortion tactics are ethical or unethical? Are any such tactics ever useful or necessary? If so, which ones, and in what situations? Have you ever had experience using distortion tactics? If so, which ones and under what circumstances? Have distortion tactics ever been used on you? If so, what were your reactions?

POWER AND POLITICS IN SOCIAL SERVICE ORGANIZATIONS

We have established that *power* is the potential ability to move people on a chosen course to produce an effect or achieve some goal. Power is an important concept regarding social service organizations. Who has power and how it's used directly affects how workers can do their jobs. Management has power over workers (including you when you get a job). However, we determined earlier that there are various types of power that don't necessarily coincide with the formal organizational chart. Therefore, a discussion of power in organizations is relevant to you for at least two reasons. First, management has the potential to empower you to do your job well. Second, as a worker you can think in terms of your own power and how you can strive to improve agency functioning. You may also develop tactics to influence people in power when advocating for clients or improved service provision. For example, you might

| **Highlight 6.3** | **Enhancing Ethical Communication in Agencies: Means to Empowerment** |

There are a number of guidelines to improve ethical interpersonal communication in agencies. These are important both for management and other staff to implement.

1. "Be honest" (Vecchio, 2006, p. 308). Simply put, honesty enhances open communication and increases trust. Colleagues are more likely to work together when they trust and like each other.

2. Practice empathy in your interpersonal work relationships (Dumler & Skinner, 2005; Vecchio, 2006). *Empathy* is the interpersonal practice not only of *being in tune* with how another person feels, but also *conveying* to that person that you understand how he or she feels (Kirst-Ashman & Hull, 2006b). People are more likely to communicate with you and feel comfortable with you if they think you understand them.

3. Workers should work at listening carefully to each other and trying to understand what each other is really trying to say (Daft & Marcic, 2006; Dumler & Skinner, 2005; Vecchio, 2006). Daft and Marcic (2006) explain that an important aspect of communication is *active listening*, "the process of asking questions, showing interest, and

occasionally paraphrasing what the speaker has said to ensure that one is interpreting accurately" (p. 515). They continue:

> Senders and receivers should make a special effort to understand each other's perspective. Managers [and supervisors] can sensitize themselves to the information receiver so they will be able to target the message, detect bias, and clarify missed interpretations. By communicators understanding each others' perspectives, semantics can be clarified, perceptions understood, and objectivity maintained. (p. 515)

4. Management should work to establish an environment that encourages a *climate of trust and openness:* "Open communication and dialogue can encourage people to communicate honestly with one another. Subordinates will feel free to transmit negative as well as positive messages without fear of retribution. Efforts to develop interpersonal skills among employees can also foster openness, honest, and trust" (Daft, 2003, p. 604; Vecchio, 2006). (Chapter 7 will discuss management approaches.)

feel that agency hours should be extended to better accommodate clients' schedules. Or you might feel clients' needs are not being met adequately in some area (for example, counseling, transportation, financial support) and you decide to advocate on their behalf. Acquisition of a power base may also be useful when requesting benefits such as a raise or select vacation times.

Types of Power

Chapter 2 discussed the five types of power that group leaders may have. These types of power also apply to people working in organizations (Champoux, 2003; Daft, 2003; Dumler & Skinner, 2005; Lussier, 2006). Sources of power include the following:

- *Legitimate power* (that attained because of one's position and vested authority)
- *Reward power* (that which stems from the ability to provide positive reinforcement and rewards to others)
- *Coercive power* (the capability of dispensing punishments in order to influence others' behavior)

- *Referent power* (that held as a result of other group members' respect and high esteem)
- *Expert power* (that based on established authority or expertise in a particular domain)

Supervisors and managers usually are given legitimate power. They also often have reward and coercive power. Anyone, including direct service workers and supervisors or managers, can develop referent and expert power. The concept of power is quite complex. Vecchio (2006) explains:

> Power is an essential feature of a manager's [or supervisor's] role. Without some degree of power, a [supervisor] . . . would find it difficult to direct the efforts of subordinates. Thus, power underlies a [supervisor's] . . . effectiveness. Subordinates also possess forms and degrees of power. For example, subordinates can control the work flow or withhold support from their [supervisor]. . . . Therefore, to some extent, each member of an organization possesses power.
>
> Because power is intangible, it is very difficult to define clearly and precisely. Also, our language has several similar terms that we tend to confuse with power, such as authority and influence. . . .
>
> Power is not always legitimate. Therefore, we speak of *authority* as the right to try to change or direct others. Authority includes the notion of legitimacy. It is the right to influence others in the pursuit of common goals agreed upon by various parties. [For example, supervisors have authority by virtue of their job titles and descriptions.] Power, in contrast, does not always pursue common goals and may, at times, be clearly directed to pursuing only a single individual's goals.
>
> Another term, *influence,* is also frequently used when discussing the notion of power. Influence tends to be subtler, broader, and more general than power. Although both influence and power can be defined as the ability to change the behavior of others, power embodies the ability to do so with regularity and ease. Influence is weaker and less reliable than power. . . . Influence relies on particular tactics and often employs face-to-face interactions. Thus, the exercise of influence tends to be more subtle than the exercise of power. (p. 124)

Determining who has power can be tricky. Sometimes, people with important titles or placement high in the organizational structure have little ability to influence and control subordinates' behavior in reality. Because people in power have the potential ability to influence your work behavior and how clients are served, it's important to know who has this power. Aldag and Kuzuhara (2005) explain:

> How can you tell . . . [who has power in an agency]? . . . Job titles may help; so may status symbols. Still, we know these things can be deceptive and that some people with a lot of power don't have fancy titles or big offices. Some other signs of managers' power include the abilities to do the following:

- Intercede favorably on behalf of someone in trouble with the organization
- Get a good placement for a talented subordinate
- Gain approval for expenditures beyond the budget
- Obtain above-average salary increases for subordinates
- Place items on the agenda at policy meetings

- Get fast access to top decision makers
- Have regular, frequent access to top decision makers
- Obtain early information about decisions and policy shifts (pp. 370–371; Kanter, 1979; Rynecki, Smith, Shanley, & Wheat, 2003).

Critical Thinking Questions 6.6

Power relationships characterize all organizations, including social services and businesses. Most of us have had work experience. Think of a job you've had. What types of power did your direct supervisor have? Who else in the organization had influence or power, and how did they use it?

Politics in Social Service Organizations

Aldag and Kuzuhara (2005) describe *organizational politics:*

> When we hear someone speak of organizational politics, we probably think of such things as "passing the buck," "apple polishing," "backstabbing," and other "dirty tricks" we use to further our selfish interests. We use the term organizational politics more broadly, to refer to activities that people perform to acquire, enhance, and use power and other resources to obtain their preferred outcomes in a situation where there is uncertainty or disagreement. Because the focus is on people's preferred outcomes, rather than organizational outcomes, this may or may not involve activities contrary to the best interests of the organization. (p. 378; Pfeffer, 1981)

Don't automatically think that organizational politics are always evil and self-serving (Aldag & Kuzuhara, 2005). Sometimes, agency problems or needs should be addressed. A policy might not be working or a supervisor might not be performing all her responsibilities. It's beyond the scope of this book to teach you *how* to advocate for positive changes, but you should be aware of organizational politics as an important aspect of human behavior in the macro social environment. For one thing, most people prefer to be somewhat "political" by avoiding "criticizing your boss in public, losing control of your emotions during meetings, or challenging sacred beliefs or values of the organization" (Aldag & Kuzuhara, 2005, p. 379). Therefore, being aware of politics may be important, "if only to be alert for the political actions of others and to avoid personal embarrassment" (Aldag & Kuzuhara, 2005, p. 379).

Dynamics Contributing to Political Behavior in Agencies   DuBrin (2002) cites at least three reasons why politics occur in organizations:

1. Organizations are by nature political. They are made up of a range of units or departments, each striving to achieve its own goals and competing

for resources. Competition is a fact of life when resources are limited or scarce. Power enhances the ability to compete.

2. Some people are more power-oriented than others. When power is limited, power-oriented workers, supervisors, or managers will often try to expand their influence. "Power-oriented managers [or supervisors] sometimes cope with the limited amount of power available by expanding their sphere of influence sideways. For example, the director of the food stamp program in a government agency might attempt to gain control over the housing assistance program, which is at the same level" (p. 242). (*Food stamps* are credits distributed through a federal program to be used like cash to purchase primarily food, plants, and seeds [Barker, 2003]. *Housing assistance* often involves rental subsidies or vouchers by which government programs assist with rent, mortgage payments, and low-rent public housing, or block grants to state and local governments for developing affordable housing [Dolgoff & Feldstein, 2003].) Some people who are extremely concerned with gaining power are characterized by "Machiavellianism, a tendency to manipulate others for personal gain" (p. 243). Such people thrive on gaining power for power's sake.

3. Decentralized organizations, mentioned in Highlight 6.1, distribute power widely to lower levels in the organizational hierarchy. Because of the lack of structure, it is logical for units to undertake organizational politics to establish their position, and maintain or gain resources to keep them going.

Using Agency Politics for Positive Change   We've indicated that as an agency worker, you may be in the position to advocate for positive change on the behalf or clients or agency personnel. The following are tactics to establish a power base within an agency setting so that you might have greater influence with decision makers.

First, conduct a *political diagnosis,* an assessment of "the location of power in an organization and the type of political behavior that is likely to happen" identifying "politically active individuals and coalitions in the organization, the amount of power they have, and the likely ways they will use their power" (Champoux, 2003, pp. 339–340).

You can pursue several strategies to identify individuals who have power; start with "the organizational chart and a description of titles and duties" (Champoux, 2003, p. 340). Then interview people in various organizational units to determine how decisions are made, who has decision-making responsibility for distributing resources, how identified people generally use their power or are likely to, and what their goals are for their performance and status within the organization.

It is also important to identify any coalitions within the agency. "A *coalition* is an alliance of individuals who share a common goal. Coalitions are also interest groups that try to affect decisions in the organization. Coalitions can have members from widely scattered parts of the organization" (Champoux, 2003, p. 341). Assessing coalitions should involve the same strategies used in assessing the power of individuals within the organization. This should help establish the agency's "political network," the system of "affiliations and alliances of individuals and coalitions" within the social service organization's environment (Champoux, 2003, p. 341).

A second tactic for enhancing power and influence involves developing contacts and relationships with people in power (DuBrin, 2002). Such people can provide you with support and information to help achieve your goals.

Third, to increase your power base, form coalitions yourself (Aldag & Kuzuhara, 2005; Vecchio, 2006). This may be as simple a thing as forming a coalition to have enough votes to get a proposal passed in a committee. Or it may involve a coalition approaching an administrator with a new idea to persuade him or her to adopt it. Involving more people tends to enhance your credibility and validity.

Fourth, get information about what's going on (Aldag & Kuzuhara, 2005). Keeping current helps you develop believable arguments on your behalf. Being knowledgeable inspires people's confidence in you.

Fifth, provide positive feedback where warranted (Aldag & Kuzuhara, 2005). Positive feedback can be given concerning others' statements, support, and performance; it should be "a straightforward and specific declaration of what the person did right" (DuBrin, 2002, p. 247). Positive feedback helps to strengthen interpersonal relationships. Persistent complainers tend to turn other people off. People with positive proposals who are known to be supportive are more easily heard.

Sixth, use assertive communication (DuBrin, 2002; Vecchio, 2006). "*Assertiveness* involves being able to state your thoughts, wants, and feelings straightforwardly and effectively. It concerns the ability to establish an appropriate stance between being too aggressive and too timid. . . . The implication is that you take both your needs and the needs of others into account" (Kirst-Ashman & Hull, 2006b, p. 155). Of course, being assertive does not mean that you should avoid tact. Always consider the communication receivers' feelings. Effective assertive communication means thinking about the best way to state your ideas at the most appropriate what time.

Highlight 6.4 describes some tactics *not* to use when engaging in agency politics.

Critical Thinking Questions 6.7

Most of us have likely had work experiences. Have you ever been in a position to observe the use of either the negative or positive tactics described above? If so, explain the circumstances. To what extent were the tactics effective? To what extent were they ethical?

| **Highlight 6.4** | **Tactics NOT to Use in Agency Politics: Problematic Unethical Behavior** |

We've noted that behavior can occur in organizations that is inappropriate and unethical. Some political tactics are designed to hurt other people. Others are intended for selfish advancement. Some tactics can ruin your reputation or have very negative consequences in the future. The following six strategies should not be used when involved in agency politics.

1. *Don't engage in "backstabbing"* (DuBrin, 2002, p. 246). Backstabbing "requires that you pretend to be nice but all the while plan someone's demise. A frequent form of backstabbing is to inform your rival's superior that he or she is faltering under the pressure of job responsibilities" (DuBrin, 2002, p. 246). People backstab to make themselves look better or more important to to get ahead in competitive situations. Backstabbing is devious, self-serving, and unprofessional. It usually results in deterioration of interpersonal relationships and the ability to function as a team. "The recommended approach to dealing with a backstabber is to confront the person directly, ask for an explanation of his or her behavior, and demand that he or she stop" (DuBrin, 2002, p. 246).

2. *Don't set up a person for failure* (DuBrin, 2002, p. 247). "The object of the setup is to place a person in a position where he or she will either fail outright or look ineffective. For example, a supervisor who the agency head dislikes might be given responsibility for a troubled department. The newly appointed supervisor cannot improve productivity, is then reprimanded for poor performance, and the negative evaluation becomes part of the person's permanent record" (DuBrin, 2002, p. 247).

At one point I was a newly promoted supervisor of a social work unit in a day treatment center for youth having serious emotional and behavioral problems. The center provided therapy and special education for troubled youth residing in the community. The program's two primary components were social services and therapy under my direction, and the school under its principal's direction. I was young and didn't know much about supervision or agency politics. For whatever reason, the school principal was not supportive of my promotion. The Director informed the principal and me (who were equals on the organizational chart) that new recording requirements of clients' progress would require twice as much time and work as before. None of the staff—teachers, teaching assistants, or social workers—would be at all happy about that news. The principal asked me to make the announcement at an all-staff meeting. I foolishly did what he told me to and made the announcement both to my social work supervisees and to his teaching staff. Everyone immediately viewed me as the bringer of bad tidings and "the bad guy," an image that persisted for months. The principal benefited in at least two ways by setting me up for failure. First, he avoided being "the bad guy" himself. Second, he enhanced his power base by making me look worse than him.

3. *Don't "divide and conquer"* (Vecchio, 2006, p. 131). This strategy "usually involves creating a feud among two or more people so that they will be continually off balance and thus unable to mount an attack against you" (Vecchio, 2006, p. 131). They are essentially kept busy fighting

CHAPTER SUMMARY

Organizational culture and organizational structure were described. Lines of authority, channels of communication, dimensions of power, and informal agency structure were examined within the context or organizational structure. Pros and cons exist for centralized and decentralized organizations.

Interpersonal communication in social service organizations was discussed. The communication sender's intent should closely match the receiver's with each other, allowing you to go about your business. Unfortunately, this tactic hurts interpersonal relationships. It also takes time and energy away from doing a good job.

I once worked in a social work department supervised by Fred. Fred's approach to supervision was control by dividing and conquering. Two of the workers, Jethrow and Davida, had been good friends for a long time. Fred told Jethrow that Davida had been criticizing his work. Fred then told Davida that Jethrow had been critical of her work. None of this was true. By disrupting Jethrow's and Davida's friendship, Fred broke up the coalition of support that they formed. In this way, Fred felt he had greater control of what went on in the department. It eventually backfired for Fred, however. A third worker, Cathy, talked both to Jethrow and Davida, who told her what Fred had been saying. Cathy subsequently told Jethrow and Davida what each other had shared. The result was that they confronted each other and discovered that Fred had been lying. They then confronted Fred, who consistently denied that he had said anything like that. Eventually, the entire department formed a coalition and sought help from the administration concerning Fred for this and many other behavioral problems. Fred was fired.

4. *Don't "exclude the opposition"* (Vecchio, 2006, p. 131). Another underhanded technique is to exclude a rival or adversary from participation in meetings, agency functions, or social events. One approach is to schedule an important decision-making meeting "when the opposition is out of town (on vacation . . .) or attending another meeting. With the opposition absent, it is possible to influence decision making or to take credit for a rival's efforts" (Vecchio, 2006, p. 131).

5. *Don't go over your supervisor's head without first exhausting all other options* (Vecchio, 2006). There are times when it might be necessary to go over your supervisor's head and complain to his or her supervisor. Some employees do this to complain about the supervisor's performance or how the supervisor is treating them. Consider the earlier example with Fred, Jethrow, and Davida when staff formed a coalition and sought help from administration. However, the staff first confronted Fred, who did not respond. The entire staff formed a coalition to address the issue the only way they knew how. Only then did they "air dirty laundry" about the department to higher levels of administration. Supervisors hate it when supervisees go over their heads and "narc" about their performance. It's much wiser to try to work out whatever the problem is internally before going outside of the department. Making an enemy of a supervisor by making him or her look bad can make your life miserable in the future. Additionally, often administration will side with the supervisor, as people in management tend to stick together. The result might be a decrease rather than an increase in your power and potential to influence.

6. *Don't throw temper tantrums* (Vecchio, 2006, p. 132). Emotional volatility may earn you the reputation of being overly emotional and overreactive. People tend to see the emotions and miss out on the content of what you're trying to communicate. You don't want to establish a reputation of being hard to work with. That will only encourage others to avoid you and not provide you with support when you need it.

impact in effective communication. The process of perception involves attention, organization, interpretation, and retention. Interpersonal barriers to communication in agencies include noise, personality factors, individual errors in perception, and lying and distortion. Specific individual perceptual errors include stereotyping, the halo effect, projection, and assumptions about ethnicity and culture. Distortion may include impression management in the forms of ingratiation, self-promotion, and face-saving. Ethical communication in agencies can be enhanced through honesty, empathy, careful listening, and a climate of trust and openness.

Power is the potential to move people on a chosen course to produce an effect or achieve some goal. Types of power include legitimate, reward, coercive, referent, and expert. It's important to understand power in organizations because people will be in positions of power over you.

Organizational politics are activities that people perform to acquire, enhance, and use power to attain goals when there is uncertainty or disagreement in the organizational environment. Dynamics contributing to political behavior in agencies include the political nature of organizations; the power-orientation of some workers, supervisors, and managers; and decentralization. Suggestions for using agency politics for positive change include conducting a political diagnosis, developing contacts, forming coalitions, being well-informed, providing positive feedback, and using assertive communication. Unethical tactics not to use in agency politics are backstabbing, setting people up for failure, trying to divide and conquer, excluding the opposition, going over your supervisor's head, and throwing temper tantrums.

Human Behavior, Management, and Empowerment in Organizations

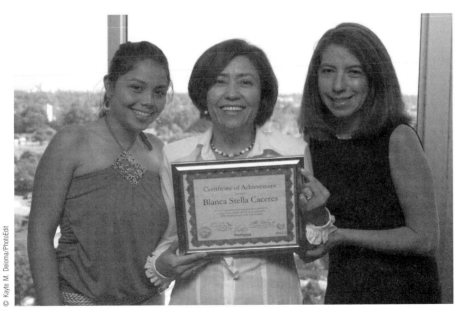

Organizations can empower their members. Awards for achievement can enhance internal environments in all types of organizations.

CHAPTER CONTENTS

*Have you ever worked in an organization or business where you heard the
following complaints or, perhaps, made them yourself?*
   "My boss is so . . ."

- *Bossy*
- *Inconsiderate*
- *Disorganized*
- *Unfair*
- *Incompetent*
- *Pea-brained*
- *Unethical*
- *Screwed up*

Critical Thinking Questions 7.1

Have you ever worked in an organization or business where you or other employees
had difficulties with a supervisor? If so, what did the problems involve? How might
they have been solved and the situation improved?

All organizations, including social service organizations, are governed
by the orientation or style of their management. Supervisors, as part of
management, function within the organizational culture and expectations.
For any variety of reasons, you yourself may have experienced having a poor
supervisor. Management in social service settings can empower practitioners
to work more effectively and efficiently, ultimately benefiting their clients.
The internal functioning of organizational systems can promote or deter
its workers' ability to perform effective interventions and link clients with
needed resources. Because management is so important for how workers
function in organizations, it is critical to understand the dynamics of
management and how they relate to worker behavior in the macro social
environment.

This chapter will:

- Explain the significance of management in social service organizations.
- Describe traditional bureaucracies, orientation discrepancies between
  social work and bureaucracies, and common behavior patterns found in
  bureaucracies.
- Critique the U.S. health care system's clash with Asian and Pacific Islander
  cultural values.
- Discuss problems frequently encountered by social service organizations.
- Describe newer approaches to management and employee empowerment,
  including constructing a culture of caring, the learning organization,
  teamwork and team empowerment, managing diversity, and client system
  empowerment by management.

- Discuss the situation encountered by women in social services management.
- Describe two examples of newer management and leadership approaches—total quality management (TQM) and servant leadership.

THE IMPORTANCE OF MANAGEMENT

Management is the "effective and efficient attainment of organizational goals through planning, organizing, leading, and controlling organizational resources" (Daft & Marcic, 2006, p. 7). Management involves how employees are thought of and treated. Management style provides important clues for understanding people's behavior in the organizational environment. Often, an organization's management approach reflects some combination of the organizational theories described in Chapter 4. Numerous bureaucracies continue to exist, with all their strengths and weaknesses, but alternative organizational perspectives and management styles are continuously being developed.

For example, management by objectives (MBO) was a popular approach used in the last quarter of the twentieth century (Albrecht, 1978). It focused on goals as the primary driving force of agency life, measuring organizational success in terms of how effectively the organization achieved these goals (Netting, Kettner, & McMurtry, 2004). MBO encouraged organizational employees to arrive at an agreement about what objectives or results they want to accomplish, specify what organizational resources each goal requires, and establish how long the goal-attainment process should take (Barker, 2003).

The following sections will address various aspects of management. First, traditional bureaucracy will be discussed. Subsequently, some problems organizations face in the macro social environment will be addressed. The remainder of the chapter will focus on new methods of management aimed at empowering workers to provide better services to clients.

WORKING IN A TRADITIONAL BUREAUCRACY

The concept of bureaucracy was introduced in Chapter 4 under classical management organizational theories. It reflects a traditional approach to management. Because it is such a commonly used concept, we will spend some time here addressing practice within bureaucracies.

What words come to mind when you hear the term "bureaucracy?" Dullness? Tediousness? Boredom? Repetitiveness? Red tape? Sludge?

For whatever reason, most of us have a terrible opinion of bureaucracies. Even one dictionary definition labels bureaucracy "a system of administration marked by officialism (lack of flexibility and initiative combined with excessive adherence to regulations in the behavior of usually government officials), red tape (official routine or procedure marked by excessive complexity which results in delay or inaction), and proliferations ([growth] by rapid production of new parts, cells, buds, or offspring)" (Mish, 1995, pp. 152, 807, 980, 933). Even reading this definition is rather dull.

As classical organizational theories propose, bureaucratic management style emphasizes the importance of a specifically designed, formal structure and a consistent, rigid organizational network of employees to make an organization run well and achieve its goals (Daft & Marcic, 2004; Hellriegel & Slocum, 2007; Hodge et al., 2003). Each employee has a clearly defined job and is told exactly how that job should be accomplished. This school of thought calls for minimal independent functioning on the part of employees. Supervisors closely scrutinize the latter's work. Efficiency is of utmost importance. How people feel about their jobs is insignificant. Administration avoids allowing employees to have any input regarding how organizational goals can best be reached. Rather, employees are expected to do their jobs as instructed as quietly and efficiently as possible.

Traditional bureaucracies are made up of numerous highly specialized units that are supposed to perform specific job tasks. In the formal structure, there is supposed to be little communication among horizontal units, that is, units of approximately equal status that perform different functions. Employees are supposed to "stick to their own business" and get their own specifically defined jobs done within their own units. That's it. Discussion is unnecessary.

Traditional bureaucracies allow very little discretion on the part of workers. Policies and procedures for how to accomplish tasks are clearly specified. In other words, what any particular worker is supposed to do in any particular situation is designated ahead of time. Employees are allowed little, if any, ability and opportunity to be able to think for themselves and make their own decisions concerning their work. They are simply supposed to follow instructions.

The policies and procedures are infinitely complex and detailed. Regardless of what new situation might come up, workers should be able to consult the "rule book" regarding how they should deal with it.

Value Orientation Discrepancies Between Workers and "The System"

Helping professionals (including social workers) have a value orientation that can clash with the traditional bureaucracy's reality (Knopf, 1979; Lewis, Lewis, Packard, & Souflee, 2001). Expecting the values of a large bureaucracy to coincide with your own simply sets you up for disappointment.

Examples of discrepancies are many. For instance, helping professionals believe that the primary goal of bureaucracies should be to serve clients, while the actual goal of bureaucracies is to survive. Helping professionals believe bureaucracies should change to meet the emerging needs of clients, while bureaucracies resist change and are most efficient when no one is "rocking the boat." Helping professionals believe bureaucracies should personalize services to each client and convey that "you count as a person," while bureaucracies are in fact highly depersonalized systems in which clients (and employees) do not count as persons but are only tiny components of a mammoth system. Highlight 7.1 lists additional conflicting orientations between helping professionals and bureaucratic systems (Knopf, 1979; Schriver, 2004).

| Highlight 7.1 | **Value Orientation Conflicts Between Helping Professionals and Bureaucracies** |

Orientation of Helping Professionals	Orientation of Bureaucratic Systems
Desire a democratic system for decision making.	Most decisions are made autocratically.
Desire that power be distributed equally among employees (horizontal structure).	Power is distributed vertically.
Desire that clients have considerable power in the system.	Power is held primarily by top executives.
Desire a flexible, changing system.	System is rigid and stable.
Desire that creativity and growth be emphasized.	Emphasis is on structure and the status quo.
Desire that communication be on a personalized level from person to person.	Communication is from level to level.
Desire shared decision making and a shared responsibility structure.	A hierarchical decision-making structure and a hierarchical responsibility structure are characteristic.
Desire that decisions be made by those having the most knowledge.	Decisions are made in terms of the decision-making authority assigned to each position in the hierarchy.
Belief that clients' and employees' feelings should be highly valued by the system.	Procedures and processes are highly valued.

Any of these differences in orientation can become an arena of conflict between helping professionals and the bureaucracies in which they work. A number of helping professionals respond to these orientation conflicts by erroneously projecting a "personality" onto the bureaucracy. The bureaucracy is viewed as being "officialism," "uncaring," "cruel," and "the enemy." A negative personality is sometimes also projected onto officials of a bureaucracy, who may be viewed as being "paper shufflers," "rigid," "deadwood," "inefficient," and "unproductive." Knopf (1979, p. 25) states:

> The HP (helping person) . . . may deal with the impersonal nature of the system by projecting values onto it and thereby give the BS (Bureaucratic System) a "personality" [It is interesting how Knopf refers to a bureaucracy as BS]. In this way, we fool ourselves into thinking that we can deal with it in a personal way. Unfortunately, projection is almost always negative and reflects the dark or negative aspects of ourselves. The BS then becomes a screen onto which we vent our anger, sadness, or fright, and while a lot of energy is generated, very little is accomplished. Since the BS is amoral [that is, the BS can be neither moral nor immoral so the concept of morality does not apply to it], it is unproductive to place a personality on it.

A bureaucratic system is neither good nor bad. It is simply a structure with certain expectations for how to carry out various tasks. However, practitioners may have strong emotional reactions to these orientation conflicts between the helping professions and bureaucracies. Common reactions are anger at the system, self-blame ("It's all my fault"), sadness and depression ("Poor me," "Nobody appreciates all I've done"), and fright and paranoia ("They're out to get me," "If I mess up, I'm gone").

Behavior Patterns in Bureaucratic Systems

Helping professionals often adopt one of several types of behavior patterns while coping with bureaucracies that don't enhance organizational effectiveness; they include "the warrior," "the gossip," "the complainer," "the dancer," "the machine," and "the executioner" (Knopf, 1979, pp. 33–36).

The Warrior   The *warrior* leads open campaigns to destroy and malign the system. A warrior discounts the value of the system and often enters into a win-lose conflict. Warriors loudly and outspokenly complain about almost everything. Because of their overt "bad attitude," warriors rarely, if ever, get promoted. In fact, the warrior generally loses and is dismissed.

The Gossip   The *gossip* is a covert warrior who complains to others both inside and outside of the agency (including clients, politicians, and the news media) about how terrible the system is. A gossip frequently singles out a few officials to focus criticism upon. Bureaucratic administrators generally hate gossips because gossips try to air internal "dirty laundry" outside of the agency. Therefore, supervisors and administrators in bureaucracies often make life very difficult for gossips by assigning them distasteful tasks, refusing to promote them, giving them very low salary increases, and perhaps, even dismissing them.

The Complainer   The *complainer* resembles a gossip, but confines complaints internally to other helping persons, to in-house staff, and to family members. A complainer wants people to agree in order to find comfort in shared misery. Complainers want to stay with the system, and generally do. Since they primarily keep their complaining secretive and internal, they usually avoid antagonizing the administration and, therefore, maintain their anonymity (and their jobs).

The Dancer   The *dancer* is skillful at ignoring rules and procedures. Dancers are frequently lonely, often reprimanded for incorrectly filling out forms, and have low investment in the system or in helping clients. However, once inside of a bureaucratic system, dancers often manage to "just get by." In essence, they are usually lazy. Dancers generally don't really cause any trouble. They just don't do their jobs very well. It generally goes against the bureaucratic principle of maintaining the status quo to exert the energy necessary to fire a dancer.

The Machine   The *machine* is a "typical bureaucrat" who takes on the orientation of the bureaucracy. A machine's intent is to abide by the official bureaucratic rules no matter what. Machines dislike conflict. To them, obeying the rules to the letter of the law is much safer. Often a machine has not been involved in providing direct services for years. Machines are frequently named to head study committees and policy groups, and to chair boards. Machines often rise to the level of their incompetence ("The Peter Principle"), where they often remain until retirement. The Peter Principle is the observation, developed by Laurence J. Peter in 1968, that "in a hierarchy employees tend to rise [in the organizational power structure] to the level of their incompetence" (Mish, 1995, p. 868).

The Executioner   The *executioner* is a tremendously enthusiastic and self-motivated individual who has managed to gain some power, status, and advancement within the bureaucratic organization. Executioners have no real commitment to the value orientations of the helping professionals or to the bureaucracy. However, they have learned how to "play the game." They have managed to hide their anger toward bureaucratic control and red tape. They have succeeded in disguising their manipulative ploys and have fooled many of those around them about their true self-centered, hostile motives. Especially when threatened, executioners attack other targeted persons within an organization with energized, impulsive vigor. An executioner abuses power by not only indiscriminately assailing and dismissing employees but also slashing services and programs.

A Final Commentary on Bureaucracies

The description of bureaucratic systems presented here stresses a number of the negatives about such systems, particularly their impersonalization. In fairness, Lewis and colleagues (2001) stress that there are some positive aspects of bureaucracy, particularly as it "provides a foundation for personnel practices that all workers appreciate" (p. 74). These include "clear job roles and performance expectations, fair treatment, and due process" (p. 74). They continue, however, that it surely doesn't focus enough on the importance of interpersonal processes and the "uniqueness" of each individual (p. 74). In a later section, this chapter will address newer, more relationship-focused management approaches.

Also note that another advantage of being part of a large bureaucracy is the existing potential for changing a powerful system to clients' advantage. In small or nonbureaucratic systems, a social worker may have lots of freedom but little opportunity or power to influence large macro systems or mobilize extensive resources on behalf of clients.

 Critical Thinking Questions 7.2

If you were to work in a traditional bureaucracy, what aspects of that bureaucracy would be most difficult for you and why? How might you cope with the problem?

Highlight 7.2 discusses problems inherent in the U.S. health care system with respect to Asian and Pacific Islander cultural values. It also proposes ways to improve its functioning to empower this macro client system.

| Highlight 7.2 | **The U.S. Health Care System, and Asian and Pacific Islander Cultural Values** |

The U.S. health care system is a huge bureaucracy reflecting many of the characteristics of traditional bureaucracies. Although management approaches do vary within its many organizational structures, strict regulations and decision-making hierarchies for health care provision tend to dominate. A problem commonly faced by such bureaucracies is the lack of cultural sensitivity. Rigid rules do not provide flexibility for adapting to culturally diverse values and needs. A major goal in social work is to enhance service provision for clients. Lack of responsiveness to clients' cultural values and belief systems can erect major barriers to receiving effective services.

McLaughlin and Braun (1999) critique the appropriateness of the U.S. health care system concerning its responsiveness to Americans of Asian and Pacific Islander (API) cultural heritage. More specifically, concerns focus on how "the system" emphasizes individual autonomy which may conflict with "collectivist decision-making norms" inherent in API cultures (p. 321). The concept *collectivist* refers to giving greater consideration to group goals, needs, and issues over those of the individual (Sue, 2006). The following discussion first describes five dimensions important in understanding API cultures with respect to involvement in the health care system. Second, three conflicts with U.S. health care policy are addressed—medical informed consent, advance directives, and decisions about nursing home placement. Third, implications for improved health care provision are proposed.

Value Dimensions in API Cultures Relating to Health Care Provision

At least five major concepts inherent in API cultures relate directly to U.S. health care provision; they include shared decision making in families, "filial piety," "silent communication," "preservation of harmony," and "delayed access but great respect" for health care (Brammer, 2004; McLaughlin and Braun, 1999, pp. 323–325; Paniagua, 2005; Weaver, 2005).

Shared Decision-Making in Families
In contrast to the individualist perspective emphasized in U.S. health care, Asian Americans and Pacific

Islanders rely on the family or larger group to make ultimate decisions about any individual member's care. In the U.S. health care system, individual patients are subject to *informed consent*. That is, physicians and health care staff must inform an individual patient about her "diagnosis, prognosis, and alternatives for treatment" (McLaughlin and Braun, 1999, p. 322). A patient then has the right to provide consent for continuation of the treatment process. In many API cultures, this assumption does not comply with values and norms. For instance, "unlike the custom among white people, for whom the individual patient is the decision maker, many Japanese and Chinese families assign decision-making duties to the eldest son. In Pacific Islander families, it may be less obvious who the decision maker is" (McLaughlin and Braun, 1999, pp. 323–324). The entire family may share duties and assume designated responsibilities like getting food. Because of the collective nature of decision making, in API cultures it is customary for "all family members" to "receive the same level of detail about the patient's diagnosis, prognosis, and treatment options" (Braun, Mokuau, & Tsark, 1997; McLaughlin & Braun, 1999, p. 324).

A Cautionary Note   Note that when speaking about any racial, ethnic, or cultural group, it is important not to overly generalize. Here we talk about general value dimensions evident in API cultures. However, individuals or families from any ethnic or racial group may embrace traditional cultural norms to various degrees. They may also experience acculturation, "the loss of traditional cultural attitudes, values, beliefs, customs, behaviors, and the acceptance of new cultural traits" (Lum, 2005, p. 101). In other words, members of a diverse group may gradually blend into and adopt the values and customs of the larger society. When thinking about a racial, ethnic, or cultural group, it is therefore important not to assume that all members comply with all cultural values or conform to the same extent. Being of German ethnic heritage does not automatically mean a person loves sauerkraut, liver sausage, and raw ground beef with onions on rye

continued

Highlight 7.2 | *continued*

bread just because these are traditional ethnic foods. The trick is to openmindedly view each person as a unique personality, yet be sensitive to the possible cultural values and beliefs that person may hold.

The other word of caution concerns differences among the many cultures included under the API umbrella. For example, "in contrast to other Asian cultures, the individual in Cambodian society is not necessarily subordinate to the family or social group," note DuongTran and Matsuoka. "Although the extended family is acknowledged, family structure is based more on the couple relationship" (1995, p. 251).

Filial Piety

A second value dimension in API cultures is *filial piety*, "a devotion to and compliance with parental and familial authority, to the point of sacrificing individual desires and ambitions" (Kirst-Ashman & Hull, 2006b, p. 414; Wong, 2005). Paniagua (2005) explains:

> Traditional Asians believe that children's primary duty is to be good and to respect their parents. Parents are expected to determine the course of their children's lives, without consulting the children about their own desires and ambitions, and any failure on a child's part to comply with parent's expectations is seen as a threat to the parents' authority. (p. 76)

Silent Communication

A third value inherent in API cultures is silent or nonverbal communication. Paniagua (2005) explains:

> Asians often respond to the verbal communications of others by being quiet and passive; they may go to a great deal of effort to avoid offending others, sometimes answering all questions affirmatively to be polite even when they do not understand the questions, and they tend to avoid eye contact. . . .
>
> Among Asians silence is a sign of respect and politeness; it also signals an individual's desire to continue speaking after making a point during a conversation (Sue & Sue, 2003). In Western cultures, eye contact during direct verbal communication is understood to imply attention and

respect toward others. Among Asians, however, eye contact is considered a sign of lack of respect and attention, particularly to authority figures (e.g., parents) and older people. (p. 77)

Therefore, much can often be learned by carefully observing silent responses and subtle nonverbal gestures. For example, it is "improper" for children "to discuss issues of death and dying with parents, yet concern by either party may be expressed by nonverbal cues such as bowing of the head or eye contact" (McLaughlin and Braun, 1999, p. 324).

API cultures value both self-control and inconspicuousness, both of which discourage the sharing of information, especially about personal issues (Kitano & Maki, 1996). For example, "the traditional Japanese culture emphasizes the importance of inner discipline and encourages the concealing of frustrations and disappointments" (Murase, 1995, p. 246). Laotian culture stresses "the need to 'save face,' which means that an individual must stay cool or keep quiet in all circumstances;" furthermore, "it is considered humiliating to point out a person's errors directly" (DuongTran & Matsuoka, 1995, p. 250; Outsama, 1977).

Preservation of Harmony

API cultures emphasize *harmony*, the importance of getting along peacefully and not causing trouble for the family (Brammer, 2004; Weaver, 2005). This concept characterizes collectivist societies. The implication, then, is "to endure hardship and pain," especially if addressing issues that might cause discomfort or disturbance for other family or group members (McLaughlin and Braun, 1999, p. 325). For example, in Vietnamese culture "harmony in interpersonal relationships is accomplished through tact, delicacy, and politeness, sometimes at the cost of honesty and forthrightness" (DuongTran & Matsuoka, 1995, p. 251). In Hawaiian culture, "contributions to unity and harmony are more valued . . . than are competitive success or self-satisfaction" (Ewalt & Mokuau, 1996, p. 260). Many values in Hawaiian culture reflect the importance of harmony and affiliation, including "generosity, graciousness, keeping promises, intelligence, cleanliness, and helpfulness" (Mokuau, 1995, p. 1795).

There also tends to be respect for clearly defined family structure and hierarchy of authority, arrangements that tend to clarify expectations and encourage predictability of behavior (Sue, 2006). For instance, Samoan culture stresses "hierarchical systems with clearly defined roles. The highly structured organization of the family defines an individual's roles and responsibilities and guides the individual in interactions with others" (Ewalt & Mokuau, 1996, p. 261).

Delayed Access But Great Respect for Health Care
API values include emphasis on family, cooperation, harmony, and aversion to causing trouble. All these contribute to avoidance of the U.S. health care system if at all possible. For Asian Americans and Pacific Islanders, "there is stigma about and shame in experiencing mental and emotional distress" (Balgopal, 1995, p. 236; McLaughlin & Braun, 1999; Paniagua, 2005). Thus, family and group members strongly prefer to deal with issues and illnesses internally within the family and avoid exposing problems to outsiders (Paniagua, 2005). For example, for Chinese people, "to share negative information outside the home is to bring disgrace on the family name"; "mental illness and retardation, criminal behavior, job failure, and even poor school grades are kept in the family" (Lum, 1995, p. 239).

When it becomes obvious to family members that the family is incapable of resolving health problems, they hesitantly turn to health care providers. For example, for Japanese Americans "any request for service" concerning mental health is of "an extraordinary nature"; "the presenting problem is likely to be a severe dysfunction beyond the coping capacity of the individual or his or her family" (Murase, 1995, p. 246). For physical illness, API families pursue external health services "only if emergency care is needed"; once that step is taken, however, group members view the physician "as a wise and benevolent authority figure" (McLaughlin and Braun, 1999, p. 325). Health care professionals are expected to make collectivist decisions, that is, those "in the best interest of the greatest number of people involved with the patient" (McLaughlin & Braun, 1999, p. 325).

Conflicts Between Cultural Values and the U.S. Health Care System
Conflicts between API cultures and U.S. health care system policy and practice focus on at least three areas—informed consent, advance directives, and decisions about nursing home placement (McLaughlin & Braun, 1999). The following discussion relates how the five value dimensions discussed above can clash with that system. The point is not to condemn the U.S. health care system, but rather to examine how it can either detract from health and well-being of Asian Americans and Pacific Islanders or empower them. The subsequent section will suggest recommendations for improvement.

Informed Consent
Four problematic issues relate to informed consent (McLaughlin & Braun, 1999). First, consider Asian Americans' and Pacific Islanders' emphasis on harmony and conforming to group wishes. Patients may feel obligated to sign consent papers presented to them when they really don't want to. The API cultural orientation is to cooperate and not cause trouble. Second, cultural norms emphasizing silence and inconspicuousness may prevent patients from voicing contrary opinions, asking questions about illnesses, and refusing to sign papers. Third, health care personnel are often unaware of how API cultural values can affect the consent process and interfere with its integrity.

Fourth, although physicians generally tell family members about a terminal illness, informing the patient about ensuing death is taboo for many Asian Americans and Pacific Islanders. Reasons can be "that the family does not want the patient to become disheartened and give up on living, that the family feels it is disrespectful to speak of such things to an elder, or that talking about death is 'polluting' or will cause bad luck" (McLaughlin & Braun, 1999, p. 330). Health care personnel thus face an ethical dilemma. Policy and professional ethics may assert that a patient be informed of a terminal diagnosis in order to discuss and weigh treatment options. However, culturally, the patient may not want to know and may well choose ignorance if given that option.

Advance Directives
A second problematic issue concerning API cultures and the health care system involves advance directives. An *advance directive* is a person's formally recognized statement signed before witnesses that

continued

Highlight 7.2 | *continued*

gives instructions for what medical alternatives should be pursued in the event that the person becomes incapable of making such choices. Two issues tend to surface here (McLaughlin & Braun, 1999). First, health care facilities are legally required to "to approach patients for copies of advance directives" (McLaughlin & Braun, 1999, p. 331). However, in Chinese, Japanese, and Hawaiian cultures, people seriously avoid discussing death for fear of inviting it or suffering negative consequences. A second issue is that it is pointless for Asian Americans and Pacific Islanders to discuss such issues because of their collectivist approach. They assume that family members will take care of those issues appropriately when the time comes anyway.

Decisions About Nursing Home Placement
Many Asian Americans and Pacific Islanders embrace filial piety and firmly believe that children should care for aging parents (Balgopal, 1995; Brammer, 2004; DuongTran & Matsuoka, 1995; Lum, 1995; McLaughlin & Braun, 1999; Murase, 1995). To them nursing home placements should be avoided at all costs. Thus, there is some tendency for API families to wait until situations reach crisis proportions before initiating possible nursing home placement (McLaughlin & Braun, 1999; Murase, 1995). Stress may escalate from economic pressure to work outside the home, caring for both children and aging parents, and increasing physical and cognitive health problems experienced during the aging process.

Interestingly, in contrast to Western culture, "many traditional API cultures expect death to occur at home and have mourning traditions that involve keeping the body at home for a number of days before burial" (McLaughlin & Braun, 1999, p. 331; Nichols & Braun, 1996). Thus, ensuing death may not spur API families to remove the dying member to a nursing or hospital facility.

Critical Thinking: Implications for an Improved Health Care System
Large service provision systems are never perfect. There are always quirks and problems because such a broad range of people are involved. Bureaucracies

have established rules to assist in their ongoing functioning. A large health care system cannot adapt itself perfectly to all its beneficiaries' needs. However, a continuous concern for social workers is the need to assess large systems' functioning, recommend improvements, and work to achieve positive changes. This is especially true in view of the U.S. population's wide range of cultural diversity.

How can the U.S. health care system become more sensitive to API and other cultures? How would you address this issue? What recommendations would you make to improve service access and provision to people of API cultural heritage? Four recommendations are proposed here.

First, training should be provided for health care personnel that sensitizes them to API cultural values and issues (McLaughlin & Braun, 1999; Yamashiro & Matsuoka, 1997). Staff should be taught to carefully observe periods of silence, nonverbal behavior, and family or group interaction for clues to understand such behavior.

Second, the health care system should encourage personnel to "begin addressing end-of-life planning issues with whole families (not just individual patients) earlier in the life course (rather than waiting until the end) and in nonhospital venues" (McLaughlin & Braun, 1999, p. 333). Agency policy should encourage staff to tune in to cultural values regarding collectivist versus individual perspectives on decision making, and work with families accordingly.

Third, the health care system should begin investigating the adoption of family-centered rather than individual-centered decision-making models for virtually any health-related decisions (McLaughlin & Braun, 1999; Mokuau, 1995). Health care personnel should seek to understand individual's and family values, and work within that value system to the greatest extent possible. The health care system should respect both the individual's and the family's right to self-determination (Ewalt & Mokuau, 1996).

Fourth, social workers should pursue ongoing advocacy for positive policy and practice changes in the health care system. Health care should respect and appreciate cultural diversity and self-determination, not pretend they don't exist.

PROBLEMS FREQUENTLY ENCOUNTERED BY SOCIAL SERVICE ORGANIZATIONS

Regardless of an agency's structural type and managerial approach, a number of obstacles can hinder social workers' ability to do their best possible job. As social service agencies struggle to provide efficient and effective services within the larger macro environment, they are often plagued by internal problems and issues. These include vagueness of goals, vagueness of process, impersonal behavior, lack of rewards and recognition, agency policy and worker discretion, and traditions and unwritten rules.

Vagueness of Goals

From a social work perspective, *accountability* is an individual worker's and the profession's responsibility to clients and the community to work effectively and achieve the goals that have been established. Individual practitioners and whole agencies are called upon to prove that their performance is productive and valuable. A major way of doing this is to define specific, measurable goals and monitor the extent to which these goals are achieved.

Superficially, this sounds good. However, think about it. How can a practitioner prove that a client has been helped? One way is to define specific behavioral goals. This takes substantial time, effort, and expertise.

For instance, if you're teaching physically abusive parents child management techniques, how do you know when you've been successful? When they can pass a written test quizzing them on specific techniques? When the parents strike their children only on the hands and rump instead of on the head? When they only strike their children once each day instead of at least a dozen times, as they did in the past? Human behavior simply is difficult to define and measure.

Evaluating the outcomes of an entire organization (or even a single program), including goals, effectiveness, and efficiency, is infinitely more difficult than evaluating the outcomes of micro or mezzo interventions. This is because of the strikingly increased number of variables involved. In order to evaluate program outcomes, first, "service content must also be made clear, with uniform definitions describing program activities. For consequences to be attributed to an activity, it is necessary to state exactly what a client has received from a given treatment or service and to determine whether that content has remained consistent over the course of the intervention" (Holland & Petchers, 1987, p. 213). This is not an easy task, although social service agencies continue to make progress in the area of defining goals despite all the difficulties involved. Effective definition, measurement, and attainment of goals enhances workers' ability to do their jobs.

Vagueness of Process

Interventions performed by a variety of individual practitioners and other staff are very difficult to measure and monitor. They are not like manufacturing machinery that punches out slabs of metal. Such slabs can be measured. Raw materials can be made uniform. Effectiveness can be evaluated in terms of the machine's accuracy and efficiency (that is, how fast and perfectly the machine can punch out slabs). In this context, unlike that of the social services, work routines are predictable, repetitive, and relatively easy to monitor and control.

Additionally, professional staff in social service organizations vary widely in terms of intervention approaches, techniques used, priorities, and personality styles. Clients probably vary even more widely in terms of characteristics and needs. Therefore, social service organizations bring multiple, immeasurable, human factors to the intervention process. Because people vary drastically more than inanimate materials like metal slabs, practitioners who work with people must have much more flexibility than metal slab punchers. That is, workers in organizations need to have some degree of discretion in working with their clients. This, in turn, makes the monitoring of the intervention process more difficult. Social service organizations must constantly strive to define the process by which they deliver services to enhance social workers' ability to function effectively.

Impersonal Behavior

The goals of accountability and efficiency can create difficulties for workers and clients. Sometimes agencies engage in behavior intended to be business-like but perceived by the workers as impersonal. It's easy, for example, for administrators to make arbitrary decisions where the workers feel left out. One agency director wanted to reduce costs such as postage and cut the time workers spent performing clerical tasks. He decided to eliminate the appointment letters that workers would type on their computers and send to clients who lacked phones. The letters told the client when the worker was planning to visit and asked the client to notify the worker if this was not satisfactory.

No one quarreled with the wish to save money, but many workers were upset because the new mandate would force them to make home visits without giving clients prior notice. To many workers this seemed inappropriate and unprofessional behavior, even a violation of clients' rights. It could also be more time consuming. The director did not share these opinions, and he overruled the workers' objections. Finally, tired of arguing social work values against business values, one worker calculated the cost of driving across the county to see a client who wasn't home. The wasted mileage cost exceeded the cost of sending out the appointment letters. After some discussion and debate, the director canceled the policy and allowed workers to send out appointment post cards once again.

Management can minimize impersonal behavior by enhancing workers' involvement in planning and decision making. It can also strive to address and improve internal channels of communication. Newer trends in management discussed later in the chapter address this issue.

Another example of impersonal behavior involves a foreign adoptions unit in a private child welfare agency. Unit staff felt like their supervisor, Keung, was disinterested in their work and their needs. Keung spent most of his time in meetings with administration. Other times, he seemed preoccupied, gave little eye contact to supervisees, and enclosed himself in his office whenever possible. By demonstrating such impersonal behavior, his staff felt he just didn't care. In reality, Keung was faced with some major issues in terms of keeping his unit intact and healthy. International political problems were causing difficulties in foreign adoptions, making many fewer children available for U.S. adoption. Keung was struggling with administration, trying not to lay off workers and instead providing transfer alternatives for them to other agency units. Keung appeared impersonal, but he was really very concerned. He was preoccupied with helping his workers keep their jobs.

Thus, workers should be sensitive to the position and needs of supervisors and administrators. The latter may indeed appear preoccupied or aloof. However, they must attune themselves to external social and economic forces that affect the entire agency and its operation. If they don't keep the agency running, no one has a job.

Lack of Rewards and Recognition

Another impediment in many organizational environments is management's failure to distribute rewards and recognition as frequently and consistently as most workers would like. In school, it is common for you to get periodic feedback on your performance. Papers are returned with comments and a grade. Exams are returned soon after they are given with the grade very evidently displayed. After each grading period, instructors give grades in each course. Many people prefer this regular system of positive reinforcement and expect something like it to exist in the agencies where they work.

Unfortunately, much of the good work that social workers do will never be recognized. It is simply not acknowledged in the busy life of the agency. Other good work will be noticed, but for many reasons no one will comment on it. Supervisors may come to take the good work for granted, not believing it needs regular reinforcement. Clients may appreciate our efforts but are too involved in their own situations to show their gratitude. Sometimes, supervisors like practitioners' performance but clients do not. For example, probation and parole workers taking clients back to court because of clients' violations are unlikely to have such clients praise their efforts. Consequently, a good guiding principle is to learn to reinforce yourself. This means you must take pride in work you do well, accepting that your work will not always be acknowledged to the extent you would like.

A guiding principle is for supervisors, managers, and even colleagues to emphasize strengths whenever possible, just as workers should do with clients. In a busy, demanding work environment, they are easily overlooked. However, the extent to which management can emphasize strengths generally enhances workers' morale and ability to function well.

Agency Policy and Worker Discretion

Agency policies and worker discretion can pose another obstruction to effective work. Practitioners may either feel squelched by policy restrictions about what they can and can't do, or floundering because policies don't provide enough guidance.

Agencies establish and operate within a system of policies that guide workers' behavior and provide direction in situations commonly encountered. For example, an agency may have a policy that requires workers to sign out when they leave the building. This policy makes it easier for supervisors, administrators, and clients needing help to know a worker's location at any given moment. In effect, it is a form of accountability and makes sense to most workers.

Many new workers feel overwhelmed with all the policies, rules, regulations, and procedures they must learn and abide by. They may think that policies control or constrain their every action. In reality, workers have enormous discretion about how they do their jobs, because policies, by their very nature, must be general enough to apply in many different situations. This means that no policy can foresee all the possible events, nuances, and complexities that arise in any given case. Policies establish general guidelines, but workers are responsible for using their discretion or judgment with specific cases. Thus, these policies do not present a real barrier to effective social work. Workers must be prepared to apply their professional knowledge and skills and cannot rely on agency policy to dictate each decision in the field.

For example, consider being a practitioner working for a family services agency that specializes in helping parents learn how to control their children's behavior. Agency policy might prescribe eight weeks to work with parents and demonstrate improvements in their children's behavior. However, you and the parents have relatively wide discretion in determining what specific behaviors to work on. Should you focus on the children's tantrums, their refusal to eat anything but pizza and Krispy Kreme double-chocolate cream-filled donuts for supper, or their almost constant nagging for attention? The decision is a matter of discretion.

It is important for management to monitor the effectiveness of policy on all aspects of agency functioning. Outdated policies should be identified and changed. Cumbersome policies should be simplified if possible. Vague policies should be clarified to provide workers with adequate direction, even in view of their need to use discretion.

Traditions and Unwritten Rules

Unobtrusive, hidden traditions and unwritten rules are other potential problems in agency environments. The written rules frequently appear in some sort of regulation manual or personnel handbook. The unwritten rules are related to the organization's informal structure reflecting who has power and who communicates with whom. As in families, the traditions and unwritten rules are often learned only through verbal exchanges with more experienced group members. Sometimes they are learned only when the novice worker inadvertently violates the rule or tradition.

A case in point was a situation that arose when a new MSW graduate, Butch Cassidy, took his first job at a huge state mental hospital. Each Wednesday afternoon at 2:00 p.m., all the social workers at the hospital gathered around a large conference table. The meeting's purpose was to improve communication among the social work staff. The hospital's social services director, Frank Enstein, and formal policy encouraged social workers to feel free at these meetings to raise issues that were causing them problems or making their jobs more difficult. Butch was confused. Frank, the supervisor of four social work units, had offered Butch a job right out of graduate school. Butch had done his first field placement at the hospital and Frank had liked the quality of his work.

Butch's direct social work supervisor, Danielle Pricklesteel, seemed distant and acted as though she resented Butch's presence. Although she was always polite and professional, Butch felt Danielle did not really want him around. Finally, Butch decided to use the next Wednesday afternoon meeting to discuss his feelings. All social work staff, supervisors, and Frank attended these meetings.

At the meeting, Butch shared his feelings with the assembled group. Danielle tactfully acknowledged she felt as though Frank had "dumped" Butch in her unit without talking to her about Butch's status beforehand. Danielle apologized for taking out her anger at Frank on Butch. Frank apologized to Danielle for not consulting her before assigning Butch to her unit. The air appeared to clear, and Butch felt much better.

After the meeting, Danielle took Butch aside and told him that she was very upset because he had brought the topic up at the meeting. She stressed, "We never discuss anything important at these meetings. We just meet because Frank likes us to get together. If you have a concern, please talk it over with me first and we'll work it out." Later, Butch learned from talking to other workers that Danielle was right. The group had an informal rule that they never discussed anything important at these meetings. To do so was to violate the workers' informal policy and expectations.

The point of this example is that informal rules and traditions can affect social workers' ability to function effectively. We learn best by observing others and asking privately about things that appear to be rules. Learning about informal rules by breaking them can be painful. The extent to which management can identify expectations and clearly communicate them to new staff enhance workers' ability to function effectively.

 ## Critical Thinking Questions 7.3

Have you ever worked in an organization or business where you experienced any of these problems—vagueness of goals, vagueness of process, impersonal behavior, lack of rewards and recognition, vague or restrictive work policies, or hidden traditions and unwritten rules? If so, what were the circumstances? How did you deal with the problem?

NEWER APPROACHES TO MANAGEMENT AND WORKER EMPOWERMENT

We've discussed bureaucracy and some of the problems inherent in bureaucracies and any organization providing social services, regardless of its management approach. We'll now turn to addressing some of the new management trends in social service and other organizations. In contrast to bureaucracy, a number of new approaches have been developing that serve to empower workers. Here we will explain five of them: constructing a culture of caring, the learning organization, teamwork and team empowerment, managing diversity, and client system empowerment within the organizational context. There are also dozens of specific methods of management. Two will subsequently be explained here—total quality management and servant leadership. Note that because all of these management trends and specific approaches focus on worker motivation, needs, and interpersonal dynamics, there's overlap in some of the concepts involved.

Constructing a Culture of Caring

Chapter 6 defined *organizational culture* as "the constellation of values, beliefs, assumptions, and expectations that underlie and organize the organization's behavior as a group" (Holland, 1995, p. 1789). Organizational culture provides guidelines and establishes expectations for how people should behave while at work (Brueggemann, 2006). Brody (2005) recommends developing a "culture of caring" in the social service agency setting. When staff feel connected with and supportive of each other, they can become a strong, cohesive force in achieving agency goals together.

Five core values characterize a caring organization (Brody, 2005). First, *job ownership* is the situation where workers feel that their job and their work performance is an important part of their identity (p. 152). They will strive hard to achieve goals and excellence in their work.

Organizations can promote job ownership by encouraging a second key value, *seeking a higher purpose* (p. 153). A caring culture encourages employees genuinely to feel that they're making a difference through their participation. It makes them feel like an integral, important part of a larger system. This can motivate them to work hard and learn new skills, not because management orders them to, but because they have a genuine desire to do so.

A third core value promoting a caring organizational culture is *emotional bonding* (p. 153). This means the organizational culture supports an environment in which people truly care about and experience a vital feeling of connection with each other. This can be especially helpful in agencies where workers experience exceptional pressures to work demanding clients.

The fourth core value is *trust,* the condition where people feel they can depend on each other to follow through on tasks and be supportive of one another (p. 153). They then don't have to waste energy on negative interpersonal interactions, conflicts, complaints, and criticisms.

Pride in one's work, the fifth core value, is the condition where workers feel high self-esteem regarding and have great respect for their accomplishments at work (p. 153). Feeling good about yourself and being proud of the job you're doing motivates you to continue doing a good job.

The Learning Organization

A second management trend related to empowering workers is the concept of the learning organization. The *learning organization* is one "in which everyone is engaged in identifying and solving problems, enabling the organization to continuously experiment, change, and improve, thus increasing its capacity to grow, learn, and achieve its purpose" (Aldag & Kuzuhara, 2005; Daft, 2003, p. 55).

Daft (2003) further explains:

> The essential idea is problem solving, in contrast to the traditional organization designed for efficiency. In the learning organization all employees look for problems, such as understanding special customer needs. Employees also solve problems, which means putting things together in unique ways to meet a . . . [client's] needs. (p. 55)

At least five primary concepts characterize the learning organization (Aldag & Kuzuhara, 2005; Daft & Marcic, 2004; Hellriegel, Jackson, & Slocum, 2002). First, power is redistributed from higher levels to lower levels in the organizational structure. Workers providing services directly to clients are given greater discretion to make their own decisions and plans. Power to develop and pursue organizational goals is distributed among all staff instead of being concentrated in management (Daft, 2007).

> *Empowerment* means unleashing the power and creativity of employees by giving them the freedom, resources, information, and skills to make decisions and perform effectively. Traditional management tries to limit employees while empowerment expands their behavior. Empowerment may be reflected in self-directed work teams, . . . job enrichment, and employee participation groups as well as through decision-making authority, training, and information so that people can perform jobs without close supervision. In learning organizations, people are a manager's primary source of strength, not a cost to be minimized. (Daft, 2003, p. 56)

A second concept involves how learning organizations nurture the development of new ideas. Employees are encouraged to be creative and share their ideas with others. Risk taking on behalf of improvement is encouraged (Daft & Marcic, 2004; Lussier, 2006). Learning organizations "encourage employees to be creative without fear of punishment if they fail. Mistakes and failure are viewed as learning experiences" (Lussier, 2006, p. 240).

Third, learning organizations emphasize the *effectiveness* of service provision to clients instead of the *process* of service provision. Clients' perceptions about services are sought out so that improvements in quality and effectiveness can be made.

Fourth, the use of multidisciplinary teams (those including representatives from a variety of fields and with a range of backgrounds) is encouraged. Teams are encouraged to make recommendations and decisions that management takes seriously and implements. Teams are charged with regularly assessing processes and procedures in order to make improvements. Thus, change occurs continuously. This contrasts strongly with traditional bureaucracies, which usually work to maintain the status quo.

Fifth, "open information" is promoted (Daft, 2003, p. 56). Daft (2003) explains: "A learning organization is flooded with information. To identify needs and solve problems, people have to be aware of what's going on. They must understand the whole organization as well as their part in it" (p. 56).

Sixth, as in a caring organizational culture, a learning organization encourages individuals to "lead because they want to serve one another as well as a higher purpose" (Aldag & Kuzuhara, 2005, p. 588). Their motivation focuses on the organization's greater good rather than on their own personal power and gain. Servant leadership, discussed later in the chapter, reflects this type of approach. (Highlight 7.3 explains four major types of leadership often identified in the context of organizational management.)

Learning Disabilities Working Against Learning Organizations Senge (1990) identifies at least six "learning disabilities" that may occur in organizations and work against learning organization culture (pp. 18–25):

- *I am my position.* This means that each worker has tunnel vision, focusing only on the tasks required in his or her position. Workers neither feel part of the greater whole nor feel that have input into the organization's vision for the future.
- *The enemy is out there.* It's not my fault. It's his. Or it's hers. Blaming others for the consequences of your own behavior works against the learning organization. People don't learn from their mistakes and improve their behavior. Blaming others only weakens interpersonal relationships.
- *The illusion of taking charge.* Sometimes it appears that organizational leaders are taking charge of situations when they lash out at others while trying to solve problems. Superficially, they look like they're in control because they're calling attention to themselves. However, people who are really in charge don't react with emotional outbursts. Rather, they carefully think issues through, assess their own conduct, and make rational decisions.
- *The parable of the boiled frog.* As unappealing as this analogy is, it paints a poignant picture. If you throw a frog into a pot of boiling water, it immediately reacts by jumping out. However, if you put a frog in cold water and gradually heat it to boiling, the frog will just stay put and come to an unfortunate end. That's because frogs have adapted to react to abrupt changes in temperature, not gradual ones. The analogy between this parable and organizational behavior is that management often reacts to a crisis or some other situation and shifts its focus on events as they

| Highlight 7.3 | **Leadership Styles** |

Leadership is "a process whereby an individual influences a group of individuals to achieve a common goal" (Northouse, 2004, p. 3). Four leadership styles will be described here—directive, supportive, participative, and achievement-oriented (House, 1971, 1996; House & Dessler, 1974; House & Mitchell, 1974; Lussier, 2006; Northouse, 2004; Williams, 2005, 2006). They are based on a theoretical approach to leadership called *path-goal theory*. Williams (2006) explains:

> Just as its name suggests, *path-goal theory* states that leaders can increase subordinate satisfaction and performance by clarifying and clearing the paths to goals and by increasing the number and kinds of rewards available for goal attainment. Said another way, leaders need to clarify how followers can achieve organizational goals, take care of problems that prevent followers from achieving goals, and then find more and varied rewards to motivate followers who achieve those goals. (p. 427)

As Northouse explains, the path-goal theory of leadership "is about how leaders motivate subordinates to accomplish designated goals."

> Path-goal theory emphasizes the relationship between the leader's style and the characteristics of the subordinates and the work setting. The underlying assumption of path-goal theory . . . suggests that subordinates will be motivated if they think they are capable of performing their work, if they believe their efforts will result in a certain outcome, and if they believe that the payoffs for doing their work are worthwhile. (Northouse, 2004, p. 123)

The following four leadership styles are based on path-goal theory:

1. *Directive leadership* "involves letting employees know precisely what is expected of them, giving them specific guidelines for performing tasks, scheduling work, setting standards of performance, and making sure that people follow standard rules and regulations" (Williams, 2005, p. 604).

2. *Supportive leadership* "involves being friendly to and approachable by employees, showing concern for them and their welfare, treating them as equals, and creating a friendly climate" (Williams, 2005, p. 604). "Leaders using supportive behaviors go out of their way to make work pleasant for subordinates" (Northouse, 2004, p. 126). "Supportive leadership . . . often results in employee job satisfaction and satisfaction with leaders. This leadership style may also result in improved performance when it increases employee confidence, lowers employee job stress, or improves relations and trust between employees and leaders" (Williams, 2005, p. 604).

3. *Participative leadership* "involves consulting employees for their suggestions and input before making decisions. Participation in decision making should help followers understand which goals are most important and clarify the paths to accomplishing them. Furthermore, when people participate in decisions, they become more committed to making them work" (Williams, 2005, p. 605).

4. *Achievement-oriented leadership* "means setting challenging goals, having high expectations of employees, and displaying confidence that employees will assume responsibility and put forth extraordinary effort" (Williams, 2005, p. 605).

Note that these categories are not mutually exclusive. People's personalities, values, and behaviors vary dramatically. Each person is unique. It is certainly possible, indeed probable, that a particular leader may reflect aspects of more than one leadership style.

 Critical Thinking Questions 7.4

What type or types of leadership do you think characterizes leaders in a learning organization?

occur. For example, an important, highly skilled employee quits. New legislation requires recording procedures radically different from the old ones. Huge funding cuts loom on the horizon. Senge (1990) would say that the major issues affecting organizations are ongoing, gradual developments. Of course, management must react to events, but managers should never lose sight of the long haul, ongoing processes, and longer-term, distant goals.

- *The delusion of learning from experience.* Hopefully, each of us learns from our experiences so that we make better, wiser choices in the future. However, after a change (such as making a policy decision or implementing a new program) is made in an organization, it often takes years to determine whether that change was effective or not. Thus, organizations don't necessarily learn from experience very quickly.
- *The myth of the management team.* Some teams (defined in Chapter 3 and discussed further in the next section) are made up of members with hidden agendas who engage in power struggles and attempted manipulation. Management should look beyond the external appearance of a team's functioning and carefully evaluate its accomplishments.

Teamwork and Team Empowerment

Chapter 3 established that a *team* is a group of two or more people gathered together to work collaboratively and interdependently with each other to pursue a designated purpose. Teams can provide a useful means of empowerment in organizations by giving the responsibility for service provision to designated groups that work together (Daft, 2007; Daft & Marcic, 2006; Lussier, 2006; Williams, 2005) . In effect, it means giving power to teams of agency workers rather than individual managers or workers. Teams can identify problems and issues, discuss potential alternatives, make decisions about how to proceed, set goals, and evaluate progress.

Specific teams might consist of groups of staff members who either provide similar services or serve the same category of clients. Teams generally meet regularly and are expected to work cooperatively together on the clients' behalf. Ongoing resolution of any conflicts occurring among team members is emphasized. Negative internal staff conflict does not benefit clients. Therefore, it is not tolerated.

Teams are most effective and empowered when used under four circumstances (Williams, 2005). First, a "clear, engaging reason or purpose" should exist for using them (p. 434). "Teams are much more likely to succeed if they know why they exist and what they are supposed to accomplish, and more likely to fail if they don't" (p. 434).

"Second, teams should be used when the job can't be done unless people work together. This typically means that teams are required when tasks are complex, require multiple perspectives, or require repeated interaction with others to complete" (pp. 434–435). Tasks requiring specific skills that can be undertaken by a single worker don't necessarily require the multiple sources of energy and ideas generated by a team.

"Third, teams should be used when rewards can be provided for team-work and team performance. Team rewards that depend on team performance rather than individual performance are the key to rewarding team behaviors and efforts" (p. 435). An agency might reward teamwork by giving the team's efforts and accomplishments public recognition in the form of praise, progress reports in an agency newsletter, plaques that can be displayed in an office. Bonuses and raises also provide means of rewarding effective teamwork.

The fourth circumstance under which teams can function well is when they have clear authority to make recommendations or implement their decisions as a result of their efforts. Teams function most effectively when left to their own devices to determine their own processes and procedures (Williams, 2005). "Unfortunately, managers can undermine teams' authority by closely monitoring their work, asking teams to change their decisions, or directly ignoring or overruling team decisions" (Williams, 2005, p. 436). Such oversight can frustrate team members and undermine team morale.

Working as a team has several advantages to working as separate individuals (LSS, 1993). First, a team allows for the presentation and sharing of many ideas, perspectives, and experiences. Second, team members have a wider repertoire of skills than any one individual. Third, the entire team should "own" its conclusions, recommendations, and results. Fourth, members can teach each other skills in addition to sharing knowledge and information.

The *team* concept should be distinguished from that of a *group*. A team is always a group, but a group might not be a team. Groups do not necessarily work cooperatively, individual roles may be unclear, participation of individual members may be hampered or discouraged, and frequently individual group members are seen as "stars" instead of cooperative co-participants (LSS, 1993, p. 18). The team perspective, on the other hand, should encourage performance of the team allowing the entire team to gain recognition and respect within the agency environment.

Managing Diversity

"Diversity exists in organizations when there is a variety of demographic, cultural, and personal differences among the people who work there" and the clients who receive services there (Williams, 2005, p. 395). Lussier (2006) reflects:

> When we talk about diversity, we are referring to characteristics of individuals that shape their identities and their experiences in the workplace. Diversity refers to the degree of differences among members of a group or an organization. People are diverse in many ways. Within the workforce, people differ in their race/ethnicity, religion, gender, age, and ability. They also differ in their military status, sexual . . . [orientation], expectations and values, lifestyle, socioeconomic status, work style, and function and/or position within the organization. (p. 242)

In contrast to traditional approaches to management, which emphasized conformity, current thought focuses on the appreciation of diversity. "*Valuing diversity* emphasizes training employees of different races and ethnicities, religions, genders, ages, and abilities to function together effectively. To be creative and innovative and to continuously improve . . . [service delivery], employees must work together . . . in an atmosphere of dignity and trust" (Lussier, 2006, p. 243).

Daft (2007) concludes: "Diversity is a fact of life for today's organizations, and many are implementing new recruiting, mentoring, and promotion methods, diversity training programs, tough policies regarding sexual harassment and racial discrimination, and new benefits programs that respond to a more diverse workforce" (p. 421).

Highlight 7.4 addresses the status of women in social services management.

Client System Empowerment by Management

We have defined *power* as the potential to move other people on a chosen course to produce an effect or achieve some goal, and *empowerment* as the "process of increasing personal, interpersonal, or political power so that individuals can take action to improve their life situations" (Gutierrez, 2001, p. 210). Chapter 1 established that a *client system* is any individual, family, group, organization, or community who will ultimately benefit from social work intervention. *Macro client systems* include communities, organizations, and larger groups of clientele with similar issues and problems. Despite typical organizational problems and wide variations in management style, social workers are responsible for client-system empowerment.

By orienting their management approaches, organizations can serve as empowerment mechanisms for large groups of clients. A major goal of social work is to enhance clients' right of choice, participation in decision making concerning their own well-being, and the availability of resources for them. A "goal of effective practice is not coping or adaptation but an increase in the actual power of the client or community so that action can be taken to change and prevent the problems clients are facing" (Gutierrez, GlenMaye, & DeLois, 1995, p. 250). How then can organizational management as a mightier force than individual practitioners encourage the empowerment of large groups of clients and citizens?

Gutierrez, GlenMaye, and DeLois (1995) identify a range of elements working for and against an agency's ability to empower large groups of clients. They selected six private social service organizations that oriented themselves to serving client "populations that have been associated with empowerment-based services" (p. 251). Empowerment-oriented intervention involves educating clients so that they understand their social environment, helping them acquire "concrete skills for surviving and developing social power," emphasizing strengths upon which to build skills, and using democratic processes to involve clients in decision making (Gutierrez et al., 1995, p. 250).

| Highlight 7.4 | **Women in Social Services Management** |

Gardella and Haynes (2004) explain the situation concerning women, social work, and social services management:

> Women represent nearly 70 percent of all paid employees in human services organizations, and more than 79 percent of social workers in the National Association of Social Workers (NASW) are women. Even so, men hold most of the managerial positions. In comparison to women in human services, men move into management earlier in their careers, are promoted faster, and earn significantly higher salaries at every occupational level. (p. 7).

The also note: Few books encourage women in human services to become leaders. . . . Management literature provides more information than inspiration for women with social work values and goals. Most research on women leaders has taken place in large corporations, where, in contrast to women in human services, nearly all the managers are affluent and white. . . .

Although corporate managers and human services managers perform many similar tasks, books by and for women corporate leaders do not address the particular challenges of leading human services organizations. Many women who advance into leadership positions must resist prejudice and discrimination in their careers, but from a social work perspective, women leaders in human services have the greater responsibility 'to strive to end discrimination, oppression, poverty, and other forms of social injustice,'[NASW, 1999] which is the professional mission of social work. (2004, p. xiii)

Management Approaches Used by Women Who Are Leaders

To explore further the dynamics of women in social services management, Gardella and Haynes (2004) invited 23 women leaders in the human services to become members in one of three focus groups, two that met face-to-face and one online. *Focus groups* are those formed to discuss some topic in depth, clarify issues, and significantly enhance understanding of the topic (Toseland & Rivas, 2005). Group members in Gardella's and Haynes' groups came from racially diverse backgrounds, and all participants had substantial leadership experience in organizations. These groups were formed to discuss the career paths

followed and the issues faced by these women as they progressed up the career ladder.

Findings revealed that group members' leadership experience reflected the theme of "inclusion," a pattern of behavior emphasizing "connection" and "collaboration" with others, "commitment" to professional values, and "optimism" (p. 102). "Inclusive leaders cultivate relationships with and among various communities and groups, using relationships to gather information, to enhance resources, and to form political alliances for their organizations" (p. 139). They took their "social responsibility" very seriously and strove to empower their clients, students, staff, organizations, and communities (p. 102). These leaders believed in "participatory decision making" and "an appreciation for diversity," which, of course coincides with a culture of caring, employee empowerment, and advocating for diversity (p. 102). "Responding to obstacles with perseverance and hope, they were optimists who learned to fit into human services organizations while also trying to change them. . . . They advanced their causes along with their careers, pursuing changes 'to make the workplace more equitable and inclusive'" (p. 103; quote from Meyerson & Scully, 1999).

Austin (2002) comments on how these findings clash with perspectives adopted by many workers and managers in human service organizations:

> Executive positions in human service organizations, as well as in much of the rest of society, are still perceived as being embedded in a White, male, heterosexual culture . . . One of the factors in the resistance of many White heterosexual men, who are otherwise reasonable individuals, to the demographic changes that are now taking place within many organizations is anxiety over the possibility of having to adapt to different expectations in organizational settings in which *it is not taken for granted* that the White, male, heterosexual culture is dominant at the executive level. Anxiety may be particularly acute in male-dominated organizations that have traditionally been organized as a hierarchical, command-and-control structure in which a gender change in leadership positions is accompanied by a change to a low-profile interactive management style. Such

continued

Highlight 7.4   *continued*

culture changes have already occurred in some human service organizations in which women predominate in executive and in policy-making roles as well as in direct service roles. (p. 349)

What Organizations Can Do To Empower Women as Leaders

What should be done to empower women as leaders in organizational settings? First, an organization's management should conduct an audit or analysis of the status of women within itself (Powell & Graves, 2003). This should go beyond counting the number of women in specific job categories:

Organization analysis also includes a cultural audit, a snapshot of the current organizational culture. It assesses the nature of the organizational culture as experienced by employees, which is not necessarily what top management thinks the culture is or should be. It also assesses how the organizational culture influences the treatment of members of different groups. Surveys, interviews, focus groups, and meetings may be used to gather information for the audit. . . . A successful audit uncovers obstacles to the full attainment of diversity goals. Obstacles may include stereotypes and prejudices that affect employees' interactions with one another and managers' decisions regarding recruitment, performance appraisals, promotions, compensation, and other employment practices. (Powell & Graves, 2003, p. 233)

A second suggestion is for an organization to establish clear-cut objectives for each management unit (Powell & Graves, 2003). "Managers will put more effort into promoting nondiscrimination, diversity, and inclusion if they are expected to meet concrete objectives in pursuit of each of these goals" (Powell & Graves, 2003, p. 233).

A third suggestion involves encouraging employee involvement in the diversity-enhancement process by establishing "employee network groups" composed of women or people with the same cultural background (Powell & Graves, 2003, p. 235). These groups can provide "career development and networking opportunities" (Powell & Graves, 2003, p. 235). However, Gardella and Haynes (2004) warn that this process can isolate women or ethnic groups of color. They indicate that "ethnic niche experience is considered marginal

experience with little relevance to the rest of the organization. Knowledge related to women or ethnic minority communities is seen as specialized knowledge, applicable only to those groups. Knowledge related to majority or mainstream groups is seen as general knowledge, applicable to all" (p. 111).

Encouraging Women in Social Work to Pursue Careers in Management

Gardella and Haynes (2004) make several suggestions for female social workers to consider in pursuing a career in organizational management or to support other women who want to do so:

- "Identify a woman leader who may be a role model for you in the future or, alternatively, who has been a role model for you in the past. Invite your role model to lunch. Ask about her career path, accomplishments, and future goals, and thank her for her example" (p. 13).
- Develop a list of your personal strengths. What qualities do you have that enhance your ability to set and achieve goals? Go over the list with a person you respect to assess its accuracy and expand it if possible.
- If you ever have the opportunity, "reach out" to another woman "as a mentor" (p. 53). Offer her support and the chance to solicit information and help from you. Help her integrate herself into a professional network where she can make additional contacts and establish her professional identity. "Mentoring relationships" are "essential" for "success" (Gibelman, 1998, p. 161).
- Think about and articulate what "personal and professional goals" you would like to achieve within "the next five years" (p. 76). Identify the "barriers and opportunities" that may confront you. Develop a strategy for how to deal with them (p. 76).
- Select a community club or professional organization and join it. This can expand both your personal and professional networks. Networking often opens up exciting opportunities.
- Meet with other women who are in professional circumstances similar to your own. You can talk about issues, provide support, and make suggestions for how to cope with problems and develop your personal and professional life.

Selected agencies included two focusing on women's services, two on people of color, one on young people, and one on older adults. The researchers interviewed both direct-service staff and administrators, using taped interviews with an established format to identify environmental variables working for and against client empowerment. They identified four obstacles to empowerment—expectations of funding sources, the macro social environment, intrapersonal issues, and interpersonal issues. Three positive supports for client empowerment included staff development, an enhanced collaborative approach, and appropriate administrative leadership and support.

Factors Working Against Client Empowerment   The first barrier to empowerment is *expectations of funding sources* (p. 252). Funding agencies do not necessarily give precedence to encouraging client participation. Involving clients in the decision-making and service provision process on a large scale takes more time and energy. More people are involved. More communication is necessary. Therefore, the empowerment process is time-consuming. Funding sources must be sensitive to the significance of empowerment. They must consider it valuable enough to pursue despite increased costs in time and money.

The second impediment to empowerment is the *social environment,* the macro context in which organizations function (p. 252). Other agencies not supportive of the empowerment concept may not encourage referrals to or from empowerment-based agencies. Likewise, competition among agencies works against client empowerment in that empowerment is best established when people and agencies work together.

Rivalry for people's time and participation in the community social environment also obstructs the client-empowerment process. Community residents and practitioners have just so much time and energy. It becomes more difficult to involve people in the empowerment process who are also integrally involved in other organizations and processes. These might include neighborhood centers, advocacy groups, professional organizations (such as the National Association of Social Workers), or Parent/Teacher organizations.

Intrapersonal issues make up the third barrier to an organization's ability to seek client empowerment (Gutierrez, GlenMaye, and DeLois, 1995, p. 253). Sometimes, the basic attributes of clients or workers interfere with the empowerment process. For example, to what extent can people with serious mental or physical disabilities participate in the empowerment process? Some practitioners express frustration at the time and energy involved in pursuing empowerment, especially when they only find limited success.

The fourth obstacle to organizational empowerment consists of *interpersonal issues* (p. 253). These involve the interactions and relationships between clients and practitioners. Some workers express serious concerns about how difficult it is to let go of their own control and direction in the intervention process. This is especially so when empowered clients choose alternatives placing their own well-being at risk. For example, a client who is a survivor of domestic violence might *choose* to return to a destructive, abusive situation. It is difficult for some workers to accept their clients' right to choice when the workers feel the choice is inherently bad.

Organizational Conditions Enhancing Client Empowerment   In contrast to the obstacles, three supports are identified for client empowerment in organizations. The first key to client empowerment is *administrative leadership and support* (p. 255). When administrators encourage the nurturance of client empowerment and practitioners feel this, "an atmosphere of empowerment" is established (p. 255).

A second support for client empowerment is *staff development* (p. 254). This includes the in-service training and other educational activities the agency provides both to empower the staff themselves and to teach staff how to incorporate approaches for empowering clients. Management should develop means of soliciting and improving client input into service provision, and teach these methods to staff.

A third support for client empowerment is an *enhanced collaborative approach* (p. 254). This involves the importance of a teamwork perspective infiltrating the agency environment. Staff understand the concepts of input and shared decision making because they're living it. They, in turn, can use these concepts to involve and empower clients. Gutierrez and her colleagues (1995) conclude that "those organizations that empower workers by creating an employment setting that provides participatory management, the ability to make independent decisions about their work, communication and support from administrators, and opportunities for skill development will be more capable of empowering clients and communities" (p. 256).

 Critical Thinking Questions 7.5

Consider the following scenario.

Yoko is furious. She is the single mother of three young children and a client at Penniless County Department of Social Services. She is currently receiving public assistance and is enrolled in a work preparation program teaching her skills in food preparation.

She has tried to see her assigned social worker Gunter eight times without success. The man is simply never there. Twice she's tried to complain to a supervisor but was cut off at the pass by secretarial sentries who adamantly declared that all supervisors were busy at the moment. They added she could make an appointment in three weeks or so.

Yoko's problem is that she discovered she hates food preparation and the training program in which she was arbitrarily placed. She wants to work and needs training, but couldn't it involve office work or sales or anything but food preparation? She has little time to make a change. She will only qualify for a few more months of assistance before she is required to work and her assistance is terminated.

Yoko doesn't know who she can turn to. The agency has no client advisory group or formal appeal process for clients to use. Clients must work through their designated worker. Yoko feels frustrated, angry, and powerless.

How might the Department of Social Services' management improve "the system" to include procedures and opportunities for Yoko's empowerment? How might she be allowed better opportunities to voice her opinions, make her own decisions, and have direct access to people in power making decisions about her?

SPECIFIC MANAGEMENT APPROACHES

We've discussed some major themes in current management thought. Now we'll turn to two of the dozens of specific management approaches being used today that apply some of these themes—Total Quality Management and servant leadership. Note that these two theoretical approaches simply provide examples of how management can be used to empower staff in organizations.

Total Quality Management[1]

The first of two specific approaches to management and leadership discussed here is *Total Quality Management (TQM)*. Developed by W. Edward Deming (1982, 1986) and others (Crosby, 1980; Feigenbaum, 1983; Juran, 1989), Total Quality Management (TQM) emphasizes organizational process, attainment of excellent quality service, and empowerment of employees (Keys, 1995b; Morrissey & Wandersman, 1995). TQM "focuses on managing the total organization to deliver quality to customers" (in the social services context, clients); important elements include employee empowerment, a focus on customer (client) satisfaction, and continuous improvement in service provision (Daft, 2003, p. 54; Hodge, et al., 2003). TQM involves both the application of systematic research and statistical analysis to determine what quality service involves, reflecting a scientific management approach, and an emphasis on human relations (Austin, 2002; Kronenberg & Loeffler, 1991; Martin, 1993). We have also established that many of the principles proposed by Theory Z (discussed in Chapter 4) apply as well.

Sashkin and Kiser (1993) explain:

> TQM means that the organization's culture is defined by and supports the constant attainment of customer satisfaction through an integrated system of tools, techniques, and training. This involves the continuous improvement of organization processes, resulting in high quality products and services. (p. 39)

Bedwell (1993) provides a more straightforward description of TQM by stating, "The essence of total quality is simple: Ask your customers what they want; then give it to them!" (p. 29).

It is beyond the scope of this book to describe in detail the implementation process of a TQM philosophy and program. However, to begin understanding how TQM is implemented and how it affects human behavior in a real agency, we will discuss a number of concepts. These include clients as customers, customer feedback, quality as the primary goal, employee empowerment, the use of team and teamwork, TQM leadership, and a culture of quality.

---

[1] The author wishes to thank the administrators for Lutheran Social Services of Wisconsin and Upper Michigan, 3200 W. Highland Blvd., P.O. Box 08520, Milwaukee, WI 53208, and Family Counseling Service 148 Prospect St., Ridgewood, NJ 07450 who readily shared their ideas and materials.

Clients As Customers   The central theme of TQM is the importance of the customer or client (Austin, 2002; Daft & Marcic, 2004). The quest for quality should be focused on what clients need and how effective and efficient they perceive service provision to be. Since staff who provide service directly to clients are central to client satisfaction, such staff are considered critical. TQM stresses that they should have high status and receive good, supportive treatment. Highlight 7.5 identifies seven interactions between workers and customers that should never occur in an organization espousing Total Quality Management.

Customer Feedback   Since customer satisfaction is paramount, agencies must solicit information from customers in order to strive for greater effectiveness (Austin, 2002; Sluyter, 1998). This can be done in a variety of ways (Albrecht, 1988; Martin, 1993). For one thing, the agency can administer customer satisfaction surveys or community surveys that solicit information from customers or residents about agency services. Staff can also conduct extensive interviews with individual customers to identify and examine their feelings. Likewise, the agency can focus on customer complaints and undertake extensive investigations. Suggestion boxes for anonymous feedback can be placed in accessible places. Finally, the agency can assemble groups of customers (focus groups) to discuss services and to make suggestions for quality improvement.

It should be emphasized that not only is customer feedback regularly solicited, but that the agency *uses* this feedback to improve its service provision. There are many ways an agency might incorporate feedback: by prioritizing client and agency needs, planning new goals, and undertaking new projects and procedures. Once again, since this book's purpose is not to teach you how to be a manager but rather how to understand and work within an organizational environment, we will not discuss these processes here.

Quality as the Primary Goal   In TQM, quality is the primary goal (Daft, 2004; Keys, 1995b; Schriver, 2004). However, quality is a difficult term to define. There is "no universally accepted definition" (Martin, 1993, p. 27). Each organization must determine for itself what quality means in terms of its own service provision.

For example, Lutheran Social Services of Wisconsin and Upper Michigan define six components of quality: "accuracy," "consistency," "responsiveness," "availability," "perceived value," and "service experience" (LSS, 1993, p. 8).

- *Accuracy* measures the extent to which actual service provision matches customers' expectations. To what extent do customers feel they are getting the services they sought and hoped to receive?
- *Consistency* is "service accuracy over time" (LSS, 1993, p. 8). Are customers consistently getting the appropriate services, or is service provision inconsistent?

Highlight 7.5	**"The Seven Sins of Service"**

Albrecht (1988) maintains the need to focus consistently on the quality of service provided to customers (or clients). He identifies "seven sins of service" that organizations commonly commit which work against maintenance and enhancement of service quality; they include "apathy," "brush-off," "coldness," "condescension," "robotism," "rule book," and "runaround" (pp. 14–16).

Of course, according to professional social work ethics, our clients or customers should always be our top priority. In an ideal world this would be so. In the real world, however, staff members are individuals with individual weaknesses and failings. These seven sins of service can and do occur. From an organizational perspective, of course, "staff" includes everyone from the agency director to various levels of administrative staff to professional social workers and other helping professionals to clerical staff to maintenance staff. Regardless of job title and responsibilities, each is, in essence, a representative of the agency. Albrecht maintains that it is absolutely essential for all staff to avoid committing any of the seven sins described below.

Of course, as professional social workers, we are supposed to be warm, empathic, and genuine. We are to always treat the customer with respect. However, these values are more difficult to maintain when we have twenty-three customers waiting in line impatiently for service, or if we absolutely have to finish by 4:30 p. m. today an eight-page report that we haven't started yet, or if we have an excruciatingly painful migraine headache. During these times, Albrecht would say that it's especially important to be vigilant about not committing any of the seven sins. Each of the seven organizational sins is explained below.

1. *Apathy.* Albrecht describes this as the "DILLIGAD" syndrome, or "Do I Look Like I Give Damn? "–à la comic George Carlin (p. 15). In other words, it's easy for staff to focus on getting their jobs over with so that they can go home and live their own lives. Apathy involves boredom with customer interactions and almost total lack of concern regarding the *quality*, usefulness, or effectiveness of the service provided.

2. *Brush-off.* This consists of getting rid of the customer by passing the buck and doing the smallest amount of work feasible. For example, a staff member might tell a customer that he can't answer her questions accurately and send her off to another department, probably on a wild goose chase.

3. *Coldness.* This "kind of chilly hostility, curtness, unfriendliness, inconsiderateness, or impatience" is intended to convey to the customer, "You're a nuisance; please go away" (p. 15). It is difficult to maintain a warm, interested interpersonal stance every minute of the day. Some customers may be hostile, feisty, or demanding, on the one hand. On the other, you as a worker may be tired, fed up, or disgusted.

4. *Condescension.* Treating customers with a disdainful, patronizing attitude implies you as the worker are more knowledgeable and, essentially, better than the customers are. When you condescend, you treat people as if they're not very bright. It might be characterized by the phrase, "Now don't you worry your stupid little head about it. I know best and I'll take care of everything. Trust me."

5. *Robotism.* When you treat each customer identically, without changes in facial or verbal expression, or ask the same questions over and over to different customers, you are not responding to individual differences. Such differences don't concern you. Your main intent is to get the job done as fast and efficiently as possible while using as little brain power as possible.

6. *Rule Book.* If you want to think as little as possible, use the rule book to give the organization's rules and regulations absolute precedence. "Go by the book" totally and completely without any hint of compromise. I once called a weight control clinic for information on exercising and maintaining my weight. A young woman answered the phone, obviously reading a boilerplate blurb about losing weight at the clinic. I asked her if the clinic also helped people *maintain* their current weight, not lose anymore. She answered by rereading the identical blurb she just had read to me. I asked her the same question two more times, after which she repeated the same blurb.

continued

Finally, exasperated, I said, "Can't you think for yourself or what?" and abruptly hung up. Although this situation does not reflect a social work context, it does exemplify the sin of rule book. The young woman answering the phone apparently was instructed to read her blurb and not say anything else. As a result, trying to get any help from her (in this case, information) was totally useless and frustrating.

7. *Runaround.* Stalling customers is a common sin. Workers tell a customer to call someone else for the information first, or to go to Window 217 and fill out the appropriate twenty-seven page form. Runaround entails using as little of your own time as possible, on the one hand, and wasting the customer's time, on the other.

- *Responsiveness* refers to timeliness of service provision. How long do customers have to wait before they get the attention and services they need? *Availability* is the ease with which customers can obtain services. To what extent are the services actually delivered to customers who request and need them?
- *Perceived value* is the extent to which customers feel the service is worth it. To what extent are the services they received worth the expense, time, and energy, and possible annoyance or frustration they experienced? To what extent is the service's value worth its total cost?
- The *service experience* sums up the total treatment experience with all of its nuances and subtleties. What is the customer's sum total evaluation of each word spoken with staff? How do customers perceive the agency, taking into account all their experiences with it. This covers each moment of interaction with the agency and each tiny aspect of their experience. For example, what was the time like that they spent sitting in a waiting room chair? How clean were those chairs, anyhow? Where they comfortable? How long were they forced to wait? How were the clients greeted when they finally met with their workers? What is their summary impression of their total treatment experience?

Individualized Definitions of Quality Each social services agency must specify its own definition of quality in the context of its own mission statement. We've established that a mission statement summarizes an agency's mission or official goals. What is the primary function an individual agency intends to accomplish? This would vary markedly between an organization composed of dozens of group homes for adults with physical disabilities to an organization aimed at curbing and preventing domestic violence, for example. The following is an example of a mission statement posed by a family counseling agency: "Recognizing the family, in all its forms, as the cornerstone of our society, Family Counseling Service of Ridgewood and Vicinity seeks to provide support and counseling to both families and individuals throughout their lives" (Family Counseling Service, 1993).

Employee Empowerment We stress repeatedly that empowerment involves providing people with authority or power so that they might have greater control over what they do. A TQM approach espouses "participative management" that empowers workers to make decisions about how to do their jobs (Dumler & Skinner, 2005; LSS, 1993, pp. 20–27; Sluyter, 1998). Participative management refers to placing the major responsibility for effective service provision on direct service workers. TQM not only emphasizes the importance of customers, but also employees in the agency units providing services directly to these customers. Likewise, other agency units providing input to direct service units are considered important because of their support to the service providers. For example, supervisory input is considered important primarily because it should aid in the service provision process.

In some ways, you might envision TQM as an upside down pyramid. In a typical bureaucratic organization, the power structure as reflected in a formal organizational chart is in the form of a triangle or pyramid. The agency director sits at the pinnacle. Below her might be assistant directors, beneath them managers, below them supervisors, and, finally, at the very bottom, the many workers. The pyramid's shape, of course, reflects the relative number of persons involved at each level. There is only one agency director. There are fewer supervisors than direct service workers. Finally, there are fewer direct service workers than there are clients. In TQM, because the client customers or consumers are given precedence, those providing service directly to them are considered, in a way, the most important. The agency's clients as customers thus form the top level of the inverted pyramid because they are considered the most significant. Right below them would be the direct service workers, beneath them the supervisors, and so on in the reverse order of the bureaucratic pyramid. The agency director and, perhaps, the board of directors would be placed at the very bottom of the inverted pyramid.

TQM emphasizes each employee's importance. Matza (1990) describes empowerment as "getting employees—especially front line employees—to take care of the customer" (p. 21).

Use of Teams and Teamwork A total quality approach espouses not only empowerment of individual employees, but also "team empowerment" (Ginsberg, 1995; LSS, 1993, pp. 20–27; Schriver, 2004). As already discussed, this involves giving the responsibility for service provision to designated groups that work together. TQM emphasizes cooperation instead of competition (Martin, 1993; Muckian, 1994).

A Total Quality Approach to Leadership Strong support and leadership from top management is critical in implementing TQM (Dumler & Skinner, 2005; Martin, 1993; Sluyter, 1998). TQM leadership must focus on the process of making all aspects of the organization's functioning excellent (Joiner & Scholtes, 1985). This includes supplying support to all agency units, especially those providing services to customers. Essentially, leaders should "serve as integrators and facilitators, not as watchdogs and interventionists" (Kanter, 1989, p. 89). Leaders often assume the latter roles in traditional bureaucracies.

Establishing a Culture of Quality   One task leaders must accomplish is the establishment of a "culture of quality" (Martin, 1993, p. 80). We've defined *organizational culture* as "the constellation of values, beliefs, assumptions, and expectations that underlie and organize the organization's behavior as a group" (Holland, 1995, p. 1789). TQM provides a very different organizational culture than the traditional bureaucracy. We have established that a culture reflecting a total quality perspective is one "characterized by teamwork, cooperation, open communication, flexibility, autonomy and empowerment"; the culture is focused on service to customers (LSS, 1993, p.74). "As all employees must be involved in the total quality approach, agency leaders must visibly demonstrate their commitment to TQM (Brown, Hitchcock, & Willard, 94, p. 3). Leaders are responsible for "changing the organizational culture from one that dwells on *status quo* to one that gets excited about change" (Bedwell, 1993, p. 30).

For example, one agency director whose private nonprofit family services organization had adopted a TQM perspective illustrated her commitment in a very concrete way. Historically, staff would park in the best spots in the parking lot each workday morning because they always got there first. Customers, who regularly got there later, would get the parking spots furthest from the building—if there were any spots left at all. Traditionally, the agency director assumed "ownership" of the best parking spot right by the agency's main door. The assistant director (#2 in the agency's hierarchy) then took the second-best spot, and so it went on down the line. The day-time janitor was assigned the very worst spot.

Reflecting the TQM philosophy, the director decided to demonstrate the importance of serving customers and giving them priority by ordering that customers should be left the very best parking spots. Staff were relegated to the worst. The director herself chose the spot in the farthest corner of the lot, next to an appallingly foul-smelling dumpster. She also rallied some of the agency's precious funds to purchase extra parking spaces for customers in a lot adjacent to the agency. She felt that customers should no longer suffer from parking scarcity problems.

Another example of how agency leaders can demonstrate their commitment to TQM principles involves a family services agency that had held its Board of Directors meetings at noon each Friday since 1946. The boardroom where their meetings were held was the only large meeting facility in the agency. Therefore, it was used for a variety of agency activities and business including staff meetings, staffings concerning individual cases, and educational activities for customers. When the agency adopted the TQM management philosophy, the board solicited and received feedback from customers. One recommendation was a stress management class that, ideally, would be held at (yes, you guessed it) noon on Fridays. Because TQM emphasizes customers' importance, the board changed its meeting time to another day and another time than noon on Friday. This was done despite some inconveniences for board members.

It should be noted that the board of directors in a traditionally bureaucratic agency would assume the topmost status in an agency. In effect, they function as the agency director's boss. In traditional bureaucracies, top leaders usually receive top priority for access to agency resources such as prime meeting space.

A Long-Term Perspective   Note that TQM takes agency leaders substantial time and resources to implement (Martin, 1993; Morrissey & Wandersman, 1995; Muckian, 1994). It takes massive effort to establish the team concept and the other aspects of TQM. An organization needs to teach its staff new roles and expectations. It is management's responsibility to organize a TQM structure, gain staff support, and educate staff about expected responsibilities and performance. Thus, it is critical for management to clarify for staff the objectives and means for achieving them, to nurture staff's faith in the total quality approach, to engender trust in its success, and to make staff feel that it is "personally worthwhile for them" (Albrecht, 1988, p. 116). Since this is not a management text, we will not address details about how management might go about this process. Rather, our intent is to familiarize you with the dynamics of human behavior in the organizational environment, including the impacts of how such organizations are managed.

   Critical Thinking Questions 7.6

What are the pros and cons of Total Quality Management? To what extent would you feel comfortable either being an employee or a manager in an organization employing Total Quality Management principles?

Servant Leadership

Another approach to the leadership aspect of management "that has received a great deal of emphasis in the leadership literature" (Northouse, 2004, p. 312) is *servant leadership*, developed by Robert Greenleaf (1970, 1977). Northouse (2004) explains:

> Servant leadership emphasizes that leaders should be attentive to the concerns of their followers and empathize with them; they should take care of them and nurture them. Greenleaf (1970, 1977) argued that leadership was bestowed on a person who was by nature a servant. In fact, the way an individual emerges as a leader is by first becoming a servant. A servant leader focuses on the needs of followers and helps them to become more knowledgeable, more free, more autonomous, and more like servants themselves. They enrich others by their presence.

In addition to serving, the servant leader has a social responsibility to be concerned with the "have-nots" and to recognize them as equal stakeholders in the life of the organization. Where inequalities and social injustices exist, a servant leader tries to remove them (Graham, 1991). In becoming a servant leader, a leader uses less institutional power and less control, while shifting authority to those who are being led. Servant leadership values everyone's involvement in community life because it is within a community that one fully experiences respect, trust, and individual strength. Greenleaf places a great deal of emphasis on listening, empathy, and unconditional acceptance of others.

In the novel *The Journey to the East*, by Herman Hesse (1956), there is an example of leadership that was the inspiration behind Greenleaf's formulation of servant leadership. The story is about a group of travelers on a mythical journey who are accompanied by a servant who does menial chores for the travelers but also sustains them with this spirits and song. The servant's presence has an extraordinary impact on the group, but when the servant becomes lost and disappears, the group of travelers falls into disarray and abandons their journey. Without the servant, they are unable to carry on. It was the servant who was leading the group. He emerged as a leader by caring for the travelers. (p. 309)

Qualities of a Servant Leader   Barbuto and Wheeler (2005, A-15) cite 11 characteristics that make one a good servant leader. Some are inherent qualities that really can't be taught. Others are behaviors that can be learned and enhanced.

1. *Calling.* Becoming a servant leader is more than just choosing that course. You must have an innate desire to forgo your own needs. Instead, you must put the well-being of others in the organization and the organization itself before yourself. You must have a genuine desire to improve the lives and functioning of workers. Therefore, it's like a calling instead of a choice.
2. *Listening.* We've established that listening is a vital communication skill. Servant leaders are exceptional listeners. They seek out information from others in the organization and strive to understand what others are trying to say.
3. *Empathy.* Empathy involves not only *being in tune* with how others feel, but also *conveying to them* that you understand how they feel (Kirst-Ashman & Hull, 2006b).
4. *Healing.* Servant leaders encourage emotional healing. They are supportive people who are easy to talk to and trust. People are naturally drawn to them.
5. *Awareness.* Servant leaders have a keen awareness of what's going on around them. They look beyond superficial appearances and explore issues and situations in depth.
6. *Persuasion.* Servant leaders are experts at using persuasion. They avoid making commands, but rather explain their views carefully and help others see their point of view.

7. *Conceptualization.* Servant leaders look at the organization's total picture and have vision about what the organization might become. They encourage others to be creative and dream of how things could or should be. Their conceptualization of the organization's operation and environment is clearly articulated to others.

8. *Foresight.* Servant leaders look ahead and prepare for what might happen in the future. Others look to them for guidance and depend on them to anticipate upcoming issues.

9. *Stewardship.* Stewardship is the condition and act of caring for the basic daily needs of others. It involves planning activities, managing processes, and helping to make other people's lives run smoothly. Stewardship involves a strong desire to serve and assist.

10. *Growth.* Servant leaders view others as being capable of growth and improvement. They maintain a positive perspective and encourage skill development and confidence building in others.

11. *Building Community.* A "*community* consists of a number of people with something in common that connects them in some way and that distinguishes them from others" (Homan, 2004, p. 9). Servant leaders encourage a sense of community among all the people who work in an organization. They urge others to work together as a part of something bigger and more important than any single individual could be.

Critical Thinking Questions 7.7

What are the pros and cons of servant leadership? To what extent would you feel comfortable either being an employee or a manager in an organization employing servant leadership principles?

CHAPTER SUMMARY

The significance of management style for workers in social services agencies was explained. Bureaucracy was explored as a traditional method of management. Orientation conflicts between professionals and the bureaucracy were discussed. Common behavior patterns within bureaucracies were identified. Orientation conflicts between the U.S. health care system and Asian and Pacific Islander cultural values were explored. Problems frequently encountered by social service organizations include vagueness of goals, vagueness of process, impersonal behavior, lack of rewards and recognition, agency policy and worker discretion, and traditions and unwritten rules.

Newer approaches to management and employee empowerment include constructing a culture of caring, the learning organization, teamwork and team empowerment, managing diversity, and client system empowerment by management. Leadership styles include directive, supportive, participative, and achievement-oriented. Management approaches used by women in social services management were discussed and suggestions for empowerment proposed. Two examples of newer management styles were explained and their major concepts identified. These include Total Quality Management (TQM) and servant leadership.

Communities in the Macro Social Environment: Theories and Concepts

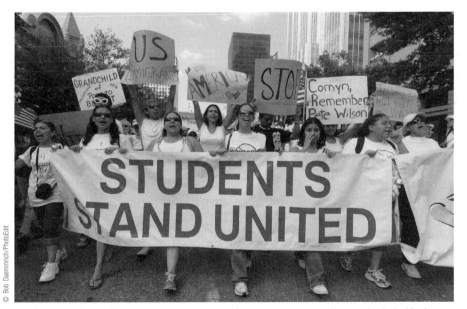

Student members of a Hispanic community demonstrate at a rally on the behalf of immigrants.

© Bob Daemmrich/PhotoEdit

CHAPTER CONTENTS

Samura had an idea. For years she had worked for an alternative school in a large city. Her clients were teenagers coming from poor socioeconomic backgrounds and, frequently, troubled families. They had experienced little scholastic success and had usually begun participating in a range of illegal activities. Samura felt these young people needed direction, support, a sense of competence, and paid work.

At the same time, Samura was concerned about the urban community, which she felt was deteriorating. She spent substantial time thinking about what could be done to help both her clients and the community in which they lived.

Finally, she came up with the idea for a community project. She met with a group of social workers from the local National Association of Social Workers chapter. Responding to her initiative, these workers formed a coalition, that is, a union of various individuals or groups who come together in order to accomplish some designated goal. Coalition members identified people with power in fifty-five local organizations and businesses. They contacted these people, solicited supportive funding, and discussed potential ideas for community improvement. Thirty-five contacts become active members in the coalition. Together coalition members raised enough money to pay 400 community young people to participate in community-enhancing projects within a designated geographical area. Projects included "building a cement basketball court for a church, rehabilitating housing, painting murals, designing puppets for a parade, developing a 'toxic tour' of the city's hazardous neighborhood, and educating residents about health issues" (Kretzmann & McKnight, 1993, p. 35).

Samura was thrilled that so many good works were performed as a result of her initiation. She also felt the young people involved learned much about what it was like to be an active, concerned, and committed community citizen.

Communities are primary settings for human behavior in the macro social environment. Understanding communities is essential for understanding why people behave as they do. This book does not try to teach *how* to do social work practice and implement changes in communities, organizations, or groups. However, it does intend to provide a *foundation* upon which to build such system-changing skills. Generalist practitioners are then better prepared to plan for and implement changes in communities to enhance people's well-being and improve their quality of life.

This chapter will:

- Define the concept of community.
- Explore several theoretical perspectives on communities, including social systems, human ecology, social-psychological, structural, functionalist, conflict, symbolic interaction, and empowerment theories.
- Describe geographical and nongeographical contexts for communities.
- Provide examples of nongeographical communities, including professional, spiritual, ethnic and racial, and those based on sexual orientation.
- Describe rural communities, including population trends, employment issues, some inherent problems, and generalist social work practice within them.

- Describe urban communities, including some inherent problems and social work practice within them.
- Explain people's membership in multiple communities.

DEFINING COMMUNITIES

A *community* is "a number of people who have something in common with one another that connects them in some way and that distinguishes them from others" (Homan, 2004, p. 9). A key feature of a community is the fact that participants share some mutual characteristic. Common features might include "location, interest, identification, culture, and/or common activities" (Fellin, 2001a, 2001b, p. 118).

Thus, communities can be of two primary types—those based on geographic vicinity and those on common ideas, interests, loyalty, and "a sense of belonging" (Martinez-Brawley, 1995, p. 539). Locality-based communities include smaller towns such as Crouch, Idaho, Eggemoggin, Maine, and Necessity, Louisiana. Larger communities include mammoth cities such as the greater Los Angeles Metropolitan Area or New York City. Still other locality-based communities include smaller portions of larger cities, such as a struggling inner-city ghetto or a posh suburban neighborhood.

Nongeographical communities are based on some commonality other than location. For example, African Americans might form a community based on racial identification, mutual history, and culture. Similarly, a community of professional social workers share common values, beliefs, and generalist practice skills. Additionally, there are "*gay communities* and *military communities* that have discernible structures and functions and that share many cultural and psychological characteristics" (Harrison, 1995, p. 560). Even scuba divers make up a community based on common interests, activities, and experiences.

A major social work perspective views communities as entities where citizens can organize or be organized in order to address mutual concerns and improve their overall quality of life. You, as a social worker, have the responsibility to examine the community macro environment in which your clients reside. Certainly, you are concerned about how specific clients will function as individuals. However, the effects of the environment in which they live, such as access to resources, cannot be ignored. Assessment of human behavior within the community context is necessary to propose solutions in your practice that address larger issues affecting a broad range of clients. Social workers can use generalist practice skills to mobilize citizens within communities in order to accomplish the goals these citizens define for themselves.

THEORETICAL PERSPECTIVES ON COMMUNITIES

Theoretical perspectives provide means to view, analyze, and understand communities. You might think of community theories as a series of different lenses, each focusing on alternate aspects or characteristics, and, thus, affording different outlooks. Viewing the same picture through a red wide-angle lens poses a distinctly different picture than looking at the same scene through a dark blue telephoto lens. Because theories may be applied either to geographical or nongeographical communities, the term *member* rather than *resident* will be used regarding people involved. The five theoretical perspectives introduced below are structural, human ecological, functional, social-psychological, and social system.

Social Systems Theories

The first theoretical perspective identified here concerning communities involves thinking of them as social systems. This view is based on systems theory, the major concepts of which were introduced in Chapter 1 and applied to organizations in Chapter 4. We defined a *system* as a set of elements that are orderly, interrelated, and a functional whole. Each community has *boundaries,* borders or margins that separate one entity from another, that define it. For example, a specific location lies within city limits or a specific county. Or you are either a member of the National Association of Bungee Jumpers or you are not. Anderson, Carter, and Lowe (1999) comment on the internal boundaries of geographical communities:

> Boundaries within the community include those between [social] institutions that differentiate tasks. [Remember from Chapter 1 that a *social institution* is an established and valued practice or means of operation in a society resulting in the development of a formalized system to carry out its purpose.] These horizontal boundaries include, for example, the uniform worn and the choice of specific colors and tasks. Firefighters' gear is adapted to their task, but it also distinguishes them from police. Their distinctive gear says, "We fight fires. We don't baptize children with our hoses, pick up garbage with our trucks, or fight off mobs with our axes and poles!"
>
> Sometimes boundaries between differentiated institutions are not so clear: Are parochial schools entitled to public funds? Should schools provide sex education? Should police conduct drug education programs? Should health clinics do AIDS testing and should they be required to report the results to federal agencies? These continue to be controversial questions in many communities. (p. 84)

The social systems perspective emphasizes analyzing how the various social *subsystems* within the community interact with each other. A subsystem is a secondary or subordinate system within a larger system. Fellin (2001a) explains the importance of examining a community's functioning from a social systems perspective:

> We are interested in examining the activities of the various social units which make up the subsystems in order to determine how well these subsystems are carrying out their community functions. The major social units within each of these subsystems are formal organizations, such as businesses, governmental units, churches, schools, health care organizations, and social welfare agencies. A significant aspect of a community social system also involves the functioning of informal groups, including families and other social groups. . . . [T]hese groups contribute to the

functioning of community subsystems, e.g., parents' activity in relations to schools, and residents' contributions to the community as a whole through civic involvement and voluntary associations. (pp. 82–83)

Viewing communities from a social systems perspective can aid you in assessing your clients' community and their involvement in that community. A social systems perspective can help you formulate a range of questions to help you assess your clients' situations and figure out what you can do to assist them among your various options *(equifinality)*. You might ask yourself what *inputs* the community has in terms of resources available to clients and other citizens. How effectively does the community process these *inputs* into *outputs* to meet its citizens' needs? Are enough resources entering the community to keep it healthy and thriving (thereby experiencing *negative entropy* and growth)? Is the community or possibly some of its *subsystems* progressing toward disorganization and *entropy*? For instance, are farmers moving out of a rural community because they can no longer make ends meet on family farms owned for generations? Are high crime rates driving residents out of a large segment of an urban community, leaving behind deserted, dilapidated shells of buildings? How do the answers to these questions affect your clients' *homeostasis*? What clues do they provide concerning what you can do on your clients' behalf? What actions might you consider taking (a form of *output* on your behalf that results in *input* into the community) to improve the community and how it affects your clients' quality of life?

Human Ecology Theories

Recall the ecological concepts reviewed in Chapter 1. A human ecology perspective of community "focuses on the relationship of populations to their environment, especially in regard to . . . how people and services are distributed" (Fellin, 2001b, p. 119). This view emphasizes how communities are complex organisms. Their members are integrally involved in transactions with each other in the surrounding social environment. How clusters of people and organizations are arranged in the community's space becomes important. Sometimes, the human ecology perspective is referred to as "the people and territory" approach (Rothman, 1987, p. 310).

Demographics, facts about population characteristics and distribution, are very important from the human ecology perspective (Rothman, 1987). Environmental issues such as pollution, depletion of scarce resources, and over-population are especially relevant.

For example, a human ecology approach might focus attention on the exodus of community residents from inner-city neighborhoods to outlying suburbs. Emphasis is placed on the relationship between people and their environment, including the resources available in that environment. Inner-city buildings might be deteriorating rapidly. Businesses and industries might be moving to new, more spacious facilities allowing for more parking, greater growth potential, better consolidation of shopping areas, and improved access for workers and consumers. Often when jobs—and hence, resources—leave an area, so do residents. People move where they can find work. The human ecology perspective might help frame subsequent questions. For example, how can the inner-city environmental deterioration be reversed to provide necessary resources and allow people to thrive there once again?

Competition, Segregation, and Integration   In addition to some basic ecological concepts identified in Chapter 1, three more terms based in human ecology that apply to community macro systems include *competition, segregation,* and *integration* (Fellin, 2001b, p. 119). *Competition* concerns how community members must compete "over the use of land" and "seek an 'advantage of place' for commercial, industrial, institutional, and residential purposes" (Fellin, 2001b, p. 119). Space and resources within communities are inevitably limited. Therefore, individuals and groups within a community must typically vie for them. Community members with greater resources and power can gain greater space and larger resources. It follows, then, that poorer residents have access only to less desirable space and significantly poorer resources. For example, richer community members can afford to acquire grander houses in the suburbs while poorer residents might be clustered in crowded urban ghettos.

Competition is often related to *social class,* the ranking of people in society based on their wealth, power, and family background. Indicators of social class usually include job type, educational level, amount of income, and typical lifestyle. People of higher social class generally have a higher standard of living than those of lower social class.

Segregation is the detachment or isolation of some group having certain common characteristics such as race, ethnicity, or religion through social pressure, restrictive laws, or personal choice. *Integration,* on the other hand, refers to the process of bringing together and blending a range of groups (including people of different races and ethnic backgrounds) into a unified, functional whole.

Such ecological concepts as competition, segregation, and integration can help you as a social worker analyze a community in terms of its fairness and support to all of its members. Fellin (2001b) explains:

> Membership in these groups affects the quality of life of people in positive and negative ways. People benefit or suffer as a result of their social positions within communities, through differential life chances, employment opportunities, access to social and material resources, and social relationships. (p. 121)

Viewing communities from a human ecology perspective helps you to focus in on the inequities and problems faced by people who have fewer resources (in effect, less energy) than others in the community. It provides a useful assessment mechanism for understanding why people act as they do within the context of the larger community macro system.

Social-Psychological Theories

A social-psychological perspective emphasizes how each community member feels about him- or herself and how they interact with others. Beyond mere structural, territorial, or functional concerns, this perspective views community members as bound together for psychological and social reasons (Martinez-Brawley, 1995). People feel they are part of a community to experience a sense of belonging, importance, and being part of "we."

One aspect, then, of a social-psychological approach involves the extent to which community members feel they have similar concerns. Do people perceive that the community has a sense of identity? Do individuals feel that they are truly a part of the community along with the other members? To what extent do community members agree about how well the community is running or how it should be run?

Another aspect of the social-psychological perspective involves individuals' sense of well-being within the community. Do people feel protected and secure? Or, do they feel they imperil themselves by just walking the streets? Are fellow community members perceived as "friends" or as "foes?"

Still another social-psychological approach to communities involves a "cultural-anthropological view" that emphasizes "attitudes, norms, customs, and behavior" (Rothman, 1987, p. 309). How do community members expect each other to behave? Which behaviors and attitudes are considered appropriate and which are not? To what extent do community members feel that they fit into the community social environment?

Martinez-Brawley (2000) notes:

> Traditional communities play an important part in defining identity . . . and stressing normative [expected] behavior. They bond the members through a strong sense of what came before or through a strong personal commitment to maintaining the culture—rituals, lore, and folklore. Ethnic group practices that emphasize a sense of who the individual is, given a role in group rituals, also function as an antidote for the sense of normlessness and confusion that often plagues modern societies. The more traditional Indian tribes in Arizona, for example, offer their members a continued sense of belonging by adherence to the rituals that have been, through the ages, a mark of tribal continuity. Among the Hopi in Arizona, even among tribe members who would be considered 'modern' because they dwell and earn a living outside the reservation, the maintenance of ritual has great significance. (p. 114)

Structural Theories

Generally, the term structure refers to how the parts of any community are organized to become one whole. Additionally, structure involves how the components of the whole relate to each other. Although a bit vague, the point is that there are many ways of viewing a community's structure, three of which we identify here.

The first structural approach is the *political-legal perspective*, which "refers to the official units designated as 'municipality,' 'township,' 'county,'

Highlight 8.1   Structural Theories and Social Action

Healy (2005) maintains that social workers adopting a structural perspective "are primarily concerned with analyzing and confronting structural injustices, particularly 'how the rich and powerful within society constrain and define the less powerful' (p. 178; Martin, 2003, p. 24). She continues that "structural social workers draw on the insights of a range of critical social work theories including . . . anti-racist and feminist social work, noting that structural social workers "promote consciousness" because the social structure may hide inequities from people (p. 178). Social workers serve as catalysts to mobilize people to change the power structure to make it more equitable.

and so forth" (Rothman, 1987, p. 309). Communities are considered "political entities" that fulfill "many political and social functions and mediate between the state as a central power and the individual" (Martinez-Brawley, 1995, p. 539). Communities, then, are smaller political subsystems within larger systems, namely, state and national governments. When thinking about such entities, concepts such as the public, taxes, and voting come to mind.

A second means of viewing communities from a structural perspective focuses on *geographical organization*. How are properties and tracks of land arranged within the community's geographical area? How are roads arranged? Is the community geographically organized like Tokyo, which developed over centuries and is composed of an endless maze of winding, confusing streets and alleys? Or, is the community structured in terms of equally square blocks of land where an address such as "South 2230 East 14791" pinpoints an exact location?

A third way of viewing the community from a structural perspective stresses *power structure*. A community can be assessed according to which of its units have the most power and influence over what happens within it. For instance, wealthier residents typically have greater power. It's likely, then, that they will exert greater influence over decisions made in the community than will the community's poorer citizens. "Power groups" within a community, notes Barker, involve members "who, because of their social status and positions, influence the decisions made on behalf of the community and who have greatest access to resources" (2003, p. 334). He notes that power group members generally include elected politicians, business executives, clergy, and other local leaders (p. 334). Highlight 8.1 addresses the relationship between structural theories and social action.

Critical Thinking Questions 8.1

In what ways are systems, human ecology, social-psychological, and structural theories similar? In what ways do they differ?

Functionalist Theories

Functionalist theories emphasize a community's purpose or function and how that community can continue working to attain that purpose. Harrison (1995) comments that "this outlook stems from the idea that to maintain itself, a society must fulfill certain social functions, such as nurturance of the young and the distribution of food and other essential resources" (p. 556). The functionalist perspective views society as "a stable, orderly system composed of a number of interrelated parts, each of which performs a function that contributes to the overall stability of society" (Kendall, 2004, p. 9; Parsons, 1951).

A functional community is one that "includes groups of people who share some common interest or function, such as welfare, agriculture, education, [or] religion" (Ross, 1967, p. 42). The primary functions of the community over time directly impact the actions a community chooses to take. For instance, historically, farming community members would assist a new neighbor in building a barn. The community's *function* focused on farming. Community *actions* were used to support that function.

Another example concerns looking at various dimensions of an individual's life in a geographical community, including family, schools, the economy, the political system, and religion. It involves "how the family provides its members with a sense of belonging, how schools provide young people with the skills they need for adult life, how the economy produces and distributes material goods, how the political system sets national goals and priorities, and how religion gives our lives purpose and meaning" (Macionis, 2005, p. 11). Each dimension of life serves some function to sustain an individual as a member of a community.

A functionalist approach also focuses on how the community has grown, acted, and matured over time. Because decisions and maneuvers change as time passes, taken collectively the actions become a process. These processes are intimately linked to a wide range of the community's structures, all serving to carry out designated functions. For example, churches of various denominations in a community may informally work together to raise funds and provide food, shelter, and clothing to the community's homeless population. More formal community structures include school boards to supervise the provision of education and social service agencies to provide services and resources (Harrison, 1995).

Manifest and Latent Functions   Not all social functions work out as they're planned. Kendall explains:

> *Manifest functions* are intended and recognized consequences of an activity or social process. A manifest function of education, for example, is to provide students with knowledge, skills, and cultural values. In contrast, *latent functions* are the unintended consequences of an activity or social process that are hidden and remain unacknowledged by participants (Merton, 1968). The latent functions of education

include the babysitter function of keeping young people off the street and out of the full-time job market and the matchmaking function whereby schools provide opportunities for students to meet and socialize with potential marriage partners. These functions are latent because schools were not created for babysitting or matchmaking, and most organizational participants do not acknowledge that these activities take place. (2004, p. 9).

Positive and Negative Social Functions   A society's functions can be either positive or negative. Positive functions serve to sustain people (Macionis, 2005). Negative functions, or *dysfunctions*, "are the undesirable consequences of an activity or social process that inhibit a society's ability to adapt or adjust" (Merton, 1968, quoted in Kendall, 2004, p. 9.) Kendall explains: "A [positive] function of education is to prepare students for jobs, but if schools fail to do so, then students have problems finding jobs, employers have to spend millions of dollars on employee training programs, and consumers have to pay higher prices for goods and services to offset worker training costs. In other words, dysfunctions in education threaten other social institutions, especially families and the economy" (p. 9).

Sometimes, trying to address and fix a social dysfunction results in unpredictable other problems. As Coleman and Kerbo note (2002):

> Things get out of whack. Even when things are going well, changes introduced to correct one imbalance may produce other problems. . . . [Education for all citizens is a valued social function. The educational system develops programs to train people for jobs. However,] educators may train too many people for certain jobs. Those who cannot find positions in their area of expertise may become resentful, rebelling against the system that they feel has treated them unfairly. Thus, 'over-education' may be said to be a dysfunction of our educational institutions. Functionalists also realize there are sometimes unintended consequences from our efforts to change society. For example, the effort to reduce the amount of drugs available on the street may work to push up the crime rate. As the supply of illegal drugs is reduced, the street price of drugs goes up, and addicts may have to commit more crimes to pay for their drug habit. (p. 12)

The functionalist perspective stresses that before making major changes in society, it is vital to analyze carefully the potential repercussions. Bad consequences or dysfunctions may result from well-intended attempts at making positive changes. Highlight 8.2 discusses the relationships among social dysfunctions, social problems, and social disorganization.

Conflict Theories

Conflict theories pose direct opposition to functionalist theories. Kendall (2004) explains:

> The conflict perspective is based on the assumption that groups in society are engaged in a continuous power struggle for control of scarce resources. Unlike functionalist theorists, who emphasize the degree to which society is held together

| Highlight 8.2 | Social Dysfunctions, Social Problems, and Social Disorganization |

Coleman and Kerbo (2002) describe the relationship between social dysfunctions, social problems, and social disorganization from a functionalist perspective:

> Functionalists see a common set of norms and values as the glue that holds groups, [social] institutions, and whole societies together. Small tribal societies in which everyone is in constant close contact usually have little difficulty in maintaining these common ideals, but as the great French sociologist Emile Durkheim pointed out, as societies have become ever larger and more complex, it has become increasingly difficult to maintain a social consensus [agreement by all of society's members about what's valued and what's not] about basic norms and values [Durkheim, 1947]. Thus, one of the major sources of contemporary social problems is the weakening of the social consensus. [A *social problem* is a social condition that is believed to be "harmful to society or to a segment of society" and "diminish the quality of human life" (Mooney, Knox, & Schacht, 1007, p. 3).] Functionalists can cite considerable evidence to show that when the social rules lose their power to control our behavior, people become lost and confused and are more susceptible to suicide, mental disorders, and drug problems.
>
>   Functionalists also feel that social problems arise when society, or some part of it, becomes disorganized. This *social disorganization* involves a breakdown of social structure, so that its various parts no longer work together as smoothly as they should. Functionalists see many causes of social disorganization: Young people may be inadequately socialized because of problems in the institution of the family, or society may fail to provide enough social and economic opportunities to some of its members, thus encouraging them to become involved in crime or other antisocial activities. Sometimes a society's relationship to its environment may be disrupted so that it no longer has sufficient food, energy, building materials, or other resources. However, in modern industrial societies, one cause of social disorganization—rapid social change—promotes all [the other social problems]. (pp. 12–13)

Leon-Guerrero adds:

> The functionalist perspective, as its name suggests, examines the functions of consequences of the structure of society. Functionalists use a macro perspective, focusing on how society creates and maintains social order. Social problems are not analyzed in terms of how "bad" it is for parts of society. Rather, a functionalist asks: How does the social problem emerge from the society? Does the social problem have a function?
>
>   . . . [For example,] [a] social problem such as homelessness has a clear set of dysfunctions but can also have positive consequences or functions. One could argue that homelessness is clearly dysfunctional and unpleasant for the women, men and children who experience it; and for a city or community, homelessness can serve as a public embarrassment. Yet, a functionalist would say that homelessness is beneficial for at least one part of society, or else it would cease to exist. Think of it, the population of the homeless supports an industry of social service agencies, religious organizations, and community groups and service workers. In addition, the homeless also serve to highlight problems in other parts of our social structure, namely the problems of the lack of a livable wage or affordable housing. (pp. 10–11)

 Critical Thinking Questions 8.2

To what extent do you think that viewing the social problem of homelessness from a positive perspective is ethical? Explain.

by a consensus on values, conflict theorists emphasize the degree to which society is characterized by conflict and discrimination. According to some conflict theorists, certain groups of people are privileged while others are disadvantaged through the unjust use of political, economic, or social power. (p. 11)

Whereas functionalists assume that society maintains itself on the basis of a configuration of stable rules and consensus, conflict theorists "see stability as a temporary and unusual state, note Robbins, Chatterjee, and Canda (2006).

> Conflict rather than consensus is assumed to be the norm, and coercion rather than cooperation is considered the primary force in social life. Conflict theorists are primarily interested in two phenomena—power and change. More specifically, they are interested in the ways that people use power to resist or create change. (p. 63)

An example of how functionalism and conflict theories starkly contrast involves how people view the law (Coleman & Kerbo, 2002). Functionalists maintain that people obey laws because they value them and know they're supposed to do the right thing. There is a social consensus that law is important to maintain the social structure. Conflict theorists, on the other hand, affirm that people avoid committing crimes because they're afraid of the negative consequences such as jail. It's not so much that they want to be "good," but rather that they want to avoid potential conflict.

Four concepts are vital dimensions of all conflict theories; Robbins and her colleagues (2006) define them from the conflict perspective:

> *Conflict* is a clash or struggle between opposing forces or interests. *Power* is the ability to control and influence collective decisions and actions. *Minority* refers to groups that have limited access to power even when they represent a numerical majority. *Change* is a transition or transformation from one condition or state to another. Change can be either rapid or slow, radical or conservative, evolutionary or revolutionary. Some conflict theories perceive change as rapid and radical while others see slow, incremental change as the norm. Change, however, is seen as normative and healthy and the central propositions listed above are at the core of most conflict [theories]. (p. 66)

Society is viewed as being composed of various competing groups. These groups are in constant conflict, grappling with each other for power and resources. Some groups such as minority groups have less access to power, which means they must struggle to get it. Such struggling results in ongoing conflict. Ongoing conflict, in turn, means constant pressures for change in the distribution of power and resources.

Class Conflict   Conflict theories can be divided into two broad categories—those focusing on "class conflict and the other on interest group conflict" (Robbins et al., 2006, p. 66). Karl Marx (1818–1883), a German philosopher, economist, and activist, began to conceptualize conflict theory based on class differences and conflict. Marx identified basic differences in *social class*, which we have established is their ranking of people in society based on their wealth, power, and family background. He proposed that society was basically divided into the "haves," those with access to wealth and power, and the "have-nots," those with little or no access to such resources. Marx theorized that the wealthy, whom he called the capitalist *bourgeoisie*, owned the factories and businesses, and ran the government. (*Capitalism* is "an economic system in which businesses are privately owned by people who operate them for profit" [Macionis, 2005, p. 12]). The bourgeoisie then wielded power over the workers, whom he called the *proletariat*, and exploited them at low wages for profit. Marx maintained that the capitalist system only resulted in the exploitation and poverty experienced by the proletariat.

Robbins and her colleagues (2006) explain the resulting conflict:

> Because a small privileged group owns the means of production and exploits others for their profit, a class struggle becomes inevitable as people struggle against exploitation. During this struggle the owners and the laborers become increasingly polarized and antagonistic toward each other. A class consciousness—an awareness of class position— develops among the bourgeoisie, who consolidate their common interests based on their need to exploit others for profit. Their economic monopoly, however, manifests itself not only in the work arena but also in the political arena. Through their consolidation of interests they transform their economic power into political power and dominate the political institutions that then become subservient to them. (p. 67)

The result is ongoing conflict between various groups in society based on their social class and the resulting access to power. Marx proposed that the only solution would be revolution and the demise of capitalism so that resources and power could be more equally distributed (Robbins et al., 2006). This, of course, has not happened.

Out of the perspective of conflict theory comes the troubling idea that capitalism encourages "corporate violence" (Mooney et al., 2007, p. 12). Mooney and his colleagues (2007) reflect:

> Corporate violence can be defined as actual harm and/or risk of harm inflicted on consumers, workers, and the general public as a result of decisions by corporate executives or managers. Corporate violence can also result from corporate negligence, the quest for profits at any cost, and willful violations of health, safety, and environmental laws (Reiman, 2004). Our profit-motivated economy encourages individuals who are otherwise good, kind, and law-abiding to knowingly participate in the manufacturing and marketing of defective brakes on American jets, fuel tanks on automobiles, and contraceptive devices (e.g., intrauterine devices [IUDs]). The profit motive has also caused individuals to sell defective medical devices, toxic pesticides, and contaminated food to developing countries. (p. 12)

 ## Critical Thinking Questions 8.3

To what extent should corporations be held accountable for the production and distribution of harmful goods nationally and internationally? In what ways should they be held accountable?

Interest Group Conflict   The second broad category of conflict theories involve those focused on conflict resulting from *contradictory values and interests among social groups* rather than among *social classes*. Such groups and coalitions may be based on race, ethnicity, gender, sexual orientation, religion, politics, or values.

For example, consider the abortion controversy. People who maintain an anti-abortion stance feel strongly that a fetus is a human being from the moment of conception when sperm meets egg. Pro-choice proponents, on the other hand, emphasize that a woman has the basic right to choose what she wants done with her own body.

Another example involves *affirmative action*, "the broad range of policies and practices to promote equal opportunity and diversity in the workplace and on campuses" (Mooney et al., 2007, p. 323). People who support affirmative action often feel that it's a necessary approach to fight discrimination against people of color, promote equality, and help level the playing field for oppressed populations. People against affirmative action often maintain that it's unfair to provide privileges unavailable to white people because that in itself is a form of discrimination.

Still another conflict-laden issue concerns same-gender marriage. People supporting it feel that marriage is a basic right regardless of sexual orientation and that it is discriminatory to deny that right to people of the same gender. On the other hand, people against gay marriage may claim that marriage, often portrayed in a biblical context, can only occur between a man and a woman.

 Critical Thinking Questions 8.4

What are the similarities and differences between functionalist and conflict theories with respect to communities?

Symbolic Interactionist Theories

Both functionalists and conflict theorists maintain a macro focus on communities and the total society. In contrast, symbolic interactionist theories emphasize using "a microlevel analysis of how people act toward one another and how they make sense of their lives. The symbolic interactionist perspective views society as the sum of the interactions of individuals and groups" (Kendall, 2004, pp. 13–14).

Leon-Guerrero (2005) explains:

An interactionist focuses on how we use language, words, and symbols to create and maintain our social reality. This perspective highlights what we take for granted: the expectations, rules, and norms that we learn and practice without even noticing. In our interaction with others, we become the products and creators of our social reality. (p. 12)

Our communities and our society, therefore, are based on how we construct and perceive what exists, what is important, and what is expected behavior. "The concept of role is central to symbolic interactionism" explain Robbins et al. (2006). "A *role* is a social category or position with a set of expected behavior patterns. Roles, however, do not exist in isolation and are, to a great extent, defined by their relationship to one another" (p. 310).

They further explain how a sense of oneself develops:

> Goffman [(1959), an early proponent of symbolic interaction] proposed that the self was constructed through dramatic interaction between the individual actor and the audience. As actors, people manage impressions of themselves in their daily interaction with others. Impression management involves presenting oneself to others in ways that are intentionally guided and controlled by the actor. The 'parts' that people play during a 'performance' are consciously constructed by the actor in an attempt to present a self that will be accepted by others. (p. 305)

Leon-Guerrero (2005) continues:

> How does the self emerge from interaction? Consider the roles that you and I play. As a university professor, I am aware of what is expected of me; as university students, you are aware of what the student role means. There are no posted guides in the classroom that instruct us where to stand, how to dress, or what to bring into class. Even before we enter the classroom, we know how we are supposed to behave. We act based on our past experiences and based on what we have come to accept as definitions of each role. But we need each other to create this reality; our interaction in the classroom reaffirms each of our roles and the larger educational institution. Imagine what it takes to maintain this reality: consensus not just between a single professor and her students but between every professor and every student on campus, on every university campus, ultimately reaffirming the structure of a university classroom and higher education. (p. 13)

Deviant Behavior   Appropriate behavior can be interpreted and learned, but so can deviant behavior. Consider drug addiction or delinquency (Leon-Guerrero, 2005). Symbolic interaction theory maintains that no one begins life as a drug addict or a delinquent. Rather, such behavior is perceived and learned. Drug addicts and delinquents learn and establish their destructive behaviors through interaction with others. They construct and view their realities to support their patterns of behavior.

Labeling Theory   *Labeling theory,* which has developed from symbolic interactionism, indicates that no behavior is inherently bad (Leon-Guerrera, 2005; Robbins et al., 2006). Rather, society determines which behaviors it considers deviant and labels them as such. Thus, when an individual is labeled as "being mentally ill" or a "criminal," these labels reposition that person "from a normal position in society to a deviant role. This role carries with it a special status and role expectations and the labeled person is expected to fulfill the role requirements note Robbins et al. (2006).

Often, these role expectations become a self-fulfilling prophecy for both the individual and the social audience. Further, labeling theorists point out that these roles are stigmatized and are usually not reversible. Thus, once labeled, the stigmatized person is rarely, if ever, allowed to resume a normal role or position in society. (p. 309)

 Critical Thinking Questions 8.5

To what extent do you agree with the comment, "Once a person is labeled as having a deviant role, that label is impossible or nearly impossible to escape"? Explain.

Empowerment Theories

Chapter 1 introduced the concepts of empowerment, strengths, and resiliency, the latter two being important aspects of empowerment theories. Chapters 2 and 4 related empowerment theory to groups and organizations respectively. The concept of empowerment was integrated throughout Chapter 7, focusing on its importance for both workers and clients in the organizational context. Empowerment is just as important in the context and understanding of communities.

We have established that empowerment involves supporting the development of self-confidence, establishing control over one's life, working together to improve the quality of life, and gaining political power to enhance input and equality. Empowerment theories support the attainment of these goals in communities. Chapter 9 explores community empowerment in greater depth.

The Strengths Perspective and Communities   The strengths perspective, which provides a basis for empowerment, focuses on community's assets rather than its problems. Here, six principles championed by the strengths perspective are applied to communities (Saleebey, 2002, pp. 14–17):

1. Each community has assets and strengths. The important thing is to identify them, then use them.
2. Community problems (for example, crime, delinquency, drug addiction, unemployment, poverty, lack of resources and services in a geographical community, and conflict among factions in a nongeographical community) may be detrimental to the community's well-being, but they can also be viewed as jumping-off points for improvement and growth. For example, if crime and delinquency are problems in a geographical community, then citizens can band together to form neighborhood watch organizations to look out for each other. (*Neighborhood watch organizations* are voluntary groups of neighborhood residents who help each other by keeping a careful eye on each other's property for potential damaging criminal activity, and report any suspicious incidents to each other and police.) Residents can work together to advocate for youths' recreational opportunities and job training to provide positive alternatives to delinquency and employment potential. Citizens can work with school personnel to educate children

| **Highlight 8.3** | **Using Resiliency to Enhance Communities: Kwanzaa As an Example** |

Chapter 1 defined *resiliency* as the ability of any size system including a community to recover from adversity and resume functioning even when suffering serious trouble, confusion, or hardship. Greene (2007) discusses how one means of strengthening and developing a community is to combine the seven resiliencies of Kwanzaa. Kwanzaa, meaning "first fruits of the harvest" in Swahili, is a week-long celebration of life, culture, and history for many African Americans (Woodward & Johnson, 1995, p. 88). Greene (2007) indicates that geographical communities and their members can become more resilient when they abide by the tenets inherent in Kwanzaa (quoted from Karenga, 1997):

1. *Umoja* (unity): believing that the community, family, nation, and ethnic group of which a person is a part may become whole

2. *Kujichagulia* (self-determination): accomplishing goals that are self-selected

3. *Ujima* (collective work and responsibility): working together to solve problems and make their community a safe and productive place

4. *Ujamma* (collective economics): building and maintaining community-based businesses and profiting from them together

5. *Nia* (purpose): planning for the future and being willing to help others to succeed

6. *Kuumba* (creativity): planning for the future and being willing to help others to succeed

7. *Imani* (faith: believing with all their heart in their people and in the righteousness of their struggle

about drugs, abuse, and prevention. Residents can work together with various facets of the community for improved services and resources.

Similarly, the strengths perspective views conflict in a nongeographical community such as a professional or special interest organization as providing the opportunity to address differences, make compromises, and collaborate to improve the community's functioning. For example, two factions in a professional organization that differ regarding preferred meeting times—mornings or evenings—may need to meet and discuss a potential compromise. This provides the opportunity for both factions to explain their needs, get information on the other's perspective, review the purpose for meetings, and make compromises that both factions can live with.

3. You never can fully realize how far a community can grow and improve itself. Instead of focusing on limitations and what a community cannot do, the strengths perspective seeks out and enhances ideas about what it can do.

4. Social workers are most effective when working together collaboratively with clients. Social workers can work with community members to identify issues, develop plans, and achieve results.

5. Each community has multiple resources. The trick is to identify them and establish ways to use them.

6. It's critical to care about the community's overall well-being and provide community members with support and help.

Resiliency, a concept introduced earlier in the book, is related to the strengths perspective. Highlight 8.3 discusses how community resiliency can be enhanced through the celebration of Kwanzaa.

Which Theoretical Perspective Is Best?

There is no answer to this question. Theoretical perspectives simply give you ways of examining things. They give you ideas about how to think and what to look for. Thinking about communities or assessing them in different ways can give social work practitioners ideas about what could be done to improve life for large groups of people in communities. Highlight 8.4 provides a summary of the theories identified here, their foundation principles, and some of their major concepts.

 Critical Thinking Questions 8.6

Of the theories portrayed in Highlight 8.4, which theories and concepts do you think have the most relevance to social work practice in communities? Explain your reasons. Which theories and concepts do you think have the least relevance? Explain.

COMMUNITY CONTEXT: NONGEOGRAPHICAL COMMUNITIES

We have established that in addition to geographical communities such as a small town or large city, a community may also be based on some commonality other than location, such as a belief system, cultural background, area of interest, or common experience. These are also referred to as "nonplace communities" (Anderson et al., 1999, p. 73). Examples include professional communities, racial-ethnic communities, religious groups, friendship networks, groups of patients experiencing common problems, and groups of workplace colleagues (Martinez-Brawley, 1995; Schriver, 2004).

Nongeographical communities can serve a number of purposes to enhance members' sense of well-being, all relating to each other (Schriver, 2004). First, they provide an arena for forming relationships where a person can receive support, encouragement, praise, and information. Relationships can provide feelings of belonging and connectedness that most people seek in one way or another. Second, non-geographical communities can also offer a sense of identity, of who they are. People can view themselves as Roman Catholics, gay men, lesbians, PC users, Mexican Americans, massage therapists, or rocket scientists, depending on the communities to which they belong. Third, nongeographical communities make people feel that they belong and are an integral part of the community even when apart from other members. You don't have to be standing next to another member to experience being part of the community. Regardless of where nongeographical community members are, their community membership and its contribution of their identity as community members remains intact.

Highlight 8.4	Comparison of Community Theories

Community Theories	Foundation Principle	Some Major Concepts
Social Systems	A system as a set of elements that are orderly, inter-related, and a functional whole.	Boundaries Subsystems Inputs/outputs Entropy Negative entropy Homeostasis Equifinality
Human Ecology	Emphasis on the relationship between populations and their environment, especially regarding how resources are distributed.	Competition Segregation Integration
Social-Psychological	Emphasis on how community members feel about themselves and on their interactions with others.	Sense of "We" Having similar concerns Sense of well-being
Structural	Emphasis on the structure of the community and how various parts are organized to make a unified whole.	Political-legal structure Geographical structure Power structure
Functionalist	Emphasis on a community's purpose or function and how the community works to continue functioning.	Functions -Manifest & latent -Positive and negative (dysfunctions) Social problems Social disorganization
Conflict	Emphasis on how groups in communities and society are in constant conflict and in a power struggle for scarce resources.	Conflict Power Minority Change Class conflict Interest group conflict
Symbolic Interaction	Emphasis on interpersonal interaction and how communities and society in general are based on people's interpretations of these interactions.	Roles Defining deviant behavior Labeling theory
Empowerment	Emphasis on supporting the development of self-confidence, increased control over personal destiny, working together, and increased political power.	Strengths Resiliency

Four examples of nongeographical communities will be presented here. These include professional communities (specifically, the National Association of Social Workers), spiritual communities, ethnic communities and communities of people of color, and communities based on sexual orientation.

Professional Communities: The National Association of Social Workers

One type of nongeographical community is a professional or special interest organization. The National Association of Social Workers (NASW) has already been mentioned several times, especially with respect to its *Code of Ethics*. Established in 1955, NASW is the major social work organization with the largest and broadest membership in the profession. Persons holding bachelor's or master's degrees in social work and students in accredited social work programs can join. It is called an "organization" and does have an internal management structure. However, like many other professional and special interest organizations, it also provides a community for members to share information concerning common issues and to provide each other with support.

Like other professional organizations, NASW fulfills at least five purposes in establishing a professional community. First, membership in such a professional organization lends credibility as a social work professional (Simpson & Simpson, 1992). Most, if not all, established professions have an organization to which members can belong. Such membership bolsters members' professional identity, helps them identify with other members, and enhances the visibility of a profession.

NASW's second purpose is to provide opportunities for networking. State, regional, and national conferences and meetings enable members to talk with each other and share news and ideas. Such meetings also provide a means for finding out about new career and job opportunities.

NASW's third purpose is to provide membership services. These include *Social Work,* a quarterly journal that addresses various aspects of practice; the *NASW News,* a national newspaper published almost monthly that focuses on relevant research, social welfare policy and service issues, and social workers' accomplishments around the country and the world; and newsletters published by some state chapters.

NASW's fourth purpose is to sponsor organized efforts for lobbying on behalf of socially responsible social welfare policies and services (Simpson & Simpson, 1992). NASW exerts influence in support of causes and political agendas concurrent with professional social work values. It has also helped states establish licensing or certification regulations for social workers.

NASW's fifth purpose is to publish policy statements on various issues (e.g., youth suicide, health care, people with disabilities, affirmative action, and environmental policy) to help guide members in their practice (NASW, 2003).

A number of other organizations reflect more specific facets or subsets of social work. Examples include the Association of Community Organization and Social Administration (ACOSA) and the National Association of Black Social Workers (NABSW).

Spiritual Communities

Religion and spirituality reflect yet another aspect of human diversity. *Religion* involves people's spiritual beliefs concerning the origin, character, and reason for being, usually based on the existence of some higher power or powers, that often involves designated rituals and provides direction for what is considered moral or right. *Spirituality,* a related concept, involves "the views and behaviors that express a sense of relatedness to something greater than the self; spirituality connotes transcendence or a level of awareness that exceeds ordinary physical and spatial boundaries" (Beckett & Johnson, 1995, p. 1393). Religion implies membership in a spiritual organization with customs, traditions, and structure. Spirituality may involve religion, or it may reflect a personal, internalized view of existence.

Gotterer (2001) explains: "For some people, religion fosters a spirituality that serves as a bastion of strength. It can provide emotional consolation, inspiration, guidance, structure and security. It can foster personal responsibility, identity, respect for ethical codes, meaningful ritual, and community building" (p. 188).

People involved in formally organized religious denominations or sects become part of that religious community. Hugen (2001 p. 11) cites five ways religion can maintain a sense of community:

- Religion serves an integrative function by establishing norms and values, making for moral character and for ethical relations with others.
- Religion serves as social control function by fostering order, discipline, and authority.
- Religion provides the individual believer with emotional support when needed.
- Religion confers on believers a sense of identity.
- Religion can serve as a source of positive physical and mental health. It can contribute to happier, more stable families, marriages, and communities.

Religion may also provide an important source of community for ethnic and racial groups. Solomon (2002) describes the church's importance for many African Americans:

No African religious cults were established in the United States during slavery. However, with the coming of Baptist and Methodist missionaries, the slaves found an avenue for the expression of emotion as well as bonds of kinship with their fellow slaves. After emancipation, the enlarged church organizations played an even more important role in the organization of the African American communities. They promoted economic cooperation for the purpose of erecting and buying churches, establishing mutual assistance and insurance companies, and building educational institutions [Leigh & Green, 1982]. As the main form or focus of organized social life, the church has been both a secular and a religious institution, a fact that may well account for its playing a broader role in African American communities than in white communities. . . .

The spiritual side of the African American church is far more personal than that of the traditional white church: God is never an abstraction apart from the here and now. He is personalized and included in daily life situations. . . . Prayer is a frequent response to everyday crisis, even by those who do not profess to any deep religious convictions. Comments like "I prayed that my husband would find a job," or "I prayed that my child would get well," may be heard. The church provides significant services in African American communities that can be utilized by creative social work practitioners seeking to enhance social functioning in those communities. For example, Leigh and Green [1982] point out that churches have served to develop leadership skills and mutual aid activities, as well as emotional catharsis for those in need of some release of emotional tensions. If social workers routinely assess the significance of the church in the lives of African American clients, they may find avenues for enhancing their service effectiveness through collaborative activity. (pp. 302–303)

As indicated, spirituality can also be expressed in ways other than those determined by formal religions. Another example is Kwanzaa, described earlier in its role of providing a source of strength and resilience. We described how Kwanzaa "emphasizes spiritual grounding" for many African Americans in their communities (Karenga, 2000, p. 62). Karenga (2000) explains its conceptualization and how it is key to a sense of community:

Kwanzaa [first celebrated in 1966] was created first as a fundamental way to rescue and reconstruct African culture in the midst of a movement for re-Africanization. It was to recover a valuable and ancient way of building family and community, shaped so it spoke to current needs and aspirations as a paradigm of possibility. Second, I created it to introduce the Nguzo Saba (The Seven Principles [noted earlier]) and to reaffirm the centrality of communitarian values in building and reaffirming family, community and culture. Kwanzaa was also created to serve as a regular communal celebration which reaffirmed and reinforced the bonds between us as African people both nationally and internationally. And finally, Kwanzaa was created as an act of self-determination as a distinct way of being African in the world. It was conceived as a cultural project, as a way to speak a special African truth to the world by recovering lost models and memory, reviving suppressed principles and practices of African culture, and putting them in the service of the struggle for liberation and ever higher levels of human life. (p. 57)

Sometimes, people's spiritual community involves a combination of religion and spirituality. Consider the First Nations people, the Lakota (Teton Sioux). (Other terms that refer to the indigenous people of North America include American Indians and Native Americans.) Brave Heart (2001) describes the spiritual orientation of the Lakota people:

For the Lakota and many other Native peoples, spirituality is an integral part of culture and of one's sense of self and worldview. Lakota spirituality is based upon the Seven Sacred Rites brought by the White Buffalo Calf Woman. . . . Inherent in this spiritual tradition are the sacredness of women, the sacred relationship with the

Buffalo Nation, the values manifested in the ceremonies of self-sacrifice for the good of others, and the importance and sacredness of relationship with all of creation. The Seven Laws (*Woope Sakowin*) of the Lakota include generosity; compassion; humility; respect for all of creation; the development of a great mind through observance, silence, and patience; bravery in the face of adversity in order to protect the nation; and wisdom. The Lakota embrace principles of *non-interference* [the concept that people should be able to make their own decisions without meddling from others (emphasis added)] and tolerance and value interdependence. Traditionally, all decisions are made with the next seven generations in mind. (p. 19)

Ethnic Communities and Communities of People of Color

People may also be part of nongeographical communities based on ethnicity or race. For example, many large cities sponsor a range of ethnic festivals such as Italian Fest, Polish Fest, or African American Fest. People who identify with their ethnic heritage may belong to an organized community group that celebrates its heritage and provides opportunities for socializing.

People may also feel part of that community based on their race. However, it may depend on the degree that an individual continues to identify with that racial group's traditional heritage and customs. *Acculturation,* as defined by Lum (2004) is

"an ethnic person's adoption of the dominant culture in which he or she is immersed. There are several degrees of acculturation; a person can maintain his or her own traditional cultural beliefs, values, and customs from the country of origin to a greater or a lesser extent" (p. 202).

For example, people initially immigrating to the United States from Mexico might maintain a strong identity with their Mexican heritage and culture when they first arrive. However, the subsequent generations may lose some of their adherence to traditional culture as they become acculturated.

Weaver (2005) describes how First Nations people often strive to maintain their sense of traditional community:

Native communities continue to exist as distinct cultural entities with many strengths. Even when federal policies interrupted values transmission, wisdom, beliefs, and practices are strengths that have survived (Long & Curry, 1998). Communities are striving to revitalize traditions through programs that teach language and culture. Many youth now participate in kindergarten or grade school immersion programs that teach language. The importance of the group reinforces socially acceptable behaviors and emphasizes the value of learning traditions (Swinomish Tribal Mental Health Project, 1991).

First Nations people of all ages are seeking and reclaiming cultural knowledge and traditions. A study of Native women (predominantly Oneida) revealed they handle multiple roles through integration and balance of traditional and contemporary feminine strengths in a positive, culturally consistent manner. Healing the spirit is done through returning to traditions to reclaim the self (Napholz, 2000). (p. 94)

Communities Based on Sexual Orientation

Communities based on sexual orientation reflect another type of nongeographical community. Chapter 1 introduced terminology used in referring to gay, lesbian, bisexual, and transgender (GLBT) people and explained the concept of homophobia. Because GLBT people live in a world that's primarily heterosexual, they frequently seek out others of the same sexual orientation. They then often can feel more comfortable, feel free to be themselves, and avoid the scrutiny of critical heterosexuals.

Hunter and Hickerson (2003) discuss the significance of community for many GLBT people:

> The lesbian and gay community is essentially based on a shared sense of identity instead of on residential areas or territories (Bernard, 1973). The solidarity of an identificational community flourishes in large part through its culture or the values, common experiences, and sentiments that it produces (Gruskin, 1999). This includes art, music, literature, and jewelry; groups and organizations, including political associations, baseball teams, and choruses; and special events including music festivals and marches. The lesbian and gay community is also a subculture of the larger American culture and thus shares many broader social values (Murray, 1992).
>
> Just as no unified American culture or community exists, no monolithic gay and lesbian culture or community exists. "Community" can mean different things to different persons, for example, being a member of the worldwide population of lesbian and gay persons versus the population of lesbian and gay persons in the San Francisco Bay area. It can mean participation in a social network, the social "scene," or the lesbian and gay institutions operating in a certain area (Saulnier, 1997). Cultural norms and behaviors also vary because of factors including social class, ethnicity, and residential area (Appleby & Anastas, 1998). Diversity is evident in large events such as Lesbian and Gay Pride Day that is celebrated every year across the United States with parades. Although "solidarity" is present in rhetoric, considerable diversity and pluralism are evident among the parade participants (Herrell, 1992). (p. 22)

Hunter and Hickerson (2003) note that GLBT people can reach out in a number of ways to become part of a community:

> In this time of expanding technology and media, LGBT persons have been able to interact with others in their groups via print publications, e-mail, and the Web. Yet, the most enduring connection of these groups remains proximity as they gather in urban areas and neighborhoods to build an infrastructure that offers not only individual support, but also public identity and a sense of pride. Intersex persons also experience these kinds of connections. (p. 29)

COMMUNITY CONTEXT: GEOGRAPHICAL COMMUNITIES

Geographical communities, the second major type of community, are based on location. "Population size, density, and heterogeneity" are the most frequent demographic variables used to characterize geographical communities (Fellin, 2001a, p. 89). Such communities are also referred to as "place communities"

(Anderson et al., 1999, p. 73). *Population size,* of course, is the total number of persons living in a designated community. The communities may be large, widely spread out farming areas or counties within an urban area.

Density is the ratio of people living within a particular space. The density of a heavily populated inner-city area is much higher than a suburb where all residences contain single families and are built on two-acre lots. Population size and density are often closely related. Extremely dense areas usually have high populations.

Heterogeneity refers to the extent to which community members have diverse characteristics. A community may vary in its level of heterogeneity depending on its residents' socioeconomic status, racial and ethnic background, or age range.

The largest communities are *metropolitan,* traditionally those with at least 50,000 people (Ginsberg, 2005; Davenport & Davenport, 1995). The U.S. Census Bureau now uses a more complex definition that divides urban areas into metropolitan and micropolitan areas (U.S. Census Bureau, 2005). *Metropolitan* areas are locales that "have a least one urbanized area of 50,000 or more inhabitants" (U.S. Census Bureau, p. 921). *Micropolitan* areas, on the other hand, are locales that "have a least one urban cluster of at least 10,000 but less than 50,000 population" (U.S. Census Bureau, p. 921). "As of November 2004, there are 361 metropolitan statistical areas and 575 micropolitan statistical areas in the United States. In addition, there are 8 metropolitan statistical areas and 5 micropolitan statistical areas in Puerto Rico" (U.S. Census Bureau, 2005, p. 921 [italics added]).

This book will consider both metropolitan and micropolitan areas as *urban* communities. Rural communities, discussed later, are generally considered as having 2,500 residents or less (Ginsberg, 2005; Johnson & Yanca, 2004). Because communities differ so widely, Highlight 8.5 identifies a number of terms that reflect some of the differences in communities that don't necessarily fit clearly the categories we've identified thus far.

Urban communities then are usually composed of many smaller neighborhoods, communities, and even smaller cities enveloping a central nucleus of social, business, and political activity. Cities making up a large metropolis may include suburban and satellite communities. Suburban communities directly adjoin large urban centers, while satellite communities are located near but not directly next to the metropolitan area.

For example, Metropolis, a large metropolitan city of two million people, comprises numerous smaller communities, including downtown Metropolis, Wauwatosa, Cudahy, and Wayside. Directly adjacent to the central Metropolis area are less densely populated suburbs with generally higher socioeconomic levels, including Mequon, Pinegrove, and Menomonee Falls. Satellite communities located thirty to forty miles from central Metropolis are Sheboygan, Oconomowoc, and Ixonia. Many people working in central Metropolis actually live in these outlying communities and commute. Suburbs and satellite communities often offer less population density, more services, and a generally higher quality of life. They also usually cost much more to live in.

| **Highlight 8.5** | **Variations in Communities** |

Communities vary widely. The following are terms used to identify some of these distinctions (Johnson & Yanca, 2004, p. 142):

1. *Small cities* are units of 15,000 to 20,000 people. They generally have internal operations with their own police department, post office, and other systems (Kirst-Ashman & Hull, 2006a). They may be satellite communities to metropolitan areas.

2. *Small towns* have between 8,000 and 20,000 people. Unlike small cities, they do not operate independently. Services are few, residents depending on the encompassing county or larger cities close by.

3. *Bedroom (or satellite) communities* usually grow up near larger urban areas. They are what the name implies, primarily residential communities where people reside, sleep, and enjoy recreational activities. Residents work in nearby urban centers that harbor businesses and industry.

4. *Institutional communities* contain "a large institution such as a state mental hospital, an educational institution, or a government site (state capital),

which is the major employer in that community" (Johnson & Yanca, 2004, p. 142). Smaller communities with large universities or prisons are other examples. Residents in such communities are dependent on the institution for their economic well-being. Most often, these are located in rural environments.

5. *Reservation communities* are areas that are recognized by the federal government where First Nations people reside. The largest concentration of their population is in California, Oklahoma, and Arizona respectively (U. S. Census Bureau, 2005). Lewis (1995) explains how tribes of First Nations peoples "are sovereign—that is, government and state laws do not apply within reservation boundaries without congressional consent" (p. 220). Thus, tribal governments control some aspects of tribal life such as law enforcement. The federal government "has a role in assisting the reservation communities by providing financial and medical services" (Kirst-Ashman & Hull, 2006a, p. 256).

Heterogeneity or the opposite, *homogeneity* (having like or similar characteristics), also comes into play. Returning to the Metropolis example above, South Metropolis, the southern portion of the central city, comprises mostly Hispanic residents; Babblebrook, a northern suburb, people of Jewish descent; Pinegrove, a western suburb, white Anglo-Saxon Protestants (WASPS); and the old fifth ward in the central city, people of Italian descent. Wayside on the east side of central Metropolis is the home of a large university and, hence, is a congregating place for intellectuals, artists, and more trendy people. It is known for great diversity in its racial, ethnic, and vocational composition.

Rural Communities

We've established that rural communities have traditionally been characterized as having 2,500 residents or less. They usually include a small town, which might consist of a grocery store, gas station, and tavern. However, such communities often do not offer a wide variety of specialized services. Residents depend on the county and neighboring towns for resources.

There are many stereotypes about rural living (Davenport & Davenport, 1995). Some think of country living fancifully as a Garden of Eden where one can withdraw from the hustle and bustle of urban life. Others harbor negative stereotypes about rural residents, often viewing them as stupid, lacking in sophistication, or being blatantly naive. Some may remember the old television sitcom and a more recent movie "The Beverly Hillbillies." The plot, if you can call it that, revolved around a family of awkward, unsophisticated rustics who struck oil, became millionaires, and moved to Beverly Hills, where they regularly made fools of themselves. Although a popular comedy at the time, such inappropriate and derogatory stereotypes do little to reflect the realities of rural life.

People in a rural social environment live under very different circumstances than those in urban areas. These conditions directly affect resource availability and, hence, the way social workers practice. Three variables tend to characterize communities in rural areas (Davenport & Davenport, 1995). First, population density is low as people either live relatively far apart or relatively few people populate the entire community area. Second, rural communities tend to be geographically distant from larger urban areas. Third, rural communities tend to be more specialized in function than urban centers, which have both population and room to achieve diversity. For example, a farming community's resources would focus on those supporting farming needs such as feed, seed, and farm implements like tractors and harvesting equipment. Such a community would probably not be able to support a gourmet jelly bean and cappuccino shop. There would be too few people to support such a specialized interest. A generic Super Duper Value grocery store offering a wide range of basic daily foods would probably achieve greater success.

Population Trends in Rural Areas   Lohmann and Lohmann (2005) report the following population trends in rural areas:

1. "The actual number of rural residents has grown slowly but steadily since the first census in 1790 right to the present" (p. xv). So, although people have steadily migrated to urban areas over the past two centuries, the total number of people living in rural areas has actually grown. The rural environment is not a desolate wilderness void of people.
2. "At the same time, the proportion of rural population has declined steadily for more than a century, and at least four states (California, New York, Florida, and Massachusetts) are now over 90 percent urban" (p. xv). So, it is indeed true that the *proportion* of urban residents has grown in comparison to rural residents. Also note that the proportion of people who work as full-time farmers is less than 1 percent, the lowest proportion ever (p. xxi).
3. "Each of those 90 percent-plus urban states (like most other large urban states) also has a rural population that, in actual numbers, exceeds the total population of the smallest state(s)" (p. xv). Therefore, even in states where the number of urban residents vastly exceeds the number of rural residents, a significant number of people still reside in rural areas.
4. "For the country as a whole, and for most states, the proportion of the rural population living outside any "organized" place (small town or village) is almost four times the number of rural people living in towns and

villages of 2,500 or less" (p. xv). Therefore, many people live in places with very low population density.

So, when we talk about the rural social environment, we're referring to a significant number of people. We've defined the rural community in terms of numbers, but looking at the microcosm of life there is much more complex. The next sections will discuss employment issues, problems faced, and generalist social work practice in rural communities

Employment Issues in Rural Communities   Lohmann and Lohmann (2005) report on the labor force participation in rural areas:

> In earlier, simpler times, labor force participation in rural areas was concentrated heavily in the so-called primary industries: fishing, mining, and most especially farming. However, we easily underestimate how long ago declines in employment in these industries began occurring and the continuing impact this has had on rural life for many decades. Historians now generally agree that the market revolution in American society that transformed farming and fishing from subsistence activity to employment probably began around 1800. Prior to that time, rural living truly may have been the fully self-sufficient way of life of a cashless existence where things were grown, made at home, or done without. But at least, since that time, rural life for most has included a strong, if sometimes minor dimension of 'store-bought goods,' and most rural communities moved from simple villages to towns where organized buying and selling occurred regularly. Only in a relative few backwoods areas was this not the case even by 1920.
>
> There is almost nowhere in the United States where urban markets and consumer goods (and accompanying jobs in sales and service occupations) do not reach today. While certainly not an unmixed blessing, as illustrated by concerns with Walmarts and MacDonalds, access to national markets is a reality of rural life. It is certainly also the case that mechanization, increased productivity and relocation of industries [many to foreign countries], particularly over the past half-century, have taken a ferocious toll on the number of traditional rural jobs. . . .
>
> And yet, through such wrenching declines in traditional rural employment, the total numbers of people living in rural areas have increased. How do rural people survive? In the case of many Native American reservations (almost all of which are located in rural areas) and other distressed communities, the answer is that many rural people barely survive and do so only on the basis of public aid and their own grit despite staggering barriers and challenges. (pp. xxiii–xxv)

The result is that many people are forced to live on "Social Security, pensions, Temporary Assistance to Needy Families (TANF), food stamps," and other cash benefits (Lohmann & Lohmann, 2005, p. xxv). Ginsberg discusses the impact of social welfare:

> In rural areas, social welfare programs are often the most important economic factor in the community. . . . [Cash benefits], along with the in-kind economic impact of the Food Stamp Program, may drive the retail industry in the community, provide much of the tax revenue, and serve as factors in real estate and other aspects of the community's economy. (pp. 7–8)

Some people in rural environments may work for businesses where they may earn near minimum wages and receive no health care benefits. Ginsberg (2005) reflects on the rural employment scene:

> Many small communities are one- or two-industry towns ("company towns"). . . . However, there are many other kind of rural community industries, such as tourism, services to retirees, and, to some extent, warehousing and manufacturing. Many smaller communities do not provide a diversity of employment, though, and young people often find that they must either find a job within the limited number of local industries or move elsewhere for work. Rural employment for well educated people is often available only in public schools, churches, colleges and universities, or social service agencies. Much employment in rural areas may also require extensive commuting. Trains and buses are not generally available in smaller towns, particularly in the South and West. Therefore, commuting is often by private automobile, which is expensive and often unreliable. Therefore, transportation resources are often considered a major deficiency in rural areas. (p. 8)

The United States Department of Agriculture (USDA) has established an identification system for work in rural areas that can give us clues about where people find employment (Olaveson, Conway, & Shaver, 2004). They classify rural counties by "economic activity and policy traits . . . Economic types are farming-dependent, mining-dependent, manufacturing-dependent, government-dependent, services-dependent, and non-specialized. The policy types are retirement-destination, federal lands, commuting, persistent poverty, and transfer-dependent (more than 25 of the population receives public funds)" (p. 12).

Other Problems and Issues Faced by Rural Communities   People have similar problems whether they live in rural or urban environments. However, there are generally fewer services available in rural areas, and those that do exist are often not readily accessible. Therefore, it's often more difficult for rural residents to get what they need. Carlton-LaNey, Edwards, and Reid (1999) explain:

> The list of problems with which rural and small town residents must cope includes poverty, lack of transportation, inadequate childcare, unemployment, substandard housing, and insufficient health care. Problems of access and adequacy, for example, remain critical issues that need to be addressed in rural social work practice. Krout (1994) noted that access problems add time and expense to service delivery efforts, ultimately discouraging both the development of new services and the expansion of existing services into rural areas. For example, rural homebound individuals who could benefit from home-delivered meals and thereby maintain independence are denied this service because it is too expensive. The cost of delivering meals to remote areas can significantly limit the amount of money available for the service itself.
>
> Health care is another significant problem. Rural areas, particularly low-income areas, are underserved because of a lack of physicians and other healthcare providers. (p. 7)

It is also important to note that access to medical specialists is limited in rural areas, often posing additional difficulties for rural residents.

Generalist Social Work Practice in Rural Communities Social workers practicing in rural communities must address at least four special issues. First, they must be true generalists who are prepared to work with individuals, families, groups, local organizations, and the community, using a wide range of skills to meet clients' diverse needs (Daley & Avant, 2004; Davenport & Davenport, 1995; Carlton-LeNay et al., 1999). We've established that because of lower population densities, rural environments usually have fewer resources.

A large metropolitan area with dense population generates lots of tax moneys and resources. Such a county can afford to support a large urban Department of Social Services that may have a huge number of workers. Large numbers enable such a department to diversify. For example, public and private social service agencies might provide specific, separate services such as substance abuse counseling, protective services for older adults, services for people with cognitive disabilities, foster care, crisis counseling for victims of sexual assault, shelter for victims of domestic violence, and so on. Urban workers may become more specialized in the problems they address depending on their assigned unit.

In contrast, rural environments usually can't sustain large social services departments with numerous workers. Rather, practitioners must use a wide range of skills to help clients address a broad arena of issues. In a single day, a rural worker may deal with child maltreatment, elder abuse, substance abuse, and foster care issues.

A second special issue for social workers in rural communities involves *interagency cooperation* (Carlton-LeNay et al., 1999, p. 10). Because fewer, more general services are usually provided by public agencies, it's critical for agencies and their staffs to work more closely together than in many urban communities. It's common for practitioners and agency administrations "to know each other and to reach out to each other regularly" to meet clients' diverse needs (Carlton-LeNay et al., 1999, p. 10). In urban areas with hundreds of available services, this may not be the case.

A third issue involving social work in rural communities is the importance placed on understanding the community, knowing its values, and developing relationships with rural residents (Daley & Avant, 2004). People living in rural communities have different life experiences than those living in bustling cities. Because there are fewer people, social interaction and relationships tend to be much more informal. Rural social workers and their family members might attend the same church or school, participate in the same civic clubs and organizations, and shop at the same grocery store as clients. Therefore, a rural practitioner must be careful to portray an image that reflects positively on his or her agency (Daley & Avant, 2004). Private lives might be more public—some say as if "living in a fishbowl" (Davenport & Davenport, 1995). For example, it would not be impressive for a social worker counseling a client with an alcohol problem to be cited in the local newspaper for driving under the influence (DUI). Highlight 8.6 addresses the ethical issue of dual relationships in rural communities.

| Highlight 8.6 | **Ethical Issues Involved in Dual Relationships in Rural Communities** |

Because of the close interpersonal nature of rural communities, there is a strong likelihood that dual relationships exist. *Dual* or *multiple relationships* occur when "a practitioner is in a professional role with a person in addition to another role with that same individual, or with another person who is close to that individual" (e.g., both social worker and neighbor, or member of the same church, temple, mosque, or synagogue) (Corey, Corey, & Callanan, 2007, p. 262). Especially in rural communities, dual and multiple relationships may be unavoidable. Watkins (2004) suggests that social workers in such situations "above all, do no harm; practice only with competence; do not exploit; treat people with respect

for their dignity as human beings; protect confidentiality; act, except in the more extreme instances, only after obtaining informal consent; [and] practice, insofar as possible, within the framework of social equity and justice" (p. 70).

It's very important for workers to separate their personal relationships from their professional to the greatest extent possible. For example, consider a worker and a client who attend the same church and serve on the same committee there. This does not mean that the worker should become "friends" with the client. That would bias the worker's objectivity and threaten the effectiveness and fairness of the worker-client relationship.

The fourth issue important for social work in rural communities involves emphasizing the strengths inherent in rural communities. Because of the informal nature of relationships, rural clients are often integrally involved with informal support systems or social networks of other people willing to help them out—sometimes referred to as *natural helping networks* (Tracy, 2002; Watkins, 2004). Such networks can include family members, neighbors, coworkers, fellow church members, community benefactors, and others not providing formal agency services who are willing to volunteer assistance.

Highlight 8.7 discusses potential advantages for social workers in rural environments.

Urban Communities[1]

Urban communities provide very different settings for generalist social work practice than rural communities. *Urban social work* is practice within the context of heavily populated communities, with their vast array of social problems, exceptional diversity, and potential range of resources. Phillips and Straussner (2002) stress how urban social workers "need to be sensitive to the situations commonly found in the cities and to be knowledgeable about the nature of urban life and the range of impact that the urban environment can have on people" (p. 20). Work in urban communities is important in view of how both the national and global population has been shifting from rural to urban settings. People often flock to cities in search of new opportunities,

---

[1] Note that many of the ideas in this section are taken from *Urban Social Work: An Introduction to Policy and Practice in the Cities* by N. K. Phillips, and S. L. A. Straussner (Boston: Allyn & Bacon, 2002), unless otherwise indicated.

| Highlight 8.7 | **Advantages for Social Workers in Rural Environments** |

Despite the challenges inherent in working in rural environments, there are often several positive aspects as well (Ginsberg, 2005). First, workers usually have greater independence because of broader job descriptions and less complex bureaucratic structures in social service organizations. This may be a great advantage for people who appreciate having discretion over what they do and how they accomplish goals. A second advantage is that it may be easier to

advance in the social services organizational power structure and get a management position. Competition may not be nearly as strong or plentiful. Third, social workers may be more likely to see the fruits of their efforts with clients more quickly and clearly. "The dearth of services and the smaller scale, which often permits rapid implementation of plans, can allow social workers to see what they have done early in their assignments" (p. 10).

higher-paying jobs, and greater access to activities and services. Many times, although hopes are high, actual opportunities are scarce or nonexistent, which results in a "disproportionate number of the poor" in the "country's largest cities" (p. 107).

Urban communities are characterized by a number of conditions (Marsella, 1998). First, population is denser and often contains diverse population subgroups (for example, ethnic, racial, cultural, age, sexual orientation). Second, urban economic conditions involve a range of industries, businesses, rent levels, and transportation availability and costs. Third, urban communities often involve a bustling tangle of concrete, traffic, noise, and questions about air quality—in sharp contrast to the more natural rural environment. Fourth, an urban lifestyle entails more condensed interaction and contact with many people. Fifth, the political situation may be intense, with many layers of bureaucracy and numerous people in "the system" who have various amounts of power. Sometimes crime, corruption, and social injustice are evident.

Watkins (2004) explains:

Urbanization brought dramatic changes in the way people interacted with each other. Individuals moved away from extended family and other primary relationships to cities where primary relationships were replaced by more role-based interactions [for example, employee, renter, customer, student]. Population density and crowding were accompanied by emotional distancing to preserve a sense of privacy and individuality. In low-income neighborhoods, needs overwhelmed the resources of neighbors. Many persons in need were new to the cities and had no support networks. Formalized or institutionalized social services were a rational response to the peculiar social patterns and needs of these urban residents. . . . However, when federal, state, and local governments increased their role in providing services, the programs were no longer tailored to a specific community. In efforts to increase efficiency and fairness, services became more bureaucratic and standardized. The new model of service delivery that developed preferred secondary, "professional" relationships and interactions that were rule- and role-based rather than more personal [and individualized]. Needy individuals were depersonalized into "clients". (p. 67)

Problems Inherent in Urban Communities   At least five problems tend to characterize urban areas more than rural areas (Phillips & Straussner, 2002). Even though "problems such as poverty, discrimination, overcrowded housing, crime and violence, homelessness, high rates of school dropouts, substance abuse, and HIV/AIDS exist in communities of all sizes," it is important to note that "they occur with greater frequency and therefore are more visible in the cities" (p. 25).

A second problem is the widespread occurrence of discriminatory behavior because of the wide variety of ethnic, racial, religious, and cultural groups living in cities. Groups may be in conflict and fighting for power and resources. Often public schools are disadvantaged because of inadequate funding, resulting in poorer buildings, libraries, laboratory equipment, and technology, as well as underpaid staff.

"Migration of people unprepared" for the pressures and demands of urban living is a third problem characterizing cities. Phillips and Straussner (2002) explain:

> With their promise of freedom and opportunity, the cities have always been mag-nets for both the adventurous and the desperate. Most people move to urban areas in search of better opportunities for work or for education, either for themselves or their families, and for many, the cities have served and continue to serve as gate-ways to success.
>
> However, some who migrate to urban areas, whether from other parts of the United States or from other countries, are faced with unemployment, under-employment, discrimination, poor housing, and language barriers. Those without families or social supports to help them make the transition to the new culture and to city life are at greater risk for poverty, social isolation, and personal and family problems. (p. 27)

As Phillips and Straussner point out, financial shortfalls or unavailability of resources make up a fourth problem characterizing urban areas:

> Some cities do not have the financial resources to provide services that would assist people in maximizing their potential, while other cities may have the resources, but do not choose to provide services, particularly for the poor. Consequently, there may be a lack of affordable, good-quality housing, or a lack of adequate police protection, schools, or recreational facilities. For example, preschool children and their parents are underserved in many urban communities. (2002, p. 28)

Because of cities' dense population, service gaps can affect huge numbers of people.

The fifth problem characterizing cities involves greater amounts of psy-chological stress. Stressors including noise, dirty streets, abandoned buildings, overcrowded housing, lack of geographic mobility, and substance abuse can impose psychological pressure and increase general anxieties (Phillips and Straussner, 2002, p. 29).

Highlight 8.8 describes some of the skills involved in urban social work practice.

| **Highlight 8.8** | **Generalist Social Work Practice in Urban Communities** |

As in other types of social work, urban social workers use micro practice skills in their work with clients in the community, including establishing and working toward goals, using effective communication and interviewing techniques, respecting client values and perspectives, emphasizing strengths, expressing empathy, and "developing self-awareness" to combat biases and effectively understand clients' perspectives (Phillips & Straussner, 2002, p. 201). Thus, "social workers need to constantly reflect on their work, talk with supervisors or consultants, discuss their concerns with colleagues, and, as students, engage in classroom discussion and exercises that promote the development of self-awareness" (Phillips & Straussner, 2002, p. 201).

Additionally, urban social workers must focus on using skills in at least four major arenas (Phillips & Straussner, 2002).

1. *Paying close attention to human diversity.* Because urban environments more likely have a wider variety of ethnic, racial, and religious backgrounds, urban social workers must be sensitive to the wide range of cultural differences, become knowledgeable about their various clients' cultures, and focus on the identification and use of clients' respective cultural and personal strengths. Urban practitioners must also be attuned to the potential discrimination experienced by people "based on race, ethnicity, culture, age, gender, religion, sexual orientation, disability, poverty, or language spoken. While historically various immigrant groups such as the Irish, the Jews, the Italians, the Chinese, and the Japanese have experienced discrimination in the United States, the most persistent discrimination today is experienced by Native Americans; blacks, including African Americans, people from the Caribbean, and people from Africa; Latinos; Asians; and people of Middle Eastern backgrounds" (p. 26).

2. *Understanding their agency environment.* Urban agencies may be large and complex, or may serve large client populations. Urban workers must understand the intricacy of their agency's power structure, who has decision-making power about what they can and can't do, and where resources are located. Large bureaucracies are often highly impersonal. They tend to emphasize following rules and regulations to coordinate their complex maze of service provision. Often workers are called on to work with other personnel they don't know. Workers must then be sensitive to other staff's roles and use good communication skills to work effectively in collaboration with other service providers. Even smaller agencies in urban settings must work within a complex interplay of numerous organizations also addressing client needs. Urban social workers must understand the functioning of other agencies serving the same clients and work carefully with other staff to coordinate service provision.

3. *Seeking resources in the external urban environment.* Urban social workers often function in a complex labyrinth of many public and private agencies, each providing specialized services in one of a broad range of areas (for example, mental health counseling, administration of public assistance, domestic violence shelter, sexual assault hotline, or adolescent pregnancy prevention). This differs from rural agencies, which frequently provide a broader range of services to a smaller population; in other words, they are less likely to specialize to the degree that urban agencies can. In their broker role, urban social workers must often seek resources in a confusing tangle of red tape and available services.

4. *Using advocacy.* Note that just because urban areas tend to have larger and more numerous services, this does not mean that there are no significant gaps in service due to limited or lacking resources. Such gaps may involve massive numbers of people. At the agency level, an urban practitioner may need to develop a coalition with colleagues and approach decision-making administrators with suggestions for

continued

Highlight 8.8 | *continued*

positive changes. On another level, public policy may not serve clients' best interests. Therefore, strategies to change legislation may include the use of letter-writing or e-mail campaigns to lawmakers, lobbying (seeking direct contact with legislators to influence their opinions), or using the mass media to publicize clients' needs and issues to gain public support for positive change.

MEMBERSHIP IN MULTIPLE COMMUNITIES

Remember that each individual is probably a member of multiple communities. You are probably a member of the university or college community, your residential community, the social work professional community, possibly a work group community, and any number of others. Involvement in multiple communities reinforces an individual's sense of belonging and expands potential access to resources and support provided by various communities. For example, the college community provides you with access to library resources and knowledge about values and skills. The residential community gives you neighborly support and potential friendship. The professional community furnishes you with information about jobs, ethical decision making, relevant legal issues, and new work skills.

    Critical Thinking Questions 8.7

In which geographical and nongeographical communities do you belong? Describe each.

CHAPTER SUMMARY

This chapter defined communities and emphasized their importance as a context for human behavior. Eight theoretical perspectives—social systems, human ecology, social-psychological, structural, functionalist, conflict, symbolic interaction, and empowerment—were discussed. Boundaries and subsystems are major concepts in systems theories with respect to communities, while other social systems concepts also apply. Competition, segregation, and integration are concepts characterizing human ecology theories.

Social-psychological theories emphasize how community members feel about themselves as belonging to a community. Structural theories emphasize how various parts of a community, such as the political-legal, geographical, and power structures, form an organized whole. Functionalist theories focus on how communities must maintain a range of functions to continue existing. Various community functions may be manifest or latent, and positive or negative (dysfunctional). Social dysfunctions are related to social problems and social disorganization. Conflict theories are based on the assumption that groups in the community are in constant conflict and a struggle to compete for scarce resources. Some conflict theories emphasize class conflict and others interest group conflict. Symbolic interaction theories focus on how norms and expectations in communities are based on interpersonal interactions and how participants perceive these interactions. Empowerment theories are built on the concepts of strengths and resiliency.

Nongeographical communities are founded on commonalities other than location. Examples provided include professional communities (in the form of professional organizations), spiritual communities, ethnic communities and communities of people of color, and communities based on sexual orientation.

Geographical communities are based on location and are often assessed in terms of population size, density, and heterogeneity. Metropolitan and micropolitan communities were defined. Rural communities are those with 2,500 residents or less. Population trends, employment issues, some inherent problems, and generalist social work practice within rural communities was discussed. Social work practice in urban communities was discussed including inherent problems and skills needed. Most people are members of multiple communities.

Assessment of Geographic Communities and Empowerment

Communities can help and empower their residents. Here Emergency Management Agency volunteers rescue a family from the roof of their Suburban trapped by flooding from Hurricane Katrina.

CHAPTER CONTENTS

Brutus, 77, lives in a rundown two-story home in an ancient residential section of Bumrap, a large metropolitan city. Chenequa, his neighbor, is very concerned about Brutus and his situation. Twice she found Brutus had fallen helplessly on the ground while walking out to get his mail. She practically had to drag Brutus into the house. Brutus has rheumatoid arthritis, which makes it very difficult to walk even with his two canes. Additionally, his eyesight is poor. Chenequa has questions about Brutus' ability to shop and cook for himself.

Brutus' wife, Olive, died two years ago after a long bout with intestinal cancer. Since her death, Brutus has remained isolated and alone. His two children live in other states and are busy with their own families and careers.

Brutus considers himself an intelligent, independent man who worked hard most of his life as an house painter. However, since his arthritis took a turn for the worse 10 years ago, he has had to stop actively working. He is now facing financial difficulties. He's experienced many years of little income and high health costs for both him and his wife. He is becoming increasingly depressed at his failing health. However, he clings doggedly to the notion he must remain in his home. To do otherwise, he thinks to himself, would mean giving up and accepting certain death. Brutus is aware of the Heavenly Happy Haven Health Care Center, the only nursing home in the area. He has sadly watched some of his friends enter it and dreads the thought of having to go himself. He misses the old days when he was an active breadwinner who loved to play stud poker and drink Miller GD.

Luckily for Brutus, Chenequa is a natural helper[1] who is concerned about her neighbors' well-being and is well acquainted with a series of neighborhood services available for older adults. Chenequa made a "neighborly visit" and forced Brutus to address his needs and situation. Although reticent at first, Brutus succumbed to her persuasive encouragement that his life could be better than it is. She emphasized he would not have to enter a nursing home if he didn't want to.

Chenequa made a number of suggestions regarding how Brutus might tap community resources. First, a local neighborhood center sponsored hot meals each weekday noon for senior residents at nominal cost. Volunteers were available to transport people like Brutus who had difficulty walking even a couple blocks. Brutus had to admit he was tiring of his repetitive diet of baked beans and sauerkraut. Hot cooked meals with some kind of meat sounded pretty good to him. Some company with others his age didn't sound that bad either. The center also sponsored a cooking group that taught citizens basic cooking techniques and provided some free canned goods and other staples.

Chenequa was also aware of a special outreach program sponsored by a local hospital that provided affordable basic medical care for seniors. Seeing a

---

[1] *Natural helpers* are "'ordinary' individuals identified by others in the community as being good listeners and helpers"; natural helpers typically "provide social support consisting of alleviation of social isolation, emotional support (encouragement, reassurance), communication activities (confidante, listening), and problem-centered services (light housekeeping, errands, transportation, cooking)" (Biegel, Shore, & Gordon, 1984, p. 97).

physician there might help Brutus deal more effectively with his arthritis, or, at least, get him some pain medication for those days when it was really bad. The local library sponsored a day periodically when practitioners from a local eye-care center volunteered their time to "screen seniors for cataracts" and provide updated eyeglass prescriptions (Kretzmann & McKnight, 1993, p. 58). The center subsequently discounted seniors' fees for new glasses.

Chenequa indicated that a local church sponsored biweekly lectures and discussion groups on wellness for senior citizens. Brutus expressed some interest in this but indicated he would rather play poker and drink beer. Chenequa noted that another church sponsored bingo parties for seniors, which held more appeal for Brutus.

Chenequa kept popping in on Brutus to see how he was doing. As a result of her efforts and his involvement with a range of neighborhood services and activities, he attained a consequentially better quality of life for a number of years. He significantly benefited from community empowerment.

Chapter 8 provided descriptive and theoretical information about communities and how they function. This chapter focuses on community empowerment. It emphasizes the importance of assessing a geographic community, not only in terms of its problems and needs, but also concerning its strengths and assets.

This chapter will:

- Examine the significance of power in communities, who has it, and why.
- Discuss the importance of citizen participation and social networks.
- Explain natural helping networks.
- Describe personal empowerment, social empowerment, and the relationship between the two.
- Provide a format for assessing communities and describe data-gathering procedures.
- Explain community building and highlight the primary principles involved.
- Explain mapping community assets and suggest methods for collecting information.
- Provide numerous examples of how individuals, groups, associations, organizations, and social institutions can work together for community empowerment.

PEOPLE AND POWER IN COMMUNITIES

As a generalist practitioner, you must understand how communities work. Accurate assessment of community functioning can provide you with a foundation to initiate community change. One aspect of communities that you must understand is power. *Power* is the potential ability to move people on a chosen course to produce an effect or achieve some goal (Homan, 2004;

Martinez-Brawley, 1995). Four concepts are important in this definition. First, power involves *potential* ability or other people's perception that power exists. Even if power is not used, the potential for use is there.

For example, a major religious leader may have the power to influence heavily a decision regarding whether to allow women in the clergy. He might have the power to make this decision independently or to exert pressure upon others to comply with his wishes. However, that same leader may choose to remain neutral on the issue and, hence, not use his potential power. Potential ability means the opportunity to use power is there, but there is no guarantee regarding whether this power will be used or to what extent it will work.

The second concept involved in the definition of power is that of *moving people on a chosen course*. People having power can influence, that is, direct or sway, people's actions, thoughts, or decisions in some desired direction. Consider a practitioner working for a public social service agency who wants that agency to earmark more resources for poor people in the community. She must somehow engender some power to obtain that end. She must write a grant for funding, persuade the agency's board of directors[2] and administrative leaders of the idea's value, or lobby with local politicians to divert funding for her proposal.

The third important concept in the definition of power involves the idea that power is used to *produce an effect or achieve some end*. The worker described above might have specific programmatic ideas about helping poor people in her community. For example, she might think a community food pantry or a homeless shelter is the best way to spend funds after they're attained.

A community's power structure involves "who holds the power and who calls the shots" within a community (Rothman, 1987, p. 312). Rothman (1987) summarizes the importance of attending to and potentially using the community power structure to effect positive change:

> An understanding of the nature of power at the community level is an important consideration for community practitioners. It enables them to determine possible allies or adversaries in relation to given courses of action, and it facilitates the design of strategies stressing either consensus or conflict in regard to a given goal. It provides ongoing guidance in the general process of community appraisal. (p. 312)

Who Has Power in Communities and Why?

At least seven rationales explain why some people in communities have greater power than others. Remember these reasons only reflect potential power. Even a person who has power may or may not get what he wants in the end. The rationales are information, wealth, reputation, high status, decision-making positions, laws and policies, and interpersonal connections.

---

[2] Chapter 3 established that a *board of directors* is a group of people authorized to formulate an organization's mission, objectives, and policies, and to oversee the organization's ongoing activities.

Information (Homan, 2004, p. 186). You might think of the old cliché "knowledge is power." Information provides insight into an issue. It might provide greater access to ideas or help one choose allies to enhance power. For example, perhaps you happen to be a great grant writer and can expertly use the Internet to locate information such as grant sources. This gives you an advantage over someone without this knowledge. It gives you greater power to achieve your goals for acquiring funds. Other examples of people whose access to information gives them power includes "newspaper editors, talk show hosts, educators, gossips, gatekeepers (those who control the flow of information to decision makers), preachers, computer wizards, and political confidants" (Homan, 2004, p. 186).

Wealth (Homan, 2004; Martinez-Brawley, 1995). Think of another old cliché, "money is power." People with lots of money have many more choices regarding how they will live their lives than poor people. Rich people can choose to live in Boca Raton, Florida, Beverly Hills, California, or Aspen, Colorado, if they want. Money provides them with that power.

Likewise, having money affects interaction with those who don't have it. People without enough money must go to other people who have money to get what they need to achieve goals. For example, people who can't afford to pay cash for a home must go to a bank or mortgage broker and apply for a loan. The lending institution has power over those requesting money. It can determine whether a potential borrower is a good credit risk or not. The lender also has the power to determine conditions for the loan, namely, how much interest the borrower must pay in order to use the borrowed money for some designated time period.

Reputation (Martinez-Brawley, 1990, 1995). People who are highly thought of have greater power to influence others than people with shoddy reputations. Consider the milk advertisements in national news magazines where famous athletes, celebrities, and even politicians pose smiling ear to ear with blatant milk mustaches. The advertisers obviously are trying to communicate nonverbally that milk is good for you. You're supposed to believe this based on the celebrities' great reputations.

Liking and respecting a person probably makes you more likely to go along with that person's ideas. This reflects one type of interpersonal power. On the other hand, a politician who you feel has lied to you or participated in some sleazy, unethical behavior probably would not command much of your attention.

High Status (Homan, 2004; Martinez-Brawley, 1990, 1995). People who have high social status can command power over those with less social status. Sometimes, such people are in professional or work positions commanding respect because of their high earnings, their degrees, the difficulty it takes to get these degrees, or their sterling accomplishments. They might be CEOs of huge corporations, supreme court justices, physicians specializing in breakthrough health care arenas, nuclear physicists, astronauts, or university presidents. Other times, people have high status because of popular political support and acclaim. At varying levels, presidents of nations, state governors, and town board chairpersons have positions assuming status because of the popular support necessary to achieve such positions.

Sometimes, conditions for enhancing power overlap. For example, an extremely wealthy automobile manufacturer with a high public profile might command power based on wealth, reputation, and resulting high status. Similarly, the director of the CIA might command power based on ready access to lots of information, popular reputation, and high status related to that position.

Decision-Making Positions (Homan, 2004; Martinez-Brawley, 1990, 1995). People holding important positions in organizational hierarchies have automatic decision-making power as part of their job descriptions. By definition, agency executive directors, company or professional organization presidents, elected politicians, and labor leaders have power and decision-making authority over those below them in their respective hierarchies. People in lower positions are dependent upon those above to make effective decisions regarding how organizations and communities are run.

Laws and Policies (Homan, 2004). Public laws and organizational policies dictate how such macro systems are organized and run. "The ability to make, interpret, and enforce the policies governing a community confers a great measure of authority" (Homan, 2004, p. 187). A law or policy can swiftly determine whether you win or lose a child custody suit or an agency grievance concerning sexual harassment. Being associated with formal legal processes gives politicians power. Greater knowledge about legal issues gives lawyers power. Ability to enforce laws gives police officers power. If the blue and red flashing lights have ever overtaken you as you were passing on a curvy rural road on the yellow line, you would be well aware of how it feels to be at the mercy of legal power. It is even worse when the middle-aged officer says, "You're getting a ticket, young lady" when the "young lady" is 47.

Connections (Homan, 2004). Interpersonal connections and affiliations with others in the community can enhance your power base. This is true concerning both large numbers of contacts and supporters, on the one hand, and fewer but more powerful contacts, on the other. Good ol' boy networks are alive and well, while good ol' girl connections are developing (Homan, 2004). When trying to change a community policy or develop a community service, soliciting others' collaboration and support can significantly strengthen a macro change effort. Other people can provide support, money, votes, information, and extended networking contacts (that is, people they know but you don't).

    Critical Thinking Questions 9.1

Think of a person in your own geographical or university community that has power. What are the sources of that power in terms of the seven described above?

CITIZEN PARTICIPATION

Individuals and people banding together in community groups can develop and wield significant power. *Citizen participation* is the dynamic, voluntary involvement of community members to address issues and concerns affecting their community and improve social policies, laws, and programs. Several aspects of this definition are significant. First, participants are voluntary, that is, they are committed to expend their efforts. Second, the focus is on the community members themselves, not on outside help. Community members work to make their own changes and improvement. Third, members are aware of issues and problems confronting the community. Often, this requires the education of community members by providing factual information and discussing specific change tactics. Fourth, citizen participation targets laws, rules, and regulations affecting the community in order to make them serve the community and its members better.

Social workers who strive to improve community macro systems often employ the concept of citizen participation. Social workers can encourage and enable community members to improve community conditions for themselves. Highlight 9.1 provides examples of how young people can contribute to their communities.

SOCIAL NETWORKS

We have established that interpersonal connections provide people with one source of power. The extent of support, both formal and informal, evident in any community usually contributes strength to community citizens. When residents work together, it's usually easier to get more accomplished than when isolated individuals work alone.

A term related to interpersonal connections is that of a social network. For any individual, a *social network* is a "formal or informal linkage of people or organizations that may share resources, skills, contacts, and knowledge with one another" (Barker, 2003, p. 405). A core concept is the establishment of communication channels with others based on common characteristics, interests, or needs.

Social networks vary according to the number of people involved, the frequency of their contact or communication with each other, how strongly members feel about being part of the network, strength of common bonds or characteristics (such as religious commitment, age, or cultural heritage), and geographic distance among members (Fellin, 2001a). An example of a formal social network is a professional association such as the American Public Human Services Organization. Formal social networks may have established membership dues, prerequisites for membership, or lists of members' names. Note that professional organizations also serve as professional communities. Social networks, however, imply more intercommunication and interaction than the concept of community. One can be a member of a professional community, for example, and have very little involvement with other members.

Highlight 9.1   The Power of Youth

Community involvement is not limited to adult residents. Creative, energetic, concerned young people can also provide great citizen participation and service. Agrest (1997) identifies a number of projects that young people could undertake.

Janet, 8, noticed some of her classmates were going without the clothes, toys, and attention she so much enjoyed. The inequities continued to bother her until age 15 when she took the initiative to visit a shelter for homeless people. There she met many children and gave them gifts of colorful crayons, markers, and paper with which they could draw. Some of the drawings, reflecting their life experiences, were intense, moving, and distressing. For the next half of a year, she continued to visit the shelter on a weekly basis, playing with and reading to the children. Then she got an idea. She organized a group at school to help her carry it out. First, she took the pictures the children had drawn and used them as illustrations on calendars. Her start-up money was about $250, most of which she had earned working part-time. She then organized her schoolmates to sell them. The two purposes were to raise money for the shelter and to educate the public about homelessness. When Janet left for college, she made certain that the club would continue. She trained officers, transferred records, and recruited a faculty advisor.

Scott, 13, was a computer whiz. He sometimes said his classmates considered him a "nerd." But, there he was giving his teachers a two-hour in-service training session on advanced computer technology. He commented that the hard thing was to get his teachers to overcome their fear of the unknown. He conducts two in-service training sessions every year but serves as a free consultant every day. Since the school system has too few resources and personnel to update teachers and train them in the latest technology, he provides the community with a great service. The teachers, in turn, can teach their new skills to their students and improve their teaching.

Jacques, 15, knew that the Special Olympics existed for people with cognitive disabilities, but he never really attended functions or helped out. Jacques was very active in high school basketball, football, and tennis. Accidentally, he found out about Unified Sports, a Special Olympics program that paired people who had a disability with those who performed actively in competitive sports. The intent was to provide opportunities for sports participation and simply to have fun. As Jacques' mother was a special education teacher, he put up a sign-up sheet in her classroom. Seven students with various learning and cognitive disabilities were interested. Jacques then recruited two friends and established the community's first Unified Sports team. Now 200 community citizens are actively involved in Unified Sports basketball, track, soccer, bowling, baseball, and tennis. Jacques still allocates 30 hours each week in a variety of sporting activities.

Yael, 17, attended a multiracial high school in which the student population was 45 percent Hispanic, 24 percent Asian, 25 percent African American, and 6 percent white. She became increasingly distressed by the serious racial tensions engulfing all aspects of school life. Racial groups put pressure on individuals including Yael not to associate across racial lines. More and more fights were breaking out. Finally, Yael had enough. She started with 6 interested people, a number which grew to over 40. Everyday they have lunch together, discussing issues and ideas. She also started publishing a newsletter where students could share their ideas and suggest improvements.

Abdu, 16, was saddened at the condition of a triangular plot of city land compressed where two city streets came together. It was scattered with junk—old refrigerators, tires, twisted pieces of metal that came from who knows what, and basic garbage. One day while reading the paper, Abdu ran across an article describing a national organization aimed at helping poor neighborhoods improve their conditions. It sparked an idea. Why couldn't he get some volunteers and money together to help fix up that miserable piece of property. Abdu worked with school officials, city administrators, other students, teachers, and community residents to completely refurbish the lot into an attractive, well-kept little park. He managed to solicit over $9,500 in donations, grants, and material contributions and helped organize volunteers to develop and use skills. Together, they seeded grass, planted shrubs, erected basketball hoops, and installed playground equipment. Thanks to Abdu's efforts, the community could be proud of its a new park.

Other social networks are informal or more casual associations. Most social networks, for example, are "individuals or groups linked by some common bond, shared social status, similar or shared functions, or geographic or cultural connection" (Barker, 2003, p. 405). Such networks are based on either interest or need and can include family, friends, neighbors, volunteers, or work groups (Barker, 2003; Fellin, 2001a). Usually, there is no formal membership list or hierarchy of authority. An example is an Internet talk group or "chat room" addressing some common interest like Christmas ornament collecting or the hottest Hawaiian fishing spots.

 Critical Thinking Questions 9.2

With what social networks are you involved? In what ways do they serve to support you?

The Relationships Among Power, Citizen Participation, and Social Networks

The concepts of power, citizen participation, and social networks often relate to each other. Community members come together in citizen participation. They form a social network of support for each other and establish their power base. They then can confront a formal power structure (for example, the mayor's office) and pressure this structure to make policies fairer and to distribute community resources more equitably.

Natural Helping Networks

One form of informal social network is the *natural helping network,* a group of nonprofessional people volunteering their time and resources to help either an individual or group of people in need (Barker, 1995; Lewis & Suarez, 1995). The emphasis here is on a network *helping* designated individuals who require resources or support instead of a group networking on the basis of some other common interest. The help usually focuses on at least two functions (Lewis & Suarez, 1995). First, the network can provide support, either emotional or in the form of resources. For example, Zebb, a young man leaving prison on parole, has a natural helping network back in his home community consisting of concerned family members and clergy. Zebb depends on his family to provide a place to live, food, clothing, and emotional support to help him get back on his feet and live independently. A second function of natural helping networks is to provide information and help connect people with other needed resources. Zebb can rely on his rabbi to help link him with potential jobs made available by other members of the synagogue.

One example of establishing a natural helping network in a community neighborhood involves a protective services worker, Olga, who "was aware that a particular neighborhood needed more day care services and had a high incidence of child abuse" (Halley, Kopp, & Austin, 1998, pp. 407–408).[3] Olga received a number of referrals to investigate alleged child maltreatment. She made numerous visits to the neighborhood and talked to many residents. Olga found out that many residents had an excellent grasp of what was happening there, including incidents of family violence and neglect. Olga thought that if she could find out about potentially explosive situations before they "blew," she could help prevent placement of many neighborhood children in foster care.

A number of residents often referred to two strong, independent community women, Lolita and Pat, as "people in the know." They were *natural helpers,* that is, " 'ordinary' individuals identified by others in the community as being good listeners and helpers"; natural helpers typically "provide social support consisting of alleviation of social isolation, emotional support (encouragement, reassurance), communication activities (confidante, listening), and problem-centered services (light housekeeping, errands, transportation, cooking)" (Biegel, Shore, & Gordon, 1984, p. 97).

Lolita and Pat, who were good friends, each managed an eight-family rental property located near a large public housing project. Apparently, community residents, including those in the project, knew that they could turn to Lolita and Pat for help and support when they were down and out. For example, one resident, Jewel, mentioned to Olga that when her 13-year-old daughter became pregnant last year, Lolita lent Jewel money for an abortion. Another neighborhood resident, Lakeesha, told Olga how Pat helped her out last year. When Lakeesha couldn't make the rent one month and was evicted from her tiny apartment, Pat let Lakeesha stay with her for a couple weeks until Lakeesha found another place to live.

Olga contacted Lolita and Pat, set up informal meetings, and talked to them about neighborhood issues. Olga slowly approached them about the possibility of becoming identified neighborhood helpers. She explained that residents would informally come to know such helpers as people to whom they could turn for help, advice, information, and support. Lolita and Pat could act as brokers to link community residents with needed daycare services and other resources aimed at combating child maltreatment. Olga emphasized that she would continue to be available to Lolita and Pat to provide information about resources or intervene in crisis situations they felt were too difficult to handle.

Both Lolita and Pat were wary at first. However, upon understanding Olga's idea more fully, Lolita was flattered. It surprised her that a person representing "the system" would recognize her in this manner. Pat was more

---

[3] This vignette is loosely adapted from one described in *Delivering Human Services: A Learning Approach to Practice* (4th ed.) by A. A. Halley, J. Kopp, and M. J. Austin (New York: Longman, 1998).

hesitant. She didn't feel she was qualified to pull off such a role. After all, Pat told Olga that she only had a high school education.

Olga, Pat, and Lolita continued to talk. They discussed how Pat and Lolita were essentially neighborhood helpers already. The new ideas Olga was suggesting were to reinforce this fact, help spread the word farther, and have Olga provide them with help from a formal institution when they needed it. Pat's and Lolita's relationship with Olga evolved and was strengthened. They effectively put the plan into action for the general betterment of community residents' health and well-being.

The extent of support, both formal and informal, evident in any community usually contributes strength to that community. When residents work together, it's easier to get more accomplished than when isolated individuals work alone.

 Critical Thinking Questions 9.3

Are you aware of any natural helping network in your community? If so, describe it and how it works.

EMPOWERMENT AND COMMUNITIES

We have established that *power* is the potential ability to move people on a chosen course to produce an effect or achieve some goal (Homan, 1995; Martinez-Brawley, 1995). We have also defined *empowerment* as the "process of increasing personal, interpersonal, or political power so that individuals can take action to improve their life situations" (Gutierrez, 2001, p. 210). It involves "an intentional, ongoing process centered in the local community, involving mutual respect, critical reflection, caring, and group participation, through which people lacking an equal share of valued resources gain greater access to and control over those resources" (Cornell University Empowerment Group, 1989, p. 2). Social workers seek to empower client systems, including individuals, families, groups, organizations, and communities, depending on who benefits from the change effort.

Social workers do not hand power over to people. Rather, they help people identify potential courses of action and make decisions about which options result in greater benefits, giving them more power over their own lives and futures. In community settings, social workers can help people become empowered in two basic ways, by achieving personal empowerment and social empowerment (Cowger & Snively, 2002, p. 108).

Personal Empowerment

People have *personal empowerment* when they can directly control what's happening in their own lives. For example, on a simple level, a person can choose whether to order a cherry-chocolate double-nut ice cream cone topped with butterscotch-flavored jimmies or a peanut butter and pumpkin cone covered in chopped walnuts. Likewise, people are empowered when they can choose in which neighborhood they want to live or which job offer to accept.

Social Empowerment

Social empowerment is the condition in the social environment where people have access to opportunities and resources in order to make personal choices and maintain some control over their environment. Personal empowerment is limited if people don't first possess social empowerment. Laws and policies often regulate people's ability to make choices. For example, people under age 18 do not have the right to vote. Thus, they do not have the social empowerment necessary to provide input for selecting government officials.

Similarly, several decades ago many southern states restricted the use of water fountains either to people of color or white people. People were not empowered in the social environment to make their own decision regarding which water fountain to use. People choosing to use the one not designated for persons with their skin color potentially subjected themselves to severe criticism, ridicule, and even physical endangerment.

Still another example involves professional women working in an agency setting. Agency decision makers follow an unspoken rule that women make ineffective supervisors and administrators because of stereotyped gender-related characteristics. For example, administrators think women get crabby when they have their periods or they aren't strong enough to back up their decisions. Thus, women in that agency are not empowered to move up the career ladder. They do not have social empowerment.

The prior examples of social empowerment or the lack thereof primarily involve opportunities. People can also gain social empowerment by having adequate access to resources. Resources and opportunity are often integrally entwined. For example, people who earn minimum wages do not have the option of buying Rolex watches and Porsches or of living across from Central Park in Manhattan (unless they're servants or enjoy rent freezes established many years ago). Likewise, consider people who live in poverty-stricken areas that provide relatively poor educational backgrounds. School systems might have extremely large class sizes, giving teachers little chance of giving students individual attention. Scarce resources result in fewer educational supplies and limited access to current technology. Because of poorer educational preparation, students attending such schools are less likely to do as well on college entrance examinations and, therefore, are less likely to be accepted into college. Additionally, the poorer people are, the more difficulty they have paying for higher education and vocational training. Statistics clearly establish that the more education you have, the higher your income is likely to be. Lack of current resources subsequently blocks the acquisition of future resources.

The Interrelationship of Personal and Social Empowerment

Individual and social empowerment are interrelated. It is often hard to determine where one leaves off and the other begins. When a person has social empowerment, it is much more possible to enjoy personal empowerment by exercising personal choice. More personal choices are available.

Community empowerment is a primary social work task. We have established that people are not isolated individuals doing whatever they want like mosquitoes buzzing around potential targets. Rather, each aspect of life depends on people's involvement in the communities, organizations, and groups encompassing them. The macro social environment sets the stage for what resources and opportunities are available. A focus on community empowerment enhances professional social workers' ability to help people gain better access to resources, opportunities, and, subsequently, choices.

ASSESSMENT OF COMMUNITIES

Essentially, there are two ways of looking at a community in order to understand it (Kretzmann & McKnight, 1993: Naparstek & Dooley, 1997; Rapp, 1998; Saleebey, 2002). First, there is the traditional focus on *community problems and needs*. This problem- or deficit-based perspective directs social workers' focus to stressing what's wrong or missing in a situation. "*Need identification* describes health and social service requirements in a geographic or social area, whereas *need assessment* is aimed at estimating the relative importance of these needs" (Siegel, Attkisson, & Carson, 2001, p. 105). (Note that the process is also referred to as *needs* assessment.)

Consider the terms "South Bronx," "South Central L.A.," or "public housing," which, for many, prompt immediate thoughts of a host of problems—gangs, poverty, substance abuse, crime, unemployment, welfare, homelessness, truancy, slums, child maltreatment, broken families, and poor health care (Kretzmann & McKnight, 1993, p. 2). An analogy is looking at a glass as being half empty instead of half full (Kretzmann & McKnight, 1993). Not only is this problem-focused perspective overwhelming, but it encourages a spectrum of segmented services each aimed at addressing some designated, isolated problem or need. Service is provided to eligible individuals who may see themselves as service consumers or victims with little or no power to control their own destiny.

For example, a Protective Services agency may see Nicole, 20, as a client who appears to be using illegal drugs and is neglecting her two small daughters. The agency's primary goal is to stop the neglect. Its purpose is to ensure survival rather than to improve Nicole's overall quality of life. Agency workers may refer Nicole to counseling, a parent effectiveness training group, or a substance abuse program, and help her receive a public assistance grant. They might threaten to place her children in foster care. However, with large caseloads, there may be little they can do to help Nicole get her G.E.D. (general education diploma or high school equivalency), seek employment with good health care benefits, find adequate daycare, locate better housing, improve her cooking and child-caring skills, or provide her with an improved social support system. With Nicole, service provision to meet specific individual needs or address designated problems is the focus.

An alternative to viewing a community and its clients from a problem-focused perspective is appraisal of and emphasis on *assets and strengths*. *Mapping assets* is an assessment of a community that emphasizes that community's "capacities, skills, and assets" instead of the community's problems and weaknesses (Kretzmann and McKnight, 1993, p. 5). This approach stresses the importance of looking at the strengths of individuals, community organizations, and social institutions[4] when analyzing any community. It helps practitioners focus on what's going right for people in a community, what resources exist, and what opportunities might be developed. Capacity building then can result. *Capacity building* "is the ability to increase the leadership and organizational skills of local people for the purpose of strengthening their own organizations and networking capacities" (Gamble & Hoff, 2005, p. 178). By identifying and focusing on a community's and its residents' assets, you can build people's capacity to empower themselves and improve their life and living conditions.

Nicole, introduced earlier, for example, has strengths including love for her children, a foundation of parenting and homemaking skills upon which to build, friends and two sisters in the community who might help and support her, completion of her sophomore year in high school, and a strong desire to keep her two little girls. Potential community organizations to which she might turn for support include an outpatient substance abuse clinic, a vocational education and job placement program, daycare centers, support groups for single mothers held at the local YWCA,[5] and a church to which she belongs. Local institutions potentially available for her and her children's use include public social services, the school system (including an adult education program), hospitals, libraries, and parks.

The following sections will discuss community assessment. First, the many dimensions of a community will be identified that will help you understand its essence and how it functions. This kind of information forms the basis for a needs assessment. The final two sections will focus on approaches concerned with community empowerment, community building and mapping assets.

---

[4] We've established that a *social institution* is an established and valued practice or means of operation in a society resulting in the development of a formalized system to carry out its purpose. Examples include "religion, the family, military structures, government, and the social welfare system" (Barker, 2003, p. 404).

[5] YWCA (Young Women's Christian Association), established more than 150 years ago, refers to organizations around the world that serve to "eliminate racism and empower women" by providing education, social activities, recreation, and other types of support (YWCA, 2006) in the pursuit of "justice, peace, health, human dignity, freedom, and care for the environment" (World YWCA, 2006).

UNDERSTANDING THE DIMENSIONS OF A COMMUNITY

There are many dimensions of a community to explore that are important to fully understand that community. Questions posed here should provide a foundation for how to identify and subsequently assess community needs. Sheafor and Horejsi (2003, pp. 241–242) propose 14 dimensions to consider.

1. *Identifying information.* Identify the names given to various parts of the community. Are different areas known for having their own characteristics? For example, if it's a larger community, is there an industrial area with several factories? Are there some neighborhoods characterized by blue-collar families and others by wealthy professionals and business people? Does one section have a university with its accompanying academic and student populations and activities? Where is the community located with respect to other communities, towns, and cities? Is it relatively isolated or close to other communities that could provide resources and services?

2. *Demographics.* What are the community's boundaries and basic demographic characteristics (Netting, Kettner, & McMurtry, 2004; Rubin & Rubin, 2001; Sheafor & Horejsi, 2003). Think about the type of community it is. This includes determining the community's *population size* (the total number of persons living in a designated community), *density* (the ratio of people living within a particular space), and *heterogeneity* (the extent to which community members have diverse characteristics). What ethnic groups live in the community? Do they speak languages other than English?

3. *History of area.* How old is the community? How has it developed over time? What changes have occurred regarding who has populated the area? Have certain groups moved away and others moved in? If so, why?

4. *Geography and environmental influences on community.* What kind of environment encompasses the community (Rubin & Rubin, 2001)? Is it in the middle of the central prairies, connected by interstate highways with other communities at great distances? Is it located on an ocean, major river, or one of the Great Lakes, where shipping and boating are primary economic and recreational activities respectfully? Is it located in the mountains where winter might cause transportation difficulties? Are there recreational areas such as parks available? To what extent is the community experiencing environmental hazards like pollution, smog, or tainted water, or deprivations like power shortages?

5. *Beliefs and attitudes.* What are the "cultural values, traditions, and beliefs" that matter to various segments of the population (Netting et al., 2004, p. 203)? What are the spiritual and political values of the various factions of community residents? What social service agencies are available in the community and how do residents receive and value them? To what extent do residents feel an integral and supported part of the community? Or do they feel isolated and alone?

6. *Local politics.* How is the government structured? For example, cities, towns, and counties can be structured quite differently in terms of who

has decision-making power and control. Are there any major issues currently under debate? For example, residents might have conflicting views regarding paying for a new middle school or rezoning a residential area to a business one.

7. *Local economy and businesses.* What businesses, factories, and other sources of employment characterize the community? Is the local economy thriving or in a major slump? Are businesses owned by local residents or huge conglomerates based in other states? What kinds of jobs exist in the community? Do people work inside the community or simply live there and work somewhere else (Rubin & Rubin, 2001)? Is there adequate public transportation for people to get to and from work? What is the unemployment rate?

8. *Income distribution.* To what extent do community residents receive cash and in-kind (goods and services) public assistance benefits? What are the median income levels for men, women, and various ethnic groups? What percentage of people live in poverty?

9. *Housing.* What are housing conditions like in the community? Is it a relatively new community with low population density. Or it is an aging, economically deprived community with a high population density and deteriorating, dilapidated housing? What are the "types of housing" characterizing the area ("for example, single-family dwellings, apartments, public housing") (Sheafor & Horejsi, 2003, p. 242)? What are average rents and costs for real estate? Is there a shortage of low income housing?

10. *Educational facilities and programs.* An educational system can be assessed in at least four ways. The first involves its context. What is the educational system like? Are schools well supported by the community, or are they experiencing funding cut after funding cut? Where and in what types of neighborhoods are schools located? Are they public, private, or charter schools? A *charter school* is a public school supported by tax dollars but allowed to be managed "(chartered) outside of the public school bureaucracy as long as it complied with specified regulations and guidelines" (Barker, 2003, p. 65).

The second way an educational system can be assessed involves its treatment of special populations of children (Naparstek & Dooley, 1997) and its attention to cultural differences. How are children with special needs treated? To what extent are programs available for preschool children to prepare them for school entry? For instance, are Headstart programs available? Are there diagnostic and treatment services available for children who have developmental disabilities? Are schools perceptive regarding the ethnic and cultural makeup of their students? Do they celebrate or discourage diversity?

A third way to assess the functioning of a community's educational system is the extent to which the school system enables students to do well (Naparstek & Dooley, 1997, p. 83). How do children typically score on standardized achievement tests compared to other communities in the United States and Canada? How well do community students compete with students from other communities in events such as science fairs, spelling competitions, and other contests? How well prepared for high school and college are students? How many students graduate and go on to college? Does elementary school provide them with a solid foundation for future levels of higher education, vocational education, and job training? What is the drop-out rate?

A fourth assessment aspect concerns a community educational system's attention to its adult residents (Naparstek & Dooley, 1997). On the one hand, to what extent do parents understand their children's development? On the other, how well do community educational programs adequately prepare adults to enter the labor force?

11. *Health and welfare systems.* A community's strengths concerning residents' health primarily involves access to and quality of care. Are there adequate numbers of health professionals and specialists? Are hospitals and clinics readily accessible to area residents? Are residents adequately covered by private insurance or public programs? Especially important is "the prevention and treatment of those conditions that afflict inner-city and poor people of color at disproportionate rates" (Naparstek & Dooley, 1997, p. 84).

What social service programs are available and where are they located? What specific types of services exist (for example, crisis intervention, substance abuse treatment, and public assistance)? How accessible and well publicized are these programs? To what extent are they adequate, or are there substantial gaps in service? To what extent are "service providers sensitive to special needs or concerns of minority and ethnic groups" (Sheafor & Horejsi, 2003, p. 242)? If the community has non-English-speaking residents, are translators available? Are "self-help groups and informal helping networks" available in the community (Sheafor & Horejsi, 2003, p. 242)?

12. *Public safety and justice system.* To what extent are "police and fire protection" adequate (Sheafor & Horejsi, 2003, p. 243)? To what extent is the environment safe? Are housing standards and codes being followed? How do community residents view "local police, courts, and correctional programs" (Sheafor & Horejsi, 2003, p. 243)? Are the public safety and justice systems sensitive to the needs and issued faced by minorities in the community?

13. *Sources of information and public opinion.* Are there "influential TV and radio stations and newspapers to which the people look for information and perspectives on current events" (Sheafor & Horejsi, 2003, p. 243)? We have established that knowledge is power. It is therefore important to ask how members of the community learn what is going on in the community as well as in the world at large (Rubin & Rubin, 2001, p. 157). Are there neighborhood organizations or other active community groups whose purposes are to keep on top of what's going on within the community? For example, are residents aware that commercial developers are planning to build a toxic waste plant in the near vicinity? Do

residents know that school classroom populations have climbed to a ratio of 1 teacher for every 45 students? Do community members know about a job training program subsidized by the County and targeting people in need?

To what extent does the community have human resources? *Human resources* are the knowledge and abilities characterizing some people that can be used to enhance other people's quality of life (Barker, 2003). Human resources are people who can act as advocates, initiators, planners, educators, leaders, and workers for positive social changes. Are there significant community political, religious, or other informal community leaders who speak for various subgroups and minorities in the population and to whom people look to for help and support?

14. *Summary assessment of community issues.* What is your overall assessment of the community's functioning? To what extent is it good or inadequate? What serious social problems (for example, "inadequate housing, inadequate public transportation, lack of jobs, youth gangs, poverty, teen pregnancy, domestic abuse, etc.") do community residents face (Sheafor & Horejsi, 2003, p. 243)? What primary "gaps" are evident in "social, health care, and educational services" (Sheafor & Horejsi, 2003, p. 243)?

 Critical Thinking Questions 9.4

How would you analyze your own community in terms of these 14 criteria? How would you summarize the information? What are your community's primary problems, needs, and strengths?

Highlight 9.2 discusses ways to gather data about a community.

COMMUNITY BUILDING

Community building, a vital concept in an empowerment approach, is the process of enhancing a community's strengths by linking community residents, community organizations, and external resources to tackle community problems and working together toward positive change (Chaskin, Joseph, & Chipenda-Dansohkho, 1998; Ewalt, Freeman, & Poole, 1998; Naparstek & Dooley, 1997, 1998). All communities obviously have problems and needs. The trick is to scrutinize potential strengths, often easily overlooked, and to get relevant entities to work together on behalf of community growth and improvement. Saleebey (2002a) explains:

Community building refers to the reality and possibility of restoring or refurbishing the sense and reality of community in neighborhoods. It involves among other things helping neighbors—individuals, families, and associations—in a

| **Highlight 9.2** | **How To Gather Data About A Community** |

There are many ways of collecting data to assess a community. Three will be introduced here that are often used in conducting a needs assessment.

First, you can hold a *community forum,* which is "an open meeting of all members of a community" (Siegel et al., 2001, p. 120). Any community member may be a valuable source of information. "The perspectives of residents concerning the accessibility, availability, acceptability, and organization of services comprise indispensable clues about the human service needs of the community as a whole" (p. 119). Although probably no individual can give you the "total picture" of what a community needs, he or she might provide some valuable insights. Getting information from a variety of residents can result in a general picture of community needs.

A second needs assessment approach is the *nominal group technique* (Siegel et al., 2001; Zastrow, 2006). Here group members are gathered and asked to silently "list their needs on paper without group discussion" so that "each member's personal views can be ascertained" without influence from the others (Zastrow, 2006, p. 94). Members are asked to write down what they feel are the community's major needs. After members have completed their list, the group leader asks them to go around one at a time and share one of their ideas with the rest of the

group. Ideas are then recorded on a blackboard, on large sheets of paper, or electronically so that they are visible to the group. After all ideas have been recorded, group members participate in a discussion regarding their feelings about the needs that have been shared. After the leader determines that discussion has been adequate, he or she asks group members to prioritize and write down what they feel are the community's most pressing needs. The leader then collects the lists and can combine them to determine the group's overall impression of community needs.

A third needs assessment approach is the *key informant technique* (Kirst-Ashman & Hull, 2006a; Siegel et al., 2001). Here 10 to 15 individuals are identified "who have extensive first-hand knowledge of the community and who either live or work in the community" (Siegel et al., 2001, p. 126). Participants might include service providers such as police officers or teachers, residents who have resided in the community a long time and have been active in community activities, and workers in community service agencies. Participants who serve as key informants are then interviewed in depth concerning their perceptions of community needs. A summary regarding their impression of community needs can subsequently be established.

community strengthen relationships with one another usually around mutually crafted projects. The idea is to replace the notion that they must be completely dependent on outside or professional organizations and institutions for help with the assumptions that they have internal assets and capacities that can be developed and used in increasing the human and social capital of the community. The upshot of this is an increase in the sense of self-efficacy and power in the individuals, families, and associations of the community—they believe that they can make things happen! (p. 241)

Naparstek and Dooley (1997) emphasize four major principles in establishing a healthy, productive, integrated community: working together, developing new allegiances working in cooperation, targeting neighborhoods, and building on neighborhood strengths.

Working Together

First, community building involves many components of a community and other systems with which it's involved working synchronously together. If community resource systems don't work together, nothing much gets done. For example, a community high school may have a strong vocational component aimed at training for and placing students in jobs upon graduation. Related components are adequate employment opportunities, affordable housing, and availability of health care. The high school's efforts are virtually useless if no adequately paying jobs for high school graduates exist in the area and no public transportation is available for workers to get to jobs located elsewhere. What good is a job if no affordable housing is available? Where would workers live? Or, how useful is it to get a young single parent of a chronically ill child a job paying minimum wages and offering no health care benefits? She wouldn't make nearly enough to cover even minimal health expenses and keep her family afloat financially anyway.

New Alliances and Cooperation

A second principle basic to community building is that it requires new alliances and cooperation. These relationships involve both those among agencies within the community and those between community agencies and external larger systems.

The first dimension of this principle, *internal cooperation* among community organizations and groups, might involve new creative ways in which they can work together to serve residents. For example, a church, YMCA,[6] and outpatient substance abuse counseling center might combine their efforts in outreach for youth. They might work together contributing staff time, resources, and space to establish a program offering a series of services. These may include drug education provided by counseling center staff at the church and YMCA, supervised social activities cosponsored by all three agencies, space provided by the YMCA for recreational activities for youth involved in both church groups and abuse counseling, and publicity developed and distributed by the church and YMCA. These three agencies have no formal connections with each other. Yet, they could potentially work together to establish a unified program available to a wide spectrum of community youth.

Another dimension of establishing new alliances in community building is *external cooperation*. This concerns how organizations and groups in the community must work well together with external macro systems in order to meet community needs. Community residents know what they need and are experts on how public resource systems work or do not work on their behalf. A high-level white male policy maker in Washington, D.C. likely has little insight into the life of a single African American mother of three who has an eleventh-grade education and lives in a tiny two-room apartment in a huge urban hub. How could that administrator know the myriad of details and problems she

[6]*YMCA* (Young Men's Christian Association), initiated over 150 years ago, refers to organizations in over 120 countries that provide a wide range of educational, recreational, social, and supportive services to community residents including "all people of all faiths, races, ages, abilities and incomes" (YMCA, 2006).

must address everyday to stay alive? There's a crack house next door. She's afraid of what would happen to her kids if they wander too near the dealers and the addicts. Prostitutes walk the streets every night. She's not certain how well her baby-sitter attends to her kids while she's at work. She can just barely make the rent and the grocery bill each week. She's afraid to tell the landlord someone broke her back window because she fears he might evict her. Sometimes, she's late with the rent and doesn't want to make any waves.

The point is that community residents usually have the best understanding about what affects their lives. They really need to provide input into decisions made far above in the bureaucratic structure that have major and sometimes ominous effects on their lives. Hence, we heavily emphasize community resident involvement and leadership.

However, major resources flow into communities from larger city, state, and national macro systems. Communities depend on these resources. Bureaucratic structures are complicated, and regulations for funding distribution complex. Communities don't have the power and influence to formulate policies and make decisions about how public funds at national and state levels are spent. Community residents and leaders generally have a more limited perspective on what's going on outside of their community and "are less likely to produce the comprehensive policy changes that are needed to address more complex realities" (Naparstek & Dooley, 1997, p. 80). Therefore, community residents and leaders must work together with decision makers in external systems to understand processes and obtain resources the community deserves.

The Importance of Targeting Neighborhoods

The third principle involved in community building is the importance of targeting neighborhoods to undertake positive change on behalf of the community. Successful macro changes "must focus on a distinct geographic area whose residents are linked by, and who identify with, a cluster of local institutions such as schools, churches, or community centers" (Naparstek & Dooley, 1997, p. 81). Chapter 10 examines more thoroughly how neighborhoods function and can empower residents.

Building on Neighborhood Strengths

Neighborhoods are central to the fourth salient principle in community building. The foundation for positive macro change rests on neighborhood strengths and assets. Neighborhood residents know the most about their needs. They have much in common in that they experience similar living conditions. The basic social work values of self-determination and empowerment dictate that neighborhood residents should have maximum choices about what happens in their own lives.

Mapping assets is a tool to prepare for community building. A subsequent section elaborates upon this approach.

MAPPING COMMUNITY ASSETS AND EMPOWERMENT

Earlier we indicated that Kretzmann and McKnight (1993) have established a capacity-building approach to community assessment called *mapping assets*. It emphasizes the community's "capacities, skills, and assets" instead of the community's problems and weaknesses (p. 5). *Assets* are potential persons, groups, and resources in a community that can help a community function and grow. It contrasts with the community-assessment approach we reviewed earlier that focused primarily on figuring out a community's problems and gaps in services. Saleebey (2002) explains mapping assets:

> Three principles define this approach. First, it is *assets and strengths based*. Community workers start with what resources are present in the community and not with what is missing, what is wrong, or what the community needs. Second, this approach to community development is internally focused. That is, it is very important to know what is going on within the community, what assets are available, and what individual and group capacities exist. The role of external factors and institutions is, for the time being, ignored. Rather the focus on the inner life of the community demonstrates the centrality of local control, local capital, local vision, and local ownership. Finally, if the first two elements of the assets-based scheme are to hold, then the process must clearly be relationship driven. If people are to be pulled into the life of the community and share their capacities, it will be done through the medium of relationship. A gift is given from hand to hand. (p. 236)

Mapping assets concerns at least two domains—"releasing individual capacities" and empowering local associations, organizations, and institutions (Kretzmann & McKnight, 1993, p. 13).

Releasing Individual Capacities

Each community resident has positive qualities and capacities that can contribute to the community's well-being. If those capacities are identified and appreciated by fellow citizens, the individual will feel like an important community member who feels a sense of connection with other citizens. Kretzmann and McKnight (1993) provide a detailed framework for assessing individual capacities that can be administered to a community resident. These capacities reflect many dimensions of abilities and skills.[7]

Health   Individuals, family members, neighbors, or volunteers can provide help to those who need it in a community. This may take the form of assisting people who are seniors, have mental illness, have physical or cognitive disabilities, or have other health problems.

---

[7]Note that the headings of *health, construction and repair, maintenance,* and *food* were taken directly from Kretzmann and McKnight (1993, pp. 19–21). Ideas presented under *administrative and interpersonal work skills,* and *assistance in daily activities* were also based on those presented in this source.

Administrative and Interpersonal Work Skills   Individuals may also have organization and office skills that could help in developing a neighborhood organization or supporting a social service or health care agency through volunteering. Such skills might include computer proficiency, budgeting, planning, telephone communication, marketing and sales, writing reports, and organizing data and records.

Construction and Repair   Being handy at building and fixing things can be helpful. Repairing buildings, improving homes, and fixing electrical and plumbing fixtures are skills that can contribute to community well-being. Consider Habitat for Humanity, an international organization whose overarching goal is "to eliminate poverty housing and homelessness from the face of the earth by building adequate and basic housing" (Habitat for Humanity, 2005). To do this, the organization solicits donations from sponsors and help from volunteers. People skilled in construction and repair have valuable assets to contribute.

Kretzmann and McKnight (1993) provide another example involving how a "group of residents in a public housing project organized and became powerful enough to gain control of their buildings." They describe how "their association took over the management and finances of the project" and how subsequently "they were able to employ residents to carry out the maintenance functions such as painting rooms, fixing broken windows, running a laundromat, etc." (p. 26). The group used information from a questionnaire addressing individuals' assets to identify who had which strengths, skills, and assets (p. 19).

Even without working within a formal structure, community residents can help their neighbors by using specific skills. Staff in one community social services organization wrote and received a grant for starting a tool library. Community residents could "take out" tools and use them for household construction and repair. They later would return them to the tool library, as they would books from a library.

Maintenance   Community residents may contribute time and effort to help maintain and clean up buildings, parks, and public facilities. For example, various groups, businesses, or families volunteer to clean up garbage along highways in Adopt-a-Highway programs. Or a group of community residents could volunteer to renovate a park area.

Food   Some people are skilled at food preparation. People can volunteer to set up, cook, barbeque, and clean up for a neighborhood picnic or other community event.

Recreation and Entertainment   Community volunteers could organize sports teams and events for youth or adults. One neighborhood organization in an impoverished community of a large city established sports teams for high school–age youth. This provided an excellent alternative to participating in illegal and idle activities. All participants were required to maintain at least a

B average in school. Volunteer coaches were supportive and worked hard at reinforcing positive behavior, not only on the court, but also in terms of conflict resolution and interpersonal skills. The tallest team member was only 6'2", which, as we know, is not very tall in the basketball world. However, the team managed to make it to and compete in the national championship against players who loomed above them. Although they didn't quite win, they became the much-applauded and well-respected underdogs. They beamed with self-confidence and pride at their accomplishments.

Some community residents may be musically talented. They can organize into an orchestra or a band and give concerts or play during parades. One neighborhood resident was highly skilled at playing the piano. She gave monthly concerts to all neighbors who were interested in attending.

Assistance in Daily Activities   There are many other arenas of life where community residents can help each other. Working parents might provide child care for each other. Or senior residents might volunteer to provide daycare for children. A resident with a car could volunteer to take another resident who doesn't have one to a doctor's appointment. One neighbor could mow another neighbor's lawn or help change the oil in his car. One community member might help another with sewing or mending clothing.

Anything Else   Potential sources of individual assets and contributions are infinite. Asking individuals what they feel their strengths are and how they could help might result in answers that never would've occurred to you.

Critical Thinking Questions 9.5

How would you assess your own individual capacities with respect to the dimensions cited above? What do you consider as your most important three assets?

Highlight 9.3 suggests ways to undertake mapping assets in a community.

Mapping Assets of Associations, Organizations, and Institutions: Forming Community Linkages

After it's determined what associations, organizations, and institutions exist in the community by using processes such as those suggested in Highlight 9.3, a list of strengths can be established for each organization. Creative ideas about how to get these systems to work together to provide services and meet needs are endless. For example, each organization may have assets including "personnel," "space and facilities," "materials and equipment," "expertise," and "economic power" (Kretzmann & McKnight, 1994, pp. 144–145). Personnel, of course, are people who are members of an organization or who work for an

| Highlight 9.3 | **Mapping Assets of Local Associations, Organizations, and Institutions: Gathering Information** |

In addition to assessing individual capacities, it is important to find out what associations, organizations, and institutions exist in the community and how they function; there are at least four ways to do this. First, look to media such as newspapers and newsletters for printed information (Kretzmann & McKnight, 1993). Service directories might be available. The internet also is an excellent source of information. Most agencies have Web pages.

A second way to find out about community services is to use the library. "Your public library has a treasure trove of information about your community, and so does your college or university library," reflects Homan (2004).

> Prepare some questions in advance. This will give the librarian a better idea of how to help you. It will also help you focus your inquiry. . . . Most librarians are very helpful. Not only do they know books and where to find them, but they enjoy helping people uncover information and discover the other wonders of their library, such as audiovisual resources, computer data banks, and much more. (p. 167)

A third way to gather information about services and organizations is to talk "to people at local institutions" such as parks and churches (Kretzmann &

McKnight, 1993, p. 113). To what groups do people belong in the community? These may be political, recreational, volunteer, or social. You can also contact individual leaders of various organizations for their insights. Finally, you can simply start conversations with people you run into as you go about your daily business (Homan, 2004). You might be sitting at the bus stop or standing in line at Wal-Mart. Informal conversation can provide you with valuable insights and ideas.

A fourth means of gathering information about services is to conduct a telephone survey (Homan, 2004; Kretzmann & McKnight, 1993). A "scientific sampling procedure" should be used so that "answers from a modest number of people can be generalized to a larger number with a specified degree of accuracy" (Rubin & Rubin, 2001, p. 181). There are several other suggestions for enhancing the effectiveness of surveys (Rubin & Rubin, 2001). Make certain that the questions are clear and that respondents can clearly understand their meaning. Only collect the information that you really need. Don't waste respondents' and your time. Make sure that the categories of answers are simple and distinct. For example, "strongly agree," "mildly agree," "mildly disagree," and "strongly disagree." Use open-ended questions carefully because you might get much too much information or information that's irrelevant.

organization. They reflect a potential for volunteer service. Space and facilities refer to rooms that are not being used all the time. An organization may give other organizations and groups access to space at unused times. An organization may also have a special space such as a gym that it could share when not in use. Materials and equipment include copying machines, writing utensils, computers, kitchens, tables, chairs, DVD equipment, and sports equipment (Kretzmann & McKnight, 1993). Any of these could be shared with other groups. Expertise means specialized knowledge or skills that also can be shared with other groups and organizations. Finally, economic power means access to resources. Organizations may have membership dues or contributions, grant money, or the ability to conduct fund-raising activities.

Community associations, organizations, and institutions can use these assets to work together with other groups and organizations to benefit community residents, both as groups and as individuals. For instance, a religious organization can provide space for Alcoholics Anonymous support group meetings or recreational activities for community youth. (*Alcoholics Anonymous* is a nationwide self-help organization, also sponsoring chapters in many other countries, that provides support, information, and guidance necessary for many recovering alcoholics to maintain their recovery process.) Similarly, a church can sponsor a fund-raising drive for a homeless shelter.

Public parks can be used in conjunction with other community groups and organizations to sponsor activities and provide space. For example, a park offered it's meeting room facility to a group of seniors for their weekly support meeting; another worked with a local museum to sponsor displays and offer crafts classes (Kretzmann & McKnight, 1993).

Schools provide communities with another source of strengths and assets; consider the following examples (Kretzmann & McKnight, 1993). A school can work with a local hospital to provide an opportunity for health professionals to offer pregnancy prevention information. A retired business executive offers to provide tutoring to students at a school. A school's chorus gives concerts to nursing home residents.

Police departments provide yet another source of community assets, as illustrated by the following examples (Kretzmann & McKnight, 1993). Police officers distribute Thanksgiving turkeys provided by a local grocery among senior and "blind neighborhood residents" (p. 249). Police provide training in tactics to reduce substance abuse at a local high school. A police department works together with local neighborhood associations to motivate "at-risk" children by rewarding them with bicycles for improved school performance (p. 247). In reaction to a crime wave in an urban community, police work with neighborhood residents to establish an information network. Residents telephone others they've been assigned to announce when safety meetings are being held in local churches.

Hospitals also provide a source of community assets (Kretzmann & McKnight, 1993). For example, a hospital works with local churches to sponsor and publicize blood pressure screenings at the religious facilities or supports a Hispanic culture festival with Hispanic neighborhood associations at a local park. Another hospital hires a person with mild cognitive disabilities to do filing in one of its administrative offices.

Community colleges and universities are yet another source of community assets (Kretzmann & McKnight, 1993). For example, faculty can provide educational presentations on any number of topics to community groups. One college established a lecture series presented each fall at a nearby nursing home. One instructor who was certified in sex education volunteered to help a residential treatment center for male adolescents with severe behavioral and emotional problems develop a sex education program. Highlight 9.4 provides a more detailed example of macro systems—including a university—working together.

 ## Critical Thinking Questions 9.6

What ways does your college or university work with individuals, groups, and organizations in the community to empower the community?

| Highlight 9.4 | A Case Example: Macro Systems Working Together |

Improving communities often requires creative thinking about how to use existing political and other public structures, residents' energy, and other resources. One example is the unlikely association between a Housing Authority in a large, well-established, southern city and a major university in that city—"a highly selective, overwhelmingly white, old-line Southern school situation in a picturesque neighborhood" (Gwynne, 1998, p. 74). The city's "government-subsidized apartments were consistently rated among the country's worst" (Gwynne, 1998, p. 74). One of the largest projects having 1,800 apartment units, ironically named Desire, was infamous as one of the worst in the country.

Gwynne (1998) explains the scenario. The Housing Authority, a 58-year-old agency, was "a political hornet's nest of patronage and chronic mismanagement" that "was so inept at making repairs that tenants routinely waited years for simple services. Hundreds of tenements were literally falling down" (Gwynne, 1998, p. 74). At its wits' end, the Housing Authority had two choices. It could either put the projects under the authority of a federal judge or find some outside agent to take control. A major university in the city turned out to be that outside agent. Many might ask, "What does a university know about running public housing projects?" Apparently, a lot.

University representatives approached the U.S. Bureau of Housing and Urban Development (HUD)

with a proposal to assist with one project. HUD and the mayor of the city took it much further and gave the university authority over 10 projects and 55,000 residents. The new association allowed for the newly appointed Housing Authority vice-president to reorganize the agency's total structure and approach.

First tasks included expelling drug dealers and criminals, drastically reducing the backlog of residents' requests for service, and dramatically improving how long it took to get repairs like plumbing leaks and broken windows accomplished. Instead of months and years, such repairs now might take days or even hours. Future plans included building new, better single-family apartment units after tearing down old, dilapidated ones.

Importantly, the university and the Housing Authority worked closely with the projects' resident association. Community residents became actively involved in running the projects where they lived. Additionally, they helped with maintenance, security, and finding residents employment.

Hundreds of university faculty and students volunteered to provide residents with tutoring and information on "health, parenting, job training, teen pregnancy and high school equivalency" (Gwynne, 1998, p. 74). The volunteers have helped hundreds of adult residents find jobs and placed hundreds of young people in basketball and other sports programs.

CHAPTER SUMMARY

This chapter focused on the importance of power in communities. It examined who tends to have power and why. Sources of power include information, wealth, reputation, high status, decision-making positions, laws and policies, and connections. The importance of citizen participation and social networks including natural helping networks was stressed. The relationships among power, citizen participation, and social networks were described.

Personal empowerment, social empowerment, and the relationship between the two were explained. Personal empowerment involves

having direct control over one's life. Social empowerment is the condition in the social environment where people have access to opportunities and resources in order to make personal choices and maintain some control over their environment.

Communities may be assessed by focusing on problems and needs, on the one hand, or strengths and assets on the other. Dimensions of a community important to understand include identifying information about the community, demographics, history, geography and environment influences, beliefs and attitudes, local politics, local economy and businesses, income distribution, housing, educational facilities and programs, health and welfare systems, public safety and justice system, sources of information and public opinion, and a summary assessment. Data can be gathered using the community forum, nominal group, and key informant techniques.

Community building focuses on working together, new alliances and cooperation, the importance of targeting neighborhoods, and building on neighborhood strengths. Community mapping assets involves identifying individual capacities, including those involving health care and assistance, administrative and interpersonal work skills, construction and repair, maintenance, food, recreation and entertainment, assistance in daily activities, and anything else you can think of. Mapping assets in community associations, organizations, and institutions involves looking at personnel, space and facilities, materials and equipment, expertise, and economic power. Sources of assets include religious organizations, public parks, schools, police departments, hospitals, and community colleges and universities. Data can be collected by consulting the media, using libraries, talking to people at local institutions, and conducting telephone surveys.

Neighborhood Empowerment

Neighborhoods and neighborhood centers can improve the quality of life in communities. Here neighborhood residents work together to paint a mural on a community center wall.

CHAPTER CONTENTS

Neighborhood residents can:

- *Start up a new radio station that plays ethnic music and discusses topics of interest to residents.*
- *Initiate a campaign to clean up and preserve the downtown riverfront area.*
- *Help entrepreneurs start up new businesses.*
- *Organize community celebrations and events.*
- *Conduct fund-raisers to support community goals and projects.*
- *Identify employers and link them with community citizens needing jobs.*
- *Develop a network of community experts that residents can contact for help in their areas of expertise (for example, electrical repair, writing, wellness, or investment).*
- *And do much more.*[1]

Because of a neighborhood's critical significance in community building and empowerment, we will discuss neighborhoods in some detail here. The subsequent section emphasizes the importance of neighborhood centers as facilitators of empowerment.

This chapter will:

- Define neighborhoods and examine how they provide a vital context for human behavior.
- Review the functions of neighborhoods and how they can enhance residents' optimal health and well-being.
- Identify the qualities of strong neighborhoods.
- Describe two approaches to examining neighborhood structure—one focusing on interpersonal interaction, identification, and connections, and the other on neighborhood groups and value implementation.
- Discuss neighborhoods, ethnicity, and social class including the strengths of ethnic and cultural solidarity, and segregation.
- Describe projects that can enhance neighborhood strengths, including murals, gardens, and community playgrounds.
- Examine processes of change in neighborhoods, including those based on the invasion-succession, life cycle, and political capacity models.
- Describe neighborhood centers and examine their origin in the settlement house movement.
- Examine the assumptions upon which neighborhood centers are based today.
- Specify the types of activities neighborhood centers can sponsor to improve living conditions for neighborhood residents.
- Provide specific examples of neighborhood and community projects reflecting empowerment.

---

[1] These ideas are based on those described by J. P. Kretzmann and J. L. McKnight in *Building Communities from the Inside Out* (Chicago: ACTA Publications, 1993).

DEFINING NEIGHBORHOODS

A *neighborhood* is a "community of place within a larger community" (Fellin, 2001a, p. 128) where residents "share certain characteristics, values, mutual interests, or styles of living" (Barker, 2003, p. 292). There are three important points to this definition. First, a neighborhood is based on a physical area. Second, neighborhoods provide places for people to reside and go about their daily living tasks. Third, neighborhood residents share something in common, such as religious affiliation, racial identity, socioeconomic status, or concerns about encroaching crime. Neighborhood is an especially important concept when talking about geographical communities because of its immediate significance to clients' lives. It is the immediate social environment in which they live, eat, sleep, and interact on a daily basis.

A geographical community may consist of a number of neighborhoods. There are several types of neighborhoods based on size (Fellin, 2001b, p. 127). An *immediate neighborhood* is one consisting of a limited number of family units and lodgings located in a relatively small area. A three-block-long city street might exemplify an immediate neighborhood. An *extended neighborhood* is larger than an immediate neighborhood and might include several square blocks. Finally, a *community neighborhood* includes 30 square blocks or even more.

Neighborhood boundaries are determined in various ways (Fellin, 2001a; Homan, 1994). Neighborhoods are based upon residents' common characteristics, values, interests, or lifestyles. Therefore, the concept of neighborhood is more complex than *x* number of square feet, homes, or blocks. For example, Hmong immigrants from Southeast Asia might relocate in the same neighborhood based on common heritage, culture, and language. The immediate neighborhood might end abruptly in the middle of an urban block where people who are not Hmong reside in the event there is little interaction or common interest between the two groups.

Likewise, consider a single-home neighborhood populated primarily by senior citizens. A government housing project for families with young children is built on the next block. The immediate neighborhood for the senior residents might end where the housing project begins if the divergent groups have little in common and virtually nothing to do with each other. You might view a neighborhood and its boundaries as how residents define it (Homan, 2004). How would you define the boundaries of your own neighborhood?

FUNCTIONS OF NEIGHBORHOODS: PROMOTING OPTIMAL HEALTH AND WELL-BEING

Neighborhoods can perform a variety of functions (Fellin, 2001a; Homan, 2004; Rubin & Rubin, 1992, 2001; Warren, 1977; Warren & Warren, 1977). First, a neighborhood can be an arena for social interaction. It can be a place where people feel comfortable and that they belong. Residents might use each other as their primary context for socializing. A neighborhood block party in

Madison, Wisconsin, comes to mind. Each year residents on three blocks of Mifflin Street banded together, obtained permission from the city, and hosted a block party where residents contribute resources and "party hearty" to celebrate the coming of spring.

A second neighborhood function is the provision of mutual aid. Residents can help each other in any number of ways. Homan (2004) reflects:

> Neighbors can provide one another with a range of practical and emotional support. Borrowing a cup of sugar, helping out in times of emergency, establishing social contact over a cup of coffee, or helping to fix a leaky toilet are some of the common forms of assistance neighbors provide to each other. The benefits of these commonplace activities, of course, extend beyond eggs and coffee and functional flushing. These connections provide psychological benefits by strengthening our attachments to a wider human community and by helping us recognize the reality and importance of our interdependence. More effectively functioning neighborhoods are more likely to offer their members the benefits of "neighboring." (pp. 445–446)

The following are other examples of mutual aid. A neighborhood in a metropolitan suburb filled with young families who have small children can provide each other child care when they need it. An urban neighborhood can form a "Neighborhood Watch" organization where residents keep a careful eye out on each others' homes to report suspicious strangers and prevent crime. In a northern suburban neighborhood, one neighbor snowplows another's driveway when the latter takes a winter vacation. This helps conceal the fact that residents aren't home and decreases their vulnerability to thieves and vandals.

A third function of neighborhoods is provision of an arena for people to communicate and share information. We have noted that information can provide power. Therefore, neighborhood residents with access to information can share that information and thereby increase their neighbors' and ultimately the neighborhood's power. For example, Harry, a neighborhood resident in a small town, has a good friend, Ernest, a town board member (the decision-making body responsible for planning town projects). Harry finds out from Ernest that the Town Board is planning to rezone a lot in the neighborhood from residential to commercial, requiring that a business and not a personal residence be built on the lot. The implication for the neighborhood is that property values may plummet. The neighborhood's property is valuable because it boasts a pleasant, laid-back residential area for families. A business in its midst implies more traffic, more congestion, and less daily living appeal. Thus, with this information Harry and his neighbors can band together, confront the Town Board, and initiate whatever action is necessary to halt the rezoning plan.

A fourth function of neighborhoods is to allow people to "assert their social status" "through the choice of a physical neighborhood" (Rubin & Rubin, 1992, p. 89). For better or for worse, a neighborhood can establish certain standards and strive to admit residents who comply with the prerequisites. A common example is a suburban neighborhood that promotes residents who are white and who have achieved a prescribed level of socioeconomic status.

Current residents can work to keep out potential residents who don't comply. High property prices and taxes can exclude people from lower socioeconomic levels. Derogatory comments and even threats can act to deter people of color from moving into such neighborhoods. Obviously, this function does little to comply with the social work values of self-determination and the right to equal opportunity. Preserving social status can be an oppressive function that can counteract optimal health and well-being for people who are excluded from neighborhoods.

Consider one such suburban neighborhood. Neighborhood residents all have one-acre lots on a lake and huge, expensive homes with intricately manicured landscaping. All the neighborhood residents are white. Typically, residents make racial slurs and steadfastly discourage people of color from becoming interested in purchasing homes or empty lots. When one resident family moved because of a job relocation, a rich single white female owner of a large trucking firm, Lullabelle, purchased the family's home. The neighbors had seen Lullabelle, who was obviously white, and thus had few, if any, negative comments to make about her. They were, however, interested in determining what Lullabelle was like and how she would "fit into" the neighborhood. Unfortunately for them, they discovered that Lullabelle was a one-sided, perpetual talker who limited herself to various complaints and excessive detail about how much money she made. Lullabelle also had numerous men friends ranging in age from about 17 to 71 frequently stay with her and roam about the property. Neighbors were mortified as these men regularly spewed forth vulgarities and felt perfectly comfortable urinating on the garage or on the faultlessly trimmed bushes. Lullabelle could afford to hire a professional landscaper to maintain her yard. Lullabelle built a small, ugly warehouse-like structure in the front yard to house her old junker cars and used appliances. She kept the remaining three "junkers" out in the driveway. Then she placed several dozen plaster of paris and wooden lawn ornaments about the property. These included the ones where the backsides of "Ma" and "Pa" bending over are viewed so that you can see their polka-dotted underwear. No, the neighborhood residents didn't want any persons of color living in their neighborhood.

A fifth function of neighborhoods is provision of an organizational and political base. Neighborhood residents may choose to join a neighborhood organization or center. Such organizations are groups formed to address common needs of or establish goals for the neighborhood. Examples of goals are cleaning up rubbish, improving the conditions of older buildings, enhancing voter registration and voting, or targeting and abolishing crack houses. This chapter later discusses neighborhood centers much more thoroughly as a means of neighborhood empowerment.

As a group, neighborhood residents may also push politicians and community decision makers to make changes on their behalf. They may advocate for heavier police protection through increased patrolling of the area, or enforcement of property requirements such as maintaining buildings' compliance with minimal codes (for example, all windows must have screens, lead paint must be removed, or outside doors must be operational).

Qualities of Strong Neighborhoods

Strong, healthy neighborhoods that support residents and enhance their quality of life have the following eight basic characteristics (Homan, 2004; Wireman, 1984):

1. A good school system with high standards, good resources, and well-trained teachers who respond to the neighborhood's cultural composition and needs.
2. Good, safe areas for children to participate in play, sports, and other positive recreational and cultural activities.
3. Effective management of children's behavior by presiding adults.
4. Ready availability of and access to good health care facilities and services, especially in times of emergency.
5. Easily accessible public or other community transportation so residents can go to work or school, access health care, and undertake other necessary activities for daily life.
6. Good availability and facilities to meet daycare and other child care needs.
7. Strong support network of families and adults to watch over children, provide support, and serve as positive role models.
8. A reasonably safe environment with low or nonexistent levels of criminal activity, hazardous environmental dangers (such as potholes in streets or bridges lacking railings), and racial conflict.

Critical Thinking Questions 10.1

To what extent does the neighborhood you live in reflect the 8 strengths mentioned here?

DESCRIBING NEIGHBORHOOD STRUCTURE

Several models or approaches have been developed to describe neighborhoods' structure and composition (Fellin, 2001a, pp. 137–140; 2001b, pp. 123–125). Such approaches focus our attention on various dimensions of neighborhoods so we can evaluate how well they provide for residents' health and well-being. Two will be described here. The first emphasizes interpersonal interaction, identification, and connections. The second approach focuses on neighborhood groups and value implementation.

Approach One: Interpersonal Interaction, Identification, and Connections

One approach to assessing neighborhoods focuses on three conditions (Fellin, 2001a, 2001b; Warren & Warren, 1977). The first is the degree of interpersonal interaction among residents. To what extent do they socialize with each

Highlight 10.1	**Communities Based on Interpersonal Interaction, Identification, and Social Connections**		

	Interpersonal Interaction	Identification with Neighborhood	Social Connectedness
Integral	High	High	High
Parochial	High	High	Low
Diffuse	Low	High	Low
Stepping-Stone	Low	High	High
Transitory	Low	Low	High
Anomic	Low	Low	Low

other and provide each other with support? The second condition is the residents' identification with the neighborhood and each other. To what extent do they identify with and feel a part of their neighborhood? The third condition involves the neighborhood's connections with the larger encompassing community. This last variable involving *social connectedness* concerns how neighborhoods have varying degrees of access to politicians who wield power, resources, needed services, and other systems in the larger community. Each of these variables can be appraised along a continuum from low to "neutral" to high (Fellin, 2001a, p. 138).

 Critical Thinking Questions 10.2

To what extent do you socialize with and get support from your neighbors? To what extent do you identify with and feel an integral part of the neighborhood where you live? To what extent is your neighborhood connected with other systems in the larger community environment? Explain your answers.

Neighborhoods can then be categorized into six basic types—integral, parochial, diffuse, stepping-stone, transitory, diffuse, and anomic—based on residents' social interaction, sense of belonging, and connections with others (Fellin, 2001a, pp. 138–139). Highlight 10.1 summarizes how each type of neighborhood reflects the degree of interpersonal interaction, residents' identification with the neighborhood, and social connectedness with other systems outside of the neighborhood.

Integral Neighborhoods   *Integral* neighborhoods are those manifesting high levels of all three conditions. Neighborhood residents are highly involved with each other. They readily identify themselves as part of the neighborhood. Espousing "positive values toward education, participation in community life, community improvement, and maintenance of law and order" can add to a neighborhood's cohesion (Fellin & Litwak, 1968, p. 79). Additionally, an integral neighborhood is clearly linked with the encompassing larger community. For example, neighborhood residents may sit on governing groups or agency boards in their town, city, or state. Or, residents may regularly write letters or editorials for the media.

Parochial Neighborhoods   A *parochial* neighborhood is one high on interaction and identification but low on community connections. In such a neighborhood, residents may interact frequently, identify with each other, and advocate for positive neighborhood goals and changes. Yet, they may have no involvement with the larger community or have access to many resources. For instance, residents in an urban Hispanic neighborhood where most residents speak only Spanish may have little opportunity or ability to communicate with decision makers in the larger community. Yet, these residents may feel very bonded with each other and be extremely supportive among themselves.

Diffuse Neighborhoods   A *diffuse* neighborhood offers residents a strong sense of neighborhood identification. However, residents experience little social interaction. They feel they do not need the neighborhood for support or help, and require low levels of connections to resources and services outside of the community. These are usually exclusive suburban neighborhoods or opulent luxury apartment buildings in urban settings. Residents may have money, power, and perceived identification with the neighborhood yet not feel interaction is essential. They already have what they need and more; therefore, they find it unnecessary to expend energy for advocacy or change.

Stepping-Stone Neighborhoods   A *stepping-stone* neighborhood is characterized by the temporary nature of residents. They may positively identify themselves with the neighborhood but have low levels of commitment to interact with other residents or to work on the neighborhood's behalf because they simply won't be there that long. Residents of stepping-stone neighborhoods often are moving up in their careers and possibly starting and raising families. Because they're "on the way up," they usually have high levels of connection with other resources and systems in the larger community environment. Their efforts are directed elsewhere than neighborhood involvement and improvement. These are poor social environments for people seeking permanent residence or social belonging.

Transitory Neighborhoods   A *transitory* neighborhood resembles a stepping-stone in terms of the transitory nature of residents. However, residents in such neighborhoods have much less access to resources and are probably not moving up in the world. They're just moving. In such a neighborhood, residents have low levels of social interaction and identification with the neighborhood.

Brief Commentary on the Nature of Neighborhoods

It should be noted that these neighborhood types are not necessarily distinct from each other. The degree to which a neighborhood has social interaction, resident identity, and community linkages vary from one to another. Thus, neighborhood types may overlap or change over time (Fellin, 2001a, 2001b).

Understanding a neighborhood can help social workers determine an intervention strategy to improve the neighborhood's functioning and enhance residents' quality of life. For example, in an anomic neighborhood, a generalist practitioner might seek to improve residents' involvement and identification with the neighborhood. One way is to identify potential community leaders who are interested and have a stake in community improvement. The worker could then help to organize residents, "provide expertise in developing leadership within the neighborhood, and promote participation by residents" (Fellin & Litwak, 1968, p. 79).

However, because of their serious needs, they frequently have high linkages with the wider community with its resources and services.

Anomic Neighborhoods   Finally, an *anomic* neighborhood is dysfunctional and provides little social support. *Anomie* is a sociological term that means "social instability resulting from a breakdown of standards and values" often involving "personal unrest, alienation, and uncertainty that comes from a lack of purpose or ideals" (Mish, 1995, p. 47). Despite residents' geographical proximity, the feeling of being in a neighborhood does not exist. It differs from a transitory neighborhood in that people may live here for long periods of time. An example of such a neighborhood is a huge urban public housing project for people with very low incomes. Gangs, guns, and drugs may infest its corridors. Many residents may feel little identification with other residents yet have nowhere else to go. They may live in constant fear, often for good reason. The larger community may provide little support.

Critical Thinking Questions 10.3

Of these six neighborhood categories—integral, parochial, diffuse, stepping-stone, transitory, diffuse, and anomic—how would you describe your neighborhood and why?

Highlight 10.2 addresses the issue of how neighborhoods don't always fall clearly into one category or another.

Approach Two: Neighborhood Groups and Value Implementation

The second approach to describing and understanding neighborhoods focuses on two dimensions—the structure and connections of formal and informal groups in neighborhoods, and how these groups implement the neighborhood's primary values. The basic idea is that formal and informal groups in neighborhoods can "play a significant role in the attainment of individual and social goals in American society" (Fellin & Litwak, 1968, p. 73). Such goals may concern "education, participation in community life, community improvement, and maintenance of social order" (Fellin, 2001a, p. 141). Fellin (2001b) explains:

> The organizational base of neighborhoods involves informal contacts and local formal organizations, such as voluntary associations. Neighborhoods can be classified in terms of both their level of organization and their capacity to implement their values, such as orientations toward education, good citizenship, and crime and violence. Recognition of the values of residents in a neighborhood is helpful for both interpersonal and community practice. For example, in areas with high rates of crime and delinquency, the social worker can assess the values of residents toward law and order and toward the tolerance of deviant behavior, and their willingness to organize to implement values to combat violence and crime. (p. 128)

Examples of informal neighborhood groups include groups based on friendship or shared caregiving for children or ailing seniors. Other organized groups might involve support groups, Neighborhood Watch organizations, or social groups such as the Red Hat Society (a nationally based organization with local groups of women who are middle-aged and older that congregate for social activities whose hallmark is the wearing of red and purple clothing; hence, the name "Red Hat").

Fellin and Litwak (1968) stress the significance of neighborhood groups:

> In the use of expertise, formal organizations provide for problem-solving most efficiently in dealing with uniform tasks, while the neighborhood group is likely to be equal to or better than the formal organization when there is no real knowledge available, when problems are simple, and when they are idiosyncratic in nature. The neighborhood can handle problems of a diffuse nature and, owing to small size and common values, can gain quick consensus for action. Thus, a variety of crisis situations can be handled by the neighborhood group, such as emergency first aid, baby-sitting, and immediate advice. (pp. 76–77)

Problems often facing neighborhoods, especially urban ones, include mobility and impersonality (Fellin & Litwak, 1968, p. 74). Mobility involves a continuous flux in a neighborhood's population. Fellin and Litwak (1968) explain: "Since it generally has been assumed that relatively permanent membership is a condition of group cohesion, the question becomes one of how well the neighborhood primary group can function when members move in and out of the group" (p. 74). A second problem, impersonality, involves lack of connection and caring among neighborhood residents. It implies deficient social interaction and even isolation from each other. Without cohesion, it's difficult for neighborhood residents to bond together and provide each other with help and support.

By strengthening neighborhood groups and their links with formal organizations, neighborhoods can address and help resolve these problems to empower residents. Social workers can enhance this process. Residents can address the problem of mobility by discussing issues openly, developing welcoming attitudes and behaviors, and using informal groups and local voluntary organizations to reach out to new residents. Neighborhoods can address the issue of impersonality by strengthening their informal group structures, associating and bonding with each other, and offering support.

 Critical Thinking Questions 10.4

What are the strengths and weaknesses of the two theories describing neighborhood structure—the first emphasizing interpersonal interaction, identification, and connections, and the second focusing on neighborhood groups and value implementation?

NEIGHBORHOODS, ETHNICITY, AND SOCIAL CLASS

Neighborhoods are often characterized by ethnicity and social class. (Fellin, 2001a, 2001b; Rubin & Rubin, 2001). Fellin (2001a) explains:

> The most common criteria used for classifying neighborhoods are social class, ethnicity, and culture. Neighborhoods may be distinguished by social class through the use of census data regarding occupational status, household income, education, and lifestyle. Residents usually refer to one or more of these factors in assigning social class names to their neighborhoods. Class names include terms such as wealthy, middle-class, working class, poor, underclass, and skid row neighborhoods. Names for ethnic neighborhoods include those of white ethnic groups, religious ethnic groups, and ethnic minority groups. Use of ethnic/cultural labels for neighborhoods usually indicates that members of a specific group are over-represented in relation to the general population, such as an African American neighborhood or a Hispanic/ Latino neighborhood. Religious or white ethnic labels are usually used when a substantial portion of the population, even if not a majority, are members of a specified group, such as Jewish, Catholic, Italian, Polish, or Irish neighborhoods. (p. 149)

Strengths of Ethnic and Cultural Solidarity

Rubin and Rubin (2001) elaborate on the strengths of community neighborhoods characterized by ethnicity, culture, and religion:

> *Solidarity communities* [emphasis added] are composed of people in the same racial or ethnic group, who share history, culture, language, or religion. Solidarity ties are usually based on birth. They are a given, not something to be created; however, definitions of who is in and who is out can evolve and may be subject to controversy. Certain orthodox Hasidic Jews who live together in urban neighborhoods define less religious Jews as not truly of the same faith and, hence, not part of their solidarity community. Slavic groups who were antagonistic to one another in Europe accepted a common cultural identity in the United States as part of their effort to unite to gain political clout (Kornblum, 1974).

Understanding linkages within solidarity communities is important if members of that group are to be mobilized. [Community organizers such as social workers identify, convene, and mobilize neighborhood residents and resources to make them responsive to unmet community neighborhood needs.] Cultural pride and ethnic identity provide the social glue that enables people to come together on issues that affect the whole group, whether or not specific individuals in the group are immediately affected. People are likely to give to charities sponsored by their solidarity group, even if the contributors don't foresee that they themselves are likely to need support. Or people of a given ethnic neighborhood may rally when a hurricane devastates their ancestral homeland, collecting food and clothes in local churches. Or those within a solidarity community may band together to support new immigrants from the old country, sponsoring them for jobs and giving them temporary shelter.

Solidarity communities reinforce their connectedness through shared rituals, holidays, festivals, and evocations of a common history. To build organizations within solidarity communities, organizers promote the art, social events, and stories that relate shared historic sufferings of the group to its current members. These stories replay past traumas and humiliations, forced migrations for Native Americans, incarceration in concentration camps for Japanese Americans during World War II, slavery for [African Americans]. By sharing these experiences and vulnerabilities, members of the solidarity community rediscover what membership entails and why future collective actions might be required. These historic, mutual experiences can be a cause for pride—we went through all this and survived—as well as a cause for rebellion. Native American organizers build solidarity within the group by narrating how the mainstream society stole Native American land and then by demanding that government restore traditional hunting, fishing, and land rights, which it had taken away.

By reframing how the past is understood, solidarity groups can turn prior humiliation into a source of pride. (pp. 102–103)

Highlight 10.3 describes three types of projects neighborhoods can undertake to build assets, the first of which emphasizes embracing one's cultural heritage and pride.

Social Class

"Attention to the social class level of neighborhoods is important for social workers, since neighborhood location and social class have a powerful effect on the resources and liabilities that affect the quality of life of neighborhood residents" (Fellin, 2001b, p. 129). The proportion of homes owned and the quality of those homes usually reflect the social class level of a neighborhood. Both social class and home ownership are related "to some combination of occupational status, household income, and educational level of members of a household" (Fellin, 2001a, p. 150). Houses and social class reflect social status. Higher social status implies greater access to resources.

| Highlight 10.3 | **Projects to Enhance Neighborhood Strengths** |

Delgado (2000) suggests at least three types of projects that community neighborhoods can undertake to enhance their strengths and assets. These include murals, gardens, and playgrounds. The idea behind such projects is for neighborhood residents to express themselves and their culture, thereby enhancing their sense of presence, cultural pride, and self-esteem.

The concept of *community built* means that a project is undertaken with the support and under the direction of a community neighborhood (Delgado, 2000, p. 75). This can mean that the entire project is completed by neighborhood residents or that the residents choose to bring in experts to complete a project. To be labeled community built, the project must meet the following 11 criteria (Arie-Donch, 1991; Delgado, 2000, p. 76): "(1) A concrete product is the end result, (2) the project is built primarily by volunteers, (3) successful completion is dependent on the participation of a wide sector of the community (the wider the better), (4) the project's scale corresponds to the size of the community to increase accessibility, (5) the project has distinct phases (a beginning, middle, and end), (6) the project develops in the community a sense of ownership, (7) the project is spatially defined, (8) the project has significance (social, political, and psychological) for the community, (9) the final form of the project reflects the needs of the community, (10) the final project can last long enough to be enjoyed by future generations, and (11) the project is permanent and creates a sense of permanence and long-term community commitment."

Murals

Large pictures painted or drawn on walls or ceilings, known as murals, can provide an important means of self-expression and cultural pride. Delgado (2000) explains:

> A mural is an art form that is expressed on a building's walls as opposed to a canvass" (Barnett, 1984). Murals represent a [neighborhood] community effort to utilize cultural symbols as a way of creating an impact internally and externally. Murals should not be confused with graffiti. A mural represents an artistic impression that is not only sanctioned by a [neighborhood] community, but often commissioned by it ("California Town Hope," 1996; Madden, 1996) and invariably involve a team of artists. Graffiti, on the other hand, represent an artistic impression (sometimes referred to as "tagging") that is individual centered and manifested on subway trains, doors, mailboxes, buses, public settings, and other less significant locations. Their content generally focuses on the trials and tribulations associated with urban living, issues of oppression, or simply a "signature" of the artist. (p. 78)

"Delgado and Barton (1998) describe six basic types of mural content. First, murals can illustrate "symbols of ethnic and racial pride" (p. 349). For example, concerning Chicanos and their pride in their history, Treguer (1992, cited in Delgado & Barton, 1998, p. 348) notes that pre-Columbian themes are common, with frequent ancient Aztec motifs (taken from or inspired by Aztec manuscripts and temples) and references to the Spanish conquest and images of the Virgin of Guadelupe, which he describes as "a cherished Mexican icon" (p. 23).

A second theme often evident in murals involves religious symbols. Delgado and Barton (1998) remark in the context of Latino culture:

> Spirituality, in the form of religion and folk beliefs, plays an important role in the lives of Latinos (Coleman, 1994; Cooper & Sciorra, 1994; Treguer, 1992). Religious and spiritual symbols often represent a community's hopes for the future, its history, and, depending on the symbols, the value it places on the metaphysical. (p. 349)

The third type of content often portrayed in murals involves "issues related to social justice" (Delgado & Barton, 1998, p. 349). This may include "scenes of police brutality, arson, alcohol and other drug abuse, prison, U.S. imperialism" and "infant mortality," scenes that Delgado and Barton characterize as "based on historical events" and "a daily reminder of the trials and tribulations" experienced by people of color in "the search for social justice" (p. 349).

A fourth theme displayed in murals involves beautification and decoration for its own sake. Murals don't have to be a statement of great social, political, or religious impact. Rather, they can serve to make a neighborhood a more pleasing and nice-looking place to live.

The fifth type of content displayed in murals concerns "homages to national and local heroes" (p. 350). Delgado and Barton (1998) explain:

> Communities of color rarely have the opportunity to honor their own. With the exception of national heroes like Rev. Martin Luther King, Jr., Malcolm X, Cesar Chavez, and so forth, many local heroes never make it into history books. Consequently, murals provide local residents the opportunities to validate their experiences through their heroes. (p. 350)

The sixth theme for a neighborhood mural involves "memorials commissioned by local residents, which may honor "a dead relative, close friend, or gang member (p. 350) "The number and extent of murals dedicated to community residents who have died," note Delgado and Barton, "can be an excellent indicator of key issues within the community," an assessment of which "can provide important data on gender, age, cause of death, as well as other information" (p. 350).

Delgado and Barton (1998) also note that mural production can provide the opportunity for neighborhood youths to develop a number of skills in the process. These include:

- "research skills" to define content
- "negotiation skills" to help neighborhood residents come to a consensus regarding what the mural should entail
- "safety consciousness and following rules"
- "teamwork"
- "starting and completing a project"
- "development of proper work habits"
- improvement of "communication skills"
- "knowledge of math and chemistry" when designing content and preparing paints
- "budgeting and scheduling abilities" when finding resources to finance the project and scheduling a plan for completion

- becoming effective contributors to the neighborhood and community by assuming responsibility as active participants in the project's completion

Gardens

Gardens in urban areas are very important (Delgado, 2000; Hynes, 1995). "Urban gardens are an essential part of an ecological system that fosters the development of community, relationships, and capacity enhancement" (Delgado, 2000, p. 88). Gardens are grown for three basic purposes (Delgado, 2000). First, they can be visually appealing. Second, people can grow gardens as a type of recreation. Third, gardens can be grown for food. Sometimes, gardens serve two or all of these purposes.

Neighborhood residents usually get together to develop a garden under four different circumstances (Delgado, 2000). A local empty or cleared plot of land might become available for their use. An institution such as a hospital, church, or school might seek a beautification project. Neighborhood residents might decide to grow a garden for residents in need. Or funding becomes available from grants or other public or private sources to support a neighborhood gardening project.

There are many benefits from community gardens. Gardens can provide opportunities for residents to work together toward a common goal. We've already noted that gardens can both provide food and improve a neighborhood's appearance. They can improve residents' sense of self-worth and self-esteem. Gardens can help people living in urban settings experience and appreciate nature.

Neighborhood House of Milwaukee, Inc., a neighborhood center located in an impoverished inner-city community, provides a good example of encouraging urban gardening and the appreciation of nature.* (Neighborhood centers established in the Settlement House tradition are described later in the chapter.) Neighborhood House's mission is to provide "social, educational and recreational activities to improve the quality of life in the community" (Neighborhood House, 2006b).

---

*Many thanks to Bradley Blaeser, Program Director of the Outdoor and Environmental Education Department and School-Age Program, Neighborhood House of Milwaukee, Inc. (2819 W. Richardson Place, Milwaukee, WI 53208-3546) for his excellent explanation of this program. Further information about Neighborhood House can be retrieved from http://www.nh-milw.org.

continued

Highlight 10.3 | *continued*

One of its programs involves Outdoor/Environ-mental Education (Neighborhood House, 2006a). The agency's property includes a "32,000 square foot outdoor habitat, including butterfly gardens, art sculptures, and pizza gardens" (where pizza ingre-dients such as tomatoes and herbs are grown) (Neighborhood House, 2006a). A primary purpose is to encourage young people's appreciation and enjoyment of nature. Children ages 6 weeks to 6 years are introduced to this habitat and encouraged to explore. The Gardening Programs offer opportunities for children and teens up to age 18 to participate in all aspects of gardening, including "choosing the plants, sprouting seeds, planting seedlings, growing plants, harvesting the vegetables, weeding the beds, adding compost to the soil [which they observe being pro-cessed right there in the garden], and . . . eating the products from the garden" (Neighborhood House, 2006b). The program also sponsors School-Age and Teen Programs that include camping and other out-door experiences at a rural site owned by the agency.

Community Playgrounds

Developing and improving "community playgrounds" can provide excellent opportunities for enhancing a neighborhood's assets. Delgado (2000) explains:

Although community playgrounds primarily target the recreational needs of children, they also fulfill other functions that rarely get noticed

in the everyday life of a community. The struc-tures can play a central role in connecting resi-dents with each other and provide an outlet for families to do some activity together that does not require the expenditure of funds. (pp. 95–96)

It is vital that neighborhood residents make their own decisions regarding what the playground should be like—what types of equipment should be included and how it should be arranged. It's crucial that the area meet the individual neighborhood's and its resi-dents' needs. Delgado (2000) likens a neighborhood's development of a playground to an old-fashioned barn raising. He continues:

Simply described, a barn raising brings all mem-bers of a rural community, regardless of age, gender, and skills, together for a concentrated period (usually one or two days) to help a fellow neighbor who has suffered some tragedy, like a fire, to build a barn. It serves to help a neighbor in need, reaffirms a community's definition of itself, and ensures the members that they do, in fact, belong to a community that cares. (p. 97)

He concludes, "Community-built playgrounds . . . reflect a community's desire to claim their own space and control the activities within this area. Thus, the presence of such playgrounds can serve as excellent indicators of a community's capacity to rally for a common good" (Delgado, 2000, p. 102).

 Critical Thinking Questions 10.5

Have you noticed any murals, neighborhood gardens, or playground development in your community neighborhood? If so, what were your thoughts about it?

Social workers are especially concerned with building assets in poorer community neighborhoods because these generally have the greatest needs. Fellin (2001a) reflects:

Studies of inner-city poverty areas show a decline in status in these neighborhoods, due to the decline in employment and increase in welfare dependency among residents, as well as the departure of upwardly mobile individuals and families (Wilson, 1996). At the same time, many working-and middle-class ethnic minority neighborhoods have been able to maintain their status because of residential stability and strong institutional supports from schools, churches, medical and social service institutions, and neighborhood voluntary organizations. Many urban neighborhoods that have become more integrated racially have managed to maintain their class status through institutional and voluntary group efforts that support integration. [*Integration* is the process of assembling diverse groups of people including different races into a cohesive whole.] (pp. 153–154)

Segregation

Segregation, the opposite of integration, is "the separation or isolation of a group through social sanctions, laws, peer pressure, or personal preference" (Barker, 2003, p. 386). Segregation may be imposed upon a group or it may be voluntary. Fellin (2001b) explains:

> Communities in the United States continue to be highly segregated (Harrison & Weinberg, 1992). The concepts of segregation and integration serve to describe these neighborhood communities, with segregated neighborhoods having a high proportion of ethnic minority and/or cultural group membership (Rusk, 1993). Empirical studies of housing patterns in North American communities continue to leave no doubt that housing segregation is due in large part to discrimination and prejudice based on race and/or ethnicity. (p. 129)

There are other rationales for the existence of neighborhoods where residents have the same racial heritage. Fellin (2001a) explains:

> Some members of ethnic minority groups prefer to reside in neighborhoods populated mainly by members of their own group. These individuals . . . reside in and are positively identified with the minority community. These neighborhoods also receive people who are unable to move into other neighborhoods due to economic factors and/or discrimination in housing. There is strong evidence that societal and community barriers to residential mobility prohibit some persons from 'leaving the "hood"' and [entering more mainstream society]. These barriers include not only financial constraints and housing discrimination, but obstacles imposed by suburban communities to new arrivals from minority groups, such as restrictive covenants and zoning ordinances. (p. 158)

 Critical Thinking Questions 10.6

Think of a large city with which you're familiar. To what extent do neighborhoods reflect ethnic, cultural, and class distinctions? To what extent is segregation apparent? What are the reasons for these conditions?

PROCESSES OF CHANGE IN NEIGHBORHOODS

By nature, systems are subject to change. Levels of input and output change. External factors affecting the system are altered. So it is with neighborhoods. Neighborhoods' social, economic, and political environments are in constant flux. People move in and out. Jobs are developed or businesses leave the area. Buildings get older and require repair. Sometimes, old buildings are torn down and new ones built. Other times, old buildings are refurbished. Still other times, old buildings rot and stagnate in deteriorating states.

Homan (2004) cites three theories that explain neighborhood change; they include the "invasion-succession," "life cycle," and "political capacity" models (pp. 447–448).

The Invasion-Succession Model

The invasion-succession model is based on the idea that conflict occurs when new groups of people reflecting certain racial, cultural, or religious characteristics move into areas already inhabited by people with different characteristics. A new group will invade and the other will withdraw. *Invasion* is "the tendency of each new group" of people coming into an area "to force existing groups out" (Kirst-Ashman & Hull, 2006a, p. 263). *Succession*, then, is "the replacement of the original occupants of a community or neighborhood by new groups" (Kirst-Ashman & Hull, 2006a, p. 263). For example, a neighborhood might first be populated by people of German descent, followed by African Americans, and later by Eastern Europeans. A concern is that "if the withdrawing group takes valuable resources from the community (for example, family income, shop ownership, political clout) before these can be effectively replaced, the neighborhood is likely to decline" (Homan, 2004, p. 448).

The Life Cycle Model

The life cycle model views neighborhood change as a decline, with a neighborhood undergoing predictable phases from birth until death. These phases include the following five (Downs, 1981; Homan, 2004).

1. A stable and viable neighborhood
2. A minor decline
3. A clear decline
4. A heavily deteriorated neighborhood
5. An unhealthy and nonviable neighborhood (Homan, 2004, p. 448).

Homan (2004) explains:

> A stable and viable neighborhood exists when no symptoms of decline have appeared and property values are rising. A period of minor decline may follow in which some minor deficiencies in housing units are visible and density is higher than when the neighborhood was first developed, but property values are stable or increasing slightly. A neighborhood in clear decline is marked by populations from lower socioeconomic groups. Renters are dominant in the housing market, and landlord-tenant relations are poor because of high absentee ownership. Other factors, such as higher density, low confidence in the area's future, and abandoned buildings, are also associated with this stage. In heavily deteriorated neighborhoods, housing is very run down and even dilapidated. Most structures require

major repair. Subsistence level households are numerous, and profitability of rental units is poor. Pessimism about the area's future is widespread. An unhealthy and nonviable neighborhood is at the final stage of change. Massive abandonment occurs, and those residents who remain are at the lowest social status and incomes in the region. Expectations about the area's future are nil. (p. 448)

The Political Capacity Model

The political capacity model perceives a neighborhood as having the ability to pass through various stages as it develops it's political viability and power (Homan, 2004; Taylor, 1979). Unlike the life cycle model, the focus is on growth rather than deterioration.

Initially, the neighborhood may be disorganized and lacking in leadership. At this stage, someone must function as a community organizer to encourage development of leadership potential in residents. The next stage involves the organizer identifying and working with a number of social institutions such as schools, churches, and clubs to develop social networking, cooperative inter-action, and emerging leadership. The following phase concerns identifying and targeting some neighborhood issues for change. The organizer eventually develops a strong network of neighborhood groups and individuals who begin working together seriously in addressing neighborhood concerns and needs. The final stage involves a neighborhood with a strong leadership and a wide-spread, inclusive social network that can independently identify neighborhood goals and work cohesively to achieve them.

 Critical Thinking Questions 10.7

What are the strengths and weaknesses of each of the three models explaining neighborhood change—invasion-succession, life cycle, and political capacity?

NEIGHBORHOOD CENTERS, EMPOWERMENT, AND THE PROMOTION OF HEALTH AND WELL-BEING

A *neighborhood center* is a community-based agency that advocates for community residents and works with them to provide a wide array of services meeting their needs; it is funded through a variety of services including grants, the United Way,[2] and various government agencies (Smith, 1995). Such services address numerous issues, needs, and developmental tasks from pre-birth to post-death. For example, a neighborhood center might offer family planning information to one family, while helping another plan a funeral (Smith, 1995).

---

[2] The *United Way* is a nationally based alliance of local agencies founded to organize and coordinate voluntary fundraising for many social agencies including those providing health, educational, or recreational services (Barker, 2003).

To understand the potential significance of neighborhood centers in the macro social environment, we will discuss three dimensions. These include a brief history of their development originating with settlement houses, a description of current services and structures and types of activities they sponsor, and a range of case examples.

Settlement Houses: A Response to Changing Social and Economic Forces

Settlement houses of the last century provided the ideological foundation for today's neighborhood centers (Smith, 1995). They developed in response to three changing social and economic forces (Garvin & Cox, 1995). The first was industrialization. Mammoth growth in manufacturing and technology brought with it a "wide range of social problems," including "problems of working hours and conditions, safety, and child labor" (Garvin & Cox, 1995, p. 65).

The second primary change was urbanization. Concurrent with the centralization of industry within urban settings was tremendous growth of urban populations. Masses of people moved from rural to urban areas on quests for work and prosperity. Unfortunately, most were forced to move into the oldest, most crowded, and least sanitary portions of cities.

The third major change during this period was explosive immigration, primarily from northwestern Europe. Immigrants brought with them their own problems. Many came from poor rural environments and had little with which to start their lives in this country. Many became ill during the immigration process. When they arrived, poverty forced many immigrants to live under poor conditions and accept whatever work they could find.

Settlement houses were "places where ministers, students, or humanitarians 'settled' (hence the name) to interact with poor slum dwellers with the purpose of alleviating the conditions of capitalism" (Smith, 1995, p. 2130). Supporters of settlement houses "wanted to be 'neighbors' to the poor and to help communities solve self-identified problems, such as day care, literacy, and citizenship" (Popple, 1995, p. 2282). Additionally, they and the people developing them "advocated for child labor laws, urban parks, women's suffrage, public housing, and public health" (Smith, 1995, p. 2130).

Settlement Houses and Generalist Social Work Practice

Settlement houses formed a strong partial foundation for generalist social work practice within communities in at least three ways, (Smith, 1995). First, the settlement house approach addressed the problems of people in an environmental context instead of focusing on individual pathology. Problems existed in the environment that created difficulties for individuals. Individuals were not viewed as the targets of blame, punishment, and change. Settlements focused on social issues and improving living conditions, especially for those who were poor or less fortunate than most.

Second, an environmental focus led naturally to an emphasis on advocacy and social reform. The macro social environment required change in order to meet people's needs.

Third, settlement houses emphasized the empowerment of people. At its most basic level, empowerment involves providing people with authority or power. The settlement house perspective viewed people as having strengths and capabilities to effect their own change. Families and neighborhoods were seen as potential vehicles for positive change. The concepts of community organization and group work developed within the settlement house context. Jane Addams and Ellen Gates Starr began, perhaps, the most famous settlement house, Hull House, in Chicago in 1889.

Yan (2004) maintains that settlement houses can provide an important source of strength to neighborhoods and communities today. He explains:

> The settlement house can provide a physical platform for dialogue. The "neutral turf" of a settlement house allows it to function as a "living room" of the neighborhood, in which all members of the community, of different generations, racial, cultural, gender and political orientation, are welcome (Hiroto, Brown, & Martin, 1997). The settlement house's physical presence in the community also represents a symbolic figure of the community. The architectural image of many settlement houses and their history of working with members of the community have been interwoven into the memories of several generations of members of the community. To newcomers in the community, the physical presence of, and the services provided by, a settlement house also provide a physical entry point for integration into the new environment. (p. 62)

Neighborhood Centers Today

Many of the social ills that settlement houses originally addressed no longer exist today. For example, child labor is illegal, and minimum requirements for workplace safety are in place. However, successful neighborhood centers organize community residents to meet new needs and demands. These include provision of daycare for working parents, preschool programs, home support for senior citizens, family counseling, substance abuse education and counseling, health services, recreational activities for children and teens, food pantries, temporary shelter, vocational assessment and employment counseling, and meeting locations for various local organizations from the Boy Scouts to Alcoholics Anonymous (Smith, 1995). Alternative names for neighborhood centers include "community center" or "multipurpose center" (Smith, 1995, p. 2131).

Whereas the initial settlement houses were run by concerned volunteers and community residents, today's neighborhood center is typically run by professionals, although volunteers are often used. The executive director or chief executive officer is usually a social worker with a master's degree (Smith, 1995).

Community Neighborhood Residents Are Key Factors Neighborhood centers are built on four assumptions (Smith, 1995). First, the core of a neighborhood center's existence and success rests on community people. It exists only to furnish service to community residents and to provide a mechanism for residents to organize themselves to get things done.

Emphasis on Community Neighborhood Assets   The second assumption upon which neighborhood centers are built is a focus on community assets. These include strengths and values that contribute to a community's progress, improvement, and development. The focus is on providing residents with what they need to survive and thrive.

For example, working single parents may require daycare and after-school care for their children in order to keep their jobs. Providing such services supports parents' strength in their capacity to work.

Senior citizens may be able to remain in their own homes if they receive minimal daily support, such as a daily hot meal delivered or someone to transport them to get groceries. A neighborhood center can build on strengths and help maximize people's potential to live independently.

Finally, a neighborhood center may sponsor a gang prevention and youth recreation program. Such a program could focus on the strengths of the community's young people. Services might include counseling children and teens concerning the legal repercussions of gang involvement and redirect their energies to other more productive social and recreational activities.

Neighborhood Centers Can Help Neighborhoods Work Together   A third assumption regarding neighborhood centers is that they are a means of unifying a neighborhood so it may work together with other neighborhood centers for the betterment of the entire community. The center can serve as the congregating place for residents to organize and hold meetings to address social, economic, and political issues. For example, several neighborhood centers could collaborate to develop "an inventory to initiate self-help, mutual support and exchange networks" for all the neighborhoods involved (Kretzmann & McKnight, 1993, p. 133). With consolidated resources, the neighborhoods could provide a wider range of services to address more specific identified needs.

One such neighborhood collective in an urban neighborhood initiated several self-help groups. These included Parents Anonymous to deal with parental stress and a Young at Heart group for victims of arthritis to discuss means of tempering lifestyles "to conserve energy and minimize arthritic pain" (Powell, 1995, p. 2119).

The collective also established a landlord assistance project where residents volunteered time and effort to help local landlords. Volunteers identified and made minor repairs on and in neighborhood homes to keep neighborhood residences operational and in compliance with local building codes. Landlords were responsible only for providing required materials at minimal costs. Prior to the landlord assistance project, landlords frequently avoided or "forgot" to make repairs and improvements, saying that it was too costly to repair old properties in low-rent neighborhoods. They threatened to allow foreclosure for unpaid taxes if upkeep became too expensive. Neighbors volunteering time significantly cut upkeep costs as landlords paid only for supplies, not for the expensive reimbursement required by skilled tradespeople.

Linkage Among Neighborhood Units   A fourth foundation principle for neighborhood centers is linkage among various facets of the neighborhood. This includes individual families, local businesses, social service departments, schools, medical centers, religious organizations, and other public resources. For example, one neighborhood center established a neighborhood-based mental health referral group (Kretzmann & McKnight, 1993). The group identified businesses supportive of providing jobs to people with mental health problems; county social workers to assess, counsel, and refer; school social workers to identify clients and provide group counseling; psychiatrists and other physicians to assess, provide, and monitor appropriate psychotherapeutic drugs; and church groups providing facilities for support group meetings and recreational space and activities. After establishing relationships with relevant service and resource providers, the referral group publicized its existence with fliers to residents and ads in local papers. Neighborhood families with members suffering from mental health problems could then contact the referral group, which, in turn, would link people with necessary resources.

Highlight 10.4 identifies a number of goals that an effective community center can accomplish.

 Critical Thinking Questions 10.8

Are you aware of or familiar with a neighborhood center in your neighborhood or campus community? If so, what types of programs does it provide? If you don't know of one, you might investigate where one exists in a town or city close to you.

Examples of Neighborhood and Community Projects: Resident Empowerment

The following are some examples of projects pursued by neighborhood centers or other local organizations (Kretzmann and McKnight, 1993):

- Residents in a public housing project identified unemployment as a major problem. They banded together and formulated job training sessions that addressed issues like developing resumes, preparing and dressing for interviews, answering questions asked during job interviews, emphasizing personal strengths, and establishing good work habits. Additionally, they developed a system for identifying job openings and referring residents to them for full- and part-time employment.

- Local chapter members of the National Association of Black Accountants volunteered time to help community residents and local businesses. They

| Highlight 10.4 | What Effective Neighborhood Centers Can Do |

Neighborhood centers can provide support to residents and improve living conditions in a number of ways (Homan, 2004):

- *Establish a positive and effective sense of self as a neighborhood and as a resident of that neighborhood.* This can be done through publicity in local papers and newsletters, announcements posted in businesses, and decals and emblems placed throughout the neighborhood.
- *Social activities and celebrations.* Neighborhood centers can sponsor picnics, cultural events, dinners, recreational activities, and entertainment to provide opportunities for positive social interaction, networking, and bonding as a community neighborhood.
- *Maintenance and clean up.* Neighborhood centers can form groups to pick up garbage, repair housing, plant trees and gardens, and rejuvenate parks, playgrounds, and other public spaces.
- *Opportunities for interpersonal interaction.* Neighborhood centers can sponsor and promote any number of chances for social interaction. These include establishing a program where seniors become foster grandparents to lonely children, sponsoring dances, providing information via newsletters about community events, and offering opportunities for residents to participate in the organization's decision-making processes.
- *Sharing resources and organizing volunteer help.* Neighborhood centers can sponsor book, toy, or tool libraries. They can identify residents' skills and link these residents with others who need help.
- *Training and education.* Neighborhood centers can provide educational and training opportunities on any number of topics ranging from how to change the oil in your car to a discussion about a work of classic literature.

- *Support for various organized groups.* Neighborhood centers can provide facilities and promote publicity for neighborhood groups, including Boy Scouts, Gamblers Anonymous, or the local theater guild.
- *Evaluating services provided by the local government.* The quality of police and fire protection can be monitored as can the neighborhood's general maintenance.
- *Protection and safety.* Neighborhood centers can initiate resident participation in crime prevention and monitoring. They can serve as advocates for environmental improvements where dangerous physical conditions exist.
- *Provision of various services.* Neighborhood centers can provide a range of services including counseling, daycare, transportation, and emergency help.
- *Collaboration with managers of public programs.* Neighborhood centers can work with local government and service providers to develop needed programs and make certain laws and local codes are enforced.
- *Housing improvement and business development.* Neighborhood centers can advocate for upholding building codes, write grants to develop small businesses to help stimulate the local economy, and encourage resident involvement in public programs providing loans and other assistance.
- *Enhancement of political clout.* Neighborhood centers can encourage residents to participate in the political process through voting and forming coalitions to advocate for positive change.
- *School improvement.* Neighborhood centers can provide feedback to local schools and work with school personnel to develop programs and improve educational processes.

assisted with business start-ups, budget development, and other accounting tasks.

- A group of neighborhood residents living in a small town determined that they needed a place to hold community events. Thus, they established a reception center in a local church basement. They used the space for a wide range of local festivities including organizational banquets, fundraising festivities, neighborhood meetings, church events, and family reunions.

- A neighborhood center's members became concerned about teens having little to do when school was out. The neighborhood had virtually no places for young people to congregate other than in alleys or on storefront sidewalks. The center's members rented a deserted warehouse and volunteered time to fix it up and make it into a recreational center. They also volunteered time to coach youth and supervise activities. In addition, they organized interested young people into a work club that emphasized identifying skills and finding part-time employment.

- One neighborhood center identified homebound senior residents' need for help plowing snow in winter and spading gardens in preparation for spring planting. Center members identified volunteers willing to participate in a mutual help program. Volunteers who did the physical labor for the older adults were called "The Earthmovers"; in return, seniors receiving help prayed for volunteers' well-being and were called "The Prayer Warriors" (p. 135). Each group's intent was to help the other.

- Residents of a suburban neighborhood concluded that they needed greater communication among themselves about community events and each other's activities. There was no local paper except one in the nearby big city, so they got little detail about issues, activities, concerns, and accomplishments in their smaller community. Starting a newsletter, *The Community Chitchatter,* a group of volunteer residents visited door-to-door soliciting subscriptions and approaching local businesses for financial backing to help with initial start-up costs. A local school allowed the group to use space for evening meetings. Volunteers formed an editorial staff that solicited news items and articles. Once the newsletter became known, neighborhood residents sent in dozens of news items. The volunteer staff was able to publish and distribute the newsletter for minimal cost.

- Community residents in St. Louis addressed the problem of teen pregnancy by establishing the Teen Outreach Program (TOP) 20 years ago (McDonald, 1998). TOP now has over 6,000 members from New York to California. The program's strategy is that "the best way to help teenage girls avoid becoming pregnant is to involve them in voluntary activity, whether or not it is explicitly designed to point out the pitfalls of early parenthood" (McDonald, 1998, p. 48). TOP aims to reinforce members' self-esteem and change the way they view the world. It emphasizes members' role in the community and the importance of caring for both others and themselves. One study found that TOP members "had 40 percent fewer pregnancies than a control group" (McDonald, 1998, p. 48). It should be noted that this does not mean that sex education is unimportant. It is way beyond the scope of this book to discuss currently raging debates about the value of sex education and what content to include.

CHAPTER SUMMARY

This chapter emphasized the importance of neighborhoods as a context for human behavior and empowerment. Neighborhoods were defined and their primary functions reviewed. Qualities of strong neighborhoods were identified.

Two approaches to describing neighborhood structure were presented. One focuses on interpersonal interaction, identification, and connections with the larger encompassing community. This model identifies six types of neighborhoods—integral, parochial, diffuse, stepping-stone, transitory, and anomic. The other approach to examining neighborhood structure stresses neighborhood groups and value implementation.

The importance of ethnicity and social class in neighborhoods was discussed. The strengths of ethnic and cultural solidarity were noted. The concept of segregation was defined and its relationship to neighborhoods introduced.

Projects to enhance neighborhood strengths include murals, gardens, and community playgrounds. Processes of change in neighborhoods include those based on the invasion-succession, life cycle, and political capacity models.

Neighborhood centers were examined and their history in the settlement house movement reviewed. Assumptions upon which neighborhood centers function were explained. These include community neighborhood residents as key factors, emphasis on community neighborhood assets, the potential for neighborhood centers helping neighborhoods work together, and the importance of linkages among various neighborhood units. The range of activities neighborhood centers can sponsor to improve residents' living conditions was identified. Specific examples of various neighborhood and community projects focusing on empowerment were presented.

Diversity, Populations-At-Risk, and Empowerment in the Macro Social Environment

The macro social environment is characterized by many kinds of diversity including that involving race, culture, and age. Here an African American grandmother enjoys pleasant interaction with her pre-kindergarten granddaughter.

CHAPTER CONTENTS

Rivera and Erlich (1995, p. 204) cite the following empowerment approaches undertaken by various racial and ethnic groups:

- *An urban African American community actively countered drug lords by undertaking an aggressive anti-drug campaign spearheaded by major community leaders.*
- *An African American teacher promised her first-grade class that she would pay for their college education if they maintained "C" averages and made it to college. She saves $10,000 each year from her modest salary to fortify the fund.*
- *"Southeast Asian communities in Boston, New York, Houston, and San Francisco have organized legal immigration and refugee task forces to help fight the arbitrary deportation of undocumented workers."*
- *Isolated, poor urban neighborhoods in major cities throughout the U.S. have "revitalized themselves through cooperatives and community development activities."*
- *"Native-American tribes are attacking problems of alcoholism through indigenous healing rituals which utilize the sweat lodge ceremony as its core. Success rates are often dramatic."*
- *Boston's Latino community has initiated an effective health care program entitled "Mujeres Latina en Action." It emphasizes the importance of extended family in health care provision and uses "a culturally and gender-sensitive model of community organization . . . to reach women in the barrios."*

Each example above reflects a creative example of empowerment for various diverse populations within the macro social environment. The responses of macro systems to people in need often cannot be categorized neatly as a community, organizational, or group effort. Rather, responses and resulting activities reflect a combination of all three types of systems. Okazawa-Rey (1998) maintains that problems ranging "from addiction and mental illness to homelessness and poverty" all involve micro, mezzo, and macro variables. A need might be identified within a community context. Organizations and their staff may participate with citizens to develop programs in response to community needs. Task groups are formed to initiate, develop, and implement ideas. Sometimes groups focusing on treatment, support, education, personal growth, or socialization are formed to meet identified needs.

This chapter provides a range of examples regarding how communities and organizations can respond to the needs of citizens who are members of diverse groups. This chapter will:

- Describe how groups including African Americans, Hispanics, GLBT people, and women are populations-at-risk.
- Discuss how the macro social environment can serve to empower each group.
- Provide case examples of empowerment in the macro social environment for each group.

- Provide examples of how spiritual communities can empower their members.
- Define developmental disabilities and identify a range of disabilities clustered under its umbrella.
- Examine the past history of how people with developmental disabilities have been treated by the macro social environment, and discuss current trends.
- Describe generalist social work practice with people who have developmental disabilities.
- Discuss avenues of legislative, community, and worker empowerment.
- Examine the macro environment's potential for empowering people with visual impairment and cognitive disabilities.

EMPOWERMENT IN THE MACRO ENVIRONMENT FOR AFRICAN AMERICANS

Consider the status of African American citizens in the United States. Leashore (1995) remarks:

> African Americans have fought and endured institutionalized racism, discrimination, and oppression . . . Amid inhumane assaults and against great odds it is remarkable that they have made substantial improvements in advancing the quality of their lives, as well as the lives of Americans in general. However, improvements for African Americans have been uneven, and African Americans continue to differ on many socioeconomic indicators when compared with whites. (p. 107)

Chapter 3 established that African American people (making up almost 12.8 percent of the U.S. population) continue to suffer a range of injustices (U.S. Census Bureau, 2005). Almost one quarter of African Americans live below the poverty level, compared to 10.5 percent of whites. Over one third of all African American children live in poverty, compared to 13.9 percent of white children. The median[1] income for African American people age 15 and older is 71.5 percent that of their white peers. African Americans are much more likely than their white peers to be incarcerated or on death row.

We have established that macro systems can develop policies and programs to enhance the well-being of various groups and populations-at-risk. Groups can be formed and services offered to address larger social issues facing African Americans that benefit individual group participants. An example presented here concerns a program assisting African American grandparents who are primary caregivers for grandchildren due to their own children's crack-cocaine abuse.

---

[1] A *median* is the middle number in any ordered list of numbers, with one half of the other numbers below it and one half above it.

Empowerment of Grandparents Who Become Primary Caregivers of Grandchildren

Gibson (2004) explains the current scenario:

> According to the U.S. Census Bureau, there are 4.5 million children under the age of 18 living in grandparent-headed households; one-third of these children have no parents present in the home. . . . African American grandmothers are coming to their grandchildren's aid in unprecedented numbers . . . , and grandparent-maintained households with neither parent present are the most economically disadvantaged. (p. 21)

Okazawa-Rey (1998) provides an example of a community response to the needs of African American grandparents who have become primary caregivers of their grandchildren. The initiating problem is one well established in the community and national scenes. Many people have become addicted to crack cocaine and are relinquishing their responsibilities as parents and productive citizens to pursue drug use. An example of a program responding to this problem is the Grandparents Who Care Support Network of San Francisco. Most members are "poor and working class, middle-aged and . . . [older adult] African-American women" (Cox, 2002; Okazawa-Rey, 1998, p. 54). They have gained custody of their grandchildren because of their own children's neglect. This is due to drug abuse, incarceration because of drug convictions, and the unwillingness to submit their grandchildren to strangers in the public foster care system.

These grandparents have found themselves in the strange and unusual circumstance of having sudden responsibility for small children at a stage in life when they feel they were done with all that. This situation can pose serious challenges, as Okazawa-Rey (1998) explains:

> Research on the issues confronting grandparents raising grandchildren reveals that these caregivers are prone to an increased incidence or exacerbation of depression and insomnia, hypertension, back and stomach problems [Miller, 1991] as well as increased use of alcohol and cigarettes [Burton, 1992]. In addition, grandparents tend to ignore their problems and the associated stresses to meet the needs of their grandchildren [Minkler & Roe, 1993]. (p. 46)

Problems are compounded with the health problems many children suffer due to poor prenatal care, drug use during pregnancy, and child neglect. These grandparents "desperately need day care, special education services, transportation, respite care, and money" (Okazawa-Rey, 1998, p. 54). To get services, they find themselves trying to negotiate the confusing maze of bureaucracies governing service provision.

Two health care workers, Doriane Miller and Sue Trupin, identified the problems and needs, and established Grandparents Who Care (Okazawa-Rey, 1998). The program is based on four philosophical principles. First, individual health problems transcend the fault of the individual. They are related to mezzo and macro conditions. Second, cultural, legal, and organizational barriers often hinder access to needed services. Third, even if people can get needed services, they may be inadequate and unable to meet needs. Fourth, empowerment at the micro, mezzo, and macro levels is necessary maintaining optimal health and well-being (Breidenstein, 2003).

The project reflects an empowerment approach as described by Cox (2002):

> The immediate goals of empowerment practice are to help clients achieve a sense of personal power, become more aware of connections between individual and community problems, develop helping skills, and work collaboratively towards social change (Gutierrez, GlenMay, & DeLois, 1995). But, the gains of empowerment do not rest only with the individual (Lee, 1994). As empowered people work together on common issues and problems, the communities in which they live become empowered, further empowering those who reside there. (p. 46)

Grandparents Who Care established a series of support groups to provide information, emotional support, and practical advice. Groups consist of 2 to 25 grandparents, are co-led by professional health care personnel (including nurses or social workers), and meet weekly for 90 minutes. Grandparents Who Care has a board of directors made up of grandparents, citizens, and concerned health care professionals who advise the organization.

Group members provide each other with support and help addressing a range of issues. For example, "when one woman faces a particular problem with her grandchild in the school system, another one will describe her dealings with this system and offer suggestions concerning the most effective ways to intercede" (Okazawa-Rey, 1998, p. 58). Members can, thus, share their experiences with each other and help work through issues. The professional co-leaders can assist the group by providing technical information about service availability, eligibility, and accessibility.

Areas of relevant interest to participants include "(1) introduction to empowerment; (2) importance of self-esteem; (3) communicating with grandchildren; (4) dealing with loss and grief; (5) helping grandchildren deal with loss; (6) dealing with behavior problems; (7) talking to grandchildren about sex, HIV/AIDS, and drugs; (8) legal and entitlement issues; (9) developing advocacy skills; [and] (10) negotiating systems" (Cox, 2003, p. 47).

Grandparents Who Care expanded its work in several macro dimensions to further empower its members. First, grandparents were trained as group leaders who go out and form new groups. In this way, the program's supportive help spread to help grandparents elsewhere in the community.

Second, Grandparents Who Care undertook political advocacy and lobbying on its members' behalf. One problem advocates addressed involved the legal difficulties grandparents experienced in receiving foster care payments. As relatives, they did not technically qualify as foster parents. Other financial support available to them was not nearly as good as that provided to unrelated foster parents. Grandparents Who Care advocates lobbied with a state legislator to pass a bill allowing grandparents to receive greater benefits.

EMPOWERMENT IN THE MACRO ENVIRONMENT FOR HISPANICS

Almost 41 million Hispanic people live in the United States (U.S. Census Bureau, 2005). The population varies immensely in terms of culture, race, and ethnic origin. Also, note that Hispanic people may also be of more than one race.

Highlight 11.1 addresses identifying terms used to describe Hispanics, and a subsequent section examines the oppression of Hispanic people in the macro environment. A discussion of empowering practices employed by Hispanic women and two case examples of how communities can empower Hispanic people follow.

Oppression in the Macro Environment

The economic and educational picture for the Hispanic population is much poorer than for whites (U.S. Census Bureau, 2005):

- There's a significantly higher percentage of families earning lower incomes and a significantly lower percentage earning high incomes compared to whites: 44.5 percent of Hispanic families have annual incomes of less than $30,000 compared to 32.9 percent of whites, while 23.6 percent of Hispanic families have annual incomes of $60,000 or more compared to 37.8 percent of whites. Greatest disparities between Hispanics and whites exist at the highest income levels.
- Almost 21 percent of Hispanic families have incomes below the poverty level, compared to slightly more than 8 percent of whites. Of Hispanic groups, Puerto Rican families (22.8 percent) are most likely to be below the poverty level, followed by Mexican families (20.9 percent) and Cuban families (12.9 percent), respectively.
- Mean (average) annual earnings for Hispanics is $25,810, compared to $38,053 for whites. The median income for Hispanic families is $34,272, compared to $55,768 for whites.
- In terms of educational attainment, 57.3 percent and 59.5 percent of Hispanic men and women, respectively, graduated from high school or attained more education, compared to 85.3 and 86.3 percent for white men and women, respectively. Only 11.8 percent of Hispanic men and 12.3 percent of Hispanic women graduated from college or attained higher levels of education, compared to 30 and 26.4 percent for white men and women, respectively.

Delgado (1997) cites three primary reasons for these demographics (p. 446). First, poverty is related to the immigrant status of many Latinos and "rapid demographic changes (high rates of female-headed households and fertility)." Second, Latinos have formed "an 'underclass' (low formal educational achievement and lack of or inconsistent employment history)." Third, Latinos manifest a lack of "market-attractive skills," preventing them from entering higher paid professions.

Highlight 11.1	**Identifying Terms**

The U.S. government's Office of Management and Budget originally coined the term *Hispanic* in 1978 for use in the census (Green, 1999). The original definition defined Hispanic as "a person of Mexican, Puerto Rican, Cuban, Central or South American or other Spanish culture or origin, regardless of race" (Green, 1999, p. 256). However, the concept is much more complex than this. For example, does this umbrella term include Brazilian people who speak Portuguese, South American Indians whose original language is not Spanish, people from the Philippines who speak Spanish, or immigrants from Spain (Green, 1999)?

An alternate term is *Latino,* which makes reference both to the Latin languages including Spanish and to Latin America. (Note that the term *Latina* is the feminine form of Latino.) However, this term omits South Americans who speak English, such as those from Belize or the Guyanas, and "people whose family roots extend to Italy, Germany, and some areas of the Mediterranean" (Green, 1999, p. 256).

Still another term often used is *Chicano,* which refers to U.S. citizens whose heritage is based in Mexico. The obvious disadvantage of this is that it focuses only on Mexico and excludes people with origins in other countries, including those that are primarily Spanish speaking.

Essentially, no one term is acceptable to all groups of people. The three primary Hispanic groups in the United States in terms of size are Mexican Americans (63% of all Hispanics), Puerto Ricans who live on the mainland (12%), and Cuban Americans (6%) (Goldenberg & Goldenberg, 2002). Other groups include those from the Dominican Republic and from other countries in Central and South America (Santiago-Rivera, Arredondo, & Gallardo-Cooper, 2002). However, for any particular family, Goldenberg and Goldenberg (2002) caution, "Socioeconomic, regional, and demographic characteristics vary among Hispanic American groups, making cultural generalizations risky" (p. 326). Santiago-Rivera, Arredondo, and Gallardo-Cooper (2002) reflect:

Perhaps no other ethnic group in the United States is as heterogeneous in its ethnicity, physical appearance, cultural practices and traditions, and Spanish language dialects as the Latino population. Latinos in the United States are a diverse group of multigenerational ... [people] from different Spanish-speaking countries as well as long-term residents in the southwest United States. All have unique social, economic, and political histories. Latino groups vary in their ancestry, blending indigenous [people originating in an area] (e.g., Aztec and Mayan) and Spanish cultural traditions and, for some Latino groups, African traditions. (p. 56)

It's important not to make stereotyped assumptions about such a diverse group. Santiago-Rivera and her colleagues (2002) continue:

Although it is not often reported, Latinos may also be of Asian heritage. The Philippine islands, conquered by Spain, were populated by people of Asian heritage. Whereas the native language of the island is Tagalog, Spanish surnames are commonplace, and in the United States, Filipinos may claim either Asian or Latino heritage. In South America and Mexico, there are settlements of Chinese families as well. Peru is one such example. (p. 23)

Longres (1995) concludes that social workers "should take the lead from the individuals, families, or communities they work with" and use the terms people prefer (p. 1215). Despite the complexity and the need to appreciate differences within this population, the terms *Hispanic* and *Latino/a* have generally been used to refer to people originating in countries in which Spanish is spoken. Here the terms Hispanic and Latino will be used interchangeably unless a specific group (e.g., Puerto Rican Americans) are discussed.

Values Often Characterizing Hispanic Families

Keeping in mind that more specific variations exist within the many subgroups, we will discuss some cultural themes important to Hispanic families in general. Hispanic heritage is rich and diverse, but the groups tend to share similarities in terms of values, beliefs, attitudes, culture, and self-perception. These include the significance of a common language, the importance of family relationships including extended family and other support systems, spirituality, and the traditional strictness of gender roles.

Significance of a Common Language The first theme important in understanding the environment for children growing up in Hispanic families is the significance of a common language. Although everyday communication among Latinos is frequently in English (Longres, 1995), "90% of Latinos in the United States continue to use the Spanish language"; therefore, social workers should "know that there is a growing population of bilingual Latinos who have varying degrees of language proficiencies in English and Spanish" (Santiago-Rivera et al., 2002, p. 121). For instance, recent immigrants may use little if any English, whereas people whose families have been here for centuries may be bilingual or lack any knowledge of Spanish. One strong implication of such diversity is the need for social workers to assess Latino clients' language history and use on an individual basis.

Arredondo and Perez (2003) point out that "language has always been made a political issue in the United States" so that many Latinos may "prefer to speak English versus Spanish" (pp. 120–121). They suggest that practitioners consider the following issues when working with Hispanic clients and communities:

1. Language use can be associated with generation in the United States. Recent immigrants may be monolingual Spanish speakers or speak English as a second language with a wide range of ability.
2. Many Latinos, particularly Mexican Americans, do not speak Spanish at all. These individuals were taught by their parents that in order to fit in and not be punished in school, as they had been, they could not learn to speak Spanish.
3. Being bilingual or speaking Spanish whenever possible can be viewed as an indication of comfort. However, speaking Spanish in the workplace has often been discouraged so as not to make "others" feel uncomfortable.
4. *Code-switching* refers to the use of Spanish and English in the same sentence [emphasis added]. Individuals engage in code-switching to emphasize a point with a particular English or Spanish word.
5. Bilingualism is an academic, psychological, social and economic asset, not a deficit. The need for Spanish-speaking professionals and workers continues to increase in all work environments in both urban and rural settings. (p. 121)

An important note is the fact that so many cultural activities and aspects of cultural pride are associated with Spanish. Consider the events and holidays (e.g., Cinco de Mayo for Mexican Americans, which refers to the celebrated day a small Mexican army defeated a French army battalion), "history and traditions, Spanish posters, and foods associated with Spanish-speaking homelands" that are so meaningful in daily cultural life (Longres, 1995, p. 1215).

The Importance of Family   A second theme reflecting a major strength in many Hispanic families is the significance placed on relationships within the nuclear and extended family, including "aunts, uncles, cousins, and grandparents, as well as close friends," referred to as *familismo* (Santiago-Rivera et al., 2002, pp. 42–43; Weaver, 2005):

> Latino families are typically large, intergenerational, and interdependent, and offer an important source of support to their members. . . . Extended family ties are highly valued and serve as a source of pride and security. . . . This emphasis on respect and responsibility to family members often leads to elderly adults both being cared for and taking on caregiving responsibilities within the family. The elderly are often cared for within the family rather than through formal social services. When nursing homes are used, family members often continue to fulfill supportive caregiving responsibilities. (Kolb, 1999; Weaver, 2005, p. 148)

Another important related concept reflecting a cultural strength is *compadrazco* (godparentage). *Compadres* (godparents) often serve as substitute parents. According to Santiago-Rivera et al., (2002), godparents "may be prominent leaders or older people who hold some position of authority and respect within the Latino community" and "play an important role in the Latino family's life and are included in all traditional celebrations. The practice of godparentage formalizes relationships between the child's parents and the *compadres* and promotes a sense of community" (p. 44).

Other vital sources of strength involve the community support systems often available to Hispanic families. These include the following:

- *Botanicas:* "Shops that sell herbs as well as records and novels in Spanish."
- *Bodegas:* "Grocery stores" that "also serve as information centers for the Hispanic community, providing such information as where folk healers can be found." (Mexican, Puerto Rican, and Cuban Hispanic cultures espouse folk healers who help people deal with physical, emotional, and spiritual difficulties).
- *Club sociales:* Settings that "provide recreation as well as links to community resources, including employment and housing." (Chilman, 1993, p. 160)

Personalismo   *Personalismo* is "a preference by Latinos for forming personal relationships with others based on a strong sense of trust, cooperation, mutual help-giving, and inclusion rather than exclusion" (Morales, 1996, p. 275). Ho, Rasheed, and Rasheed (2004) explain:

> Along with the concept of *familismo,* Latinos define their self-worth in terms of those inner qualities that give them self-respect and earn them the respect of others

[emphasis added]. They feel an inner dignity *(dignidad)* and expect others to show respect *(respeto)* for that dignity. Personalismo is also a cultural trait that reflects a collectivisitic worldview (Levine & Padilla, 1980) in which there is a great deal of emotional investment in the family. Positive interpersonal interaction will help to maintain mutual dependency and closeness for a lifetime. Hence, great importance is given to those positive interpersonal and social skills to facilitate warm, close relationships. (p. 152)

This value can provide a natural predisposition for practice in neighborhoods and communities where people work together and are concerned about each other.

Machismo and Marianismo Morales (1996) describes the concepts of *machismo* and *marianismo*:

> *Machismo* refers to a man's responsibility to provide for, protect, and defend his family. His loyalty and sense of responsibility to family, friends, and community make him a good man. The Anglo-American definition of *macho* that describes sexist, male-chauvinist behavior is radically different from the original Latino meaning of *machismo,* which convened the notion of "an honorable and responsible man."
>
> *Marianismo* refers to the responsibility of a woman to provide for, protect, and nurture her family and to value motherhood strongly. Her self-sacrificing dedication to the family and motherhood is viewed with great esteem and is expected of Latinas. The term comes from the biblical Virgin Mary (Maria) and refers to her purity and sanctity in relation to the family and her influence in maintaining high moral and ethical standards. (p. 274)

Santiago-Rivera and her colleagues (2002) reflect: "There is considerable debate over the extent to which Latinos adhere to traditional gender roles in contemporary U.S. society. Although evidence suggests that gender roles are undergoing transformation, the complexities surrounding this phenomenon are far from clear-cut" (p. 51).

Weaver (2005) indicates that "although distinct gender roles exist, it is important to recognize that not all Latinas fit these roles to the same extent," and gives the following example:

> Latinas are often stereotyped as passive and submissive, but many changes have taken place in marriages and families in the last decade. Many Latinas now work outside the home and may wield decision-making power about family finances. It is important to understand evolving gender roles within Latino families. (p. 146)

Today over 58 percent of Hispanic women are in the workforce compared to 64 percent of African American women and 59 percent of white women, respectively (U.S. Census Bureau, 2004). From a strengths perspective, Hispanic women function as socializers, educators, and promoters of values and beliefs within family systems. Hispanic couples vary widely in terms of who assumes decision-making power and responsibility for family support, as do couples in any other ethnic or racial group. Other factors to consider that influence gender roles include educational level, income, location, history in this country, verbal communication, and family structure (Santiago-Rivera et al., 2002).

Spirituality   A third theme characterizing many Hispanic families is the importance of spirituality and religion. Weaver (2005) explains:

> Spirituality has a fundamental shaping influence on the lives of many Latinos. Catholicism is a defining force of family and gender roles for Latino people.... Latino Catholicism revolves around the concepts of life and death. This fatalistic belief system emphasizes that God will provide. There is a pervading sense that much of what happens is beyond an individual's personal control. Most Latinos are Roman Catholic, but many espouse beliefs and practices influenced by indigenous and African belief systems. (p. 147; Santiago-Rivera et al., 2002)

Negroni-Rodriguez and Morales (2001) give the following examples of such folk beliefs including:

Espiritismo (among Puerto Ricans): "The belief in spirits. Everyone is believed to have spirits of protection, and these can be increased by performing good deeds and decreasing evil. Latinos who ascribe to *espiritismo* believe that loved ones can be around in spirit after death and can lead one's life in times of difficulties. *Espiritistas* (spiritist healers) communicate with spirits and can be incarnated by them. Healing can take place with prescribed folk healing treatment (p. 135)."

Curanderismo (among Mexican Americans and other Central and South Americans): The practice of curing "physical, emotional, and folk illnesses. *Curanderos/as* are healers who use a range of treatments, such as herbal remedies, inhalation, sweating, massage, incantations, and *limpieza* (a ritual cleansing) (p. 135)."

Santeria (among Cuban Americans): Practices that combine "African deities with Catholic saints. The *santeros/as* are priests who function as healers, diviners, and directors of rituals (p. 135)."

 ## Critical Thinking Questions 11.1

People of color have a long history of discrimination in the United States (Delgado, 1997). How has discrimination and lack of appreciation for diversity negatively affected Hispanic people? How might obstacles to progress be demolished and improvements be made?

Case Examples Involving Empowerment for Hispanics

There are many ways communities can empower Hispanic people. The next section reviews some research regarding Hispanic women's perceptions of their means of successfully helping to empower their communities. The subsequent two sections provide case examples of empowerment—one involving Latina-owned beauty parlors and the other community assets assessment conducted by Latino youths.

Hispanic Women Empower Communities   Lazzari, Ford, and Haughey (1996) studied 21 Hispanic women who were active in social service related employment and volunteer activities in a variety of Colorado communities. An old stereotype portrays "Hispanic men as macho and Hispanic women as passive and subservient" (Lazzari, et al., 1996, p. 198; Melville, 1980). This research paints quite a different picture. The women interviewed were involved in activities that included "performing tasks for others (for example, teaching translating, connecting with resources), performing tasks for oneself to service others (for example, becoming certified in domestic violence counseling, developing leadership skills, learning Spanish), and performing tasks in groups to help others (for example, networking grassroots organizing , participating in decision making)" (Lazzari et al., 1996, p. 200).

These women indicated that factors supporting and sustaining them "in their extensive amount of community involvement included seeing the need, feeling personal satisfaction, receiving support from others, and having personal beliefs and obligations" (such as a sense of responsibility or spiritual beliefs) (Lazzari, et al., 1996, p. 201). It is the social worker's task to identify such strong potential actors in community development, help them, and work with them on the behalf of communities.

   ## Critical Thinking Questions 11.2

In what ways do these Hispanic women's perceptions concerning empowering communities differ from traditional male approaches?

Case Example: Latina-Owned Beauty Parlors and Empowerment   We have established that there are many ways to empower people in communities. Some might not be that obvious. For example, one study of Puerto Rican–owned grocery stores and restaurants found that such small businesses can serve their communities in ways far beyond selling food. They can:

- Furnish credit and cash checks when necessary.
- Provide information about community issues and events.
- Supply information about what's going on in their homeland.
- Provide informal counseling to people in crisis.
- Furnish information about relevant, available social services.
- Help community residents interpret and fill out government forms.
- Provide "cultural connectedness to the homeland through the selling of videotapes, publications," etc. (Delgado, 1997, p. 447).

Targeting beauty parlors might not be the first approach that comes to mind when trying to empower a community. However, Delgado (1997) pursued this idea by identifying Latina-owned beauty parlors in Lawrence, Massachusetts, and interviewing their owners. Some findings were similar to those cited above concerning the expanded community roles of small businesses. Although no social service agency had approached any of the owners to solicit their involvement in formal community service roles such as task force or advisory board member, most owners expressed interest in assuming such leadership roles. Owners understood the impacts of the community's problems ("most notably alcoholism and family violence") on their customers and their families, and recognized the need to address these issues (Delgado, 1997, p. 449).

This research emphasizes the significant roles that small businesses such as beauty parlors can play in communities. Social workers who intend to strengthen communities can use innovative strategies to do so. Delgado (1997) suggests that social workers and social service organizations can pursue "sponsoring workshops for small business development, contracting with small businesses for goods and services whenever possible, and facilitating the provision of consultation for owners (p. 450). Delgado notes that such efforts benefit both the businesses and the larger community:

> Latino small businesses can be organized into coalitions to increase their visibility, advocacy, purchase of supplies, and so forth. In turn, owners are an excellent community resource to be tapped for agency boards, advisory committees, task forces, and commissions. (p. 450)

Case Example: Latino Youth Conduct a Community Assets Assessment   We have emphasized the importance of using community strengths to empower communities. Delgado (1998a) describes a project conducted by New Bridges (Nuevo Puente), an agency established by a Center on Substance Abuse Prevention grant. The grant targeted at-risk youth "who are vulnerable to, or likely to be harmed by, a specific medical, social, or environmental circumstance" such as substance use, truancy, delinquency, depression, or suicide (Barker, 1995, p. 28). New Bridges' purpose is to identify and recruit natural helping resources to participate in substance abuse prevention activities. Other facets of New Bridges include provision of "cultural and educational activities"; opportunities to learn about "the effect of substance abuse on individuals, families, and communities; and training "to carry out school and community education on alcohol, tobacco, and other drugs" (Delgado, 1998a, pp. 204–205).

New Bridges hired six girls and four boys to conduct a community strengths assessment of a 40-block urban community. Interviewers asked representatives of business establishments questions about type of business, when it initially opened, availability of contact people, social services provided (if a social services agency), and "willingness to collaborate with schools and agencies on community projects" (Delgado, 1998a, p. 205). Goals were to "provide youths with an appreciation of community strengths, raise school and human services agency awareness of community assets, and develop an assets directory" (Delgado, 1998a, p. 205).

Results indicated that "the use of Latino adolescents in community asset assessments offers much promise" for social work (Delgado, 1998a, p. 210). Although this assessment was conducted via a grant-created community agency, Delgado (1998a) presents a number of suggestions for implementation of community asset assessments. He suggests doing so through community schools because there is natural access to youth, including those at-risk.

First, school social workers can recruit youths to identify "potential student leaders, candidates for peer education programs, and possible projects involving natural support systems" (Delgado, 1998a, p. 209). For example, the young people involved in the New Bridges project decided they wanted to go on a trip and finance it by sponsoring a car wash. They asked identified Latino businesses to contribute a small amount of money (such as a nickel or a quarter) for each car washed. In return, the youth listed sponsors' names on a billboard to provide publicity for them. This is a good example of how a community can work together to enhance relationships among various facets (that is, this group of young people and local businesses) to reach mutually positive goals (that is, financial backing for the trip and positive publicity for the businesses).

A second idea for using assets assessment is for schools to invite interested business owners from the community in to talk about how they started their businesses. In this way owners could provide positive role models for young people and sow some seeds about career possibilities and goals.

A third idea for using the community assets assessment is to use information gathered to sponsor special school projects. Extra credit might be assigned to investigate community strengths in a social studies course. Students might videotape interviews with interested community residents or community service representatives. They might then share these tapes with other students or even social service agencies to provide education about social issues or cultural strengths.

Critical Thinking Questions 11.3

In what ways might a project such as New Bridges serve to enhance young people's self-esteem and why?

EMPOWERMENT FOR GAY, LESBIAN, BISEXUAL, AND TRANSGENDER PEOPLE THROUGH POLITICAL ACTION ORGANIZATIONS

Chapter 1 introduced the concepts of sexual orientation, the expression of gender, and a number of related terms. It defined *sexual orientation* as sexual and romantic attraction to persons of one or both genders.

Elze (2006) explains the historical context facing gay, lesbian, bisexual, and transgender (GLBT) people:

> The history of gay, lesbian, bisexual, and transgender people in America is a history of oppression and resistance. Since colonial times, gender-variant people, and people who love and sexually desire those of the same sex, have been imprisoned, executed, witch-hunted, pilloried [placed in a frame with hands and head locked in as a means of public embarrassment], confined in asylums, fired, excommunicated, disinherited, evicted, extorted, entrapped, censored, declared mentally ill, drugged, and subjected to castration, hormone injections, clitoridectomy [surgical removal of the clitoris], hysterectomy [surgical removal of the uterus], ovariectomy [surgical removal of the ovaries], lobotomy [surgical cutting of the nerves connecting the brain's two frontal lobes], psychoanalysis, and aversive therapies such as electroshock and pharmacologic shock. (p. 43)

A *political action organization* is based on the concept of a social action group. It is an organization that conducts "coordinated efforts to influence legislation, election of candidates, and social causes" (Barker, 2003, p. 330). Changing legislation and social policy on the behalf of GLBT people can involve the provision of due and equal rights, the purging of discrimination, and the enhancement of overall well-being.

The National Association of Social Workers *Code of Ethics* states that "Social workers should not practice, condone, facilitate, or collaborate with any form of discrimination on the basis of ... sexual orientation" (NASW, 1999, 4.02). It continues that "social workers should act to prevent and eliminate domination of, exploitation of, and discrimination against any person, group, or class on the basis of ... sexual orientation" (NASW, 1999, 6.04d). It is the ethical obligation of social workers to advocate on the behalf of GLBT people so that they have the right to self-determination and equal treatment under the law.

Important Issues for GLBT People

Many issues concerning GLBT people require attention, six of which are mentioned here (Barusch, 2006; Messinger, 2006). They include the need for nondiscrimination laws, the recognition of same-sex relationships, family policies for GLBT parents, harassment and violence against GLBT people, housing, and employment.

Need for Nondiscrimination Laws First, there is a need for nondiscrimination laws. Although debates are currently taking place at the state level, there is no federal legislation prohibiting discrimination against GLBT people in "public and private employment, public accommodations, insurance practices, housing, credit, and education" (Barusch, 2006; Berger & Kelly, 1995, p. 1071; Elze, 2006). A few states have laws securing some of these rights. In lieu of a federal law, political action organizations can work to establish laws enhancing rights at the state and local levels.

Recognition of Same-Sex Relationships   A second issue involves the recognition of same-sex relationships, particularly the legalization of gay marriage. The possibility is being hotly debated at local, state, and national levels. As of February 2006, 18 states had passed constitutional bans on gay marriage, and more were considering doing so (Buchanan, 2006). In June, 2006 the U.S. Senate failed to pass a constitutional amendment banning gay marriage for the second time, despite President George W. Bush's avid support (Kellman, 2006; Murray, 2006). Only one state, Massachusetts, has legalized gay marriage, although Washington state is considering doing so at the time of this writing (Buchanan, 2006; Rosenberg, 2006). National polls conducted in mid-2006 by CNN, Gallup, and FOX News found that 55 to 58 percent of those asked felt gay marriage should not be legalized (PollingReport.com, 2006). Inability to marry denies GLBT couples, among many other things, potential income tax, health insurance, and Social Security (upon death of a spouse) benefits in addition to decision-making rights when partners are seriously ill and are unable to make decisions for themselves.

Family Policies for GLBT Parents   A third issue involves family policies for GLBT parents. Thirty percent of same-sex couples have children under the age of 18 living in their households; of those who have children, over half (56 percent) have two or more living with them (Gay Demographics, 2006). Some research proposes that about "30 percent of all lesbian and bisexual female parents have been threatened with loss of custody. Fathers, known sperm donors, female co-parents, grandparents and other relatives all have the potential of bringing custody challenges against lesbian mothers" (Cahill, Ellen, & Tobias, 2002, p. 74, cited in Messinger, 2006, p. 441). Only in the District of Columbia is sexual orientation prohibited from being a determining factor in custody and visitation decisions (Cahill et al., 2002; Messinger, 2006).

Harassment and Violence Against GLBT People   A fourth area threatening the rights of GLBT people involves harassment and violence. Messinger (2006) explains:

> Hate crimes legislation at the state and federal levels is designed to impose additional penalties for certain crimes that are based on ... [spiteful ill will] toward some element of a person's identity, specifically an identity of a population that is oppressed. While all but five states have some sort of hate crimes legislation, only seven states have statutes against hate crimes that are based on prejudice toward gender expression, and twenty-nine states have statutes against hate crimes that are based on prejudice toward sexual orientation ... The federal statute used to prosecute hate crimes does not include sexual orientation or gender expression as protected categories. ... GLBT activists have been working with friendly politicians to pass federal hate crimes legislation that would include sexual orientation and gender expression (pp. 444–445).

Housing　A fifth area of concern involves housing, as Messinger (2006) explains:

> Most GLBT families have no legal remedy if they encounter discrimination in purchasing or renting a dwelling. There is no federal law banning discrimination in housing that is based upon sexual orientation or gender expression, though ten states and the District of Columbia ban discrimination on the basis of sexual orientation (Cahill et al., 2002). (Messinger, 2006, p. 448)

Employment　A sixth issue relevant to GLBT people involves employment. According to Messinger (2006), "A cursory review of employment law reveals that most GLBT people have no protection from harassment and discrimination in the workplace" (p. 449). She explains that an executive order issued in 1998 "does ban discrimination based on sexual orientation in federal agencies (other than the military) but does not include employment protection for transgender people (Cahill et al., 2002, pp. 166–168)." And, she continues, the situation at the state and local levels is little better:

> In 2002 twelve states and the District of Columbia prohibited discrimination on the basis of sexual orientation in both the public and the private sectors, while nine states banned discrimination only in the public sector (Cahill et al., 2002, pp. 166–168). More than two hundred cities, towns, and counties have laws prohibiting discrimination based on sexual orientation, although they differ as to whether they apply to public and/or private agencies. Two states, along with thirty-three municipalities, explicitly ban discrimination in public agencies on the basis of gender identity (Cahill & Jones, 2001; Currah & Minter, 2000). This still leaves many GLBT people without protections. (p. 449)

Critical Thinking Questions 11.4

What are your personal views concerning each of the six issues mentioned concerning GLBT people? Explain.

Political Action Organizations

Political action organizations working on the behalf of GLBT people to address these and other issues can function in at least three ways. These include providing direct support to political candidates, educating the public to gain support, and conducting legislative advocacy (Barker, 2003; Messinger, 2006).

Providing Support to Political Candidates　Political action organizations can identify and support the campaigns of political candidates advocating for GLBT rights. Haynes and Mickelson (2003) describe candidate selection:

> Because it is not unusual for a political candidate to slant a position on a particular issue in order to gain the support of specific groups, often it becomes

necessary to determine how a politician really stands on issues that may not be of major campaign interest. In the case of incumbents, the best measurement is action already taken. Consequently, to give a clearer picture of the candidate's position on certain issues, PACs often prepare and publicize a record of the candidate's votes on relevant pieces of legislation—sometimes referred to as the "report card." (p. 155)

Questions can be posed. To what extent did the candidate support GLBT rights in the past? What is the candidate's verbal stance and/or voting record on such issues as anti-hate legislation and gay marriage?

Because political campaigns cost money, a primary means of supporting political candidates is through financial support. This is often done by forming and working through a *political action committee (PAC)*, a group whose purpose is to raise money and provide support for designated political candidates (Barker, 2003; Haynes & Mickelson, 2003). A PAC can participate in any number of fund-raising activities, from bake sales to walk-a-thons to direct solicitation for financial support.

Political action organizations can also provide candidates support by endorsing them. The "PAC can endorse the candidate by stating that the membership organization (for example, the NASW [National Association of Social Workers]) recommends that social workers vote for that candidate" (Haynes & Mickelson, 2003, p. 158). Haynes and Mickelson (2003) elaborate:

> Services and support can be offered [by a PAC], including mailing and telephone lists. Candidates are aware that the endorsement alone will not guarantee membership votes, but mailing lists and telephone numbers facilitate the candidate's ability to reach PAC members and to gain their support and labor. . . .
>
> A PAC can recruit and assign volunteers from its membership to assist candidates, thereby increasing the effect of the endorsement. PACE [Political Action for Candidate Endorsement, NASW's political action component] has found this to be most effective because candidates have discovered that social workers have excellent campaign skills. Social workers listen well, are organized, are trained to take a broad perspective, and can work well with a variety of individuals (Wolk, 1981). Some candidates enlist social workers as campaign managers. Also after an election, social workers often are hired as aides to work out constituent problems. (pp. 159–160).

Educating the Public to Gain Support   A political action organization can work to influence public opinion to enlighten citizens about GLBT issues and mobilize citizens to vote on GLBT people's behalf. Citizens support politicians who, in turn, formulate laws that govern our macro social environment. Social workers can urge voters to critically think about issues of self-determination and expand their perceptions about human rights with respect to GLBT people.

In order to educate effectively, it's first important to define the issues and know the relevant facts (Hoefer, 2003). Myths and stereotypes that support prejudice against gay and lesbian people must be identified and disputed. The following facts should be emphasized (Morrow, 2006):

- Sexual orientation is "an innate orientation," not "a lifestyle choice" (p. 4). Significant research supports a strong biological component in the development of sexual orientation. "The term *sexual orientation* is more appropriate than the term *sexual preference*," explains Morrow.

> *Preference* implies ease and simplicity of choice or selection, while *orientation* more accurately connotes the innate essence of a person's intimate and affectional nature. Perhaps the best way to understand the role of choice in relation to sexual orientation is that people must choose whether to embrace or reject whatever is their essential orientation. (p. 4)

- Sexual orientation is a normal facet of human diversity. Chapter 1 established that the expression of gender is a complex concept. Van Wormer, Wells, and Boes (2000) explain that in a homophobic society that has much anxiety about sexuality, "sexual expression is often perceived as dirty, disgusting, and lustful, particularly same-sex sexuality (p. 89). They continue:

> Although sexual behaviors are similar across sexual orientations, the assumptions are that gay males and lesbians engage in homosexual behaviors that differ vastly from heterosexual behaviors when, in fact, sexual behaviors that people engage in are more appropriately deemed as human sexual behaviors. Gay men and lesbians do differ sexually from their heterosexual counterparts in that they are less goal oriented, communicate more, use more erotic words, [and] do not let interruptions ruin the mood ... Gays and lesbians more often include pleasure, intimacy, and emotions into their definitions of sexuality than do heterosexuals. (p. 89)

- GLBT people are just as likely to be good parents as heterosexual people (Barusch, 2006). Good parenting skills have no relationship to sexual orientation. GLBT parents are not more likely to molest children. In reality, 80 percent of all child molesting is done to young girls by heterosexual men who usually are people trusted and close to them (for example, a father, stepfather, or brother) (McAnulty & Burnette, 2003; Patterson, 1995). Heterosexual men are 11 times more likely to be child molesters than gay men (McCammon, Knox, & Schacht, 2004; Moser, 1992). There is no indication that gay or lesbian parents will cause their children to have a nonheterosexual orientation (Barusch, 2006; Morales, 1995). Children growing up in families with gay or lesbian parents are just as psychologically healthy as children growing up with heterosexual parents (Barusch, 2006; Laird, 1995; Woodman, 1995).
- Same-sex couples "develop long-term, committed relationships" just like heterosexual couples do (Morrow, 2006, p. 6). Relationships are complex. Just as heterosexuals, GLBT people may enter permanent relationships or may have a series of shorter-term relationships. However, GLBT people lack the social and legal supports provided to married heterosexuals.

Legislative Advocacy   *Advocacy* is the practice of actively intervening on the behalf of clients so that they get what they need (Kirst-Ashman & Hull, 2006b). *Legislative advocacy* is the process of influencing legislators to support legislation promoting specific goals. *Lobbying* is the practice of seeking "direct

| Highlight 11.2 | **Empowerment of GLBT People Through Special Social Services** |

There are many ways social services can respond to the needs of GLBT people. Special social services can be developed to lessen oppression and educate the general public about the need for gay rights. Mann (1997) identifies projects including a national organization and two community initiatives pursuing these ends on their behalf.

The Bridges Project sponsored by the American Friends Service Committee (AFSC), a Quaker organization, serves as a "national clearinghouse" to provide "information, resources, referrals and assistance to LGBT and their allies nationwide" (Mann, 1997, p. 96). The project serves to "support the formation of new youth-led organizations; enable mainstream organizations to effectively accept their LGBT youth; work with adult LGBT groups to include LGBT youth as leaders within their organizations; refer individuals and groups to sources that can help answer questions; and link groups working on similar issues" (pp. 96–97).

A second example of how special services can be developed to address issues is the Rural Transportation Program "sponsored by the State of Nevada's Bureau of Disease Control and Intervention Services" (Mann, 1997, p. 98). The program's purpose is to assist HIV-positive people who live in rural areas in transporting themselves to medical or social services appointments in urban areas. The program provides a credit card to eligible service recipients that can be used to pay "for transportation related purchases by the consumer and/or a family member, a friend, or volunteer assisting the consumer"; purchases can include "gas, oil, windshield wiper fluid, anti-freeze, food, water, sodas and juices" (Mann, 1997, p. 99).

A final example of how a community has developed special services to meet lesbian and gay persons' needs is Beyond the Closet, a rural central Oregon organization. Its goals are to educate citizens, advocate for lesbian and gay rights, and provide support where needed (Mann, 1997). The organization has achieved the following accomplishments:

> the organizing of the premiere gay and lesbian lecture series in rural Oregon; the facilitation of a meeting between area clergy and Beyond the Closet spokespersons; . . . and the organization of several events such as a "queer" book sale and film series, concerts by out lesbian performers, and the distribution of radio, television and printed interviews and opinions regarding issues relevant to the LGBT community. (Mann, 1997, pp. 99–100)

access to lawmakers to influence legislation and public policy"; the expression originated when people seeking to influence lawmakers met with them in the lobbies of legislative houses (Barker, 2003, p. 253). Political organizational members can lobby legislators or testify before legislative committees to educate decision makers about issues and encourage them to vote in GLBT people's best interest. The same principles involved in the earlier discussion concerning educating the general public also apply here.

An example of a political action organization activity is to establish a statewide telephone network where members contact designated other members who in turn would initiate their own designated telephone contacts and so on. Before legislative decisions are made, members can alert each other to the issues via the network. Members can then exert immediate pressure upon legislative decision makers by writing letters, emailing, or phoning in their pleas advocating for whatever GLBT rights issue had current legislative attention.

We've established that empowerment can be pursued in many ways. Highlight 11.2 provides examples of programs empowering GLBT people through special social services.

EMPOWERMENT IN THE MACRO ENVIRONMENT FOR WOMEN

Lorber (2005) comments on the status of women:

> As a *social institution* ["an established and enduring pattern of social relationships" (Mooney et al., 2007, p. 4)], gender determines the distribution of power, privileges, and economic resources [emphasis added]. Other major social statuses combine with gender to produce an overall stratification system, but gender privileges men over women in most social groups.
>
> Through parenting, the schools, and the mass media, gendered norms and expectations get built into boys' and girls' sense of self as a certain kind of human being. Other social statuses, such as racial ethnic identification and religion, are similarly socially constructed and reproduced, but gender is so deeply embedded that it is rarely examined or rebelled against. By the time people get to be adults, alternative ways of acting as women and men and arranging work and family life are literally unthinkable. (p. 242)

Many facts support the existence of oppression for women:

- The median income of women who work full-time is 77 percent of what men earn (U.S. Census Bureau, 2004).
- Women of color are significantly more disadvantaged than white women. Hispanic women earn less than African American women, and both groups earn less than white women (U.S. Census Bureau, 2004).
- For all races, women earn significantly less than men do at every educational level. The average annual earnings for women with a bachelor's degree or more are about 64 percent of what men with an equivalent education earn. Similarly, the average annual income for women with a high school education is about 72 percent of what correspondingly educated men earn (U.S. Census Bureau, 2004).
- Women are clustered in low paying supportive occupations such as clerical workers, teachers, and service workers while men tend to assume higher paying occupations such as managers, professionals, and construction workers (National Committee on Pay Equity, 2003; U.S. Census Bureau, 2003).
- Women earn significantly less than men in the same job category doing the same work (Ruth, 2001; Sapiro, 2003).
- Women are significantly more likely to be poor than men (Sapiro, 2003).
- Women of color are significantly more likely to be poor than white women (Renzetti & Curran, 2003).
- Similar disparities prevail in the household:

> Women perform more household work than men do, with the figure averaging out at around two-thirds. The other third tends to be shared by men and children, with female children performing a greater amount of housework than male children. In addition, men tend to overestimate the work they do in the home and women underestimate it ... [Additionally, women and men tend to do different kinds of tasks where women] "do the repetitive, ongoing, daily

kinds of tasks, and men are more likely to perform the less repetitive or seasonal tasks. ... Women are much more likely to 'multitask' or perform a series of tasks simultaneously. This means, for example, that they might be folding laundry at the same time that they are feeding the baby, or are cooking dinner at the same time that they are vacuuming. (Shaw & Lee, 2004, pp. 324–325)

 ## Critical Thinking Questions 11.5

What are the reasons for these differences in income, employment, poverty, and contribution to household work? To what extent do you feel women are oppressed and why?

Because women are an oppressed population-at-risk, it is social workers' responsibility to work in the macro environment for positive change. Chapter 2 introduced a number of feminist principles that can be applied to the treatment of women by macro systems. These include using a gender lens, the end of patriarchy, empowerment, consciousness raising, the personal is political, the importance of process, unity in diversity, and validation. The following section presents a case example for empowering at-risk pregnant women.

Empowering At-Risk Pregnant Women

Prenatal care is critically important for mothers and infants. Balsanek (1998, p. 411) cites a number of facts:

- Approximately 25 percent of pregnant women do not receive adequate prenatal care.
- The number of women receiving no prenatal care at all is accelerating.
- Women who are "young, poor, unmarried, relatively uneducated, uninsured, or living in inner cities or rural areas" are likely to receive the poorest prenatal care. These women are thus *at-risk* of problems and complications.
- Women who receive less than adequate prenatal care are significantly more likely to have infants with low birth weights and a range of disabilities.

Shared Beginnings, a Denver program, provides a good example of how various facets of a community have come together to address this issue (Balsanek, 1998). Initial consciousness raising occurred through extensive media coverage of the problem, alerting the public to the fact that increasing numbers of poor, single, and young mothers failed to seek or receive prenatal care. The project was spearheaded by a concerned volunteer philanthropist who brought citizens, social services representatives, health care personnel, and potential financial backers together to initiate the project. Fund-raising projects included a luncheon program supported by influential community members and solicitation of financial donations.

Participants involved in the project established five basic program goals. The first was to educate the community concerning the importance of prenatal health care and to alter attitudes on health care's behalf. A second goal was the initiation of a "Sharing Partners" program where volunteer paraprofessionals would go out into the community to educate residents about prenatal care and encourage them to use services (p. 414). The third goal was to establish an ongoing agency complete with director, administrative assistant, and volunteer coordinator to oversee progress. The fourth was the creation of a "Baby Store" located in a local hospital where "coupons could be redeemed for new baby care items to reinforce health care appointment attendance before the baby is born and immunizations after the baby is born" (p. 414). The final goal was to integrate a research component to evaluate the program's effectiveness and provide suggestions for improvement. In summary, "Shared Beginnings represents a grassroots approach to providing the community support that poor and at-risk families need to raise healthy children" (p. 418).

SPIRITUAL COMMUNITIES AND EMPOWERMENT

We've established that *spirituality* "includes one's values, beliefs, mission, awareness, subjectivity, experience, sense of purpose and direction, and a kind of striving toward something greater than oneself" (Frame, 2003, p. 3). Chapter 8 addressed the importance of spiritual values and religion for many African Americans and First Nations people. The following two case examples reflect how spiritual communities can empower their members. First, an African American spiritual community serves as a safe haven for its youth. Second, a Navajo spiritual and cultural community empowers its senior citizens through the provision of spiritually and culturally sensitive care to nursing home residents.

A Spiritual Community as a Haven for African American Youth

A common theme in the lives of many African Americans involves strong religious beliefs and a close relationship with the church, especially an African American church (Diller, 2004; Dhooper & Moore, 2001; Paniagua, 1998). Many African American families consider the church to be a part of the extended family, providing similar nurturance and support (Paniagua, 1998). Dhooper and Moore (2001) explain:

> The African American church continues to address not only the religious and spiritual needs of the individual, family, and community, but also their social needs. It serves as a coping and survival mechanism against the effects of racial discrimination and oppression and as a place where African Americans are able to experience unconditional positive regard. (p. 101)

The following is an example of how social workers can help enhance a community's functioning, in this case, an African American spiritual community in Utah. Social workers can serve as human resources in a wide range of capacities. First, a study is discussed that explores the values and opinions of the spiritual community's members. Subsequently, a project is described that demonstrates how social workers can creatively work with a spiritual community to help meet its needs.

Haight (1999) conducted an ethnographic study targeting African American youth belonging to the First Baptist Church in Salt Lake City, Utah. The church was established over 100 years ago by " 'a Baptist Prayer Band,' a group of African Americans who, excluded from worshipping in the white churches, met in one another's homes" (p. 247). Haight (1998) notes that "African American Utahns, like African Americans in other parts of the country, experience racial discrimination in employment, housing, education, and everyday social interactions" (p. 248). African Americans are a tiny minority in Utah. Additionally, most of the Utah population belongs to the Church of Jesus Christ of Latter-Day Saints, a tightly knit spiritual community that sponsors a wide realm of social and cultural activities for its members.

Extensive interviews with First Baptist Church members revealed a local environmental context for children that was "negligent at best and virulently racist at worst" (p. 249). Of special concern was the perceived "negative expectations" of white educators in the public school system (p. 249). In response, First Baptist Church members felt the church's spiritual community provided a safe haven where children could learn about their cultural heritage in a safe, supportive environment. Emphasis was placed on "helping children understand the relevance of, and then apply, biblical concepts to their own lives" (p. 252). Additionally, children were strongly encouraged to participate in ongoing learning activities. One illustration is that children were expected to respond to a series of "call-and-response sequences." Haight gives an example: "When the teacher said that they would no longer be fishermen, but that they would be fishers of ———?, the class responded that they would be fishers of men" (p. 253). In this way, each individual was expected to actively participate. The nurturing spiritual community provided children with an environment where they could develop resilience to cope with any rejection, isolation, or discrimination they experienced in the external environment. Church members also placed great importance on positive, supportive relationships between adults and children.

Along with First Baptist Church leaders, social workers initiated and developed "an intervention, informed by knowledge generated through the ethnographic study, to support the development of children's resilience" (p. 253). This intervention strategy was the establishment of a "Computer Club" (p. 254). First Baptist Church members "both prioritized educational achievement and identified school as problematic for African American children" (p. 254). Furthermore, children's computer literacy was perceived as "a specific area of need, and learning more about computers as an opportunity that children and families would embrace" (p. 254). Thus, members felt that enhancing children's competence in using computers was a valuable goal. Although the Computer Club's primary focus was educational computer games, student volunteers from a local university also participated with children in a range of activities, including field trips, parties, picnics, computer-generated art shows, African dance groups, and a gospel choir (p. 254). The activities provided a healthy atmosphere for students and children to enjoy mutual experiences, share ideas, and develop positive relationships.

The workers portrayed in this example first explored the values and strengths of the community and then worked together with community members toward a mutually desirable goal. The process was based on mutual respect and cooperation. Haight (1998) concludes that

> the ability of social workers to develop knowledge of cultural beliefs and practices relevant both to African American communities in general and to the unique African American communities in which they are practicing is critical to the development of ethnic-sensitive social work interventions such as the Computer Club. (p. 255)

The Navajo Community, Spirituality, and Respect for Older Adult Members

The Navajo community traditionally has maintained a rich fabric of spiritual beliefs intertwined with its cultural traditions and values. It is a community because of its intricate interpersonal relationships, sense of identity, and recognition of members' belonging regardless of where they reside. Many Navajos live on the Navajo reservation, a large geographical community located in the south central Colorado Plateau including parts of Arizona, New Mexico, and Utah.

An ongoing theme in social work practice is the importance of responding to diverse ethnic, cultural, and spiritual values and needs. This example portrays how the Navajo community has responded to meet the needs of aging members in ways differing from commonly held European Caucasian traditions. First, values focusing on spiritual beliefs and family centrality are discussed. Subsequently, a Navajo community's nursing home's responsiveness to meeting Navajo residents' needs is explored.

Traditional Navajo elders, referred to here as "Grandparents," adhere to cultural values that differ from European Caucasian traditions. For one thing, Mercer (1996) explains that

> traditional Navajo religion deals with controlling the many supernatural powers in the Navajo world. Earth Surface People (living and dead humans) and Holy People (supernatural beings) interact. ... Navajos abide by prescriptions and proscriptions (taboos) given by the Holy People to maintain harmony with others, nature, and supernatural forces. ... The goal of traditional Navajo life is to live in harmony and die of old age. If one indulges in excesses, has improper contacts with dangerous powers, or deliberately or accidentally breaks other rules, then disharmony, conflict, evil, sickness of body and mind, misfortune, and disaster result. (pp. 182–183)

Thus, when an imbalance occurs, a person may become sick, which can be attributed to "infection by animals, natural phenomena, or evil spirits such as ghosts (*chindi*) and witches" (p. 183). Preventive ceremonies can address the root of the illness, involve the appropriate Holy People, seek to restore harmony, and avoid ill fortune. "As major social and religious events involving entire communities, ceremonies are a major investment of time and resources for the afflicted person, extended family, and clan" (p. 183).

Another primary traditional value in Navajo life is the importance placed on the extended family. Referred to as a clan, such families include a much more extensive membership than that of grandparents, parents, and children. The Navajo community has "over 60 clan-based kinship groups." A related concept is the importance of the *hogan,* or home, as the center of Navajo family life.

Mercer (1996) explored the treatment of senior Navajo people, the Grandparents, who reside in the Chinle Nursing Home, a nonprofit agency whose Board of Directors is composed solely of Navajos. She investigated how treatment for Grandparents in the Chinle home differed from typical treatment provided outside of the reservation. She found that, essentially, the Chinle home emphasized the importance of spiritual values and *cultural care,* "the learned and transmitted values and beliefs that enable people to maintain their well-being and health and to deal with illness, disability and death" (Leininger, 1990, 1992; Mercer, 1996, p. 186).

Mercer (1996) found that culturally and spiritually sensitive care is applied in at least six major areas: "communication; clan associations and social structure; personal space, modesty, privacy, and cleanliness; traditional food; dying and death; and cultural rituals" (pp. 186–188).

1. *Communication.* Few Navajo Grandparents are fluent in English, so translators are used. Such translation is done with great sensitivity, as often the Navajo language has no word that means exactly what an English word does. Additionally, sensitivity is important while listening, as interrupting a speaker is considered extremely rude.

2. *Clan associations and social structure.* Clan associations are very important to Navajo people. Upon introduction, Navajos traditionally announce their clan membership. Nursing home staff are sensitive to the fact that Grandparents would often have many visitors from their clan who traveled great distances at significant cost.

3. *Personal space, modesty, privacy, and cleanliness.* The Grandparents value personal space. They often find it difficult and uncomfortable to sleep in the high nursing home beds, having been accustomed to mattresses or sheep skins on the floor. Staff comply with Grandparents' wishes to sleep where they want and usually find that Grandparents eventually adjust to sleeping in beds.

   Grandparents value modesty and privacy. Therefore, communal showering is a problem. Rather, Grandparents often prefer sweat baths, which they feel cleanse them both physically and spiritually. The nursing home provides saunas to simulate these sweat baths and offers showers to residents twice each week.

Finally, Grandparents often prefer sleeping in their daytime clothes rather than changing into nightgowns or pajamas. Staff allow Grandparents to sleep in whatever they want. In due time, most come to choose night clothes.

4. *Traditional food.* Grandparents prefer "grilled mutton [meat of a mature sheep], mutton stew, fry bread, corn, fried potatoes, and coffee" (p. 187). In response, nursing home staff serve lamb three times a month and usually bake fresh bread. Staff also encourage family members to bring foods the Grandparents prefer (that is, those that comply with health-related dietary constraints).

5. *Dying and death.* "Traditional Navajo people have many restrictions regarding contact with the dead. They do not talk about death, believing that discussing death may 'bring it to you'" (p. 187). Navajo families will usually move a dying person to a nearby brush shelter to avoid having death occur in the *hogan.* In the event of a home death, that *hogan* is usually deserted and even demolished.

Traditionally, people touching a dead body followed specific rituals to avoid taboos. Similarly, most Grandparents and staff want to avoid touching a dead person or a dead person's clothing. Usually, a dying Grandparent is transferred to a hospital so that death will not occur in the nursing home. If a death does occur there, cleansing rituals are performed before other residents inhabit the room.

Because of their aversion to talking about death, no Grandparents will discuss such issues as living wills or power of attorney. Staff respect this value and do not pressure residents to do so.

6. *Cultural rituals.* In order to hold cultural rituals, a *hogan* was constructed near the Chinle home and is made available for ceremonies and prayers that remain important aspects of Grandparents' lives.

The point here for social workers is the importance of understanding, appreciating, and respecting the values inherent in any spiritual community. Practice should then focus on emphasizing clients' strengths and meeting clients' needs within their own value system.

EMPOWERMENT OF PEOPLE WITH DEVELOPMENTAL DISABILITIES

Bill, 35, has always lived with his parents. He has an energetic, upbeat personality and a moderate cognitive disability. His favorite activity is delivering mail as a volunteer to staff and patients at a local hospital. This is a bit tricky as he can't read. However, hospital staff, who appreciate his efforts and enthusiasm, have established a special color coding system to help him through the delivery process. Hospital staff all know him, watch for him, and assist him in carrying out his task.

Bill loves wearing the special red vest declaring him an official deliverer of the mail. He enjoys talking to patients and staff, and considers himself an integral part of the hospital environment.[2]

The hospital environment identified above provides an empowering organizational environment for Bill, an adult with a cognitive disability. People enjoy Bill's presence, support him, and include him in daily hospital life. Bill feels like he belongs.

A primary goal of social work education is "to formulate and implement social policies, services, and programs that meet basic human needs and support the development of human capacities" (CSWE, 2001, I.A.). Social workers strive to enhance people's living conditions in their social environment to make it as comfortable and supportive as possible. To do this social workers should advocate for "policies, services, and resources" that empower "populations-at-risk" and "promote social and economic justice" (CSWE, 2001, I.A.).

People with developmental disabilities are a population-at-risk, as they likely experience more difficulties in daily living, discrimination, and lack of adequate services to address their disabilities. Therefore, social workers must maintain sharp awareness of how the macro social environment affects people with developmental disabilities, their choices, and their behavior (Rothman, 2003). Communities and organizations in the macro social environment can serve to promote or deter their optimal well-being. Bill's example above shows how an organization in a community has adapted itself to empower Bill. Means of empowerment in organizational and community environments for people with developmental disabilities is the primary theme of the remainder of this chapter. This topic is given significant attention here because of its importance to practitioners and because it often receives minimal coverage in other social work textbooks.

Defining Developmental Disabilities

Five attributes characterize people with developmental disabilities (DeWeaver, 1995; DiNitto, 2005; Freedman, 1995; Maryland Developmental Disabilities Council, 2006; P.L. 101–496, 104 Stat. 1191, 1990). First, the disability is both severe and chronic, resulting from some mental or physical impairment. Second, the disability occurs before age twenty-two. Third, the conditions are likely to be permanent. Fourth, the disability "results in substantial functional limitations in three or more of the following areas of major life activity: (i) self-care, (ii) receptive and expressive language, (iii) learning, (iv) mobility, (v) self-direction, (vi) capacity for independent living, and (vii) economic self-sufficiency" (P.L. 101–496, 104 Stat. 1191, 1990). Fifth, a developmental disability demonstrates the need for lifelong supplementary help and services.

Examples of developmental disabilities are cognitive disabilities (formerly referred to as mental retardation), cerebral palsy, epilepsy, orthopedic problems, hearing impairment or deafness, visual impairment or blindness, and

---

[2] This vignette is loosely adapted from one described by J. P. Kretzmann and J. L. McKnight in *Building Communities from the Inside Out* (Chicago: ACTA Publications, 1993).

| **Highlight 11.3** | **Terms for People with Cognitive Disabilities** |

Note that the technical medical diagnosis for cognitive disabilities is still *mental retardation*. As legislation also uses that term, it will not go away. Because of the term's negative connotations, a preferred term is *cognitive disabilities*. We need to choose some specific term so we know what type of developmental disability we're talking about. The term *developmental disability* is much too broad as it comprises the various disabilities identified below.

An empowerment perspective focuses on abilities, not on retardation. It is also important to refer to people with cognitive disabilities as *people* before referring to any disability they might have. For example, referring to them as *mentally* or *cognitively challenged* people tends to emphasize the disability because the disability is stated first. Our intent is simply to respect their right to equality and dignity. As there is no easy answer, we will continue using the term cognitive disabilities here.

autism (DeWeaver, 1995). Each results in serious implications for living in the macro social environment that will be discussed below.

Cognitive Disabilities   *Cognitive disabilities* involve a condition defined by three criteria. First, there is "significantly subaverage general intellectual functioning (Criterion A) that is accompanied by significant limitations in adaptive functioning in at least two of the following skill areas: communication, self-care, home living, social/interpersonal skills, use of community resources, self-direction, functional academic skills, work leisure, health, and safety (Criterion B). The onset must occur before age 18 years (Criterion C)" (American Psychiatric Association [APA], 2000, p. 41). Highlight 11.3 discusses the use of terms to refer to this population-at-risk.

The first criterion for cognitive disabilities concerns scoring significantly below average on standard intelligence tests. The second criterion involves adaptive functioning, which the APA defines as

> how effectively individuals cope with common life demands and how well they meet the standards of personal independence expected of someone in their particular age group, sociocultural background, and community setting. Adaptive functioning may be influenced by various factors, including education, motivation, personality characteristics, social and vocational opportunities, and the mental disorders and general medical conditions that may coexist with Mental Retardation. Problems in adaptation are more likely to improve with remedial efforts than is the cognitive IQ, which tends to remain a more stable attribute. (APA, 2000, p. 42)

Individuals with cognitive disabilities, to some degree, are unable intellectually to grasp concepts and function as well and as quickly as their peers. It is estimated that between 1 and 3 percent of the population have cognitive disabilities (Goldenring, 2004).

Cerebral Palsy   *Cerebral palsy* is a disability involving problems in muscular control and coordination resulting from damage to the brain before it has matured, that is, before or during birth. Problems include lack of balance, problems walking, paralysis, weakness, uncontrolled or restricted movements, and psychological impairment, depending on where the brain damage occurred

(DeWeaver, 1995; Hallahan & Kauffman, 2003). It should be emphasized that people with cerebral palsy may experience only motor impairment, with cognitive ability being unaffected.

Seizure Disorder   *Seizure disorder* (often referred to as *epilepsy*) is an abrupt change in one's conscious state that may involve unconsciousness, convulsive and/or jerky motor activity, or sensory distortions (DeWeaver, 1995; Hallahan & Kauffman, 2003). Seizures are caused by sudden bursts of electrical activity in some brain cells causing reaction in other brain cells. Epilepsy can result from virtually any type of injury inflicted on the brain, including insufficient oxygen, chemical imbalances, infections, or physical damage (Hallahan & Kauffman, 2003).

Orthopedic Problems   *Orthopedic problems* "involve difficulties in the functioning of muscles, bones, and joints" (DeWeaver, 1995, p. 714). Although there is no neurological impairment, orthopedic problems result in inability to move about normally. Usually, difficulties involve "the legs, arms, joints, or spine, making it difficult or impossible for the child to walk, stand, sit, or use his or her hands" (Hallahan & Kauffman, 2003, p. 428). These problems may have genetic origins, or they can result from injury, disease, accidents, or other developmental disorders (Hallahan & Kauffman, 2003).

Hearing Impairment   *Hearing impairment* is a general concept indicating a hearing loss that can range from mild to extremely severe (Hallahan & Kauffman, 2003). At the extreme, a person who is deaf has no ability to hear sound and process information through hearing. Depending on its severity, a hearing impairment can seriously influence an individual's ability to speak, communicate, and learn (DeWeaver, 1995).

Visual Impairment   *Visual impairment* is difficulty in perception compared to the norm that is experienced through sight. Many people have a mild visual impairment correctable by glasses or contact lenses. People of special concern here are those whose vision cannot be corrected and therefore experience significant functional limitations. Legal blindness is "clinically measured visual acuity of 20/200 or less in the better eye or a visual field of 20 degrees or less after optimal correction" (for example, with eyeglasses or contact lenses) (Asch, 1995, p. 2463). Hallahan and Kauffman (2003) explain that "the fraction 20/200 means that the person sees at 20 feet what a person with normal vision sees at 200 feet (Normal visual acuity is thus 20/20.)" They further explain that "the inclusion of a narrowed field of vision in the legal definition means that a person may have 20/20 vision in the central field but severely restricted peripheral vision" in the outer field of sight (p. 344).

Autism   *Autism* is characterized by at least four conditions (APA, 2000; DeWeaver, 1995; Hallahan & Kauffman, 2003). The first is intense inner directedness and problems such as inability to participate in normal communication and social interaction. Second, people with autism have difficulties communicating with others. Third, they often demonstrate repetitive self-stimulating movements such as waving a hand in front of their eyes for a long period of time. Fourth, they may experience an intense obsession with objects, a limited range of interests that can capture their attention, and a compulsive need for predictability and sameness (for example, they won't tolerate a piece of furniture being moved).

It should be emphasized that people differ markedly in the extent to which they experience each of these conditions. Additionally, there is a range of disorders in the autistic spectrum. Hallahan and Kauffman (2003) explain:

> Traditionally, autism is said to be a *pervasive developmental disorder* (PDD) with onset before age three [emphasis added]. [PDD is a "severe developmental disorder characterized by abnormal social relations, including bizarre mannerisms, inappropriate social behavior, and unusual or delayed speech and language" (p. 520).] Related disorders may be diagnosed later, and often there is uncertainty at first about just what disorder the child has. Autistic spectrum disorder implies a qualitative impairment of social interaction and communication. It also is often characterized by restricted, repetitive, stereotyped patterns of behavior, interests, and activities. Besides autism, autistic spectrum disorders include the following:
>
> - *Asperger syndrome (AS),* or Asperger's disorder—much like mild autism, but usually without significant delays in cognition and language [For example, a person with AS might do reasonably well in school and be fairly adept at communication. However, that person might also find it difficult establishing 'normal' interpersonal relationships in addition to feeling the compulsive need to control his or her environment.]
> - *Rett's Disorder*—normal development for five months to four years, followed by regression and mental retardation
> - *Childhood disintegrative disorder*—normal development for a least 2 and up to 10 years, followed by significant loss of skills
> - *Pervasive developmental disorder* not otherwise specified (PDD-NOS—pervasive delay in development that does not fit into any of the other diagnostic categories (p. 376)

 Critical Thinking Questions 11.6

Do you know of anyone who has one of these developmental disabilities? If so, which one? Describe the person's characteristics. What kinds of support does the person need and get? What difficulties, if any, does the person experience? What are the person's strengths and how can they be used to empower the person?

Multiple Disabilities   Any individual may experience a number of disabilities at the same time (Freedman, 1995; DeWeaver, 1995). A person with cognitive disabilities may also have an orthopedic problem or epilepsy (Freedman, 1995). A developmental disability may originate in some genetic disorder or from a problem occurring before, during, or after birth (DeWeaver, 1995). It may also result from problems derived from some combination of these conditions.

TREATMENT OF PEOPLE WITH DEVELOPMENTAL DISABILITIES YESTERDAY AND TODAY: QUESTS FOR SOCIAL AND ECONOMIC JUSTICE

Because of the difficulties experienced by people with developmental disabilities, community support systems and available agency resources are extremely important. How community residents and macro-level decision makers view people with developmental disabilities has tremendous implications concerning the latter's quality of life. To more fully understand the macro social environment's impacts, Mary (1998) describes how community attitudes and resulting social policies have changed over recent decades.

Prior to the Late 1960s

Until the late 1960s, community treatment and public policy emphasized individual pathology. The medical model formed the basis for conceptualizing developmental disabilities. People were considered "patients," with caregivers focusing on individual diagnoses and the resulting problems (Mary, 1998, p. 249). Many people with developmental disabilities were placed in large state or regional institutions where they received custodial care and were kept clean and safe. These times obviously did not foster the current strong professional values of client self-determination and empowerment.

The 1970s and 1980s

The 1970s to early 1980s saw significant changes in how people with developmental disabilities were viewed. Principles becoming important, especially for people with cognitive disabilities, were "normalization," deinstitutionalization, "individual program planning," and "the developmental model" (Mary, 1998, p. 249).

Normalization *Normalization* is the belief "that every individual, even the most disabled, should have an educational and living environment as close to normal as possible" (Hallahan & Kauffman, 2003, p. 519). Prior to the late 1960s, people with developmental disabilities were placed out of sight and mind in obscurely located institutions. During the 1970s and 1980s, however, communities and organizations started viewing such people as clients who had a right to live as normally as possible. Clients now had rights. This approach "shifted much of the problem from the individual to the environment" (Mary, 1998, p. 250). Instead of focusing on people's negative diagnoses, emphasis was placed on the importance of the social environment for an individual's quality of life.

Deinstitutionalization A parallel concept to normalization is *deinstitutionalization*, the process of providing services and care for people within their own communities rather than in institutional settings. Their residences included "both large and small intermediate care facilities and group and family care homes" (Mary, 1998, p. 250). Sometimes, these facilities are referred to as community-based residential facilities (CBRFs). As explained earlier, this concept assumes that the more people with developmental disabilities can be assimilated into the community and live "normal" lives, the better their quality of life will be.

Although the thought to deinstitutionalize services was good and there were many successes, there were also significant problems. For one thing, clients simply being placed in the community did not necessarily mean integration or acceptance in that community (Mary, 1998). It did not mean automatic attitude readjustments on the part of community residents to alter their old stereotypes and unfounded fears about people with developmental disabilities.

Another problem with deinstitutionalization concerned inadequate community resources and services. Institutions were expensive, but so were community-based services. People could get lost and be severed from service provision altogether. Frequently, community-based services were furnished "by a complex and often fragmented set of local and state agencies" providing an unevenly distributed conglomeration of public and private services (Freedman, 1995, p. 722). Service provision could be confusing to clients and their families, as some services were available to the general public and others only to those with specific disabilities (DeWeaver, 1995). (Sometime, try calling the Social Security Office to get some specific information about a case. See how well you understand what's going on—and you're a current or future social worker at that.) Other criticisms of deinstitutionalization included people being discharged too quickly and sometimes inappropriately (for example, without adequate planning or resources for continued community service provision) (DeWeaver, 1995).

Individual Program Planning   Social workers, often functioning as case managers, developed *individual programs,* a second principle espoused in the 1970s and 1980s. (A *case manager* is a designated person who seeks out services, plans how they might be delivered, coordinates service provision, and monitors progress on the behalf of a client, usually one having ongoing multiple needs [Kirst-Ashman & Hull, 2006b].) Such individual programs emphasized people's environments and intervention results that would enhance people's functioning within those environments. Intervention stressed helping people with disabilities "achieve their maximum potential in the least restrictive setting possible" (Mary, 1998, p. 150). The concept of *least restrictive environment* concerns the encouragement of clients to enjoy as much freedom and make as many decisions for themselves as they can. This concept is related to normalization and deinstitutionalization. People living in the community should be more likely to live "normal" lives and make their own decisions than those living in institutional care. Program evaluation for organizational effectiveness was also stressed.

The Developmental Model   The fourth important concept during 1970s and 1980s was that treatment should be based on a *developmental model* that espoused a continuum of service. People received services depending on the intensity and type of their needs. People with developmental disabilities were *clients* whom professionals assessed in terms of their needs. These professionals then determined necessary services depending on where the clients fell on the developmental continuum of service. You might picture a ruler. If a client was assessed as functioning at the 6.25-inch point, then that client would receive the services appropriate for that exact point. Likewise, a client at the 10-inch point would receive services designated for that level of assessment. Emphasis was not placed on the individual as a unique personality, but rather on the assessed level of need and the designated services available to address that need.

Often, clients' needs change over time. One assumption was that many clients made progress toward greater independence in a step-by-step process. A client had to master one skill first before attempting a more difficult one. For example, a young woman with mild cognitive disabilities might start out living in a group home where she could learn basic housekeeping, cooking, and self-care skills, including shopping and paying bills. She might then move to an apartment complex or boarding house for people with cognitive disabilities. Houseparents or residential caregivers would not be living with her, but they would be available in another apartment to help her with problems or questions. Eventually, the woman might achieve enough self-care mastery to live on her own or with a roommate.

Other clients' needs change over time but require increasing levels of help and assistance. A person with a deteriorating orthopedic problem involving his knees might require increasingly more intensive help as he loses mobility. Depending on his assessed state of need at any point in time, in the 1970s and 1980s he would receive a designated level of service.

The 1990s and Beyond: Consumer Empowerment

The 1990s brought with them a significantly greater emphasis on individual choice and personalized planning for people with developmental disabilities than there was in earlier decades (Freedman, 1995; Mary 1998; Raske, 2005; Rothman, 2003). Essentially, such an emphasis laid the foundation for an empowerment approach. Before, people with developmental disabilities were *clients* whom professionals assessed and provided services prescribed for their level of functioning. There was relatively little variation of service provision at the assessed level. Today's perspective reflects four new important concepts—consumers, choice, innovation, and family support.

Clients as Consumers Today, Mary (1998) stresses that practitioners should assume a much more individualized approach and summarizes two principles involved. First, "services are driven by client needs, and clients are viewed as *consumers* with choices" (p. 253). The term *consumer* implies greater power and choice than does the term client. Consumers choose their purchases or resource providers within a competitive market rather than having someone else make these choices for them. Second, "service delivery mechanisms allow for innovative provision of supports to help children stay with families, and adults live as independently as possible" (p. 253). Innovation is stressed to develop unique avenues of service provision in response to individual needs.

Emphasis on Choice   One key word here is *choice*. Here the ruler concept explained earlier no longer applies. Rather, clients are encouraged to assess the choices available and decide what supports they want and what goals they wish to pursue.

Consider Bertram, 44, a quadriplegic whose condition is the result of a congenital spinal cord malformation. Instead of professionals assessing his capabilities and designating where it is best for him to live, he can make that decision himself. With practitioners and other caregiving professionals' input regarding what resources and services are available, Bertram can determine the environment providing him with what he perceives as the highest quality of life. Of course, his choices are influenced by his own capabilities and the resources available. It is impossible for Bertram to live in an apartment alone with no supportive help. His viable choices might include living in a nursing home or a group home for people with severe physical disabilities, staying in an apartment with the necessary supportive attendants, or living with his family whose members would serve as primary caregivers (assuming, of course, that they were willing to do so).

 Critical Thinking Questions 11.7

If you were Bertram, what alternative would you prefer? What do you think your major concerns would be?

Another example is Heriberto, who has cerebral palsy resulting in major difficulty controlling his arm movements. With professional help and practice, he has learned to dress himself if his clothes have zippers and no buttons. However, it takes him over an hour each time and leaves him physically exhausted. A personal care attendant can do the job in about four minutes. Heriberto might choose to have the attendant help him dress even though this option reflects less independence. His choice might be in his best interest to save him substantial time and energy (Renz-Beaulaurier, 1998).

 Critical Thinking Questions 11.8

If you were Heriberto, what choice do you think you would make for yourself and why?

Highlight 11.4 poses some words of caution about emphasizing choice.

| Highlight 11.4 | **Words of Caution About Choice** |

Mackelprang and Salsgiver (1996) caution that practitioners "not be too quick to assume that consumers already have knowledge and abilities rather than recognizing that they may need assistance to develop their strengths" (p. 12). They continue by presenting an example involving Jim, 28, who had suffered traumatic brain injury. Although this is technically not a developmental disability—because injury occurred after age 22—it still illustrates concepts commonly addressed when working with people who have developmental disabilities. While residing in an independent living center, Jim initially sought help with financial planning. While his counselor, an MSW student, helped him with budgeting issues, it became apparent that Jim was also experiencing difficulty in his marriage. Because Jim did not specifically seek help concerning his marriage, the student decided not to interfere with those issues. Because of his head injury, Jim lacked insight into the depths of his relationship problems. By the time Jim began to understand how badly his marital situation had deteriorated, his wife had divorced him and retained custody of their adolescent daughter.

Mackelprang and Salsgiver (1996) suggest:

This case illustrates the conflict between absolute self-determination and the need to sometimes impose professional intervention. Although some would argue against any change in Jim's intervention, a social work approach would have allowed for broader intervention and ultimately may have been more empowering to Jim and his family. (p. 13)

Innovation   A vital word in today's approach toward working with people with developmental disabilities is *innovation,* the initiation, development, and application of new ideas. Innovative service provision may involve a totally unique combination of services depending on what an individual wishes to accomplish. In other words, "consumers define their own vision of the future— where they want to live, learn, work, and recreate—in a community that they define" (Mary, 1998, p. 253).

For example, Emmaline, 7, has spina bifida, "a condition in which the spinal column fails to close properly" (Hallahan & Kauffman, 2003, p. 118). The split may occur at any point along the bones supporting the spinal column; the unprotected spinal nerves may be exposed and damaged, resulting in paralysis below that point (Hallahan & Kauffman, 2003). Emmaline has an individualized service plan designed to meet her unique needs. She can live at home with an innovative combination of supports. A motorized wheel chair maximizes her mobility. Family counseling provides her parents with information and help in responding to Emmaline's special needs. A wheelchair-accessible van provides her with transportation to and from school. A teacher's aid assists her with any help she needs in completing school assignments. Designated medical staff help Emmaline and her family meet her special health and surgical needs.

Family Support   One other important concept in current service provision for people with developmental disabilities is *family support* (Freedman, 1995; Mary 1998; Rothman 2003). Family members often need special resources and help to respond to the extraordinary needs of people with developmental disabilities. For example, parents with a young child having a developmental disability may experience stresses including "stigmatized social interactions, the prolonged burden of care, the lack of information about the disability and behavioral management issues, and grieving" (Freedman, 1995, p. 725).

Family members' strengths must be identified and fortified. Examples of strengths include good communication skills, sincere caring and consideration for each other, effective organizational and planning skills, a strong social network of friends and relatives, spiritual involvement with clergy and religious groups, and adequate financial resources.

Current Emphasis on the Empowerment Approach

The empowerment approach continues to reflect our most current perspective on service provision for people with disabilities (Mackelprang & Salsgiver, 1999; Rothman, 2003). It focuses on what people can do, not what they cannot. Pfeiffer (2005) discusses the misconceptions about disability:

> (1) Disability is not a tragedy; (2) disability does not mean dependency; (3) disability does not mean a loss of potential, productivity, social contribution, value, capability, ability, and the like; (4) disability is a natural part of life, everyone's life; and (5) there is as much variation between people with disabilities as between people in general.
>
> In other words, disability does not mean grief, guilt, and bitterness. People with disabilities are not courageous, noble, and brave any more than any one else. People with disabilities can be very sexual and sensual. People with disabilities can be very good parents. People with disabilities are not poor unless they are unemployed. People with disabilities are not ignorant unless they were segregated from mainstream education and even then many are quite brilliant in spite of so-called special education. People with disabilities do not have to be with "their own kind," whatever that means. (p. 38)

 Critical Thinking Questions 11.9

What are your reactions to these statements about the misconceptions of disability? To what extent do you automatically respond positively or negatively to them? Explain why.

Rothman (2003) addresses the empowerment of individuals with disabilities:

> The empowerment model assists clients to achieve their potential and to promote changes in their environment and in social policy that will promote social justice (Lee, 1996, p. 230).
>
> Society has described the person with disabilities as a "victim" or a "tragedy" with which one must cope. Critiques of this assumption present the concept that (1) disability is not always as disastrous a condition for the individual as . . . people [without disabilities] think and that (2) it is not the disabling condition itself, but societal reactions to it that create difficulties and victimize the . . . person [with a disability] (Black, 1994, pp. 409–410).

Highlight 11.5	## Case Example: Discrimination Against People with Developmental Disabilities

Shapiro (1995) cites the example of Sandra, a 35-year-old woman with Down's Syndrome, who was recently denied a heart-lung transplant even though insurance covered the $250,000 necessary for the operation. Down's syndrome is a congenital type of mental retardation "characterized by moderate to severe mental retardation, slanting eyes, a broad short skull, [and] broad hands with short fingers" (Mish, 1995, p. 349). The two hospitals approved for conducting this type of surgery "made issue of her intelligence and rejected her" (Shapiro, 1995, p. 59). One hospital administrator allegedly said, "We do not feel that patients with Down's syndrome are appropriate candidates for heart-lung transplantation" (Shapiro,

1995, p. 59). Others at the hospitals indicated that they doubted she could maintain the rigorous medical requirements involved in taking medication and monitoring her health after the operations.

Sandra and her doctor strongly disagree with these allegations. Sandra has bussed tables in a public cafeteria, lives in her own apartment, and has "testified eloquently before committees" on the behalf of people with developmental disabilities (Shapiro, 1995, p. 59). Sandra already had assumed responsibility for taking various medications and monitoring her blood pressure every day. Publicity compelled the hospitals to reconsider her plea. Without the surgery Sandra only had a few years to live.

   ## Critical Thinking Questions 11.10

To what extent do you feel Sandra's treatment was fair? What do you think should or should not be done?

> Redefining disability to focus not on what is "wrong" with the individual but rather on what limits his or her ability to function in society moves us away from the medical model and toward a more social work-appropriate model that involves the full range of both individual and environmental assessment that is an essential part of the social work processes (Black, 1994, pp. 396–397).
>
> The strengths assessment is an especially useful tool in working with the empowerment model of practice. By focusing on the client's strengths, the worker can help the client to motivate and to see himself or herself as actor, rather than acted upon. Empowerment practice involves the worker in helping the client to act, rather than in acting on his or her behalf. (pp. 210–211)

Rothman (2003) continues by discussing an empowerment approach with respect to people with disabilities as a community:

> The empowerment model for communities is an extension of the empowerment model for individuals and is built upon the same foundations: that human dignity and respect are an essential part of optimal functioning, and that oppression, exclusion, and discrimination undermine self-esteem. On this broader level, empowerment focuses on supporting a feeling of group competence, connectedness, and the group's ability to effect change for the good of all of the members of the group. The skills, abilities, and personal characteristics of each member of the group are used together to promote and achieve the mutually determined goals. (p. 226)

People with developmental disabilities continue to suffer widespread discrimination (Karger & Stoesz, 2006). Highlight 11.5 describes a case example of discrimination against a person with disabilities.

Generalist Social Work Practice with People Who Have Developmental Disabilities

May (2003) comments on how people with disabilities are treated differently than other populations-at-risk:

> Great effort is expended to ensure that everyone understands the value of diversity (read "deviation") in contemporary U.S. Culture. Not so when disability is the issue. Here, the focus is on "restoring" the person who is labeled "disabled" so he or she no longer deviates from normative expectations. There is no systematic effort to identify sources of pride or to instill positive connotations on being "disabled."
>
> The implications for social workers and other intentional helpers are profound and require a "working with" orientation with the ... client [who has a disability] versus a "working on" orientation. From this "working with" perspective, the client system is not merely the collection of difficulties or clinical symptomatology, but is one component of an interactive system that may produce impairment. Solutions, then, are not to be found solely in the person with the disability, but in the larger social environment. (p. 84)

Social workers often must use brokering, case management, and advocacy skills to provide effective services. *Brokering* is the linkage of clients (consumers) to needed resources. *Case management* is the process of organizing, coordinating, and maintaining "a network of formal and informal supports and activities designed to optimize the functioning and well-being of people with multiple needs" (Moxley, 1989, p. 21). Obviously, many people with developmental disabilities require an innovative range of services to maximize self-determination and pursue an optimal quality of life. The key here is coordinating and monitoring services so that clients with ongoing or changing needs get these needs met.

Advocacy is "the process of working with and/or on behalf of clients (1) to obtain services or resources for clients that would not otherwise be provided, (2) to modify ... policies, procedures, or practices that adversely affect clients, or (3) to promote new legislation or policies that will result in the provision of needed resources or services" (Hepworth et al., 2006, p. 428). There is usually no problem when adequate resources and services are available. However, in reality, this is usually not the case. When clients are not getting their needs met, it is the practitioner's responsibility to advocate on their behalf. Resources may require redistribution. Policies may require change and improvement. New services may need development.

One facet of advocacy is helping clients advocate for themselves when they are capable instead of doing everything for them (Mackelsprang & Salsgiver, 1999). This is another form of client empowerment. For example, it might be easy for Kofi, a social worker, to advocate for his client Thanasi, 38, who has *muscular dystrophy*. This condition is "any of a group of hereditary diseases characterized by a progressive wasting of the muscles" (Mish, 1995, p. 766). Thanasi was diagnosed with the disease at age 12. Although Thanasi can take a few steps by herself, it is very difficult for her and she usually uses a motorized wheelchair. Balance is difficult, as she has lost eight of her toes from the disease.

She has little strength in her arms and hands and so accomplishes tasks such as writing and eating very slowly. As muscles deteriorate, her voice is weakening, so she tries to do most of her necessary talking earlier in the day when she is stronger. Thanasi is a strong, independent person who prides herself in accomplishing her goals. For example, she has earned a bachelor's degree in accounting and is able to work part-time at her own pace.

Thanasi lives in a group home where Kofi is the social worker with other people who have physical disabilities. Thanasi has several issues to address, including some funding glitches and the need for a new wheelchair and other medical equipment. Kofi talks to Thanasi about these needs and eagerly volunteers to make the calls, write the letters, and advocate on her behalf. He is taken aback when Thanasi responds with a dour look on her face and then avoids eye contact with him. He asks her what's wrong. She hesitantly responds that she would much rather do it herself, although she admits she probably needs help negotiating the complicated maze of services. Kofi suddenly grasps the issue like being hit by a two by four. He backs off and volunteers to help find out who she needs to contact and what information she needs to present. Although it will be much slower for her to advocate for herself than for him to do it, the process will empower her. Tofi decides it's best for him to support her in her advocacy efforts instead of performing the primary advocacy role himself.

Examples of Positive Legislation: Empowerment through Social and Economic Justice

Two positive pieces of legislation passed in the 1990s are of special significance for people with developmental disabilities in terms of improving access to resources in the macro social environment (DeWeaver, 1995; Segal, 2007). First, the Americans with Disabilities Act of 1990 (ADA) intends to provide people with physical or mental disabilities "access to public areas and workplaces" and to blast away barriers keeping these people isolated from "the mainstream of public life" (Smolowe, 1995, p. 54). The ADA defines people with disabilities as those who have substantial physical or mental difficulties that significantly hinder at least one primary life activity, have an established record of such hindrances, or are regarded by other people as demonstrating such difficulties (Asch & Mudrick, 1995; Kopels, 1995). Impairments include those that

> substantially limit major life activities such as seeing, hearing, speaking, walking, breathing, performing manual tasks, learning, caring for oneself, and working. An individual with epilepsy, paralysis, HIV infection, AIDS, a substantial hearing or visual impairment, mental retardation, or a specific learning disability is covered, but an individual with a minor, nonchronic condition of short duration, such as a sprain, broken limb, or the flu, generally would not be covered. (U.S. Department of Justice, 2002)

The act also forbids discrimination against people "with a record of a disability" such as "cancer or mental illness," and against people perceived of as having a disability such as those "with a severe facial disfigurement" (U.S. Department of Justice, 2002). "About twenty percent of the U.S. population have disabilities that limit their ability to work" (Karger & Stoecz, 2006, p. 94).

ADA Requirements   ADA provisions help people with disabilities in at least two major ways. First, it "prohibits discrimination in all employment practices, including job application procedures, hiring, firing, advancement, compensation, training, and other terms, conditions, and privileges of employment" and "applies to recruitment, advertising, tenure, layoff, leave, fringe benefits, and all other employment-related activities" (U.S. Department of Justice, 2002).

The ADA's second major thrust requires that "workplaces and public facilities provide 'reasonable accommodation" and accessibility for people with disabilities" (Segal, 2007, p. 110; U.S. Department of Justice, 2002). This means that "discriminatory practices, such as environmental and telecommunication barriers, need to be replaced with accessible structures in instances where cost would not be prohibitive" (DePoy & Gilson, 2004, p. 100).

The ADA "has legitimized the idea that the fundamental problems facing people are less medical than social and structural" (Renz-Beaulaurier, 1998, p. 81). It redefines problems as belonging to the *community*, not people with disabilities living in the community. For example, "the problem of how to get up the steps (problem within the individual) changes to how to get a ramp installed (problem outside the individual)" (Renz-Beaulaurier, 1998, p. 80).

Jansson (2005) reports on some of the ADA's "remarkable improvements" for people with disabilities:

> Elevators and ramps were added to most public buildings. Work accommodations were provided by public and private employers, including use of computer-assisted technologies, flexible work assignments, and special training programs. Lifts were placed in buses, as were reserved seats. Kitchens and bathrooms were redesigned in housing units. (p. 335)

Countering this view, Karger and Stoecz (2006) indicate:

> Despite the ADA and other federal laws, discrimination is still widespread against people with disabilities. For instance, most buildings still do not meet the needs of ... [people with physical disabilities] in terms of access, exits, restrooms, parking lots, warning systems, and so forth. Many apartment complexes and stores continue to be built without allowing for the needs of people with disabilities. The struggle for full integration remains an ongoing battle. (pp. 96–97)

 Critical Thinking Questions 11.11

To what extent do you think the ADA has been successful in fighting discrimination and increasing access to people with disabilities? Do you know anyone with a disability? If so, what is that person's opinion?

Supreme Court Decisions and the ADA   As you know, Supreme Court decisions can shape the application of policy and refine how it's interpreted. DiNitto (2005) summarizes recent court activity concerning the ADA and the rights of people with disabilities:

> With a more conservative Supreme Court, White House, and Congress, recent decisions have diluted the ADA. Between 1999 and 2003 rulings have favored business defendants rather than plaintiffs. In a number of cases, the court has concluded that individuals whose impairment can be corrected with medication or eyeglasses are not "truly disabled" and therefore are not entitled to protection against employment discrimination under the ADA. The "catch-22" is that some people are not "disabled enough" to receive protection under the ADA, but they are disabled enough to be refused a job or fired from a job because their physical or mental limitations, in the employer's opinion, keep them from safely and/or effectively fulfilling job requirements. (p. 183)

For example, Barusch (2006) elaborates:

> Two 1999 cases, [including] *Sutton v. United Airlines* ... introduced the notion of "corrective" or "mitigating" measures to narrow the definition of disability. In the Sutton case, two sisters who had applied for jobs as airline pilots were turned down because they did not meet the airline's uncorrected vision requirement. The court rejected their complaint, holding that with assistive devices (glasses) they could perform other jobs and so did not meet the ADA definition of disability. [Yet they still couldn't be hired as pilots because they had to wear glasses.] (pp. 249–250)

 ## Critical Thinking Questions 11.12

To what extent do you think the court's finding in the *Sutton v. United Airlines* case was fair? Explain your reasons.

DiNitto (2005) continues:

> To date courts have ruled against individuals with visual impairments, high blood pressure, carpal tunnel syndrome, and liver disease, and a stroke victim. In a Tennessee case, a judge ruled that a 9-year-old with spina bifida ... did not have a disability as defined by the ADA and therefore was not permitted to keep her service animal. The U.S. Supreme Court has supported a strict definition of disability, indicating that it must interfere with essential tasks such as brushing one's teeth or washing one's face.
>
> Plaintiffs are also filing ADA law suits against states, but they are losing and states are winning based on the notion of "sovereign immunity" provided under the 11th Amendment to the U.S. Constitution. This amendment holds that it is unlawful to sue a state without the state's permission; consequently, individuals with disabilities have been denied punitive damages in suits against negligent states. For example, in the Garret decision (a ruling on two cases), Patricia Garret was denied punitive damages when she sued her employer, a state hospital, for demoting her after being diagnosed and treated for breast cancer; and Milton Ash was denied damages he sought from his state employer for not providing reasonable workplace accommodations for his asthma condition. (pp. 184–185)

One positive note involves the *L. C. & E. W. v. Olmstead* case decision by the Supreme Court in 1999. Hayashi (2005) explains:

> L. C. and E. W. were patients in a state psychiatric hospital in Georgia. They challenged their placement in an institutional setting rather than in a community-based program. The Supreme Court decided that unnecessary institutionalization of individuals with disabilities is discrimination under the ADA, and that the state must provide services in the most integrated setting appropriate to individual clients. (p. 49)

Developmental Disabilities Assistance and Bill of Rights Act of 1990   A second major piece of legislation other than the ADA is the Developmental Disabilities Assistance and Bill of Rights Act of 1990, amended in 2000, which accomplished several things (DeWeaver, 1995). First, it renewed funding for four major grant programs on behalf of people with developmental disabilities. Second, it increased the total estimated "number of people with developmental disabilities," thereby acknowledging that more resources are necessary. Third, it "indicated that a substantial portion of people with developmental disabilities remained unserved or underserved" (p. 716). Importantly, the law also called for advocacy on the behalf of people with developmental disabilities. It requires provision of adequate services so that people might attain their optimum potential, quality of life, and independence as integral members of the community. The 2000 amendments increased the range of services people with disabilities could access and broadened the availability of services to people who are blind or deaf (DiNitto, 2005).

COMMUNITY SUPPORT AND EMPOWERMENT

Communities and organizations in the macro environment can offer resources and support to people with developmental disabilities in at least two major ways. First, mandated federal and state legislation can provide for programs available to community residents with developmental disabilities. The last sections reviewed two major pieces of federal legislation passed on the behalf of this population. Second, community residents can work together to establish their own innovative resources within the community.

Some examples of how to make progress through legislation, direct community support, and social work advocacy are presented below. The populations-at-risk addressed include people with visual impairment and those with cognitive disabilities.

LEGISLATIVE EMPOWERMENT FOR PEOPLE WITH VISUAL IMPAIRMENT

Asch (1995) describes some of the legislation and services available in the macro environment for people with visual impairment. The Rehabilitation Act of 1973 and its 1992 amendments approve reimbursement for some services provided by agencies for people with visual impairment specifically designated to help this population. One difficulty, however, is that individual states may define blindness however they wish. States, then, may choose to limit service provision only to those people with severe impairment or total blindness.

Other examples of supportive legislation are two 1930s laws that provide special employment opportunities for blind people. The Wagner-O'Day Act (P.L. 75-739) "established a system of sheltered workshops" and the Randolph-Sheppard Act (P.L. 74-734) "gives blind people preference in obtaining employment as operators of vending facilities on federal properties" (Asch, 1995, p. 2465). Sheltered workshops provide "a protected and monitored work environment" for people who have trouble functioning more independently (Barker, 1995, p. 346).

Additionally, people who are legally blind, unemployed, and have assets falling below prescribed levels may receive Supplemental Security Income (SSI). SSI is "a federal program that provides monthly case payments to poor individuals and couples who are elderly, disabled, or blind" (Meyer, 1995, p. 2379). Benefits are provided on the basis of need instead of one's work history.

Several pieces of legislation make reading material more accessible for people with visual impairment. For example, the 1931 Pratt-Smoot Act (P.L. 71-787) established a Library of Congress program that later formed the foundation for regional centers providing Braille and recorded materials to people with visual impairment.

Community Empowerment for People with Visual Impairment

Laws and mandated programs may make some resources available. However, communities themselves can also enhance and make easier the lives of people with visual impairment. Community groups and government units can disseminate information concerning the issues addressed and strengths inherent in people with visual impairment. These people and their families "need accurate information about laws, services, and alternative techniques for performing household tasks, reading, writing, traveling, and the like that people customarily imagine cannot be handled without vision" (Asch, 1995, p. 2466). Communities can sponsor self-help groups where people with visual impairment can come together, discuss issues, provide each other with ideas, and find support. Schools who have students with visual impairment can make it a point to educate parents about services, resources, and aids. Schools can encourage students with visual impairment to participate in sports, recreation, and other extracurricular and educational activities just as children with perfect vision do.

Even such a basic thing as ensuring that public buildings use braille next to the floor indicator buttons on elevators is very helpful. Esther, a student with a visual impairment comes to mind. She attended a state university renowned for its support of and services for students with disabilities. Esther felt that the campus focused its attention on serving people with physical disabilities involving mobility and viewed people with visual impairment as less significant. All buildings and classrooms had been readily accessible for as long as anyone could remember. She advocated for years to have braille information installed in elevators throughout the campus with little response by university administration. After persistent pressure, she finally was able to make her point and all elevators were furnished with braille directions.

Empowerment for People with Visual Impairment and Social Work Practice

Social workers can serve as important advocates in their communities and agencies to provide needed services for people with visual impairment. People initially dealing with visual impairment in themselves or another family member will need time to adjust to the situation and cope with its ramifications. Social workers can help people realize that the long cane ("a mobility aid used by individuals with visual impairment who sweep it in a wide arc in front of them"), a guide dog, human guides, recorded information, adapted computers, and other technological devices (such as reading machines that convert print into spoken words) can help people organize home, work, and social lives in an effective, efficient, although different, manner (Kallahan & Kauffman, 2003, p. 357; see also Asch, 1995).

COMMUNITY EMPOWERMENT FOR PEOPLE WITH COGNITIVE DISABILITIES

Because people with cognitive disabilities constitute the largest proportion of people with developmental disabilities, and because they are the most likely to use services provided by state agencies, we will spend considerable time discussing them (Freedman, 1995). As with people who have visual impairment, legislation provides some support and programs for people with cognitive disabilities who qualify for such services. Funding for people with cognitive disabilities comes from a range of sources depending on whether individuals fulfill eligibility criteria often related to their income level. For example, Supplemental Security Income (SSI) may be available to people with cognitive disabilities "whose income and assets are below designated levels" (Meyer, 1995, p. 2381).

Communities can creatively develop resources and programs to integrate people with cognitive disabilities and enhance their quality of life. For instance, one state has a Community Options Program (COP) funded at the state level that "provides assessments, case plans, and community services as an alternative to nursing home placements" (ARC Milwaukee, undated, b, p. 2).

ARCs and Related Resources Can Empower People and Enhance Quality of Life

One excellent example of how a community can use a support system for people with cognitive disabilities is an organization called ARC. Historically known as the Association for Retarded Citizens, ARCs now are established in communities throughout the United States. The following discussion focuses specifically on ARCs. However, the types of services ARCs provide can certainly be sponsored by other organizations and community groups.

Typically funded through a variety of sources including donations by private citizens, corporations, local service clubs, foundations, and by government service contracts, ARCs provide a wide range of services. They reflect a creative alliance of public services, private contributions, and community groups to provide services for this population-at-risk. Potential services include information and referral service, help lines, noninstitutional residential opportunities, vocational and employment programs, support services, intervention advocacy, volunteer programs, and recreational activities.

Information and Referral Service and Help Lines

An information and referral service "informs people about existing benefits and programs and the procedures for obtaining or using them" and "helps people find other appropriate resources and sources of help" (Barker, 1995, p. 187). A help line is an information and referral system based on telephone contact. Persons requiring information about services, laws, or issues related to a specific problem or population, in this case, cognitive disabilities, call a trained professional who connects them with the appropriate resource or provides them with necessary information. Many ARCs develop an extensive computerized system that can quickly identify relevant linkages between questions, needs, information, and resources.

Provision of Noninstitutional Living Opportunities

One type of resource that can help people with a disability maintain maximum independence and self-determination is linkage with noninstitutional living opportunities. As we discussed earlier in the context of deinstitutionalization, the intent is to place people in the least restrictive setting possible. These placements include adult family care homes where clients reside in the home of caregivers who supervise and care for them. Another setting is a group home or community-based residential care facility (CBRF). Residents often are selected on the basis of having similar needs, such as required levels of supervision and support. For example, one CBRF might have residents capable of taking care of personal needs and working at a sheltered workshop. Another CBRF might have clients who require a higher level of supervision where staff must provide more direct input concerning how they dress, eat, and interact.

Other even more independent supported living options include living with a roommate or by oneself in an apartment. Some limited supervision and assistance such as help with paying bills or arranging transportation to work is usually needed in these cases.

Vocational and Employment Opportunities

ARCs are also quite creative regarding provision of vocational and employment opportunities. They can assist people in gaining community employment by preparing clients for the expectations of employment, assisting in placement, helping employers restructure jobs to maximize clients' abilities to complete job tasks, and providing job coaching concerning basic work skills (such as getting to work on time and following supervisory instructions).

Individuals may also gain employment in more structured settings such as sheltered workshops. One ARC agency developed an employment program where clients made and finished ceramic gifts for special occasions such as weddings and graduations. Another ARC organization developed a work setting where clients manufactured pillows for a major national airline.

People who are unable to function in more demanding settings may receive "day services"; these aim to "maximize an individual's independent functional level in self-care, physical and emotional growth, mobility and community transportation, socialization, recreation, leisure time, and education and prevocational skills" (ARC Milwaukee, undated, a, p. 2).

Other Support Services

Support services can have many facets. Organizations can provide outreach support services to clients in their own homes that involve instruction in daily living skills, budgeting and financial management, transportation, parenting skills, and personal issues including interpersonal interaction, leisure activities, self-esteem, and assertiveness. Respite care programs provide caregiving services to parents or other caregivers of persons with cognitive disabilities. Caregivers can take some time off from responsibilities to give them a break and refresh their efforts. Family services geared to senior caregivers can provide support to aging caregivers who find it increasingly difficult to provide the same level of care they could in the past. For example, because of increasing strength limitations an aging caregiver might find it much more difficult to assist a person with a severe disability in dressing himself. Family services for senior caregivers can also provide support during crises, such as a caregiver experiencing her own acute health problems. They can also be used to assist caregivers in long-term planning for and with the person who has the disability. A common concern of aging caregivers is what will happen to the individual with a disability when the caregiver can no longer assume that function.

Support groups are another support mechanism, and they can focus on many different issues. Parent support groups "provide parents with an opportunity to get together and share stories, concerns and achievements with other parents who are experiencing similar circumstances" (ARC, undated, a, p. 2). Support groups for seniors with disabilities can give them opportunities to share concerns, discuss suggestions, and talk about how to maximize their quality of life.

Advocacy

Intervention advocacy "is designed to respond to the needs of persons with disabilities and their families when serious problems arise affecting legal rights, safety and health, financial security, or access to community resources" (ARC, undated, c, p. 2). The service system is complicated and clients along with their families may find it very difficult to negotiate (DeWeaver, 1995). Advocacy is often necessary to link clients with services they need and deserve. Advocacy is also essential when needed services don't exist.

Using Community Volunteers

There are numerous ways in which volunteers can help ARC programming. These include performing clerical duties and answering the phone, caring for small children while parents attend support groups, serving as a matched "friend" with a person who has a disability to provide support and encouragement, giving support via telephone to persons needing intermittent help, participating in fundraising activities, assisting at supervision of events such as group outings, and helping with household upkeep and maintenance (ARC, undated, c).

Providing Recreational Activities

Recreational activities and functions provide still another means of enhancing the quality of life for people with disabilities. Examples include ongoing athletic programs, support for Special Olympics, and operation of a summer camp where groups of clients of any age group can interact socially, work on crafts, participate in games and plays, learn appreciation for nature, increase leisure skills, and gain confidence in expressing themselves (ARC, undated, c).

 Critical Thinking Questions 11.13

Do you know a person with a cognitive disability? If so, to what resources does that person have access? What resources does that person need, but doesn't get? What are the reasons for any unavailability of resources?

Highlight 11.6 provides a case example of how a community supports and fails to support a person with a cognitive disability in some of the areas discussed above.

Highlight 11.6   A Case Example: A Community Helps and Hinders Hiroshi, a Person with Cognitive Disabilities

Consider Hiroshi and how the environment both succeeds and fails to support him. Hiroshi, 58, lives in a midwestern town of about 8,000 people in a rural farming community. Hiroshi has mild cognitive disabilities. He graduated from high school but only because in those days students like him were passed on whether they could perform the work or not. He is very proud of the high school ring he purchased at graduation. The macro environment, especially the school system, did not serve him well. Instead of receiving special services and training that might now be available, the system basically ignored him and passed him on through.

A major problem for Hiroshi is his speech. He has difficulty forming words, and he takes considerable time to structure his sentences. His comprehension of verbal communication is good, however, and he has an excellent sense of humor. His difficult speech often fools people who don't know him well into thinking he is much less competent than he really is. Speech therapy may have helped if it had been available when he was young.

Hiroshi works at a sheltered workshop in addition to working six hours per week as a janitor at Bertha's Butter Burgers. Hiroshi has a strong work history. For almost 20 years, he worked at a local tanning factory hauling deer hides from one area to another as they proceeded through the leather-making process. It was gruesome, backbreaking work. The place was doused with various chemicals. When Hiroshi got home, he was exhausted. At the time, he was living with his father, who cooked for him, did his laundry, and helped him with other daily living tasks.

Work at the tanning factory had not been without its problems. Once Hiroshi confessed to his relatives a story about another "guy at work" who liked to pick on him. Hiroshi had lots of experience being picked on. The guy liked to draw a knife and tease Hiroshi, pretending to cut him. Once, he made quite a slit in Hiroshi's right hand. Hiroshi's confession involved payback time. One night after work, he slit all "the guy's" tires. The guy, who was fired shortly thereafter, never did find out who did it.

Hiroshi was a saver. He would wear the same pair of polyester pants for years, until the threads in the hem seams gave way. Although Hiroshi made little more than minimum wage, he put almost all of it in savings. When the plant closed and he was laid off, he had accumulated over $40,000. Investing with the help of his brother Egbert and a slick certified financial planner brought his assets to almost $200,000 by the time he turned 58. Unfortunately, this prevented him from receiving public assistance and resources because he did not meet various programs' means tests. Means tests involve using established criteria to evaluate clients' financial resources and to decide whether they're eligible for service.

When his father died, with Egbert's help Hiroshi was able to live in and pay rent for his own apartment. He told Egbert he preferred living alone to living with a roommate. One of Hiroshi's strengths was his strong relationship with Egbert and his family although they lived inconveniently about 185 miles away. Hiroshi didn't see his family as often as he liked since buses were deregulated and federal regulations no longer required companies to sponsor less popular

More Examples of Community Integration for People with Cognitive Disabilities

Kretzmann and McKnight (1993) cite a number of situations regarding how adults with cognitive disabilities can be mainstreamed[3] and integrated as

---

[3] *Mainstreaming* is "bringing people who have some exceptional characteristics into the living, working, or educational environments to which all others have access" (Barker, 1995, p. 221). Examples of such special groups include people with cognitive and other developmental disabilities.

runs. Egbert and his wife were periodically forced to endure a gravely dull three-hour trip through flat farmland to pick Hiroshi up and another three hours to drive him home.

A major strength in Hiroshi's life was his involvement with the local Center for People with Developmental Disabilities, an agency that did not have a means test. In its sheltered workshop, Hiroshi felt productive and established many social contacts. As one of the highest functioning clients, he achieved significant social status. At the center's periodic social dances, he was quite accomplished and admired. Hiroshi also had a knack for taking pictures and videos, which he did regularly at the center's events. The center sponsored or cosponsored numerous events including Special Olympics, bowling tournaments, picnics, and outings to movies in nearby towns. Hiroshi was extremely proud of a Volunteer's Award Plaque he received from the center for all of the conscientious time he spent photographing and videorecording events.

At the center he was assigned a case manager, Cornelia, who evaluated his daily living skills. She linked him with a trainer who tried to teach him how to cook. However, Hiroshi didn't like to cook so ended up subsisting mostly on TV dinners. It might be noted that Egbert who had superior intelligence did not "know how" to boil water. He didn't like to cook either. Cornelia also helped coordinate any other supportive services Hiroshi might need with Egbert and his family.

Although Cornelia and Egbert tried to encourage Hiroshi to manage his own finances and checkbook, this was too difficult for him. Hiroshi didn't like making computations or sending checks, and he typically made significant mistakes. When mail-ordering gifts for family members, he would always send cash despite the risk of losing it. Egbert finally gave up and determined that it was easier just to keep track of Hiroshi's finances himself than to keep after Hiroshi on a regular basis.

Another major community strength was the support Hiroshi received from his church. He attended services regularly and was involved in a group called The Sunday Evening Club, consisting of adult church members who met every other Sunday for a pot-luck dinner and a chance to socialize or hear speakers.

Hiroshi's work at Bertha's was helpful in terms of making him feel useful and conserving his savings. However, the six-hour weekly work allocation was minimal. The management could have given him many more hours if they had not viewed him as an inadequate, "retarded" person. The town provided no public transportation, so Hiroshi had to walk to get anywhere, including two miles to work.

In summary, community strengths for Hiroshi include the Center for People with Developmental Disabilities; its sheltered workshop; his case manager, Cornelia, who oversees Hiroshi's care; public recognition by receiving a Volunteer's Award; his spiritual involvement at church; his job at Bertha's; and strong connections with his family despite the fact that they lived so far away. For Hiroshi, weaknesses in the community include the history of inattention to his needs through decades of absent service, the community residents who demeaningly made fun of him whenever they had the chance, inadequate involvement in his paid work environment, and lack of public transportation. In some ways, Hiroshi's community environment supported and integrated him, thereby enhancing his quality of life. In other ways, lack of community support served to hinder his ability to live the most useful, productive, and happy life possible.

part of a large urban community. The following four are adapted from their ideas:

1. Perry, 28, thrives at playing games. Perry's neighbor acquainted him with the local Boys Club. He now volunteers there regularly, teaching children games and supervising their activities.
2. Felicita, 22, spends most weekdays at a day program with other people who have cognitive disabilities. She passes much of her time coloring and watching other residents. She is an exceptionally warm person who will light up with a dazzling smile when spoken to or given any attention. One

of the day program staff introduced her to a local daycare center to see if she could help out there.

At first, the day program staff always accompanied her and provided some supervision. Now she goes to the daycare center by herself several times a week. The children love her and her attention. She always has time to listen to what they have to say and give them a hug when needed. They realize she's different than their other teachers because sometimes they have to help her out in completing activities. They don't care. They love her anyway.

3. Joe, 68, lives in a group home. He loves to bowl. Julietta, a member of the area's neighborhood association stopped by one day to see if there was anything the association could do for Joe and the other residents. She found out about Joe's desire to bowl and remembered that a local church had a Thursday night bowling league. She talked to the team members and asked them if they would consider including Joe on their team. They were a bit hesitant, as they took bowling very seriously and played desperately to win. They were even more hesitant when they discovered Joe was not a very good bowler. However, Joe was obviously ecstatic about being on the team. Team members worked out a rotation system where Joe could periodically bowl but his score was omitted from the final total. Joe continued to beam as he proudly wore his Beaver's Bowling Buddies T-shirt.

4. Norma, 35, is a pleasant, soft-spoken, shy woman who had lived with her senior parents. She and her parents would often shop at a small local drug store and gift shop across the street from their modest home. Myrtle, who owned the store, got to know and like Norma and her family. Myrtle was concerned that Norma rarely got out of the house except for shopping and other errands with her parents. She started taking Norma out for lunch or a movie every other week or so. Although a busy businesswoman, Myrtle enjoys her time with Norma and feels Norma really appreciates it. She harbors some growing fears about what will happen to Norma when her parents die. Myrtle has become part of Norma's natural helping network.

 ## Critical Thinking Questions 11.14

Of these examples of how to integrate people with cognitive disabilities into the community, which do you feel are most creative and why? Can you think of any other creative ways to integrate people with cognitive disabilities? If so, describe them.

There are many ways community residents can discover and invent to help people with cognitive disabilities. Help can be given by formal groups such as ARCs or Social Service Departments, or by concerned individuals such as neighbors and fellow church members. The key is concern for the well-being of other community members, sensitivity to their needs, and the willingness to contribute precious energy on the behalf of others in need.

CHAPTER SUMMARY

This chapter focused on a range of services and resources that can be developed to meet the needs of and empower diverse populations and populations-at-risk. Four diverse groups were addressed. Empowerment for African Americans was discussed. An example was presented of providing support for grandparents of substance-abusing children who had custody of grandchildren.

Basic terms referring to the Hispanic population were defined and the oppression of the Hispanic population discussed. Values often characterizing Hispanic families include the significance of a common language, the importance of family, personalismo, machismo and marianismo, and spirituality. Hispanic women's perspectives on community empowerment were identified. Case examples were presented focusing on empowerment approaches using Latina-owned beauty parlors and Latino youth conducting a community assets assessment.

The importance of GLBT people's empowerment was stressed. Important issues include the need for nondiscrimination laws, recognition of same-sex relationships, family policies for GLBT parents, harassment and violence against GLBT people, housing, and employment. Political action organizations can provide support to political candidates, educate the public to gain support, and conduct legislative advocacy. Examples of empowerment though special social services were provided.

The oppression of women in the macro environment was addressed. A case example of grassroots empowerment involved developing a program for at-risk pregnant women.

The potential of spiritual communities for empowering their members was identified. Case examples included a spiritual community as a haven for African American youths and how a Navajo community empowered its senior residents through spiritually and culturally sensitive treatment in a nursing home.

The necessity of empowering people who have developmental disabilities was emphasized. Developmental disabilities were defined. They include cognitive disabilities, cerebral palsy, seizure disorders, orthopedic problems, hearing impairment, visual impairment, and the autistic spectrum. People may have multiple disabilities.

A history of how people with developmental disabilities have been treated over time was discussed. Major concepts involved in their treatment were explained. In the 1970s and 1980s, these included normalization, deinstitutionalization, individual program planning, and the developmental model. During the 1990s, clients as consumers, the emphasis on choice, innovation, and family support were stressed. Current emphasis is on the empowerment approach.

Generalist social work practice with people having developmental disabilities was described. Important tasks include brokering, case management, and advocacy. The Americans with Disabilities Act of 1990 and the Developmental Disabilities Assistance and Bill of Rights of 1990, along with its 2000 amendments, were discussed. Legislative and community empowerment with people who have visual impairment and cognitive disabilities was examined. For people with cognitive disabilities, ARCs and related resources can provide information and referral services in addition to help lines, noninstitutional living opportunities, vocational and employment opportunities, advocacy, the help of community volunteers, recreational activities, and other supportive services.

12 CHAPTER | Social Justice and the Global Community

Social injustice and poverty characterize much of the world. Pictured here are young beggar children in Karachi, Pakistan.

© Ilyas Dean/The Image Works

CHAPTER CONTENTS

"We have become rich countries of poor people"[1]
"Back to work for the world's investors"[2]
"Success of Turkey talks 'vital to whole world'"[3]
"Russia and China 'stay committed' over Tehran"[4]
"A British press veteran builds a European empire"[5]
"The west must address the roots of Islamic struggle"[6]
"US mortgage banks look for European funding"[7]
"Singapore's security laws cast a shadow over global economic meeting"[8]
"World financial markets changed utterly by September 11"[9]

Each of the above is a headline found in a major national newspaper, *The Financial Times,* over the course of two days. What do you think they all have in common? Each, in its own way, refers to the integral way our world is interconnected. Neither we nor citizens in any other country are isolated entities able to do whatever we please. The point is that we live in a global environment that is interconnected in a complex web of social, economic, and political policies.

Brueggemann (2006) paints a disturbing picture of this world:

If we could shrink the earth's population to a village of precisely 200 people, with all the existing human ratios remaining the same:

57 Asians

21 Europeans

14 from the Western Hemisphere, both north and south

8 Africans

52 would be female

48 would be male

70 would be non-White

30 would be White

70 would be non-Christian

30 would be Christian

89 would be heterosexual

11 would ... [have a same-gender sexual orientation]

---

[1] This is a headline in the Financial Times, Friday, September 8, 2006 on page 11.

[2] This is a headline in the Financial Times, Friday, September 10, 2006 on page 6.

[3] This is a headline in the Financial Times, Friday, September 8, 2006 on page 3.

[4] This is a headline in the Financial Times, Friday, September 8, 2006 on page 4.

[5] This is a headline in the Financial Times, Friday, September 8, 2006 on page 6.

[6] This is a headline in the Financial Times, Friday, September 8, 2006 on page 11.

[7] This is a headline in the Financial Times, Friday, September 8, 2006 on page 23.

[8] This is a headline in the Financial Times, Friday, September 10, 2006 on page 4.

[9] This is a headline in the Financial Times, Friday, September 10, 2006 on page 12.

6 (all from the United States) would possess 59% of the world's wealth

80 would live in substandard housing

50 would suffer from malnutrition

1 would have a college education

1 would own a computer

70 would be unable to read or write

If you have food in the refrigerator, clothes on your back, a roof overhead, and a place to sleep, you are richer than 75% of the world's people. If you have money in the bank, in your wallet, and spare change in a dish someplace, you are among the top 8% of the world's wealthy. If you woke up this morning with more health than illness, you are more blessed than the million who will not survive this week. If your parents are still alive and still married, you are very rare, even in the United States and Canada. If you have never experienced the danger of battle, the loneliness of imprisonment, the agony of torture, or the pangs of starvation, you are more fortunate than 500 million people in our global society. (pp. 457–458)

This chapter intends to expand your perspective from a local, state, and national one to a global one. The international macro environment affects every citizen on earth. We will address some of the global issues we all face, explore the concept of social justice, and discuss international social work. Specifically, this chapter will:

- Describe the context of the global environment in which we live.
- Define social justice and stress its significance for international social work practice.
- Discuss the social issues of poverty and economic justice, global conflict, and the forced migration of people in need.
- Define community development and discuss its theoretical foundations.
- Discuss and provide examples of community development practice.
- Describe social development.
- Examine a feminist perspective on global development.
- Define and explain international social work.
- Identify and describe international social work and social welfare organizations.
- Define international nongovernmental organizations and provide examples.
- Discuss social work values and cross-cultural values in global perspective.
- Identify some of the cultural differences existing in organizational contexts.

WE LIVE IN A GLOBAL MACRO ENVIRONMENT

We have emphasized the importance of social workers understanding their macro environment in order to practice effectively. We've discussed how social workers practice within organizational environments. Organizations exist in the context of neighborhoods and communities. Communities subsist in a state government environment, subject to state rules, regulations, and laws. Individual states, the District of Columbia, and Puerto Rico, in turn, exist within the national environment of the United States and must function under federal directives. The macro environment doesn't stop there, which is no news flash. The United States is part of a complex global network that is intricately involved with other countries economically, politically, and socially (Finn & Jacobson, 2003). *Globalization* is the "process of global integration in which diverse peoples, economies, cultures, and political processes are increasingly subjected to international influences" (Midgley, 1997a, p. xi). In other words, it means that what happens in one part of the world directly influences what happens in other parts (Brueggemann, 2006, p. 458).

A friend of mine investing for retirement recently mentioned that in the past he had been very hesitant to invest in international stocks because he felt safer sticking to investments at the national level. He said a stockbroker friend of his told him, "Good luck. Almost everything's involved internationally now. Finding good investments at the national level is almost impossible." Although that might be a bit of an exaggeration, the point is that we live in a global environment with a global economy. We face soaring gasoline prices, the threat of terrorism, and global warming (which most claim is due to human activity and carbon dioxide emissions) on a daily basis. Isolation is no longer a viable option for your country or for you.

In a global economy, what social and economic forces impact one nation may well result in repercussions in many other nations. Hokenstad and Midgley (1997) explain:

> Social work is one of many players in the response to these realities of global interdependence. The scope of global poverty and the intensity of ethnic conflict require first political and economic responses by nations and international organizations. Global challenges require action on many levels by many actors. Nevertheless, these are problems that are directly related to social work commitment and expertise. Social workers at the local level are directly involved with the implications of international realities by working with refugees or helping displaced workers. At the national level in many countries, the profession is active in promoting economic and social justice policy. Internationally, social work organizations are increasingly active in combating human rights violations. Thus, it is essential for social workers to have an international perspective and understanding to be effective practitioners in today's world. (pp. 3–4)

Link, Ramanathan, and Asamoah (1999) assert that "through building a global perspective, [social work] students can add insights about the human condition and more adequately understand, analyze, and predict human behavior" (p. 31). They provide an example of the 18th Street Gang members in Los Angeles, whose families originated in El Salvador and who maintain an ongoing cultural connection with that country. Link and his colleagues (1999) stress how a global perspective helps social workers, recognize how artificial it is to see national borders as separations between micro or macro systems. . . . These disenfranchised young people are frequently rounded up and deported to El Salvador, where they pick up with another branch of their gang so that their interactions are seamless despite the structural efforts of immigration and law enforcement to disband or break them (DeCesare, 1993). (p. 31)

We have established that social work's mission "is to enhance human well-being and help meet the basic human needs of all people, with particular attention to the needs and empowerment of people who are vulnerable, oppressed, and living in poverty" (NASW, 1999). We have also ascertained that the National Association of Social Workers (NASW) *Code of Ethics* states that "social workers should advocate for resource allocation procedures that are open and fair. When clients' needs can be met, an allocation procedure should be developed that is non-discriminatory and based on appropriate and consistently applied principles" (NASW, 1999, 3.07b). We have indicated that the Code instructs,

> Social workers should promote the general welfare of society, from local to global levels, and the development of people, their communities, and their environments. Social workers should advocate for living conditions conducive to the fulfillment of basic human needs and should promote social, economic, political, and cultural values and institutions that are compatible with the realization of social justice. (NASW, 1999, 6.01)

Three key concepts inherent in these quotes are the terms *global, advocate,* and *social justice.* A *global* focus concerns looking beyond your immediate local, state, and even national environment. A basic social work value is the importance of focusing on human rights issues around the world, not just those affecting you in your own backyard. We have defined *advocacy* as the act of speaking up, pushing for change, or pleading the causes of clients and those in need (Hoefer, 2006). Finally, *social justice* involves upholding the condition that in a perfect world all citizens would have identical "rights, protection, opportunities, obligations, and social benefits" regardless of their backgrounds and membership in diverse groups (Barker, 2003, pp. 404–405). Thus, it is social workers' responsibility to attend to and advocate for social justice on a global basis.

Social justice is one of the six core values identified in the NASW *Code of Ethics* (NASW, 1999). (Highlight 12.1 summarizes the six values.) The Code explains:

> Social workers pursue social change, particularly with and on behalf of vulnerable and oppressed individuals and groups of people. Social workers' social change efforts are focused primarily on issues of poverty, unemployment, discrimination, and other forms of social injustice. These activities seek to promote sensitivity to and knowledge about oppression and cultural and ethnic diversity. Social workers strive to ensure access to needed information, services, and resources; equality of opportunity; and meaningful participation in decision making for all people.

| Highlight 12.1 | Six Core Ethical Values for Social Workers |

The NASW Code of Ethics identifies the following six core values (NASW 1999):

1. *Service*—Providing help, resources, and benefits so people can achieve their maximum potential
2. *Social justice*—Upholding the condition that in a perfect world all citizens would have identical "rights, protection, opportunities, obligations, and social benefits" regardless of their backgrounds and membership in diverse groups (Barker, 2003, pp. 404–405)
3. *Dignity and worth of the person*—Holding in high esteem and appreciating individual value

4. *Importance of human relationships*—Valuing "the mutual emotional exchange; dynamic interaction; and affective, cognitive, and behavioral connections that exist between the social worker and the client to create the working and helping atmosphere" (Barker, 2003, p. 365)
5. *Integrity*—Maintaining trustworthiness and sound adherence to moral ideals
6. *Competence*—Having the necessary skills and abilities to work effectively with clients

GLOBAL ISSUES AFFECT US ALL

Developing a global focus means becoming aware of the issues facing the human population in the 21st century. From a social work perspective, global problems are everyone's problems. We have established that it is the ethical obligation of social workers to do what they can to help solve them. Out of the multitude of social problems that should be addressed, we will arbitrarily choose three to identify here. These are poverty and economic inequality, global conflict, and forced migration of people in need.

Poverty and Economic Inequality

Poverty is the condition where people maintain "a standard of living below the minimum needed for the maintenance of adequate diet, health, and shelter" (Eitzen & Zinn, 2003, p. 180). Poverty concerns lack of access to adequate resources. There are a number of terms related to poverty. "*Income* refers to the amount of money a person makes in a given year. *Wealth* is the total value of that person's assets: real estate and personal property, stocks, bonds, cash, and so forth" (Coleman & Kerbo, 2002, p. 222).

The Complexity of Defining Poverty   Poverty is not a perfectly clear-cut concept. Leon-Guerrero (2005) remarks:

> *Absolute poverty* refers to a lack of basic necessities, such as food, shelter, and income. *Relative poverty* refers to a situation in which some people fail to achieve the average income or lifestyle enjoyed by the rest of society. Individuals in this category may be able to afford basic necessities, but they cannot maintain a standard of living comparable to other members of society. (p. 224)

In the United States, the Social Security Administration (SSA) establishes an "*official poverty line* based on what it considers the minimal amount of money required for a subsistence level of life" (Eitzen & Zinn, 2003, p. 180).

However, this has been criticized as underestimating the extent of poverty in the United States. The formula was initiated in 1955, at which time people spent about one third of their income on food (Mooney et al., 2007). Although the index is adjusted each year, the amount of money necessary for adequate food is still multiplied by three based on the 1955 formula. Costs of food, however, have not risen nearly as fast as the costs of other necessary costs of living such as housing, fuel, and transportation. It is estimated that families now spend only one-fifth of what they need to live on food instead of one-third (Schiller, 2004). The implication is that the poverty line really should be five times the amount necessary for food instead of three. This would result in a significantly higher official poverty line and significantly more people officially living "in poverty." Using the current method, the U.S. Census Bureau indicates that 12.7 percent of the U.S. population lives below the poverty level (U.S. Census Bureau, 2005).

The Widening Gap in the United States   Another facet of economic inequality in the United States involves the widening gap between the very rich and very poor (Coleman & Kerbo, 2002; Macionis, 2005; Mooney et al., 2007). Among all industrial nations, the United States has the largest gap between rich and poor (Mooney et al., 1007). Macionis (2005) explains:

> The highest-earning 20 percent of U.S. families (with income of at least $94,151 a year and averaging about $160,000) received 47.7 percent of all income. At the other end of the hierarchy, the lowest-paid 20 percent (with income below $20,000 a year and averaging $14,021) received just 4.2 percent of all income. In short, the high-income families earn more than ten times as much as the low-income families. Put another way, the highest-earning 20 percent of families earn almost as much as the remaining 80 percent of families combined. (p. 28)

   ## Critical Thinking Questions 12.1

Where do you stand personally in terms of your overall wealth? What factors in your own background contributed to your current financial status and your potential future financial status?

One study found that if average workers' pay had kept up with the increases in Chief Executive Officers' (CEOs') pay, workers would be earning $184,000 a year (Murphy, 2004). In 1974, CEOs made 44 times what the average worker did, and in 2003 they made 301 times that (Murphy, 2004).

Other demographic variables affect a U.S. citizen's potential to be in poverty. Females and people of color are significantly more likely to be poor. For example, African American households have one-tenth the total net worth of white households (Texeira, 2005).

Poverty levels also vary by state. For example, 5.7 percent of the population fall below the poverty line in New Hampshire, whereas over 17 percent do so in Arkansas, Mississippi, and New Mexico (Mooney et al., 2007).

Critical Thinking Questions 12.2

What are the reasons for the widening gap in wealth in the United States? Can or should something be done about it? If so, what?

Global Poverty   Poverty is defined differently depending on where in the world you are. Mooney and her colleagues (2007) describe the situation:

> The World Bank sets a "poverty threshold" of $1 per day to compare poverty in most of the developing world [in the past, referred to as "third world"], $2 per day in Latin America, $4 per day in Eastern Europe ..., and $14.50 per day in industrial countries (which corresponds to the income poverty line in the United States). [The *World Bank's* formal name is the International Bank for Reconstruction and Development. Headquartered in Washington, DC, it has branches around the world that make loans and provide economic consultation to countries that have low per capita incomes and lack resources.] Another poverty measure is based on whether individuals are experiencing hunger, which is defined as consuming less than 1,960 calories a day. (p. 185)

Mooney and her colleagues (2007) indicate that "South Asia has the greatest number of people living in poverty, and sub-Saharan Africa has the highest proportion of people in poverty" (p. 187).

Cox and Pawar (2006) summarize:

> Poverty, with its associated problems such as infant mortality, malnutrition, and vulnerability, is commonly regarded as the world's most serious problem. Depending on how poverty is defined and measured, no one would dispute the claim that, at the very least, approximately one in every three of the world's people lives in poverty. This is partly because many people around the globe exist so close to the poverty line that any one of a number of common occurrences, even at a minor level, will push them into poverty. Such occurrences include economic changes, such as increases in inflation rates ["an increase in the volume of money and credit relative to available goods and services resulting in a continuing rise in the general price level" (Mish, 1995, p. 498)], deteriorating trade arrangements, or reductions in a government's subsidies of basic necessities; ecological changes, such as deterioration of the environment or depletion of essential food sources; social conflict within a nation or war between nations; demographic changes through migration or natural increase; and natural disasters that destroy people's homes and livelihoods. (p. 51)

Problems Related to Poverty   Numerous other problems, of course, are related to poverty. If people don't have the resources, they may not be able to get many of the things they need to survive and thrive. These related problems include hunger, homelessness, unsafe water supplies, and lack of health care, among many others, all of which are beyond the scope of this text. They all are serious issues that social workers around the world must address.

Critical Thinking Questions 12.3

What are the reasons for such extreme global poverty? What can or should be done to help?

Global Conflict

Cox and Pawar (2006) summarize the state of conflict in this and the past century:

> A reading of any global history reveals the extremely common inability of social groupings, nations, and empires to live at peace with their neighbors. In pursuit of territory, booty of all kinds, slaves, power, and status, conflict at all levels has been a significant aspect of the human story. The last century witnessed two of the worst wars known to history, and since the end of the Cold War in 1989 the scourge of civil war has intensified alarmingly. In recent times, the world has been experiencing upwards of 30 civil wars at any one time, with very high casualty figures, especially among civilians.
>
> A major goal of the UN [United Nations] is world peace, yet its work and that of national governments and regional associations, along with that of many organizations of civil society, have together failed to do more than perhaps contain many situations. Only when we add together the widespread consequences of conflict on people's personal lives and social contexts, economic conditions, physical infrastructure, and the environment, do we begin to appreciate the enormity of this global problem. Yet because conflict once again has many causes, it seems difficult for the international community to significantly reduce the impact of conflict in the foreseeable future. Finally, it has become clear in recent times that rebuilding a society after conflict is a complex, hugely expensive, and extremely difficult undertaking. (p. 52)

 Critical Thinking Questions 12.4

To what extent do you or did you support the United States invasion and occupation of Iraq? What are your reasons? What were the consequences for the United States? The Iraqi people? Other nations around the globe?

Forced Migration of People in Need

It is estimated that about 50 million people worldwide are displaced from their community of origin, although they would prefer to have remained at home (Cox & Pawar, 2006). Cox and Pawar (2006) explain why:

> One inevitable consequence of extreme poverty, widespread social conflict, serious natural disasters, ecological degradation, and low levels of development is that many people are forced to leave their usual place of abode and seek refuge, assistance, or a better future elsewhere. (p. 53)

Ahearn (1995) describes some of the terms used when discussing these populations:

> *Displaced people* are those people who have been uprooted within their own country. [This often occurs during wars when one religious or ethnic sect takes over and displaces another sect elsewhere.] *Refugees* are people who have crossed national boundaries in search of refuge. The United Nations defines refugees as people who flee to another country out of a fear of persecution because of religion,

political affiliation, race, nationality, or membership in a particular group. *Immigrants* are those individuals who have been granted legal permanent residence in a country not their own. *Migrants* are those people usually workers, who have temporary permission to live in a country, but plan to return to their country of origin. *Illegal aliens* are people who migrate illegally to another country. (p. 771)

Many people from other countries may receive or need social services. Padilla (1999) reports:

Immigrants make up a significant segment of U.S. society. Moreover, immigration to the United States is characterized by steady growth, dramatic changes in ethnic composition, and declining socioeconomic levels. In 1990 the proportion of immigrants in the total U.S. population was almost 9 percent (Edmonston & Passel, 1994). Over 7 million people immigrated during the past decade, reflecting consistent increases over previous decades (Borjas, 1994), and these increases are expected to continue. By 2040 one in four Americans will be an immigrant (first generation) or the child of immigrants (second generation), and by 2010 children of immigrants will account for 22 percent of the school-age population (Fix & Passel, 1994). (p. 590)

People with different national origins often find it difficult to integrate themselves into the mainstream culture. This is intensified when the use of different languages is a factor (Gushue & Sciarra, 1995). Finding employment, accessing adequate housing, and "fitting into" the social fabric of neighborhoods and communities can be difficult. Kamya (2001) cites "social isolation, cultural shock, cultural change, and goal-striving stress as four significant experiences" newcomers often face (p. 607). They may have difficulties understanding new behavioral expectations imposed on them, interacting effectively with others in the new culture, and achieving the goals they had hoped for.

 Critical Thinking Questions 12.5

What do you think the United States policy should be toward people migrating illegally across the southern boarder?

COMMUNITY AND SOCIAL DEVELOPMENT

What should be done in response to the turbulence and many issues faced by the global community? How can resources be distributed more equitably and enhanced social justice attained? Community development provides one positive avenue to help communities and nations in need.

Rivera and Erlich (2001) state:

Community Development refers to efforts to mobilize people who are directly affected by a community condition (that is, the "victims," the unaffiliated, the unorganized, and the nonparticipating) into groups and organizations to enable them to take action on the social problems and issues that concern them. A typical feature of these efforts is the concern with building new organizations among people who have not been previously organized to take social action on a problem (emphasis amended). (p. 256; Erlich & Rivera, 1981; Fisher, 1984)

Community development involves helping people in a designated geographic who share cultural values and experience similar social and economic conditions; goals are to improve living conditions and enhance residents' quality of life in the social environment by using a planned change process (Harrison, 1995).[10] "Development involves growth, maturation, and strengthening" (Harrison, 1995, p. 555). Theory "provides practitioners with a coherent way to organize the variables that have a bearing on their work" (Kramer & Specht, 1983, p. 19). We have defined a *community* as "a number of people who have something in common with one another that connects them in some way and that distinguishes them from others" (Homan, 2004, p. 9). A key feature of a community is the fact that participants share some mutual characteristic. Common features might include "location, interest, identification, culture, and/or common activities" (Fellin, 2001a, 2001b, p. 118). The following section describes the theoretical functions of community that provide a context for community development.

Theoretical Functions of Communities

An important theoretical perspective on communities that serves as a foundation for community development involves the functionalist perspective introduced earlier in Chapter 8. Warren (1983), one of the leading early theorists on communities, cited five basic functions that communities should serve:

1. "*Production-distribution-consumption* relates to local participation in the process of producing, distributing, and consuming those goods and services that are a part of daily living and access to which is desirable in the immediate locality" (pp. 28–29). People need access to goods such as food, clothing, and housing, in addition to services like police and fire protection. In various communities around the world, this function is seriously obstructed.

2. "*Socialization* involves a process by which society or one of its constituent social units transmits prevailing knowledge, social values, and behavior patterns to its members" (p. 29). People in communities, which may be local or national, are socialized regarding expectations for behavior and "appropriate" values. One primary method of socialization is education, which is sorely lacking in many areas of the world.

3. "*Social control* involves the process through which a group influences the behavior of its members toward conformity with its norms" (p. 29). The first thing that comes to mind might be the government with its branches of police and courts. However, "many other social units, including the

---

[10] Planned change as described in Chapter 1 involves engagement, assessment, planning, implementation, evaluation, termination, and follow-up.

family, the school, the church, and the social agency, also play a part" (p. 29). As of this writing, a critical issue in Iraq concerns who maintains social control. Is it the occupying U.S. government, the newly formed Iraqi government, or the various terrorist ethnic and religious groups fighting those in power?

4. *"Social participation"* concerns the involvement of citizens in social, political, and economic processes. Various social entities provide avenues for social participation including churches and religious organizations, "businesses, government offices,... voluntary and public health and welfare agencies,... family and kinship groups, friendship groups, and other less formal groupings" (p. 29). From a global perspective, various local and national communities limit social participation based on gender, or ethnic or religious status. Social participation is often a primary goal in achieving social justice.

5. *Mutual support* involves encouragement, assistance, caring, and cooperation among people in communities (p. 29). "Traditionally, such mutual support, whether in the form of care in time of sickness, exchange of labor, or helping a local family in economic distress, has been performed locally very largely under such primary-group auspices as family and relatives, neighborhood groups, friendship groups, and local religious groups" (p. 29). Today, many mutual support functions, at least in wealthier industrialized nations, have been assumed by public welfare departments, private health and welfare agencies, governmental and commercial insurance companies, and other formalized organizational structures (p. 29).

 Critical Thinking Questions 12.6

How does the community in which you live fulfill the five functions mentioned here? If something is lacking, how might community functioning be improved?

Community Development Practice

Three basic principles characterize practice when undertaking community development practice (Harrison, 1995). First, because community development emphasizes citizen participation, community development practice generally focuses on improving the *functioning* of the community. This usually targets the functions described above rather than significantly transforming and reorganizing formal structures in the community (including organizations and political structures). Second, however, community development most frequently involves improving the functioning of organizations in the community so that they might undertake their functions and serve citizens more effectively and efficiently. Third, it is critical to establish goals that residents have in common and mutually support. Community development must progress within the value structure of the community's people. Values and priorities vary dramatically from one culture or location to another. A subsequent section addresses the issue of cross-cultural value differences.

Examples of Community Development   Midgley and Livermore (2004) provide examples of community development in Africa:

> In many African countries, social workers have mobilized local people to engage in small-scale agricultural activities, construct rural bridges and feeder roads, establish cooperative enterprises [a program owned and run by people receiving its services], and accumulate community assets. These projects have a direct and positive impact on economic development. Community built and owned feeder roads provide easier access to the markets in larger towns and ensure that farmers get their produce to these markets in a timely way. Community development has also been used to assist women to engage more effectively in agricultural activities and microenterprises [such as small businesses] and to become economically independent.
>
>   Community development has . . . been used to promote social welfare projects that . . . contribute to economic development. Throughout Africa, local people have collaborated with both governmental and nongovernmental agencies to build community centers, schools and clinics, sanitary and other public health facilities, and to provide safe drinking water. The use of community development to provide safe drinking water in many rural areas in Africa has been particularly impressive. Many communities that relied on rivers, streams, and marshes were exposed to the hazard of being infected with waterborne diseases. Community participation has been vital in providing access to clean drinking water. Village people have played an important role by providing labor for the construction of wells and channeling clean water to local communities from unpolluted mountain springs. (pp. 124–125)

Sowers and Rowe (2007) provide other examples of community development in Carmelita (Guatemala), Ghana, and Indonesia:

> In Carmelita, the Guatemalan government has established 13 locally managed forest concessions [governmental grants of land for specified use] in the jungle village. The cooperative that works the 130,000-acre concession in the rain forest consists of 56 impoverished families from the jungle village. The concessions are logged in accordance with rules laid down by the Forest Stewardship Council, a nonprofit organization based in Bonn, Germany. Environmental organizations credit the approach with reducing deforestation and protecting watersheds and wetland areas while providing a steady income for local residents (Replogle, n.d.). . . .
>
>   The Ghana Community School Alliances Project, a community-mobilization initiative funded by USAID, fosters community participation in more than 300 primary schools throughout Ghana to build an environment of mutual respect, responsibility, and action among community members, schools, and education administrators as they work to meet the learning needs of Ghanaian children. [USAID, the United States Agency for International Development, is "the principle U.S. agency to extend assistance to countries recovering from disaster, trying to escape poverty, and engaging in democratic reforms" (USAID, 2006).] In addition, the project trains district-level education managers to use data for decision making at the local level (Educational Development Center, n.d.). . . .

In the aftermath of the December 2004 Indian Ocean tsunami, Mercy Corps field managers quickly mobilized local workers to rebuild schools, clean up water systems, and repair commercial fishing boats. [Mercy Corps is a charitable organization founded in 1979 that focuses on relief assistance and "long-term solutions to hunger and poverty" (MercyCorps, 2006).] Through innovative cash-for-work programs, tsunami survivors earned income to support their families and reclaim their lives (Mercy Corps. n.d.). (p. 220)

 Critical Thinking Questions 12.7

What is your opinion regarding FEMA's (Federal Emergency Management Agency) handling of the Hurricane Katrina disaster in New Orleans? What could have been done to improve effectiveness and efficiency?

Social Development

A term related to community development is social development, initially coined when the British Colonial Office began promoting economic development in the British colonies following World War II . *Social development* is "a process of planned social change designed to promote people's welfare within the context of a comprehensive process of economic development" (Midgley, 1994, p. 3). Three words are particularly significant in the definition—*planned, comprehensive,* and *economic* (Lowe, 1995, p. 2171). First, social development must be *planned* and the government integrally involved in its implementation. Second, the plan is *comprehensive,* meaning that it encompasses multiple systems and dimensions in the community. All social welfare providers should be involved. Third, social development includes *economic* aspects as essential components in the planning and implementation process. Economic development should enhance social gains, and vice versa. Social development involves both such economic aspects as availability and quality of jobs, and also enhanced standard of living and availability of social services. "Social welfare programs should be investment-oriented, and . . . enhance people's capabilities to participate in the productive economy" (Midgley, 1999; Midgley & Livermore. 2004, p. 118). For example, effective programs might seek "to generate employment, raise incomes, and ensure that workers receive living wages" (Midgley & Livermore. 2004, p. 118).

Wetzel (2004) provides an example where economic development in the social development process had a successful impact on social conditions:

Probably the world's most successful economic development program is the Grameen Bank of Dhaka, Bangladesh, founded in 1976 by Muhammad Yunus, an economist who was making loans for commercial banks. (Grameen means "rural" or "village" in English.) Yunus was appalled by the living conditions of people in rural Bangladesh, the second poorest nation in the world. He was struck especially by the severe situation of women who are in a particularly precarious position when they are abandoned or divorced. They have no means of livelihood, and their families will not allow them to return to their homes. Consequently, the self-esteem of these women is as impoverished as their economic . . . [resources]. Banks would not grant them loans without collateral guarantees, so Yunus decided to become a personal benefactor to the region for micro-enterprises for low-income women. His credit union was opened to men as well, but 77 percent of the loans continue to be granted to women. Their payback rate has proven to be even better than their male counterparts. Because people without . . . [economic resources] seldom have access to credit, the Grameen model requires the group members themselves to become the collateral, promising to pay any outstanding debt that is not paid by the grantee [any individual who does not repay the loan]. It has seldom been necessary to do so. (pp. 108–109)

Consequently, the Grameen model has been used successfully in developing and industrialized countries to help impoverished people (Rosenberg, 2000). Success has been attributed to three aspects—an emphasis on enhanced "self-esteem," "group support," and "collaboration in reaching . . . goals" (Wetzel, 2004, p. 109).

Highlight 12.2 describes a feminist perspective on global development that can be used both in community and social development.

Distorted Development   Midgley (1997b) explains how sometimes economic development does not significantly improve social conditions:

Distorted development occurs through a mismatch between economic and social development. The problem in many countries is not an absence of economic development but rather a failure to harmonize economic and social objectives and to ensure that the benefits of economic progress reach the population as a whole.

Conditions of distorted development are widespread in the Third World. Perhaps the most dramatic examples have occurred in Latin America, where rates of economic growth have been impressive but where poverty and deprivation are . . . [widespread]. Despite a significant degree of economic development, housing standards are inadequate, the distribution of income and wealth is highly skewed, investments in education and the social services are low, and rates of unemployment and underemployment are high. Similar examples are found in Africa and Asia, particularly in countries where economic prosperity has been achieved through exploiting natural resources. In these nations, mineral wealth has provided high standards of living for a small minority of the population but left the majority in conditions of poverty.

Distorted development also persists in industrial countries such as the United Kingdom and the United States despite their high level of economic development. In these countries significant sections of the population do not benefit from economic growth. Distorted development is manifested in high rates of poverty in decayed inner-city areas and deprived rural communities. Inner cities are increasingly devastated in both physical and social terms. Here poverty, unemployment, crime, family disintegration, violence, drug use, and social deprivation are most marked. (pp. 13–14)

INTERNATIONAL SOCIAL WORK

International social work is "international professional practice and the capacity for international action by the social work profession and its members. International social work has four dimensions: internationally related domestic practice and advocacy, professional exchange, international practice,

Highlight 12.2 | # A Feminist Perspective on Global Development

Wetzel (1995) discusses the importance of women's mental health on a global level as a necessity to maintain their optimal well-being. She cites several standards based on feminist principles that should govern the development of programs for women around the world. For each she provides an international example. Although programs may vary, they should address the improvement of women's self-concepts, increasing their ability to act assertively on their own behalves, and enhance supportive relationships.

Standard 1. "Raising consciousness regarding gender roles and the importance and worth of every female" (p. 181). Work that is traditionally "women's work" should be respected and appreciated as work just as traditional "men's work" (work outside of the home) is respected. The rights and emotional well-being of women deserve respect.

Filomena Tomaira Pacsi, a women's social action group in Peru, provides an example. The issue addressed the plight of the wives of rural miners who were traditionally belittled and abused by their spouses. *Filomena* consisted of a group of urban women from Lima who worked with these rural women "to reduce their feeling of isolation (negative aloneness), enhance their solidarity (positive connectedness), encourage social action, and increase their self-perception and sense of worth by recognizing how important their roles are to their husbands, children, and communities (p. 182). Wetzel (1995) elaborates:

> The urban women of *Filomena* joined with these rural women to raise their consciousness and change their lives. When the mines were being

closed without notice, the rural women encouraged their husbands and families to make sacrifice marches hundreds of miles to the city. With the help of *Filomena,* the women of Lima began to realize how important they were to the mining struggle. The rural women took charge of the marches, feeding their families in community kitchens and providing education for their children along the way. The women also took responsibility for health care, surveying the needs of children and arranging for mobile health units staffed by paramedics . . .

> The presence of the urban women of *Filomena,* in the words of the rural women of the mines, brought them 'tremendous joy, sweeping them off their feet.' The solidarity and spirit of the two groups of women spread to the rural women's husbands, who stopped being violent toward their wives and showed them newfound respect. Respect for the rural women's roles was enhanced by bonding among the women and the recognition of their organizational expertise. It was the women who taught their husbands to advocate for better working conditions rather than to settle for their poor circumstances. The women opened their husbands' eyes to the responsibilities of companies and the rights of human beings in their employ. (p. 182)

Standard 2. "Forming interdisciplinary professional partnerships with poor women and training indigenous [those originating in the community] *trainers to serve their own communities"* (p. 182). It's

---

    | ## Critical Thinking Questions 12.8

To what extent do you agree with these three feminist principles? How valuable did the principles seem in implementing the three programmatic examples?

---

and international policy development and advocacy" (Healy, 2001, p. 7). International social work involves adopting a global focus whether working in one's own country or in an international context. It also means establishing the global goal of firmly establishing social work as a respected profession around the world (Cox & Pawar, 2006). The following content elaborates upon the four dimensions inherent in international social work.

important for professionals from various backgrounds to work together with poor women to train them. These poor women then, in turn, can return to and help their own communities by providing training for the women there.

The Women in Development Consortium of Thailand was a program co-sponsored by three Thai universities in conjunction with York University in Canada. The project, called "Train the Trainers," was undertaken by "Friends of Women, an interdisciplinary group of professional women and a few men who . . . [were] kindred spirits. These women and men . . . [were] devoted to working in partnership with low-income female factory workers who . . . [were] exploited. Using a nonhierarchical participative group approach, the professional facilitators train[ed] selected leaders from the factory, who in turn train[ed] the other female factory workers, hence, the Train the Trainer program title."

The training included five parts. First, the participants' feelings of isolation were addressed and their connectedness as a potentially supportive group emphasized. Most participants originated in rural areas and traveled to work in the relatively better economic urban environment. The second part of training involved health concerns in an industrial setting including "chronic exhaustion from devastating working conditions" (p. 182). The third training segment addressed participants' individual economic issues such as "personal incomes and expenses, analyzing their situations in the context of their poor status" (p. 182). Feminist labor lawyers and educators led the fourth phase where labor laws and rights were discussed. Collective bargaining and lobbying in the political arena were also explained. The fifth

training unit concerned a "synthesis" of all that participants had learned. Connections between personal and social problems and economic and political concerns were clearly identified, and the necessity of working individually and collectively for social change was emphasized (p. 183). The process resulted in participants' enhanced self-esteem and vision concerning what they might be able to achieve. Participants could then return to their factory environments and share what they learned with other workers.

Standard 3. "*Teaching women that both personal development and action, as well as collective social development and action, are essential if their lives are to change for the better*" (p. 186). We have identified feminist principles that stress how consciousness raising, an enhanced perception of one's life circumstances, and an increased understanding of self are extremely important for women. We have also emphasized that, according to feminist theories, the personal is political. Personal development is fine, but it must coincide with political and social action. Only then can conditions be improved and social justice be attained for all women.

An example of a program adopting this standard is *Stree Mukti Sanghatana,* a group that uses street theater to raise consciousness and advocate for women's rights in Bombay, India. Dramatic performances, entertainment, and other visual media such as posters serve as conduits to convey information and identify issues. Examples of performances include *No Dowry, Please; We Will Smash the Prison;* and *A Girl is Born;* all of these performances "address traumatic examples of female subordination" (p. 187).

1. *Internationally related domestic practice and advocacy.* The first dimension inherent in the definition of international social work concerns advocating for domestic policy that supports international social justice. It also means educating others about international issues to solicit their support on behalf of global social justice. This is true for social workers practicing primarily in the United States, Canada, Puerto Rico, the Caribbean, and anywhere else in the world.

   One way of practicing international social work in one's own country includes "international adoption" (Turner, 2001, p. 4). From our perspective, "*international adoptions* are those in which children are brought from other countries and placed with adoptive couples in the United States" (Crosson-Tower, 2004, p. 342). Another way of practicing international social work here is by "working with refugees or immigrants" (Turner, 2001, p. 4).

2. *Professional exchange.* The second dimension of international social work involves developing international arrangements and structures to encourage travel among countries and communication among professional colleagues. Various international social work and related organizations are discussed later in the chapter. These organizations sponsor conferences and serve as clearinghouses for information and ideas concerning global issues. Other positive avenues of professional exchange include international field internships sponsored by social work programs, volunteer activities in international helping organizations, and international social work faculty exchange programs.

Turner (2001) provides an example of a professional exchange concerning Robert Wiles, who was a graduate student at the University of Calgary (Turner, 2001). He entered a three-month practicum where he was involved in "the development of the practicum component of the Associate Degree in Social Work at the University College of Belize" (p. 5). He emphasized:

> "My experience in Belize was outstanding," ... [stated] Robert. "Certainly, the opportunity to work within another country was an incredible privilege, but being and living there was an intense learning experience. Beyond the classroom and university setting, interacting and learning about another culture was the most beautiful part of the experience." (p. 5)

3. *International practice.* Practicing in other countries can involve a wide range of social work activities, including participating in community development activities, working directly with individuals, families, and groups, assuming management positions, and assisting in policy development. Ways of getting your foot in the door for international social work positions include volunteering for or getting a job in a global social welfare organization such as CARE (a humanitarian organization dedicated to combating global poverty) or Save the Children (a humanitarian organization committed to helping children in need around the world and improving their potential for a better quality of life) (Brueggemann, 2006). Examples of potential paid positions include child protection officer, program director, education specialist, regional HIV/AIDS director, training manager, global challenge coordinator, community campaigns and organization manager, advocacy and policy advisor, and campaigner (CARE, 2006; Oxfam, 2006).

Note that it's important to be prepared to face and overcome possible hurdles when practicing in other countries. These include potential resistance on the part of indigenous citizens; funding shortages; lower salaries; different certification, licensing, and credentialing regulations; and language barriers (Turner, 2001).

4. *International policy development and advocacy.* International social work involves supporting positive policy development and advocacy in the pursuit of social justice at the global level. An aspect of international social work includes joining and actively working for global organizations

just as one would a national organization. These organizations often encompass "coalitions of people who are concerned about peace, environment, labor, housing, hunger, and social justice" (Verschelden, 1993, p. 768). Supporting global organizations seeking positive humanitarian policy changes such as the United Nations is another facet of this dimension.

The National Association of Social Workers (NASW) recently became "a member of InterAction, a large alliance of U.S.-based international development and humanitarian nongovernmental organizations" (NASW, 2005, p. 1). Being a member of NASW indirectly supports InterAction's humanitarian efforts.

INTERNATIONAL SOCIAL WORK ORGANIZATIONS

We've discussed organizations and communities in various contexts. When addressing the global community, it's important to understand how international organizations function within it. International social work organizations that actively engage social workers around the globe include the International Federation of Social Workers (IFSW) and the International Association of Schools of Social Work (IASSW). Two other international organizations that have values closely related to social work are the International Council on Social Welfare (ICSW) and the International Consortium for Social Development (ICSD) (Brueggeman, 2006).

International Federation of Social Workers (IFSW)

Established in 1956, the IFSW "is a global organisation striving for social justice, human rights and social development" through the support of effective social work practice and "international cooperation between social workers and their professional organisations" (International Federation of Social Workers [IFSW], 2006). It focuses on improving "the quality of life," "achievement of social justice," and the development "of human potential" for people around the globe (IFSW, 2006). It is especially involved in "protesting human rights violations" (Hokenstad & Midgley, 1997, pp. 4–5).

The IFSW consists of five regions—Africa, Asia and the Pacific, Europe, Latin America and the Caribbean, and North America. It publishes a monthly newsletter for members. The IFSW also sponsors regional and global conferences to teach skills, train educators to teach in various areas related to social justice, and provide a forum for the discussion and development of ideas for addressing critical global issues. Regional 2007 conferences included a European Conference in Parma, Italy, and a Pan-African Conference in Kampala, Uganda. The 2008 global conference is being held in Salvador de Bahia, Brazil. The IFSW also "promotes Human Rights by publishing statements on human rights issues and related matters and by raising awareness within the profession about the profession's commitment to its Human Rights heritage (IFSW, 2006). It has also developed an "International Policy on Human Rights" to provide guidance concerning human rights issues to social workers and organizations around the world. (The IFSW's home website is http://www.ifsw.org.)

International Association of Schools of Social Work (IASSW)

The IASSW is a "worldwide association of schools of social work," "related educational programmes, and social work educators"; it "promotes the development of social work education throughout the world, develops standards to enhance [the] quality of social work education, encourages international exchange, provides forums for sharing social work research and scholarship, and promotes human rights and social development through policy and advocacy activities" (International Association of Schools of Social Work [IASSW], 2006). It also serves as a consultant to the United Nations.

The IASSW is based on humanitarian values and the quest for social justice on the behalf of oppressed populations. It holds a biennial conference for social work educators, publishes a member newsletter, provides representation at the United Nations, co-sponsors with the IFSW and the ICSW (discussed below) the journal *International Social Work*, sponsors various committees and task forces, and funds "small cross-national projects in social work education" (IASSW, 2006). (The IASSW's home website is http://www.iassw-aiets.org.)

Other Global Organizations Dedicated to Social Welfare and Social Justice

Established in 1928, the International Council on Social Welfare (ICSW) is an international nongovernmental organization whose membership includes local and national organizations in over 50 countries (International Council on Social Welfare [ICSW], 2006). (Highlight 12.3 describes international nongovernment organizations.) The ICSW's membership consists of "tens of thousands of community organizations which work directly at the grass-roots with people in poverty, hardship or distress" (ICSW, 2006). The ICSW collects relevant information and dispenses it to various community groups, governments, and other organizations; provides training and support for members and other organizations; assists in policy development; sponsors global and regional meetings; publishes papers and reports on issues; and advocates for oppressed populations (ICSW, 2006). (The home website is http://www.icsw.org.)

The International Consortium for Social Development (ICSD) consists of "practitioners, scholars, and students in the human services" and "serves as a clearinghouse for information on international social development" (International Consortium for Social Development [ICSD], 2006). The ICSD seeks to improve economic and social conditions in various parts of the world by building on community strengths, improving distribution of economic resources, encouraging peace, and fighting discrimination (ICSD, 2006). It links skilled members with communities and governments in need, offers opportunities for training and curriculum development, and provides a forum

| **Highlight 12.3** | **International Nongovernmental Organizations** |

An *international nongovernment organization (INGO)* is a nonprofit agency whose purpose is to address designated social problems and issues (Cox & Pawar, 2006, p. 61). It is usually funded privately through such sources as donations and grants. An INGO's activities at the international level include advocating for human rights, assisting in economic development, providing education to citizens, helping people address crises, monitoring governments' treatment of their citizens, and providing consultation to national governments (Barker, 2003). Examples of goals include helping refugees relocate and providing assistance in reconstruction after a crisis such as a hurricane, earthquake, or war (Cox & Pawar, 2006). One of the oldest, most famous INGOs is the *International Red Cross,* originating in 1863 (Cox & Pawar, 2006). It is "concerned with the alleviation of human suffering and the promotion of public health and civil rights" (Barker, 2003, p. 362). However, "many Christian humanitarian organizations, Jewish welfare agencies, and the American Medical Association were founded even earlier" (Beigbeder, 1991; Cox & Pawar, 2006).

Amnesty International provides another example of an INGO (Brueggemann, 2006). It is a global movement that "operates around the world, mobilizing an international base of human rights advocates who question individual states about their human rights practices and provide material resources and legal services for victims of human rights abuse" (Amnesty International [AI], 2006a; Brueggemann 2006, p. 478). For example, one issue Amnesty International is addressing at the time of this writing concerns the United States' treatment of people being detained because of suspected involvement in the "war on terror." Amnesty International is demanding that the U.S. government "clarify the fate and whereabouts of all people who have been secretly detained and guarantee fair trials for all people in its custody" (AI, 2006c). Another example of an issue Amnesty International is currently addressing involves Papua New Guinea. Amnesty International has brought global attention to the "government's ongoing failure to tackle violence against women ... [which has] resulted in this violence becoming so pervasive that it impedes national development and contributes to the spread of HIV/AIDS (AI, 2000c)." Gang rapes, knife attacks on wives, beating and sexual abuse of girls and torture and murder of female sorcerers are only a few of the many frightening incidents frequently cited in the national media (AI, 2006b). (Amnesty International's home website is http://web.amnesty.org.)

for the development and application of new ideas. (The ICSD's home website is http://www.iucisd.org.)

SOCIAL WORK VALUES AND CROSS-CULTURAL VALUES IN GLOBAL PERSPECTIVE

"Social work practice does not follow the same patterns in all parts of the world. The form of social work that develops in any society is shaped by the prevailing social, economic, and cultural forces" (Doel & Shadlow, 1996; Sowers & Rowe, 2007, pp. 29–30). Therefore, it's of critical importance to view and understand community development within the context of the society where it's happening.

Sowers and Rowe (2007) maintain that "social work has been profoundly influenced by Western thought, values, and views" (p. 30; Sacco, 1996). They continue:

Arising from the dominant Western cultural point of view, human needs are based on the assumption that each individual needs a decent standard of living, education, housing, medical care, and social services, and that the provision of universal

Highlight 12.4 | Cultural Differences in an Organizational Context

Dubrin (2002) cites four cultural differences in the context of working with and in large organizations (Hofstede, 1980, 1993; Kennedy & Everest, 1991). These also are significant when working effectively with organizations in the community environment and with community citizens. It's essential to establish goals with community residents that fit well with their own value systems. It's also crucial for people commencing community development to be aware of their own value orientations so as not to impose them on people in the community.

1. *Individualism versus collectivism. Individualism* is "a mental set in which people see themselves first as individuals and believe that their own interests take priority. *Collectivism,* at the other end of the continuum, is a feeling that the group and society receive top priority. . . . Highly individualistic cultures include the United States, Canada, Great Britain, Australia, and the Nether-

lands. Japan, Taiwan, Mexico, Greece, and Hong Kong are among the countries that strongly value collectivism" (Dubrin, p. 330).

Sowers and Rowe (2007) comment concerning differences in how individual importance is perceived:

"For instance, within the African context, traditional African thinking understands human nature and human flourishing as a network of life forces that emanate from God and end in God, who is the source of all life forces. For many Africans, personhood is attainable only in community and the single most important concept within African traditional life is the inclusion of all into the community (Senghor, 1966; Setiloane, 1986). Traditional Native American teachings hold that mental, physical, and spiritual disease is caused by disharmony within the individual, or by disconnection from the family, community, nature, or the greater universe. Working out an

services would lead to the elimination of poverty, the advancement of underprivileged groups, and the narrowing of gaps in income, education, and employment (Barretta-Herman, 1994). (p. 30)

Verschelden (1993, pp. 766–767) proposes the following as fundamental global social work values that transcend cultural and national differences:

1. Primary importance of the individual
2. Respect and appreciation for differences
3. Commitment to social justice and the well-being of all in society
4. Willingness to persist despite frustration

Some research indicates that the last three are generally held by social workers around the globe; however, the first is addressed quite differently depending on the culture (Rowe, Hanley, Moreno, & Mould, 2000; Sowers & Rowe, 2007). Social workers must respond to the diverse cultural values of the societies in which they work. The ways in which individuals expect to be treated and the ways they prioritize their values vary from one culture to another. Highlight 12.4 identifies some cultural differences that must be taken into account when undertaking community development.

  Critical Thinking Questions 12.9

How would you describe yourself concerning these four value dimensions and why?

understanding of human beings and personal development that incorporates cultural conceptions and beliefs is critical to effective social work practice, particularly in a global context" (p. 30).

2. *Materialism versus concern for others* (Dubrin, p. 331). "*Materialism*" is the value that material things and money are extremely important, much more so than humanitarian or spiritual pursuits. There is also a tendency to emphasize, "Me, Me, Me" rather than focus on other people's needs and issues. In contrast, *concern for others* refers to genuine, active concern for other people's well-being and a focus on the importance of interpersonal relationships. As Dubrin notes, "Materialistic countries include Japan, Austria, and Italy. The United States is considered to be moderately materialistic... Scandinavian nations all emphasize caring as a national value (p. 331).

3. *Formality versus informality*. According to Dubrin, "A country that values *formality* attaches considerable importance to tradition, ceremony, social rules, and rank. At the other extreme, *informality* refers to a casual attitude toward tradition, ceremony, social rules, and rank. . . . [People] in Latin American countries highly value formality, such as lavish public receptions and processions. Americans, Canadians, and Scandinavians are much more informal (p. 331).

4. *Urgent time orientation versus casual time orientation*. "Dubrin notes that "individuals and nations attach different importance to time. People with an *urgent time orientation* perceive time as a scarce resource and tend to be impatient. People with a *casual time orientation* view time as an unlimited and unending resource and tend to be patient. Americans are noted for their urgent time orientation. They frequently impose deadlines and are eager to get started doing business. Asians and Middle Easterners, in contrast are [much more] patient." (p. 331).

WHAT YOU CAN DO ON THE BEHALF OF GLOBAL SOCIAL JUSTICE

There are at least five things that you can do to address and enhance social justice on a global basis. First, vote for political candidates who appreciate the importance of global cooperation to address human rights issues and solve social ills (Verschelden, 1993). Second, you can continue to become more knowledgeable about global issues and educate others including legislators about the issues' significance (Verschelden, 1993). Third, you can become politically involved yourself by actively participating in political debate and working to support political candidates (Shaefor & Horejsi, 2003). You might even decide to run for office yourself. Fourth, you can join organizations, several of which were mentioned earlier, that seek to help needy and hurting people around the world. Fifth, you can volunteer your time to support the work of international helping organizations. Sixth, you can become a macro practice social worker participating in community development in the international context.

CHAPTER SUMMARY

We live in a global environment. Globalization is the "process of global integration in which diverse people, economies, cultures, and political processes are increasingly subjected to international influences" (Midgley, 1997a, p. xi). The concepts—global, advocate, and social justice—are critical aspects of social work's global perspective.

Poverty and economic inequality are major problems in the United States and the rest of the world. Poverty is a complex term to define. The gap between rich and poor is widening in the United States. Global poverty and its related problems is a major concern internationally. Global conflict is also rampant. Forced migration of people in need results in numerous potential problems.

"Community development refers to efforts to mobilize people who are directly affected by a community condition into groups and organizations to enable them to take action on the social problems and issues that concern them" (Rivera & Erlich, 2001, p. 256). Important concepts in the conceptualization of community development are production-distribution-consumption, socialization, social control, social participation, and mutual support. Community development practice emphasizes improving community functioning. Social development is a concept related to community development that emphasizes comprehensive, planned change that has major economic impacts in addition to improving social conditions. Distorted development can occur where economic conditions improve, but social conditions do not.

A feminist perspective on global development involves "raising consciousness regarding gender roles and the importance and worth of every female"; "forming interdisciplinary professional partnerships with poor women and training indigenous trainers to serve their own communities"; and "teaching women that both personal development and action, as well as collective social development and action, are essential if their lives are to change for the better" (Wetzel, 1995, pp. 181–186).

International social work is "international professional practice and the capacity for international action by the social work profession and its members. International social work has four dimensions: internationally related domestic practice and advocacy, professional exchange, international practice, and international policy development and advocacy" (Healy, 2001, p. 7). International social work and social welfare organizations include the International Federation of Social Workers, the International Association of Schools of Social Work, the International Council on Social Welfare, and the International Consortium for Social Development. International non-government organizations are nonprofit agencies whose purpose is to address designated social problems and issues. Examples include the International Red Cross and Amnesty International.

Fundamental social work values that transcend cultural and national differences include: "respect and appreciation for differences"; "commitment to social justice and the well-being of all in society"; and "willingness to persist despite frustration" (Verschelden, 1993, pp. 766–767). Social workers should be attuned to the cultural differences in international organizations and communities that focus on "individualism versus collectivism"; "materialism versus concern for others"; "formality versus informality"; and "urgent time orientation versus casual time orientation" (Dubrin, 2002, pp. 330–331).

References

Abramovitz, M. (1995). Aid to families with dependent children. In *Encyclopedia of social work* (Vol. 1, pp. 183–194). Washington, DC: NASW Press.

Abramovitz, M. (1997). Temporary assistance to needy families. In *Encyclopedia of social work supplement*, (19th ed., pp. 311–330). Washington, DC: NASW Press.

Administration for Children & Families (ACF). (2006). *Welfare reform reauthorized*. Retrieved on June 27, 2006, from http://www.acf.hhs.gov/opa/spotlight/welfarereauthorized.htm.

Agrest, S. (1997, December 15). Kids who care. *Time*, Special Report, unnumbered inset.

Ahearn, F. L. Jr. (1995). Displaced people. In R. L. Edwards (Eds.), *Encyclopedia of social work* (19th ed., Vol. 1, pp. 771–780). Washington, DC: NASW Press.

Albrecht, K. (1978). *Successful management by objectives: An action manual*. Englewood Cliffs, NJ: Prentice Hall.

Albrecht, K. (1988). *At America's Service*. New York: Warner Books.

Aldag, R. J., & Kuzuhara, L. W. (2005). *Mastering management skills*. Mason, OH: South-Western.

American Psychiatric Association. (2000). *Diagnostic and statistical manual of mental disorders: Text revision DSM-IV-TR* (4th ed.). Washington, DC: Author.

Amnesty, International (AI). (2006a). *About AI*. Retrieved on September 8, 2006, from http://web.amnesty.org.

Amnesty, International (AI). (2006b). *Papua New Guinea: Culture and resources no excuse for violence against women*. Retrieved on September 8, 2006, from http://news.amnesty.org/mavp/news.nsf/print/ENGASA340072006.

Amnesty, International (AI). (2006c). *USA: Government must end all secret detention and guarantee fair trials*. Retrieved on September 8, 2006, from http://news.amnesty.org/mavp/news.nsf/print/ENGAMR511432006.

Anderson, J. (1997). *Social work with groups: A process model*. New York: Longman.

Anderson, R. E., & Carter, I., & Lowe, G. R. (1999). *Human behavior in the social environment: A social systems approach* (5th ed.). New York: Aldine De Gruyter.

Appleby, G. A., & Anastas, J. W. (1998). *Not just a passing phase: Social work with gay, lesbian, and bisexual people*. New York: Columbia University Press.

Arie-Donch, T. (1991). *A guide to community built projects: Organizing techniques for making your community self-help projects a success*. Unpublished manuscript.

Arredondo, P., & Perez, P. (2003). Counseling paradigms and Latina/o Americans: Contemporary considerations. In F. D. Harper, & J. McFadden (Eds.), *Culture and counseling: New Approaches* (pp. 115–132). Boston: Allyn & Bacon.

Asch, A. (1995). Visual impairment and blindness. In *Encyclopedia of social work* (Vol. 3, pp. 2461–2468). Washington, DC: NASW Press.

Asch, A. & Mudrick, N. R. (1995). Disability. In *Encyclopedia of social work* (Vol. 1, pp. 752–761). Washington, DC: NASW Press.

Austin, D. M. (1995). Management overview. In *Encyclopedia of social work* (Vol. 2, pp. 1642–1658). Washington, DC: NASW Press.

Austin, D. M. (2002). *Human services management: Organizational leadership in social work practice.* New York: Columbia.

Bales, R. F. (1950). *Interaction process analysis: A method for the study of small groups.* Cambridge, MA: Addison-Wesley.

Balgopal, P. R. Asian Americans Overview. In *Encyclopedia of Social Work* (Vol. 1, pp. 231–238). Washington, DC: NASW Press.

Ball, S. & Lipton, B. (1997). Group work with gay men. In G. L. Greif & P. H. Ephross (Eds.), *Group work with populations at risk.* New York: Oxford University Press, 259–277.

Balsanek, J. (1998). Addressing at-risk pregnant women's issues through community, individual, and corporate grassroots efforts. In P. L. Ewalt, E. M. Freeman, & D. L. Poole (Eds.), *Community building: Renewal, well-being, and shared responsbility.* Washington, DC: NASW Press, 411–419.

Barbuto, Jr., J. E., & Wheeler, D. W. (2005). *Becoming a servant leader: Do you have what it takes?* Lincoln, NE: University of Nebraska-Lincoln Extension, Institute of Agriculture and Natural Resources, A-15 General.

Barker, R. L. (1995). *The social work dictionary.* Washington, DC: NASW Press.

Barker, R. L. (2003). *The social work dictionary* (5th ed.). Washington, DC: National Association of Social Workers.

Barnett, A. W. (1984). *Community murals: The people's art.* Philadelphia: Art Alliance Press.

Barretta-Herman, A. (1994). Revisioning the community as provider: Restructuring New Zealand's social services. *International Social Work, 37* (1), 7–21.

Barusch, A. S. (2006). *Foundations of social policy: Social justice in human perspective* (2nd ed.). Pacific Grove, CA: Brooks/Cole.

Beckett, J. O., & Johnson, H. C. (1995). Human development. In R. L. Edwards (Eds.), *Encyclopedia of social work* (19th ed., Vol. 2, pp. 1385–1405). Washington, DC: NASW Press.

Bedwell, R. T., Jr. (1993). Total quality management: Making the decision. *Nonprofit World, 2* (3), 29–31.

Beigbeder, Y. (1991). *The role and status of international humanitarian volunteers and organisations.* Dordrecht, The Netherlands: Martinus Nijhoff.

Berger, R. J., & Kelly, J. J. (1995). Gay Men Overview. In *Encyclopedia of social work* (Vol. 2, pp. 1064–1075). Washington, DC: NASW Press.

Bernard, J. (1973). *The sociology of community.* Glenview, IL: Scott, Foresman.

Biegal, D. E., Shore, B. K., & Gordon, E. (1984). *Building support networks for the elderly.* Beverly Hills: Sage.

Black, R. B. (1994). Diversity and populations at risk: People with disabilities. In F. Reamer (Ed.), *The foundations of social work knowledge.* New York: Columbia University Press.

Blackless, E., et al. (2000). How sexually dimorphic are we? Review and synthesis. *American Journal of Human Biology, 12,* 151–166.

Blythe, B., & Reighoffer, A. (2000). Assessment and measurement issues in direct practice in social work. In P. Allen-Meares & C. Garvin (Eds.), *The handbook of social work practice* (pp. 551–564). Thousand Oaks, CA: Sage.

Borjas, G. J. (1994). The economics of immigration. *Journal of Economic Literature, 32,* 1667–1717.

Brammer, R. (2004). *Diversity in counseling.* Belmont, CA: Brooks/Cole.

Braun, K. L., Mokuau, N., & Tsark, J. (1997). Cultural themes in health, illness, and rehabilitation for Native Hawaiians: Observations of rehabilitation staff and physicians. *Topics in Geriatric Rehabilitation, 12,* 19–37.

Brave Heart, M. Y. H. (2001). Lakota—Native people's spirituality. In M. Van Hook, B. Hugen, & M. Aguilar (Eds., pp. 18–33), *Spirituality within religious traditions in social work practice.* Belmont, CA: Brooks-Cole.

Breidenstein, J. L. (2003, Spring). Grandparents raising grandchildren. *The New Social Worker, 10* (2), 5–7.

Breton, M. (2004). An empowerment perspective. In C. D. Garvin, L. M. Gutierrez, & M. J. Galinsky (Eds.), *Handbook of social work with groups* (pp. 58–75). New York: Guilford.

Bricker-Jenkins, M., & Lockett, P. W. (1995). Women: Direct practice. In R. L. Edwards (Ed.), *Encyclopedia of social work* (19th ed., Vol. 3, pp. 2529–2539). Washington, DC: NASW Press.

Bridgewater, D. (1992). A gay male survivor of antigay violence. In S. H. Dworkin & F. J. Gutierrez (Eds.), *Counseling gay men and lesbians: Journey to the end of the rainbow* (pp. 219–230). Alexandria, VA: AACD Press.

Brody, R. (2005). *Effectively managing human service organizations* (3rd ed.). Thousand Oaks, CA: Sage.

Brown, M. G., Hitchcock, D. E., & Willard, M. L. (1994). *Why TQM fails and what to do about it. Soundview Executive Book Summaries, 16* (5), 1–8.

Brueggemann, W. G. (2006). *The practice of macro social work* (3rd ed.). Belmont, CA: Brooks/Cole.

Buchanan, W. (2006, Feb. 15). *San Francisco same-sex marriage still a hot topic: Weddings in S. F. city hall made debate national.* Retrieved on June 17, 2006, from http://sfgate.com/cgi-bin/article.cgi?f=c/a/2006/02/15/BAGCJH 8FGP1.DTL.

Burrell, G., & Morgan, G. (1979). *Sociological paradigms and organizational analysis.* London: Heinemann.

Burton, L. M. (1992). Black grandparents rearing children of drug-addicted parents: Stressors, outcomes, and social service needs. *Gerontologist, 32,* 744–751.

Butler, S., & Wintram, C. (1992). *Feminist groupwork*. Thousand Oaks, CA: Sage.

Cahill, S., Ellen, M., & Tobias, S. (2002). *Family policy: Issues affecting gay, lesbian, bisexual, and transgendered families*. New York: National Gay and Lesbian Task Force Policy Institute.

Cahill, S., & Jones, K. T. (2001). *Leaving our children behind: Welfare reform and the gay, lesbian, bisexual, and transgender community*. New York: National Gay and Lesbian Task Force Policy Institute.

California town hopes eye-catching murals will put it on map. (1996, November 10). *New York Times*, p. 24.

Capuzi, D., & Gross, D. R. (2006). Group work: Elements of effective leadership. In D. Capuzi, D. R. Gross, & M. D. Stauffer, M. D. (Eds.), *Introduction to group work* (4th ed., pp. 57–88). Denver: Love.

Capuzi, D., Gross, D. R., & Stauffer, M. D. (2006). *Introduction to group work* (4th ed.). Denver: Love.

CARE. (2006). *CARE*. Retrieved on September 10, 2006, from http://www.care.org.

Carlton-LaNey, I. B., Edwards, R. L., & Reid, P. N. (1999). Small towns and rural communities: From romantic notions to harsh realities. In I. B. Carlton-LaNey, R. L. Edwards, & P. N. Reid (Eds.), *Preserving and strengthening small towns and rural communities* (pp. 5–12). Washington, DC: NASW Press.

Carr, E. S. (2004). Accessing resources, transforming systems: Group work with poor and homeless people. In C. D. Garvin, L. M. Gutierrez, & M. J. Galinsky (Eds.), *Handbook of social work with groups* (pp. 360–383). New York: Guilford.

Carroll, C., Bates, M., & Johnson, C. (2004). *Group leadership: Strategies for group counseling leaders* (4th ed.). Denver: Love.

Carroll, J. L. (2005). *Sexuality now*. Pacific Grove, CA: Brooks/Cole.

Center on Budget and Policy Priorities (CBPP). (2006, May 9). *Implementing the TANF changes in the Deficit Reduction Act: "Win-win" solutions for families and states*. Retrieved on June 27, 2006, from http://www.cbpp.org/5-9-06tanf.htm.

Champoux, J. E. (2003). *Organizational behavior: Essential tenets* (2nd ed.). Mason, OH: South-Western.

Chaskin, R. J., Joseph, M. L., & Chipenda-Dansokho. (1998). Implementing comprehensive community development: Possibilities and limitations. In P. L. Ewalt, E. M. Freeman, & D. L. Poole (Eds.), *Community building: Renewal, well-being, and shared responsibility* (pp. 17–28). Washington, DC: NASW Press.

Child Welfare League of America (CWLA). (2006, February 1). *Analysis and summary of Deficit Reduction Act*. Retrieved on June 27, 2006, from http://www.cwla.org/printable/printpage.asp.

Chilman, C. S. (1993). Hispanic families in the United States: Research perspectives. In H. P. McAdoo, Ed.), *Family ethnicity: Strength in diversity*. Newbury Park, CA: Sage.

Cohen, R. (1979). Neighborhood planning and political capacity. *Urban Affairs Quarterly*, 14 (3), 337–362).

Coleman, J. W., & Kerbo, H. R. (2002). *Social problems* (8th ed.). Upper Saddle River, NJ: Prentice-Hall.

Coleman, S. (1994, December 11). Mission's marvelous murals if you go … *The Boston Glove*, p. B1.

Compton, B. R., Galaway, B., & Cournoyer, B. R. (2005). *Social work processes* (7th ed.). Belmont, CA: Brooks/Cole.

Cooper, M., & Sciorra, J. (1994). *R.I.P. memorial wall art*. New York: Henry Holt.

Corcoran, K. (1997). Managed care: Implications for social work practice. In *Encyclopedia of social work supplement* (19th ed., pp. 191–200). Washington, DC: NASW Press.

Corey, G. (2004). *Theory & practice of group counseling* (6th ed.). Belmont, CA: Brooks/Cole.

Corey, M. S., & Corey, G. (1997). *Groups process and practice* (5th ed.). Pacific Grove, CA: Brooks/Cole.

Corey, M. S., & Corey, G. (2006) *Groups: Process and practice* (7th ed.). Belmont, CA: Brooks/Cole.

Corey, G., Corey, M. S., & Callanan, P. (2007). *Issues and ethics in the helping professions* (7th ed.). Belmont, CA: Brooks/Cole.

Cormier, S., & Hackney, H. (1999). *Counseling strategies and interventions* (5th ed.). Boston: Allyn & Bacon.

Council on Social Work Education (CSWE). (2001). *Educational policy and accreditation standards*. Alexandria, VA: Author.

Cowger, C. D., & Snively, C. A. (2002). Assessing client strengths: Individual, family, and community empowerment. In D. Saleebey (Ed.), *The strengths perspective in social work practice* (3rd ed., pp. 106–123). Boston: Allyn & Bacon.

Cox, C. B. (2002). Empowering African American Custodial Grandparents. *Social Work*, 47 (1), 45–54.

Cox, D., & Pawar, M. (2006). *International social work: Issues, strategies, and programs*. Thousand Oaks, CA: Sage.

Cox, E. O. (1991). The critical role of social action in empowerment oriented groups. In A. Vinik & M. Levin (Eds.), *Social action in group work* (pp. 77–90). New York: Haworth.

Crooks, R., & Baur, K. (2005). *Our sexuality* (9th ed.). Belmont, CA: Wadsworth.

Crosby, P. (1980). Quality if free. New York: Mentor.

Crosson-Tower, C. (2004). *Exploring child welfare: A practice perspective* (3rd ed.). Boston: Allyn & Bacon.

Currah, P., & Minter, S. (2000). *Transgender equality: A handbook for activists and policymakers*. New York: National Gay and Lesbian Task Force Policy Institute.

Daley, M. R., & Avant, F. L. (2004). Rural social work. In T. L. Scales & C. L. Streeter (Eds.), *Rural social work: building and sustaining community assets* (pp. 34–42). Belmont, CA: Brooks/Cole.

Daft, R. L. (2003). *Management* (6th ed.). Cincinnati, OH: South-Western.

Daft, R. L. (2001). *Organization theory and design* (7th ed.). Cincinnati, OH: South-Western.

Daft, R. L. (2004). *Organization theory and design* (8th ed.). Cincinnati, OH: South-Western.

Daft, R. L. (2007). *Organization theory and design* (9th ed.). Cincinnati, OH: South-Western.

Daft, R. L., & Marcic, D. (2004). *Understanding management* (4th ed.). Cincinnati, OH: South-Western.

Daft, R. L., & Marcic, D. (2006). *Understanding management* (5th ed.). Cincinnati, OH: South-Western.

DeCesare, D. (1993, March). El Salvador: War, poverty and migration: A photo essay. *Fellowship, 59* (3).

Delgado, M. (1997). Role of Latina-owned beauty parlors in a Latino community. *Social Work* 42 (5), 445–453.

Delgado, M. (2000). *Community social work practice in an urban context: The potential of a capacity-enhancement perspective.* New York: Oxford.

Delgado, M., & Barton, K. (1998, July). Murals in Latino communities: Social indicators of community strengths. *Social Work, 43* (4), 346–356.

Delgado, M., & Barton, K. (1999). Murals in Latino communities: Social indicators of community strengths. In P. L. Ewalt, E. M. Freeman, A. E. Fortune, D. L. Poole, & S. L. Witkin (Eds.), *Multicultural issues in social work: Practice and research* (pp. 229–244). Washington, DC: NASW Press.

DeLois, K. A. (1998). Empowerment practice with lesbians and gays. In L. M. Gutierrez, R. J. Parsons, & E. O. Cox, *Empowerment in social work practice: A sourcebook,* 65–72.

Denhardt, R. B., Denhardt, J. V., & Aristigueta, M. P. (2002). *Managing human behavior in public and nonprofit organizations.* Thousand Oaks, CA: Sage.

DePoy, E., & Gilson, S. F. (2004). *Rethinking disability: Principles for professional and social change.* Belmont, CA: Brooks/Cole.

DeWeaver, K. L. (1995). Developmental disabilities: Definitions and policies. In *Encyclopedia of social work* (Vol. 1, pp. 712–720). Washington, DC: NASW Press.

Dhooper, S. S., & Moore, S. E. (2001). *Social work practice with culturally diverse people.* Thousand Oaks, CA: Sage.

Diller, J. V. (2004). *Cultural diversity: A primer for the human services* (2nd ed.). Belmont, CA: Brooks/Cole.

DiNitto, D. M. (2005). *Social welfare: Politics and public policy* (6th ed.). Boston: Allyn & Bacon.

Doel, M., & Shardlow, S. (1996). Introduction to the context of practice learning: An overview of key themes. In M. Doel & S. Shardlow (Eds.), *Social work in a changing world: An international perspective on practice learning.* Brookfield, VT: Arena Ashgate.

Dolgoff, R., & Feldstein, D. (2003). *Understanding social welfare* (6th ed.). Boston: Allyn & Bacon.

Downs, A. (1981). *Neighborhoods and urban development.* Washington, DC: The Brookings Institution.

DuBrin, A. J. (2002). *Fundamentals of organizational behavior* (2nd ed.). Mason, OH: South-Western.

Dumler, M. P., & Skinner, S. J. (2005). *A primer for management.* Mason, OH: South-Western.

DuongTran, Q., & Matsuoka, J. K. (1995). Asian Americans: Southeast Asians. In *Encyclopedia of Social Work* (Vol. 1, pp. 249–255). Washington, DC: NASW Press.

Durkheim, E. (1947). *Division of labor in society.* Glencoe, IL: Free Press.

Dworkin, S. H. (2000). Individual therapy with lesbian, gay, and bisexual clients. In R. M. Perez, K. A. DeBord, & K. J. Bieschke (Eds.), *Handbook of counseling and psychotherapy with lesbian, gay, and bisexual clients* (pp. 157–181). Washington, DC: American Psychological Association.

Edinburg, G. M., & Cottler, J. M. (1995). Managed care. In *Encyclopedia of social work* (Vol. 2, pp. 1635–1642). Washington, DC: NASW Press.

Edmonston, B., & Passel, J. S. (1994). Ethnic demography: U.S. immigration an ethnic variation. In B. Edmonston & J. S. Passel (Eds.), *Immigration and ethnicity* (pp. 1–30). Washington, DC: Urban Institute Press.

Education Development Center. (n.d.). *Ghana community school alliances (CSA) project.* Retrieved on August 27, 2005, from http://main.edc.org/Search/viewProject.asp?ProjectID=2485.

Eitzen, D. S., & Zinn, M. B. (2003). *Social problems* (9th ed.). Boston: Allyn & Bacon.

Elze, D. E. (2006). Oppression, prejudice, and discrimination. In D. F. Morrow & L. Messinger (Eds.), *Sexual orientation & gender expression in social work practice: Working with gay, lesbian, bisexual, & transgender people* (pp. 43–77). New York: Columbia University Press.

Emery, S. E., & Trist, E. L. The causal texture of organizational environments. *Human Relations,* 18 (1), 21–32.

Engelhardt, B. J. (1997). Group work with lesbians. In G. L. Greif & P. H. Ephross (Eds.), *Group work with populations at risk.* New York: Oxford University Press, 278–291.

Erhlich, J. L., & Rivera, F. G. (1981). Community organization and community development. In N. Gilbert & H. Specht (Eds.), *Handbook of the Social Services* (pp. 472–489). Englewood Cliffs, NJ: Prentice Hall.

Evans, K. G. (1996). Chaos as opportunity: grounding a positive vision of management and society in the new physics. *Public Administration Review,* 56, 491–494.

Ewalt, P. L., & Mokuau, N. (1996). Self-determination from a Pacific perspective. In P. L. Ewalt, E. M. Freeman, A. E. Fortune, D. L. Poole, & S. L. Witkin (eds.). *Multicultural issues in social work: Practice and research.* Washington, DC: NASW Press, 255–268.

Families.com, LLC. (2006). Social exchange theory. Retrieved on May 17, 2006 from http://issues.families.com/social-exchange-theory-1532-1535-iemf.

Fatout, M., & Rose, S. R. (1995). *Task groups in the social services.* Thousand Oaks, CA: Sage.

Feigenbaum, A. (1983). *Total quality control* (3rd ed.). New York: McGraw-Hill.

Fellin, P. (2001a). *The community and the social worker* (3rd ed.). Belmont, CA: Brooks/Cole.

Fellin, P. (2001b). Understanding American communities. In J. Rothman, J. L. Erlich, & J. E. Tropman (Eds.), *Strategies of community organization* (3rd ed., pp. 118–132).

Fellin, P. & Litwak, E. (1968). The neighborhood in urban American society. *Social Work* 13 (3), 72–80.

Finn, J. L., & Jacobson, M. (2003). *Just practice: A social justice approach to social work.* Peosta, IA: Eddie Bowers.

Finnegan, D. G., & McNally, E. B. (1996). Chemical dependency and depression in lesbians and gay men: What helps? *Journal of Gay and Lesbian Social Services,* 4 (2), 115–129.

Fisher, R. (1984, Summer). Community organization in historical perspective: A typology. *The Huston Review,* 8.

Fisher, R. (2001). Social action community organization: Proliferation, persistence, roots, and prospects. In J. Rothman, J. L. Erlich, & J. E. Tropman (Eds.), *Strategies of community intervention* (6th ed., pp. 350–363). Itasca, IL: Peacock.

Fix, M., & Passel, J. S. (1994). *Immigration and immigrants: Setting the record straight.* Washington, DC: Urban Institute.

Frame, M. W. (2003). *Integrating religion and spirituality into counseling: A comprehensive approach.* Belmont, CA: Brooks/Cole.

French, J. R., & Raven, B. (1968). The bases of social power. In D. Cartwright, & A. Zander (Eds.), *Group dynamics: Research and theory,* (pp. 259–269). New York: Harper & Row.

Gamble, D. N., & Hoff, M. D. (2005). Sustainable community development. In M. Weil (Ed.), *The handbook of community practice* (pp. 169–188). Thousand Oaks, CA: Sage.

Gardella, L. G., & Haynes, K. S. (2004). *A dream and a plan: A women's path to leadership in human services.* Washington, DC: NASW Press.

Garvin, C. D. (1987). Group theory and research. In *Encyclopedia of social work* (Vol. 1, pp. 683–696). Washington, DC: NASW Press. Silver Spring, MD: National Association of Social Workers.

Garvin, C. D., & Cox, F. M. (1995). A history of community organizing since the Civil War with special reference to oppressed communities. In J. Rothman, J. L. Erlich, & J. E. Tropman (Eds.), *Strategies of community intervention* (pp. 64–99). Itasca, IL: Peacock, 64–98.

Garvin, C. D., & Reed, B. G. (1995). Sources and visions for feminist group work: Reflective processes, social justice, diversity, and connection. In N. Van Den Bergh, N. (Ed.), *Feminist practice in the 21st century* (pp. 41–69). Washington, DC: NASW Press.

Gay Demographics. (2006). *Percent of households with children under 18 years.* Retrieved on June 17, 2006, from http://www.gaydemographics.org/USA/PUMS/nationalintro.htm.

Germain, C. B., & Gitterman, A. (1995). Ecological perspective. In *Encyclopedia of social work* (Vol. 1, pp. 816–824). Washington, DC: NASW Press.

Gibbs, L., & Gambrill, E. (1999). *Critical thinking for social workers: Exercises for the helping profession* (Revised ed.). Thousand Oaks, CA: Pine Forge.

Gibelman, M. (1998, Summer). Women's perceptions of the glass ceiling in human service organizations and what to do about it. *Affilia,* 13 (2), 147–165.

Gibson, P. A. (2004, Fall). Religious expressions of African American Grandmother caregivers: Social work's role with church communities. *Arete,* 28 (1), 21–37.

Gilbert, N., & Terrell, P. (2005). *Dimensions of social welfare policy* (6th ed.). Boston: Allyn & Bacon.

Ginsberg, L. (1995). Concepts of new management. In L. Ginsberg & P. R. Keys (Eds.) *New management in human services,* (2nd ed.) (pp. 1–37). Washington, DC: NASW Press.

Ginsberg, L. H. (2005). Introduction: The overall context of rural practice. In L. H. Ginsberg (Ed.), *Social work in rural communities* (4th ed., pp. 1–14). Alexandria, VA: Council on Social Work Education.

Gitterman, A. (2004). The mutual aid model. In C. D. Garvin, L. M. Gutierrez, & M. J. Galinsky (Eds.), *Handbook of social work with groups* (pp. 93–110). New York: Guilford.

GlenMaye, L. (1998). Empowerment of women. In L. M. Gutierrez, R. J. Parsons, & E. O. Cox (Eds.), *Empowerment in social work practice: A sourcebook* (pp. 2–51). Belmont, CA: Brooks/Cole.

Goffman, E. (1959). *The presentation of self in everyday life.* Garden City, NY: Doubleday.

Goldberg Wood, G., & Middleman, R. R. (1989). *The structural approach to direct practice in social work.* New York: Columbia.

Goldenring, J. (2004, January 4). *Mental retardation.* Retrieved on May 22, 2005, from http://nlm.nih.gov/medlineplus/ency/article/001523.htm.

Goldlenberg, H., & Goldenberg, I. (2002). *Counseling today's families* (4th ed.). Belmont, CA: Brooks/Cole.

Gotterer. R. (2001). The spiritual dimension in clinical social work practice: A client perspective. *Families in Society,* 82 (2), 187–193.

Graham, J. W. (1991). Servant-leadership in organizations: Inspirational and moral. *Leadership Quarterly,* 2 (2), 105–119.

Greene, R. R. (2007). A risk and resilience perspective. In R. R. Greene (Ed.), *Social work practice: A risk and resilience perspective.* Belmont, CA: Brooks/Cole.

Greenleaf, R. K. (1970). *The servant as leader.* Newton Centre, MA: Robert K. Greenleaf Center.

Greenleaf, R. K. (1977). *Servant leadership: A journey into the nature of legitimate power and greatness.* New York: Paulist.

Gruskin, E. P. (1999). *Treating lesbians and bisexual women: Challenges and strategies for health professionals.* Thousand Oaks, CA: Sage.

Gummer, B., & Edwards, R. L. (1995). The politics of human services administration. In L. Ginsberg & P. R. Keys (Eds.) *New management in human services,* (2nd ed.) (pp. 57–71). Washington, DC: NASW Press.

Gushue, G. V., & Sciarra, D. T. (1995). Culture and families: A multidimensional approach. In J. G. Ponterotto, J. M. Casas, L. A. Suzuke, & C. M. Alexander (Eds.), *Handbook of multicultural counseling* (2nd ed., pp. 586–606). Thousand Oaks, CA: Sage.

Gutheil, I. A., & Congress, E. (2002). Resiliency in older people: A paradigm for practice. In R. R. Green (Ed., pp. 40–52), *Resiliency: An integrated approach to practice, policy, and research.* Washington, DC: NASW Press.

Gutierrez, L. M. (2001). Working with women of color: An empowerment perspective. In J. Rothman, J. L. Erlich, & J. E. Tropman (Eds.), *Strategies of community intervention* (6th ed., pp. 209–217). Itasca, IL: Peacock.

Gutierrez, L. M., GlenMaye, L., & Delois, K. (1995). The organizational context of empowerment practice: Implications for social work administration. *Social Work,* 40, 249–257.

Gutierrez, L. M., & Lewis, E. A. (1999). *Empowering women of color.* New York: Columbia.

Gwynne, S. C. (1998, March 9). Miracle in New Orleans. *Time,* 74.

Habitat for Humanity. (2005). 2005 annual report: Respecting our past, building for the future. Retrieved on July 21, 2006, from http://www.habitat.org/giving/report/2005/annual_report_2005.pdf.

Haight, W. L. (1999). "Gathering the spirit" at First Baptist Church: Spirituality as a protective factor in the lives of African American children. In P. L. Ewalt, E. M. Freeman, A. E. Fortune, D. L. Poole, & S. L. Witkin (eds.). *Multicultural issues in social work: Practice and research.*

Washington, DC: NASW Press, 245–255.

Hallahan, D. P., & Kauffman, J. M. (2003). *Exceptional learners: Introduction to special education* (9th ed.). Boston: Allyn & Bacon.

Harrison, R. J., & Weinberg, D. H. (1992, April). *Racial and ethnic segregation in 1990.* Washington, DC: U.S. Bureau of the Census.

Harrison, W. D. (1995). Community development. In R. L. Edwards (Ed.), *Encyclopedia of social work* (19th ed., Vol. 1, pp. 555–562). Washington, DC: NASW Press.

Harvey, A. R. (1997). Group work with African-American youth in the criminal justice system: A culturally competent model. In G. L. Greif & P. H. Ephross (Eds.), *Group work with populations at risk* (pp. 160–174). New York: Oxford University Press.

Hasenfeld, Y. (1983). *Human service organizations.* Englewood Cliffs, NJ: Prentice-Hall.

Hasenfeld, Y. (1984). Analyzing the human service agency. In F. M. Cos, J. L. Erlich, J. Rothman, & E. Tropman (Eds.), *Tactics and techniques of community practice.* Itasca, IL: Peacock, 14–26.

Hayashi, R. (2005). The environment of disability today: A nursing home is not a home. In G. E. May & M. B. Raske, M. B. (Eds., pp. 45–70), *Ending disability discrimination: Strategies for social workers.* Boston: Allyn & Bacon.

Haynes, K. S., & Mickelson, J. S. (2003). *Affecting change: Social workers in the political arena* (5th ed.). Boston: Allyn & Bacon.

Healy, K. (2005). *Social work theories in context: Creating frameworks for practice.* New York: Palgrave.

Healy, L. (2001). *International social work: Professional action in an interdependent world.* New York: Oxford University Press.

Hellriegel, D., & Slocum, J. W., Jr. (2007). *Organizational behavior* (11th ed.). Mason, OH: South-Western.

Hellriegel, D., Jackson, S. E., & Slocum, Jr., J. W. (2002). *Management: A competency-based approach* (9th ed.). Cincinnati, OH: South-Western.

Hepworth, D. H., Rooney, R. H., Rooney, G. D., Strom-Gottfried, K., & Larsen, J. (2006). *Direct social work practice: Theory and skills* (7th ed.). Belmont, CA: Brooks-Cole.

Herek, G. M., Gillis, R. J., & Cogan, J. (1997, May). *Study offers "snapshot" of Sacramento area lesbian, gay and bisexual community.* Available at http://psychology.ucdavis.edu/rainbow/default.html.

Herrell, R. K. (1992). The symbolic strategies of Chicago's gay and lesbian pride parade. In G. Herdt (Ed.), *Gay culture in America: Essays from the field* (pp. 225–252). Boston: Beacon Press.

Hesse, H. (1956). *The journey to the East.* London: P. Owen.

Hiroto, J. M., Brown, P., & Martin, N. (1997). *Building community: The tradition and promise of settlement houses.* New York: United Neighborhood Houses of New York.

Ho, M. K., & Rasheed, J. M., & Rasheed, M. N. (2004). *Family therapy with ethnic minorities* (2nd ed.). Thousand Oaks, CA: Sage.

Hodge, B. J., Anthony, W. P., & Gales, L. M. (2003). *Organization theory: A strategic approach* (6th ed.). Upper Saddle River, NJ: Prentice-Hall.

Hodge, J. L., Struckmann, D. K., & Trost, L. D. (1975). *Cultural bases of racism and group oppression.* Berkely, CA: Two Riders Press.

Hoefer, R. (2006). *Advocacy practice for social justice.* Chicago: Lyceum.

Hofstede, G. (1993, Spring). A conversation with Geert Hofstede. *Organizational Dynamics,* 50–54.

Hofstede, G. (1980). *Culture's consequences: International differences in work-related values.* Thousand Oaks, CA: Sage.

Hokenstad, M. C., & Midgley, J. (1997). Realities of global interdependence: Challenges for social work in a new century. In M. C. Hokenstad & J. Midgley (Eds.), *Issues in international social work: Global challenges for a new century* (pp. 1–10). Washington, DC: NASW Press.

Holland, T. P. (1995). Organizations: Context for social services delivery. In *Encyclopedia of social work* (Vol. 2, pp. 1787–1794). Washington, DC: NASW Press.

Holland, T. P., & Petchers, M. K. (1987). Organizations: Context for social service delivery. In *Encyclopedia of social work* (18th ed., Vol. 2, pp. 729–736). Silver Spring, MD: National Association of Social Workers.

Homan, M. S. (2004). *Promoting community change: Making it happen in the real world* (3rd ed.). Belmont, CA: Brooks/Cole.

Homans, G. C. (1950). *The human group.* New York: Harcourt Brace Jovanovich.

House, R. J. (1971). A path-goal theory of leader effectiveness. *Administrative Science Quarterly, 16,* 321–328.

House, R. J. (1996). Path-goal theory of leadership: Lessons, legacy, and a reformulated theory. *Leadership Quarterly, 7* (3), 323–352.

House, R. J., & Dessler, G. (1974). The path-goal theory of leadership: Some post hoc and a priori tests. In J. Hunt & L. Larson (Eds.), *Contingency approaches in leadership* (pp. 29–55). Carbondale: Southern Illinois University Press.

House, R. J., & Mitchell, R. R. (1974). Path-goal theory of leadership. *Journal of Contemporary Business, 3,* 81–97.

Hugen, B. (2001). Spirituality and religion in social work practice: A conceptual model. In M. Van Hook, B. Hugen, & M. Aguilar (Eds., pp. 1–17), *Spirituality within religious traditions in social work practice.* Belmont, CA: Brooks-Cole.

Hunter, S., & Hickerson, J. C. (2003). *Affirmative practice: Understanding and working with lesbian, gay, bisexual, and transgender persons.* Washington, DC: NASW Press.

Hynes, H. P. (1995). *A patch of Eden: America's inner-city gardeners.* White River Junction, VT: Chelsea Green.

International Association of Schools of Social Work (IASSW). (2006). *About IASSW: Overview.* Retrieved on September 8, 2006, from http://www.iassw-aiets.org.

International Consortium for Social Development (ICSD). (2006).

About ICSD. Retrieved on September 8, 2006, from http://www.iucisd.org/about.htm.

International Council on Social Welfare (ICSW). (2006). *ICSW: Who are we?* Retrieved on September 8, 2006, from http://www.icsw.org.

International Federation of Social Workers (IFSW). (2006). *Welcome to IFSW.* Retrieved on September 8, 2006, from http://www.ifsw.org.

Ivey, A. E., & Ivey, M. B. (2003). *Intentional interviewing and counseling: Facilitating client development in a multicultural society* (5th ed.). Belmont, CA: Brooks/Cole.

Jansson, B. S. (2003). *Becoming an effective policy advocate* (4th ed.). Pacific Grove, CA: Brooks/Cole.

Jansson, B. S. (2005). *The reluctant welfare state: American social welfare policies: past, present, and future* (5th ed.). Belmont, CA: Brooks/Cole.

Johns, G. (1996). *Organizational behavior: Understanding and managing life at work,* (4th ed.). New York: HarperCollins.

Johnson, D. W., & Johnson, F. P. (1997). *Joining together: Group theory and group skills.* Boston: Allyn & Bacon.

Johnson, L. C., & Yanca, S. J. (2004). *Social work practice: A generalist approach* (8th ed.). Boston: Allyn & Bacon.

Joiner, B. L., & Scholtes, P. R. (1985). Total quality leadership vs. management by results (pp. 1–9), Madison, WI: Joiner Associates, Inc.

Juran, J. (1989). *Juran on leadership for quality: An executive handbook* (4th ed.). New York: McGraw-Hill.

Kamya, H. G. (1999). African immigrants in the United States: The challenge for research and practice. In P. L. Ewalt, E. M. Freeman, A. E. Fortune, D. L. Poole, & S. L. Witkin (Eds.), *Multicultural issues in social work: Practice and research* (pp. 605–621). Washington, DC: NASW Press.

Kantner, R. M. (1979, July-August). Power failure in management

circuits. *Harvard Business Review,* 31–54.

Karenga, M. (1965). *Kwanzaa: Origin, concepts and practice.* Los Angeles: Kawaida Publications.

Karenga, M. (1997). *Kwanzaa: A celebration of family, community and culture.* Los Angeles: University of Sankore Press.

Karenga, M. (2000). Making the past meaningful: Kwanzaa and the concept of sankofa. In S. L. Abels (Ed.), *Spirituality in social work practice: Narratives for professional helping* (pp. 51–67). Denver, CO: Love.

Karger, H. J., & Stoesz, D. (2006). *American social welfare policy: A pluralist approach* (5th ed.). Boston: Allyn & Bacon.

Katzenbach, J., & Smith, D. (1993). *The wisdom of teams.* Cambridge, MA: Harvard business School Press.

Kazdin, A. E. (2001). *Behavior modification in applied settings* (6th ed.). Belmont, CA: Wadsworth.

Keene, J. (2006, February 3). The House narrowly passes the Deficit Reduction Act of 2005. Retrieved on June 27, 2006, from http://www.imakenews.com/eletra/mod_print_view.cfm?this_id=526167&u=csac&issue.

Kellman, L. (2006, June 7). *Gay marriage ban falls short of majority.* Retrieved on June 17, 2006, from http://abcnews.go.com/Politics/wireStory?id=2049175.

Kendall, D. (2004). *Social problems in a diverse society* (3rd ed.). Boston: Allyn & Bacon.

Kennedy, J., & Everest, A. (1991, September). Put diversity in context. *Personnel Journal,* 50–54.

Kettner, P. M., Moroney, R. M., & Martin, L. L. (1999). *Designing and managing programs: An effectiveness-based approach* (2nd ed.). Thousand Oaks, CA: Sage.

Keys, P. R. (1995a). Japanese quality management techniques. In L. Ginsberg & P. R. Keys (Eds.), *New management in human services,* (2nd ed.) (pp. 162–170).

Keys, P. R. (1995b). Quality management. In *Encyclopedia of social work* (Vol. 3, pp. 2019–2025). Washington, DC: NASW Press.

Kirk, G., & Okazawa-Rey, M. (2004). *Women's lives: Multicultural perspectives* (3rd ed.). New York: McGraw-Hill.

Kirst-Ashman, K. K. (2007). *Introduction to social work and social welfare: Critical thinking perspectives*. Belmont, CA: Brooks/Cole.

Kirst-Ashman, K. K., & Hull, G. H., Jr. (1997). *Generalist Practice with Organizations and Communities*. Chicago: Nelson-Hall.

Kirst-Ashman, K. K., & Hull, G. H., Jr. (2006a). *Generalist practice with organizations and communities* (3rd ed.). Belmont, CA: Brooks/Cole.

Kirst-Ashman, K. K., & Hull, G. H., Jr. (2002). *Understanding generalist practice* (3rd ed.). Belmont, CA: Brooks/Cole.

Kirst-Ashman, K. K., & Hull, G. H., Jr. (2006b). *Understanding generalist practice* (4th ed.). Belmont, CA: Brooks/Cole.

Kitano, H. H. L., & Maki, M. T. (1996). Continuity, change, and diversity: Counseling Asian Americans. In P. B. Pederson, J. G. Draguns, W. J. Lonner, & J. E. trimble (Eds.), *Counseling across cultures*, (4th ed.). Thousand Oaks, CA: Sage, 124–145.

Knopf, R. (1979). *Suviving the BS (Bureaucratic System)*. Wilmington, NC: Mandala Press.

Kolb, P. J. (1999). A stage of migration approach to understanding nursing home placement in Latino families. *Journal of Multicultural Social Work,* 7 (3/4), 95–112.

Kopels, S. (1995). The Americans with Disabilities Act: A tool to combat poverty. *Journal of Social Work Education* 31 (3), 337–346.

Kornblum, W. (1974). *Blue collar community*. Chicago: University of Chicago Press.

Kramer, R. M., & Specht, H. (1983). *Readings in community organization practice* (3rd ed.). Englewood Cliffs, NJ: Prentice-Hall.

Kretzmann, J. P., & McKnight, J. L. (1993). *Building communites from the inside out: A patth toward finding and mobilizing a community's assets*. Chicago, IL: ACTA Publications.

Krippner, S. (1994, Summer) Humanistic psychology and chaos theory: The third revolution and the third force. *Journal of Humanistic Psychology,* 34 (3), 48–61.

Kronenberg, P., & Loeffler, R. (1991). Quality management theory: Historical context and future prospect. *Journal of Management Science & Policy Analysis,* 8, 203–221.

Krout, J. (1994). Community size differences in senior center resources, programming, and participation. *Research on Aging,* 16, 440–462.

Lad Lake, Inc. (Undated). Mission statement. Dousman, WI: Author.

Lad Lake, Inc. (2005). *Small steps: 2005 annual report*. Dousman, WI: Author.

Laird, J. (1995). Lesbians: Parenting. In *Encyclopedia of social work* (Vol. 2, pp. 1604–1616). Washington, DC: NASW Press.

Lauffer, A., Nybell, L., Overberger, C., Reed, B., & Zeff, L. (1977). *Understanding your social agency*. Beverly Hills: Sage.

Lazzari, M. M., Ford, H. R., & Haughey, K. J. (1996). Making a difference: Women of action in the community. *Social Work* 41 (2), 197–205.

Leashore, B. R. (1995). African Americans overview. In R. L. Edwards (Ed.), *Encyclopedia of social work* (19th ed., Vol. 1, pp. 101–115). Washington, DC: NASW Press.

Lee, J. A. B. (1994). *The empowerment approach to social work practice: Building the beloved community*. New York: Columbia.

Lee, J. A. B. (2001). *The empowerment approach to social work practice: Building the beloved community* (2nd ed.). New York: Columbia.

Lee, J. B. (1996). The empowerment approach to social work practice. In F. Turner (Ed.), *Social work treatment: Interlocking theoretical approaches*. New York: Free Press.

Leigh, J. W., & Green, J. W. (1982). The structure of the Black community: The knowledge base for social services. In J. W. Green (Ed.), *Cultural awareness in the human services* (pp. 106–107). Englewood Cliffs, NJ: Prentice Hall.

Leininger, M. M. (1990). Historic and epistemologic dimensions of care and caring with future directions. In J. Stevenson (Ed.), *American Academy of nursing* (pp. 19–31). Kansas City, MO: American Nurses Association Press.

Leininger, M. M. (1992). *Cultural care diversity and universality: A theory of nursing* (Publication No. 15-2401). New York: National League for Nursing Press.

Leon-Guerrero, A. (2005). *Social problems: Community, policy, and social action*. Thousand Oaks, CA: Pine Forge.

Levine, E., & Padilla, A. (1980). *Crossing cultures in therapy: Pluralistic counseling for the Hispanic*. Belmont, CA: Brooks/Cole.

Lewin, K. (1951). *Field theory in social science*. New York: Harper & Row.

Lewin, K., Lippitt, R., & White, R. K. (1939). Patterns of aggressive behavior in experimentally created social climates. *Journal of Social Psychology* (10), 271–299.

Lewis, E. A., & Suarez, Z. E. (1995). Natural helping networks. In *Encyclopedia of social work* (Vol. 2, pp. 1765–1772). Washington, DC: NASW Press.

Lewis, J. A., Lewis, M. D., Packard, T., & Souflee, Jr., F. (2001). *Management of human service programs*. Belmont, CA: Brooks/Cole.

Lewis, R. G. (1995). American Indians. In R. L. Edwards (Ed.), *Encyclopedia of social work* (Vol. 1, pp. 216–225). Washington, DC: NASW Press.

Link, R. J., Ramanathan, C. S., & Asamoah, Y. (1999). Understanding the human condition and human behavior in a global era. In C. S. Ramanathan & R. J. Link (Eds.), *All our futures: Principles and resources for social work practice in a global era* (pp. 30–51). Belmont, CA: Brooks/Cole.

Lohmann, R. A. (1997). Managed care: A review of recent research. In R. L. Edwards (Ed.) *Encyclopedia of social work: Supplement 1997* (19th ed., pp. 200–213). Washington, DC: NASW Press.

Lohmann, R. A., & Lohmann, N. (2005). Introduction. In N. Lohmann & R. A. Lohmann (Eds.), *Rural social work practice* (pp. xi–xxvii). New York: Columbia.

Long, C. R., & Curry, M. A. (1998). Living in two worlds: Native American women and prenatal care. *Health Care for Women International, 19* (3), 205–215.

Longres, J. F. (1995). Hispanics overview. In *Encyclopedia of social work* (Vol. 2, pp. 1214–1222). Washington, DC: NASW Press.

Loprest, P. J. (2003). *Fewer welfare leavers employed in weak economy.* Retrieved on January 12, 2005, from http://www.urban.org/urlprint.cfm?ID=8550.

Lorber, J. (2005). *Gender inequality: Feminist theories and politics* (3rd ed.). Los Angeles: Roxbury.

Lowe, G. R. (1995). Social development. In R. L. Edwards (Ed.), *Encyclopedia of social work* (19th ed., Vol. 3, pp. 2168–2173). Washington, DC: NASW Press.

Lum, D. (1999). *Culturally competent practice: A framework for growth and action.* Pacific Grove, CA: Brooks/Cole.

Lum, D. (2003). *Culturally competent practice* (2nd ed.). Pacific Grove, CA: Brooks/Cole.

Lum, D. (2004). *Social work practice and people of color: A process-stage approach* (5th ed.). Belmont, CA: Brooks/Cole.

Lum, D. (2005). *Cultural competence, practice stages, and client systems: A case study approach.* Belmont, CA: Brooks/Cole.

Lussier, R. N. (2006). *Management fundamentals: Concepts, applications, skill development* (3rd ed.). Belmont, CA: Brooks/Cole.

Macionis, J. J. (2005). *Social problems* (2nd ed.). Upper Saddle River, NJ: Prentice-Hall.

Mackelprang, R., & Salsgiver, R. (1999). *Disability: A diversity model approach in human service practice.* Belmont, CA: Brooks/Cole.

Mackelprang, R. W., & Salsgiver, R. O. (1996). People with disabilities and social work: Historical and contemporary issues. *Social Work, 41* (1), 7–14.

MacKinnon, C. A. (1982). Feminism, Marxism, method, and the state: An agenda for theory. *Signs, 7* (3), 515–544.

Madden, J. (1996, November 14). Offending art: Graffiti on Beverly walls attracts attention, criticism. *Salem Evening News,* pp. A1, A10.

Marsella, A. J. (1998, June). Urbanization, mental health, and social deviancy. *American Psychologist, 53* (6) 624–634.

Martin, J. (2003). Historical development of critical social work practice. In J. Allan, B. Pease, & L. Briskman (Eds.), *Critical social work: An introduction to theories and practice* (pp. 17–31). Crows Nest, Sydney: Allen and Unwin).

Martin, J. L. (2003, July). What is field theory? *The American Journal of Sociology, 109,* i1 p. 1 (50). Retrieved on May 17, 2007, http://infotrac.thomsonlearning.com.

Martin, L. L. (1993). *Total quality management in human service organizations.* Newbury Park, CA: Sage.

Martinez-Brawley, E. E. (1995). Community. In *Encyclopedia of social work* (Vol. 1, pp. 539–548). Washington, DC: NASW Press.

Martinez-Brawley, E. E. (2000). *Close to home: Human services and the small community.* Washington, DC: NASW Press.

Marx, J. D. (2004). *Social welfare: The American partnership.* Boston: Allyn & Bacon.

Mary, N. L. (1998). Social work and the support model of services for people with developmental disabilities. *Journal of Social Work Education, 34* (2), 247–260.

Maryland Development Disabilities Council. (2006). *Developmental Disabilities Assistance and Bill of Right Amendments of 2000.* Retrieved on August 10, 2006, from http://www.md-council.org/about/add_act.html.

Mattaini, M. A., & Meyer, C. H. (2002). The ecosystems perspective: Implications for practice. In M. A. Mattaini, C. T. Lowery, & C. H. Meyer (Eds.), *Foundations of social work practice: A graduate text* (3rd ed., pp. 3–24). Washington, DC: NASW Press.

Matza, B. R. (1990). Empowerment: The key management skill of the 90s. *Retail Control, 58* (11), 20–23.

May, G. E. (2005). Changing the future of disability: The disability discrimination model. In G. E. May & M. B. Raske, M. B. (Eds., pp. 82–98), *Ending disability discrimination: Strategies for social workers.* Boston: Allyn & Bacon.

McAnulty, R. D., & Burnette, M. M. (2003). *Fundamentals of human sexuality: Making healthy decisions.* Boston: Allyn & Bacon.

McCammon, S. L., Knox, D., & Schacht, C. (2004). *Choices in sexuality* (2nd ed.). Cincinnati, OH: Atomic Dog Publishing.

McDonald, M. (1998, January 5). How to reduce teen pregnancy: Voluntary community service. *U. S. News & World Report,* 48–49.

Mclaughlin, L. A., & Braun, K. L. (1999). Asian and Pacific Islander cultural values: Considerations for health care decision-making. In P. L. Ewalt, E. M. Freeman, A. E. Fortune, D. L. Poole, & S. L. Witkin (eds.). *Multicultural issues in social work: Practice and research.* Washington, DC: NASW Press, 321–336.

Meenaghan, T. M. (1987). Macro practice: Current trends and issues. In *Encyclopedia of social work* (Vol. 2, pp. 82–89). Silver Spring, MD: National Association of Social Workers.

Mercy Corps. (2006). *History.* Retrieved on September 10, 2006, from http://www.mercycorps.org/aboutus/overview/686.

Mercy Corps. (n.d.). *Restoring lives in Indonesia.* Retrieved on August 27, 2005, from http://www.mercycorps.org.

Merton, R. K. (1968). *Social theory and social structure* (enlarged ed.). New York: Free Press.

Messinger, L. (2006). Social welfare policy and advocacy. In D. F. Morrow & L. Messinger (Eds.), *Sexual orientation & gender expression in social work practice: Working with gay, lesbian, bisexual, & transgender people* (pp. 427–459). New York: Columbia University Press.

Meyer, D. R. (1995). Supplemental security income. In *Encyclopedia of social work* (Vol. 3, pp. 2379–2385). Washington, DC: NASW Press.

Meyerson, D. E., & Scully, M. (1999). *Tempered radicalism: Changing the workplace from within*

(CGO Insights No. 6). Boston: Simmons Graduate School of Management, Center for Gender in Organizations.

Midgley, J. (1994). Defining social development: Historical trends and conceptual formulations. *Social Development Issues,* 16 (3), 3–16.

Midgley, J. (1999). Growth, redistribution and welfare: Towards social investment. *Social Service Review,* 77 (1), 3–21.

Midgley, J. (1997a). Social work and international social development: Promoting a developmental perspective in the profession. In M. C. Hokenstad & J. Midgley (Eds.), *Issues in international social work: Global challenges for a new century* (pp. 11–26). Washington, DC: NASW Press.

Midgley, J. (1997b). *Social welfare in global context.* Thousand Oaks, CA: Sage.

Midgley, J., & Livermore, M. (2004). Social development: Lessons from the global south. In M. C. Hokenstad & J. Midgley (Eds.), *Lessons from abroad: Adapting international social welfare innovations* (pp. 117–135). Washington, DC: NASW Press.

Miller, D. (1991, November). *The "grandparents who care" support project.* Paper presented at the 44th Annual Meeting of the Gerontological Society of America, San Francisco.

Minkler, M., & Roe, K. M. (1993). *Grandmothers are caregivers: Raising children of the crack cocaine epidemic.* Newbury Park, CA: Sage.

Mish, F. C. (Editor-in-Chief). (1995). *Merriam Webster's Collegiate Dictionary* (10th ed.). Springfield, MA: Merriam-Webster, Inc.

Mokuau, N. (1995). Pacific Islanders. In *Encyclopedia of Social Work* (Vol. 3, pp. 1795–1801). Washington, DC: NASW Press.

Money, J. (1987). Sin, sickness, or status: Homosexual gender identity and psychoneuroendocrinology. *American Psychologist,* 42, 384–399.

Mooney, L. A., Knox, D., & Schacht, C. (2007). *Understanding social problems* (5th ed.). Belmont, CA: Wadsworth.

Morales, E. (1996). Gender roles among Latino gay and bisexual men. In J. Laird & R-J. Green (Eds.), *Lesbians and gays in couples and families: A handbook for therapists* (pp. 273–297). San Francisco: Jossey-Bass.

Morales, J. (1995). Gay men: Parenting. In R. L. Edwards (Ed.), *Encyclopedia of social work* (19th ed., Vol. 2, pp. 1085–1095). Washington, DC: NASW Press.

Morrissey, E., & Wandersman, A. (1995). Total quality management in health care settings: A preliminary framework for successful implementation. In L. Ginsberg & P. R. Keys (Eds.), *New management in human services,* (2nd ed.) (pp. 171–194).

Morrow, D. F. (2006). Sexual orientation and gender identity expression. In D. F. Morrow & L. Messinger (Eds.), *Sexual orientation & gender expression in social work practice: Working with gay, lesbian, bisexual, & transgender people* (pp. 3–17). New York: Columbia University Press.

Moser, C. (1992). Lust, lack of desire, and paraphilias: Some thoughts and possible connections. *Journal of Sex and Marital Therapy,* 18, 65–69.

Moxley, D. P. (1989). *The practice of case management.* Newbury Park, CA: Sage.

Muckian, M. (1994). TQM bumps and bruises. In *Business* (June), 20–35, 39.

Murase, K. (1995). Asian Americans: Japanese. In *Encyclopedia of Social Work* (Vol. 1, pp. 241–249). Washington, DC: NASW Press.

Murphy, B. (2004, October 10). If worker pay kept pace with CEOs, it would be $184,000. *Milwaukee Journal Sentinel,* A1.

Murray, S. (1992). *Components of gay community in San Francisco.* In G. Herdt (Ed.), Gay culture in America (pp. 107–146). Boston: Beacon Press.

Murray, S. (2006, June 8). *Gay marriage amendment fails in senate.* Retrieved on June 17, 2006, from http://www.washingtonpost.com/.

Naparstek, R. J., & Dooley, D. (1997). Community building. In *Encyclopedia of social work supplement* (19th ed., pp. 77–89). Washington, DC: NASW Press.

Naparstek, R. J., & Dooley, D. (1998). Countering urban disinvestment through community-building initiatives. In P. L. Ewalt, E. M. Freeman, & D. L. Poole (Eds.), *Community building: Renewal, well-being, and shared responsibility* (pp. 6–16). Washington, DC: NASW Press.

Napholz, L. (2000). Balancing multiple roles among a group of urban midlife American Indian working women. *Health Care for Women International,* 21 (4), 255–266.

National Association of Social Workers. (2005, February). Association joins global coalition. *NASW News,* 1.

National Association of Social Workers. (1999). *NASW code of ethics* (amended). Washington, DC: Author.

National Association of Social Workers. (2003). *Social work speaks: National Association of Social Workers policy statements 2003–2006.* Washington, DC: Author.

National Committee for Pay Equity. (2003). Questions and answers on pay equity. In A. Kesselman, L. D. McNair, & N. Schniedewind (Eds.), *Women: Images and realities* (3rd ed., pp. 192–195). Boston: McGraw-Hill.

Negroni-Rodriguez, L., K., & Morales, J. (2001). Individual and family assessment skills with Latino/Hispanic Americans. In R. Fong & S. Furuto (Eds.), *Culturally competent practice: Skills, interventions, and evaluations* (pp. 132–146). Boston: Allyn & Bacon.

Neighborhood House of Milwaukee, Inc. (2006a). *Mission and vision statements.* Retrieved on August 2, 2006, from http://www.nh-milw.org/about_nh/mission/mission.html.

Neighborhood House of Milwaukee, Inc. (2006b). *Outdoor/environmental education.* Retrieved on August 2, 2006, from http://www.nh-milw.org/programs/naturecenter/naturecenter.html.

Netting, F. E., Kettner, P. M., & McMurtry, S. L. (2004). *Social work macro practice* (3rd ed.). Boston: Allyn & Bacon.

Netting, F. E., & O'Connor, M. K. (2003). *Organization practice: A social worker's guide to understanding human services.* Boston: Allyn & Bacon.

Nichols, R., & Braun, K. L. (1996). *Death and dying in five Asian and Pacific Islander cultres: A preliminary study.* Honolulu: University of Hawaii, School of Public Health, Center on Aging.

Nobles, W. W. (1976). African consciousness and black research: The consciousness of self. In L. M. King, V. Dixon, & W. Nobles (Eds.), *African philosophy: Assumption and paradigms fore research on black persons* (pp. 163–174). Los Angeles: Fanon Center.

Norman, E. (2000). Introduction: The strengths perspective and resilience enhancement—a natural partnership. In E. Normal (Ed.), *Resiliency enhancement: Putting the strengths perspective into social work practice* (pp. 1–16). New York: Columbia.

Northouse, P. G. (2004). *Leadership: Theory and practice* (3rd ed.). Thousand Oaks, CA: Sage.

Okazawa-Rey, M. (1998). Empowering poor communities of color: A self-help model. In L. M. Gutierrez, R. J. Parsons, & E. O. Cox (Eds.) *Empowerment in social work practice: A sourcebook.* Pacific Grove, CA: Brooks/Cole.

Olaveson, J., Conway, P., Shaver, C. (2004). Defining *rural* for social work practice and research. In T. L. Scales & C. L. Streeter (Eds.), *Rural social work: Building and sustaining community assets* (pp. 9–20). Belmont, CA: Brooks/Cole.

Orren, D., Smith, R., Norlin, J. M., & Chess, W. A. (2006). *Human behavior and the social environment: Social systems theory* (5th ed.). Boston: Allyn & Bacon.

Outsama, K. (1977). *Laotian themes.* New York: Center for Bilingual Education.

Oxfam. (2006). *Oxfam.* Retrieved on September 10, 2006, from http://www.oxfam.org.uk.

Padilla, Y. C. (1999). Immigrant policy: Issues for social work practice. In P. L. Ewalt, E. M. Freeman, A. E. Fortune, D. L. Poole, & S. L. Witkin (Eds.), *Multicultural issues in social work: Practice and research* (pp. 589–604). Washington, DC: NASW Press.

Paniagua, F. A. (1998). *Assessing and treating culturally diverse clients: A practical guide* (2nd ed.). Thousand Oaks, CA: Sage.

Paniagua, F. A. (2005). *Assessing and treating culturally diverse clients: A practical guide* (3rd ed.). Thousand Oaks, CA: Sage.

Parsons, R. J., Gutierrez, L. M., & Cox, E. O. (1998). *Empowerment in social work practice: A sourcebook* (pp. 3–23). Belmont, CA: Brooks/Cole.

Parsons, T. (1951). *The social system.* New York: Free Press.

Parsons, T., Bales, R. F., & Shils, E. A. (Eds.). (1953). *Working papers in the theory of action.* New York: Free Press.

Patterson, C. J. (1995). Lesbian mothers, gay fathers, and their children. In A. R. D'Augelli & C. J. Patterson (Eds.), *Lesbian, gay and bisexual identities over the lifespan: Psychological perspectives* (pp. 262–290). New York: Oxford.

Perez-Koenig, R. (2000). The Unitas extended family circle: Developing resiliency in Hispanic youngsters. In E. Norman (Ed.), *Resiliency enhancement: Putting the strengths perspective into social work practice* (pp. 143–153). New York: Columbia.

Perrow, C. A. (1961). The analysis of goals in complex organizations. *American Sociological Review*, 26 (6), 856–866.

Pfeffer, J. (1981). *Power in organizations.* Marshfield, MA: Pitman.

Pfeiffer, D. (2005). The conceptualization of disability. In G. E. May & M. B. Raske, M. B. (Eds., pp. 25–44), *Ending disability discrimination: Strategies for social workers.* Boston: Allyn & Bacon.

Phillips, M. H., & Cohen, C. S. (2000). *Strength and resiliency themes in social work practice with groups.* New York: Columbia.

Phillips, N. K., & Straussner, S. L. A. (2002). *Urban social work: An introduction to policy and practice in the cities.* Boston: Allyn & Bacon.

Pippard, J. L., & Bjorklund, R. W. (2003). Identifying essential techniques for social work community practice. *Journal of Community Practice*, 11 (4), 101–116.

PollingReport.com. (2006). *Law and civil rights.* Retrieved on June 17, 2006, from http://www.pollingreport.com/civil.htm.

Poole, D. L. (1995). Health care: Direct Practice. In *Encyclopedia of social work* (Vol. 2, pp. 1156–1167). Washington, DC: NASW Press.

Popple, P. R. (1995). The social work profession: History. In *Encyclopedia of social work* (Vol. 3, pp. 2282–2292). Washington, DC: NASW Press.

Poulin, J. (2005). *Strengths-based generalist practice* (2nd ed.). Belmont, CA: Brooks/Cole.

Powell, G. N., & Graves, L. M. (2003). *Women and men in management* (3rd ed.). Thousand Oaks, CA: Sage.

Powell, T. J. (1995). Self-help groups. In *Encyclopedia of social work* (Vol. 3, pp. 2116–2123). Washington, DC: NASW Press.

Publia, B., & House, R. M. (2006). Group work: Gay, lesbian, and bisexual clients. In D. Capuzi, D. R. Gross, & M. D. Stauffer, M. D. (Eds.), *Introduction to group work* (4th ed., pp. 515–547). Denver: Love.

Rapp, C. A. (1998). *The strengths model: Case management with people suffering from severe and persistent mental illness.* Oxford University Press: New York.

Raske, M. (2005). The disability discrimination model in social work practice. In G. E. May & M. B. Raske, M. B. (Eds., pp. 99–112), *Ending disability discrimination: Strategies for social workers.* Boston: Allyn & Bacon.

Redmond, H. (2002, March 18). A social worker's outlook on the managed care crisis. *Social Work Today*, 22–23.

Reiman, J. (2004). *The rich get richer and the poor get poorer.* Boston, MA: Allyn & Bacon.

Renz-Beaulaurier, R. (1998). Empowering people with disabilities:

The role of choice. In L. M. Gutierrez, R. J. Parsons, & E. O. Cox (Eds.), *Empowerment in social work practice: A sourcebook* (pp. 73–84). Pacific Grove, CA: Brooks/Cole.

Renzetti, C. M., & Curran, D. J. (2003). *Women, men, and society* (5th ed.). Boston: Allyn & Bacon.

Replogle, J. (n.d.). *Village in Guatemalan rain forest thrives with ecological logging: Lumber sold in U.S. through program that certifies wood.* Retrieved on August 27, 2005, from http://www.sfgate.com/cgi-bin/article.cgi?f=/c/a2005/08/22/MNGJKEBBIVI.DTL&hw=Guatemalan+rain+forest&sn=007&sc=426.

Resnick, H., & Patti, R. J. (Eds.). (1980). *Change from within: Humanizing social welfare institutions.* Philadelphia: Temple University Press.

Riley, D. P. (1995). Family life education. In *Encyclopedia of social work* (Vol. 2, pp. 960–965). Washington, DC: NASW Press.

Rivera, F. G., & Erlich, J. L. (1995). Organizing with people of color: A perspective. In J. E. Tropman, J. L. Erlich, & J. Rothman (Eds.), *Tactics and techniques of community intervention* (3rd ed.). Itasca, IL: F. E. Peacock, 198–213.

Rivera, F. G., & Erlich, J. L. (2001). Organizing with people of color. In J. Rothman, J. L. Erlich, & J. E. Tropman (Eds.), *Strategies of community intervention* (pp. 254–269). Itasca, IL: Peacock.

Robbins, S. P., Chatterjee, P., Canda, E. R. (2006). *Contemporary human behavior theory* (2nd ed.). Boston: Allyn & Bacon.

Robert, H. M. (1971). *Robert's Rules of Order Revised.* New York: William Morrow.

Rose, S. D. (1986). Group methods. In F. H. Kanfer & A. P. Goldstein (Eds.), *Helping people change: A textbook of methods* (3rd ed., pp. 437–469). New York: Pergamon Press.

Rose, S. D. (1998). *Group therapy with troubled youth: A cognitive-behavioral interactive approach.* Thousand Oaks, CA: Sage.

Rosenberg, D. (2006, June 12). *Politics of the altar: GOP leaders are putting gay marriage back on the agenda. Will voters repond?* Retrieved on June 17, 2006, from http://www.msnbc.msn.com/id/13121953/site/newsweek.

Rosenberg, T. (2000, October 26). Looking at poverty, seeing untapped riches. *New York Times,* p. A34.

Ross, M. G. (1967). *Community organization: Theory, principles, and practice* (2nd ed.). New York: Harper & Row.

Rothman, J. (2001). Approaches to community intervention. In J. Rothman, J. L. Erlich, & J. E. Tropman (Eds.), *Strategies of community intervention* (pp. 27–64). Itasca, IL: Peacock.

Rothman, J. (1987). Community theory and research. In *Encyclopedia of social work* (Vol. 1, pp. 308–316). Silver Spring, MD: National Association of Social Workers.

Rothman, J. C. (2003). *Social work practice across disability.* Boston: Allyn & Bacon.

Rowe, W., Hanley, J., Moreno, E. R., & Mould, J. (2000). Voices of social work practice: International reflections on the effects of globalization. *Canadian Social Work, 2* (1), 65–87.

Rubin, H. R., & Rubin, I. S. (2001). *Community organizing and development* (3rd ed.). Boston: Allyn & Bacon.

Ruscio, J. (2006). *Critical thinking in psychology* (2nd ed.). Belmont, CA: Wadsworth.

Rusk, D. *Cities without suburbs.* (1993). Baltimore: Johns Hopkins University Press.

Ruth, S. (2001). *Issues in feminism: An introduction to women's studies* (5th ed.). Mountain View, CA: Mayfield.

Rynecki, D., Smith, T., Shanley, M., & Wheat, A. (2003, August 11). Field guide to power. *Fortune,* 126–127.

Sacco, T. (1996). Towards an inclusive paradigm for social work. In M. Doel & S. Shardlow (Eds.), *Social work in a changing world: An international perspective on practive learning.* Brookfield, VT: Arena Ashgate.

Saleebey, D. (2002a). Community development, neighborhood empowerment, and individual resilience. In D. Saleebey (Ed.), *The strengths perspective in social work practice* (3rd ed., pp. 228–246). Boston: Allyn & Bacon.

Saleebey, D. (2002). Introduction: Power in the people. In D. Saleebey (Ed.), *The strengths perspective in social work practice* (3rd ed., pp. 1–22). Boston: Allyn & Bacon.

Santiago-Rivera, A. L., Arredondo, P., & Gallardo-Cooper, M. (2002). *Counseling Latinos and la familia: A practical guide.* Thousand Oaks, CA: Sage.

Sapiro, V. (2003). *Women in American society: An introduction to women's studies* (5th ed.). Boston: McGraw-Hill.

Sarri, R. (1987). Administration in social welfare. In *Encyclopedia of social work* (Vol. 1, pp. 555–562). Washington, DC: NASW Press.

Sashkin, M., & Kiser, K. J. (1993). *Putting total quality management to work: What TQM means, how to use it and how to sustain it over the long run.* San Francisco: Berrett-Koehler.

Saulnier, C. F. (1997). Alcohol problems and marginalization: Social group work with lesbians. *Social work with groups, 20,* 37–59.

Schiller, B. R. (2004). *The economics of poverty and discrimination* (9th ed.). Upper Saddle River, NJ: Pearson Prentice Hall.

Schriver, J. M. (2004). *Human behavior and the social environment* (4th ed.). Boston: Allyn & Bacon.

Schopler, J. H., & Galinsky, M. J. (1995). Group practice overview. In *Encyclopedia of social work* (Vol. 2, pp. 1129–1142). Washington, DC: NASW Press.

Schulz, A. J., Israel, B. A., & Lantz, P. (2004). Assessing and strengthening characteristics of effective groups in community-based participatory research partnerships. In C. D. Garvin, L. M. Gutierrez, & M. J. Galinsky (Eds.), *Handbook of social work with groups* (pp. 309–325). New York: Guilford.

Senge, P. (1990). *The fifth discipline: The art and practice of learning organizations* (New York: Doubleday/Currency.

Senghor, L. S. (1966). Negritude. *Optima*, 16, 1–8.

Sentiloane, G. M. (1986). *African theology: an introduction*. Johannesburg: Skotaville.

Shapiro, J. P. (1995, September 11). *U. S. News & World Report*, 59.

Shaw, S. M., & Lee, J. (2004). *Women's voices, feminist visions: Classic and contemporary readings* (2nd ed.). Boston: McGraw-Hill.

Sheafor, B. W., & Horejsi, C. R. (2003). *Techniques and guidelines for social work practice* (6th ed.). Boston: Allyn & Bacon.

Shulman, L. (1992). *The skills of helping: Individuals, families, and groups*, (3rd ed.). Itasca, IL: F. E. Peacock.

Siegel, L. M., Attkisson, C. C., & Carson, L. G. (2001). Need identification and program planning in the community context. In J. E. Tropman, J. L. Erlich, & J. Rothman (Eds.), *Tactics & techniques of community intervention* (4th ed., pp. 105–129). Itasca, IL: F. E. Peacock.

Segal, E. A. (2007). *Social welfare policy and social programs: A values perspective*. Belmont, CA: Brooks/Cole.

Simpson, C., & Simpson, D. (1992). *Exploring careers in social work*. New York: Rosen.

Slattery, J. M. (2004). *Counseling diverse clients: Bringing context into therapy*. Belmont, CA: Brooks/Cole.

Sluyter, G. V. (1998). *Improving organizational performance: A practical guidebook for the human services field*. Thousand Oaks, CA: Sage.

Smith, R. F. (1995). Settlements and neighborhood centers. In *Encyclopedia of social work* (Vol. 3, pp. 2129–2135). Washington, DC: NASW Press.

Smolowe, J. (1995, July 31). Noble aims, mixed results. *Time*, pp. 54–55.

Solomon, B. B. (2002). Social work practice with African Americans. In A. R. Morales & B. W. Sheafor (Eds.), *The many faces of social work clients* (pp. 295–315). Boston: Allyn & Bacon.

Sowers, K. M., & Rowe, W. S. (2007). *Social work practice & social justice: From local to global perspectives*. Belmont, CA: Brooks/Cole.

Staples, L. H. (2004). Social action groups. In C. D. Garvin, L. M. Gutierrez, & M. J. Galinsky (Eds.), *Handbook of social work with groups* (pp. 344–359). New York: Guilford.

Stauffer, M. D., Pehrsson, D. E., & Briggs, C., A. (2006). Groups in mental health settings. In D. Capuzi, D. R. Gross, & M. D. Stauffer, M. D. (Eds.), *Introduction to group work* (4th ed., pp. 355–383). Denver: Love.

Strong, B., DeVault, C., Sayad, B. W., & Yarber, W. L. (2005). *Human sexuality: Diversity in contemporary America* (5th ed.). Boston: McGraw-Hill.

Sue, D. W. (2006). *Multicultural social work practice*. Hoboken, NJ: Wiley.

Sue, E. W., & Sue, D. (Eds.). (2003). *Counseling the culturally different: Theory and practice* (4th ed.). New York: John Wiley.

Sundel, M., & Sundel. S. S. (2005). *Behavior change in the human services: Behavioral and cognitive principles and applications* (5th ed.). Thousand Oaks, CA: Sage.

Swinomish Tribal Mental Health Project. (1991). *A gathering of wisdoms, tribal mental health: A cultural perspective*. LaConner, WA: Swinomish Tribal Community.

Taylor, R. (1979). Black ethnicity and the persistence of ethnogenesis. *American Journal of Sociology*, 84, p. 6.

Texeira, E. (2005, April 10). Great gap in wealth remains between races in America. *Milwaukee Journal Sentinel*, 23A.

Toseland, R. W., & Rivas, R. F. (1995). *An introduction to group work practice* (2nd ed.). Needham Heights, MA: Allyn & Bacon.

Toseland, R. W., & Rivas, R. F. (2005). *An introduction to group work practice* (5th ed.). Boston: Allyn & Bacon.

Tracy, E. M. (2002). Working with and strengthening social networks. In A. R. Roberts & G. J. Greene (Eds.), *Social workers' desk reference* (pp. 402–405). New York: Oxford.

Treguer, A. (1992). The Chicanos—Muralists with a message. *UNESCO Courier*, 45, 22–24.

Tully, C. T. (2001). *Lesbians, gays, and the empowerment perspective*. New York: Columbia University Press.

Turem, J. W. (1986). Social work administration and modern management technology. *Administration in social work*, 10 (3), 15–24.

Turner, G. (2001, Winter). The puzzling world of international social work careers. *The New Social Worker*, 4–7.

USAID. (2006). *About us*. Retrieved on September 10, 2006, from http://www.usaid.gov/about_usaid/.

U. S. Census Bureau. (2005). *Statistical abstract of the United States: 2006*. Washington, DC: U. S. Department of Commerce.

U. S. Census Bureau. (2004). *Statistical abstract of the United States: 2005*. Washington, DC: U. S. Department of Commerce.

U. S. Census Bureau. (2003). *Statistical abstract of the United States: 2005*. Washington, DC: U. S. Department of Commerce.

U. S. Department of Justice. (2002, May). *Americans with Disabilities Act questions and answers*. Retrieved on August 10, 2006, from http://www.usdoj.gov/crt/ada/q%26aeng02.htm.

van Soest, D., & Garcia, B. (2003). *Diversity education for social justice: Mastering teaching skills*. Alexandria, VA: Council on Social Work Education.

van Voorhis, R. M. (1999). Feminist theories and social work practice. In R. R. Greene (Ed.), *Human behavior theory and social work practice* (2nd ed., pp. 351–387). New York: Aldine de Gruyter.

van Wormer, K. (2004). *Confronting oppression, restoring justice: From policy analysis to social action*. Alexandria, VA: Council on Social Work Education.

van Wormer, K., Well, J., & Boes, M. (2000). *Social work with lesbians, gays, and bisexuals: A strengths perspective*. Boston: Allyn & Bacon.

Vecchio, R. P. (2006). *Organizational behavior* (6th ed.). Mason, OH: South-Western.

Verschelden, C. (1993). Social work values and pacifism: Opposition to war as a professional responsibility. *Social Work,* 38 (6), 765–769.

Vourlekis, B. S. (1999). Cognitive theory for social work practice. In R. R. Green (Ed., pp. 173–205), *Human behavior theory and social work practice* (2nd ed.). New York: Aldine de Gruyter.

Waller, M. (2002). *TANF reauthorization: Options and Opportunities.* Presentation to the U.S. Conference of Mayors Annual Meeting, June 15, 2002. Retrieved on January 1, 2005, from http://www.brook.edu/es/urban/speeches/20020615waller.htm.

Walsh, J. (2006). *Theories of direct social work practice.* Belmont, CA: Brooks/Cole.

Warren, E. (1977). The functional diversity of urban neighborhood. *Urban Affairs Quarterly,* 13 (2), 151–179.

Warren, R. (1983). A community model. In R. M. Kramer & H. Specht (Eds.), *Readings in community organization practice* (pp. 28–36). Englewood Cliffs, NJ: Prentice-Hall.

Warren, R., & Warren, D. I. (1977). *The neighborhood organizers handbook.* South Bend: University of Notre Dame Press.

Watkins, T. R. (2004). Natural helping networks: Assets for rural communities. In T. L. Scales & C. L. Streeter (Eds.), *Rural social work: Building and sustaining community assets* (pp. 65–76). Belmont, CA: Brooks/Cole.

Weaver, H. N. (2005). *Explorations in cultural competence: Journeys to the four directions.* Belmont, CA: Brooks/Cole.

Wetzel, J. W. (1995). Global feminist zeitgeist practice. In N. Van Den Bergh (Ed.), *Feminist practice in the 21st century* (pp. 175–192). Washington, DC: NASW Press.

Wetzel, J. W. (2004). Mental health lessons from abroad. In M. C.

Hokenstad & J. Midgley (Eds.), *Lessons from abroad: Adapting international social welfare innovations* (pp. 93–116). Washington, DC: NASW Press.

Wheelan, S. A. (1999), *Creating effective teams: A guide for members and leaders.* Thousand Oaks, CA: Sage.

Williams, C. (2006). *Effective management* (2nd ed.). Mason, OH: South-Western.

Williams, C. (2005). *Management* (3rd ed.). Mason, OH: South-Western.

Wilson, W. J. (1996). *When work disappears: The world of the new urban poor.* New York: Knopf.

Wireman, P. (1984). *Urban neighborhoods, networks, and families: New forms for old values.* Lexington, MA: Lexington Books.

Wolk, J. L. (1981). Are social workers politically active? *Social Work,* 26 (4), 283–288.

Women Work! (2006, May 24). *TANF reauthorization that works.* Retrieved on June 27, 2006, from http://www.womenwork.org.

Wong, J. (2005). Asian Pacific Islanders. In K. L. Guadalupe & D. Lum (Eds.), *Multidimensional contextual practice: Diversity and transcendence* (pp. 388–429). Belmont, CA: Brooks/Cole.

Woodman, N. J. (1995). Lesbians: Direct practice. In *Encyclopedia of social work* (Vol. 2, pp. 1597–1604). Washington, DC: NASW Press.

Woodword, K. L., & Johnson, P. (1995, December 11). The advent of Kwanzaa: Will success spoil an African-American fest? *Newsweek,* 88.

Workworld.org. (2006). Temporary assistance for needy families (TANF): Overview. Retrieved on June 27, 2006, from http://www.workworld.org/wwwebhelp/temporary_assistance_for_needy_families_tanf_htm.

World YWCA. (2006). *Women leading change.* Retrieved on July 20,

2006, from http://www.worldywca.info.

Yalom, I. D. (1985). *The theory and practice of group psychotherapy* (3rd ed.). New York: Basic Books.

Yamashiro, G., & Matsuoka, J. K. (1997). Help-seeking among Asian and Pacific Americans: A Multiperspective Analysis. *Social Work,* 42, 2, 176–186.

Yan, M. C. (2004). Bridging the fragmented community: Revitalizing settlement houses in the global era. *Journal of Community Practice,* 12 (1/2), 51–69.

Yessian, M. R., & Broskowski, A. (1983). Generalists in human service systems: Their problems and prospects. In R. M. Kramer & H. Specht (Eds.), *Readings in community organization practice* (pp. 180–198). Englewood Cliffs, NJ: Prentice-Hall.

YMCA. (2006). *Welcome to the YMCA.* Retrieved on July 20, 2006 from http://www.ymca.net.

YWCA. (2006). *Eliminating racism, Empowering women.* Retrieved on July 20, 2006, from http://www.ywca.org.

Zastrow, C. H. (2006). *Social work with groups: A comprehensive workbook* (6th ed.). Belmont, CA: Brooks/Cole.

Zastrow, C., & Kirst-Ashman, K. K. (2004). *Understanding human behavior and the social environment* (6th ed.). Belmont, CA: Brooks/Cole.

Zhang, W. (2003). Use with care: Culturally incorrect attending can be rude. In A. E. Ivey & M. B. Ivey, *Intentional interviewing and counseling: Facilitating client development in a multicultural society* (5th ed.). Belmont, CA: Brooks/Cole.

Name Index

Index